Frommer's®
Turkey

My Turkey

by Lynn A. Levine

WHEN MY COLLEGE ROOMMATE ONCE TOLD ME THAT SHE WOULD BE vacationing in Turkey, in my youthful ignorance I thought to myself, *How does she pick these places?* (expletive deleted) Little did I know then that shortly thereafter I would enter into one of the most stimulating portions of my life, destined to become a life-long student of all things Turkic, Anatolian, and Ottoman.

Upon my first step off the plane, I was immediately swept off my feet by Turkey: by the kindhearted warmth of the people, the profound richness of an incomparable cultural mosaic, the grandeur of monumental empires, and the artistry present in centuries-old traditional crafts. Narrowing down the selection of photographs to provide a mere taste of what you might experience there was one of the greatest challenges of writing this book. But my soul warms just looking at them, and I hope that your snapshot memories of Turkey will do the same for you one day.

© Images&Stories/Alamy

In contrast to the scripted mass seaside celebrations taking place all along the Turkish coast, the historically preserved cobblestone village of **ALACATI (left)** is a jewel of the Turkish Aegean. Oddly enough, it's juxtaposed opposite the windsurfing wonderland over at Alacati's bay, a playground that attracts daredevils, sportsmen, and free spirits. When the sun goes down, the scents of jasmine, bougainvillea, and honeysuckle fill the breeze, and there's nothing quite like spoiling yourself at a free table beckoning along the picturesque main drag to sooth your sunburn.

What Mark Twain so fondly referred to as "the rustiest old barn in heathendom" is a monumental icon for the city of Istanbul, the defunct Byzantine Empire, and modern-day Orthodox Christianity. The sense of humility created is as striking today as it was more than a thousand years ago—standing below the bull's-eye of the soaring dome, you may half expect this substantial heap of masonry to collapse on your very head. But for nearly 1,500 years, the **AYASOFYA (above)** perseveres in its embodiment of the indomitable spirit of human ingenuity and advancement.

While the march of modernization has caught up with the "downtowns" of **CAPPADOCIA (left)** bringing with it trendy cafes, boutique spa hotels, and ubiquitous Wi-Fi access, the region still remains primarily pastoral. Mercedes-Benzes must defer to the pace of the village donkey, the de facto beast of burden for hauling farmer to field and produce to market. While visiting Cappadocia, you'll be awed by the sight of 1,001 "fairy chimneys" rising from the landscape, and ancient cities carved many levels underground.

Ancient civilizations often relied upon the high ground for self defense, and the ancient city of Pergamon is one of the loftier of Anatolian hilltop fortress kingdoms. Today, the altitude is but a minor hurdle to those wishing to visit. While catching your breath at the summit, expect to have your breath taken away again by the monumental remains of one of the West's greatest civilizations. The **TEMPLE OF TRAJAN (above)** stands high above the Lower City and contemporary Bergama, with expansive views of the Bergama Plain.

© Robert Landau/Royalty-Free/Corbis/Jupiterimages

Getting up to the **FORTRESS AT KEKOVA (above)** may not seem like much of a physical stretch, but the grade is steep and the path up is congested. The reward? One of the most memorable views of this or any trip: Lycian tombs jutting above the waterline, and Kekova Island and Bay as seen through the lens of the fortress parapets.

Like the most exclusive haunts of the truly rich and perhaps famous, the palace section of the **ÇIRAĞAN PALACE HOTEL KEMPINSKI (right)** is well beyond the reach of mere mortals (like me). Most guests of the hotel are satisfied with the lavish Bosphorus-front room in the modern section. Imagine my surprise one day, while snooping around the crystal banisters and gold leaf, to find myself surrounded by NBA executives in one of the sumptuous meeting rooms. Who'd have thought that royalty would become marketable to the masses?

© John Warburton-Lee Photography/Alamy

Strolling through the Ottoman-era **EGYPTIAN SPICE MARKET** (right), you may wonder, *How many aphrodisiacs does one need?* One day, it's stuffed dried figs bearing the sign TURKISH VIAGRA. Another, pistachios steeped in honey qualify as the magic pill. As if the air scented with mint, cinnamon, and saffron wasn't enough to whet your shopping appetite . . .

On the storied **GALATA BRIDGE** (below), dozens of resident fishermen brace themselves against the rails, fishing rods aloft. You simply can't get more picturesque, particularly at sunset as the floodlights begin, one by one, to illuminate the minarets of the historic peninsula in the background.

Imagine a society where the all-powerful male figure lorded over a stable of pliant slaves and servants, where his every desire, be it culinary or carnal, was sated by comely lasses from the four corners of the empire or a coterie of able chefs. The inner sanctum of sultanic power that was **TOPKAPI PALACE** was almost literally a no-man's land of mystery and intrigue, enclosed by superlative levels of opulence characterized by precious tiles, gold, silver, ivory, and silks.

Frommer's®

Turkey

5th Edition

by Lynn A. Levine

Here's what the critics say about Frommer's:

"Amazingly easy to use. Very portable, very complete."

—*Booklist*

"Detailed, accurate, and easy-to-read information for all price ranges."
—*Glamour Magazine*

"Hotel information is close to encyclopedic."

—*Des Moines Sunday Register*

"Frommer's Guides have a way of giving you a real feel for a place."
—*Knight Ridder Newspapers*

WILEY

Wiley Publishing, Inc.

About the Author

Lynn A. Levine is author of *Frommer's Istanbul* and has contributed to a number of other titles, including *Frommer's Italy from $90 a Day* and *Frommer's Southeast Asia*. Her work has appeared in the *Boston Globe, Elle, MSNBC/Newsweek Budget Travel, Travel Holiday,* and the *UN Chronicle*. When not writing about travel, she is a communications consultant for UNICEF, the UNDP, and IFAW. She also runs the website www.talkingturkey.com.

Published by:

Wiley Publishing, Inc.

111 River St.
Hoboken, NJ 07030-5774

ISBN: 978-0-470-24761-7
Editor: Jamie Ehrlich
Production Editor: Michael Brumitt
Cartographer: Roberta Stockwell
Photo Editor: Richard Fox
Production by Wiley Indianapolis Composition Services

Front cover photo: Ephesus: Low angle view of female statue in the Library of Celsus
Back cover photo: Three young women posing in front of the camera in traditional dress

For information on our other products and services or to obtain technical support, please contact our Customer Care Department within the U.S. at 800/762-2974, outside the U.S. at 317/572-3993 or fax 317/572-4002.

Wiley also publishes its books in a variety of electronic formats. Some content that appears in print may not be available in electronic formats.

Manufactured in the United States of America

5 4 3 2 1

Contents

5 Çanakkale, Gallipoli & the Troad   170

6 The Central & Southern Aegean Coasts (Greater Izmir)   188

7 The Turquoise & Mediterranean Coasts   255

8 Cappadocia & the Interior   331

List of Maps

Acknowledgments

Special thanks are in order for a handful of incredibly wonderful and supportive individuals. Thanks to Sırma, Sıla, Aydın, Suha, Süleyman, and Hakan for their professional assistance and personal friendship. Each has been instrumental in supporting me in my work on this guide and in introducing me to the soul of Turkey. Warm thanks also go out to the people and the country of Turkey for exposing me to countless true friendships made during the course of working in Turkey.

An Invitation to the Reader

In researching this book, we discovered many wonderful places—hotels, restaurants, shops, and more. We're sure you'll find others. Please tell us about them, so we can share the information with your fellow travelers in upcoming editions. If you were disappointed with a recommendation, we'd love to know that, too. Please write to:

Frommer's Turkey, 5th Edition
Wiley Publishing, Inc. • 111 River St. • Hoboken, NJ 07030-5774

An Additional Note

Please be advised that travel information is subject to change at any time—and this is especially true of prices. We therefore suggest that you write or call ahead for confirmation when making your travel plans. The authors, editors, and publisher cannot be held responsible for the experiences of readers while traveling. Your safety is important to us, however, so we encourage you to stay alert and be aware of your surroundings. Keep a close eye on cameras, purses, and wallets, all favorite targets of thieves and pickpockets.

Other Great Guides for Your Trip:

Frommer's Istanbul
Frommer's European Cruises & Ports of Call
Frommer's Greek Islands

Frommer's Star Ratings, Icons & Abbreviations

Every hotel, restaurant, and attraction listing in this guide has been ranked for quality, value, service, amenities, and special features using a **star-rating system.** In country, state, and regional guides, we also rate towns and regions to help you narrow down your choices and budget your time accordingly. Hotels and restaurants are rated on a scale of zero (recommended) to three stars (exceptional). Attractions, shopping, nightlife, towns, and regions are rated according to the following scale: zero stars (recommended), one star (highly recommended), two stars (very highly recommended), and three stars (must-see).

In addition to the star-rating system, we also use **seven feature icons** that point you to the great deals, in-the-know advice, and unique experiences that separate travelers from tourists. Throughout the book, look for:

Finds	Special finds—those places only insiders know about
Fun Fact	Fun facts—details that make travelers more informed and their trips more fun
Kids	Best bets for kids and advice for the whole family
Moments	Special moments—those experiences that memories are made of
Overrated	Places or experiences not worth your time or money
Tips	Insider tips—great ways to save time and money
Value	Great values—where to get the best deals

The following **abbreviations** are used for credit cards:

AE	American Express	DISC	Discover	V	Visa
DC	Diners Club	MC	MasterCard		

Frommers.com

Now that you have this guidebook to help you plan a great trip, visit our website at **www.frommers.com** for additional travel information on more than 4,000 destinations. We update features regularly to give you instant access to the most current trip-planning information available. At Frommers.com, you'll find scoops on the best airfares, lodging rates, and car rental bargains. You can even book your travel online through our reliable travel booking partners. Other popular features include:

- Online updates of our most popular guidebooks
- Vacation sweepstakes and contest giveaways
- Newsletters highlighting the hottest travel trends
- Podcasts, interactive maps, and up-to-the-minute events listings
- Opinionated blog entries by Arthur Frommer himself
- Online travel message boards with featured travel discussions

What's New in Turkey

If thoughts of a slow international economy and ongoing insurgencies in Afghanistan and Iraq are holding you back, rest assured: Turkey has more than gracefully weathered the storm. The nation's economic growth rivals that of China, while tourism is up, up, up, for the first time in several years. So in spite of somewhat inflated prices in comparison to previous years (bordering on shocking in Istanbul), Turkey still presents itself as one of the best, safest, *easiest,* and all-around rewarding destinations in the region.

PLANNING YOUR TRIP   For complete planning information, see chapter 2.

Getting There   Although the paint is barely dry on the Atatürk International Airport, its international terminal underwent renovations in 2007. It must be a result of the pressure created by increased arrivals and departures, because Turkish Airlines has spread out to the little-known **Sabiha Gökçen Airport,** located on the outskirts of Istanbul on the Asian side of the Bosphorus. Flights are for now mostly domestic, but budget-minded visitors may want to look into service offered by **Pegasus** (from London, Bologna, and Vienna), **Easyjet** (from London), **Condor** (from Amsterdam), and **Myair** (from Milan). Keep in mind that the bus ride into town will add an additional 90 or so minutes to the trip.

Visitor Information, Entry Requirements & Money   Entry visas for holders of American passports now cost $29 for admission to what is fast becoming one of the globe's top destinations. Visas for Canadians now cost US$60, Brits pay £10, and the fee for Aussies is up to A$68. Kiwis get in for free. Helping to make the visa fees a bit less painful, Turkey will be lowering its VAT rate, beginning in 2008, from 18% to 8%. New for this edition is the inclusion of conversion rates for both the U.S. dollar and the British pound. Since the last installment of this book, the dollar has plummeted from 1YTL = US$1.35 down to US$1.15.

Getting Around   Rising prices are not the only consequence of the current frenzy surrounding Turkish tourism. Renewed demand translates to the emergence of new (and old) ferry services. In the summer of 2007, **Deniz Cruise & Ferry Lines** (www.denizline.com.tr) announced Istanbul-to-Bodrum cruises. Istanbul-to-Izmir excursions were organized through the summer of 2007. There is also a new passenger ferry service from Istanbul to Bursa. As a result of the inflow of cash from tourism and foreign direct investment, the government has invested in infrastructure projects that have brought Turkey's motorways up to European standards.

ISTANBUL   For complete coverage of Istanbul, see chapter 4.

Getting Around   A number of domestic airline start-ups are giving the standards a run for their money. These include **Pegasus** (serving Izmir and Kayseri from

Istanbul; www.flypgs.com), IZair (Istanbul to Izmir; www.izair.com.tr), and Atlasjet (serving Istanbul, Ankara, Antalya, Bodrum, Çanakkale, Izmir, and so on; www.atlasjet.com.tr), with fares as low as 45YTL (US$39/£17).

A flurry of **restoration** and **city renewal** projects are underway in Istanbul. **Istiklal Caddesi** is now completely repaved with flat marble blocks. **Galip Dede Sokak,** leading down from Tünel to the Galata Tower, is no longer dangerous going; instead, it's been newly paved with modern cobblestones and the sidewalks have been widened. Streets all over the city that were formerly dusty and potholed messes have also been newly cobbled. One major improvement is the completion of the **tramway** all the way up to Kabataş, next to Dolmabahçe Palace. This, together with the new **funicular** connecting Kabataş with Taksim Square, makes getting around the city (particularly between the Old City and the New) a snap (albeit a crowded one). It also completes the public transport network connecting Atatürk Airport with the city. Still another **funicular** was completed over in the neighborhood of Eyüp, making that haul up the hill from the base of Pierre Loti Caddesi. Construction of the **Marmaray Project,** a 76km (47-mile) rail that at its center will include a much-awaited connection from Taksim to the airport, is moving along as best as it can, given the most recent developments. In the process of construction, workers unearthed the groundbreaking remains of a **Theodesius-era port at Yenikapı** and **pre-classical artifacts at Sirkeci.** Word of the discovery reverberated throughout the international archaeology community; at last count, archaeologists had uncovered 24 shipwrecks—the highest concentration of wrecks in the world. The wooden broad-beamed boats still have much of their cargo in them.

Safety   Perhaps it's indicative of economic growth, or of increased tourism creating more opportunity, but Istanbul seems to be experiencing a new level of petty crime. It's seeped into the otherwise pastoral neighborhood of Sultanahmet, where previously, crimes were committed by glorified gigolos with a wink and a smile. Not so now. Men walking alone are now at high risk of being mugged in dark byways, and contents of purses are routinely disappearing. It seems as though the Big Bad City has arrived in the quiet, leafy green neighborhoods of Istanbul's Old City. Take all the precautions you would take visiting any major international metropolis. See p. 35.

Where to Stay   Those huge corporate names like Marriott, InterContinental, Radisson, and Starwood just couldn't sit by and watch the little boutique hotels (many of them enterprises created by current and reformed carpet sellers) scoop up all the hotel profits. The result is a sobering addition of more than 70 big-name hotels under construction in 2007 alone. Some highlights: The **Apricot Hotel** (© 0212/638-1658), which was forced to find new digs due to a change in building ownership, is now in a more charming spot around the corner. Several new boutique hotels have opened in the Sultanahmet district of Istanbul, including the very special **Sultanhan** (© 0212/516-3232) and the **Ottoman Hotel** (© 0212/513-6150). The **Four Seasons** (© 0212/638-8200) in Sultanahmet somehow got permission to construct an annex at the back of its property. The dig (inevitably an archaeological excavation) is under way. By publication of this guide, the paint should probably be dry on the new **Four Seasons the Bosphorus,** whose debut has been eagerly anticipated since our last edition. **Les Ottomans** (© 0212/359-1500) will be giving all of these new luxury properties a run for their money—though with only 10 units,

its exclusivity is more than guaranteed. Bringing new style to the back streets of Beyoğlu is the **Misafir Suites** (© 0212/249-8930), a seven-unit hideaway with studiolike apartments that any city-dweller would covet. Meanwhile, two old horses, the **Pera Palas** and the palace section of the eminent **Çırağan Palace,** are undergoing extensive renovations and should be reopened by the time you read this. See "Where to Stay" in chapter 4 for more information.

Where to Dine   Rising prices in Turkey have not stopped the middle and upper classes from packing tables as fast as restaurants can open. A number of outstanding and creative kitchens have popped up since our previous edition. **Mikla** is the most recent undertaking of celebrity chef Mehmet Gürs (© 0212/293-5656). **House Café** (© 0212/259-2377) has emerged as a popular franchise phenomenon (p. 101). The proletariat-friendly **Saray Muhallebiçileri** (© 0212/292-3434) has opened a number of new locations around the city, in addition to its current location on Istiklal Caddesi, in the space opposite its original location (p. 103). The cleanup of the streets around Taksim has pumped new life into **Kurabiye Sokak** (parallel to Istiklal Cad. on the Tarlabaşı side), which is now host to a cluster of simple and inexpensive restaurants, both old and new. One standout is **Parsifal** (© 0212/245-2588), serving an inventive all-vegetarian menu (p. 103).

What to See   Among the frenzy of restoration projects going on around the city, the splendid **Byzantine mosaics** on the second-floor gallery of the Ayasofya were just recently cleaned. There's now an extra entrance fee to the upper gallery, in addition to the museum admission (p. 108). The largest collection of sarcophagi in Turkey, hidden for the last 25 years in storage, is now on display in the **Northern Wing of the Istanbul Archaeology Museum** (© 0212/520-7740),

which was inaugurated in 2007 (p. 114). On the less cerebral end of exploring Istanbul, the **Süleymaniye Hamamı** (© 0212/519-5569) recently opened to the public but take heed: It's coed (p. 128).

Shopping   Two new shopping malls have opened their doors, aiming for the upmarket crowd. The **shops at Istinye** recreate an upscale village atmosphere above the Bosphorus. And down in Nişantaşı, the new indoor **City Mall** aims to target Istanbul's version of those who shop on Madison Avenue or in Knightsbridge (p. 150).

AROUND THE SEA OF MARMARA & THE NORTH AEGEAN   For complete information on this region, see chapter 5.

Bursa   Getting There   New ferry service began in April 2007 from Istanbul's Yenikapı docks to Güzelyalı, about 7 miles from Bursa (p. 158).

Çanakkale   Where to Stay   As long as the beer flows when the Aussies are in town, apparently they're not too selective about where they stay. Thus, Çanakkale's tradition of cement-block hotels. The exception is the new **Kervansaray** (© 0286/217-8192), a newly renovated former judge's mansion just steps from the clock tower (p. 164). For this edition, we are including wider coverage of Turkey's northwestern Aegean **Troad,** an as-of-yet undiscovered region hidden in plain sight. Step back into the era of Troy by visiting **Alexander Troas** and **Assos,** both attached to wonderfully backward little villages, and the idyllic **Bozcaada Island,** just off the coast (p. 183).

THE CENTRAL & SOUTHERN AEGEAN COASTS   For complete information on this region, see chapter 6.

Izmir   Getting There   Izmir Airport inaugurated its **new international terminal** in September 2006. The new facility has already increased Izmir's capacity for additional flights, including by charter airlines, and passengers. On the ground, a state-of-the-art **multilane toll "beltway"** road encircling metropolitan Izmir is now complete.

Getting Around   The improvement projects just keep coming with Izmir's new **metro,** which consists of one line running between Bornova, a residential suburb to the northeast of town, to Üçyol just south of Konak. Future extensions are in the works.

Where to Stay   With its growth as a major commercial center, Izmir now also has a whole new string of first-class hotels to show for its stint as a rising star. Commanding the best chunk of real estate for hotels in town is the new (delayed from Nov 2007 and now scheduled to open Mar 2008) **Swissôtel Grand Efes** (© 0232/483-9761). This majorly business-minded hotel caters to convention tourism, but single travelers may still get lost in there yet (p. 198). Opposite the Swissôtel and also awaiting its debut in 2008 is the Swiss-owned **Mövenpick,** a five-star business hotel for those with a three-star budget (p. 198). The **Kordon Hotel** (© 0232/425-0445) opened in April 2007 on the waterfront wharf facing Pasaport, and the views and pedestrian access to the rest of the city couldn't be any better (p. 197). With its lipstick-like tower rising above the district of Incıraltı, the **Crown Plaza** (© 0232/292-1300) has charisma to spare, with a thermal spring below (and now in the spa), as well as an authentic waterfront neighborhood experience (p. 197).

Çeşme Peninsula   Getting There   The completion of the **toll road** into Çeşme and the reengineering and relocation of a few traffic patterns resulted in a **move of the bus station** to its current location up the road from the main harbor (p. 204).

Where to Stay   The **Sheraton Çeşme** (© 800/325-3535) completely redid its spa to create a sublime, Asian-inspired eden of relaxing treatments, sensual scents, and soothing decor (p. 209).

What to Do   Over in **Ilica,** a new marina provides direct access to the sea (no beach) and a series of semi-immersed iron ladders beckons to those wishing to head right in (p. 206).

Sardis   This ancient city has now been added to the guide. What a fantastic site; sorry we took so long (p. 211)!

Selçuk   Getting There   Train service connecting Selçuk with Izmir (and eventually the airport) has been suspended until construction on the new Izmir metro is complete.

Where to Stay   The new **Hotel Bella** (© 0232/892-3944) opposite the flood-lit entry portal to St. John's Basilica is like a breath of fresh air in the unchanging landscape that is Selçuk. The hotel is modest yet typical of the Turkish soul you look for in shopping for accommodations (p. 225).

What to Do   The recently founded **Crisler Institute** (© 0252/892-8317) picks up the mantle of Turkish explorations and cultural understanding where researcher and archaeologist B. Cobbey Crisler left off. The institute is a labor of love for Crisler's widow, Janet, who through collaboration with the Austrian Institute of Archaeology offers lectures on the most up-to-date findings at Ephesus (p. 218).

Bodrum   Getting There   Deniz Cruise & Ferry Lines embarks upon an Aegean journey from Istanbul in summertime (p. 238).

Visitor Information   With plenty of expats and regular holiday-goers, the *Bodrum Observer,* the area's newspaper start-up (Jan 2006), seems to have a built-in audience. It tackles local issues like the problem of wildfires, as well as handy information for the tourist.

Where to Stay A whole slew of new, luxurious hotels is staking out inlets and bays all over the peninsula. The newcomers covered here are the **Kempinski Barbaros Bay** (© 0252/311-0303), the **4Reasons** (© 0252/385-3212), **Ev** (© 0252/377-6070), and **Adahan** (© 0252/385-4759). See p. 250.

What to Do In a resort where beach clubs exude hip, **Bianca Beach** (www. biancabeach.com) in Türkbükü is the ticket. Oversize draped beds and sumptuous decor create a decadent dance of beachfront seduction (p. 246). When not lounging waterside, perhaps a dive (or ride via mini-submarine) to the recently sunken boat decommissioned from the Turkish navy might do the trick (p. 245).

THE TURQUOISE & MEDITERRANEAN COASTS For complete information on this region, see chapter 7.

Marmaris Getting There A record number of private and charter airlines are now offering direct international service into Dalaman. **Onur Air** (www.onurair. com.tr) flies direct from London and Birmingham; **SunExpress** (www.sunexpress.com.tr) also serves the London-Dalaman route. Other European-based charter airlines flying into Dalaman are **Easyjet** (www.easyjet.com), **Monarch Airlines** (www.flymonarch.com), **Thomas Cook** (www.flythomascook.com), and **British Midland** (www.flybmi.com). See p. 234.

Fethiye Where to Stay One of the newer (and more sublime) exclusive properties, the **Oyster Residences** is actually two separate properties, one in the bull's-eye of Ölüdeniz and one up in the natural forests in Faralya. (For reservations contact **Exclusive Escapes** in the U.K. at © 0208/605-3500.) Recently opened in the new frontier of Faralya is **Su Değirmene** (www.natur-reisen.de) and in uncharted Yanıklar, the architectural and eco-friendly **Pastoral Vadı** (www.pastoral vadi.com). See p. 283.

Where to Dine The village of Kayaköy, up in a mountain valley above Fethiye, is growing up so fast. Two new additions have popped up to accommodate the village's more mature (not necessarily old) tastes. The **Kaya Wine House** (© 0252/ 618-0454) serves wines produced in small, private vineyards, while the wine cellar at the **Levissi Garden** (© 0252/ 618-0108) has a wider selection (p. 277).

Kalkan Where to Stay After years of faithful service, the **Kalkan Han** is transforming itself from a guesthouse to condominiums. We're sad to see it go. We've found an excellent replacement: the **Hotel Rhapsody** (© 0242/844-2575), a stylish boutique hotel above the harbor, which makes us feel better about just about everything (p. 296).

Kaş Where to Stay Where do city dwellers go when they retire? Preferably somewhere like the **Diva Residence** (© 0242/836-4255), a perfect Mediterranean retreat—but as its owners (p. 306).

What to Do In October 2006, underwater archaeologists constructed a replica of the **Uluburun shipwreck** and sunk it off the coast of Kaş. The *in situ* wreck is now a popular dive destination (p. 295).

Antalya Getting There Just like over in Dalaman, Antalya's airport now has a **new international terminal,** with direct flights from an increasing number of cities abroad. Airlines include **British Airways** (© 0870/850-9850 in the U.K.), SunExpress (© 0232/444-0797 in Turkey), the U.K.-based charter **Thomas Cook** (www.thomascookairlines.co.uk), **Onur Air** (© 0242/330-3432 in Antalya), the Istanbul-based **Atlasjet** (© 0216/444-3387), and **Fly Air** (© 444-4359). See p. 257.

What to Do Antalya's Sand Sculpture exhibition is a whimsical celebration of artistry in sand. Over in Belek, **golfing** enthusiasts are eagerly awaiting the opening of **LykiaLinks** (www.lykiagroup. com), the first course in Antalya designed to overlook the Mediterranean. Also new in the world of Turkish golf are the new PGA-approved courses over at the shiny new and palatial **Kempinski Hotel The Dome** (© 0242/710-1300; p. 321). To the west of Antalya, at the base of Mount Olympos, is a gateway to heaven in the form of the new cable car—the second longest in the world. The cable car ends up at a mountaintop restaurant, but will eventually be met by ski lifts (p. 322).

Where to Stay   The new **Marmara Antalya** (© 0242/249-3600) opened in the summer of 2006, touting their "anything, anytime" theme (p. 323).

CAPPADOCIA & THE INTERIOR For complete information on this region, see chapter 8.

Where to Stay   Just when you think that Ürgüp has topped off with new hotels, along comes something special like the **Serinn** (© 0384/341-6076).

Located in the quiet hilltop neighborhood of Esbelli, the Serinn overlays a modern art concept onto troglodyte living (p. 340).

What to Do   With a course of nets dotting the meadows in Üçhisar Valley, **Cross Golf** (© 0384/271-2351), opened in 2007, adapts the game of golf to the local environment (p. 334).

ANKARA   For complete information on this region, see chapter 9.

Getting There   Ankara's Esenboğa Airport is another of Turkey's airports to get a new modern terminal, with an annual capacity of 10 million passengers, up from 2 million. Now there are more direct international flights than ever, including **BMI** (www.flybmi.com), with flights from London Heathrow (p. 368).

What to Do   The trend in Turkey toward **historic preservation** is ramping up. The **fortress ramparts and castle,** the **Temple of Augustus,** and the **Roman Baths** are among the many ambitious projects begun by the Ministry of Culture to steward Turkey's precious patrimony into the future (p. 376).

1

The Best of Turkey

First-time visitors to Turkey (or anywhere, for that matter) often leave home with preconceived notions about what their destination will be like. But Turkey represents many, often contradictory things: It's ancient and modern, Westernized and Oriental, religious and secular, wondrous and ordinary, familiar and exotic. But there is one undeniable common denominator, and that is that Turkey, and the Turkish people, know how to do hospitality. This from a population in which 20% of the people live below the poverty line and yet the native language has no word for "bitter."

Turkey is a unique country: a rich, layered and magical world full of history, culture, gastronomy, humanity, and commerce—increasingly Europeanized yet (notwithstanding the über-cosmopolitan center that is Istanbul) still unspoiled and innocent. In the heartland, people are still pleasantly surprised and proud of the fact that people come to visit from far and wide.

Yet it wasn't until recently that Turkey's tourism industry finally began reaping the rewards appropriate for the custodian of three world empires, countless potent kingdoms, and a dazzling 8,333km (5,178-mile) coastline. This geographic and cultural bridge boasts more Greek ruins than Greece, more Roman archaeological sites than all of Italy, and—in Antalya alone—more resort hotels than all the coast of Spain. Turkey is also a major custodian of sacred sites revered by Christians, Jews, and Muslims alike, and of invaluable artifacts of early Greek civilization, Byzantine majesty, and Ottoman supremacy. Business is now booming, the middle class is spending, and cities are growing and expanding. Foreign direct investment and receipts from skyrocketing levels of tourism are creating opportunity, advancement, and progress not seen in Turkey in centuries. Dirt roads are now paved; single-lane asphalt roads have doubled in width; and new superhighways now serve Istanbul, Ankara, and Izmir. Turkey is also directing an unparalleled amount of funding into the country's cultural sites, exposing "secondary" archaeological sites to the light of day while increasing the visibility and longevity of the A-list sites.

Meanwhile, foreigners are descending on Turkey as if it were going out of business. Istanbul, Antalya, Ankara, and Cappadocia witnessed in 2007 as much as a 20% increase in arrivals from 2006. Parallel to this new—and renewed—popularity in Turkey as a travel destination is that Europeans, and particularly Brits, are profiting by unprecedented strength in their respective currencies, and where there's demand, there are both higher prices and growth. Hotels that once quoted prices in U.S. dollars switched to the symbol of the € in Istanbul, Cappadocia, and in other popular regions, and to the British pound sterling on the Mediterranean coast. For visitors wielding euros, Turkey is still very much an affordable destination, and for Brits, it's a veritable bargain basement. But for Americans paying in the pathetic dollar, Turkey is anything but the bargain it used to be. So is all of this dynamism worth it?

Absolutely. But you'll need to find the right balance. Traveling off-season will give you the strongest bargaining power, and you may have to forego that sunrise balloon ride over Cappadocia. But if you go, I guarantee that you'll soon see why people in the know just can't get enough of Turkey.

1 The Most Unforgettable Travel Experiences

- **Taking a *Hamam:*** The Turkish bath, rising out of the Islamic requirement of cleanliness, is not just practical, it's a minivacation. A good *hamam* experience includes the proper traditional ambience and a heavy-handed scrubbing. For historical value and pomp, you can't beat the coed **Süleymaniye Hamamı** (p. 128). If the royal treatment is your thing, you can try to get an appointment at **Les Ottomans** (p. 94). The lounge area of the men's section in the **Yeni Kaplıca** (p. 166) in Bursa is fabulously decorated with some of the most gorgeous wood details; you'll feel like royalty. The Queen Mother of all luxury *hamams,* however, is the skylit and picture-windowed marble *hamam* at the **Ada Hotel** (p. 249) in Türkbükü, outside of Bodrum, *by candlelight.*

- **Taking a Boat Ride up the Bosphorus:** Nowhere else in the world can you cross to another continent every 15 minutes. Connecting trade routes from the East to the West, it's no surprise that any conqueror who was anybody had his sights set on the Bosphorus. Float in the wake of Jason and the Argonauts and Constantine the Great, and enjoy the breezes, the stately wooden manses, the monumental Ottoman domes, and the fortresses that helped win the battle (p. 78).

- **Sharing Tea with the Locals:** Tea is at the center of Turkish culture; no significant negotiation takes place without some. But more than commerce, tea stops the hands of time in Turkey; it renews the bonds of friends and family. Having tea is inevitable,

as is the invitation to share a glass with a total stranger. Accept the invitation: There's more in the glass than just a beverage.

- **Soaking in a Thermal Pool:** Sometimes Turkey seems like one big open-air spa; chemically rich waters bubble up from below while frigid spring water rushes down from above. The **Çeşme Peninsula** seems like one big hot bath, and a whole slew of brand-new luxury facilities are willing to accommodate (see "Highlights of the Çeşme Peninsula," in chapter 6). In the Sacred Pool of Hierapolis at the **Pamukkale Thermal** (p. 235), you swim amid the detritus of ancient civilizations as sulfur bubbles tingle your skin. Bursa's **Çelik Palas Hotel** (p. 164) has a domed pool hot enough to make your knees weak. Down the road at the **Kervansaray Termal Hotel** (p. 164), the pools of running water are enclosed in a 700-year-old original *hamam.*

- **Exploring the Covered Bazaar:** Nobody should pass through Turkey without spending a day at the mother of all shopping malls. The atmosphere crackles with the electricity of the hunt—but are you the hunter or the hunted? The excitement is tangible, even if you're on the trail of a simple pair of elf shoes or an evil-eye talisman. It's the disciplined shopper who gets out unscathed. See "Shopping," in chapter 4.

- **Cruising the Turquoise Coast:** Words just don't do this justice. Aboard a wooden gulet (traditional broad-beamed boat), you drift past

Turkey

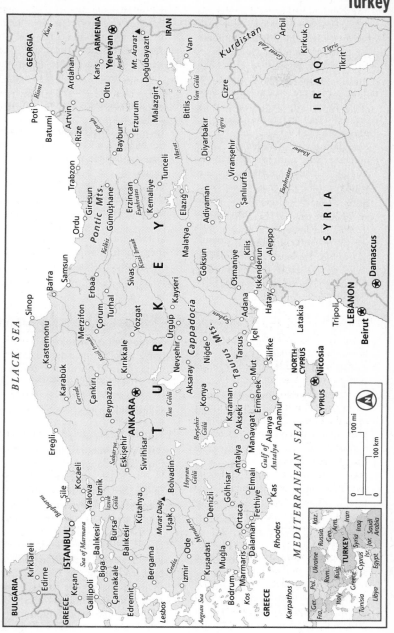

majestic mountains, undiscovered ruins, and impossibly azure waters, as the sun caresses your skin from sunrise to sunset. In this environment the morning aroma of Nescafé takes on an almost pleasant quality when enjoyed on deck, anchored just offshore a pine-enclosed inlet. By 9am you're diving off the rail and cursing the day it all has to end. See "All About the Blue Voyage" on p. 42.

- **Paragliding over Ölüdeniz:** There's no better place in the world than the surging summit of Babadağ for this wildly exhilarating and terrifying sport. For 15 brief minutes, you're flying high above the magnificent turquoise waters of Ölüdeniz with the mountains in the foreground. The safety factor? Not to be underestimated, but that nice body of water should break your fall. See "Fethiye & Ölüdeniz," in chapter 7.

- **Ballooning over Cappadocia:** Watch this surreal landscape change character right before your eyes: In a matter of minutes, the sun rises over the cliffs, valleys, and ravines, and colors morph from hazy blue to orange, pink, and finally yellow. The capper? A post-flight champagne breakfast. See "Exploring the Region," in chapter 8.

- **Spending the (Hopefully Romantic) Night in a Cave:** The ceilings are low, the light is dim, and there are niches in the wall for your alarm clock—this is the troglodyte life as the Cappadocians lived it for thousands of years. Some of these "cave hotels" are rudimentary, others extravagant; but all are cool in summer, warm in winter, and as still as the daybreak. See chapter 8.

2 The Best Small Towns

- **Assos:** Both hilltop and waterfront, Assos (known interchangeably by the name of the modern village on site, Behramkale) is a picturesque slice of the Turkish Aegean that is fast fading into oblivion. The ancient ruins and village life intermingle, while the fishing port below welcomes weary travelers with lovely little quay-front hotels and a fabulously tiny stretch of sand. See "Assos," in chapter 5.

- **Alaçatı:** A hilltop mound of windmills and 800-year-old Selçuk barrelhouses guard the entrance to the tiny Aegean village of Alaçatı. So close to the sea, and yet so far . . . See "Highlights of the Çeşme Peninsula," in chapter 6.

- **Şirince:** Originally a sanctuary for Greeks in the dying days of Ephesus, this dense hillside of preserved houses enclosed within a landscape of grape orchards is the perfect antidote to an overdose of archaeological sites. A bottle of local wine enjoyed amid the atmosphere of a former schoolhouse helps the medicine go down, too. See p. 224.

- **Gümüşlük:** The chance to walk on water—or nearly so—thanks to the sunken city walls of ancient Myndos—what more could one want? How about an undiscovered enclosed bay, a beach, and waterfront fish shacks. See "Bodrum," in chapter 6.

- **Karmylassos/Kayaköy:** Haunting panoramas of lives interrupted blanket the hillside of this once-thriving Greek settlement, abandoned during the 1924 population exchange between Turkey and Greece. Rather than reinhabit the houses—now crumbling and roofless—local Turkish residents have settled in the rolling and fertile plains of the surrounding valley. See p. 276.

- **Kaleköy:** Also known as Simena, this seaside village clings to the side of the rock more efficiently than its sunken neighbors. With only 300 inhabitants living practically on top of one another, the town is too small to even have a street; a haphazard nonsystem of paths weaves around the village houses. There's no such thing as trespassing—it's just blissfully simple. See "Kaş," in chapter 7.

- **Ayvalı:** The smell of apricots permeates the village as the harvest blankets the roofs of the flat-topped houses. Down in the valley is an almost eerie grouping of cave facades that retain the curvy lines of the smooth cave surfaces. At sunset, the sound of drums in the distance and the image of village women baking the evening meal's bread in ancient rock ovens create an unforgettable vision of rural life. See p. 338.

3 The Best Ruins & Archaeological Sites

- **Troy:** It's taken archaeologists more than a century to try and undo the damage done by Heinrich Schliemann. There's still a way to go, but the progress made here in the past 10 years alone is remarkable. Troy is quite a sight. See "Troy," in chapter 5.

- **Pergamum:** Pergamum was once one of the most influential societies in the ancient world. Only traces of its greatness remain—but high atop the hillside, the acropolis still sings the songs of the wind through its broken pillars. The theater is the most extraordinary remnant of this forgotten society, clinging stubbornly to the side of a hill that overlooks a fruitful and expansive plain. See "Bergama & Pergamum," in chapter 6.

- **St. John's Basilica** (Selçuk): Most of the marble or cut-stone ruins you'll see in Turkey are ankle-high, a shadowy evocation of what once was. That's why the preserved redbrick walls of St. John's Basilica create such a pleasantly unexpected surprise. This holy site retains the soul of its original purpose; pilgrims gather around the presumed saint's tomb in an unabashed atmosphere of goodwill. See p. 224.

- **Sardis:** Famed for its synagogue (impressively restored and preserved), the Jewish community's place of worship was hardly the main attraction when the city was the capital of ancient Lydia or splendid outpost of the Roman Empire. The intact shops, remnants of the bath house, and soaring gymnasium walls cover just a small portion of the 290-acre expanse that was Sardis. See p. 211.

- **Ephesus:** Ephesus is among the best-preserved ancient sites in the Mediterranean, rivaled only by Pompeii. Frankly, it's humbling to see how efficiently life functioned before the advent of mechanized whatnots. The partially reconstructed Library of Celsus, the newly excavated portions of the terraced housing, and the strangely evocative Public Latrine are a few highlights of this sprawling, marble-strewn site. See "Selçuk & Ephesus," in chapter 6.

- **Ancient Theatre** (Hierapolis): The acoustics are as great down in the pit as they were 3,000 years ago. The extreme upper tiers overlook the great expanse of ancient Hierapolis—and now, thanks to UNESCO, unobstructed views of Pamukkale's whitening terraces. See "Pamukkale & Hierapolis," in chapter 6.

- **Aphrodisias:** Blessed by the proximity of nearby quarries of white and blue-gray marble, it's no wonder that this ancient city hid an unprecedented quantity of sculpture. The site itself also preserves an unusually concentrated collection of grand Hellenistic monuments. See "A Side Trip to Aphrodisias," in chapter 6.

- **Lycian Tombs:** Expertly carved into inaccessible vertical cliffs to resemble a classical temple, the Lycian tombs and sarcophagi are mysterious and dramatic, with their Gothic headdresses perched above the ghosts of royalty. The best spots to see them? Dalyan, Kaunos, Myra, and while boating the pristine waters of Kekova Bay. See "Boat Trips to the Sunken City," in chapter 7.

- **Cappadocia Monasteries and Underground Cities:** What do you get when you combine an amazing feat of engineering and artistry in fresco? You get ancient painted chapels—arches, pilasters, and all—carved into rock, and a hideaway for the earliest Christians fleeing from persecution. See chapter 8.

- **Yazılıkaya:** The stony lineup of cone-headed deities at this sacred Hittite shrine is undeniably more impressive in person than in pictures. The true mystery is who was the first to discover Chamber B, a room of enigmatic carved reliefs inconspicuously hidden inside a jagged chasm in the rock? See p. 383.

4 The Best Museums, Mosques & Churches

- **Blue Mosque** (Istanbul): This landmark mosque assumes a stance of authority over Sultanahmet Park. Just under the dome, hundreds of stained-glass windows sparkle like jewels. The blue of the mosque actually changes to yellow, orange, and red, depending on the time of day and the entrance you choose to use. See p. 110.

- **Ayasofya** (Istanbul): When faced with the dome of this masterpiece, it's tempting to mimic the actions of Mehmet the Conqueror almost 600 years ago and drop to your knees in a gesture of utter humility. The sensation is increased by the low level of filtered light that finds its way in, temporarily blinding you to everything except the source of illumination. See p. 84.

- **Topkapı Palace** (Istanbul): Perspective check—this was once somebody's *house.* Actually, it was the home of a whole lot of people—up to 5,000 at a time, all in the service of one man. Six hundred years of Ottoman history, and it's all behind these grand ornamental gates. See p. 116.

- **Istanbul Archaeology Museum** (Istanbul): This is one of those must-see museums that all too many overlook. It's actually the largest museum in the country, chronicling in stone both the life of Istanbul and of Byzantium's emperors. Recovered artifacts date back to 6000 B.C. (as of the time of this writing) and proceed through the centuries. A separate building houses the Museum of the Ancient Orient, exhibiting artifacts obtained during the course of the Ottoman period. See p. 159.

- **St. Savior in Chora** (Istanbul): An empire's devotion to the faith is mirrored in the opulence of the finest preserved collections of **Byzantine mosaics** just about anywhere. See p. 127.

- **Ephesus Museum** (Selçuk): Not all of the treasures of Ephesus were smuggled out of the country to end up in Western museums. There's certainly enough here to keep you busy for a while; the explanations are succinct and the labeling clear. Now you'll finally know the story behind those omnipresent souvenir statues of the little god Beş. See p. 216.

- **Bodrum Underwater Archaeology Museum:** The only one of its kind, the Underwater Archaeology Museum displays the vast findings from the discovery of a pre-14th-century shipwreck. All the more amazing, because when divers stumbled on it, all they were looking for were a few sponges. See p. 243.

- **Underground Cities of Derinkuyu & Kaymaklı:** In Cappadocia, not everyone got a room with a view—at least not if your life was at stake. These multilevel cave cities, thought to date back to the 2nd century B.C., have supported up to 20,000 people at once in times of danger and religious persecution (though some speculation puts the number closer to 60,000). Clamber through the surprisingly intricate warren of passageways and

living quarters where entire villages thrived in safety and darkness for months at a time. But claustrophobes beware—it's very dark and sometimes very snug. See p. 354.

- **Open-Air Museums of Zelve & Göreme:** When you live amid a landscape composed primarily of porous volcanic tufa, it doesn't take long before you realize, "Hey, I could make a great house out of this stuff." In Göreme you'll see cave churches decorated with stunning medieval frescoes; the ingenious structures at Zelve are more a window into daily living, troglodyte-style. See p. 339 and 345.

- **Museum of Anatolian Civilizations** (Ankara): It's rare that a museum has the material to catalog a culture's backbone from beginning to end—but here, it happens. Looking for prehistoric cave paintings of Cappadocia's volcanoes? Got it. How about detailed archives of commerce from 2000 B.C.? Got that, too. See p. 375.

5 The Best Beaches

Most of Turkey's best beaches have been snatched up by big hotel chains or full-service entertainment beach clubs—leaving less-than-stellar public alternatives. Thankfully, those big operations can't fit everywhere, so there are still enough charming patches of sand to go around. Either way, you will most likely find yourself on a strip of sand (or pebbles) where use of a lounge chair will cost you at minimum 3€ ($4.35/£2.15) per day. The bonus: Hotels and beach clubs (even the small ones) have snack bars, watersports, and clean toilets; and for the most part, the beaches have been left in their natural states.

- **Alaçatı Bay** (Çeşme Peninsula): The small beach here opens up to an enormous bay blessed with lofty winds—paradise for windsurfers. The high

winds are attributed to the sizable stretch of shallow water and the absence of anything obstructing it. The beach is backed by hills, hills, and more hills, all topped by dry, barren brush. See "Highlights of the Çeşme Peninsula," in chapter 6.

- **Pırlanta Beach** (Çeşme Peninsula): Pırlanta, which means "diamond" in Turkish, describes the creamy whiteness of this sandy stretch of the peninsula. The beach is long and wide and faces the open Aegean. It's also easily accessible by *dolmuş* (minivan-type public transportation) from Çeşme's town center. See "Highlights of the Çeşme Peninsula," in chapter 6.

- **Altınkum Beach** (Çeşme Peninsula): The golden-colored sand from which the beach takes its name is located in a relatively hard-to-find spot at the southernmost tip of the peninsula. Luckily, this only serves to keep this public park blissfully empty and undervisited. Because this beach faces the open sea, the water is a refreshing few degrees cooler than elsewhere on the peninsula. See "Highlights of the Çeşme Peninsula," in chapter 6.

- **Ayayorgı Beach** (Çeşme Peninsula): This is not a beach per se, but a few narrow concrete piers jutting out over the water. Nevertheless, Ayayorgı is a charming spot, hidden in an overgrowth of orange and olive groves and open to a small and intimate cove. See "Highlights of the Çeşme Peninsula," in chapter 6.

- **Türkbükü** (Bodrum Peninsula): Still waters embraced by the shoreline of twin villages characterize this part of the peninsula. The jet set may need to find alternative haunts now that the mayor has announced the dismantling of all of the private access beach clubs. By the time you read this, the magical destination of Türkbükü may have opened up its shoreline to the common man. See "Bodrum," in chapter 6.

- **Ölüdeniz Beach** (Ölüdeniz): The posters just don't do it justice. On one end is the great expanse of Belcekız Beach, enclosed by the brittle silhouette of Babadağ and the landing pad for paragliders sporting jet-propulsion packs. And on the beach is the jaw-dropper, the Blue Lagoon made real: still waters in no less than three shades of turquoise. See "Fethiye & Ölüdeniz," in chapter 7.

- **Butterfly Valley** (Fethiye): After reaching the Blue Lagoon—the holy grail of Turkish beaches—it seems odd to want to go elsewhere. But the Fethiye area abounds with stunning scenery. If you can tear yourself away

from the main event, take the 30-minute boat ride to Butterfly Valley, a sandy paradise hewn out of a soaring gorge. See "Fethiye & Ölüdeniz," in chapter 7.

- **Iztuzu Beach** (Dalyan): There are strict rules of conduct here: Iztuzu Beach is a national preserve and breeding ground for the Caretta Caretta, or loggerhead turtle. But at night, after the crowds have gone home, you can watch the lights move out to sea, or listen to the sounds of home life glide over the river from a nearby fishing village. Just don't wander too close to the waterline, and on behalf of the turtles, stay away from the off-limits areas. See "Dalyan & Kaunos," in chapter 7.

- **Kaputaş Beach** (near Kalkan): Hundreds of years ago, a huge chasm opened up the side of the mountain face. The gorge has dried up, but what's left is Kaputaş Beach, a small, sandy patch 400 steps down from the highway that feels like the middle of nowhere. From here, it's just a short swim to some nearby phosphorescent caves. See "Kalkan," in chapter 7.

- **Patara Beach** (near Kalkan): Eighteen kilometers (11 miles) of beach backed by dunes and marshlands—need I say more? The Mediterranean rises to the challenge in the summer, when it turns a deep shade of blue. See "Kalkan," in chapter 7.

- **Konyaaltı** (Antalya): The newly developed waterfront in center-city Antalya breathes new life into a seaside resort that risked second-rate status. Miles of pebble beaches, waterfront promenades, meandering lawns, cafes, and activities make this one of Turkey's most coveted destinations. Bodrum, look out! See "Antalya," in chapter 7.

6 The Best One-of-a-Kind Places to Stay

- **Çırağan Palace** (Istanbul; *800/ 426-3135* in the U.S., 800/363-0366 in Canada, 0800/868-588 in the U.K., 800/623-578 in Australia, 0800/446-368 in New Zealand, or 0212/258-3377 in Istanbul): More than just Istanbul's poshest hotel, the Çırağan Palace is a destination in its own right. The grandeur of the lobby—tinted by light coming through the stained glass and imbued with the fragrance of fresh roses—hardly prepares you for what's to come. Expect regal gardens, a delicious Bosphorus-side pool, flawless service, and big fluffy beds. Make sure you splurge for that sea view, or all bets are off. See p. 93.

- **Four Seasons Hotel** (Istanbul; *800/332-3442* in the U.S., or 0212/638-8200): Nothing drives home the magnitude of this hotel's history more than to watch a former political prisoner once incarcerated here break down and cry in the hallway. Some original tile and marble details were preserved in the renovation, and you might encounter the rough etchings of an inmate's name in one of the columns. But these days the unqualified opulence of this grand hotel couldn't be further from its bread-and-water past. The new (anyone's guess in 2008) **Four Seasons the Bosphorus** promises the royal treatment—centered around the Atik Paşa mansion. See p. 94.

- **Les Ottomans** (Istanbul; *0212/ 359-1500*): You'll find rooms truly fit for royalty here—that is, if you can get a reservation. Every detail, from the chandeliers, to the salon chairs, to the bedding, is a unique creation that underlines this very personalized place. See p. 94.

- **Ada Hotel** (Türkbükü, Bodrum Peninsula; *0252/377-5915*): If you're looking for quintessential Turkish elegance, the Ada Hotel's got it, and more. Characteristic, stylish, romantic, and utterly memorable, all rolled into a boutique experience on the hillside above the trendy yet serene outpost of Türkbükü. See p. 249.

- **The Marmara Bodrum** (*0252/ 313-8130*): Deluxe, sleek, and breathtakingly situated—the Marmara sometimes feels more like an art gallery than a hotel, though infinitely more inviting. In your spare time, slink an hour in the hotel spa's saltwater flotation tank. See p. 248.

- **Hillside Su** (Antalya; *0242/249-0700*): The over-the-top, snow-blinding white design concept is sleek and razor-sharp in its wit. See p. 323.

- **Aboard a Gulet** (the Turquoise Coast): The blazing August sun gives way to a mild summer night, and you wake up at dawn with your shipmates on the rear deck of the gulet, covered in fresh morning dew. There's nothing like sleeping under the stars in a cove along the shores of the Mediterranean. See "All About the Blue Voyage," on p. 42.

- **A Cappadocian Cave Hotel** (Cappadocia): Truly, where else could sleeping in a cave be so sweet? The secret is out, and every year the hotels entice you with more and more romance. I'm convinced, but I'm preaching to the converted. See chapter 8.

7 The Best Stuff to Bring Home

- **Carpets & Kilims:** No matter how lame your bargaining skills, it's still cheaper than Bloomingdale's—and boy, do they look good unrolled under (or on) your coffee table. Turkey's tribal carpets and kilims represent a cultural tradition that goes back for centuries. The symmetrical designs we're most accustomed to are found in rugs from **Kayseri** and Hereke—the latter traditionally boasts the most exquisite silk-on-silk showpieces.

- **Ottoman Books & Rare Prints:** The Ottomans were masters of calligraphy, embellishing the page with dust from sapphires, lapis lazuli, gold, and other gems. Miniatures generally represent scenes from the life of a sultan and his family, with colorful shades to give the page life. One of the most valuable of originals or reproductions is the *tugra,* the sultan's elaborately ornate and personal seal. The **Sahaflar Çarşısı** in Istanbul is the best place to find these treasures, as are the streets near **Tünel** in Beyoğlu. See "Shopping" in chapter 4.

- **Turkish Delight:** This gummy, marshmallowy treat made of dried nuts, fruits, syrup, and cornstarch is a national favorite. I personally hate the stuff, but to each his own. It's known as *lokum* in Turkish—a word also used to refer to a voluptuous woman. The best *lokum* is available at **Hacı Bekir** in Istanbul (see "Shopping" in chapter 4), but you can find it at the Egyptian Bazaar or in practically every *pastane,* or souvenir shop.

- **Pottery & Ceramics:** These arts thrived under the Ottomans, whose skilled craftsmen perfected the coral red and cobalt blue of the Iznik tile. No one has ever been able to reproduce the intensity of these colors,

until now. The only authentic reproductions come out of the **Iznik Foundation**'s workshop and showroom in Iznik (see "Bursa: Gateway to an Empire" in chapter 4), which has a branch in Istanbul (see "Shopping" in chapter 4). Ordinary but equally stunning porcelain designs on white clay come from Kuthaya and are sold throughout Turkey.

- **Turkish Textiles:** Check the manufacturer's label on your fine linens, terry-cloth supplies, and cotton T-shirts. I bet you didn't realize it, but Turkey exports a huge amount of textiles, supplying the raw materials for well-known retailers such as OP, Calvin Klein, Walt Disney, and XOXO. **Bursa** and **Pamukkale** are both famous for the quality of their goods; many Istanbul residents head to one of these towns to stock up on plush towels and terry-cloth robes. (Good-quality pieces can be had for under 7YTL/$6.10/£2.80.) Bursa is also famous for its silks. See "Bursa: Gateway to an Empire," in chapter 4, and "Pamukkale & Hierapolis," in chapter 6.

- **Copper:** Turks use copper for everything, probably because it looks so good (particularly the white copper). Tea servers with triangular handles pass you by countless times a day; the wide copper platters that double as tables represent typical Turkish style. Those shiny white bowls you see in a *hamam* are copper, too. For the best prices and selection, head to **Çadırcılar Caddesi,** near the Grand Bazaar (see "Shopping" in chapter 4), or **Bakırcılar Çarşısı,** near the citadel in Ankara (see "Shopping" in chapter 9).

- **Gold & Silver:** The price by weight is the same, but with labor so cheap

The Best Turkey Websites

The **Web** makes it simple to do additional research before you leave home. The following sites provide a range of information:

- **www.kultur.gov.tr** is the official site of the Turkish Ministry of Culture, and an excellent source for information and links to the country's major arts events.
- **www.tourismturkey.org** is the website of the Ministry of Tourism.
- **www.turkishdailynews.com** and **www.turkishpress.com**, the sites for Turkey's two English-language dailies, allow you to plug in to real-time issues.
- **www.mymerhaba.com** is for expatriates by expatriates, but it's useful to eavesdrop on them, too.
- **http://cat.une.edu.au** is a handy little resource which compiles information on all archaeological work being conducted in Turkey.
- **www.byzantium1200.com** provides an illustrated anthology of Byzantine sites in Istanbul.
- **www.istanbul2010.org** is the go-to site for all things cultural happening in Istanbul leading up to the city's reign as cultural capital of Europe.
- **www.tavairports.com** is operated by the company that manages Turkey's major airports.

you're bound to get a deal. Shopping thoroughfares glitter with the stuff— some of it attractive, some of it hideous. The **Istanbul Handicrafts Center** (see "Shopping" in chapter 4) has an atelier where an artisan crafts his own work. In **Ürgüp** (see "Ürgüp," in chapter 8), many of the pieces have local precious stones. Museum gift shops are also great sources of unique jewelry.

- **Foodstuffs:** The exoticism of the East is in full bloom at Istanbul's **Egyptian Spice Bazaar,** where you can find over five different types of saffron at prices that will ensure you

take home a sample of each. Although this isn't Tuscany, you won't know it by the quality of the olive oil; head to the local supermarket and stock up on a few bottles. The smoothest and most delicious is bottled by Komili. See "Shopping" in chapter 4.

- **Meerschaum Pipes:** Carved from the magnesium silicate found primarily in Eskişehir, these ivory-colored pipes are hollowed out and polished to mimic playful or grotesque images. The pipes are sold in most souvenir shops and make fun, frolicsome showpieces.

2

Planning Your Trip to Turkey

You've decided to experience for yourself the beauty, history, and hospitality of Turkey. What do you need to know before you go? All the basics are outlined in this chapter: the when, why, and how of traveling to, in, and around Turkey.

1 The Regions in Brief

Turkey really is where it all began. Although Greece gets the credit for having sown the seeds of Western civilization, for the most part this took place (with a good bit of help, too) on what is now Turkish soil. In Turkey, not only do you bear witness to the ancient nomadic civilizations with minor credits in the Old and New testaments, but you also have the opportunity to experience the absurdly rich cultural and historical mosaic laid by the ancient Greek, Persian, Selçuk, Byzantine, and Ottoman empires. Turkey is also the quintessential destination for sybarites: As an eastern Mediterranean country, it gives you the pearly sands of Iztuzu Beach, the turquoise waters of Lycia, the ski slopes of Uludağ, and the thermal springs of Bursa and Çeşme.

Turkey forms a natural bridge between two continents, occupying the westernmost point of Asia while attached to Europe by way of Thrace (the northwesterly region separated from the Asian continent by the Bosphorus Straits, the Sea of Marmara, and the Dardanelles). Turkey is surrounded by four seas: the Black Sea to the north separating Turkey from Russia, Ukraine, and Romania; the Aegean to the west; the Mediterranean to the south; and the Sea of Marmara. European borders are shared with Bulgaria and

Greece, with whom it still has maritime disputes; and in many resort towns along the Turkish coastline, you can skip a stone to the nearest Greek island. To the east and south, Turkey shares borders with Georgia, Armenia, Iran, Iraq, and Syria.

Persistent concerns about the political stability in the eastern and southeastern regions of Turkey, combined with a rudimentary tourist infrastructure, have discouraged all but the most intrepid tourists from venturing to these scenic and historically significant regions. For this reason, this guidebook does not include the regions of the southeast and east. (Space constraints require the exclusion of the Black Sea Coast as well.) Instead, this guidebook focuses on the bang-for-your-buck absolute musts for a first-time visit to Turkey's western half. Inevitably, the first time won't be your last.

ISTANBUL & ENVIRONS

Many people go to Istanbul expecting an Eastern, exotic city. While it's true that Istanbul is undeniably Asian in the way it operates, most visitors are surprised to find a familiar and infinitely inviting European metropolis. Home to three mighty empires and coveted by others for its strategic hold over access in and out of the Black Sea, Istanbul is truly the original *Jewel in the Crown*. The city itself has one foot in Europe and the other in Asia—the only place in the world where a ferry can transport you to a different continent every 15 minutes. The grandeur of the **Blue Mosque** and the **Ayasofya,** the opulence of **Dolmabahçe Palace,** the echo of intrigue behind the walls of **Topkapı,** and the soulful wail of the muezzin's call to prayer from one of the hundreds of graceful minarets all have the power to transport you to another era, an exotic culture, and another way of looking at the world.

But Istanbul, like any complex and important international city, is more than just the sum of its monuments. The outdoor tables of the **Kumkapı** district come to life with singing and dancing, fresh sea bass, and fried calamari, while craftsmanship and commerce vie for business almost everywhere you turn. The lush tea gardens of **Sultanahmet,** the gentrified **coffeehouses** of Galata, the dingy back-alley streets of **Eminönü** teeming with men and women in various layers of modern or Islamic dress, the crush of low-income weekenders lazing along the **Golden Horn,** and the bustle of the jewel-encrusted upper crust in the expensive and exclusive shops of **Nişantaşı**—all are genuine and undisputable facets of this complex city. Two months, let alone 2 days, would never be enough to discover it all.

Surrounded by water and served by multiple ferry and hydrofoil services, Istanbul can easily be a base for 1- or 2-day excursions to Bursa, Gallipoli, and Troy (see below), or even overnight flights to Cappadocia or Ephesus (unfortunately, leaving little time to visit the latter). Closer to home are the beach towns of the Black Sea and the popular getaways of the Princes' Islands.

AROUND THE SEA OF MARMARA & THE NORTH AEGEAN COAST

Any army with visions of presiding over Seraglio Point seems to have camped out in this region. Attached to the base of Mount Uludağ sits the city of **Bursa,** whose eminence as the first capital of the Ottoman Empire earned the city a host of **monumental tombs.** Seeing the final resting place of such a density of dead sultans is not the only reason to go there, however. Bursa is important for its Selçuk and early Ottoman architecture, and is famous for its natural **thermal springs;** no visit to the town would be complete without taking a dip in a hot mineral pool or mud bath.

A pilgrimage to the silent cliffs of the **Gallipoli Peninsula** is especially poignant for Australians and New Zealanders, who sent their boys off to one of the bloodiest campaigns of World War I. Here Turkish and Anzac (Australian and New Zealand Army Corps) units dug into trenches, exchanged cigarettes, and fought to the death. The charming fishing and port town of **Çanakkale** is primarily used as a base for excursions to Gallipoli and fills up beyond capacity with beer-drinking backpackers from Down Under every year on April 25 for the multiple, daylong memorial services commemorating Anzac Day.

Troy is Troy. Everybody says it's disappointing but nobody ever passes it by. That's the dilemma—where else can you get this close to Homer's *Iliad*, to Agamemnon, to Achilles, and to Warner Bros.' own rendition of the Trojan Horse?

Principal Hellenistic center and later a thriving Roman province, **Pergamum** (also accepted as Pergamon in written documentation), enjoyed an era of prosperity that endured for almost 400 years. Just on the outskirts of modern-day **Bergama,** Pergamum boasts one of Turkey's finest archaeological sites in the

Acropolis, with its **Temple of Athena,** the remnants of the **great library,** the **Altar of Zeus,** the spectacular hillside **theater,** and the **Agora.** The **Asklepion** was the world's first medical center, using groundbreaking techniques in healing such as bathing, dieting, exercise, and dream therapy. Down the road is the crumbling but impressive **Red Basilica,** originally a temple honoring Serapis (known in Egypt as Osiris), later to become a Byzantine church and one of the seven churches of Asia Minor mentioned by St. John in the Book of Revelation.

THE CENTRAL & SOUTHERN AEGEAN COASTS

Izmir, the third-largest city in Turkey and the most important port on the Aegean, is typically a stopover on the way in or out of the airport, or as a base for visits to Ephesus and Pamukkale. If you've planned a day in town, take a picturesque seaside walk along the **Kordon** in Alsancak or mill around **Konak Square** to see the ornate architecture of the **clock tower**—the symbol of Izmir.

Only an hour away is the **Çeşme Peninsula,** site of expansive sandy beaches, scenic coves, historic ruins, and the many thermal springs from which it takes its name. The charming little seaside town of Çeşme is essentially the last sane stop before getting on the hedonistic highway of the Turquoise and Mediterranean coasts.

Kuşadası is the first in a long line of boisterous beach resort towns and a required stop on the cruise-ship circuit because of its convenient proximity to Ephesus. Because there is nothing of significant historical value in Kuşadası, much of the local travel business is geared toward getting you out of town; and, the archaeological ruins of **Didyma, Miletus,** and **Priene** are an easy day trip away. If you do stick around, a few noteworthy beaches in and around town offer an array of watersports options as well as several enchanting tea gardens within the castle walls.

No trip to Turkey is complete without a firsthand look at the breathtaking **limestone travertines of Pamukkale,** restored to their original luster through the efforts of UNESCO. Although it is no longer possible to shed your footwear and stroll along the snow-white terraces, the sheer magnitude of this enormous calcium formation is astounding. The Romans seem to have always established cities near curative waters, and the remains of the city of **Hierapolis,** along with its baths, acropolis, and theater, are all located on-site.

The most important Roman center in the Asian Provinces and one of the best-preserved antique civilizations in the world, **Ephesus** is the most frequented tourist destination in all of Anatolia. Visitors flock here for the **Library of Celsus,** the **Marble and Arcadian Ways,** and the **Great Theatre,** along with an impossible legacy left to the ancient city through centuries of Greek, Roman, and Byzantine daily life.

The town of **Selçuk** is usually snubbed by visitors to Ephesus, and the few who do stop in usually make a beeline for the archaeological findings in the **Ephesus Museum,** the **House of the Virgin Mary,** and the mysterious remains of the **Temple of Artemesion. St. John's Basilica,** built by Justinian in the 6th century in honor of John, who came to Ephesus in the company of the Virgin Mary, should be included on every faith tour to Turkey; the **Isabey Mosque,** exemplifying Muslim acceptance of the Christian and Jewish prophets, is also worth a visit. A side trip to the former Greek winemaking village of **Şirince** offers another view of typical Turkish life, and the nearby beaches of **Pamucak** are there for anyone going through beach withdrawals.

After 10 years of merciless tourism, the whitewashed hillside and unspoiled bays that make up **Bodrum** are still revered by the Turks as *the* place to vacation. It's the original disembarkation point for the romanticized *Mavi Yolculuk,* or **Blue Voyage,** a watery retreat with no distractions but pine cliffs, still expanses of water, and endless days of blissful tranquillity.

Beyond the infamous and cutting-edge nightlife of Bodrum's center, Bodrum offers the ruins of the ancient **Mausoleum** (though now a sad shadow of its former self), and the **Underwater Archaeological Museum,** the only museum in the world of its kind and keeper of the oldest known shipwreck, dating to the 14th century B.C. The museum is housed in the **Castle of St. Peter,** a 15th-century fortress built by the Knights of St. John. The castle is perched above the twin bays of Bodrum, presenting breathtaking views from every vantage point. It is also here that the tours for daily and weekly boat excursions pick up momentum.

THE TURQUOISE & MEDITERRANEAN COASTS

The Aegean meets the Mediterranean at the tip of the Datça Peninsula, the rugged and mountainous outpost west of Marmaris. The Blue Voyage continues in the craggy inlets and crystalline waters around **Datça, Hisarönü, Türünç, İçmeler,** and **Marmaris,** in short daylong versions or full weeklong gulet cruises (the traditional broad-beamed boat), departing from **Netsel Marina,** arguably the best marina in the eastern Mediterranean.

If you've skipped the Blue Voyage, be sure to at least plan a day trip along the **Dalyan River** to see the enigmatic **Lycian rock-cut tombs,** to walk along the protected beaches of **Iztuzu** where the loggerhead turtles lay their eggs, and to mingle with the goats in the ancient city of **Kaunos.**

Not just a turnaround port for cruises back to Marmaris, **Fethiye** and its surroundings make up one of the most enchanting spots on the Mediterranean. A stroll past the marina promenade reveals the ancient city of **Telmessos,** with its limestone **rock tombs,** its **amphitheater,** and the old city, characterized by narrow streets and squares lined with shops, coffeehouses, and restaurants. The surrounding area is also a paradise for nature lovers and athletes alike. An 8km (5-mile) drive through mountainous terrain brings you to **Ölüdeniz Beach,** set below the splendor of **Babadağ,** which provides paragliders with the perfect conditions for a wondrous flight. Down the beach are the pristine waters of the **blue lagoon** from which *Ölüdeniz* (dead sea) takes its name. A detour off the road between Ölüdeniz and Fethiye brings you to the abandoned Greek village of **Kayaköy,** a haunting reminder of the population exchange of 1923. The untouched **Butterfly Valley,** accessible only by boat, is a nature lover's dream, where during the months of April and May the bright red Tiger butterfly breaks free of its cocoon. **Saklıkent Gorge** is another wonder of natural design, with torrents of icy water carving an extraordinary path through the rock. The ancient historic sites along this part of the coast, including **Tlos, Xanthos, Letoon,** and **Patara,** which boasts an unbroken 13km (8-mile) sandy beach, are some of the richest and best preserved in the region.

Often mistaken for a fishing village, **Kalkan** is a glossy seaside village nestled at the foot of the Taurus Mountains. Nearby **Kaputaş Beach** is a breathtaking result of a gorge in the making, and the beaches of **Patara** are only 20 minutes away.

When all of the tourists left for Kalkan, the charming fishing village of **Kaş** was left much the way it was before the tourists chewed it up and spit it out. The tourist infrastructure has remained, and you will find a quiet town dotted with a few **Lycian tombs,** a 6th-century-B.C. **amphitheater,** and lots of pleasant shopping. Kaş is also the departure point for active excursions like kayaking, mountain biking, diving, and canyoning, as well as the must-do day trip to the sunken city of **Kekova,** which makes stopovers at the ancient village of **Simena,** now a fishing village of some 300 inhabitants. The nearby town of **Demre** lies shoulder to shoulder with the ancient Lycian city of **Myra,** and it was here that the bishop of Myra left his legacy and came to be known as **St. Nicholas.** The ancient site of **Olympos,** with its "fire-breathing" **Chimaera,** lies halfway between Kaş and Antalya, and few take the time to follow the oleander-laden and winding road down from the highway to this waterfront outpost.

Eastward, beyond the rocky coves of Lycia, are the pearly sand beaches of Turkey's Turquoise Coast. **Antalya** is the Mediterranean coast's main port city, as well as Turkey's principal holiday resort. The citadel walls of the **Kaleiçi** district enclose a typically Ottoman residential neighborhood, providing a majestic backdrop to the marina below. Nearby are the ancient ruins of **Termessos,** easily visited as a day excursion from anywhere along the Gulf of Antalya.

CAPPADOCIA & THE INTERIOR

Arriving into **Cappadocia** is as much like getting a part as an extra in *Lost in Space* as you can get. The phallic **"fairy chimneys"** were formed by thousands of years of rugged winds and rain, and in fact, the same type of erosion continues today. In **Üçhisar, Göreme,** and **Ürgüp,** not only can you ogle the **rock caves** from afar, but you also can actually sleep in one. In the valleys of Cappadocia, you can visit some of the hundreds of incredible **frescoed chapels** and **cave churches** from the Iconoclastic and Byzantine eras. The troglodyte cities of **Derinkuyu** and **Kaymaklı** present a sobering image of persecution, where Christians, along with their livestock, hid hundreds of feet below ground, and where a detour down a dark tunnel will teach you just how dark dark can really be.

Beyond the wonder of Cappadocia is the industrial town of **Kayseri,** holding particular interest for scholars of Selçuk art and architecture.

ANKARA

The capital of Turkey since 1923 and the administrative center of the country, Ankara is nothing if not clean, modern, and efficient. Lacking in the kind of history that attracts visitors to Istanbul, Ankara merits at least a trip to **The Museum of Anatolian Civilizations,** one of the best museums of its kind, displaying a comprehensive collection of treasures from the beginning of the history of man as we know it. The **Atatürk Mausoleum** is Turkey's equivalent of the Kennedy Memorial, honoring a forward-thinking man without whom modern Turkey would now be a Greek colony. Left over from an earlier era are the **Column of Julian,** the **Temple of Augustus,** and the **Roman Baths.** A visit to the old **citadel** or dinner within the castle walls should be part of any itinerary in Ankara.

Ankara is also an excellent base for excursions to **Hattuşaş,** home to the great Hittite kingdom for more than a thousand years, and the nearby sanctuary of **Yazılıkaya.**

2 Visitor Information & Maps

Everyone's first stop for comprehensive information on Turkey as well as visa requirements should be the Turkish Embassy website specific to one's country (**www.turkey.org** or **www.tourismturkey.org** in the U.S., **www.turkishembassy.com** in Canada, **www.turkishembassy.org.au** in Australia, and

www.gototurkey.co.uk in the U.K.). The Embassy also administers a "consulate online" in English at **www.tr consulate.org** providing up-to-date information and, although completely unnecessary, visas in advance of arrival.

The Turkish Ministry of Culture (**www.kultur.gov.tr**) has an excellent website that contains cultural information, events, regional resources, and current-events articles. Two other great sights for current information are **www.gate toturkey.com**, which also puts out *The Gate* magazine available in Istanbul airports, and **www.mymerhaba.com**, created by expats for expats living in Turkey.

In the U.S., the **Turkish Government Tourist Office** has a presence in both New York City and Washington, D.C.: at 821 United Nations Plaza, New York, NY 10017 (© **212/687-2195**), and at 2525 Massachusetts Ave., Suite 306, Washington, DC 20008 (© **202/612-6800**), where you can stock up on maps, brochures, ferry schedules to Greece, and access to practical information via an interactive computer database.

TURKISH EMBASSIES & CONSULATES

IN THE U.S. For residents of Maryland, Virginia, Washington, D.C., West Virginia, and The Bahamas: Turkish Embassy, 2525 Massachusetts Ave. NW, Washington, DC 20008 (© **202/612-6700**; fax 202/612-6744; consular section: © 202/612-6741; fax 202/319-1639; www.turkey.org).

For residents of Alabama, Arkansas, Louisiana, Missouri, New Mexico, Oklahoma, Tennessee, and Texas: Turkish Consulate, 1990 Post Oak Blvd., Suite 1300, Houston, TX 77056 (© **713/622-5849**; fax 713/623-6639).

For residents of Alaska, Arizona, California, Colorado, Hawaii, Idaho, Montana, Nevada, Oregon, Utah, Washington State, Wyoming, and the Pacific Islands: Turkish Consulate, 6300 Wilshire Blvd., Suite 2010, Los Angeles, CA 90048 (© **323/655-8832**; fax 323/655-8681; www.trconsulate.org).

For residents of Illinois, Indiana, Iowa, Kansas, Michigan, Minnesota, Mississippi, Nebraska, North Dakota, Ohio, South Dakota, and Wisconsin: Turkish Consulate, 360 Michigan Ave., Suite 1405, Chicago, IL 60601 (© **312/263-0644**; fax 312/263-1449).

For residents of Connecticut, Delaware, Florida, Georgia, Kentucky, Maine, Massachusetts, New Hampshire, New Jersey, New York, North Carolina, Pennsylvania, Rhode Island, South Carolina, Vermont, and Puerto Rico: Turkish Consulate, 821 United Nations Plaza, New York, NY 10017 (© **212/949-0160**; fax 212/983-1293).

IN CANADA Turkish Embassy, 197 Wurtemburg St., Ottawa, ON K1N 8L9 (© **613/789-4044**; fax 613/789-3442; www.turkishembassy.com). Also, Turkish Embassy Tourism Section, 360 Albert St., Suite 801, Ottawa, ON K1N 8L9 (© **613/789-4044**; fax 613/789-3442).

IN AUSTRALIA & NEW ZEALAND Turkish Embassy, Canberra, 6 Moona Place, Yarralumla, ACT 2600 (© **02/6234-0000**; fax 02/6273-6592; www.turkishembassy.org.au).

IN THE U.K. Turkish Embassy, 43 Belgrave Sq., London SW1X 8PA (© **020/7393-0202**; fax 020/7393-0066; www.turkishembassylondon.org). The Turkish Consulate General is at Rutland Lodge, Rutland Gardens, Knightsbridge SW7 1BW (© **020/7589-0360**; fax 020/7584-6235). The Turkish Culture and Tourism Office is at 170–173 Piccadilly, London W1J 9EJ (© **020/7629-7771**; fax 020/7491-0773; www.gototurkey.co.uk).

3 Entry Requirements

VISAS

An entry visa is required for citizens of the U.S. ($29 for a single entry for stays up to 3 months), Canada (US$60 or 45€ on arrival valid for 90 days and multiple entries), the U.K. (£10 on entry; £50 in advance for multiple entries up to 3 months), and Australia (A$68 on arrival), while a valid passport is sufficient for citizens of New Zealand.

There is no need to acquire an entry visa prior to departure, because obtaining one on arrival is a no-brainer (go to the visa window next to and before clearing customs and fork over the required cash); besides, in many cases it will be more expensive if you apply for one in advance. (See "Arriving at the Airport," later.)

MEDICAL REQUIREMENTS

There are no special medical requirements for entry into Turkey.

CUSTOMS

For information on what you can bring into and take out of Turkey, go to **"Customs"** in the **"Fast Facts"** section of this chapter.

4 When to Go

After a decade of some ups and mostly downs, Turkey's tourism industry is galloping at a nice clip, thank you very much. Almost 10 international hotel chains opened properties in Istanbul in 2007 alone, and the Hilton group is planning 25 additional hotels in Turkey in the coming years. So basically, if you're looking for a quiet bargain, the window of opportunity has long since passed. For the inconvenience of traveling on full flights, staying in hotels booked to capacity and paying top dollar for almost everything (except where the dollar sign has changed to the euro or British pound sterling), visitors will be greeted by a country of intriguing contradictions positively overflowing with optimism for a more prosperous future.

Turkey's Average Daytime Temperature (°F/°C)

	Jan	Feb	Mar	Apr	May	June	July	Aug	Sept	Oct	Nov	Dec
Antalya												
Temp. (°F)	50	52	55	61	68	77	82	82	77	68	59	54
Temp. (°C)	10	11	13	16	20	25	28	28	25	20	15	12
Izmir												
Temp. (°F)	48	50	52	61	68	77	82	81	73	64	59	50
Temp. (°C)	9	10	11	16	20	25	28	27	23	18	15	10
Istanbul												
Temp. (°F)	41	43	45	54	61	70	73	73	68	61	54	46
Temp. (°C)	5	6	7	12	16	21	23	23	20	16	12	8
Ankara												
Temp. (°F)	32	34	41	52	61	68	73	73	64	55	46	36
Temp. (°C)	0	1	5	11	16	20	23	23	18	13	8	2

Nevertheless, the seasonal ebbs and flows of tourism in Turkey follow some general patterns. The absolute best time to go is during the "shoulder season" months of April, May, mid- to late September, and October, when families send their kids

Travel Tip

Tickets for the main events around town can be purchased through Biletix (© 0216/556-9800; www.biletix.com) as well as at the following hotel concierge desks: Divan, Swissôtel, Four Seasons, Ritz-Carlton, Hyatt, Radisson SAS, Marmara, and Marmara Pera.

back to school, museum sites are less crowded, and the heat is pleasantly balmy. You might even need a sweater for the early morning chill or late-evening breezes, especially in Istanbul and on the steppes. Cappadocia is a great destination for rafting in the spring as well as for the autumn colors, while hiking, biking, and camping around the coastal villages are great spring or fall diversions.

Prices peak during high season, which loosely refers to July, August, and the first half of September, when the azure coastlines teem with sun-and-fun seekers. It can get excruciatingly hot during these months, especially in the hellish humidity of Antalya—perfect for a beachside or cruising vacation, but positively infernal under the blazing sun reflected off of the white stone and marble of archaeological sites.

In the winter the coastal towns shut down like a submarine before a descent, although things tend to miraculously reopen (at high-season pricing) for the Christmas and New Year's holidays. Cappadocia takes on an otherworldly wonderland aspect covered with a dusting of snow, but icy conditions may ruin a horseback-riding trek. Also, the hilltops of the Gallipoli Peninsula can get very wet and windy, so a pilgrimage to the battlegrounds may be best planned for the summertime.

CALENDAR OF EVENTS

Listed here is a selection of events wacky, weird, or wonderful enough (or all three) to go out of your way for. It would be impossible to list all of the local or regional festivals—besides, this book doesn't attempt to list all of Turkey's tourist destinations. But once arrived, keep your ear to the ground for colorful happenings such as the traditional *mesir* festival in Manisa, the International Pamukkale Song Competition, the Hittite Festival in Çorum, the Rose Festival in Isparta, the Golden Pistachio Festival in Gaziantep, and the Javelin games in Konya. For more information on these localized festivities, contact the tourism office in the corresponding region.

Islam follows the lunar calendar, which is shorter than the Gregorian calendar by 11 days. The result is that Muslim religious holidays fall on different dates each year. The dates for religious holidays listed here are accurate for 2008 and 2009.

For an exhaustive list of events beyond those listed here, check http://events.frommers.com, where you'll find a searchable, up-to-the-minute roster of what's happening in cities all over the world.

January

Camel Wrestling Festival, Selçuk. Did you know that as the temperature drops, a camel's aggression level rises? This event, scheduled erratically in January or February, provides a natural, if not inhumane, tension release as much for the poor beasts as for the testosterone-heavy locals nervously betting against the odds. The camels' mouths are bound to prevent biting, and 14 rope bearers stand by in case the scene starts to get out of hand. The last one to remain standing or in the ring wins. Sometime in January or February; dates vary.

March

Festival of Victory, Çanakkale. This festival celebrates the Turks' successful defense of the Dardanelles against invading British warships during World War I. Performances by the traditional Ottoman army *mehter* band, with its imposing cacophony of cymbals, horns, and percussion, can only suggest the terror instilled by the approaching Ottoman army. March 18.

April

International Istanbul Film Festival, Istanbul. This festival lasts 2 weeks, from the last Saturday of March to mid-April, offering movie buffs the rare opportunity to view Turkish movies with English subtitles. For schedules and tickets, contact travel agencies in Istanbul (© **0212/334-0700; www.istfest.org**). Early April.

Tulip Festival, Istanbul. The Tulip, widely accepted as having been imported from Holland and cultivated by an appreciative Turkish 17th-century society, is celebrated annually in Istanbul.

National Sovereignty and Children's Day, Istanbul and Ankara. This day celebrates the anniversary of the first Grand National Assembly, which met in Ankara in 1920 and was later decreed by Atatürk as Children's Day. The day is marked by parades and processions by schoolchildren. Banks and public offices are closed. April 23.

Anzac Day, Çanakkale. A trip to the Gallipoli Peninsula has become a sort of pilgrimage for Australians and New Zealanders indoctrinated into the folklore of the failed Allied invasion of the Straits. Memorial ceremonies begin at dawn and are staggered throughout the morning. Keep in mind that Çanakkale is bursting at the seams with Down-Unders who, although solemn and respectful by day, let loose in the bars at night. April 24 and 25.

International Music Festival, Ankara. Home of the country's first conservatory, symphonic orchestra, opera, ballet, and theater, Ankara shows the world its importance as a major cultural center each year during this international event. There are orchestral performances, chamber music, and Turkish contemporary artists playing traditional and folk music from all over the world. For schedules and tickets, contact the Sevda-Cenap & Music Foundation, Tunali Hilmi Sok. 114/26 (© **0312/427-0855;** www.ankarafestival.com). Late April to mid-May.

May

Festival of Culture and Art, Selçuk and Ephesus. The best part about this local festival is the use of the Great Theatre at Ephesus as a venue for some of the concerts and theatrical presentations. First week of May.

Youth & Sports Day. Atatürk arrived in Samsun on this day in 1919, which signifies the beginning of the Independence War. Students nationwide participate in athletic games, gymnastic events, and parades. May 19.

Fatih Festivities, Istanbul. This festival commemorates the conquest of Byzantium in 1453 by Sultan Fatih Mehmet with local celebrations. May 29.

June

Antalya Sand Sculpture Exhibition. Several dozen sand-sculpture artists convene from more than 14 countries to create temporary fantasies of oriental lore in sand. The exhibition takes place at a beach to be determined annually. For information, log on to www.prosandart.com. Mid-June through September.

Aspendos Opera and Ballet Festival. Live performances in the spectacular (now open-air) Theatre of Aspendos, the best-preserved theater of antiquity. For information, call © **0312/309-1409** or fax 0312/310-7248. June through July.

International Istanbul Music Festival. This world-class festival features big names in classical, opera, and ballet. Past artists have included La Scala Philharmonic, the Royal Coincertgebouw Orchestra, the Tokyo String Quartet, Itzhak Perlman, Idil Biret, and Burhan Öçal. For schedules and tickets, contact the Istanbul Foundation for Culture & the Arts (© **0212/293-3133;** www.istfest.org). Mid-June to mid-July.

International Izmir Festival. Not to be outdone by either Istanbul's numerous international festivals or the popular draw of Antalya's Aspendos Theatre venue, Izmir has proudly sponsored its own artistic extravaganza for more than 22 years (23, in 2009). A sampling of past feature productions include Sophocles's *Electra,* performed at the Celsus Library at Ephesus; the Royal Philharmonic Orchestra performance at Ephesus's Great Theatre; and the Izmir State Classical Turkish Music Chorus singing at the Alaçatı open-air theater in Çeşme. Tickets can be purchased at a number of box offices in Izmir, Bodrum, and Çeşme; for information go to www.iksev.org. Mid-June to mid-July.

Kırkpınar Oil Wrestling Tournaments, Edirne (Sarayiçi) and in villages around the country. This revered national sport involves the fittest of Turkish youth and astonishing amounts of olive oil to prevent the opponent from getting a good grip. The event is usually accompanied by a colorful market and fair. Late June/early July.

July

Cabotage Day. This maritime festival commemorates the establishment of Turkey's sea borders. Major ports with marinas usually celebrate with yacht races and swimming competitions. For more information, contact the Tourist Information Office of the town you will be visiting. July 1.

International Jazz Festival, Istanbul. Performances are held at various locations around the city. For schedules, dates, and tickets, contact the Istanbul Foundation for Culture & the Arts (© **0212/293-3133;** www.istfest.org).

Folklore and Music Festival, Bursa. One of Turkey's best folk-dancing events of the year, this festival features dance groups from around the country, lasts 1 week, and includes concerts and crafts displays. For more information and specific dates, contact the Bursa Foundation of Culture, Art, and Tourism (© **0312/427-1853**) or the Bursa Tourism Information Office (© **0224/251-1834**). Last 2 weeks in June through first week in July.

August

Assumption of the Virgin Mary, Ephesus. A special Mass conducted by the archbishop of Izmir celebrates the Assumption at the house of Mary. August 15.

Zafer Bayramı (Victory Day). This national holiday commemorates the decisive victory over the invading Greek armies during the War of Independence in 1922. Parades run through the main streets, and if you go soon, you may still brush elbows with some surviving vets. August 30.

International Ballet Festival, Bodrum. "Easy on the eyes" is an understatement when referring to the open-air dance performances staged under the warm glow of the night-lit castle of St. Peter. The annual festival hosts troupes from around the globe. Ticket sellers are ubiquitous on concert days; for advance information contact the

Bodrum tourist office (© **0312/324-2210;** www.devoperable.gov.tr/bodrum.html). Last 2 weeks in August.

International Mountain Biking Festival, Cappadocia. The Delta Bike Club celebrates the marriage of bicycles and monastic pathways with their annual mountain festival. The setting offers unbeatable peaks and valleys formed of ancient volcanic tufa, and various levels of difficulty (© **0312/223-6027;** www.deltabisiklet.com). End of August.

September

International Istanbul Biennial. The Istanbul Foundation for Culture and Arts puts on this major visual arts event organized around a current political or philosophical theme. Artists are selected from over 45 countries, whose innovative exhibitions are displayed around town, in clever venues like 500-year-old warehouses, deconsecrated churches and synagogues, and even commuter ferries (**www.iksv.org**). September 12 to November 8, 2009.

Şeker Bayramı (or Ramadan Baramı) is a 3-day celebration punctuating the end of Ramadan. The evening revelry reaches its peak during the last 3 evenings. Presents and sweets are given to the children (*şeker* means sugar in Turkish), and the Turkish Delight industry makes a killing. September 30 to October 3, 2008; September 19–22, 2009.

October

Akbank Jazz Festival. This 2-week-long festival brings the blues simultaneously to Istanbul, Ankara, and Izmir. Now in its 17th season, the festival hosts world-renowned performers in the cities' most atmospheric venues (© **0212/252-3500;** www.akbanksanat.com). Last 2 weeks in October.

Golden Orange Film Festival. For 44 years, Antalya has been the host of the Altın Portakal (Golden Orange) Film Festivali, Turkey's version of the Oscars. But with the 2005 inauguration of the Eurasia Film Festival, the combined event has made international waves and attracted the likes of Francis Ford Coppola, Sophie Marceau, and Miranda Richardson (© **0212/244-5251;** www.altinportakal.org.tr). Mid-October to mid-November.

Cumhuriyet Bayramı (Republic Day). This event celebrates the proclamation of the Republic of Turkey in 1923. Parades, public speeches, and firework displays are just a few of the organized events, but the Turks do their own celebrating as well. October 29.

November

Yachting Week, Marmaris. A star-studded international boating crowd gathers here to set sail for the Aegean or the Mediterranean. For information, call © **0252/455-3636,** or fax 0252/455-3650. First week in November.

Anniversary of Atatürk's Death. Turkey comes to a grinding halt at exactly 9:05am, when the population pays its respects to the father and founder of the Republic. Rather than a moment of silence, the streets and waterways echo with the blare of car horns and foghorns. Atatürk-related activities are planned for the day, such as conferences, speeches, and exhibitions, in addition to a memorial concert at the Atatürk Cultural Center's opera house. November 10.

December

Festival of St. Nicholas, Demre. Santa Claus actually lived on the Mediterranean, as bishop of Myra in the 4th century. A festival and symposium are held at the Byzantine church that honors old St. Nick. Early December.

Mevlana Festival, Konya. Whirling Dervishes believe that spiritual union with God is achieved through the *sema,* a trance-inducing dancing rite. The mystical ballet is shared with the public during this December festival, providing a window into one of Turkey's most precious cultural treasures. Book your tickets early, either through a travel agent or by contacting Konya's Tourism Information Office (© **0332/351-1074**). The week leading up to December 17.

Kurban Bayramı. In the Koranic version of an old favorite, it was Abraham's son Ismael, not Isaac, who was spared the knife. Kurban Bayramı celebrates Abraham's willingness to sacrifice his son, with 4 days of feasting and a death sentence to an alarming number of sheep the likes of which one only sees around Thanksgiving. In fact, the 4-day festival of sacrifice is the culmination of the Hajj (holy pilgrimage), and much of the meat is given to the poor. December 7–11, 2008; November 27 to December 1, 2009.

5 Getting There

BY PLANE

Partnerships among international airlines have blurred the lines of air travel, and changing market demands force airlines to continually adapt or change their services. Check with your travel agent or with the airlines directly for specific services.

FROM THE UNITED STATES & CANADA Turkish Airlines (© **800/ 874-8875;** www.turkishairlines.com) and **Delta Airlines** (© **800/221-1212;** www. delta.com) offer the only direct nonstop service to Istanbul from the U.S. Delta provides direct service from Atlanta (ATL) and New York (JFK). Turkish Airlines flies direct to Istanbul's Atatürk Airport (IST) from New York and Chicago (ORD). Meanwhile, Turkish Airlines announced that it would be instituting direct flights to Istanbul from Washington, D.C., in 2008, so keep your eyes open for this new service. These airlines are just the tip of the iceberg; most major international airlines flying to Istanbul offer flights from U.S. cities much too numerous to inventory, either as part of their own network or in partnership with an American airline. Choosing one involves a change of planes in the airline's home country hub, but this slight inconvenience is often accompanied by cheaper, more comparable fares.

Note: The following telephone numbers are for the U.S. and Canada. Log on to the airline websites for your local contact number. **Air France** (© 800/237-2747; www.airfrance.com), **Alitalia** (© 800/223-5730; www.alitalia.com), **Austrian Airlines** (© 800/843-0002; www.austrianair.com), **British Airways** (© 800/247-9297; www.british-airways. com), **Continental** (© 800/231-0856; www.continental.com), **Iberia** (© 800/ 574-8742; www.iberia.com), **KLM/ Northwest** (© 800/255-2525; www.nwa. com), **Lufthansa** (© 800/645-3880; www.lufthansa.com), **Swiss International** (© 877/359-7947; www.swiss.com), **United** (© 800/UNITED-1 [864-8331]; www.united.com), and **US Airways** (© 800/428-4322; www.usairways.com) all provide service to Istanbul. In addition, Lufthansa flies to Ankara (ANK) and Antalya (AYT), and Austrian Airlines flies to Ankara. More often than not, Turkish Airlines will provide the connecting flights to other Turkish destinations.

There are currently no direct flights to Turkey from Canada, but negotiations are on for Turkish Airlines to establish direct service, so keep your eyes open for this development. For now, **Air France, Alitalia, British Airways, Delta, KLM/ Northwest,** and **Lufthansa** all provide connecting service out of Toronto (YYZ). From Montreal (YUL), flights are available on **Air France, Alitalia, British Airways, Delta, Iberia, Northwest,** and **Lufthansa** (© 800/563-5954). Vancouver (YVR) is serviced by **British Airways, KLM/ Northwest** (via Seattle), and **Lufthansa.**

FROM THE UNITED KINGDOM

The only nonstop service to Istanbul out of London is provided by **British Airways** (© 0845/773-3377) and **Turkish Airlines** (© 20/7766-9300), which also flies nonstop from Manchester (© 161/ 489-5287). **Air France** (© 0845/082-0162), **Alitalia** (© 0870/544-8259), **Austrian Airlines** (© 0845/601-0948), **KLM/Northwest** (© 08705/074-074), **Lufthansa** (© 0845/7737-747), and **Olympic** (© 8706/060-460) offer connecting service through their home ports, providing service from many other major cities in the U.K. as well. There are also charter airline options. **Onur Air,** Şenlikköy Mahallesi Çatal Sok. 3 Florya (© **0212/663-9176;** www.onurair.com. tr), offers service from several U.K. cities into Dalaman (DLM), Bodrum (BJV), Izmir (ADB), and Antalya (AYT) via Istanbul; and from various cities throughout Europe. **SunExpress** (© **0232/444-0797;** www.sunexpress.com.tr) flies twice-weekly from London's Stansted Airport to Izmir in summer only. **British Airways** (© **0870/850-9850** in the U.K.; www.britishairways.com) flies direct from Gatwick to Izmir 4 days a week.

FROM AUSTRALIA & NEW ZEALAND

There are few choices for connecting flights to Turkey. In partnership with Turkish Airlines, **Qantas** (© 13-13-13 in Australia, 64-9/357-8900 in Auckland) will get you from Sydney,

Auckland, and Brisbane, connecting you to a Turkish Airlines flight into Istanbul. **Olympic Airways** (© 612/9251-2044 in Australia) has overnight flights from Sydney and Melbourne via Athens. Other flights from Sydney are offered on **British Airways** (© 1300/767-177 in Australia; 0800/274-847 in Auckland), **Singapore Airlines** (© 612/9350-0100), **KLM/ Northwest** (© 008/221-714), and **Lufthansa** (© 1300/655-727). From New Zealand, Singapore Airlines flies out of Auckland and New Plymouth; from Australia, British Airways flies out of Brisbane and Melbourne; and Lufthansa services Brisbane.

ARRIVING AT THE AIRPORT

IMMIGRATION & CUSTOMS CLEARANCE Visa windows are conveniently located adjacent to the immigration line at the port of entry; simply proceed to the visa counter *before* you get in the immigration line, and have your money ready—cash only, please. Visas obtained on entry can be paid in U.S. dollars, euros, or British pound sterling.

GETTING THERE BY TRAIN

Direct trains from Europe depart daily from Bucharest and Budapest and take about 27 and 40 hours, respectively—and that's without any border delays. It is your responsibility to obtain visas where required (either transit or tourist, depending on your travel plans) for every border that you will cross. If you're coming from Greece, trains leave regularly for Alexandropolis, where you must go through customs. You can catch a bus to Istanbul from the Alexandropolis train station. Depending on how long you get hung up at the border, it can take anywhere from 6 to 8 hours to get to Istanbul.

6 Money

It's always advisable to bring money in a variety of forms on a vacation: a mix of cash, credit cards, and traveler's checks.

You should also exchange enough petty cash to cover airport incidentals, tipping, and transportation to your hotel; you can

What Things Cost in Istanbul

Daytime taxi from airport to Sultanahmet	16YTL ($14/£6.40)
Nighttime taxi from airport to Sultanahmet	24YTL ($21/£9.60)
Havaş bus from airport to town	9YTL ($7.85/£3.60)
Double at Çırağan Palace with sea view	$765–$1,015 (£383–£508)
Double at the Apricot Hotel	59€–79€ ($86–$115/ £42–£56)
Dinner for one at the Four Seasons	50YTL ($44/£20)
Dinner for one at a *köftecisi* around town	15YTL ($13/£6)
Bosphorus cruise (round-trip) on public ferry	12.50YTL ($11/£5)
Bosphorus cruise with tour group	30YTL ($26/£12)
Ticket on bus, tram, or metro	1.30YTL ($1.15/50p)
Admission to Topkapı Palace and all exhibits	30YTL ($26/£12)
Taxi from Sultanahmet to Taksim	10YTL ($8.70/£4)
Glass of tea at Meşale tea gardens	2YTL ($1.75/80p)
Glass of tea in a carpet shop	Free

easily withdraw money upon arrival at an airport ATM located in the arrivals terminal.

Making the handling of Turkish money even easier, on January 1, 2005, the Turkish Central Bank lopped six zeros off a currency that saw phenomenal inflation in the past decade or so. But those were the old days. With a national economic growth rate rivaling that of China's, Turkey's economy is stronger than it's ever been. Meanwhile, those millionaire banknotes of yesteryear have been replaced with the New Turkish Lira (*yeni turk lirası,* or YTL). Banknotes come in denominations of 1, 5, 10, 20, 50, and 100YTL, while coins, called the New Kuruş, come in 1, 5, 10, 25, and 50 kuruş pieces. There is also a 1YTL coin. As of this writing, 1YTL cost about 40p, while the U.S. dollar had plummeted from 1.35YTL (where it hovered for the previous two editions of this book) to 1.25YTL. Prices quoted in this book are based on these rates of exchange. Both conversions appear in this book, but

because there is no consistency to which currency prices are quoted in Turkey (£, YTL, $), the currency in which the original fees were quoted appear first in the listings, followed by the conversion into £ and/or $ (1€=$1.45 or 71p). In cases where conversions don't add up, it's because prices were quoted in multiple currencies at the time of research. Oh, and I also round off (to the nickel/5 pence for amounts under 10 and by the dollar or pound for amounts over 10).

Until about 2 years ago, local prices were frequently quoted in U.S. dollars. But the weakness in the dollar has prompted a shift to the euro, which has resulted, for Americans at least, in a remarkable loss of value. Hotel rooms previously costing $80 per night now cost 80€, or $116, with no commensurate upgrade in services. *Note:* Where applicable, the dollar or pound is exchanged to the euro in this book based on a rate of $1.45=1€ and £1=1.40€.

Although I have tried to be as accurate as possible in quoting prices in this book, please be aware that there are a number of things working against me. Obviously, the fluctuation of exchange rates plays an enormous role. But equally capricious is the erratic nature of on-the-spot price quotes and market demand. Recent shocks in petroleum prices have also resulted in titanic increases in the cost of transportation in Turkey. Finally, don't be surprised if prices change in the time between when I research and write this book and when you read it—the time lag, given that this is a biennial guide—could be up to 2 years.

ATMS

For years, the easiest way to get money away from home was to head to the friendly neighborhood ATM. Unfortunately, a recent innovation by U.S.-based banks has been to charge a commission of up to 5% on withdrawals *in addition to the per-transaction fee of $3.* On principle, I'll probably just carry around cash, but for those of you willing to succumb to endless, creative bank fees, all cities and major tourist destinations in Turkey have bank machines on the Cirrus (© **800/ 424-7787;** www.mastercard.com) and PLUS (© **800/843-7587;** www.visa. com) networks.

Among the most reliable of the local banks are **Akbank, Türk İş Bankası, Garanti Bankası, Yapı Kredi Bankası,** and **Ziraat Bankası.** Ask whether you need a new personal identification number (PIN), as most ATMs in Turkey accept numbered passwords only, and some limit their input to four digits. Also, be aware that the ATMs are often fickle or empty, so always carry around alternatives in the form of cash or traveler's checks for emergencies.

CREDIT CARDS & DEBIT CARDS

Private bank accounts are not the only method where banks have been creative with mining additional fees. Purchases on credit card accounts are now also subject to a percentage fee, usually around 5%. In an annoying twist, these very same credit cards offer some of the more competitive exchange rates. It's up to you to do the math, though. Nevertheless, it's highly recommended that you travel with at least one major credit card. You must have a credit card to rent a car, and hotels and airlines usually require a credit card imprint as a deposit against expenses. Debit cards are also a commonly acceptable form of payment in most establishments.

TRAVELER'S CHECKS

In Turkey, as in many other European countries, local merchants are loath to accept traveler's checks, as banks charge large fees to cash them out. Banks tend to charge high commissions or hide the commission in higher rates, as do the exchange offices around town. Hotels are most amenable to exchanging your traveler's checks, but hotel exchange rates are notoriously unfavorable. The post office will probably be your best bet for exchanging them for cash.

You can buy traveler's checks at most banks. Most are offered in denominations of $20, $50, $100, $500, and sometimes $1,000. Generally, you'll pay a service charge ranging from 1% to 4%.

The most popular traveler's checks are offered by **American Express** (© **800/ 807-6233,** 800/221-7282 for cardholders; this number accepts collect calls, offers service in several foreign languages, and exempts Amex gold and platinum cardholders from the 1% fee); **Visa** (© **800/ 732-1322;** AAA members can obtain Visa checks for a $9.95 fee—for checks up to $1,500—at most AAA offices or by calling © **866/339-3378**), and **Master-Card** (© **800/223-9920**).

Be sure to keep a copy of the traveler's checks serial numbers separate from your checks in the event that they are stolen or lost. You'll get a refund faster if you know the numbers.

Another option is the new **prepaid traveler's check cards,** reloadable cards that work much like debit cards but aren't linked to your checking account. The **American Express Travelers Cheque Card,** for example, requires a minimum deposit ($300), sets a maximum balance ($2,750), and has a one-time issuance fee of $14.95. You can withdraw money from an ATM ($2.50 per transaction, not including bank fees), and the funds can be purchased in dollars, euros, or pounds. If you lose the card, your available funds will be refunded within 24 hours.

7 Travel Insurance

The cost of travel insurance varies widely, depending on the cost and length of your trip, your age and health, and the type of trip you're taking, but expect to pay between 5% and 8% of the vacation itself. You can get estimates from various providers through **InsureMyTrip.com.** Enter your trip cost and dates, your age, and other information for prices from more than a dozen companies.

Before you do all this, though, check your existing insurance policies and credit card coverage. You may already be covered for lost luggage, canceled tickets, or medical expenses.

MEDICAL INSURANCE

Although it's not required of travelers, health insurance is highly recommended. Most health insurance policies cover you if you get sick away from home—but check your coverage before you leave.

Good policies will cover the costs of an accident, repatriation, or death. Packages such as **Europ Assistance**'s **"Worldwide Healthcare Plan"** are sold by European automobile clubs and travel agencies at attractive rates. **Worldwide Assistance Services, Inc.** (© 800/777-8710; www.worldwideassistance.com) is the agent for Europ Assistance in the United States.

If you're ever hospitalized more than 150 miles from home, **MedjetAssist** (© 800/527-7478; www.medjetassistance.com) will pick you up and fly you to the hospital of your choice in a medically equipped and staffed aircraft 24 hours a day, 7 days a week. Annual memberships are $225 individual, $350 family; you can also purchase short-term memberships.

Canadians should check with their provincial health plan offices or call **Health Canada** (© 866/225-0709; www.hc-sc.gc.ca) to find out the extent of their coverage and what documentation and receipts they must take home in case they are treated in Turkey.

8 Health

STAYING HEALTHY

There are no severe health risks in travel to Turkey, nor are vaccinations required. It's still a good idea to use common sense in traveling to the more rural areas, although I confess that I rarely follow my own advice, below, and *usually* do just fine.

GENERAL AVAILABILITY OF HEALTHCARE

Visitors experiencing unexpected illness in Turkey can feel fairly confident in the healthcare he or she will receive. In general, the quality of care will be better in the major cities such as Istanbul, Ankara, Bodrum, and Izmir than in the heartland. For a list of English-speaking physicians practicing in Turkey, contact your embassy or consulate.

COMMON AILMENTS

DIETARY RED FLAGS **Food poisoning and diarrhea** are probably the most prevalent illnesses associated with travel to Turkey. Although water from the tap is chlorinated and generally safe to drink, even the locals drink bottled water. Resist the temptation to drink fresh running spring water, even if you see people lined up filling empty bottles. (*Please* take my word on this.) Avoid unpasteurized dairy products and shellfish during the hot summer months, and maintain a healthy suspicion of street vendors. In the event that you become ill, drink plenty of (bottled) water and remember that diarrhea usually dissipates on its own. Pepto-Bismol (bismuth subsalicylate) can often prevent symptoms, but if the problem becomes truly inconvenient, pharmacists are generally sympathetic and bilingual, and will be able to provide an effective remedy. (**Ercefuryl** works wonders.)

BUGS, BITES & OTHER WILDLIFE CONCERNS   Although the persistence and tenaciousness of Turkish **mosquitoes** might cause you to suffer, it is unlikely that malaria will. The high-risk areas are southeastern Anatolia and the Cukurova/Amikova areas, regions that because of political considerations are not covered in this book. Keep in mind that you're more likely to catch deadly mosquito-borne diseases in your own backyard than abroad. If you are experiencing symptoms, seek prompt medical attention while traveling as well as for up to 3 years after your return. Don't forget to pack a proven insect repellent (especially for those nights camped out on the deck of the gulet).

Rabies is endemic in parts of Turkey, and joggers have been known to be bitten by infected strays. But this is extremely rare. Best to stay away from the animals altogether, advice that, given the sweet temperaments of the street dogs and cats, I myself am incapable of following. If you're concerned, consult your doctor for pre-exposure immunization.

WHAT TO DO IF YOU GET SICK AWAY FROM HOME

Any local consulate can provide a list of area doctors who speak English. If you do get sick, you may want to ask the concierge at your hotel to recommend a local doctor, even his or her own. This will probably yield a better recommendation than any information number would. Local doctors advertise their services through discreet signs near their offices, and most speak English. If you can't find a doctor who can help you right away, try the **emergency room** of one of the private hospitals under "Fast Facts," p. 55.

If you suffer from a chronic illness, consult your doctor before your departure. Pack **prescription medications** in your carry-on luggage, and carry them in their original containers, with pharmacy labels—otherwise they won't make it through airport security.

Healthy Travels to You

The following government websites offer up-to-date health-related travel advice.

- **Australia:** www.dfat.gov.au/travel
- **Canada:** www.hc-sc.gc.ca/index_e.html
- **U.K.:** www.dh.gov.uk/PolicyAndGuidance/HealthAdviceForTravellers/fs/en
- **U.S.:** www.cdc.gov/travel

9 Safety

STAYING SAFE

Newbie Western travelers to Turkey are often plagued by worries over safety: It is a Muslim country, after all, and there is a war going on nearby, right? Well, no, actually. Yes, Turkey's population is mostly Muslim, but I don't need to remind you that all Muslims aren't terrorists, do I? Tsk tsk, if I may. Indeed, I guarantee that one of the first impressions that will overwhelm you upon arriving in Turkey is its complete and utter normalcy.

Second, there's a war going on, right? Sure, but it's 1,000 miles (1,609km) away as the crow flies. And as we've all so regrettably learned, distance doesn't contain conflict, and the violence in Iraq menaces us all just as much in London, Toronto, and New York as it does in Istanbul.

Okay, but what about the PKK? Sigh. Radicals committed to violence (in this case, right-wing Kurdish nationalists) are attacking Turkish soldiers in the southeast of the country (the main reason for which this book only covers the western half). Infrequently, the violence erupts beyond these borders. In my opinion, such an attack targeting foreign tourists would be a strategic mistake; still, it might be a good idea to check in with your appropriate travel advisories. In the U.S., log on to **http://travel.state.gov/travel**; in the U.K., **www.fco.gov.uk**; in Canada, **www.voyage.gc.ca**; in Australia, **www.smartraveller.gov.au**; and in New Zealand, **www.safetravel.govt.nz**.

DEALING WITH DISCRIMINATION

Most first-time travelers to Turkey are somewhat apprehensive about safety issues. The Western media hasn't exactly painted a rosy picture of Turkey—or of Muslims, for that matter. The first thing to realize is that Turkey is the model for democratic secularism in the Middle East, and although predominantly Muslim, it is merely fanatic about maintaining a separation of church and state. So business goes on as usual, with Turks drinking alcohol (or not), going to mosque (or not), and living life pretty much the same as you and me. Furthermore, as Islam preaches tolerance and acceptance, you may be surprised to feel more comfortable being Jewish in Istanbul than in, say, Columbus, Ohio.

People frequently ask me if Turkey is safe for women. Absolutely, but that doesn't mean that all you sistahs out there should throw common sense to the wind while on holiday. For more specifics, see the box "Important Tips for Single Women Travelers" on p. 36. Also, check out the award-winning website **Journeywoman** (www.journeywoman.com), a "real-life" women's travel-information network where you can sign up for a free e-mail newsletter and get advice on everything from etiquette and dress to safety. The travel guide *Safety and Security for Women Who Travel* by Sheila Swan and Peter Laufer (Travelers' Tales Guides), offering common-sense tips on safe travel, was updated in 2004.

Terrorism is on everybody's mind when considering a trip abroad, but in Turkey, where Turks have 20 years of experience fighting terrorists, flare-ups are now the exception rather than the rule. The only time you will get a glimpse of the existence of anything out of the ordinary is in the metal detectors at the entries of some five-star hotels or when traveling by domestic airline. Before boarding, each passenger must single out and identify his or her baggage from the lineup of luggage at the foot of the aircraft. (With any luck, no orphaned bags will be left over.)

Theft is a concern when staying home as much as when traveling. Just display as

Tips Important Tips for Single Women Travelers

Bait and Switch It's hard to believe, but in the major tourist areas of Turkey, particularly in the streets of Sultanahmet, an entire industry thrives on the acquisition and manipulation of emotions for economic gain. Foreign women, receptive, even eager, for new and exotic experiences, are just ripe for the picking, and although less-than-attractive ones are particularly vulnerable, any single girl with cash in the bank and foreign nationality is a target.

Sultanahmet is filled with professional "gigolos" practiced in the art of courtship and persuasion. The better ones come armed with scripts; the statements "You foreigners don't know how to trust anyone!" and "You foreigners think that we (Turks) are all thieves and barbarians" effectively disarm even the most remotely liberal.

Inevitably the topic of how bad things are economically will be carefully broached: how he can't pay his bills, how worried he is over his debts, and how any moment the authorities will repossess his furniture. Some invent elaborate stories of woe, and before you know it, the woman is offering—no, insisting—that he accept her help.

Some seducers even take this kind of behavior to its limits by pursuing the game as far as the wedding contract. But the most deplorable of the lot have been known to forge the marriage certificate with the assistance of those in the neighborhood even less scrupulous than themselves.

But this kind of behavior doesn't represent all of Turkey, and overall, women traveling alone in Turkey are treated with an almost exaggerated courtesy. In some cases, a woman will be in a better position to experience the openness of the Turkish people than if traveling en masse. With all of this warmth and hospitality, it's difficult to know how to temper one's

much caution in Istanbul's covered bazaar as you would at the train station of your nearest metropolitan city. And don't be deceived by the relative idyllic quiet of Istanbul's Sultanahmet neighborhood, as professional thievery is reaching new heights. Of course, it only takes one jerk to ruin your vacation. Typically, you're a target if you look like a tourist and carelessly fumble through your wallet in crowded areas like the train station or the ferry depot. Have your money ready beforehand and keep your handbag zipped up tight and your eyes open. Don't walk anywhere alone at night (this warning includes men). Beware of anyone who brushes up against you, even seemingly pious women in chadors (full-length veils) and adorable little kids straight out of *Oliver Twist.* Don't leave any valuables in your hotel room unless it's in the room safe. Hang on to your passport.

GAY & LESBIAN TRAVELERS

The fact that homosexuality is legal in Turkey is an interesting result of centuries of segregation of the sexes, veneration of female virtue, and lazy afternoons spent in the *hamam* (Turkish bath). Nevertheless, we're talking about a fairly conservative culture, so discretion is advisable, even if Turkish men are into more public instincts toward friendliness without affirming the general opinion among the more conservative class of Turks that all Western women are prostitutes. Even an innocent greeting or seemingly harmless camaraderie can be misinterpreted, so it's important to find a balance between polite formality and the openness that North American, European, and Australian women find so normal.

Dining   Practically speaking, no matter how modern the country may seem on the surface, don't be surprised if you're the only female in a restaurant. Eateries often have an *aile salonu* (family salon), an unintimidating dining area provided for men, women, couples, and anyone else not wishing to dine among groups of smoking, drinking, mustached Turks.

Dress   However Westernized Istanbul has become, wearing cutoff cheek-revealing shorts and a spandex midriff top is in bad taste. In the resort areas of the Aegean and Mediterranean seas, the economy of tourism seems to have won out over the local mores, but bathing topless is still insensitive. In Anatolia the sight of bare legs can cause a stir, so be sure to cover up on those long drives into the interior. In Istanbul, especially in the more modern neighborhoods, dress is modern, even racy, but when visiting the more traditional neighborhoods like Sultanahmet or Fatih, modesty will at least broadcast a different message to those likely to leer. Chances are you'll be visiting at least one mosque, and to enter, your shoulders, legs, and head must be covered. It's a nice idea to carry around a scarf, but all mosques provide some type of head covering. For more information on issues of safety in Turkey, see the "Safety" section on p. 35.

displays of affection with each other than with their wives.

The International Gay and Lesbian Travel Association (IGLTA; © 800/ 448-8550 or 954/776-2626; www.iglta. org) is the trade association for the gay and lesbian travel industry, and offers an online directory of gay- and lesbian-friendly travel businesses and tour operators.

Many agencies offer tours and travel itineraries specifically for gay and lesbian travelers. **Above and Beyond Tours** (© 800/397-2681; www.abovebeyond tours.com) are gay Australia tour specialists. San Francisco–based **Now, Voyager** (© 800/255-6951; www.nowvoyager. com) offers worldwide trips and cruises, and **Olivia** (© 800/631-6277; www. olivia.com) offers lesbian cruises and resort vacations.

Gay.com Travel (© 800/929-2268 or 415/644-8044; www.gay.com/travel or www.outandabout.com) is an excellent online successor to the popular *Out & About* print magazine. It provides regularly updated information about gay-owned, gay-oriented, and gay-friendly lodging, dining, sightseeing, nightlife, and shopping establishments in every important destination worldwide. British travelers should click on the "Travel" link at **www.uk.gay.com** for advice and gay-friendly trip ideas.

The Canadian website **GayTraveler** (**gaytraveler.ca**) offers ideas and advice for gay travel all over the world.

The following travel guides are available at many bookstores, or you can order them from any online bookseller: *Spartacus International Gay Guide, 35th Edition* (Bruno Gmünder Verlag; www.spartacusworld.com/gayguide) and *Odysseus: The International Gay Travel Planner, 17th Edition;* and the *Damron* guides (www.damron.com), with separate, annual books for gay men and lesbians.

SENIOR TRAVEL

Members of **AARP,** 601 E St. NW, Washington, DC 20049 (© **888/687-2277;** www.aarp.org), get discounts on hotels, airfares, and car rentals. AARP offers members a wide range of benefits, including *AARP The Magazine* and a monthly newsletter. Anyone over 50 can join.

Many reliable agencies and organizations target the 50-plus market. **Elderhostel** (© **800/454-5768;** www.elderhostel.org) arranges worldwide study programs for those aged 55 and over. **ElderTreks** (© **800/741-7956,** or 416/558-5000 outside North America; www.eldertreks.com) offers small-group tours to off-the-beaten-path or adventure-travel locations, restricted to travelers 50 and older.

Recommended publications offering travel resources and discounts for seniors include: the quarterly magazine *Travel 50 & Beyond* (www.travel50andbeyond.com) and the bestselling paperback *Unbelievably Good Deals and Great Adventures That You Absolutely Can't Get Unless You're Over 50 2007–2008, 17th Edition* (McGraw-Hill), by Joan Rattner Heilman.

FAMILY TRAVEL

Turks love kids, making travel with one a delight for all involved. And kids seem to love scrambling around ancient ruins, exploring underground cisterns (especially the ones with water in them); kids even get carried away in the Grand Bazaar. Almost all tourist services (hotels, ferryboats) offer some kind of discount for children, usually 50% of the full price for children 6 to 12, while kids under 6 generally get loads of freebies. Unfortunately, this discount does not apply to admission tickets to museums and sites for preteens.

You'll save a load of dough thanks to the Turkish tradition of providing breakfast with the room. Many hotels catering to the seaside vacationer offer (or automatically include) breakfast and dinner (called "half-board"); kids usually get the same reduced rate in this case as well. To locate accommodations, restaurants, and attractions that are particularly kid-friendly, refer to the "Kids" icon throughout this guide.

Recommended family-travel websites include **Family Travel Forum** (www.familytravelforum.com), a comprehensive site that offers customized trip planning; **Family Travel Network** (www.familytravelnetwork.com), an online magazine providing travel tips; and **Travel WithYourKids.com** (www.travelwithyourkids.com), a comprehensive site written by parents for parents offering sound advice for long-distance and international travel with children.

10 Staying Connected

TELEPHONES

Public telephones with the Türk Telekom logo can be found around town. To make a call, simply purchase a prepaid phone card at the post office (PTT) or at a private vendor around town (who will charge a small markup). There are two types of phone cards, with no difference in the amount of talking time you get for your money. The older type of card operates through a magnetic strip. These are sold in 30, 60, or 100 units. The second, **Smart Card** telephone system, also available at the post office, operates using a superior chip technology and is sold in units of 50, 100, 200, and 350. You'll need at least 100 units to make an international call. Public telephones that accept the Smart Card also operate using personal credit cards.

The following access numbers will connect you with a U.S. operator for credit card or collect calls: AT&T (✆ 00/800-12277), MCI (✆ 00/800-11177), and Sprint (✆ 00/800-14477).

The dialing codes for calling your home country are 001 for the United States and Canada, 0044 for the United Kingdom, 0061 for Australia, and 0064 for New Zealand.

Dial local calls by using the seven-digit phone number; if dialing out of town, you must include 0 plus the city code. When calling a cellphone (identifiable by the 0531, 0532, 0533, 0534, 0535, and 0536, and so on, exchanges), you must include the zero. When dialing any number in Turkey from abroad, drop the zero. Istanbul has two city codes: 216 for the Asian side and 212 for the European side.

CELLPHONES

Just because your cellphone works at home doesn't mean it'll work everywhere in the world. Nevertheless, most cellphone subscribers should have no trouble sending or receiving calls in Turkey. The exception is the American subscriber; thanks to the fragmented U.S. cellphone system, it's not a *fait accompli* that an American-based cellphone service will do you any good in Turkey. Thanks to Turkcell's ample stable of international roaming partners, U.K. users of T-Mobile, Orange, O-2, Vodafone, and Hutchison; Australian users of Singtel Optus, Telestra, Vodafone Pacific, and Hutchison 3G;

Canadian users of Rogers Wireless and Microcell; and U.S. users of AT&T Mobility, Cincinnati Bell Wireless, Commnet Wireless, Jasper Wireless, T-Mobile, and Alltel, should experience seamless service. Still, it's a good bet that your phone will work in major cities, but take a look at your wireless company's coverage map on its website before heading out.

A good alternative to the high cost of roaming is to bring/buy a GSM standard dual-band cellphone with you and buy a prepaid, no-contract SIM card. **Turkcell** and **Avea** are the two telecommunications giants in Turkey; both sell SIM cards for about 15YTL ($13/£6), which includes 100 units' worth of calling. Additional units can be purchased at any of these companies' franchises (and there are many): The cost of 100 units is 15YTL ($13/£6), 250 units cost 34YTL ($30/£14), and 500 units cost 62YTL ($54/£25). Cards holding units of 25, 50, and 1,000 are also available.

VOICE OVER INTERNET PROTOCOL (VOIP)

If you have Web access while traveling, you might consider a broadband-based telephone service (in technical terms, **Voice over Internet protocol,** or **VoIP**) such as Skype (www.skype.com) or Vonage (www.vonage.com), which allows you to make free international calls if you use their services from your laptop or in a cybercafe. The people you're calling must also use the service for it to work; check the sites for details.

INTERNET & E-MAIL
WITHOUT YOUR OWN COMPUTER

Most hotels now provide free Internet as part of the hotel's services. ISDN lines are also becoming standard equipment in better hotels. Wireless access is even becoming quite prevalent. If you and 20 other people are relying on the hotel

Frommers.com: The Complete Travel Resource

It should go without saying, but we highly recommend **Frommers.com,** voted Best Travel Site by *PC Magazine.* We think you'll find our expert advice and tips; independent reviews of hotels, restaurants, attractions, and preferred shopping and nightlife venues; vacation giveaways; and an online booking tool indispensable before, during, and after your travels. We publish the complete contents of over 128 travel guides in our **Destinations** section covering nearly 4,000 places worldwide to help you plan your trip. Each weekday, we publish original articles reporting on **Deals and News** via our free **Frommers.com Newsletter** to help you save time and money and travel smarter. We're betting you'll find our new **Events** listings (http://events. frommers.com) an invaluable resource; it's an up-to-the-minute roster of what's happening in cities everywhere—including concerts, festivals, lectures, and more. We've also added weekly **podcasts, interactive maps,** and hundreds of new images across the site. Check out our **Travel Talk** area featuring **Message Boards** where you can join in conversations with thousands of fellow Frommer's travelers and post your trip report once you return.

computer, there's still bound to be an Internet cafe nearby, and dirt cheap to boot. An hour of Internet use costs anywhere from $1.25 to $8, depending on where you are. For dinosaur dial-up users, AOL's local access number in Istanbul is ⓒ **0212/234-6100.** AT&T Business Internet Services can be accessed at ⓒ **0212/399-0001** and 399-0050. Both charge supplementary connection fees.

WITH YOUR OWN COMPUTER

More and more hotels, resorts, airports, cafes, and retailers are going Wi-Fi (wireless fidelity), becoming "hot spots" that offer free high-speed Wi-Fi access or charge a small fee for usage. Wi-Fi is even found in campgrounds, RV parks, and even entire towns. Most laptops sold today have built-in wireless capability. To find public Wi-Fi hot spots at your destination, go to **www.jiwire.com**; its Hotspot Finder holds the world's largest directory of public wireless hot spots.

Wherever you go, bring a **connection kit** of the right power and phone adapters, a spare phone cord, and a spare Ethernet network cable—or find out whether your hotel supplies them to guests.

For information on electrical currency conversions, see "Electricity," in the "Fast Facts" section at the end of this chapter.

11 Special-Interest Trips

CULTURAL TOURS

Turkey is, essentially, one big open-air museum, and it would be difficult not to have a learning experience while traveling in such a historically rich country. For their Turkey trips, **Intrepid Travel** (ⓒ **877/847-8192** in the U.S.; www. intrepidtravel.com) manages to effectively combine authentic experiences with an optimal cultural overview.

If you're looking for luxury without compromising the authenticity of your Turkish experience, **INCA** (ⓒ **510/420-1550;** www.incafloats.com) provides nature and cultural adventures.

If you're planning to drag along unwilling offspring, try booking through **Thomson Family Adventures** (© 800/262-6255 or 617/864-4803; fax 617/497-3911; www.familyadventures.com) for kid-friendly trips without adult compromise. Thomson takes an added interest in your children, establishing departure dates according to the school calendar, and they provide fun educational activities prior to departure.

Depending on your commitment to the educational aspect of your vacation, you may want to connect with one of the outfitters geared specifically toward this type of travel. **IST Cultural Tours** (© 800/833-2111) organizes painstakingly researched tours for the traveler who's looking for a more in-depth cultural experience, and a partnership with the History Channel ensures a high level of quality. **Far Horizons** (© 800/552-4575; www.farhorizon.com) offers eight archaeological tours for small groups, including a 10-day voyage by sea. Tours hook up with local professionals like archaeologists, scientists, and experts as guides. In 1994, archaeologist and professor Peter Sommer (**Peter Sommer Travels,** © 1600/861-929 in the U.K.; www.petersommer.com) set out from Troy on foot to walk the 2,000-mile path taken by Alexander the Great. His 19-day tour, aptly named In the Footsteps of Alexander the Great, retraces this trajectory and includes a short gulet cruise through some of the more scenic of the country's turquoise waters. His gulet tour of the Carian coastline makes the most of the Blue Cruise and of many of the region's off-the-beaten-track highlights.

Using a local travel agent can make anybody a bit skittish, but expert in the region is the English-proficient **Credo Tours** (© 0212/254-8175 in Istanbul; fax 90-212/237-9670; www.credo.com.tr), specializing in creating theme tours on special request. A recent program organized visits to select fine-arts galleries and exhibitions during the 2007 Biennale. Faxes and e-mails are answered within 24 hours, and there is no request that is too unusual.

BOAT TRIPS (aka THE BLUE VOYAGE)   Club Voyages, 43 Hooper Ave., Atlantic Highlands, NJ 07716 (© 888/842-2122 or 732/291-8228; fax 732/291-4277), bent over backwards to accommodate my absurd itinerary, and I've later learned that this individualized attention is due not only to a love of and commitment to the trade and to Turkey, but also because owners/operators Pat and Kemal are sincerely caring people. They specialize in high-end quality private charters with or without crew, with the possibility of land tour add-ons or land-only packages.

Blue Voyage (© 800/818-8753 or 414/392-0146; www.bluevoyage.com) has all the gulet charter options, as well as a three-cabin boat they've added to their fleet. Depending on availability, the boats can be chartered for as few as 2 days and for as little as $575 per day if you're willing to travel in May or October.

Any of the travel agents in this book can help you arrange a boat trip. Highly recommended are **Credo Tours** (© 0212/254-8175 in Istanbul; fax 90-0212/237-9670; www.credo.com.tr) and Argeus (© 0384/341-4688 in Cappadocia; www.argeus.com.tr), who can provide the optimum amount of service to best tailor your trip to your needs. Two heavy hitters in bareboat and gulet charters are **Aegean Yachting** (© 0252/316-1517; fax 0252/316-5749) and **Gino Group** (© 0252/412-0676; fax 90-252/412-2066).

V-GO Tourism Travel Agency, based in Fethiye, Fevzi Çakmak Caddesi (between the marina and the Yacht Club; © 0252/612-2113; www.boatcruise turkey.com), arranges 3-, 4-, and 7-day

All About the Blue Voyage

The *Mavi Yolculuk,* or "Blue Voyage," emerged in the late 1920s, when Cevat Şakir Kabaağaçlı, a dissident political writer whose "punishment" was exile in Bodrum, began cruising visiting friends around the idyllic Gulf of Gökova. Today tooling along the Turkish Mediterranean coastline is one of the highlights of any trip to Turkey, and in some cases, the only way to visit the small fishing villages and islands of the southwestern coast. But to do it right, you should plan in advance and know your options.

The traditional Turkish sea excursion is either by the traditional wooden broad-beamed gulet, or sleek yacht cruiser. Hiring a **private yacht** (or bareboat charter) is a popular choice for those with sailing proficiency and a taste for independence and adventure. Captained yachts are also available as an option. But so are captained and crewed gulets, which typically accommodate 8 to 12 people (or more) and come equipped with many modern conveniences.

In addition to chartering the entire gulet, it is also possible to charter a cabin on an individual basis. This last option, however, is riddled with pitfalls, not the least of which can be safety concerns. Generally, the gulets used for individual cabin charters didn't make the first cut for that season, thanks to torn cushions, faded decks, clogged toilets, smelly cabins, and a boat that should have been sent out to pasture long ago. Many tour operators and yacht agents have responded by acquiring and chartering out their own gulets, so check at the time of booking to make sure you'll be on one of these more recent acquisitions. If your booking agent can't or won't give you specific information about the boat you'll be on, be prepared for the worst, and negotiate a discount in advance if the gulet you were promised gets substituted at the last minute.

The most popular gulet cruises depart from Marmaris and ply the waters to Fethiye and back, stopping at (conditions permitting) Cleopatra's Baths, Dalyan, Kaunos, Istuzu Beach, and Ölüdeniz. See if you can get your agent

cruises departing from Fethiye or Olympos. Information (including rates) and pictures of their substantial fleet of broad-beamed gulets, ranging in age and level of luxury, can be viewed on their website.

You can go the extra nautical mile on a Blue Voyage by signing up with a reputable sailing school. **Gökova Yachting,** based in Netsel Marina in Marmaris (©/fax **0252/413-1089;** www.gokova sailing.com), is the only licensed international sailing school where students can advance through the five levels of sailing proficiency from beginner to racer. Yacht master Cumhur (Jim) Gökova presides over one of the newest fleets in the Mediterranean and also handles bookings directly. Tuition is 600€ per person per week and covers one proficiency level of instruction.

CULINARY TOURS Only a true foodie can appreciate the rewards of planning a vacation with a special emphasis on the eating habits of a country. In Turkey, where much of the language and expressions refer back to the kitchen, to book you an excursion out of Marmaris in the opposite direction (to Datça) or start in Finike and loiter around Kekova Bay.

Weeklong gulet cruises commonly depart on Sunday mornings (boarding Sat nights) and last 1 week, although it's also possible to arrange mini-cruises departing from anywhere your heart desires. A typical weeklong Blue Voyage will run you anywhere from 350€ ($508/£250) and up per person, with as much as 70% added on for a single supplement. Meals are usually included, but all drinks, even water, are extra (but available and reasonably priced onboard). Boats may come equipped with air-conditioning, but even on a private and comparatively luxurious boat, the generator, and thus the A/C, gets shut down at night.

Although most Turkish boat operators offer their services directly to the public, every travel agent and his brother has a friend in the boat business. The problem is wading through all of the brokerage options, especially when the ship's captain lists his boat with multiple agencies. The best way to ensure quality in booking your gulet or yacht cruise is to use one of the reputable local tour brokers that I recommend under "Boat Trips," above. Through long-standing relationships and extensive scrutiny of the boats, these brokers/tour operators can ensure a level of quality, as well as act as your agent in the event of unexpected developments. You will also have the added insurance of dealing with an outfitter working to protect you and your investment. Be an informed buyer and get a detailed description of the boat, keeping in mind that vessels need a complete renovation at least every 5 years. Also, decide whether a hose attachment to the sink faucet is sufficient as a shower or whether you require an enclosed stall. Finally, flush toilets (as opposed to the hand-pump type) are considered a luxury.

But look, the cabin charter is not all bad news. There's really no way to ruin a week of tooling around turquoise waters with a culturally and linguistically diverse passenger list. Hold your nose and just dive in.

---

there's no better way to get to the heart of this culture. Kathleen O'Neill's **Culinary Expeditions in Turkey** (© **415/437-5700** in the U.S.; fax 925/210-1337; www.turkishfoodandtravel.com) provides a gateway to the tradition, hospitality, and gastronomy of Turkey through "eating expeditions" that focus on the food of Turkey's eastern Mediterranean, either in the region of Gaziantep or cruising along the Turquoise coast.

ACTIVE VACATIONS Gorp Travel (© **877/440-4677;** www.gorp.com) offers the greatest variety of choices, with excursions organized around trekking, watersports, and cycling. Gorp is also one of many U.S. booking agents for **The Imaginative Traveler** (© **800/225-2380;** www.imaginative-traveller.com), the U.K.'s leading adventure tour company.

Not for the faint of thigh, **Great Explorations** (© **800-242-1825;** www.great-explorations.com), based in Canada, runs fairly hard-core combo cycling and Blue Cruise tours along the coast from Bodrum, through Datça, to Dalyan, and along the coast to Kaş, Fethiye, and Olympos on its way to Antalya. Check their website for details and departure dates.

Argeus Tourism & Travel, based in Ürgüp, Istiklal Cad. 13 (© **0384/341-4688;** fax 0384/341-4888; www.argeus. com.tr), is the most qualified local company for tailor-made tours and packages in Cappadocia, and the exclusive representatives for REI activities in Turkey. Guides are knowledgeable and enthusiastic. **Middle Earth Travel,** Gaferli Mahallesi, Cevizler Sokak, Göreme (© **0384/271-2559;** www.middleearthtravel.com), targets the hardiest of independent adventure travelers, with 6-day to 2-week treks into the Kaçkar Mountains, an 8-day climb up Mount Ararat, 2-day volcano climbs, and organized expeditions along the Lycian Way and St. Paul's Trail (see chapter 7).

If river sports are more your speed, **Medraft** (based in Antalya; © **0242/312-5770;** www.medraft.com) combines off-the-beaten-track travel with rafting trips in the canyons around Antalya and overnights at their rustic "Mountain Lodge." Medraft also runs a 9-day rafting trip into the Kaçkar region along the Black Sea coast. They also send their expert sportsmen to lead cycling adventures and jeep safaris to these regions.

Clients of **Cappadocia Tours** based in Ürgüp (© **0384/341-7485;** fax 0384/341-7487; www.cappadociatours.com) leave Turkey with a deeper attachment to the country thanks to a grass-roots approach that moves beyond the museums. In addition to the must-sees of Cappadocia, they also lead safari tours into the mountains, to waterfalls, and to off-the-beaten-track villages and little-explored underground cities.

In the past few years, Turkey has caught the **golfing fever,** and it seems that everybody with a hankering and disposable greens fees wants to get in on the act. A number of developers have recognized the investment potential, and this year (2008), the number of courses in Turkey is expected to hit 21, up from 11 in 2005. Most of these courses are located in the province of Antalya, taking advantage of the mild Mediterranean winter months. For more information, consult chapter 7 or log on to www.bookyour golf.com.

SPA VACATIONS

It's obvious by the glossy brochure published by the Ministry of Tourism that Turkey recognizes the value of the country's natural thermal resources. But it's only recently that entrepreneurs have stepped up to the plate with suitably deluxe facilities that provide alternatives to the medicinal or blue-collar environments of some of the country's older centers. Even if Istanbul is your only destination in Turkey, the *embarras de richesses* of deluxe spas will keep your skin smooth, your muscles supple, and your head clear. (For more details, pick up a copy of *Frommer's Istanbul.*)

In the hot springs-rich peninsula of **Çeşme** (see chapter 6, "The Central & Southern Aegean Coasts [Greater Izmir]"), a luxury thermal spa is now the rule rather than the exception. The **Altın Yunus** was the first, and now five-star properties with thermal-rich waters include the **Süzer** and the new **Sheraton Çeşme,** which gears its high-tech thermal center to nothing more ambitious than treatments for pure pleasure. The **Sheraton Voyager** in Antalya features a high-tech wellness center (p. 324).

Two other traditional centers for thermal treatments are **Bursa** and **Pamukkale** (see chapter 6).

In Bodrum **The Marmara Otelı** (p. 248) converted five rooms into a center geared toward complete self-indulgence. The spa offers stone therapy, a "fat attack" sea-mud body pack, and the ultimate endorphin high: 60 minutes of weightless relaxation in its state-of-the-art flotation tank.

EXCURSIONS INTO EASTERN TURKEY

For the first time in more than 20 years, eastern Turkey is enjoying an extended period of calm, and slowly but surely, destinations that previously came with State Department warnings are appearing in tour brochures. Make no mistake, however—as far as creature comforts go, it's still the Wild West out east. Alas, publisher's directives about page limits constrain me from elaborating on such wondrous destinations as **Zeugma, Antioch, Mt. Nemrut,** and **Lake Van.** Instead, I can highly recommend **Credo Tours**

(© **90-212/254-8175;** fax 90-212/237-9670; www.credo.com.tr) for your foray into Turkey's eastern and southeastern provinces.

Another reputable outfitter experienced in the east is **Fez Travel** (© **90-212/516-9024;** fax 90-212/638-8764; www.feztravel.com), run by a group of Australians who made a name for themselves with a hop-on-hop-off circuit of Turkey's hot spots. These trips, top-heavy with Australian backpackers, are geared more toward the budget end of travel. Meanwhile, many tour operators based in Göreme, in Cappadocia, run overnight bus tours to Mount Nemrut, mostly utilized by backpackers.

12 Getting Around

BY CAR

Driving through Turkey is a great way to travel independently with the utmost of freedom. This is even more the case now that the road conditions have improved dramatically in recent years. Turkey has been pouring investment into road infrastructure, including the establishment of the multilane toll roads around Istanbul, Ankara, and Izmir and the widening of major provincial thoroughfares. In fact, except for the road signs (which on the toll collection booths are now also in English), you'll almost think you were driving in Europe.

But getting to a destination is different than being there. Cities are increasingly implementing one-way traffic systems, and the traffic police are becoming unmistakably enthusiastic over performing their jobs. The shortage of parking makes these one-way roads even more of a challenge; think about arriving, overshooting your destination, and getting ushered all the way back out to the main road into town.

Avis (© **800/230-4898,** 800/272-5871 in Canada; www.avis.com) has locations

in all major cities, at most airports, and at select hotels and resorts. If you reserve a car before you go, you can take advantage of their **On Call** program (© **800/297-4447** *in advance of your trip* for access numbers in Turkey; have your confirmation or reservation number ready), which provides 24-hour, toll-free assistance for physicians, lost baggage, prescriptions from home, and mechanical problems. **National Car Rental** (© **800/227-7368;** www.nationalcar.com) has outlets pretty much everywhere, too, with rates comparable to those of Avis. Other options are **Budget** (© **800/527-0700,** 800/268-8900 in Canada; www.budget.com), with limited outlets in Turkey, and **Sixt** (© **0216/318-9040** in Turkey; www.sunrent.com), with 20 locations throughout Turkey.

BY PLANE

After one too many 12-hour hauls on a non-air-conditioned bus with unrelenting piped-in ethnic music and the pungent odors of lemon cologne and BO, you may prefer to spend your next full day of travel waiting around an airport cafe rather than in a bus seat. **Turkish**

A Note on Distances

The concept of precision is a foreign one in Turkey. "Not far" is a relative term and "just over there" indicates a point in the distance as the crow flies. Similarly, when comparing the travel literature on distances between towns, you'll notice a glaring absence of consistency. Please note that although all distances in this book have been confirmed using official maps and brochures, you might be looking at a different source than the one I got the mileage from.

Airlines (© **800/874-8875** in the U.S., 207-766-9300 in London, 0212/663-6300 in Istanbul; www.turkishairlines.com) provides regular domestic service within Turkey, with major hubs in Istanbul, Ankara, and Izmir. The recent arrival of **Onur Air** (© **0212/663-9176** in Istanbul; www.onurair.com.tr) and **Fly Air** (© **0212/444-4359** in Istanbul; www.flyair.com.tr) has created some healthy competition in Turkey's domestic air transportation industry. Onur Air flies from Istanbul to Ankara, Izmir, Antalya, and Kayseri, to name just a few destinations, while Fly Air flies from Istanbul to Izmir and Bodrum. One-way domestic fares on Onur Air or Fly Air will cost around $60, while passage on Turkish Airlines will cost you slightly more, around $79. You can book flights last-minute at one of the airline offices or through an officially recognized travel agent. These days, with flights into Istanbul consistently full, it's a good idea to plan ahead. Although it's still possible to fly last-minute, try to book your domestic seats as much in advance as possible, especially if your travel falls during one of the *bayrams* (religious holidays).

Those with more of a jet-setting mentality can charter domestic flights through **Marinair** (© **0212/663-1829**; www.bonair.com.tr, in Turkish only), providing service from Istanbul to Bodrum/Türkbükü, Çeşme, Dalaman, Göcek, and Kaş. Travel time is approximately 1½ hours, and fares hover around $2,500 to $3,000.

BY TRAIN

In the years leading up to World War I, Turkey's railroads developed thanks to the "generosity" of German and British government-supported ventures sucking up to an as-yet neutral potential ally. These entrepreneurs recognized the value of old stone, making not-so-convenient detours in the track-laying to valuable archaeological sites. The result was a uselessly meandering system highly efficient at carting away priceless archaeological finds, enriching both foreign museums and the pockets of these "part-time engineers." The Pergamum Altar is now in the Pergamon Museum in Berlin; King Priam's treasures were whisked out of Troy, passing through Berlin's Hermitage Museum and on to Moscow's Pushkin Museum, while many treasures from the Temple of Artemis are now housed in the British Museum. The only exception to an across-the-board recommendation to stick to the buses is with regard to the night train from Istanbul to Ankara. Although the bus is faster by about 3 to 4 hours, skyrocketing bus fares are making the train the choice of many. Besides cheaper fares, a bunk on the sleeper car will have you arriving fresh and ready to go on arrival (minus the shower; the cars come with sink only). For information on timetables and fares, log on to **www.tcdd.gov.tr**.

BY BUS

Traveling by bus brings up images of greasy-haired, guitar-toting rebels lifted from the pages of a Jack Kerouac novel.

Turkey has taken the grungy image of bus travel and brought it to new heights of comfort and respectability. There are several categories of bus travel: municipal buses, the local *dolmuş,* long-distance buses, and short-distance minibuses.

In big cities like Istanbul, Ankara, Izmir, and Antalya, **municipal buses** provide a cheap way to get around, if you can actually figure out how. Destinations are posted on the windshield, but it's always a good idea to ask the driver if he's going your way before getting on. Getting on in the middle of a bus route can be confusing, but there's always the ubiquitous good Samaritan there to steer you in the right direction. In Istanbul the modern green buses are for commuters with debit tokens only, while the used-up old orange buses are for everybody else; tickets can be purchased from the cashier onboard.

Another popular and economic way of getting around is the *dolmuş,* essentially a minivan with passenger seats. The best description of these little group taxis is in the translation: *dolmuş* in English means "stuffed." The *dolmuş* follows a set route, stopping and starting to pick up passengers until no one else will fit in it. The main stops are posted on the windshield and you pay according to the distance that you go, usually under 75¢. This system works well in and around small towns; drivers will politely honk as they drive to see if you want to get on, and routes are direct to the places you want to go. *Dolmuşes* do run on Sunday, so don't let those crafty taxi drivers convince you otherwise.

In major metropolitan areas such as Istanbul, the process is a bit more complicated, even for the locals. The best way to avoid an inner-city trip to nowhere is to board at one of the *dolmuş* stands marked by a blue "D" and take it to the final destination (preferably the same destination as yours). Fares are usually posted and

rarely exceed 3.50YTL ($3.05/£1.40) per ride. It's also acceptable to pay the driver before you get off, so you can enjoy a bit of spontaneity as well. *Dolmuşes* stop running in the early evening, so in the outlying areas, make sure you've got a way back to the hotel.

Long-distance buses are an integral part of the Turkish culture, probably because there are often few alternatives for inter-city travel other than renting a car.

The major bus companies in Turkey (*Note:* Phone numbers beginning with 444 are national toll-free numbers and can be dialed from anywhere in Turkey) are **Ulusoy** (*©* **444-1888;** www.ulusoy. com.tr/eng), **Varan** (*©* **0212/251-7474;** www.varanturizm.com), **Kamil Koç** (*©* **444-0562;** www.kamilkoc.com.tr), **Uludağ** (*©* **0212/245-2795**), **Metro** (*©* **444-3455**), and **Pamukkale** (*©* **444-3535;** www.pamukkaleturizm.com.tr), with the first two costing nearly double the other companies.

All have counters at the local bus station *(otogar)* as well as offices conveniently located around town. The better bus companies offer free shuttle service between the ticket office and your bus at the *otogar.*

If you're on a more relaxed timetable, it's just as easy to show up at the *otogar;* with competition stiff for your business, the bus companies that provide service to your destination will most certainly find you. Take your time and don't be bullied into buying a ticket from the first guy who hooks you in, because his bus may not be the first one to leave for your destination.

If you're like me, you believe it should take approximately 3 hours to cover 322km (200 miles). Gauge at least 40% more time on the bus than what you figure it would take you to get there by car.

Water and soft drinks are served on the bus; if you're lucky, you'll get a little

Tips Don't Let Taxi Drivers Take You for a Ride

There is a certain amount of control you give up when entering a taxi in a strange city. Your safest bet is to have your hotel concierge phone for the taxi rather than you flagging it down. (In Istanbul, under no circumstances should you hire a taxi off the street in front of the Ayasofya.) Some hotels and taxi companies have agreements that award the company repeat business in exchange for honesty and accountability at no extra charge to the passenger. Still, the risk that absolute ignorance of a location will be rewarded with a circuitous route is fairly high. Knowing in advance that there's nothing you can do about it is usually enough to let you sit back and relax. But there still are a few things to look out for to avoid being scammed.

Check to see that the meter is running, and that the correct rate applies. The less expensive day rate _(gunduz)_ alternately flashes with the metered fare and applies from 7am to midnight, but crafty taxi drivers will push the night _(gece)_ rate button to increase the fare. If you've caught a driver in the act, threaten to summon the police, or get out of the cab.

Beware of the "bait and switch" routine, whereby the driver takes your 10YTL banknote (worth about $8.70/£4) and accuses you of having given him a 1YTL note. You can avoid this by holding on to the banknote until you've received your change. Also, note that 1YTL notes are blue-toned and 10YTL notes are orange.

For longer distances or drives outside of the city limits, taxis usually have a list of set rates. Be sure you've discussed these in advance, as you may be able to negotiate a discount (though it's doubtful). A final word: Don't get into a cab expecting bad things to happen. Just be a smart customer.

---

kid-size breakfast cake to tide you over until the next feeding. A sprinkle of cologne is part of the Turkish culture, but better the brand that smells of baby oil and talcum powder than the one that stinks like Lemon Pledge. Rest stops are made at erratic intervals, but there's usually enough time at one of the pickup and drop-off points for a quick dash to the Turkish toilet. (Let the man onboard know you'll be right back!)

Except on rare occasions (and in my case, total cluelessness), unacquainted men and women do not sit together on the bus. My grievance with this tradition is more practical than unprogressive: Old Turkish ladies tend to be hefty and spill out onto the adjacent seat, while it is common practice for Turkish mothers to save a bus fare by seating her 6-year-old son on her lap for the 6-hour trip.

13 Tips on Accommodations

Hotels in Turkey are classified by a government-designated star system that apparently was established in the Neolithic era, so booking a five-star hotel in Turkey doesn't necessarily guarantee the comfort and amenities of an equivalently rated establishment in a major city. Roughly, stars are awarded for the presence of amenities like fitness centers or conference space, so a worn-out old five-star with moldy bathroom tile might rate higher than a brand-new sky-lit gem with nothing to offer but basic clean rooms, stunning balconies, and a pool.

Unless stated otherwise, all rates quoted in the hotel reviews in this book include breakfast and tax. Many hotels rely exclusively on solar power, which sounds great until you get in a cold shower at sunrise. This is increasingly rare, however, as many establishments are installing backup generators for "24-hour hot water." Power outages are an unavoidable part of daily life, and because the water supply operates on an electric pumping system, there will be no water for the duration of the outage, usually only a couple of hours. In the sweaty heat of the summer, this is where the neighborhood *hamam* comes in handy.

Typical hotel rooms in Turkey seem to have more rooms with twin beds, so unless you specify that you want a double "French" bed, you and your partner will feel like a couple out of a 1950s sitcom. Fitted sheets seem to be an anomaly in Turkey, so if you're a restless sleeper, expect to get a view of the mattress in the morning. Ask for an extra sheet if there's nothing between you and the blanket, as bed-making habits in Turkey vary from hotel to hotel. And not even the Four Seasons Hotel in Sultanahmet will spare you from the startling blare of the neighborhood's muezzin at sunrise. TVs are generally a standard feature in rooms, but even a TV with a satellite hookup will limit you to BBC World, CNN, and endless hours of cycling tournaments. Local programming is at least captivating, with reruns of *Guys and Dolls* or *The Terminator* in Turkish. Another interesting media feature in the room is a built-in radio with centrally piped-in music. There is generally a choice of up to three channels, and if you don't like the music, I discovered

that calling down to the reception for special requests was effective.

Another standard characteristic of hotels rated three stars or lower (Turkish rating) is the "Roman shower"—essentially a showerhead on the wall and a drain in the floor. In some cases, you'll get a square enamel stall basin and a shower curtain, and practiced proficiency with the hand-held showerhead will eventually ensure the least amount of leakage on the bathroom floor. Be aware, too, that an ongoing problem of not just the older hotels is the rapidity in which a clear drain will get clogged. I've kept recommendations of these hotels to the exceptional minimum.

During the in-between seasons, many hotels, operating with heating systems programmed to run during the winter months only, may leave you out in the cold. In the absence of central heat, many special-category hotels simply provide standing electric heaters. If you're prone to cold, make sure your hotel offers heat.

All hotels provide laundry and dry-cleaning services, seeing to it in the process that they make a huge profit on the transaction. Depending on the establishment, expect to pay anywhere from 3€ to 7€ ($4.35–$10/£2.15–£5) per item for ordinary laundry. At under $5 a load, a local laundromat is a cheap alternative, as long as you don't mind borrowing the hotel iron. Another service offered by all five-star hotels is babysitting, arranged by the hotel through reputable outside agencies.

Also, it is imperative to note that except in rare cases (like full occupancy, which is happening a lot lately), the room rates provided in the listings are "rack rates," fictional prices that are almost never quoted—not even to the most desperate last-minute walk-in. It is more likely than not that a rate will adjust itself anywhere from 10% to 50% (or more!) at the time of booking, depending on the season and how hungry the owner is. This doesn't mean that hoteliers have become market hagglers; it simply means that the prices listed for hotels are inextricably tied to the market. Parents with kids will be pleased to learn that children 6 and under, and in some cases 12 and under, stay free.

In order to increase business, hotels in Turkey make rooms available at absurdly low rates to travel agents so that they will provide them with business on a regular basis. Ironically, a recent, yet not yet pervasive, development has been for hotels to undercut these agents with their own Web rates. Therefore, it is up to the buyer to do the legwork. But buyer beware: Not all travel sites advertising cheap hotels on the Web are equally reputable, so I recommend that you stick to the local travel agencies recommended in this guide (or those recommended to you by friends and relatives). For a list of charming hotels beyond those recommended in this guide, log on to **www.nisanyan.net** (run by the owners of the Nişanyan houses in Şirince;

see chapter 6) and use the "Search Hotel" function. Be aware, however, that all of the hotels listed on this site pay a subscription fee and therefore may not be as wonderful in person.

SURFING FOR HOTELS

In addition to the online travel booking sites **Travelocity, Expedia, Orbitz, Priceline,** and **Hotwire,** you can book hotels through **Hotels.com, Quikbook** (www.quikbook.com), and **Travelaxe** (www.travelaxe.net). Two other great resources for locating affordable hotels are **www.venere.com** and **www.hostelworld.com**, which in addition to youth hostels lists a number of respectable pension options.

HotelChatter.com is a daily webzine offering smart coverage and critiques of hotels worldwide. Go to **TripAdvisor.com** or **HotelShark.com** for helpful independent consumer reviews of hotels and resort properties.

It's a good idea to **get a confirmation number** and **make a printout** of any online booking transaction.

14 Recommended Books & Films

Because Turkey is the custodian of a past so densely packed with history's most critical eras, if you don't do your homework before you go, you'll wind up simply wandering through pretty piles of rocks and stone.

BOOKS

At the very least, pick up a copy of *A Traveller's History of Turkey* (Interlink Books, 1998), by Richard Stoneman, a readable overview of Turkey's history from A to Z that will fit in your back pocket. Take it with you, as Stoneman provides a handy reference of ancient sites in the appendix.

The definitive modern interpretive work on the history of Turkey is by the renowned Middle East historian, Bernard Lewis, in *The Emergence of Modern*

Turkey (Oxford University Press, 2001). First published in 1961, the latest edition addresses current issues confronting Turkey, including involvement in NATO, Middle East politics, E.U. accession, and the recent and increased presence of political Islam in Turkish politics.

A Short History of Byzantium (Vintage Books, 1998), John Julius Norwich's condensed version of a three-volume epic, actually entertains while faithfully covering the life of one of the most enduring empires on earth. *Ottoman Centuries: The Rise and Fall of the Turkish Empire* (Harper Perennial, 1979), by Lord Kinross, has established itself as the definitive guidebook on Turkey during the Ottoman Empire. In a thoroughly readable prose, Kinross leads you through history while providing the contexts for understanding

Turkey today. Another book by Kinross is *Atatürk, the Rebirth of a Nation* (titled *Atatürk: A Biography of Mustafa Kemal, Father of Modern Turkey* in the U.S. and currently out of print), also respected as *the* handbook on the man who single-handedly reconstructed a nation. Also see Andrew Mango's more recent *Atatürk* (John Murray Publishers, 2004).

Constantinople: City of the World's Desire, 1453–1924 (St. Martin's Griffin, 1998), by Philip Mansel, provides an accurate and colorful history of the Ottoman Empire while sprinkling the pages with attention-grabbing little morsels of lesser-known trivia. *Turkey Unveiled: A History of Modern Turkey* (Overlook Press, 2000) was written by Hugh and Nicole Pope, two journalists working for the *Wall Street Journal* and *Le Monde,* respectively. In *Turkey Unveiled,* the Popes give us insights into the most divisive issues of Turkey today. A more recent analysis of modern problems and trends in Turkey written from a Western insider's point of view is provided by Stephen Kinzer, former Istanbul bureau chief of the *New York Times,* in *Crescent and Star: Turkey Between Two Worlds* (Farrar, Straus & Giroux, 2002).

Keep your eyes peeled in used-book stores both at home and in Turkey for old versions of George Bean's series, *Lycian Turkey, Aegean Turkey, Turkey's Southern Shore,* and *Turkey Beyond the Maeander* (last published by John Murray Ltd., 1989–90), which comprise the master-work collection of archaeological guide-books on Turkey, but are unfortunately out of print. Filling the void is the new and improved printing of Dr. Ekrem Akurgal's *Ancient Civilizations and Ruins of Turkey* (Net Turistik Yayınlar San. Tic. A.Ş. Istanbul, 2001), first printed in 1969 and currently the definitive guide-book to archaeological sites in Turkey.

Walking is a great way to see rural Turkey, and Kate Clow shows you the way in her books. *The Lycian Way* (Upcountry Ltd., 2005) is a detailed mapping out of the ancient footpaths and roads between Fethiye and Antalya, with details on the history, archaeological sites, and wildlife along the way. She's even considerate enough to let us know how out-winded we can expect to get. A collection of 20 maps is included, so although the full trek would take at least 4 to 6 weeks, you can use this guidebook for a less ambitious day trip. For information on the trail, log on to **www.lycian way.com**. Also, check out *St Paul Trail* (Upcountry Ltd., 2004), which is just as detailed, with color photos and maps chronicling the way taken by St. Paul on his missionary journeys through Asia Minor.

World War I buffs will want to show up on the battlefields at Gallipoli armed with a copy of Tim Travers's *Gallipoli 1915 (Battles & Campaigns)* (Tempus Publishing, 2004). The newly released (Viking Penguin, 2007) *The Anzacs: Gallipoli to the Western Front* is historian Peter Pedersen's account of the Anzacs' participation in the war, mixing in diary excerpts and official records into the narrative.

Coverage of terrorist actions committed by militant Muslims has prejudiced much of the Western world against anything Islamic, causing many tourists to Turkey to be unnecessarily apprehensive. *Teach Yourself Islam* (McGraw-Hill, 1996), by Ruqaiyyah Maqsood, gets to the soul of the religion by providing explanations of beliefs and analyzing the purposes behind the rituals in a straightforward and absorbing manner. *What Went Wrong?: Western Impact and Middle Eastern Response* (Oxford University Press, 2001), a balanced and scholarly work by Bernard Lewis, guides readers through the transformation of Islam from a cultural, scientific, and economic powerhouse to a significantly tarnished underdog. Finish off this reading list with *What's Right with Islam: A New Vision for Muslims and the West* (HarperOne, 2004), in which Feisal Abdul Rauf argues how the violence perceived by the West to be at the heart of terrorism has, in fact, nothing to do with religion and everything to do with economics and politics.

Jeremy Seal's *A Fez of the Heart: Travels Around Turkey in Search of a Hat* (Harcourt, 1996) and Mary Lee Settle's *Turkish Reflections: A Biography of a Place* (Touchstone Books, 1992) are two excellent travelogues that have established themselves as de facto reads for anyone interested in Turkey. *Turkish Reflections,* although accused of being outdated, succeeds in providing an accurate portrayal of the Turkish people and vivid images of the physical landscape. Interesting little snippets of trivia are sprinkled throughout the text and are especially entertaining as supplements to a historical perspective, but as a read, may be more suitable for post-voyage reminiscences. In *A Fez of the Heart,* Jeremy Seal succeeds in capturing the sights and smells of his destinations while ostensibly on the hunt for the legacy left by the fez. Seal tosses in bits of history while you're not looking and throws in unexpected episodes of hilarity that will garner you unwanted attention in public places.

For Orhan Pamuk, *Istanbul: Memories and the City* (Alfred A. Knopf, 2005) is a (tedious) personal reflection on life growing up in the "melancholy" of an Istanbul in transition. Descriptions of faded apartment buildings, and the tension between tradition and convention are as much a self-portrait as a window into the city at the crossroads of civilization.

For a modern woman's view of what it's like to work, live, and travel in Turkey, pick up the recently compiled and released *Tales from the Expat Harem: Foreign Women in Modern Turkey* (Seal Press, 2006). It's a compilation of essays, stories, and travelogues by various non-Turkish women.

In fiction, obviously, the most insightful reads will be those books written by native Turks, and in recent years, several Turkish authors have created mesmerizing works of fiction set within a vivid Turkish reality. Orhan Pamuk made quite a splash well before he won himself a Nobel Prize in 2006 for literature. His novels include *The White Castle* (Vintage, 1998), *The Black Book* (Harvest Books, 1996), *The New Life* (Vintage, 1998), *Snow* (Vintage, 2005), and *Istanbul: Memories of a City* (Knopf, 2005). Irfan Orga's *Portrait of a Turkish Family* (Hippocrene Books, 1989) is a poignant account of a simple Turkish family caught between the Ottoman Empire and Atatürk's Republic. Journalist and leading satirist Aziz Nesin spent much of his life in prison, where he penned a large portion of his highly biographical essays— colorful images of growing up in a traditional Turkish family at the beginning of the 20th century.

FILMS

The Turks rigorously resent the unfair characterization of Turkish people in the 1978 film *Midnight Express,* a movie that has been accused of encouraging prejudices in Westerners. They point out that the movie was financed by Greek cinema magnate Kirk Kerkorian and filmed using actors of predominantly Greek and Armenian origin—two nations notorious for their bad blood with Turkey. Nevertheless, it's a movie classic, it did win an Oscar, and it *was* set in Istanbul.

Topkapı (1964) is an amusing movie about a plot to steal the famous dagger from the Palace Treasury, and co-stars Peter Ustinov. The movie remake is currently in production in and around Istanbul; it's being billed as the sequel to both *Topkapı* and *The Thomas Crown Affair* and stars Pierce Brosnan and Angelina Jolie.

Gallipoli (1981), with a young, spell-binding Mel Gibson, is a movie classic that brings the World War I battle down to a human level. This movie is a must-see for anyone making the trip to the battlegrounds.

FAST FACTS: Turkey

American Express Amex has finally gone mainstream in Turkey, and American Express credit cards are now widely accepted. Before you go, you may want to log on to the travel area of the Amex website for special offers, including hotels and restaurants, in Turkey. Türk Express is the official representative of Amex Travel Related Services in Turkey, at Cumhuriyet Cad. 91/1 Elmadağ in the Hilton Hotel (© 0212/230-1515). American Express also provides a toll-free access number within Turkey for Global Assist (© 0312/935-3601).

ATM Networks Banks on the Cirrus or PLUS network include Akbank, Garanti Bankası, Yapı Kredi Bankası, and Ziraat Bankası. See also the section on ATMs under "Money," earlier in this chapter.

Business Hours The reality is that if there are customers, the shops will stay open. Official hours of operation for shops are Monday through Saturday 9:30am to 1pm and 2 to 7pm, but I've yet to find a store closed at lunchtime, and increasingly, shops are opening on Sunday afternoons. Visitors to Istanbul take note that the Grand Bazaar and the Egyptian Spice Market are both closed on Sunday. Museums and palaces are generally open Tuesday through Sunday from 9:30am to 5 or 5:30pm, while the closing day for palaces is Tuesday, Thursday, or both. Banks are open Monday through Friday from 8:30am to noon and 1:30 to 5pm. Government offices are open Monday through Friday 8:30am to 12:30pm and 1:30 to 5:30pm.

Car Rentals See "Getting Around," p. 45.

Cashpoints See "ATM Networks," above.

Currency See "Money," p. 30.

Customs **What You Can Bring Into Turkey** The Turkish government has established a list of items that may be brought into the country duty-free. In addition to personal effects, travelers are permitted one video player, one pocket computer, one portable radio/tape player, one pair of binoculars (no night vision allowed), one camera and five rolls of film, one typewriter, personal sporting equipment, necessary medical items, gifts not exceeding $300, spare car parts, and various other relatively improbable items for the average tourist. (A complete list is available through the Turkish Embassy website.) Sharp instruments and weapons may not be brought into the country without special permission (diving and camping knives included). Obviously, the importation, buying, selling, and consumption of marijuana and other narcotics is *strictly* forbidden. You shouldn't need to watch *Midnight Express* to figure that one out.

What You Can Take Home from Turkey For valuables purchased during your stay, be prepared to provide receipts or other proof of purchase—particularly for that large prize silk Hereke—to avoid problems with Turkish Customs when you leave and to aid in declarations in your home country. Forget about having your carpet salesman lie on the official Certificate of Origin, because the U.S. immigration police are prepared to consult their little carpet blue book if you try to slip through without paying up. Be aware that the authentic 16th-century porcelain soup tureen that you bought or those authentic ancient coins attached to your new necklace are either fake or unable to make the journey with you; it is illegal to take antiquities or anything of historical value out of the country. To enforce this, the Turkish government requires that anything dating to the end of the 19th century be authenticated by a museum official before its exportation can even be considered. It is also illegal to carry out tobacco seeds and plants, or hides, skins, or clothing made from wild animals. For items dating prior to the 20th century, permission plus a certificate of authenticity from a museum official is needed. Minerals require special documentation obtainable from the General Directorate of Mineral Research and Exploration in Ankara (© **312/287-3430**; in Turkish only: www.mta.gov.tr).

Drinking Laws The separation of mosque and state in Turkey ensures that the consumption of alcohol remain a personal choice. However, the pendulum of tolerance for those who drink has swung back under the current government led by Erdoğan. Taxes on imported wines and spirits went through the roof, creating a financial disincentive for anyone with a hankering for a vodka tonic (for example). Furthermore, many government-owned establishments (restaurants operated by a municipality, for example) and those establishments owned by hard-core conservatives simply do not serve alcohol. (In a compromise, Hünkar Lokantası, the famous Istanbul restaurant, only serves alcohol to foreigners.)

Practically speaking, the legal age for purchase and consumption of alcoholic beverages is 18, although people under the age of 18 can drink (non-distilled beverages only) when accompanied by a parent. Beer, wine, and spirits are widely available for purchase. Also, although winemaking was historically an activity pursued by non-Muslim natives of Anatolia, the shift to wine production by the Turks began shortly after the establishment of the Republic, and in the past few years, Turkish wines have continued to surprise (and impress).

Driving Rules Seat belts are compulsory, and the driving age is 18. Helmets are compulsory for motorcycles; motoring offenses result in an on-the-spot fine. In case of an accident, leave the vehicle where the incident occurred and call the police (© **155**). See "Getting Around," p. 45.

Electricity The standard is 220 volts, and outlets are compatible with the round European two-prong plug. Laptops are generally self-regulating, but check with your manufacturer before plugging in. You may be able to leave your hair dryer at home, as most hotel rooms come equipped with at least a weak one.

Embassies & Consulates All embassies are located in the nation's capital, Ankara. Many of these have consulates in Istanbul, while a few even have extra representation in destinations where large numbers of nationals holiday. The embassy of **Australia** is at Uğur Mumcu Cad. 88/7, Gaziosmanpaşa (© **0312/459-9500**; www.turkey.embassy.gov.au). There is also a consulate in Istanbul. See website for complete listing. The embassy of **Canada** is Cinnah Cad. 58, Çankaya (© **0312/409-2700**; www.cic.gc.ca). The embassy of **Ireland** is Uğur Mumcu Cad. 88/3, Gaziosmanpaşa (© **0312/446-6172**; http://foreignaffairs.gov.ie). Ireland has an Honorary Consulate in Istanbul. See website for complete listing. The embassy of **New Zealand** is at Iran Cad. 13/4, Kavaklıdere (📞 **0312/467-9054;** www.nzembassy.com). New Zealand maintains an Honorary Consulate in Istanbul. See website for details. The embassy of the **United Kingdom** is at Şehit Ersan Cad. 46/A, Çankaya (📞 **0312/455-3344;** www.britainusa.com). The U.K. also has a British consulate in Istanbul.

Emergencies For fire dial 📞 **110;** for general first-aid emergencies (ambulance included) dial 📞 **112.** For other health services or to call for a private ambulance in Istanbul: International Hospital Ambulance (📞 **0212/663-3000**); Istanbul Health Services (European side 📞 **0212/247-0781;** Asian side 📞 0216/302-1515). In Ankara call Bayındır Hospital Ambulance (📞 **0312/287-9000**), or call Özel Ambulans Servisi (📞 **0312/425-1565**).

Gasoline (Petrol) At press time, in Turkey, the cost of gasoline (also known as petrol) is abnormally high, at around 1.7YTL per liter, or just under $5 per gallon. Taxes are already included in the printed price (thankfully). One U.S. gallon equals 3.8 liters or .85 imperial gallons. Gas stations are plentiful and are called Petrol Ofisi.

Holidays The official holidays are New Year's Day (Jan 1), Independence and Children's Day (Apr 23), Youth and Sports Day (May 19), Victory Day (Aug 30), and Republic Foundation Day (Oct 29). Banks, public offices, and schools are closed for these national holidays. Although a secular state, most Turks also celebrate Şeker Bayramı, a 3-day celebration punctuating the end of the feast of Ramadan (Sept 2-Oct 1, 2008; Aug 22-Sept 21, 2009), and Kurban Bayramı (Dec 7–10, 2008, Nov 27–30, 2009), a 4-day feast honoring Abraham's willingness to sacrifice his son to God. All Islamic holidays follow a lunar calendar and thus fall on different dates every year: Banks, governmental offices, and most shops are closed on these days. For more information on holidays see "Calendar of Events," earlier in this chapter.

Hospitals For other health services or to call for a private ambulance in Istanbul: International Hospital Ambulance (📞 **0212/663-3000**); Istanbul Health Services (European side 📞 **0212/247-0781;** Asian side 📞 0216/302-1515). In Ankara call Bayındır Hospital Ambulance (📞 **0312/287-9000**), or call Özel Ambulans Servisi (📞 **0312/425-1565**). For general first-aid emergencies (ambulance included) dial 📞 **112.** Contact information in emergencies is also listed in the appropriate chapter.

Internet Access Turkey is one of the most connected countries around. Most hotels (even the pensions) have wireless, and at the very least, there will be a computer for use by guests. Internet cafes are also plentiful.

Legal Aid Foreigners and tourists get the benefit of the doubt in most every run-in with the law, but there are some things you just can't talk your way out of. If you're caught speeding, expect to pay dearly and on the spot. For real trouble, contact your embassy or consulate for assistance and ask for their list of private law firms catering to English-speaking foreigners.

Lost & Found Be sure to tell all of your credit card companies the minute you discover your wallet has been lost or stolen and file a report at the nearest police precinct. Your credit card company or insurer may require a police report number or record of the loss. Most credit card companies have an emergency toll-free number to call if your card is lost or stolen; they may be able to wire you a cash advance immediately or deliver an emergency credit card in a day or two. Visa's U.S. emergency number is ℂ 800/847-2911 or 410/581-9994. American Express cardholders and traveler's check holders should call ℂ 800/221-7282. MasterCard holders should call ℂ 800/307-7309 or 636/722-7111. For other credit cards, call the toll-free number directory at ℂ 800/555-1212.

Mail The PTT (post office), hard to miss with its black and yellow signs, offers the usual postal services, in addition to selling tokens *(jeton)* and phone cards for the phone booths located in and around the post office and in most public places. Postcards cost 35¢ (20p) to Europe and 70¢ (35p) to all other continents. The PTT also has currency exchange and traveler's check services; in major tourist areas PTT kiosks are strategically located for emergency money needs. For express deliveries or shipping packages, the PTT operates an *acele posta servisi* (or APS), but for your own sense of security, you'd better stick with the old reliable UPS or DHL.

Maps The tourist information office should be your first stop in every destination for local maps, which are detailed and free. The only difference between the free maps and the commercial ones, available in bookstores and tourist boutiques, is that the latter are usually illustrated with icons of important sites, so you don't inadvertently stroll by the Blue Mosque without realizing it.

Measurements See the chart on the inside front cover of this book for details on converting metric measurements to U.S. equivalents.

Newspapers & Magazines The *Turkish Daily News* and the *Turkish Press* are Turkey's most widely circulated national English-language papers providing local, national, and international news. Both have websites (www.turkishdaily news.com and www.turkishpress.com). The Turkish newspapers, *Zaman* and *Hürriyet,* also have English-language websites (www.zaman.com and www. hurriyet.com.tr). In the larger cities, the *International Herald Tribune, USA Today,* and Britain's *Financial Times* are widely available, although they're generally light on local news. The *Guide Istanbul* is a good resource for events in town (free in most five-star hotels), with interesting features and essential local listings. *Cornucopia* is a more upscale English-language glossy featuring articles on Turkish art, history, and culture, while Turkish Airlines' *Skylife* and the airport's own *Gate1* shouldn't be overlooked for monthly exhibits and performances as well as features on destination-related topics.

Passports **For U.S. Residents:** Whether you're applying in person or by mail, you can download passport applications from the U.S. Department of State website at http://travel.state.gov. To find your regional passport office, check the U.S. Department of State website or call the toll-free number of the National Passport Information Center (ℂ **877/487-2778)** for automated information.

For Canada Residents: Passport applications are available at travel agencies throughout Canada or from the central **Passport Office,** Department of Foreign Affairs and International Trade, Ottawa, ON K1A 0G3 (ℂ **800/567-6868;**

www.ppt.gc.ca). *Note:* Canadian children who travel must have their own passport. However, if you hold a valid Canadian passport issued before December 11, 2001, that bears the name of your child, the passport remains valid for you and your child until it expires.

For Ireland Residents: You can apply for a 10-year passport at the **Passport Office,** Setanta Centre, Molesworth Street, Dublin 2 (© **01/671-1633;** www.irl gov.ie/iveagh). Those under age 18 and over 65 must apply for a 3-year passport. You can also apply at 1A South Mall, Cork (© **021/272-525),** or at most main post offices.

For Residents of Australia: You can pick up an application from your local post office or any branch of Passports Australia, but you must schedule an interview at the passport office to present your application materials. Call the **Australian Passport Information Service** at © **131-232,** or visit the government website at www.passports.gov.au.

For New Zealand Residents: You can pick up a passport application at any New Zealand Passports Office or download it from their website. Contact the **Passports Office** at © **0800/225-050** in New Zealand or 04/474-8100, or log on to www.passports.govt.nz.

For Residents of the United Kingdom: To pick up an application for a standard 10-year passport (5-yr. passport for children under 16), visit your nearest passport office, major post office, or travel agency or contact the **United Kingdom Passport Service** at © **0870/521-0410** or search its website at www.ukpa. gov.uk.

Police Dial © **155** in the case of theft or in the event of a car accident, as you will need to fill out a police report for administrative and/or insurance purposes.

Safety See "Safety," earlier in this chapter.

Smoking A local saying goes something like this: "Eat like a Turk, smoke like a Turk," which roughly translates to "If you're a nonsmoker, tough luck." In theory, smoking is prohibited on public transportation, in movie theaters, in airports, and the like. But realizing the hardships of driving a bus, bus companies allow the drivers to smoke. This is a good time to work on tolerance, and remember to pack Visine and to sit upwind at outdoor cafes.

Taxes The value-added tax (VAT or sales tax) in Turkey is called the KDV; in 2008, the Turkish government is cutting taxes charged to the tourism sector by 10%, from 18% to 8%. Don't expect to see this rebate hit your wallet anytime soon: It's unlikely that hotel rates will adjust downward to reflect this change. Meanwhile, alcohol is now taxed (by alcoholic content) at a rate that could make even an alcoholic think twice before ordering a drink. Stick to Turkish brands (or drink raki rather than white wine), and if you're going to splurge in a wine shop, ask the store owner to provide you with the special VAT Refund Invoice, which must then be validated at the Customs Office at the airport prior to departure.

Telegraph, Telex & Fax Most hotels have **fax machines** available for guest use (be sure to ask about the charge to use it). Many hotel rooms are even wired for guests' fax machines.

Time All of Turkey adheres to **Eastern European Time (EET),** which is Greenwich Mean Time +2. To make it easier: When it is noon in New York, it is 7pm in Istanbul. Daylight saving time, when clocks are set 1 hour ahead of standard time, is in effect as **Eastern European Summer Time (EEST)** from 1am on the second Sunday in March to 1am on the first Sunday in November.

Tipping Indispensable as a supplement to an already low wage, gratuities are a way of life in Turkey and are often expected for even the most minor service. Try to keep small notes handy and follow these guidelines: Give the **bellhop** 50 kuruş to 1YTL (45¢–87¢/20p–40p) per bag; leave at least an additional 10% of the restaurant bill for your **waiter;** reward your **tour guide** with 10€ to 20€ ($15–$29/£7.15–£14) for a job well done; thank the **captain** of your gulet with about 50€; and give the **attendant** in the Turkish bath 3€ to 5€ ($4.35–$7.25/ £2.15–£3.55) *before* the rubdown. Shows of appreciation are also expected from your **chambermaid,** your **barber** or **hairdresser,** and an **usher** who has shown you to your seat.

Toilets There are two types of waste repositories in Turkey—the traditional toilet and the Turkish toilet, that dreaded porcelain contraption in the floor. Traditional toilet bowls are equipped at the rear with a tube for running water operated by a faucet located on the wall to the right of the tank, allowing for quick cleanups after every use. Many Turks and Europeans swear the Turkish toilet is hygienically superior; but having stepped in more unidentifiable liquids than I care to remember, I'm not convinced. In any case, you'll be thankful for those footrests and might even master the art of avoiding backsplash. The floor-level faucet and bucket are also for quick wash-ups (probably the reason the floor is wet); in both cases, toilet paper is for drying. Flushing the toilet paper is sometimes hazardous to the life of the plumbing, but generally when this is the case, there will be a sign above the tank requesting that you dispose of it in the nearby wastebasket. My advice? Lift your skirts high, hang on to the cuffs of your pants, and *always* carry tissues.

Visas For information about Turkish visas go to **www.mfa.gov.tr/mfa** and click on "Consular Information." Or go to one of the following websites:

Citizens of **Australia** and **New Zealand** can obtain up-to-date visa information from the Embassy of the **Turkish Republic Canberra,** 6 Moonah Place, Yarralumla, ACT 2600 (© 02/6273-6592), or by checking **www.turkishembassy. org.au.** **British** subjects can obtain up-to-date visa information by calling the **Turkish Embassy** (© 020/7393-0202) or by visiting the "Consulates and Visas" section of the Turkish Embassy London's website at **www.turkishembassylondon. org.** **Canadians** can obtain up-to-date visa information by calling the Turkish Embassy at 197 Wurtemburg St. Ottawa, ON (© 613/789-4044), or by logging on to the embassy website at **www.turkishembassy.com.** Citizens of the **United States** are served by one of five regional consulates. For residents of Maryland, Virginia, Washington, D.C., West Virginia, and The Bahamas: Turkish Embassy, 2525 Massachusetts Ave. NW, Washington, DC 20008 (© **202/612-6700;** fax 202/612-6744; Consular Section: © 202/612-6741; fax 202/319-1639; www. turkey.org). For residents of Alabama, Arkansas, Louisiana, Missouri, New Mexico, Oklahoma, Tennessee, and Texas: Turkish Consulate, 1990 Post Oak Blvd.,

Suite 1300, Houston, TX 77056 (© **713/622-5849**; fax 713/623-6639). For residents of Alaska, Arizona, California, Colorado, Hawaii, Idaho, Montana, Nevada, Oregon, Utah, Washington State, Wyoming, and the Pacific Islands: Turkish Consulate, 6300 Wilshire Blvd., Suite 2010, Los Angeles, CA 90048 (© **323/655-8832**; fax 323/655-8681; www.trconsulate.org). For residents of Illinois, Indiana, Iowa, Kansas, Michigan, Minnesota, Mississippi, Nebraska, North Dakota, Ohio, South Dakota, and Wisconsin: Turkish Consulate, 360 Michigan Ave., Suite 1405, Chicago, IL 60601 (© **312/263-0644**; fax 312/263-1449). For residents of Connecticut, Delaware, Florida, Georgia, Kentucky, Maine, Massachusetts, New Hampshire, New Jersey, New York, North Carolina, Pennsylvania, Rhode Island, South Carolina, Vermont, and Puerto Rico: Turkish Consulate, 821 United Nations Plaza, New York, NY 10017 (© **212/949-0160**; fax 212/983-1293).

3

Suggested Turkey Itineraries

This chapter gives you a rough outline of what you can reasonably see in 1 or 2 weeks in Turkey. Here I make all the tough decisions for you (except for one; you'll need to choose between Ephesus and Cappadocia). If the idea of letting someone else plan your entire trip takes the wind out of your sails (and I can't blame you), you still might peruse this chapter to see my recommendations for exactly *how much* you can see here in this amount of time.

1 The Best of Turkey in 1 Week

Frankly, 1 week isn't enough time to explore very much of anything anywhere, let alone Istanbul, the seat of three former world empires. And that doesn't include the 2 days spent on international travel (assuming you had to cross an ocean to get here). Because all of Turkey's major sights are scattered to the four corners of the country—and getting from one to the next will involve either a flight, a long car or bus ride, or both—a scant 7 days will force you to make some hard choices, and you'll have to hustle at high speed during what traditionally should be "downtime." With 1 week, expect to have barely enough time to cover the basics of Istanbul and one other destination. Because boat captains now regularly offer 3- and 4-day "Blue Cruises," you just may be able to squeeze in one of these, although if you do, you'll surely be compromising any hopes of experiencing the heart and soul of Turkey by sequestering yourself on the (albeit magnificent) coastal seas.

That said, an oft-asked question is "Should I go to Ephesus or Cappadocia?" It's a true dilemma: Go to Ephesus, the ancient port city and home to early Christianity's most venerated icons—or head to Cappadocia, where all weird and wonderful rock formations *not* carved by nature were hollowed out for sheer secular and profane necessity. My answer is usually in the form of a question: "Why do you want to go to Ephesus?" Weed out the underlying sense of biblical enormity, and it's just another major archaeological must-see, right? So if the appeal is purely archaeological, and if you've been to Rome or seen Pompeii, then I'd have to tout Cappadocia as unique enough to win hands-down. Happily, with more than just 1 week (or high energy and lots of commitment), you can actually do both. So, depending on your interests and the answer to my question above, below are suggestions for both a 1- and 2-week itinerary.

Day ❶: Arrive, off and Running in Istanbul ☆☆☆

Most transatlantic flights arrive in **Istanbul** ☆☆☆ in the late morning, so after you check in to your hotel and have a quick nap and a shower, it's time to head out. Spend the first afternoon getting acquainted with the old city of Sultanahmet, beginning with a good orientation point, the **Hippodrome** ☆ (p. 112). You might duck into a local **tea garden** for a bite to eat (avoid the touristy ones closest to the Hippodrome). Then go directly to the Sultanahmet Mosque, better known as the **Blue Mosque** ໖໖໖ (p. 110). Follow this up with a walk through the imposing **Ayasofya** ໖໖໖ (p. 84), stopping along the way for a quick peek into the **Haseki Sultan Hamamı** (p. 129), now a beautifully restored space used by the Ministry of Tourism as a fixed-priced carpet shop (see "Shopping" in chapter 4). Next stop is the ancient underground **Yerebatan Cistern** ໖໖ (p. 128) across the street at Yerebatan Caddesi. If you haven't yet run out of daylight, scoot over to the **St. Savior in Chora** church ໖໖໖ (p. 127) for some of the finest Byzantine mosaics anywhere—and plan to stay for dinner. (**Asitane** restaurant ໖໖໖ is located in the Kariye Hotel adjacent to the museum; p. 100.)

Day ❷: Topkapı Palace ໖໖໖ and the Grand Bazaar ໖໖໖

Begin day 2 fresher and better prepared for an exhausting morning poking around **Topkapı Palace** ໖໖໖ (p. 116), and don't you dare skip out on the **Treasury** ໖໖໖ (p. 118)—although if you're pressed for time or money, you can definitely skip the tour of the **Harem** ໖໖, which departs at regular intervals. Instead, head back to the first courtyard, where you'll find access to the Istanbul **Archaeology Museum** ໖໖ (p. 159). Few visitors take the time to visit this impressive collection of ancient and even famous artifacts (for example, the **Treaty of Kadesh,** signed by Pharaoh Ramses and the Hittite King), but I *highly* recommend this one and add that everyone I've ever sent here has thanked me for the tip. When you finally do exit the palace grounds, turn right immediately outside the main gate out along **Soğukçeşme Sokağı** (p. 140) for a walk through a typical 19th-century Ottoman neighborhood. Go down the hill and pick up the tram at the nearby Gülhane stop

(you'll have to cross the main avenue to get the correct tram) and take it to the Beyazit stop near one of the entrances to the **Grand Bazaar** ໖໖໖ (p. 141). If you ever get out of this shopping labyrinth, there's a sound-and-light show in **Sultanahmet Park** under the Blue Mosque on summer nights at 9pm (the language of the display rotates daily), after which you can grab dinner at one of the numerous rooftop restaurants mentioned in chapter 4.

Day ❸: A Day on the Bosphorus, and an Ottoman Band

Set out early in the morning for a daylong cruise up the **Bosphorus** (p. 138), allowing yourself at least an hour to explore the **Egyptian Spice Bazaar** ໖໖໖ (p. 141) and neighboring **Yeni Cami** (p. 132) before you board at the nearby ferry docks. If you're concerned about time, take a half-day guided sightseeing tour, which includes a stop at the Egyptian Bazaar, an informed description of the sights along the Asian and European shores, and a visit to **Rumeli Castle** (p. 139), which wraps up around lunchtime. If you take the guided tour, spend the remainder of the afternoon walking the length of Istanbul's main artery, on **Istiklal Caddesi** (p. 142) and poking in and around the back streets of **Beyoğlu.** If possible, arrange this afternoon exploration around the 3pm performance of the mighty **Mehter Band** ໖໖໖ in the **Military Museum** ໖໖ up in Harbiye (walking distance from Taksim Square or a short taxi ride; p. 133). If you miss the 3pm English performance, the whole thing repeats in Turkish at 3:30pm. Then, if you allow yourself one unexpected itinerary stop in Istanbul, make it this: From the Military Museum, take a taxi up to the modern and trendy seaside village of **Ortaköy** (just above the Çırağan Palace), where you'll find restaurants, cafes, and sidewalk vendors under the Bosphorus bridge (p. 142). Reward yourself with a relaxing dinner at one of the many places on the quay, or head back to Beyoğlu for a meal at one of the classic *meyhanes* (taverns) of the *Balıkpazarı* (fish bazaar).

For the rest of your week in Turkey, you're faced with the big question: "Ephesus or Cappadocia?" I'm outlining a plan for both:

PLAN A:

Day ❹: The Ancient Site of Ephesus ✸✸✸

Take a domestic flight to Izmir, and using either Selçuk or Kuşadası as your base, spend the day visiting the archaeological site of **Ephesus** ✸✸✸, the **Ephesus Museum** ✸✸✸, the **Temple of Artemis** ✸, **St. John's Basilica** ✸✸✸, and the **House of the Virgin Mary** ✸✸✸. If you have your own car, have dinner up in the village of **Şirince** ✸✸.

See the "Selçuk & Ephesus" section, beginning on p. 212, for all listings.

Day ❺: Pamukkale's Travertine Terraces ✸✸

You'll need a whole day for a visit to **Pamukkale** ✸✸, which should include a visit to the **travertines** ✸✸ and the archaeological site of **Hierapolis** ✸✸, plus a dip in the effervescent **Sacred Pool** ✸✸✸. If you've got your own wheels, stop along the way at the impressive ruins of **Aphrodisias** ✸✸.

See the "Pamukkale & Hierapolis" section, beginning on p. 233, for all listings.

Day ❻: Three Greek Sites

Dedicate the day to exploring the more neighboring ancient sites of **Priene** ✸✸, **Miletus** ✸✸, and **Didyma** ✸✸ (p. 230) on a leisurely drive down to **Bodrum** ✸✸✸.

Day ❼: Bodrum and Beyond

On your last day in Turkey, you'll have to decide whether you want to relax on a beach or maintain your holiday in the fast lane. Either way, you should schedule a visit to the **Underwater Archaeology Museum** ✸✸✸, located in the conspicuous and imposing **St. Peter's Castle** ✸✸✸. And although there's not much left of the supposedly wondrous **Mausoleum of Halicarnassus,** you'll have to do some impressive tap-dancing to explain to your friends why you didn't go. (It'll be quick, I promise.) Do both of these things early, to leave plenty of time to drive out to **Gümüşlük** ✸✸, the as-of-yet unspoiled waterside village and site of submerged ancient ruins. There's a tiny beach there too, although better beaches are located all along the peninsula, particularly around Yalıkavak and Turgutreis. (If you prefer a beach closer to home, head over to the crowded resort beaches at Gümbet, the bay adjacent to downtown Bodrum.)

See the "Bodrum" section, beginning on p. 238, for all listings.

Or you might be tempted by the landscape of Cappadocia:

PLAN B:

Day ❹: Cappadocia's Fairy Chimneys and Monastic Caves ✸✸✸

Take an early domestic flight to **Cappadocia** ✸✸✸. If you're arriving in Kayseri, it's about an hour's drive into any of the towns in the region. Rent a car and begin your visit in the rock-cut monastery of **Zelve Valley** ✸, being careful not to slip during one of the more challenging cave climbs (climbing not obligatory). Depart Zelve, following signs for the **open-air museum of Göreme** ✸✸✸, with its frescoed churches and fairy chimneys. Follow the road into the modern section of the village, and have a bite to eat at the Orient Restaurant. Spend some time in the bazaar behind the *otogar,* and then head out for a visit to the rock city of **Üçhisar** ✸✸✸. Climb up to the top of the fortress for a splendid panoramic view of the entire region, second only to a sunrise balloon ride, do some shopping at the base of the fortress, and then head back to your hotel for some old-fashioned Turkish conversation and a glass of tea.

See chapter 8 for all listings.

Day ❺: Cappadocia's Underground Cities

Set out early in the morning for the **underground cities** ✿✿✿ of Kaymaklı and Derinkuyu, where you will work up an appetite ascending and descending hundreds of underground steps. Drive the short distance to Belisırma, one of the access points for entry into the **Ihlara Valley** ✿. Before setting out on your hike, stop at one of the combination restaurant-and-camping sites for a rustic riverside lunch. After lunch, head over to the village of **Güzelyurt** ✿, wander through the valley, and poke through the village's own underground city. Finish up with dinner at the open buffet at the Kaya Hotel in Üçhisar, unless your hotel offers dinner on the premises.

See chapter 8 for all listings.

Day ❻: Cappadocia: Land of Beautiful Horses

Experience the **valleys of Cappadocia** ✿✿✿ firsthand with a horseback-riding tour or a hike through the valleys. Have lunch at the Greek House in Mustafapaşa and spend the rest of the day around **Avanos** hunting for ceramics or shopping in Ürgüp for carpets, traditional

keepsakes, or silver. Try to manage your time so that you're in town for the 9pm showing of the **Whirling Dervishes** at the 12th-century **Sarıhan** caravansary.

See chapter 8 for all listings.

Day ❼: Ankara: Pre- and Post-Republican

Take this day to drive to and visit **Ankara,** from where you can arrange to fly home via Istanbul. Begin your time in Ankara around the ancient **citadel** ✿, starting with the remarkable **Museum of Anatolian Civilizations** ✿✿✿ (which also has a great gift shop). A few steps up the hill opposite the entrance to the fortress is the restored **Çengelhan,** the 16th-century caravansary now housing the **Rahmi Koç Science Museum.** Spend an hour wandering around the inside of the citadel, then head left outside the entrance you came in through, and work your way through the copper, antiques, and carpet shops on the steeply cobbled streets heading to the daily market on **Çıkrıkçılar Caddesi.** From the bottom of Çıkrıkçılar Caddesi you will find yourself back in the heart of Ulus. From here, take a taxi to the Atatürk Mausoleum and Museum at **Anıtkabir** ✿✿. Once finished, have dinner at one of the restaurants off of Tünalı Hilmi, and then call it a day.

See chapter 9 for all listings.

2 The Best of Turkey in 2 Weeks

Follow the suggestions for the 1-week itinerary for the first week. Then assess how much time and energy you want to put into travel and what your travel goals are. Outdoor activities, historic ruins, and extraordinary natural sites converge along **the coast between Antalya and Fethiye,** which is where I recommend you spend the remainder of your stay. If you're arriving from "Plan B" (Cappadocia), you can start your Turquoise Coastal Tour in Antalya (the drive takes about 5½ hours from Cappadocia; you can also fly via Istanbul) and follow these suggestions beginning with day 14 and working backward. Or fly into Dalaman beginning at the top, in Fethiye. In either case, you'll lose a day, unfortunately, either at the airport or on the road.

Day ❽: Fly & Drive to Fethiye

Assuming you have any time left over after your travels, spend the day wandering around the old city of **Fethiye,** shopping, eating, and taking a *hamam* break. Visit the **Roman theater** and the rock-cut **Lycian tombs** ★★ of ancient Telmessos. Have dinner at Meğri Restaurant in the center of the old town, and then have a drink at Türkü Evi, a characteristic Turkish pub.

See the "Fethiye & Ölüdeniz" section, beginning on p. 272, for listings.

Days ❾ & ❿: Blue Waters and Stunning Scenery

Take a few hours in the National Park area (**Ölüdeniz, or the Blue Lagoon** ★★★), where you can swim in the lagoon that graces the cover of every tourism brochure on Turkey's Mediterranean. From the waterfront of **Belcekız Beach** ★★★, hop on one of the few daily boat taxis for the half-hour trip to **Butterfly Valley** ★★★, where you can either test out another beach or hike back toward the head of the gorge and the waterfalls. If you abhor crowds (and have a car or scooter), drive up past the ghost village of Kayaköy to the secluded and stunning **Gemiler Beach** ★★★. On the way back, stop off at **Kayaköy** ★★★ for a haunting sunset, and then grill your own wild boar in the garden restaurant of Cin Bal. On day 10, take the **"12-Island Tour"** ★★, a daylong minicruise to watery caves and breathtaking coves where you can swim ashore for a close-up view of abandoned ruins—or, if you've had enough of beautiful blue waters, take this opportunity to visit the 18km (11-mile) gorge of **Saklıkent** ★★.

See the "Fethiye & Ölüdeniz" section, beginning on p. 272, for listings.

Days ⓫, ⓬, ⓭ & ⓮: The Lovely Lycian Coast

Leave Fethiye early to allow time to explore the ruins of **Xanthos** ★★ and **Patara** ★★ (and perhaps spend a few hours on **Patara Beach** ★★ on your way east). There are a number of points along the coast that are worthy of a stopover; these are generally limited by the location of your hotel. I recommend an overnight in **Kaş** ★★, **Olympos** ★★, or, if you can hold out for a late arrival after a full day of exploration, **Antalya** ★. Places to stop along the way? There's **Kekova Bay** ★★★, where ancient Lycian tombs tumble into the sea. Take a boat taxi over to the idyllic village of **Kale** ★★ (ancient Simena) for a lunch of fresh fish with your feet dangling in the reeds, and a short walk up to the castle. Olympos is another one of my favorite destinations, located on the outskirts of the small beachfront village of **Çıralı** ★★. It's also a good starting place for a short walk along the **Lycian Way.** An afternoon picnic and stroll through ancient Roman ruins are even more delightful than imaginable at **Phaselis** ★★★, where a pine tree forest meets a particularly lovely trio of harbors. Finish up in **Antalya** ★★, either with some last-minute shopping in the meandering streets of **Kaleiçi,** in the **Antalya Museum** ★★★, or curled up on a cushion at one of the choice beach clubs now lining the pebbled waterfront of **Konyaaltı** ★★★.

See chapter 7 for all listings.

4

Istanbul

Rarely will a visit to Turkey exclude the chaotic and glorious wonder that is **Istanbul** ✦✦✦. Istanbul is home to a layering of civilization on civilization, of empire built on empire. It's as momentous as Rome, as captivating as Paris, and as exotic as Bangkok. It is all of the praises one can imagine while being simultaneously the opposite.

As the riches of Istanbul increase, urban modernization projects erase a past that—illustrated by the discovery of Theodosius's port at present-day Yenikapı—threaten the historical record pretty much any time anyone puts a shovel to the ground.

And now to the necessary clichés: As the only city on earth to straddle two continents and literally the city of civilization's desires, Istanbul is an enduring symbol of greatness. It has endured attempted or successful conquests down the historic dateline by Xerxes, Darius, Alexander the Great, the Romans, the Visigoths, the Huns, the Crusaders, the Arab raiders, and the Ottomans. In more recent centuries, Russia also had its eye on the prize of Istanbul, covetous of control of the Bosphorus Straits and free passage from the Black Sea into the Mediterranean and the trade routes beyond. Even today, hundreds of thousands of sometimes oversize and hazardous ships stream up and down this epic waterway as they make their way through the center of both a city and a nation.

The parade of civilizations converges on the historic peninsula, also known as Old Stamboul or the Old City. It is the capital of empires and a religious center, the heart of the Greek Orthodox Church and for centuries the Islamic faith. Istanbul is the custodian of one of the world's most important cultural heritages and home to some of the world's most opulent displays of art and wealth. A stroll through the neighborhoods that make up the historic peninsula will reveal the foundations of ancient Rome and Byzantium, with gilded mosaics like those in the Ayasofya and St. Savior in Chora or the more modest peristyle (open court with porticos) of the Great Palace. The Ottoman dynasty redirected the city's fortunes into the imperial majesty of undulating domes and commanding minarets, and the sumptuous mystique of Topkapı and Dolmabahçe palaces. Fatih Mehmet II was himself astounded at the beauty of the city he had finally conquered, and he as well as subsequent sultans fixated on replicating the symbolic splendor of the Ayasofya in what has become a panorama of monumental imperial mosques.

Across the Golden Horn is the modern heart of the city, heir to the future of the country, pulsating with all the electricity of a cutting-edge international metropolis. While the political capital of Ankara sits safely in the heartland, this part of Istanbul is Turkey's center for art, entertainment, music, cuisine, education, and yes, even international diplomacy. Meanwhile, in anticipation of its upcoming 2010 reign as Cultural Capital of Europe, Istanbul is undergoing an unprecedented frenzy of modernization. The ambitious

Frommer's Favorite Istanbul Experiences

- **Experiencing the *Hamam* (Turkish Bath):** Go for broke and sign up for the skin sloughing and massage.
- **Hearing a Performance of the Ottoman Mehter Band:** The underappreciated Military Museum in Harbiye puts on two half-hour daily performances of what was once the avant-garde of the fearless and brutal Ottoman army.
- **Having a Drink in the Courtyard of the Old Prison Walls:** The former house of nightmares is now the gardens of the Four Seasons Hotel, where you can relax over a raki (aniseed-flavored spirit) and admire the lookout towers.
- **Eating Your Way Through Ortaköy:** The neighborhood is particularly vibrant on a summer evening, with the lights twinkling beneath the Bosphorus Bridge. The streets behind the mosque are a food fair of Turkish fast food, or choose a spot at one of the many popular cafes.
- **Soaking Up the Atmosphere at the Pierre Loti Café:** The views of the Golden Horn from this hilltop make the trip to Pierre Loti worth the detour. Take a walk through the picturesque cemetery adjacent to the cafe.
- **Taking a Tour Through Dolmabahçe Sarayı:** The members of the tour group are almost as entertaining as the tour itself. The great equalizer has to be the plastic blue booties mandatory for admittance into the palace, but a look at the palace's crystal staircase and superb *hamam* will remind you of the divide between the haves and the have-nots.
- **Wandering the Streets Between the Egyptian Spice Market and the Grand Bazaar:** It's just as much fun outside as it is inside the markets, where purveyors of produce set their prepared foods out on the streets for the local lunch crowd. Bring wet wipes.

Marmaray railway project, spanning the entire province of Istanbul and passing beneath Istanbul's storied waterways, is making steady progress. The city's internal transport network has gone from a disjointed conglomerate of disconnected services to a coherent and efficient system in less than a decade. And you'll be hard-pressed to *avoid* wireless connectivity here.

Meanwhile, Istanbul has simultaneously made a commitment to preserving its past. Excavations are under way at Yenikapı, Sirkeci and Üsküdar, a result of the excavations going on related to the transport project. Museums are investing in celebrity-level exhibits showcasing highlights of Turkey's heritage, while forgotten neighborhoods such as Süleymaniye, Balat, Cihangir, and Galata are being preserved, restored, and transformed into desirable historic neighborhoods. It's enough to make a guidebook writer's head spin.

Amidst this blitzkrieg of modernization, Istanbul's past endures. Istanbul comprises a long list of polar opposites that creates an exotic, complex, and utterly monumental stew. It's enchanting, it's infuriating, and it's irresistible.

- **Hunting the Labyrinthine Corridors of the Grand Bazaar:** When the sales-man turns away from you in disgust, you've learned the bottom price for that item. Find another stall selling the same thing and conclude the transaction in the old-fashioned Turkish way: with a handshake and a "güle güle" (goodbye).
- **Crossing the Galata Bridge on Foot from Karaköy to Eminönü:** Fishermen line the railings above, while dinner (or tea, or backgammon) is served below as the majestic and inspiring silhouettes of the Süleymaniye, Rüstem Paşa, and Yeni Camii loom in the distance. If you're there after sunset, you'll get to see seagulls circling the minarets.
- **Taking a Cruise up the Bosphorus:** This time-honored boat trip crosses from Europe to Asia and back again every 15 minutes. Float in the wake of Jason and the Argonauts, Constantine the Great, and others, and imagine the battles that took place between these shores.
- **Dining at Asitane:** Overload on kebaps (kabobs) and *köfte* (meatballs). Most restaurants bill themselves as "Ottoman," but few of them can actu-ally boast of having translated the recipes from the kitchens of Topkapı.
- **Noshing Waterside at Eminönü:** For 12 to 14 hours a day, fresh fish is grilled quayside and on the boat, presented for a spectacular 3YTL ($2.60/£1.20) by a scruffy fishmonger in traditional costume. Grab your sandwich and step aside; the condiments are to the right on the railing. Or if walking tours have got you dog-tired, grab a seat at the crowded **Tarihi Galata Balik Evi** (with your back to the Egyptian Spice Bazaar, it's on the left side of the bridge), which churns out the highest inventory of "fish between the bread."

1 Orientation

ARRIVING

BY PLANE

Istanbul's **Atatürk International Airport** (© 0212/663-6400; www.ataturkairport.com) is Turkey's primary hub for airline traffic in and out of the country (followed by Ankara and Izmir), located in the Istanbul suburb of Yeşilköy. (For information on flights into Istanbul, see "Arriving at the Airport," in chapter 2.) The modern airport has a 24-hour pharmacy, a clinic, and a kids' playroom (freeing you up to shop or get a mas-sage). There are also two tourist information desks; several car-rental desks (including Avis, Sixt, Hertz, Budget, Europcar, and National); Türkiye Iş Bankası for on-the-spot money changing; and an ATM compatible with the Cirrus, PLUS, Visa, and Master-Card networks, all located on the lower level of the International Arrivals terminal.

At the time of this writing, most hotels have been competing for your business by offering additional services such as free pickup at the airport. In the absence of this perk, a taxi into Sultanahmet from Atatürk Airport should cost around 16YTL

⊘ Value Airport Transport on the Cheap

Many hotels are now offering free pickup at the airport from both Atatürk International and Sabiha Gökçen airports. Check to see if yours is one of them.

($14/£6.40) and a ride into Taksim around 25YTL ($22/£10), depending on traffic and whether or not you got the scenic route. Alternatively, there is the reliable and convenient **Havaş shuttle bus** (toll-free: ℭ **444-0487**) every 30 minutes from just outside the airport exit to Taksim (9YTL/$7.85/£3.60; 40 min.) as well as the cheaper and rarer green municipal bus no. 97 (1.30YTL/$1.15/50p). It's unlikely that guests heading to the deluxe hotels along the Bosphorus will be taking public transportation; nevertheless, Havaş also runs a shuttle from Atatürk Airport to the entrance of Akmerkez at Etiler (10YTL/$8.70/£4; 45 min.).

If you're on a budget and want to fully embrace independent travel, take advantage of the newly completed train connection between the airport (entrance is downstairs next to the international arrivals terminal; 1.30YTL/$1.15/50p) and Zeytinburnu, where you can connect above ground to the tramway into the historic part of the city (stops include Beyazit, Cağağoglu, Sultanahmet, Gülhane, Sirkeci, and Eminönü). You can also ride all the way to Kabataş (with stops at Karaköy, Tophane, and Findikli; from the last stop, there's a brand-new funicular transporting passengers up one of Istanbul's steeper hills to Taksim). The whole trip costs 1.30YTL/$1.15/50p if you use the Akbil; otherwise it'll be 1.30YTL per transfer and will take a little over an hour. Check out the handy online map of Istanbul's system of trains, trams, and metro at www.iett.gov.tr (look for "Harita," or map). Trains (metro, tramway, funicular) run, approximately, from 6am to midnight.

Visitors arriving via London, Bologna, Vienna, Amsterdam, and Milan now have the option of flying one of a number of budget airlines into Istanbul's **Sabiha Gökçen Airport** (ℭ **0216/585-5000;** www.sgairport.com), about 25 miles from the center of Istanbul. At the time of this writing, these included Pegasus from London, Bologna, and Vienna; Easyjet from London (Luton Airport); Condor from Amsterdam; and Myair from Milan.

There are Hertz and Decar rental desks in the international terminal of Sabiha Gökçen airport; Avis has a presence over in the domestic terminal. The on-site Türkiye Iş Bankası has both a currency exchange desk as well as an ATM on the Cirrus network.

Getting into town from Pendik, where Sabiha Gökçen is located, will require a bit more effort than from the more centrally located Atatürk Airport. A taxi all the way into Taksim will run in the neighborhood of 26YTL ($23/£10; add about 12YTL/$10/£4.80 if Sultanahmet is your destination). **Havaş** runs four lines from the airport; the ones we are concerned with go to Taksim (central; 1 hr.; 9.50YTL/ $8.25/£3.80), Levent (good access to hotels on the Bosphorus; 1 hr.; 9.50YTL/ $8.25/£3.80), and Bostanci (accessible to establishments on the Asian side; 1 hr.; 7YTL/$6.10/£2.80).

Alternatively, the **Haydarpaşa-Gebze Train,** running from Pendik's station to Istanbul's Haydarpaşa on the Asian side, will get you at least halfway to your final destination (39 min.; 1.30YTL/$1.10/50p). From Haydarpaşa, it's an easy taxi ride to hotels in Üsküdar or Kadıköy (the likeliest neighborhoods for those choosing to stay on this

Istanbul at a Glance

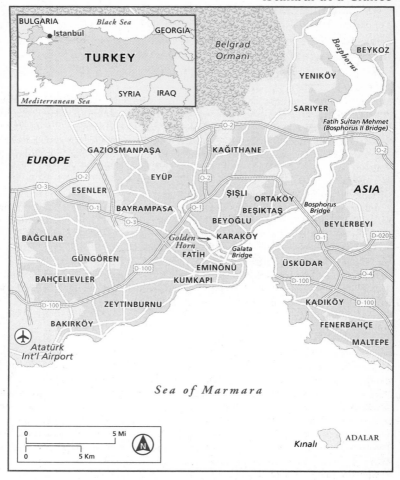

side of the Bosphorus). For those staying in or around Taksim or Eminönü, hop on a ferry to either Karaköy (for hotels in Beyoğlu, Taksim or Beşiktaş) or Eminönü (for hotels in Sirkeci, Sultanahmet, Cankurtaran or Beyazit). For more information, see "The Ferry & Seabus," below. By now you're probably soggy as old toast, so I recommend a cab for the final leg, or prearrange with your hotel for a pickup.

BY TRAIN

Sirkeci Station (© **0212/527-0050**) has been serving train passengers arriving (and departing) Istanbul from European cities for well over a century and has served as a model for railway stations throughout central Europe. A tram stop is immediately outside the station entrance, but don't rely on this if you're first arriving, as there is no ticket kiosk at this stop. Taxis are available, but note that during rush hour, the main road outside the entrance to the train station is a parking lot.

The **Haydarpaşa Station** in Kadıköy on the Asian side (*©* **0216/336-0475**) is the end of the line for trains arriving from Anatolia; there's a ferry landing just outside the station with service to Eminönü, Karaköy, Yenikapı, Avcılar, and Bakırköy.

VISITOR INFORMATION

In addition to offices at the airport (*©* **0212/663-0798**) and in Sirkeci Train Station (*©* **0212/511-5888**), you may stumble upon a tourist information office in one of the many tourist hubs around town. The location in Sultanahmet Meydanı (*©* **0212/518-1802**) is pretty handy, as are the ones in the Hilton Hotel Arcade (*©* **0212/233-0592**), in Beyazit Meydanı (near the Grand Bazaar; *©* **0212/522-4902**), and at the Karaköy Seaport (*©* **0212/249-5776**). If you're out and about and encounter trouble (pickpockets, scams, muggings), contact the passably multilingual Tourism Police at *©* **0212/527-4503** or 528-5369, or stop in at Yerebatan Cad. 6, in Sultanahmet.

A good majority of the airlines with a presence in Turkey can be found on or around Cumhuriyet Caddesi in Taksim. The major airlines for this book's audience are **American Airlines** (*©* 0212/219-8223; Halaskargazi Cad. 121—a continuation of Cumhuriyet Cad., Harbiye), **British Airways** (*©* 0212/317-6600; Büyükdere Cad. 209, Levent—nowhere near Taksim), **Delta Airlines** (*©* 0212/310-2000; Teşvikiye Cad. 103/4, Teşvikiye), **Lufthansa** (*©* 0212/315-3434; Dereboyu Cad. Özsezen İş Merkezi C Blok Esentepe—also nowhere near Taksim), **Singapore Airlines** (*©* 0212/232-3706; Halaskargazi Cad. 113, Harbiye), and **Turkish Airlines** (*©* 444-0849 toll-free, *©* 0212/465-3000 at the airport, and *©* 0212/252-1106 in Taksim; Cumhuriyet Cad. Gezi Dükkanları Sok. 7).

CITY LAYOUT

Istanbul is the only city in the world on two continents, split down the middle by the mighty Bosphorus Straits. To the east of the waterway is the **Asian side**, a predominantly residential retreat with little of the chaos of its European counterpart. The modern business district of Taksim and the historic peninsula of the Old City occupy the **European side** of the Bosphorus, separated by the picturesque **Golden Horn** estuary and connected by a number of bridges and by ferry. While the major sightseeing draw is over in the **Old City** (aka the **historic peninsula, Sultanahmet, Old Istanbul**), you should plan to give at least equal time to the modern heart of Istanbul, essential in gaining a balanced picture of the many facets of the city.

HOW TO FIND AN ADDRESS   Addresses in Turkey name the major thoroughfare followed by a logical walk-through of the smaller avenues until you get to the actual street address. Of course, in villages, where there are no major thoroughfares, you'll see a lot of the word *mahalle(si)*, which means, roughly, neighborhood. For example, if you're trying to find the Hotel Avicenna, located at Mimar Mehmet Ağa Caddesi, Amiral Tafdil Sok. 31–33, Sultanahmet/Istanbul, isolate the Sultanahmet neighborhood on the map of Istanbul and look for Mimar Mehmet Ağa Caddesi, one of the main arteries. Next, look for a cross street by the name of Amiral Tafdil Sokağı and you will find the hotel at numbers 31–33. (In this case, the hotel takes up two old Ottoman houses.) In many cases, there is another number after the street address following a slash (/), which specifies the floor on which a place is located—usually in the case of apartments, Internet cafes, offices, and other entities not located on the ground floor. Another handy word is *karşısı*, which means *across from*, as in *Isabey Camii karşısı*

Serin Sokak, Selçuk (across from the Isabey Mosque on Serin St., in Selçuk). Where the less orienting *"mahalle"* is in operation, just ask. Really.

In Istanbul, particularly on the repaved Istiklal Caddesi, there are two types of number plates for addresses: the old blue ones and the new red ones. For example, the address of an establishment may be listed as 51r or 33b.

Free maps are available at any tourist information office (until they run out). Also available for purchase in bookstores are maps with clear and easily identifiable main attractions, but the smaller streets are left nameless, if included at all. None of the maps mentioned above are 100% accurate, but you may not even notice because signs are posted everywhere for museums, hotels, and restaurants, and there will be plenty of people on the street offering to give you a hand. Asking directions is part of the local culture and a great way to get local tips.

ISTANBUL'S NEIGHBORHOODS IN BRIEF

Spread over two continents, the sprawling muddle that is Istanbul-the-city comprises nearly 100 square miles of history. The city of Istanbul is part of the province of Istanbul—think New York, New York—but seeing as how this is a city guide, we will mainly concern ourselves with the four central districts of **Beyoğlu, Beşiktaş, Eminönü,** and **Fatih,** plus throw in the highlights of the Bosphorus—both the European and Asian sides—because not to do so would be remiss.

The European and Asian sides of the city are bisected by the churning north-south artery that is the Bosphorus Straits. Strategic waterway and stuff of legends, the Bosphorus connects the nations of the Black Sea with the coveted trade routes of the Mediterranean.

The European side of Istanbul is itself separated by the estuary known in English as the Golden Horn and in Turkish as the Haliç. Bordering the south of the Golden Horn are the districts of Eminönü and Fatih, neatly enclosed by what remains of the Byzantine era defensive walls. These two districts make up the historic peninsula (aka Old Stamboul, Old Istanbul, and Rome of the East). To the north of the Golden Horn are Beyoğlu and Beşiktaş, a hodgepodge of ancient and modern, of historic and progressive.

So as not to confuse readers with a short description of every corner of Istanbul, it's important to know that neighborhoods generally bear the name of a major landmark like the mosque that served the quarter, and that neighborhood delineations are anything but clear-cut. Below is a liberal selection of areas ranging from the "must see" to "off the beaten track," but this list is by no means exhaustive.

European Side: Old Istanbul

The historic peninsula, home to the remnants of classical, Roman, Byzantine, and Ottoman eras, is now known as the modern-day district of **Eminönü.** The neighborhoods within the boundaries of the ancient city walls are oriented around the famed seven hills in an area of nearly 22 sq. km (8½ sq. miles). Eminönü also refers to the neighborhood and transportation hub at the base of the Galata Bridge (a decided lack of creativity in naming ports, neighborhoods, districts, cities, and provinces is a running theme throughout Turkish geography and a source of frustration for visitors). Here

is where you'll find ferries to just about everywhere, a metropolitan bus and *dolmuş* hub, the Egyptian Spice Bazaar, the Yeni and Rustem Paşa mosques, as well as a frenetic warren of passageways and back streets that wind their way uphill through local shops to the Grand Bazaar. Just steps to the east is the Sirkeci train station (final stop of the legendary Orient Express); here you'll find a bustling hub of people with places to go. It's easier to find more affordable food and lodging around this neighborhood than the more popular adjacent neighborhood of Sultanahmet. The easternmost tip of the peninsula known as Sarayburnu (literally translated as "palace point") is where Topkapı Palace presides over the strategic convergence of the Marmara Sea, the mouth of the Bosphorus, and the Golden Horn.

At the heart of the district is the neighborhood of **Sultanahmet**, centered around the Hippodrome, political arena, and present-day public space. Anchoring the historic center of the city are the Blue Mosque and the Ayasofya, two massive and magnificent edifices challenging each other from opposite ends of Sultanahmet Park. Bordering Sultanahmet to the southeast is the as-of-yet still characteristically residential quarter of **Cankurtaran**, named for the train station stop at Ahırkapi Gate and for all intents and purposes absorbed under the umbrella heading of Sultanahmet.

To the southwest of Sultanahmet along the Marmara Sea and along the ancient Sea Walls is **Kumkapı**, destination of local fishermen and home to the city's fish market and a dense cluster of touristy fish restaurants.

Eminönü is divided by the main avenue of **Divanyolu** (whose name changes to Yeniçeriler Cad. and then Ordu Cad. as it runs westward to the district of Fatih). Paving what was formerly the ceremonial entrance to the Great Palace, Divanyolu begins (or ends, if you were the emperor) at Sultanahmet Park, running westward through the neighborhoods of **Çemberlitaş** (former site of the Forum of Constantine and close to the Nuruosmaniye entrance to the Grand Bazaar), **Beyazit** (built on the ruins of the Forum of Theodosius and named for the Beyazit Mosque Complex), and Laleli. North and west of Beyazit is the neighborhood of **Süleymaniye** (after the mosque complex of the same name).

Back at Divanyolu (now Ordu Cad.), the road splits just as it enters the **district of Fatih** at **Aksaray;** the tramway, which follows Divanyolu, continues along the southernmost avenue (Millet Cad., aka Türgüt Özal Cad.), while the northern fork becomes the major thoroughfare of Vatan Caddesi (aka Adnan Menderes Bulv.).

The district of **Fatih** is named after the Fatih Mosque and complex built by and for Mehmet the Conqueror immediately after the conquest. It was constructed on the site of the Havariyun, the second-most revered Byzantine church after the Ayasofya, which was ravaged by earthquakes and fire. The district was prominent in the Byzantine and Ottoman eras, evidenced by the great number of monuments that dot this now bustling working-class conglomeration of diverse (including some fundamentalist) neighborhoods.

From north to south beginning at the Golden Horn are the twin quarters of **Fener** and **Balat**, Ottoman-era enclaves where Armenian, Greek, and Jewish immigrants first settled. This combined quarter is thick with the crumbling remains of monumental Byzantine palaces, synagogues, schools, and mosques. It's even the home of the Eastern Orthodox Patriarchate.

Several of the defunct Byzantine defensive gates still stand guard over the surrounding neighborhoods which now bear these names. Edirnekapı is the gateway to the Church of San Savior in Chora or Kariye Camii, while Ayvansaray sits at the base of the Old Galata Bridge near the remains of the Blachernae Palace and sections of the land walls.

Fatih's southeasternmost point is the busy port of **Yenikapı**, the departure point for seabuses to Bursa, the Marmara islands, and the southern shores of the Marmara Sea. Construction is currently taking place in Yenikapı for one of the metro stations for the in-progress Marmaray project, with extraordinary archaeological discoveries being made there.

Following the southern Marmara Sea shoreline is the **Sahil Yolu** (or the coastal road). This main thoroughfare connects the Old City with the airport and suburbs. The last neighborhood of interest as the road heads out of Fatih is **Yedikule** (translation: "Seven Towers"), the fortress constructed by Fatih Mehmet the Conqueror incorporating the earlier Theodesian land and sea walls. Almost no one goes to this neighborhood or museum, which is why you should go. There are fewer and fewer places like this in Istanbul these days.

While not within the district boundaries laid out above, I need to mention one more neighborhood on the southern banks of the Golden Horn. Located just northwest of the Haliç Bridge (above Fener and Balat) is the quarter of **Eyüp,** named for the Prophet Mohammad's warrior companion and standard-bearer, and one of the holiest figures in Islam, Eyüp Sultan. Tradition holds that Eyüp was slain in battle on this hill; the site, marked by a mosque complex and tomb, is now a point of pilgrimage for Muslims.

European Side: Beyoğlu, Beşiktaş & the Bosphorus villages of Europe and Asia

If the Old City is the jewel of empires, then the landmass on the opposite side of the Golden Horn is its crown.

The unwieldy district of **Beyoğlu** is subdivided, at least colloquially, into a mosaic of characteristic quarters. Beyoğlu is home to a more modern blend of culture, religion, and politics than on the other side of the Golden Horn. This triangle of Istanbul is connected to the Old City by the Galata Bridge (at Eminönü and the opposite port of Karaköy) and via the Atatürk Bridge.

The fortified area between the Atatürk and Galata bridges and extending up from the shoreline to the Galata Tower encloses one of Istanbul's more characteristic (and now gentrified) neighborhoods, known as **Galata.** Istanbul's earliest pre-classical settlements were found in and around Galata, today a hodgepodge of steeply sloping streets radiating from the tower. Where Karaköy and Galata merge, you'll find a wealth of architectural monuments left by the European communities that thrived here during the Ottoman period, as well as a small community of street urchins and—on the fringes—at least one brothel.

At the bottom of Galata Hill (and technically absorbing it) is **Karaköy,** a functionally messy and exhilarating transport hub. It's worth a visit for its local eateries, along with a number of significant monumental Ottoman constructions. Recent additions include the Istanbul Modern, as well as the leafy tea gardens and waterpipe cafes of **Tophane.**

At the summit of Galata Hill is **Tünel,** which also refers to the very short and very old one-stop funicular called Tünel. To make matters worse, both the upper and lower entrances of the funicular are called Tünel—thus, to avoid confusion, I refer to the area around the upper entrance as Upper Tünel and the lower, Lower Tünel, or Karaköy.

Radiating around Upper Tünel (as part of Beyoğlu also referred to as Beyoğlu) are turn-of-the-19th-century Belle Époque buildings—including a high density of foreign consulates—of 19th-century **Pera.** Pera recalls a bygone era of wealth, entitlement, and gaiety. Today, strolls along the Grand Rue de Pera have evolved into nightly walks down the same artery now known as Istiklal Caddesi.

Lining the steep slopes southeast of Istiklal Caddesi is the steep-stepped Renaissance quarter of **Çihangir.** Amidst the interwoven and alternating monikers of Taksim and Beyoğlu are antiques shops and artistic shops on and around **Cukurcuma.** These combined neighborhoods attract artists, diplomats, expat journalists, and just plain commuters along its streets full of gentrified cafes, restaurants, bars, and antiques boutiques.

If Beyoğlu is the heart and soul of modern Istanbul, then Istiklal Caddesi is its lifeline. This hectic shopping street bisects the district north from Tünel to the modern, pulsating, chaotic nucleus of the city known as **Taksim Square,** Istanbul's equivalent to New York's Times Square. Standing at the center is a statue of Atatürk and the founding fathers of Turkey, representing on one side the War of Independence and on the other the Republic. The Atatürk Cultural Center (Atatürk Kültür Merkezi)—there is talk of tearing the hideous but much-loved thing down—houses the State Opera and Ballet, and serves as a sometimes venue for the Biennale. The area is yet another commuter hub, a business center, and an open-air food court. A concentration of full-service, high-rise hotels targeting businesspeople makes the area around Taksim a convenient place to stay. The location is also connected to a transportation network that includes the Metro, a recently restored cable car/tramway along Istiklal Caddesi, a plethora of municipal buses, and a daunting network of *dolmuşes* (minibuses).

As the city and even the country's center, Taksim Square and the neighborhoods on its fringe are thick with nightclubs, seedy bars, and Internet cafes, attracting the indigents and pilferers of Istanbul. The neighborhood of **Tarlabaşı,** located on the opposite side of Tarlabaşı Caddesi, is home to a high density of crumbling architectural gems, but it's also where you'll find Istanbul's subculture of transvestites, criminal indigents, and prostitutes, newly displaced from the now-hip neighborhood of Cukurcuma. Steer clear for now, but watch this space, as gentrification may be on the way.

The city gets increasingly more elite the farther north of Taksim you go. Immediately to the north (and inland) of the square is the business district of **Harbiye,** which sidles up to the fashionable shopping neighborhood of **Nişantaşı,** a pleasant cross between New York's SoHo and Madison Avenue (this latter is technically in the district of Şişli, but never mind). Boutiques along **Teşvikiye** Caddesi and the smaller side streets of the neighborhood are stocked with high-quality merchandise in elegant settings, with major names like Mudo, Emporio Armani, Vakko, and Beyman.

Maçka can be considered Istanbul's Wall Street, while the neighborhoods become more residential the farther away from Taksim you go. Maç sits just north/east of Taksim Square and is known as Istanbul's Convention Valley because of the conference center and business hotels there.

Beşiktaş (the district, that is) refers to the Bosphorus-front area above Beyoğlu. It was made popular by a long string of sultans, paşas, and empresses who constructed European-style palaces all along the historic Straits, including Dolmabahçe, Yıldız,

> **Fun Fact   Did You Know?**
>
> Beşiktaş, meaning "cradle stone," is named after the crib in which Jesus was born, which was thought to have been brought here by early Christians.

and Çırağan palaces. The better hotels are scrambling for this prime real estate; the new Four Seasons will be open by the time this book hits the stands, while the stylish new Radisson SAS has already established itself as a favorite. Not to be outdone by Eminönü, **Beşiktaş** is also a bustling shopping, port, and transport hub neighborhood.

To the north is the uptown village with the downtown feel—**Ortaköy,** which sits at the base of the Bosphorus Bridge. It's a tiny triangle of narrow cobblestone streets enlivened by bohemian shops and cafes. All of these streets converge on the open plaza of Ortaköy Square, with postcard views of Ortaköy Mosque, ferryboat pier, and Bosphorus Bridge.

The waterfront northward becomes a picturesque chain of fishing coves transformed into bourgeois residential neighborhoods as far north as the Black Sea mouth of the Bosphorus. These include **Aravutköy, Bebek, Rumeli Hisarı, Emirgan, Istinye, Tarabya, Sariyer,** and **Rumeli Kavağı.** You can visit these by hopping on a local bus or sightsee from the bow of a Bosphorus ferry.

The Asian Side

The Asian side is a quiet and predominantly upper-class residential area that, incredibly, has more European character than the European side. The districts of **Kadıköy** and **Üsküdar** are interspersed with a smattering of architecturally outstanding mosques, monuments, and synagogues. While covering a lot of territory worthy of a

student of architecture, there's nothing so remarkable that you need to forfeit a day on the opposite shores. Many visitors include a midday stop at **Anadolu Kavağı** halfway through the Bosphorus cruise (see "Take a Quick Cruise," below) for lunch and perhaps a walk up to where one can enjoy a panorama of both the Marmara and Black seas—but the charm of this fisherman's village has recently been compromised by summer tourists all descending there with the same idea.

The tree-lined section along **Bağdat Caddesi** is frequently touted as a shopping destination, but frankly has nothing exceptional to offer a foreigner accustomed to a cosmopolitan shopping day out.

Beylerbeyı Sarayı, the summer palace of the sultans, commands the right banks of Üsküdar above the Bosphorus Bridge. Combine a visit to Beylerbeyı with lunch at one of the more charming boat landings (**Çengelköy** is famous for its cucumbers and persimmons, while people flock to **Kanlica** for yogurt from heaven). Or on Tuesday, you can spend a few hours wandering through the Salı Pazarı ("Tuesday Bazaar" near the Kadıköy landing), and then tell everyone you spent the afternoon in Asia.

Because of the phenomenal views from the newer hotels (which also provide complimentary boat-shuttle service to the European side), Asia might actually be a reasonable place to hang your hat, particularly if it's a wedding veil.

2 Getting Around

BY PUBLIC TRANSPORTATION

Transportation in Istanbul is like the Internet: It's anonymous, indispensable, and completely decentralized. Implemented with little thought to how one service might be integrated with another, the network of buses, minibuses, funiculars, ferries, catamarans, subways, trains, tramways, and trolley cars will certainly get you where you're going, but you may have to take all of them to get there. Buying a transit pass will make it a bit easier (see "Transport Made Easy with the Akbil," below); otherwise, you'll have to pay a fare for each leg.

THE BUS   Metropolitan buses in Istanbul are frequent, comprehensive, and economical. They're easy—if you know your way around, that is! The final destination of the bus is indicated above the front windshield, with a selection of major stops listed on the side of the bus next to the entrance (admittedly not much help if you aren't familiar with the basic layout of the city). Always check with the driver before getting on to make sure the bus is going in the direction you need, and once boarded, ask your neighbor frequently when to get off. Some of the more useful hubs are at Eminönü, Taksim, and Beşiktaş. Tickets are sold at the major hubs or on the bus—if your bus doesn't have a "cashier" onboard, there's an informal system whereby you can pay the driver, who will in turn hand you his own personal Akbil to use (this earns the driver about 5Ykr per cash-paying customer). Buses run, roughly, from 6 or 6:30am until around 11pm or midnight.

THE DOLMUŞ   The main *dolmuş* stands are located in Taksim, Sirkeci, and Aksaray, and connect to points all over the city. Dolmuşes are often more direct than metropolitan buses and cheaper than taxis, cutting down on time and leaving more money in your pocket. When boarding, tell the driver your destination, and ask how much it will be *(ne kadar?)*. For shorter distances, 3YTL ($2.60/£1.20) should cover it. The driver will drop you off at your destination, but if you want to get off sooner, say *"inecek var"* ("this is my stop") or *"inmek istiyorum, lütfen,"* the short version of "I want to get off" with a "please" stuck on the end.

THE TRAMWAY   When the tram from Eminönü to Zeytinburnu was built and inaugurated in 1991, the planners had overlooked one very important detail: money collection. Passengers rode for free for 1 year while the system installed booths and printed tickets. The system has grown up quite a bit since then; the city recently extended the tramway from Eminönü all the way to Kabataş (just below Dolmabahçe Palace) and added an underground funicular that hoists passengers up the hill to Taksim in just 110 seconds. This collective service cuts trips between Taksim and Sultanahmet down to around 15 minutes (with transfers), while destinations in between (Egyptian Spice Bazaar stop: Eminönü; Grand Bazaar stop: Çemberlitaş or Beyazit;

Tips   We'll Tell You Where to Go

Not sure how to get where you're going? The transport arm of the Istanbul municipality operates a great website, www.iett.gov.tr. With information in English, you can find all of the routes for the whole range of transport options. You can also plug in your starting point to find out which lines stop there.

Tips Transport Made Easy with the Akbil

True to its name (Akbil means "smart ticket"), this refillable plastic contraption offers both convenience and savings for an initial deposit of 6YTL ($5.20/£2.40; keep your receipt so that you can get your deposit back before you leave). Buses, the tramway, the streetcar, the metro, and seabuses (not the ferries, which are privately owned) have been outfitted to accept the Akbil, available for purchase (and refills) at booths displaying the Akbil logo in Taksim Square, Eminönü, and Aksaray. In addition to the per-ride savings for trips requiring multiple transfers, the Akbil will get you a savings of around 10% per ride. And better still, one Akbil can be used by multiple travelers in a group. Preloaded Akbils can also be purchased for a day (7.50YTL/$6.55/£3), weekly (40YTL/$35/£16), 15-day (60YTL/$52/£24), or monthly (100YTL/$87/£40).

Istanbul Modern stop: Tophane) are just a token away. The cost per ride is 1.30YTL/$1.15/50p; if you pay with an Akbil (see "Transport Made Easy with the Akbil," below) the cost of transfers is included. Token *(jeton)* booths are located at the entrance to the turnstiles; Akbils can be purchased/refilled at selected stops including Sultanahmet, Eminönü, and Taksim.

THE HISTORIC TROLLEY Just when you feel that your feet are ready to fall off, you hear the jingle of the life-saving streetcar. The trolley, now plying fresh tracks on newly laid cobblestones along Istiklal Caddesi, connects Taksim and Tünel for a mere 1.30YTL/$1.15/50p. It makes three intermediary stops: at Hüseyn Ağa Camii, at Galatasaray High School/Flower–Fish Market, and in Beyoğlu at Nutru Sokak (in front of the Turkiye Iş Merkezi).

THE FUNICULAR The underground subway known as Tünel connects the sea-level neighborhood of Karaköy near the Galata Bridge with the lofty neighborhood of Beyoğlu (at the end of Istiklal Cad.). Tünel trains run Monday through Saturday from 7am to 9pm and Sunday from 7:30am to 9pm.

A second funicular was completed in 2006, providing a much-needed lift to those down at the docks of Kabataş (near Dolmabahçe Palace) up the very steep hill to Taksim. The trip, which takes a fleeting 110 seconds, costs 1.30YTL ($1.15/55p).

THE METRO/UNDERGROUND Istanbul's modern underground currently connects Taksim with Levent (Akmerkez is only a short cab ride away). On the way it makes stops in Osmanbey (walking distance to Nişantaşı), Şişli/Meçidiyeköy (a commercial center), and Gayrettepe (more commerce). The metro is open from around 6:30am until midnight and costs 1.35YTL ($1.15/55p) per ride.

The metro extension connecting the airport to town is now complete, providing access at Yenikapı (just outside the airport) to Aksaray via a roundabout route by way of the *otogar* (bus station). If your destination is Sultanahmet, exit the metro at ground level, transfer to the tramway, which is but a short walk away, and hop on any train marked EMINÖNÜ.

THE FERRY & SEABUS **Istanbul City Ferry Lines,** Şehir Hatları Vapurları (main © 0212/244-4233; port offices: Bostancı © 0216/361-3087; Kabataş © 0212/243-3756; Kadıköy © 0212/336-2198), runs commuter ferry service between the Europe and Asia sides and to the nearby Princes' Islands. Some of the more useful

---

Tips Take a Quick Cruise

Two years ago, a cheeky young entrepreneur hired a crew of expert craftsmen to replicate a traditional sultan's imperial caique—fake gild, velvet, and all. The result is a kitschy and delightfully touristy ride up the Bosphorus, the way the royals used to do it. Sultan Kayıkları (*(* 0212/265-7802; www.sultankayiklari.com) has expanded to three motorized boats (the oars are for show) and now operates three different tours. Instead of craning your neck over the side of a crowded clunker, a maximum of 30 passengers each get a front-row seat to the turning of the Ottoman centuries, sea spray and all.

Two of the three tours on offer (the third is a "Palace Tour" for groups) are quick excursions of up to an hour, no stops allowed. Choose between the tour of the straits from Dolmabahçe to the Bosphorus Bridge and back (58YTL/$50/£23) or the tour of the Golden Horn (45YTL/$39/£18). Boats depart from different docks and have differing schedules; reservations are required.

For a do-it-yourself Bosphorus cruise, take the ferry departing from Eminönü Pier #3 (10:35am daily and 1:35pm summers only) for the 2-hour zigzag excursion up to Anadolu Kavağı. The ferry makes stops at all of the main docks on both the European and Asian side (10 each), giving passengers the option of jumping ship early. Many visitors stay on until the last stop at Anadolu Kavağı (which can now confidently be called a tourist trap), docking for lunch at one of the many restaurants specializing in fish. Avoid the crush and disembark at one of the lesser visited villages like Emirgan, Bebek, Kanlica, and Çengelköy (for now); then either catch a direct ferry back or wait for the return of the ferry you started on (it departs Anadolu Kavağı at 3pm and in summer at 5pm). A one-way ticket on the ferry costs 7YTL ($6.10/£2.80); a round-trip costs 13YTL ($11/£5.20). For updated information and schedules, log on to www.ido.com.tr.

---

shuttles depart from Eminönü to Kabataş, Üsküdar, Karaköy, and Haydarpaşa, this last crossing indispensable for transfers to the train and points east. A one-way fare to points within Greater Istanbul (not including the Princes' Islands, which is nominally higher) costs 1.30YTL/$1.15/50p and you can pay with the Akbil.

The faster seabuses are run by the **Istanbul Deniz Otobüsleri** (website in Turkish and English at **www.ido.com.tr** or in Istanbul call their national toll-free line at *(* 444-4436) and provide convenient service to the Asian side plus the Marmara Islands, Bursa, and Yalova. A one-way fare, for example, from Kabataş to Bostancı is 4.50YTL ($3.90/£1.80). To contact the port offices directly, the numbers are Bakırköy *(* 0212/560-7291; Bostancı *(* 0216/410-6633; and Kabataş *(* 0212/249-1558.

The ferry that takes the time-honored cruise up the Bosphorus leaves from Eminönü, stopping at Beşiktaş (near the Dolmabahçe and Çırağan palaces) on its crisscross pattern up the channel. Fares and daily departure times (7YTL/$6.10/£2.80; departing 10:35am and 1:35pm; confirm times, as they may change) are posted on or near the ticket window. (See "Take a Quick Cruise," below.)

Long-distance ferries or the faster seabuses provide transportation to the Princes' Islands (from Eminönü and Kabataş) and to points along the southern coast of the Marmara Sea. If you're interested in traveling by car to cities along the Marmara region (for example, Bursa, Çanakkale, İzmir, and points south), the easiest and quickest way is to take a ferry from Mudanya (for Bursa) or Bandırma (for Çanakkale and the Northern Aegean). The trips take 75 minutes and 1 hour, 45 minutes, respectively. For information on fares and schedules for the ferries, contact **Istanbul City Ferry Lines,** Şehir Hatları Vapurları (© **0212/244-4233**). For seabuses, consult the **Istanbul Deniz Otobüsleri** website (in Turkish and English) at **www.ido.com.tr** or in Istanbul call their national toll-free line at © **0212/444-4436** (or contact the port offices directly: Bakırköy © 0212/560-7291, Bostancı © 0216/410-6633, Kabataş © 0212/249-1558, and Yenikapı © 0212/516-1212).

BY CAR

With traffic getting denser and more aggravating on an hourly basis, having a car in Istanbul is the surest method for going nowhere. In the rare event that traffic moves smoothly, do you really think you know where you're going? Can you read signs in Turkish? Do you know what a "Cevreyolu" is? And once you get there, where are you going to park? If you do decide to disregard better judgment and good counsel (and the fact that traffic enforcement in Turkey has become rather unforgiving, given the potential revenues), or if you're only planning to pick up the car and drive out, here's some basic information:

The major car-rental companies in Istanbul are **Avis** (www.avis.com), **Sixt** (www.e-sixt.com), **Hertz** (www.hertz.com), **National** (www.nationalcar.com), **Budget** (www.budget.com), and **Alamo** (www.alamo.com). All have desks at Atatürk International Airport, as well as locations in town. Meanwhile, Hertz and Decar (www.decar.com.tr) have desks in the international terminal at Sabiha Gökçen Airport, while Avis has one in the domestic terminal. Check your national website (i.e., www.avis.co.uk) for deals; at press time, the price for a compact car was about $60/£30 per day.

BY TAXI

Taxis are plentiful in Istanbul and are more likely to hail you than vice versa. **Avoid taxis that congregate around the main tourist spots** like Topkapı Palace, Ayasofya, and at the cruise-ship landing in Karaköy—these are the ones adept at performing a bait-and-switch with large banknotes or setting the meter to the higher nighttime rates. Better to have your hotel call a cab for you, where the hotel agrees to give the taxi stand business only as long as the drivers remain aboveboard (not always a foolproof system, as drivers' employment status can change). Similarly, when out and about, pop into the nearest hotel and have the receptionist call a taxi for you. A taxi from Sultanahmet to Taksim will cost between 10YTL ($8.70/£4) and 14YTL ($12/£5.60), depending on traffic levels and distance, while nighttime rates (midnight–6am) are 50% higher. For more information, see "Don't Let Taxi Drivers Take You for a Ride," in chapter 2.

FAST FACTS: Istanbul

American Express Türk Expres is the official representative of Amex Travel Related Services in Turkey, at Cumhuriyet Cad. 47/1, 3rd floor, Taksim (© **0212/235-9500**). The worldwide customer assist service center number is © **00800/4491-4820**. Amex also provides a toll-free number within Turkey for Global Assist (© **0312/935-3601**).

Babysitters Most of the larger hotels provide some type of child-care service for a fee, be it an on-site nanny or a babysitter referral.

Climate Istanbul has seen temperatures ranging from 0°F to 104°F (–18°C–40°C), but it's unlikely that you'll encounter such extremes. Summer lasts roughly from mid-June to mid-September. The city sees a sloshy 27 inches of rain annually, mostly between October and March. In spite of the cold temperatures that sweep in from the Black Sea in winter, large accumulations of snowfall are a rarity, although light dustings do occur.

Consulates The **American Consulate** is located at Kaplıcalar Mevkii 2, Istinye (© 0212/335-9000). The **British Consulate** is back in its original, pre-terrorist bombing location at Mesrutiyet Cad. 34, Tepebşı (Beyoğlu; © 0212/334-6400; fax 0212/334-6401). The **Australian Consulate** is at Askerocağı Cad. 15, Şişli (© 0212/243-1333).

Courier Services The post office (PTT) offers an express mail service *(acele posta servisi),* while you may feel safer with old reliables such as DHL (© 0212/444-0040), Federal Express (© 0212/444-0505), TNT (© 0216/425-1700), or UPS (© 0212/444-0033). The latter has a convenient office location at Küçük Ayasofya Cad. Aksakal Sok. 14, Sultanahmet.

Dentists If Istanbul's new tooth hospital (toll-free at © 0212/444-0DIS or 327-4020; www.dentististanbul.com) in Beşiktaş can't solve your oral problems, then the Koç American Hospital in Nişantaşı (© 0212/311-2000) and the International Hospital in Yeşilyurt (© 0212/663-3000) provide emergency dental services by English speakers. For a selected list of private practitioners, log on to http://turkey.usembassy.gov/docistanbul.html.

Emergencies Local emergency numbers are: fire © 110, police © 155, and ambulance © 112. Emergencies may also warrant a call to Medline (© 0212/444-1212, 24 hr. a day), a private company equipped to deal with any medical crisis, including ambulance transfers (cost varies according to distance), lab tests, and home treatment. The International Hospital (see "Hospitals," below) also provides ambulance services.

Hospitals For optimal local emergency care, put yourself in the hands of one of the reputed private hospital facilities: The new Koç American Hospital, Güzelbahçe Sokağı Nişantaşı (© 0212/311-2000); Metropolitan Florence Nightingale Hospital, Cemil Aslangüder Sok. 8, Gayrettepe (© 0212/288-3400); the International Hospital, Istanbul Cad. 82, Yeşilköy (© 0212/663-3000); the German Hospital, Sıraselviler Cad. 119, Taksim (© 0212/293-2150); and the Balat Jewish Hospital, Hisarönü Cad. 46–48, Fatih (© 0212/635-9280) are just a few of the establishments with reliable English-speaking staff. Don't forget that payment is required at the time of treatment.

Newspapers & Magazines For local and national information, The *Turkish Daily News* gives a basic rundown of the day's headlines. If you have access to the Internet, log on to www.zaman.com, the bilingual website of *Today's Zaman,* the Turkish-language national paper. For local listings, the *Guide Istanbul* and

Time Out Istanbul contain essential listings for tourists. Both are available at newsstands; the former is provided free at some hotels.

Pharmacies Pharmacists in Turkey are qualified to provide some medical services beyond filling prescriptions, such as administering injections, bandaging minor injuries, and suggesting medication. Local pharmacies (called *eczane*) operate on a rotating schedule so that one is always open for emergencies; each pharmacy posts the schedule in the window, called Nöbetçi.

Restrooms Public restrooms are located all around town, in addition to those in public buildings such as museums. "Toll money" in Istanbul costs about 25Ykr (20¢/10p), which occasionally includes a bonus handful of toilet paper. Flushing the toilet paper can sometimes be hazardous to the plumbing; when this is the case, you will usually see a sign above the tank requesting that you dispose of it in the nearby wastebasket.

Taxes There is a flat 18% VAT (value-added tax) incorporated into the price of almost everything you buy, although news is that this will be lowered to 8% for tourist services. While generally included, note that some hotels charge this tax over and above room rates. Taxes for luxury goods are higher, as is the tax on alcoholic beverages (the current government frowns on such un-Islamic vices).

3 Where to Stay

For someone new to the sprawling mass that is Istanbul, one of the first questions to ask is "Where's a good place to set up base camp?" In previous editions, I unreservedly directed my readers to the historic bull's-eye that is Sultanahmet, where old dilapidated homes converted into "Special Category" hotels created the perfect gateway to an authentic past. However, there have been three very important developments in this neighborhood in the past few years. First, because of unrelenting demand, hotels here—the majority of which are run by people with absolutely no experience in hospitality—formerly charging $20 (£10) for a room now charge $218 (£107) and up, for absolutely no added value. Let me put this further into perspective: The luxury five-star hotel Ceylan InterContinental (reviewed later) has advance-purchase Internet rates from 176€ ($255/£126) *with a Bosphorus view.* Second, given the enormous profit margins that a hotel can bring in, it seems as if everyone has gotten in on the act—transforming what was a market of family-run houses into a sea of mass-produced, soulless "boutique hotels." Finally, and most disappointingly, the hassling by carpet salesmen and their ilk has reached new levels; last time I stayed in town several hotel guests opted for the safety of the hotel lobby rather than brave the irritating and stressful storm of harassment. It is therefore with a heavy heart that I recommend this neighborhood only with the admonition to book through a reputable agent and stay vigilant (for formal and informal crime). Instead, I recommend that you base yourself in Beyoğlu, where hotels are managed by people schooled in hotel management (and not carpet sales), and the food and nightlife are better anyway. And with the new, efficient transport system connecting Taksim and Sultanahmet, you can spend the day wandering around the Old City and in under 20 minutes be back in time for a decent meal.

The price of hotel rooms listed here generally includes breakfast and tax, although a few higher-priced hotels charge these on top of the room rate. The price categories listed in this section are to be used mainly as guidelines due to the market-driven nature of the industry. It's not uncommon, for example, for a room listed at 250€ ($363/£179) a night to sell for significantly less via the Internet, through an agency, or if you ask nicely. For this reason you may find fewer options under the "Inexpensive" or "Moderate" headings below.

THE OLD CITY
VERY EXPENSIVE

Eresin Crown Hotel 𝒜𝒜   During the building of the Eresin, workers uncovered Byzantine floor mosaics, marble columns, and a cistern, artifacts later identified as belonging to the women's quarters of Justinian's Great Palace. Altogether, the hotel recovered, registered, and now exhibits 49 historically significant museum pieces dating to the Hellenistic and Byzantine times, giving this hotel a "boutique museum" quality. Rooms in this quality hotel are well appointed, with bonus touches like window seats, plaster friezes, and Jacuzzis. From its enormous rooftop terrace, the Eresin also boasts one of the most magnificent panoramic views of Old City in Sultanahmet.

Küçük Ayasofya Cad. 40, 34400 Sultanahmet, Istanbul. ℂ **0212/638-4428.** Fax 0212/638-0933. www.eresin sultanahmet.com.tr. 59 units. 275€–325€ ($399–$471/£196–£232) double; 400€–600€ ($580–$810/£870–£429) suite. AE, MC, V. **Amenities:** 2 restaurants; 2 bars; business center; 24-hr. room service; laundry service; dry cleaning; elevator. In room: A/C, satellite and cable TV, minibar, hair dryer, safe.

Four Seasons Hotel 𝒜𝒜𝒜   Voted by *Travel + Leisure* in 2007 as Europe's best hotel, this Turkish neoclassical building located in the heart of Sultanahmet was originally a dilapidated prison for political dissidents. Much of the original marble and tile were retained and recycled into the hotel's present-day, five-star interior design. Rooms have plush furniture purchased from local vendors; the architect even stayed true to tradition by applying paint as they did in the Ottoman palaces—with a spatula. The opulent and luxurious bathrooms all have separate toilet cabins, and the king-size beds are amazingly comfy. Plus, almost all of the rooms have views of something fabulous. The hotel is also reaping the rewards of its newly opened sister property, the Four Seasons the Bosphorus. Guests of this hotel may use the considerable amenities of the other, and it's even possible to divide your stay among the two—the staff will pack up your room and lay it out precisely where you left it in the new space.

Tevkifhane Sok. 1, 34110 Sultanahmet, Istanbul. ℂ **800/332-3442** in the U.S., or 0212/638-8200. Fax 0212/638-8210. www.fshr.com. 65 units. High season 395€–1,050€ ($573–$1,523/£282–£750) double and suites; B&B rates are higher; rates lower Nov–Mar. AE, DC, MC, V. Complimentary valet parking. **Amenities:** Restaurant; 2 bars; fitness room; Jacuzzi; sauna; wired and wireless Internet access throughout hotel; shopping arcade; 24-hr. room service; laundry service; dry cleaning; nonsmoking rooms; elevator. In room: A/C, satellite TV w/pay movies, minibar, hair dryer.

EXPENSIVE

Arena Hotel   The three-story hotel located in an unpolished corner of Sultanahmet just steps behind the Hippodrome occupies a restored Ottoman house that has remained in the same family for over 80 years. The owner has retained traditional touches such as family heirloom furnishings and "grandmother Gül's caftan" in the lobby's salon. Rooms feature charming Ottoman-style decor, wood floors, and classic Turkish rugs, but the rickety stall showers (reminiscent of the two-star pensions I've stayed at in Rome) indicate that the bathrooms need updating. There are two suites,

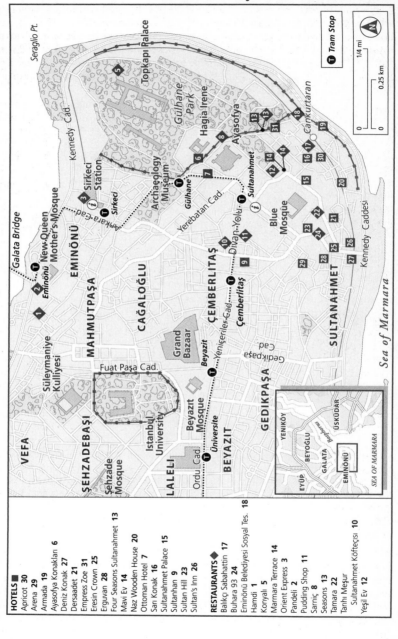

The Old City Hotels & Restaurants

HOTELS ■
Apricot **30**
Arena **29**
Armada **19**
Ayasofya Konakları **6**
Deniz Konak **27**
Dersaadet **21**
Empress Zoe **31**
Eresin Crown **25**
Erguvan **28**
Four Seasons Sultanahmet **13**
Mavi Ev **14**
Naz Wooden House **20**
Ottoman Hotel **7**
Sarı Konak **16**
Sultanahmet Palace **15**
Sultanhan **9**
Sultan Hill **23**
Sultan's Inn **26**

RESTAURANTS ◆
Balıkçı Sabahattin **17**
Buhara 93 **24**
Eminönü Belediyesi Sosyal Tes. **18**
Hamdi **1**
Konyalı **5**
Marmara Terrace **14**
Orient Express **3**
Pandeli **2**
Pudding Shop **11**
Sarnıç **8**
Seasons **13**
Tamara **22**
Tarihi Meşur
Sultanahmet Köfteçisi **10**
Yeşil Ev **12**

each with a balcony, the only two tubs in the house, and a flatscreen TV. Better yet, there's a little *hamam* (reservations required) on the basement level.

Küçükayasofya Mah. Şehit Mehmet Paşa Yokuşu Üçler Hamam Sok. 13–15, 34400 Sultanahmet, Istanbul. ℂ 0212/458-0364. Fax 0212/458-0366. www.arenahotel.com. 27 units. 150€–180€ ($218–$261/£107–£129) double; 200€ ($290/£143) suite. Special Internet rates according to availability. AE, DC, DISC, MC, V. Limited hotel parking on street. **Amenities:** Restaurant; Turkish bath for 10€ ($15/£7.15) extra; 24-hr. room service; laundry service; dry cleaning; elevator. *In room:* A/C, satellite TV, minibar, hair dryer, safe.

Ayasofya Konakları   In the 1980s, the state-run Turkish Touring and Automobile Club set off a craze for historic preservation when it restored a handful of clapboard Ottoman mansions on the historic, cobblestoned Soğukçeşme Street. Back then, the collection of pension-style rooms saw a veritable stampede of illustrious visitors. After more than 20 years and commensurate wear and tear (plus a new manager), the pension has grown into its stately skin: Rooms have been restored without sacrificing their original character and many have benefited by a number of additional comforts (including air-conditioning and TV). The *konakları* also enjoy one of the city's most characteristic settings, sandwiched between the imperial outer wall of Topkapı Palace and the Ayasofya, and encompass open-air garden and terrace cafes, and an expansive garden that surrounds a wonderful orangery.

Soğukçeşme Sok., 34400 Sultanahmet, Istanbul. ℂ 0212/513-3660. Fax 0212/514-0213. www.ayasofyapensions. com. 64 units. 150€–180€ ($218–$261/£107–£129) double; 280€ ($406/£200) suite. AE, MC, V. **Amenities:** Restaurant; 2 bars; 24-hr. room service; laundry service; dry cleaning.

Mavi Ev (Blue House) ✿   If the Blue House weren't actually painted blue, one would think the name came from the fact that the hotel is practically attached at the hip to the Blue Mosque, a stone's throw away. This hotel is a fine example of modern Turkish elegance, with its tile floors, carpets, stained glass, and understated details. Most of the rooms have stall showers, while suites have Jacuzzis. The rooftop restaurant (and bar) is especially noteworthy, if not for the food, then for the back-door viewing of the sound-and-light displays above the Blue Mosque (summer months only). The entire effect is enchanting, and you couldn't get a better view of the domes if you were standing right on top of them.

Dalbastı Sok. 14, 34400 Sultanahmet, Istanbul. ℂ 0212/638-9010. Fax 0212/638-9017. www.bluehouse.com.tr. 27 units (25 with shower). 140€ ($203/£100) double; 220€ ($319/£157) suite. Rates lower in winter. MC, V. Public parking across the street. **Amenities:** Restaurant; bar; wireless Internet; 24-hr. room service; laundry service; dry cleaning; elevator. *In room:* A/C, cable TV, minibar, hair dryer.

Sultanahmet Palace Hotel ✿   Designed in the style of a garden villa, this hotel features Byzantine-style hand-carved moldings above Roman terra-cotta flooring, a grand marble central staircase below a half-cylinder stained-glass dome, courtyards, and terrace fountains, and breathtaking views in summer of the Marmara Sea from the breakfast terrace. The Blue Mosque creates a fourth wall in the street-side rooms, a view so impressive that you won't mind the brutal dawn awakening. Rooms on the third floor are disappointingly small, so when reserving, try to nab a second-floor room or one of the suites, which include two new deluxe rooms (nos. 309 and 310), each with a modern bathroom and Jacuzzi. In all of the other rooms, each small bathroom doubles as a marble-clad mini-*hamam* (no tubs; shower heads are provided for convenience); plus-size visitors and creatures of habit might want to think twice before booking this hotel. Not everybody can adapt to the bathroom setup, though, and sadly, a glitch in the heating system prevents the *hamams* from producing any heat.

Torun Sok. 19, 34400 Sultanahmet, Istanbul. ℂ 0212/458-0460. Fax 0212/518-6224. www.sultanahmetpalace. com. 36 units. Nov–Mar 143€ ($207/£102) double, 193€ ($280/£138) suite. AE, MC, V. Free parking next door. **Amenities:** Restaurant; 24-hr. room service; laundry service; dry cleaning; elevator. *In room:* A/C, satellite TV, minibar, hair dryer, Turkish bath.

Sultanhan Hotel ★★
Muted echoes of guests' comings and goings bounce off the gracious marble walls of the lobby of this brand-new hotel, located steps away from the Grand Bazaar and tramway. The elegance extends to the rooms, which are larger than what you might find at one of the many neighborhood "boutique hotels." All rooms have bathtubs and oversize TVs, and some even have sculpted entry archways. The hotel also has one of the most spectacular rooftop views in all of the historic peninsula, offering a completely unobstructed panorama of *both* the Blue Mosque and the Hagia Sofia.

Piyer Loti Cad. 15, Çemberlitaş, Istanbul. ℂ 0212/516-3232. Fax 0212/516-5995. www.sultanhanhotel.com. 40 units. 230€ ($334/£164) double. MC, V. **Amenities:** Rooftop restaurant; bar; Turkish bath (50€/$73/£36); sauna; wireless Internet throughout hotel; 24-hr. room service; laundry service; dry cleaning; nonsmoking rooms; elevator. *In room:* A/C, cable TV, dataport, minibar, hair dryer, safe.

MODERATE

Dersaadet Oteli ★ Finds
In Turkish, Dersaadet means "place of felicity and beauty"—an appropriate designation for this handsome hotel fashioned in the style of a 19th-century Ottoman house. The parquet floors and the deep wooden details lend grace to the simple rooms, most of which have a view of the Marmara Sea and Asian side. A couple of the bathrooms have showers and sinks jerry-rigged into the original small spaces, but all units are different, so ask ahead what to expect, or go for broke and simply opt for the recently renovated honeymoon-worthy Penthouse Suite. The rooftop terrace offers stunning views of the Blue Mosque and Marmara Sea.

Kapıağası Sok. 5, 34400 Sultanahmet, Istanbul. ℂ 0212/458-0760. Fax 0212/518-4918. www.dersaadethotel.com. 16 units. 105€ ($152/£75) double; 115€ ($167/£82) sea-view double; 150€–220€ ($218–$319/£107–£157) suite. 10% discount for payment made in cash. MC, V. Free parking in adjacent lot. **Amenities:** Bar; 24-hr. room service; laundry service; dry cleaning; elevator. *In room:* A/C, satellite TV, minibar, hair dryer.

Erguvan Hotel Istanbul ★
This is one of those new boutique hotels I spoke about above. The four-story building located just below the ancient retaining wall of the Hippodrome is fresh and welcoming. Rooms retain either the original parquet or laminate, and an unobjectionable vanilla-pudding-colored paper covers the walls. Half of the rooms have bathtubs, a rarity on this side of town, and every window in the place is double-glazed, whether it needs it or not (it really doesn't, unless you haven't gotten the hang of sleeping through that dawn call to prayer). The manager made a point of mentioning that the building was reconstructed in compliance with Istanbul's new earthquake code, a fact I'm not sure made me feel better or not. Pay an additional 15€ ($21/£11) and you'll get a sea-view room.

Aksakal Cad. 3, 34400 Sultanahmet, Istanbul. ℂ 0212/458-2784. Fax 0212/458-2788. www.erguvanhotelistanbul. com. 22 units. 145€ ($210/£104) double. Free pickup from airport for stays of 3 days or longer. MC, V. **Amenities:** Rooftop restaurant and bar in summer only; Internet point; wireless throughout hotel; 24-hr. room service; laundry; dry cleaning; elevator. *In room:* A/C, cable TV, minibar, hair dryer, safe.

Hotel Armada
Located on the outer edges of Sultanahmet in Cankurtaran near the Ahırkapı Gate, the Hotel Armada is a true four-star hotel that makes a good choice for groups. (Individuals who decide to stay here should realize that it's a short yet uphill walk to all major sights.) It boasts an expansive lobby cafe, an atmospheric bar,

and one of the best rooftop terraces anywhere in the neighborhood. Rooms are decorated in "Ottoman style" simplicity, with wooden chair rails, decorative painted flowers, and subdued fabrics. The bathrooms are small but functional, with a negligible amount of wear and tear around the edges. A buffet breakfast is served in a delightful penthouse atrium adjacent to the terrace (the restaurant dining room), and the fish restaurants of Kumkapı are within walking distance (as is Balıkçı Sabahattin restaurant; see "Where to Dine" later in this chapter). Weekend guests may want to request a room away from the evening entertainment activities to insulate themselves from the late-night echoes through the marble staircases.

Ahırkapı Sok. (just behind Cankurtaran), 34400 Sultanahmet, Istanbul. © 0212/638-1370. Fax 0212/518-5060. www.armadahotel.com.tr. 110 units. 85€–100€ ($123–$145/£61–£71) double. Breakfast 9€ ($13/£6.45). Rates are exclusive of VAT. AE, DC, MC, V. Parking. **Amenities:** 2 restaurants; 2 bars; wireless Internet throughout; 24-hr. room service; laundry service; dry cleaning; elevator. *In room:* A/C, satellite TV, minibar, hair dryer, safe.

Hotel Empress Zoe ☆☆
Empress Zoe overlooks the crumbling remnants of the oldest *hamam* in the city. Access to the rooms is via a narrow circular iron staircase—good to know if traveling light wasn't on this trip's agenda. If you do hurt your back on the way up, you'll be pleased to find extremely comfortable beds when you make it to your room. The hotel combines five separate houses, and rooms range from charming doubles with Byzantine- or Anatolian-style murals, to a variety of garden and penthouse suites. Because of the configuration, secluded courtyards and panoramic terraces unexpectedly appear around almost every corner. The rooftop bar is warmly draped in deeply colored Turkish *kilims* and blankets, and there's a fireplace for those crisp winter evenings. *Note:* Because of the construction of the Four Seasons annex, there are no longer any views facing north to the Ayasofya.

Akbıyık Cad. Adliye Sok. 10, 34400 Sultanahmet, Istanbul. © 0212/518-2504. Fax 0212/518-5699. www.emzoe. com. 26 units. 105€ ($152/£75) double; 120€–225€ ($174–$326/£86–£161) suite. MC, V. **Amenities:** 3 bars; non-smoking rooms. *In room:* A/C, hair dryer, safe.

Hotel Sarı Konak ☆☆ (Finds)
It's easy to see why visitors choose to stay in this small family-run establishment. Bahattin and his son Umit roll out the red carpet for everyone. The rooms are simple but charming; the bathrooms are spotless and functional; and air-conditioning comes in half the rooms—the other half have ceiling fans. TVs were recently installed in the majority of the rooms, including the new suite, which also has high-speed Internet access and a Jacuzzi. The building next door was recently renovated into a multiroom, apartment-style annex, offering the opportunity for a real "local" experience. Breakfast is served to the soothing trickle of the garden courtyard's water fountain against the backdrop of an ancient Byzantine wall.

Mimar Mehmet Ağa Cad. 42–46, 34400 Sultanahmet, Istanbul. © 0212/638-6258. Fax 0212/517-8635. www. sarikonak.com. 17 units. 89€–129€ ($129–$187/£64–£92) double; 179€ ($260/£128) suite. Rates lower off season. AE, MC, V. **Amenities:** 2 bars; 24-hr. room service; laundry service; dry cleaning; elevator. *In room:* A/C.

Hotel Sultan Hill
In 2006, this building was little more than desiccated beams retaining, but for the grace of god, the shape of a house. Today, this brand-spanking-new replacement of the 18th-century Ottoman house previously on the site is a small but gracious bed-and-breakfast located so centrally that you'll practically trip over the Blue Mosque, the Hippodrome, and the Küçükayasofya on your way out the hotel's door. Rooms, all of which have showers, are a bit tight but are set up to be as comfortable as possible. The ground-floor breakfast rooms opens out onto a courtyard

with an inviting traditional Turkish lounging corner. The hotel also makes best use of the requisite rooftop terrace.

Tavukhane Sok. 19, Sultanahmet, Istanbul. ⓒ **0212/518-3293.** Fax 0212/518-3295. www.hotelsultanhill.com. 17 units. 50€ ($73/£36) single; 70€–75€ ($102–$109/£50–£54) double; 100€–120€ ($145–$174/£71–£86) triple and family room. MC, V. **Amenities:** Roof terrace bar; wireless Internet throughout hotel; 24-hr. room service; laundry service; dry cleaning. *In room:* A/C, cable TV, minibar, hair dryer, safe.

Naz Wooden House   For anyone interested in sleeping in a room all wrapped up in the history of Byzantium, this is the place. The hotel is built directly into the ancient city walls, so chances are you'll be ducking under a Roman archway or sleeping under an expansive brick vault. Spaces are commensurately small and showers are of the closed sliding-stall variety, but it's all very charming and historic. When Naz is booked up (there are only seven rooms, after all), the management encourages you to stay at one of their sister properties, the Deniz Konak or the Sultan's Inn (both listed below).

Akbiyik Degirmeni Sok. 7, 34400 Sultanahmet, Istanbul. ⓒ **0212/516-7130.** Fax 0212/518-5453. 7 units. 70€–110€ ($102–$160/£50–£79) double. MC, V. **Amenities:** Rooftop terrace bar; laundry service; dry cleaning. *In room:* A/C, cable TV.

Ottoman Hotel Imperial Istanbul ⓕ *(Value)*   Originally connected to the adjacent Caferağa Medresi below (where it served as a dormitory for students), this building was later converted to a hospital and then in 1972, a hostel. As of 2006, the hotel, which sits opposite the Ayasofya, joins the list of brand-new, Ottoman-influenced small hotels. Rooms are comparatively large, although the bathrooms, outfitted with albeit new European sit-in bathtubs, are a bit tight. Behind the hotel is an unexpected garden patio (restaurant) that sits above the undulating domes of Caferağa Medresi. During summer's eves, the hotel hosts a lone whirling derviş and hands-on *ebru* demonstrations.

Caferiye Sok. 6/1, 34400 Sultanahmet, Istanbul. ⓒ **0212/513-6150.** Fax 0212/512-7628. www.ottomanhotel imperial.com. 50 units. 89€–129€ ($129–$187/£64–£92) double; 129€ ($187/£92) suite. AE, DC, MC, V. **Amenities:** Restaurants; bar; concierge; business services; wireless Internet; 24-hr. room service; laundry service; dry cleaning; nonsmoking rooms; elevator. *In room:* A/C, satellite TV, dataport, minibar, coffee/tea station, hair dryer, safe.

INEXPENSIVE

Apricot Hotel ⓕ *(Finds) (Value)*   Because of a contract glitch, the Apricot was forced to move from its original location to an even more charming building on a parallel street. Although there are fewer rooms, they are prettier, larger, and better appointed. Indeed, the Apricot's owner, Hakan, has created the perfect example of why inexpensive doesn't have to mean cheap. The building provides an exclusive, stylish, and homey atmosphere at competitive (and fixed) prices with amenities such as Jacuzzis (in two rooms), *hamams* (two other rooms), and balconies (three rooms). With only six rooms, you'd better call now.

Amiral Tafdil Sok. 18, 34400 Sultanahmet, Istanbul. ⓒ/fax **0212/638-1658.** www.apricothotel.com. 6 units. 59€–79€ ($86–$115/£42–£56) per room. MC, V (add 5% to the room rate). No traveler's checks. **Amenities:** Bar; wireless and Internet point. *In room:* A/C, cable TV, wireless Internet, minibar.

Deniz Konak   This hotel at the fringes of Sultanahmet (near Küçük Ayasofya Camii and Kumkapı) is owned by the same people who run the Naz Wooden House and the Sultan Inn. All their properties are small and charming, bed-and-breakfast-type places with various pros and cons. The main attraction of the Deniz Konak is the breathtaking views of the Marmara Sea. Alas, these very same sea-facing views come at a price:

the commuter train just below (so much for the double-glazed windows). All of the rooms facing the sea have a small bonus balcony, for 20€ ($28/£14) extra (no extra charge for the train). Guests have the option of taking breakfast at the Sultan Inn across the street, which was actually a bit more ample than the one at the Deniz Konak when I visited. All of the major sites are within easy walking distance (mostly up gentle slopes), but perhaps just a bit farther than one might want.

Küçük Ayasofya Cad. Çayıroğlu Sok. 14, 34400 Sultanahmet, Istanbul. ⓒ **0212/518-9595.** Fax 0212/638-3922. www.denizkonakhotel.com. 15 units. 40€–60€ ($58–$87/£29–£43) double. Add 20€ ($29/£14) for room with view. Rates reflect seasonal fluctuations. Rates skyrocket over the New Year. MC, V. **Amenities:** Laundry service; dry cleaning. *In room:* A/C, cable TV, minibar.

Sultan's Inn   This little hotel, a sister property of the Deniz Konak and Naz Wooden House (both above), is basic without being dull. Sparsely decorated rooms nevertheless have Turkish touches and all rooms have modern baths with showers. The rooftop terrace garden benefits from views of the Küçük Ayasofya Mosque, just a stone's throw away.

Küçük Ayasofya Sok., Mustafapaşa Sok. 50. ⓒ **0212/638-2562.** Fax. 0212/518-5453. www.sultansinn.com. 17 units. 50€–100€ ($73–$145/£36–£71) double. MC, V. Rates reflect seasonal fluctuations. **Amenities:** Bar; 24-hr. room service. *In room:* A/C, cable TV, minibar, hair dryer, safe.

BEYOĞLU
VERY EXPENSIVE

Ansen 130 𝕽𝕽 (Finds)   There seems to be an endless demand for upgraded rooms in Istanbul. Ansen 130, inserted in a restored 19th-century architectural jewel, fills this need by offering 10 positively cavernous rooms that any bachelor looking for an apartment would kill for. Light wood and laminate dominate the decor, which is punctuated with more beige and a bit of black in the sofa, bedspread, and electronics. Bathrooms have pleasantly chunky hardware, and there's a kitchenette with everything you'll need for a long or short stay except for the groceries. Ansen 130 has a ground-level bar that is popular even among nonguests, a cigar/wine bar next door, and a restaurant that's made *Time Out Istanbul's* top 15.

Meşrutiyet Cad., Ansen 130, 34430 Tepebaşı. ⓒ **0212/245-8808.** Fax 0212/245-7179. www.ansensuites.com. 10 units. 350€–500€ ($508–$725/£250–£357) suites. See website for weekly and monthly rates. MC, V. **Amenities:** Restaurant; 2 bars; meeting room for 20; 24-hr. room service; laundry; dry cleaning; elevator. *In room:* A/C, satellite TV, wireless and Ethernet Internet, kitchenette w/minibar, hair dryer, safe.

Ceylan InterContinental 𝕽𝕽   In 1996 the Istanbul Sheraton morphed into the Ceylan InterContinental, making way for yet another luxury five-star hotel. Unfortunately, the existing concrete-and-glass monolith exterior didn't change its shape in the process. But structures like these are meant to please the eye from the inside, and that it does. The central glass-and-marble staircase sets the stage for just the right amount of pomp for the hotel's "international clientele." The rooms are plush and elegant, each with an armchair, desk, and loveseat to create a homey feel. If you book via the Internet, you can get rates as low as 176€ ($255/£126). And it's all just a few steps away from the bustle of Taksim Square.

Asker Ocağı Cad. 1, Taksim, Istanbul. ⓒ **0212/231-2121** or 800/327-0200 in the U.S., 0181/847-2277 in the U.K., 008/221-335 in Australia, or 0800/442-215 in New Zealand. Fax 0212/231-2180. www.interconti.com. 390 units. 450€ ($653/£321) double; 1,000€ ($1,450/£714) and up suite. Breakfast and tax not included. AE, MC, V. Garage parking. **Amenities:** 3 restaurants; 3 bars; patisserie; outdoor pool; state-of-the-art health club; Turkish bath; Jacuzzi; sauna; tanning salon; wireless Internet; shopping arcade; salon; 24-hr. room service; laundry service; dry cleaning; nonsmoking rooms; elevator. *In room:* A/C, satellite and cable TV and in-room movies, dataport, minibar, hair dryer, safe, bathtub.

Beyoğlu Hotels & Restaurants

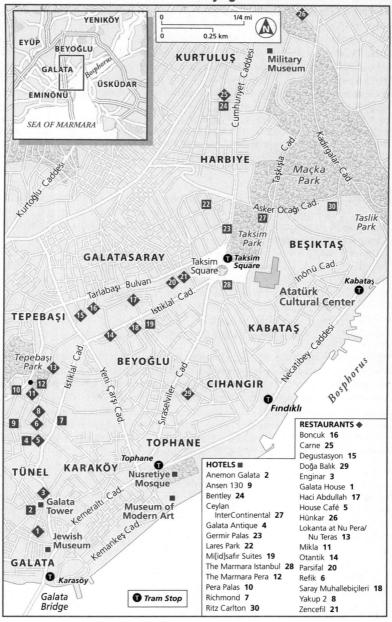

SEA OF MARMARA

YENIKÖY
EYÜP
BEYOĞLU
GALATA
ÜSKÜDAR
EMINÖNÜ
Bosphorus

0   1/4 mi
0   0.25 km

KURTULUŞ

Military Museum

Cumhuriyet Caddesi

HARBIYE

Taşkışla Cad.
Maçka Park
Kadırgalar Cad.

Asker Ocağı Cad.

Taksim Park

Taslik Park

BEŞIKTAŞ

GALATASARAY

Taksim Square

Taksim Square

İnönü Cad.

Kabataş

Tarlabaşı Bulvarı

Istiklal Cad.

Atatürk Cultural Center

TEPEBAŞI

KABATAŞ

Kurtoğlu Caddesi

Tepebaşı Park

Istiklal Cad.

BEYOĞLU

Yeni Çarşı Cad.

Sıraselviler Cad.

CIHANGIR

Necatibey Caddesi

Bosphorus

Fındıklı

TOPHANE

Tophane

KARAKÖY

Nusretiye Mosque

Museum of Modern Art

TÜNEL

Galata Tower

Jewish Museum

GALATA

Karasöy

Galata Bridge

Kemeraltı Cad.

Kemankeş Cad.

🚊 Tram Stop

HOTELS ■
Anemon Galata **2**
Ansen 130 **9**
Bentley **24**
Ceylan InterContinental **27**
Galata Antique **4**
Germir Palas **23**
Lares Park **22**
Mi[id]safır Suites **19**
The Marmara Istanbul **28**
The Marmara Pera **12**
Pera Palas **10**
Richmond **7**
Ritz Carlton **30**

RESTAURANTS ◆
Boncuk **16**
Carne **25**
Degustasyon **15**
Doğa Balık **29**
Enginar **3**
Galata House **1**
Haci Abdullah **17**
House Café **5**
Hünkar **26**
Lokanta at Nu Pera/ Nu Teras **13**
Mikla **11**
Otantik **14**
Parsifal **20**
Refik **6**
Saray Muhallebiçileri **18**
Yakup 2 **8**
Zencefil **21**

89

The Marmara Istanbul ✸✸✸   The Marmara is an excellent choice for those traveling for business or pleasure, particularly for its towering location above Taksim Square. In fact, the hotel became so popular that they opened a second one, **The Marmara Pera,** down the street. The Taksim Square hotel's got everything necessary for an exclusive visit to Istanbul, including spacious bathrooms and spectacular views. The recently renovated Club Floor specifically pampers business travelers with 24-hour floor supervision, complimentary breakfast, and in-room fax and coffee service.

Taksim Sq., Taksim, Istanbul. ✆ **0212/251-4696.** Fax 0212/244-0509. www.themarmarahotels.com. 377 units. 166€–196€ ($241–$284/£119–£140) double; 232€–275€ ($336–$399/£166–£196) Club Floor standard and suites; 490€–636€ ($711–$922/£350–£454) business and executive suites. Special weekend packages available. AE, MC, V. Ticketed parking lot below. **Amenities:** 3 restaurants; 3 bars; cafe/patisserie; outdoor swimming pool; state-of-the-art health club; spa treatments; Jacuzzi; sauna; wireless Internet; shopping arcade; salon; 24-hr. room service; laundry service; dry cleaning; nonsmoking rooms; executive floor; elevator. *In room:* A/C, satellite TV, dataport, minibar, hair dryer, safe, bathtub.

Pera Palas Hotel   In its heyday, the Pera Palas represented the Francophilia that had taken hold over the Ottoman Empire. It was built in 1892 as lodging befitting the exclusive passengers of the Orient Express, and accordingly the hotel's very own Orient Bar became a meeting place for drama and intrigue. The star-studded guest list includes Agatha Christie (who wrote *Murder on the Orient Express* in room no. 411), Atatürk (room no. 101, where he spent the days preceding the Gallipoli campaign, should remain intact), Jacqueline Kennedy Onassis, Greta Garbo, Edward VIII, Josephine Baker, and Mata Hari. This well-worn and beloved time capsule is currently under wraps as it undergoes what will be a 2-year process of renovation and restoration. Completion is expected in late 2009.

Meşrutiyet Cad. 98–100, 80050 Tepebaşı, Istanbul. ✆ **0212/251-4560.** Fax 0212/251-4089. www.perapalas.com.

Ritz-Carlton Istanbul ✸✸✸   The modern glass monolith that houses the Ritz-Carlton has marred the skyline above Dolmabahçe Palace for years, eliciting criticism at almost every turn. But the hotel's opulence and luxury make it forgivable. The hotel strives for a niche alongside that of the other multi-starred hotels with exotic massage treatments or premier health center and fitness packages. Standard rooms are spacious, with large picture windows that let in plenty of light, and suites that benefit from lovely parquet flooring and splendid views of the Bosphorus. Also, somewhere under all those pillows and bolsters, the beds are decadently high and plush. Bathrooms have bathtubs and separate showers, heated towel warmers, scales, handmade tiles, and designer soaps. The *hamam* is the one of the most luxurious in town.

Elmadağ Askerocağı Cad. 15, 80200 Şişli, Istanbul. ✆ **0212/334-4444.** Fax 0212/334-4455. www.ritzcarlton.com. 244 units. 250€–425€ ($363–$616/£179–£304) double; 550€–6,500€ ($798–$9,425/£393–£4,643) suite. AE, DC, MC, V. Indoor parking garage. **Amenities:** 2 restaurants; 3 bars; movie theater; indoor swimming pool; health club; spa; Turkish bath; Jacuzzi; sauna; concierge; tour desk; car-rental desk; shopping arcade; salon; 24-hr. room service; massage; babysitting; laundry service; dry cleaning; nonsmoking rooms; executive floor; elevator. *In room:* A/C, satellite TV, dataport, minibar, hair dryer, safe, bathtub.

EXPENSIVE

Bentley Hotel ✸ *(Finds*   Off the tourist radar yet only a 10-minute walk to Taksim is this tribute to minimalist Milanese design. The Bentley has already fast become a favorite of the fashionista and publishing crowd, thanks to a combination of high-tech amenities, great aesthetics, and convenient proximity to the trendy SoHo-like section of Nişantaşı. Each of the seven floors contains two standard rooms, two ample singles, and two suites (one a corner), while the two penthouse suites enjoy the additional bonus of a private, semi-wraparound terrace. All rooms are decorated with a sleek and spare palette of white, beige, and black, offering top-quality electronics, Internet connections, and even an espresso machine.

Halaskargazi Cad. 75 (opposite the Military Museum), 80220 Harbiye, Istanbul. © **0212/291-7730.** Fax 0212/291-7740. www.bentley-hotel.com. 14 units. 240€–280€ ($348–$406/£171–£200) double; 400€–800€ ($580–$1,160/£286–£571) suite. AE, DC, MC, V. **Amenities:** Restaurant; bar; fitness room; sauna; concierge; meeting facilities; 24-hr. room service; laundry service; dry cleaning; elevator. *In room:* A/C, satellite TV/VCR, CD player, fax, dataport, minibar, coffeemaker, hair dryer, safe.

Germir Palas Hotel   Wooden wainscoting, faux Chippendale sofas, and Parisian-style cityscapes of Istanbul make stepping into the Germir Palas like stepping back in time to 19th-century Paris. The hotel's elegant style is a direct result of the Germir family's other enterprise: As owners of a textile business, they've coordinated warm floral wallpaper with leafy green and beige fabrics to create a warm and welcoming atmosphere. Rooms are comparatively small, so if possible, book one of the seven corner rooms, which are slightly bigger but sacrifice the view. Bathrooms are spacious and all come equipped with full bathtubs. The lobby-level brasserie-style bar is a great meeting place; the hotel also offers two basement-level conference rooms.

Cumhuriyet Cad. 17, 80090 Taksim, Istanbul. (C) 0212/361-1110. Fax 0212/361-1070. www.germirpalas.com. 49 units. 180€ ($261/£129) double. AE, MC, V. **Amenities:** Restaurant; bar; concierge; tour desk; car-rental desk; 24-hr. room service; massage; babysitting; laundry service; dry cleaning; nonsmoking rooms; elevator. *In room:* A/C, satellite TV, minibar, hair dryer, safe, bathtub.

Mısafır Suites ✦✦✦   Dutch-born Joost and his partners waited 4 years for the drug addicts and squatters to vacate the derelict building they purchased before razing it and starting from scratch. The inside was gutted leaving the facade, while the basalt floors, marble baths, and artistic textiles are new and chic. The rooms are enormous (as are the baths, which are stocked with products from L'Occitaine). Rooms include king-size beds, twin sofas flanking oversize circular ottomans, and long conveniently placed upholstered benches. It's all very smart, very well planned out, and very, *very* delightful. The restaurant has a hip vibe and top-notch creative cuisine. Airport pickup is included in the price.

Gazeteci Erol Dernek Sok. 1, 34430 Beyoğlu (from the Ağa Mosque on Istiklal, turn down Sadir Alışık Sok.). (C) 0212/249-8930. Fax 0212/249-8940. www.misafirsuites.com. 7 units. 200€–250€ ($290–$363/£143–£179) suites. AE, MC, V. **Amenities:** Restaurant; bar; concierge; wireless Internet throughout; 8am–midnight room service; laundry; elevator. *In room:* A/C, satellite TV, DVD player, wireless Internet, minibar, coffee/tea station, hair dryer, safe.

MODERATE

Anemon Galata ✦   The restoration of this 19th-century neighborhood gem was at the forefront of the revival of Galata. The building enjoys a front-row seat to the neighborhood plaza at the base of the commanding Galata Tower. The hotel itself offers sophisticated old-world style and in-room architectural features such as original crown moldings and ceiling frescoes. Wall-to-wall carpeting (which I barely tolerate) and staid decor in the rooms do the building less than full justice, but the upside of all that sound-sucking upholstery is that you certainly won't hear the neighbors. For the best views, pick a room on the third floor or above.

Büyükhendek Cad. 11, 80020 Kuledibi, Istanbul. (C) 0212/293-2343. Fax 0212/292-2340. www.anemongalata.com. 27 units. 125€–150€ ($181–$218/£89–£107) double. Rates include free airport transfers. AE, MC, V. **Amenities:** Panoramic rooftop restaurant; bar; concierge; 24-hr. room service; laundry service; dry cleaning; elevator. *In room:* A/C, satellite TV, minibar, hair dryer, safe.

Galata Antique Hotel   A clean, inexpensive option in this part of town is hard to find, but the Galata Antique provides a friendly and convenient one. The hotel is located just down the street from the British embassy and a few steps away from the entrance to Tünel and Istiklal Caddesi. The building was designed by the French architect Vallaury in 1881 and still retains some 19th-century charm in its caged elevator and carved wooden arches. The rooms are basic, tasteful, and elegant, and the bathrooms, although recently redone with fresh tile, are a bit disappointing due to the sparse sink and shower setups. The entrance to the hotel sits in the middle of a flight of exterior steps, so the Galata Antique may not be appropriate for everyone. However, the central location is ideal.

Meşrutiyet Cad., Nergis Sok. 10, 80090 Beyoğlu, Istanbul. (C) 0212/245-5944. Fax 0212/245-5947. www.galata antiquehotel.com. 27 units. 110€ ($160/£79) double; 150€ ($218/£107) suite. MC, V. **Amenities:** Bar; concierge; 24-hr. room service; laundry service; dry cleaning; elevator. *In room:* A/C, satellite TV, minibar, hair dryer.

Lares Park   Modern, luxurious, and architecturally appealing. Not what you'd expect from the fringe streets around Taksim (yet). A standard unit offers plenty of room to move around, while newer "deluxe" rooms are even bigger and recently redesigned. The Presidential suite, meanwhile, gets you a duplex with fridge, clothes washer, dishwasher, microwave, and CD deck. The health club is a haven of relaxation, with patio-style lounge chairs set around a large indoor area with swimming pool, Jacuzzi, and juice bar. It contains a fitness center and a tempting Turkish bath, and you don't have to pay a cent extra to use any of it (though you do for a massage). The location right smack in the center of a commercial center is far enough away from the minarets of Sultanahmet to permit an uninterrupted night's sleep.

Topçu Cad. 23, 80090 Taksim, Istanbul. (C) 0212/254-5100. Fax 0212/256-9249. www.laresparkhotel.com. 179 units. 109€–119€ ($158–$173/£78–£85) single; 130€ ($189/£93) double and deluxe; 200€–500€ ($290–$725/£143–£357) suite. Rates higher April–Oct, Christmas, and New Year's Day. AE, MC, V. **Amenities:** Restaurant; bar; cafe/patisserie; indoor swimming pool; fitness room; Turkish bath; Jacuzzi; sauna; business center; 24-hr. room service; laundry service; dry cleaning; elevator. *In room:* A/C, satellite TV w/pay movies, minibar, hair dryer, safe.

The Marmara Pera 🏨🏨 The sister property of the Marmara Istanbul hit the ground running in 2005. It occupies a tower flanked by the Pera Palas Hotel and one of my favorite restaurants, Lokanta, in the heart of the more vibrant section of Beyoğlu. And in spite of its 200 rooms, the hotel actually feels like a boutique property, as spaces are kept to manageable scale and the decor is understatedly trendy. The architect even saved the original tile paving where possible. Splurge the extra 50€ ($73/£36) or so for a sea-view room—it'll be worth it. A patisserie, bar, and restaurant are on the ground floor, plus the independently owned Mikla (see "Where to Dine," below), which occupies the top two levels of the hotel with the best views.

Meşrutiyet Cad., Derviş Sok. 1, Tepebası, Istanbul. (C) 0212/251-4646. Fax 0212/249-8033. www.themarmarahotels. com. 200 units. 115€–190€ ($167–$276/£82–£136) double; 345€ ($500/£246) suite. Breakfast and taxes not included. AE, MC, V. **Amenities:** Rooftop restaurant; bar; rooftop pool; fitness center; business center; four meeting rooms; wireless Internet; laundry; dry cleaning; elevator. *In room:* A/C, satellite TV, wireless and dataport, minibar, hair dryer, safe, bathtub.

INEXPENSIVE

Richmond (Value The location of this Belle Epoque hotel couldn't be better. It's located close to the lively cafes and restaurants of Beyoğlu/Tünel, but remains accessible to Taksim, Galata, Karaköy, and the tramway to the Old City with a minimum of effort. It's a bit older than the snazzy new deluxe boutique hotels mushrooming around Taksim Square, but nevertheless a good value. Standard rooms have all of the necessary trappings above wall-to-wall carpeting. The newer rooms have parquet floors, sea views, and more space. The rooftop restaurant-and-bar is atmospheric and blessed with great views. Breakfast is served in the cozy brick cellar, but that's only in the unlikely event that you make it past the hotel's patisserie without stopping on your way down.

Istiklal Cad. 445, Tünel. (C) 212/252-5460. Fax 212/252-9707. www.richmondhotels.com.tr. 206 units, all with tub. 79€–120€ ($115–$174/£56–£86) double. AE, MC, V. **Amenities:** Bar; concierge; wireless Internet; 24-hr. room service; laundry service; dry cleaning; elevator. *In room:* A/C, satellite TV, dataport, minibar, hair dryer, safe.

ALONG THE BOSPHORUS
VERY EXPENSIVE

Çırağan Palace Kempinski Istanbul 🏨🏨🏨 Residence of the last Ottoman sultans, the hotel that you see today actually comprises two buildings: the faithfully restored stone-and-marble sultan's palace (housing the VIP suites) and the modern five-star deluxe hotel. Both stand majestically on the shores of the Bosphorus, presiding over a magnificent collection of sculpted lawns, marble gates, a waterside swimming pool, and even a putting green. Hard to believe that a little over a decade ago, the Çırağan was a burned-out shell of its current and former splendor. The guest list reads like a who's who of international royalty, all lining up for a Bosphorus-view room (not all get one). The alternative is a park-view room (clearly not as good), but this is just more incentive to partake of the anything-but-common areas.

Çırağan Cad. 84, 80700 Beşiktaş, Istanbul. © **800/426-3135** in the U.S., 800/363-0366 in Canada, 0800/868-588 in the U.K., 800/623-578 in Australia, 0800/446-368 in New Zealand, 0212/258-3377 in Istanbul. Fax 0212/259-6686. www.ciraganpalace.com. 316 units. $500–$765 (£250–£383) park-view double; $765–$1,015 (£383–£508) sea-view double; $1,058–$3,234 (£529–£1,617) hotel suite. Breakfast and tax not included. Double weekend rates available. AE, DC, MC, V. **Amenities:** 3 restaurants (review for Tuğra p. 104); numerous bars; indoor and outdoor swimming pools; putting green; health club; fitness room; Turkish bath; Jacuzzi; sauna; concierge; car-rental desk; meeting facilities; shopping arcade; salon; 24-hr. room service; babysitting; laundry service; dry cleaning; nonsmoking rooms; palace section; elevator. *In room:* A/C, satellite TV w/pay movies, dataport, minibar, hair dryer, safe.

Four Seasons Bosphorus 🏛🏛🏛   Eagerly anticipated for well on 4 years now, the new Four Seasons on the Bosphorus is going to keep us in suspense just a little bit longer. But since we are all familiar with the Four Seasons, I'm going to preemptively award it three starsIt is expected to be up and running by the time this book hits the stores and in time for the 2008 summer season. As a result, I can only speak of this hotel in generalities: The hotel complex is composed of the restored and stately Ottoman Atik Paşa mansion, amid 2 regrettably practical modern blocks. (If the Çırağan can get away with it, then why not the Four Seasons?) Apart from that tiny criticism, the hotel aims to be—in the model of Four Seasons everywhere—a practically flawless center of hospitality and service. East-facing rooms in the paşa's mansion benefit from spectacular, head-on views of the Bosphorus. The heated outdoor pool sits seamlessly adjacent to the seafront, and a private dock provides convenient access, via the hotel's speedboat service (or one's private yacht), to key points around the city (or to nowhere—whichever is one's pleasure).

Çırağan Cad. 28, 34349 Beşiktaş. © **0212/638-8200.** Fax 0212/638-8210. www.fourseasons.com/bosphorus. 166 units. Contact hotel for rates. AE, MC, V. **Amenities:** 2 restaurants; 3 bars; banquet facilities; cinema; indoor and outdoor swimming pools; fitness room; "Urban" spa; Turkish bath; sauna; concierge; business center w/translation services; meeting facilities; wired and wireless Internet; 24-hr. room service; massage; laundry service; dry cleaning; elevator; handicapped accessible; parking. *In room:* A/C, satellite TV/VCR, CD/DVD player, fax, Internet, minibar, hair dryer, safe.

Hotel Les Ottomans 🏛🏛🏛 *Moments*   This lavish hotel is *the* talk of the town, and only the most overused (but apt) superlatives can be used to describe it. My apologies in advance. Let's start by saying that the powerhouse behind the hotel villa, Ahu Aysal, spared no expense (upward of $60 million) in the reconstruction of the former Muhzinzade Mehmet Paşa wooden mansion that stood on this site (the exterior is an exact replica). The result is a sumptuous, 10-room (plus one; Ahu lives on the top floor) . . . palace? abode? Shangri-La? In the creation of the hotel, Ms. Aysal employed the renowned Turkish interior designer Zeynep Fadillioğlu, as well as feng shui expert Yap Cheng Hai, to ensure that the hotel conformed to principles of harmony. Feeling a bit unworthy upon my visit, I found the hotel to be opulent without being ostentatious. It's just what you'd imagine of a modern royal palace—gilded calligraphic friezes, antique ivory inlay, magnificent silk fabrics—and of course, let's not forget the plasma TVs (some suites have as many as three). The hotel's spa is one of the best in town.

Muallim Naci Cad. 68, 34345 Kuruçeşme, Istanbul. © **0212/359-1500.** Fax 0212/359-1540. www.lesottomans.com. 10 units. 800€–3,500€ ($1,160–$5,075/£571–£2,500) suite, single or double. Rates include breakfast and use of minibar but exclude taxes. AE, MC, V. **Amenities:** 2 restaurants; bar; banquet facilities; cinema; outdoor swimming pool; fitness room; Caudalie spa; Turkish bath; sauna; concierge; business center w/translation services; meeting facilities; wireless Internet; 24-hr. room service; butler service; massage; laundry service; dry cleaning; elevator; handicapped accessible; pet friendly; parking; doctor; dietician. *In room:* A/C, satellite TV/VCR, CD player, fax, free Internet, minibar, coffeemaker, hair dryer, safe.

EXPENSIVE

Radisson SAS Bosphorus Hotel ⭐ In January 2006, this piece of waterfront real estate adjacent to the artsy neighborhood of Ortaköy became one of the newer additions to the European Bosphorus. The target audience is business travelers, Turkish weekenders, and anyone else in the market for good design, seamless comfort, and a boutique experience. The hotel features a grassy "beach" and a spa offering a variety of treatments. There's a parking garage adjacent to the hotel, which is just steps away from the Ortaköy docks and some of the best nightlife the city has to offer.

Çırağan Cad. 46, 34349 Ortaköy. ⓒ **0212/310-1500.** Fax 0212/310-1515. www.radissonsas.com. 180€ ($261/£129) double; 280€–650€ ($406–$943/£200–£464) suite. AE, MC, V. **Amenities:** Restaurant; bar; fitness room; spa; Turkish bath; sauna; concierge; meeting facilities; wireless Internet; 24-hr. room service; laundry service; dry cleaning; elevator; handicapped accessible; pet friendly; parking. *In room:* A/C, satellite TV/VCR, CD player, fax, free Internet, minibar, coffeemaker, hair dryer, safe.

ON THE ASIAN SIDE

A'jia ⭐⭐ The contemporary design of this sleek and stylish romantic getaway brings this traditional Ottoman *yalı* into the 21st century. The property was originally the stately mansion of the Turkish journalist and politician Ahmet Rasim. In the 1970s, the house was converted into an elementary school (in fact, students still drop by to have a look). A tour of the rooms revealed accommodations ranging from sublime to otherworldly: ergonomic king-size beds, oversize goose-feather pillows, oversize bathtubs, and picture windows for optimal Bosphorus views. The mezzanine suite (with the tub next to the bed) is host to many a romantic interlude; the management recently obliged a guest by pasting rose petals on the glass to spell out "Will you marry me?"

Ahmet Rasim Paşa Yalısı, Çubuklu Cad. 27, Kanlıca, Istanbul. ⓒ **0216/413-9300.** Fax 0216/413-9355. www.ajia hotel.com. 16 units. 250€–750€ ($363–$1,088/£179–£536) rooms and suites. AE, MC, V. **Amenities:** Restaurant; bar; Bosphorus waterfront sun deck; airport pickup upon request; private complimentary boat shuttle; meeting facilities; wireless Internet; 24-hr. room service; butler; in-room Thai massage; private parking. *In room:* A/C, satellite TV, DVD player, wireless Internet, minibar, hair dryer, safe.

Sumahan ⭐⭐⭐ Converted from a structure originally used for the production of *soma* (grain alcohol, today more benignly called ethanol) to an idyllic retreat, the Sumahan (aptly named with *soma* and the Turkish word *han* for building) is a prime example of functional architectural preservation. Mark and Nedret Butler met while studying architecture in America. When the Turkish State began proceedings to expropriate the land (owned by Nedret's family) in the 1970s, the Butlers, by then settled into their lives in Minneapolis, entered into a 30-year bureaucratic saga that ended in them relocating back to Istanbul. The rest is a story fit for *Architectural Digest,* with significant input from the Butlers' interior designer daughter, Yaşa. Apart from the understated luxury of the spaces, the highlights include duplexes, baths swathed in the same Marmar marble found in Topkapı and Dolmabahçe, and a studied forethought to even the placement of soap. The hotel provides three complimentary shuttles per day to the Kabataş docks. There are also commuter boats from the Çengelköy docks (200m/656 ft. away) to Eminönü two times daily.

Kuleli Cad. 51, 34684 Çengelköy, Istanbul. ⓒ **0216/422-8000.** Fax 0216/422-8008. www.sumahan.com. 20 units. 280€–490€ ($406–$711/£200–£350) suites Apr–Nov; rates slightly lower in winter. AE, MC, V. **Amenities:** 2 restaurants;

bar; Turkish bath; meeting facilities; library; Internet point; wireless and wired Internet; 24-hr. room service; laundry service; dry cleaning; babysitting; handicapped accessible; elevator. *In room:* A/C, satellite TV, CD/DVD player, minibar, hair dryer, safe.

NEAR THE AIRPORT

Airport Hotel   Located on the grounds of Istanbul's Atatürk Airport, this is a sure-fire way to make sure you don't miss that flight. It's also a godsend on long layovers, because you don't even have to exit Customs to check in to your room. Not surprisingly, the hotel attracts lots of business travelers—the business center and executive meeting rooms make sure of that—but even the most sun-kissed vagabond will enjoy breakfast views of the runway. Rooms are pleasingly bright, airy, and unusually spacious, and offer high-tech amenities like TVs that show flight details and Internet access. The hotel also offers rooms at hourly rates (for naps on long layovers and such) and a well-appointed fitness room for those crack-of-dawn workouts.

Atatürk Havalimanı Dış Hatlar Terminali, Yeşilköy, Istanbul. 🕐 0212/465-4030. Fax 0212/465-4730. www.airport hotelistanbul.com. 85 units. 140€–180€ ($203–$261/£100–£129) air-side double; 150€–220€ ($218–$319/ £107–£157) land-side double. Hourly rates available. AE, MC, V. **Amenities:** Bar; fee-based fitness room; wireless Internet throughout; 24-hr. room service; laundry service; dry cleaning; elevator. *In room:* A/C, satellite TV w/pay movies, minibar, hair dryer, safe.

4 Where to Dine

For the most part, 90% of the restaurants in the Old City are sadly lacking, and although you can forgive an eatery a less-than-stellar meal at lunchtime, I for one can't forgive the extortion. Instead, I recommend you sample the honest home cooking at the various innocuous *lokantas* (dives with steam tables), particularly along Pierloti Caddesi, between the Hippodrome and Cağaloğlu and in the working streets around the Grand Bazaar, or grab a taxi to some of the restaurants I've starred in this section.

Another popular option is the neighborhood of Kumkapı, on the southern tip of the historic peninsula, a year-round carnival crammed with typical tavernas which benefits directly from the fish market across the highway. Appropriately, Kumkapı translates to "sand gate"; pick the restaurant with the most people or the freshest-looking fish, and hold on to your valuables, as the dimly lit surrounding streets attract the worst petty thieves.

SIRKECI & EMINÖNÜ
INEXPENSIVE

Hamdi Et Lokantası KEBAPS   Hamdi's southeastern kebaps will never come close to Develi's, but this is a good alternative to the overpriced mediocrity of Pandeli Lokantası only steps from the entrance to the Spice Market. The restaurant's popular terrace views of the Galata Tower and Golden Horn add to the convenience of the location, and you can move to the cozy *şark* (Oriental-style seating area) for your after-dinner

---

Tips Summer Dining Alfresco

Restaurant dining rooms resemble ghost-town eateries in the summer, but if you just continue up the steps, you'll see why. Istanbul is a city of rooftop terraces, and summer dining is almost exclusively enjoyed high above the city accompanied by warm breezes and breathtaking panoramas.

cup of coffee or tea. Specialties of the house include the *erikli kebap*, minced meat from a suckling lamb where all of the fat has been cooked out, and the showcase *testi kebap*, a stew of diced meat, tomatoes, shallots, garlic, and green pepper cooked over an open fire and served tableside by breaking the terra-cotta pot (minimum 10 people, advance orders required). Hamdi caters to vegetarians with the vegetable kebap, spiced with parsley and garlic; don't pass up the *yuvarlama*, a flavorful yogurt soup with tiny rice balls served only at dinnertime.

Tahmis Cad. Kalçin Sok. 17 (set back behind the bus depot), Eminönü. ℭ 0212/528-0390. Reservations required for dinner. Dress smart. Appetizers and main courses 6YTL–18YTL ($5.20–$16/£2.40–£7.20). MC, V. Daily 11am–midnight. Closed 1st day and last 3 days of Ramadan.

Orient Express Cafe *(Finds* TURKISH/OTTOMAN   Located next to track no. 1, the Orient Express restaurant—a real find—is proof that you don't have to pay an arm and a leg for white tablecloths, good food, and nostalgia. The elegant niches with their large stained-glass window insets and the handsome clapboard ceiling take you back at least a century, although the decorator would have done well to scrap the enormous *Shining Time Station* oil-on-canvas on the wall.

The limited but satisfying menu relies heavily on lamb, with a tender lamb shoulder as the pride of the chef. Craving eggplant, I ordered the *beğendili kebap*, cubes of flavorful beef atop a bed of eggplant purée (or was that ambrosia?). The crème caramel was a formidable substitute to an empty coffer of rice pudding, and the service was black-tie and flawless.

Sirkeci Train Station, Sirkeci. ℭ 0212/522-2280. Appetizers and main courses 5YTL–22YTL ($4.35–$19/£2–£8.80). MC, V. Daily noon–11pm.

Pandeli Lokantası *(Overrated* TURKISH   Pandeli is one of those neighborhood traditions that lives on more for its location and longevity than for anything particularly outstanding about the restaurant. Pandeli was opened in 1901 by a Greek of Turkish descent and has become a local institution ever since its arrival on the upper level of the Egyptian Spice Bazaar. It's a popular place among businessmen on expense accounts as much as for bazaar shoppers looking for a place to eat. If you nab a table in the main room facing the ancient blue Iznik tiles and windows overlooking the bazaar, you can watch the human traffic come and go.

Mısır Çarşısı 1, Eminönü (immediately inside the entrance to the Egyptian Bazaar). ℭ 0212/527-3909. Main courses 9YTL–18YTL ($7.85–$16/£3.40–£7.20). MC, V. Mon–Sat 11am–4pm.

IN & AROUND SULTANAHMET
VERY EXPENSIVE
Balıkçı Sabahattin ☆☆☆ FISH   One of the few consistently good, high-quality restaurants in a neighborhood of amateurs, Balıkçı Sabahattin is still cranking out top-quality treasures from the sea for eager fans. Meals are served alfresco on the cobbled streets in summer. When the air turns crisp, diners fill the many rooms of this restored 1927 house. Don't pass up the tahini ice cream, and what you can't finish you can feed to one of the hungry kittens milling about. When the weather chills up (or if you came too late for an outdoor table), meals are served inside a restored old Ottoman house on the fringes of Sultanahmet.

Cankurtaran, Sultanahmet (behind Armada Hotel). ℭ 0212/458-1824. Appetizers and main courses 2.50YTL–35YTL ($2.20–$30/£1–£14) and up for fish by weight. V. Daily noon–3pm and 7–10:30pm.

Sarnıç *(Overrated)* FRENCH/TURKISH   The setting for this restaurant, an old Roman cistern tucked away behind the Ayasofya, is nothing less than dramatic. The flickering light of 500 candles bounces off the iron grillwork, the lofty brick domes, and the stone pillars, while the crackling of the fire in the massive stone chimney (an inauthentic but effective addition) supplies more romance than a girl can handle. It's hard to believe that only a few years ago, before the Turkish Touring and Automobile Association bought and restored it, the cistern served as a greasy old auto repair shop.

The menu, created by the longtime chef who cut his teeth at an older incarnation of the Sheraton Hotel, marries traditional French entrees like beef bourguignon with standard Turkish grills. But while the service is good and the ambience is great, my experience there was (twice) reminiscent of a large institutional wedding (except for the marinated beef salad, which was truly memorable). Perhaps then, it is a hit-or-miss thing.

Soğukçeşme Sok., Sultanahmet. ℂ **0212/512-4291.** Reservations required. Dress smart. Appetizers and main courses 10YTL–50YTL ($8.70–$44/£4–£20). AE, MC, V. Daily 6pm–midnight; lunch available for groups only.

Seasons Restaurant 𝄐𝄐𝄐 MEDITERRANEAN   Rated no. 1 in Zagat's "Best of Europe" since the book first came out, The Four Seasons' restaurant continues to be a favorite, not only for expats and foreign visitors, but for locals as well. There are menus for breakfast, lunch, and dinner, each adapted to seasonal offerings approximately every 3 months. The *izgara levrek madalyon* (medallions of grilled sea bass) seems to be a recurrent theme, served with a ragout of vegetables, yellow tomatoes, a beet reduction, and chive essence; you can also find Oriental-leaning dishes such as seared scallops with shrimp rolls and ginger.

Four Seasons Hotel, Tevkifhane Sok. 1, Sultanahmet. ℂ **0212/638-8200.** Reservations required. Dress smart. Appetizers and main courses 14YTL–38YTL ($12–$33/£5.60–£15). AE, DC, MC, V. Daily 6:30–11am, noon–3pm, and 7–11pm.

EXPENSIVE

Konyalı Topkapı Sarayı Lokantası 𝄐 TRADITIONAL TURKISH/OTTOMAN   Diners at Topkapı are treated to a stunning stopover and a short walk through history. Don't confuse the more casual cafeteria with the formal restaurant, the latter being where all the culinary action is. Konyalı has been serving celebrity royalty for more than 100 years, and it's got the black-and-white photographs to prove it. Some of the specialties of the house are their *börek*, the slow-cooked tandır lamb, and orange baklava. Konyalı recently opened a second location at the Kanyon shopping center in Levent.

Topkapı Palace, Sultanahmet. ℂ **0212/513-9696.** A la carte main courses 9YTL–32YTL ($7.85–$28/£3.60–£13). AE, MC, V. Wed–Mon 10am–4pm.

Yeşil Ev 𝄐 FRENCH/TURKISH   Located in one of the first reconstructed replicas of an Ottoman mansion in Sultanahmet, the Yeşil Ev restaurant takes full advantage (in the summertime) of the luxurious setting provided by the enclosed garden and grand fountain. The Ottoman/French menu includes a decent duck a l'orange, the one-time selection of choice for the visit of France's prime minister. Although reputed as one of the top restaurants in Istanbul, meals here sometimes get mixed reviews. The elegant orangery is open in good weather only (in winter for groups of eight or more), and on a balmy summer's eve, you won't even notice the check.

Kabasakal Cad. 5, Sultanahmet. ℂ **0212/517-6785.** Dress smart. Appetizers and main courses 8YTL–28YTL ($6.95–$24/£3.20–£11) and up for prawns and fish. AE, MC, V. Daily noon–11pm.

MODERATE

Marmara Terrace Restaurant NOUVELLE TURKISH   With massive domes of the Blue Mosque towering over the rooftop terrace restaurant, the chef doesn't really have to work too hard to draw a crowd. Regrettably, the terrace is only open on appropriately balmy evenings June through September; the rest of the time, there's a lovely enclosed street-side cafe or an indoor lobby-level dining area. The appetizer of mixed mezes is a tasty and innovative sampler consisting of carrot rolls with yogurt, seafood with smoked salmon and shrimp, cold vegetables, and Ottoman spring rolls with cheese and potatoes. Traditional main courses include lamb chops and the Ottoman-style *köfte*.

In the Mavi Ev (Blue House), Dalbastı Sok. 14, Sultanahmet. ℭ **0212/638-9010**. Reservations suggested. Appetizers and main courses 5YTL–25YTL ($4.35–$22/£2–£10). AE, MC, V. Daily noon–11pm.

INEXPENSIVE

Buhara 93 TURKISH   For some pretty good, cheap, basic Turkish fare, Buhara is an old reliable. I tend to stick to the *ev yemekleri* (home cooking)—the dishes stewed and displayed in the window. The menu narrows to serve only kebaps during Ramadan.

Nakilbent Sok. 15A, Sultanahmet. ℭ **0212/518-1511**. Menu 3YTL–10YTL ($2.60–$8.70/£1.20–£4). MC, V. Daily 9am–10pm.

Eminönü Belediyesi Sosyal Tesisleri *(Value (Finds* TRADITIONAL TURKISH The security guards sporadically stationed at the gated entrance aren't exactly an inviting presence, but this is indeed one of the neighborhood's finds. It's actually a combined tea garden and restaurant, placed strategically on an outdoor terrace that makes up part of the ancient Byzantine fortress wall. There's a small building situated at the back of the grounds, containing a dining room serving traditional Turkish meals. And because it's owned by the municipality—presumably the reason for the guards—this destination is bone dry (no alcohol). I recommend this place regularly for anyone looking for an authentic, atmospheric, and hassle-free meal at the right price.

Ahırkapı Iskele Sok. 1, Cankurtaran (near the Armada Hotel, under the train tracks at the Dede Efendi entrance to the neighborhood from the sea road). ℭ **0212/458-5415**. Appetizers and main courses 4YTL–14YTL ($3.50–$16/£1.60–£5.30). MC, V. Daily 11am–midnight.

The Pudding Shop *(Overrated* TURKISH   In its heyday, The Pudding Shop was an obligatory stop on the "hippie trail," a starting point for restless vagabonds from the West on their way through the exotic East. With its anti-establishment clientele, it wasn't long before it gained the reputation of ground zero for drug dealings and other unsavory business propositions. In Oliver Stone's *Midnight Express,* Billy Hayes gives up his cab-driver supplier here. Today The Pudding Shop fades into history alongside the other fast-food restaurants on Divanyolu Caddesi, with fluorescent backlit menu displays and stacks of expat publications.

Divanyolu Cad. 6 (across from the tram), Sultanahmet. ℭ **0212/522-2970**. Appetizers and main courses 4YTL–13YTL ($3.50–$11/£1.60–£5.20). MC, V. Daily 8:30am–10pm or later.

Tamara *(★ (Finds (Value* TURKISH/REGIONAL   The stars have so far aligned for this relatively new upstart. The menu features an unusually broad selection of kebaps, *pides,* and salads. Still, my advice is to order one of the stewlike regional dishes. One such delight was *keldoş,* a delicious concoction of lentils and beef a la Van, in Eastern Turkey. Or the *orman* (forest) kebap—a stew of lamb, chick peas, potatoes, and carrots. The narrow entry and large steam pans conceal a clean and comfortable open-air dining room at the rear (enclosed in winter).

Küçükayasofya Cad. 6, Sultanahmet. ⓒ 0212/518-4666. Appetizers and main courses 2YTL–14YTL ($1.75–$12/ 80p–£5.60). MC, V. Daily 9am–11pm.

Tarıhı Meşhur Sultanahmet Köfteçısı ☆☆ *Kids* *Value* KÖFTE   This little, quality dive on the main drag has been around longer than Turkey has been a republic, and after one bite it's easy to see why. It's hard to imagine a simple meatball as delectable as the ones made here, but if you're not convinced, there's not much in the way of an alternative. (They also serve lamb *şiş* for 9YTL/$7.85/£3.60, but it's beside the point, as *köfte* is the main event here) Side dishes are limited to white beans or a shepherd's salad (tomato, cucumber, onions, and chili peppers). Top the meal off with the *irmik helvası,* a modestly sweet semolina comfort food beloved by Turks.

Divanyolu Cad. 12/A, Sultanahmet. ⓒ 0212/513-1438. Köfte 7YTL ($6.10/£2.80). No credit cards. Daily noon–10pm.

THE OLD CITY: NEAR THE LAND WALLS

Asitane ☆☆☆ *Value* OTTOMAN   Clearly, it was good to be the sultan, if he indeed ate at all like I do when I visit Asitane. From records of meals at Topkapı Palace (sans quantities), the chef of Asitane has succeeded in re-creating 200 palace recipes plus about 200 original Ottoman-style recipes. The *etli elma dolması* (apple stuffed with lean diced lamb, rice, currants, pistachio, and rosemary) still makes my mouth water—the only regrettable thing is that I'll probably never eat it again, because the menu changes each season. There's a menu in honor of Fatih Sultan Mehmet (the Conqueror) May through June, while vegetarian main-course selections are on the menu year-round.

In the Kariye Oteli, Kariye Camii Sok. 18 (adjacent to the Church of St. Savior in Chora), Edirnekapı. ⓒ 0212/534-8414. Reservations suggested. Dress smart. Appetizers and main courses 10YTL–30YTL ($8.70–$26/£4–£12). AE, DISC, MC, V. Daily noon–midnight.

Develi Restaurant ☆☆☆ SOUTHEASTERN KEBAPS   Develi's success may have translated into a blossoming of sister locations around the country, but no matter how good the others may be, this Develi maintains a level of consistency and fabulousness worthy of more than what a simple star rating will allow. For their regional specialties, they follow outstanding recipes from the Gaziantep region of southeastern Turkey— this translates roughly as *blisteringly spicy.* Adventurous eaters should order the fiery *çiğ köfte,* beefy meatballs combined with every spice in the book, rolled up into flat little meatballs served raw in a soothing lettuce leaf. Other notable menu items include the *muhamara,* a delectable purée of bread, nuts, and chickpeas; the *findik lahmacun,* a thin-crust pizza made Turkish-style with chopped lamb; or the lamb sausage-and-pistachio kebap. Leave room for the *künefe,* a warm slab of baklava dough oozing cheese, dipped in syrup, and covered with crushed pistachio nuts. The rooftop terrace is stupendous in the summer, and there's a nonsmoking room for indoor wintry evenings.

Balıkpazarı, Gümüşyüzük Sok. 7, Samatya (ⓒ 0212/529-0833), and Tepecik Yolu 22, Etiler (ⓒ 0212/263-2571). Reservations required. Dress smart. Appetizers and main courses 4YTL–20YTL ($3.50–$17/£1.60–£8). MC, V. Daily noon–midnight.

TAKSIM SQUARE TO TÜNEL
VERY EXPENSIVE
Mikla ☆☆☆ MEDITERRANEAN   Located on the top two floors of the new Marmara Pera hotel, Mikla is the newest hit of the Istanbul Yiyecek Icecek A.S. ("eat

drink") ventures, which include the now defunct Downtown and the very popular Lokanta (at Nu Pera in winter and at rooftop as Nu Teras in summer). The Swedish-born chef, Mehmet Gürs, is somewhat of an Istanbul celebrity by now; he settled in Istanbul in the '90s and has made all of the kitchens he's touched turn to gold. Reservations are hard to come by and the wait for a table is long; the management makes it easy with the upstairs bar-front seat views of the lights of the Old City. Raw grouper makes an outstanding appetizer, followed by the whole roast beef tenderloin for two. Try to leave space for the memorable pistachio and tahini ice cream.

Mesrutiyiyet Cad. 167–185, Tepebaşı. ℂ 0212/293-5656. Appetizers and main courses 17YTL–55YTL ($15–$48/£6.80–£22). AE, MC, V. Daily noon–3:30pm and 6–11:30pm.

EXPENSIVE

Hacı Abdullah TRADITIONAL TURKISH Politicians, businessmen, families, and out-of-towners have been coming to Istanbul's first licensed restaurant for over a century. The recipes reflect the best of traditional Turkish cuisine, serving substantial stews, whole artichokes baked with vegetables in olive oil, and their signature dish, the lamb shank with eggplant. Lining the walls are enormous glass jars filled with fruit compotes made on the premises and incorporated into the chef's proud desserts, such as quince marinated in syrup or the sweetbread custard topped with figs, apricot, pistachio, and coconut. For those wishing to celebrate with a glass of wine, Hacı Abdullah unfortunately serves no alcohol.

Sakizağacı Cad. 17, Beyoğlu. ℂ 0212/293-8561. Reservations suggested. Appetizers and main courses 9YTL–33YTL ($7.85–$29/£3.60–£13). MC, V. Daily noon–10:30pm; later on weekends.

House Café CAFE In 2002, a little cafe opened in a house in Nişantaşı. But the creative (and enormous) soups, sandwiches, and salads gained a following until House Café burst at the seams. There are now three locations (the other two are in Teşvikiye and Ortaköy) along with a solid and successful Istanbul brand. I barely made a dent in my lentil salad with purslane and goat cheese in truffle oil, although I may have had I not sunk my fork into my companion's huge and unexpectedly authentic Italian (not the Turkish kind) pizza. A handful of tiny tables line the cobbled alley, while indoors is a well-styled yet cozy space.

Asmali Mescit 9/1, Tünel. ℂ 0212/245-9515. Atiye Sok. Iskeçe Apt. 10/1, Teşvikiye. ℂ 0212/259-2377. Salhane Sok. 1, Ortaköy. ℂ 0212/227-2699. Appetizers and main courses 17YTL–30YTL ($15–$26/£6.80–£12). AE, MC, V. Mon–Thurs 8am–10:30pm; Fri–Sat 8am–11pm; Sun 8am–9:30pm (bar until 2am Mon–Sat and 11pm Sun).

MODERATE

Boncuk 👁👁 (Value TURKISH/ARMENIAN Located on a side street off the Galatasaray Fish Market, this small rustic *meyhane* is the one restaurant on this saturated stretch that is consistently full. Boncuk serves delicacies such as fried brains (mmm . . .) and stuffed spleen, but thankfully there's a variety of more recognizable hot and cold mezes like *kızır*, flavorful and spicy *bulgur* balls, and *topik*, an Armenian specialty made of chickpea paste around a nucleus of onions and currants. Because availability is seasonal, try not to be too disappointed when the waiter informs you that your choice is not on the menu that day.

Nevizade Sok. 19, Beyoğlu. ℂ 0212/243-1219. Appetizers and main courses 4YTL–20YTL ($3.50–$17/£1.60–£8) and up for fish. No credit cards. Daily noon–midnight.

Degustasyon Lokantası (Overrated MEZES/FISH Degustasyon serves a huge selection of mezes, and not just the usual selection of eggplant purée (which is phenomenal) and *ezmel*/pepper paste. Here you'll get some Armenian recipes, such as the fava loaf, thrown in with Turkish traditional dishes. It's just as full of life as the other nearby *meyhanes*, but slightly classier. And obviously, in deference to the location, the restaurant serves a good selection of fish. So why overrated? Because the last time I ate there (anonymously), the manager inflated the bill (but I busted them). See? It can happen anywhere.

Balıkpazarı, Beyoğlu. ℂ **0212/292-0667.** Appetizers 4YTL–6YTL ($3.50–$5.20/£1.60–£2.40); main courses 8YTL–16YTL ($6.85–$14/£3.05–£6.10) and up for fish. MC, V. Daily 11am–1am or later.

Doğa Balık 𝄡𝄡 FISH   People's eyes light up at the mention of this highly popular restaurant, positioned on the rooftop (top floor in winter) of the Zurich Hotel in the newly arrived expat-heavy neighborhood of Çihangir. But the view is almost beside the point here. The very freshest fish of the season is served here: amply sized bonito *(palamut)* or turbot *(kalkan)* costing upward of 30YTL ($26/£12) per kilo. While the fish is delectable, the real attraction here is the overwhelming selection of mezes. There are 30 varieties of wholesome forest greens all guaranteed to make you moan with pleasure: from nettles, to feverfew, to purslane, to "goat food." Don't miss the nongreen mezes, in particular the *mercemek köftesi* (lentil balls), and the monkfish salad. Indeed, load up on the appetizers and skip the main course.

Akarsu Yokusu Cad. 44–46, Çihangir (follow Siraselviler Cad. down from Taksim Sq. and turn left when you reach the mosque). ℂ **0212/293-9143.** Appetizers and main courses 5YTL–16YTL ($4.35–$14/£2–£6.40); fish by weight. MC, V. Daily noon–1:30am.

Refik 𝄡 BLACK SEA SPECIALTIES   Tucked into a back street in Beyoğlu, Refik is unassuming, even unimpressive, from the outside. But this little restaurant has been an institution in the neighborhood since its inception in 1954. Success lies equally with the unfailing quality of the ingredients and the pride that goes into the preparation. The earliest shifts arrive at 6am to start the preparations for a menu that is distinct to the Black Sea region and therefore heavy on dishes with black cabbage.

The *hamsibuğulama* (fish steamed in season) along with the *arnavut ciğeri* (sautéed Albanian liver and onions) are house specialties, as is the *kara lahana dolması* (stuffed cabbage). Mezes change seasonally, and in the summer, tables spill onto the narrow street. ***Bonus:*** A ventilation system sucks the cigarette smoke up and away from diners.

Sofyalı Sok. 10–12, Tünel. ℂ **0212/243-2834.** Reservations required. Appetizers and main courses 6YTL–14YTL ($5.20–$12/£2.40–£5.60); fish sold by weight. AE, DC, MC, V. Daily noon–10:30pm.

Yakup 2 TURKISH MEYHANE   The regular clientele keeps coming back to this Istanbul meyhane for the consistently good traditional Turkish mezes, kebaps, and fair prices. The decor is nothing to speak of, and the best you can say about the expansive outdoor terrace is that it's outside. But the quality of the food is first rate.

Asmalı Mescit Mah. 35–37. ℂ **0212/249-2925.** Appetizers and main courses 6YTL–19YTL ($5.20–$17/£2.40–£7.40) and up for fish. MC, V.

INEXPENSIVE

Otantik 𝄢ids TRADITIONAL ANATOLIAN   For a special night out, Turks head to their favorite *et* or *balık* (meat or fish) restaurant, ready to splurge for dishes they themselves rarely cook at home. But then, in contrast to these celebratory outings, someone realized how delicious "poor man" home-style recipes can also be. Here, the menu includes *hıngal* (potato dumplings served with yogurt), *otantik yuvarlama çorba* (spicy lentil-based vegetable soup), and *keşkek* (a familiar-tasting dish of cream of wheat with pieces of chicken), along with various types of *gözleme* (filled pancake), pilaf, and kebaps at extremely fair prices. The restaurant has four floors, each with its own traditional style, and the room in the fourth-floor annex sits right over the inner atrium of the Beaux Arts Çiçek Pasajı.

Istiklal Cad. 170 (next to the entrance to the Çiçek Pasajı). ℂ 0212/293-8451. Appetizers and main courses 5YTL–13YTL ($4.35–$11/£2–£5.20). No credit cards. Daily 8am–midnight.

Parsifal *(Finds* VEGETARIAN The formerly derelict and now reclaimed Kurabiye Street is now home to an increasing number of tiny little restaurants. This one, however, is a standout. The menu is entirely vegetarian—the type of vegetarian that keeps you coming back for more. Some of the creative dishes are broccoli ograten (sic), chard lasagna, black-eyed bean salad with walnut, and stuffed artichoke dolma. It distinguishes itself from Zencefil across the street, because while Zencefil is healthy, it's not veg.

Kurabiye Sok. 9A (the parallel st. to Istiklal). ℂ 0212/245-2588. Lunch menu to 8.50YTL ($7.40/£3.40); dinner menu slightly higher. MC, V. Daily noon–11pm.

Saray Muhallebiçileri *(Value* PATISSERIE/KEBAPS People have been flocking to Saray Muhallebiçileri since its establishment in 1949, and a look in the window will tell you why. The colorful array of desserts lures you off the street and into this patisserie—but with such a huge choice and exceedingly low prices, you'll find it difficult to decide on any one thing. Rice-pudding addicts should definitely not pass up this opportunity, although the chocolate pudding is irresistible as well. This is also a good place to try the *tavukgögsü*, a sweet gummy pudding made with chicken. There are now a number of franchises all over the city; the one in Eminönü has a cafeteria, prepared foods, and the expected wide array of sweets.

Istiklal Cad. 102–104, Beyoğlu. ℂ 0212/292-3434. Appetizers and main courses 4YTL–9YTL ($3.50–$7.85/£1.60–£3.60). MC, V. Daily 6am–1:30am.

Zencefil HEALTHY FOOD Billed as a vegetarian cafe (in spite of the chicken with leeks on the menu), this spot serves up wholesome fare worthy of its healthy designation. Homemade bread with herb butter accompanies every meal, which might be a big healthy salad, an ample slice of quiche, or Indian stew with exotic spices and vegetables. Menus have been skillfully translated into English—which is useful, because pumpkin pie probably isn't in your basic Turkish dictionary, and it's too good to miss. Zencefil will be moving to a new location across the street at an undetermined date in the future; if it's not where I say it is, just look across the street.

Kurabiye Sok. 3, Taksim. ℂ 0212/244-4082. Main courses 6YTL–12YTL ($5.20–$10/£2.40–£4.80). MC, V. Mon–Sat 9am–11pm.

AROUND THE GALATA TOWER

Enginar TURKISH PUB As with much of the history of Galata, no one knows for sure what comprised the first building on this site; but turn the clock back 100 years and envision these bright "new" stones (additions to foundations that could date back 400 yrs.) as an Italian bank, then later as a coffeehouse for the neighborhood Jewish community, and most recently as an Akbank. With its attractive lighting and interior resembling an old warehouse, Enginar is a comfortable and quiet place for a drink, and the food, seemingly simple by the looks of the menu, is quite good, too, although the portions are miniscule. Try their vegetable crepe for a lighter lunch, or go for broke with the ginger steak.

Şah Kapısı Sok. 4/A, Galata (continue straight down Istiklal Cad. to the Galata Tower; the cafe is on your right). ℂ 0212/293-9697. Appetizers and main courses 5YTL–20YTL ($4.35–$17/£2–£8). MC, V. Daily 10:30am–12:30am.

Galata House ☆ *Finds* GEORGIAN   Hidden along the steep slopes of Galata's historic streets, this little restaurant, the brainchild of an architect/city planner and his wife, occupies a row house that served as the British jail at the beginning of the 1900s. The coziness of the dining rooms—three small salons and an outdoor upper balcony—belies the building's earlier purpose, except for the few preserved squares of plaster etched by prisoners during periods of extreme boredom. At first, the menu selections appear Turkish but arrive with an unexpected twist of flavor: The menu reaches into Caucasian territory, with Georgian dumplings, blini and borscht, chicken and pea salad with yogurt and dill. Potential visitors should take note, however, of the steep incline of the streets in this neighborhood (wear rubber soles!), and that this particular street is often unlit.

Galata Kulesi Sok. 61, Galata (follow Kuledibi Sok. from the Galata Tower). ℂ 0212/245-1861. Appetizers and main courses 8YTL–16YTL ($6.95–$14/£3.20–£6.40). MC, V. Tues–Sun noon–midnight.

NIŞANTAŞİ

Carne *Kids* KOSHER MEDITERRANEAN   The menu is kosher at Carne, recently relocated from Ortaköy to its present location in Harbiye. Leaning heavily on classic ingredients of the Mediterranean, Carne puts out mouthwatering dishes such as entrecôte or grilled rack of lamb with smoked eggplant, bell pepper, rosemary, and lamb glaze. The list of appetizers does little to leave room for the main course, as who can resist a plate of salmon tartar or falafel served with your choice of hummus or tomato sauce? There are also plenty of vegetarian options on the menu.

Halaskargazı Cad. Uzay Apt. 53, Şişli. ℂ 0212/241-8585. Reservations suggested for dinner. Appetizers and main courses 7YTL–34YTL ($6.10–$30/£2.80–£14). MC, V. Mon–Thurs and Sun noon–11pm; Fri noon–4pm; Sat 7:30–11pm.

Hünkar ☆☆ OTTOMAN   This Istanbul institution was founded in the neighborhood of Fatih in 1950. The Fatih location has since closed, but the restaurant's loyal following ensured its survival in Nişantaşı, with a second branch in Etiler. Istanbullus wax lyrical over the traditional Turkish and Ottoman cooking served here. Hünkar is famous for its *beğendili kebap* and roast lamb. Their warm *irmik helvası* (semolina dessert) is the model for all others. The Nişantaşı location fills up with local professionals at lunchtime; the homey Etiler location has an outdoor trellised sidewalk cafe.

Mim Kemal Öke Cad. 21/1, Nişantaşı. ℂ 0212/225-4665. Reservations suggested. Appetizers and main courses 7YTL–15YTL ($6.10–$13/£2.80–£6). AE, MC, V. Daily 11am–11:30pm.

ALONG THE BOSPHORUS

Tuğra ☆☆☆ OTTOMAN   This place has become a legend in itself with its innovative synthesis of foods from the entire Ottoman Empire. Tuğra is the epitome of fusion food, so much so that its Turkish clientele comments that the traditional Ottoman dishes taste unfamiliar. Dishes include a delicious mackerel and red mullet dolma and a marinated lamb loin grilled with yogurt, tomato, and spicy butter sauce. It's possible to drop upward of 200YTL ($174/£80) per person on dinner and a few gin and tonics, but if you don't drink and you order a la carte, you can at least expect an exceptional dining experience without the heart failure.

Çırağan Palace Hotel Kempinski Istanbul, Çırağan Cad. 84, 80700 Beşiktaş. ℂ 0212/258-3377. Reservations required. Dress smart. Appetizers and main courses 18YTL–45YTL ($16–$39/£7.20–£18). AE, DC, MC, V. Daily 7–11pm.

5 What to See & Do in Istanbul

Istanbul is a city that has successfully incorporated a rich past into a promising future—no small feat considering the sheer magnitude of history buried under those cobblestone streets. Three of the greatest empires in Western history each claimed Istanbul as their capital; as a result, the city overflows with extraordinary sites all vying for equal time. Conveniently, all of the top sights are located on or immediately around Sultanahmet Park, but that by no means is an indication that there's nothing worth seeing outside of that neighborhood.

SUGGESTED ISTANBUL ITINERARIES

IF YOU HAVE 1 DAY   Stick to the Sultanahmet district; begin your tour chronologically at the Hippodrome, and work your way through the centuries with a visit to the Ayasofya, the Yerebatan Cistern, and the Blue Mosque. Spend the afternoon exploring the treasures of Topkapı Palace (start from the last courtyard, so you can have lunch at Konyalı right away, and don't blow off the Istanbul Archaeology Museum, although you will want to). If there's any time left, make a beeline to the Grand Bazaar (9–7pm; closed Sun), where you'll have but a few short hours to hone your bargaining prowess. After the Grand Bazaar closes, head over to the nearby Süleymaniye *hamam,* which stays open until 11pm. After you've been peeled and pressed, have dinner at Develi or Asitane, and call it a day well spent. *Note:* The Grand Bazaar is closed on Sundays, while most of the museums listed here are closed on Mondays.

IF YOU HAVE 2 DAYS   Spend the first day following the 1-day itinerary. On day 2, start the day at St. Savior in Chora museum. Then from there, either (1) head up to Pierre Loti for a rest stop of coffee or tea overlooking the storied Golden Horn, and then wander through the Ottoman cemetery and Eyüp, or (2) stroll through the as-of-yet ungentrified (but not for long) neighborhoods of Fener and Balat, densely dotted with Byzantine churches and buildings, synagogues, and the Greek Patriarchate. In the afternoon, find your way (by bus or taxi) to the streets in and behind the Egyptian Spice Bazaar, then walk across the Galata Bridge, and meander around the streets up to the Galata Tower. If your feet are still hanging on, continue up along Galip Dede Caddesi and the Istiklal Caddesi, stopping to take in the Çiçek Pasajı, the Balık Pazarı, the Avrupa Pasajı, and Fransiz Sokağı. Continue up Istiklal Caddesi to Taksim (or take the nostalgic trolley), and treat yourself to dinner at one of the recommended restaurants in this chapter, or combine dinner with some live Turkish music at one of the authentic "Turkish Houses" on Hasnun Galıp Sokak.

IF YOU HAVE 3 DAYS   Follow the 2-day itinerary for days 1 and 2, and then set out early on day 3 for a daylong cruise up the Bosphorus. If you're concerned about time, take a half-day guided sightseeing tour, which wraps up around lunchtime (they usually include a stop at the Egyptian Spice Bazaar, an informed description of the sights along the Asian and European shores, and a visit to Rumeli Castle), or hop on the 1½-hour quickie ride up the Bosphorus in the kitschy Sultan's Kayıkları. If you've opted for the do-it-yourself Bosphorus cruise, disembark at Çengelköy on the Asian side, have lunch at the ferry landing (or at Kordon, in the Sumahan Hotel *©* **0216/ 321-0473,** or at the adjacent del Mare *©* **0216/422-5762**), and then take a ferry back to Kabataş docks. From there, either take the underground funicular up to Taksim and work your way up to the Military Museum in time for the 3pm performance

Istanbul Attractions

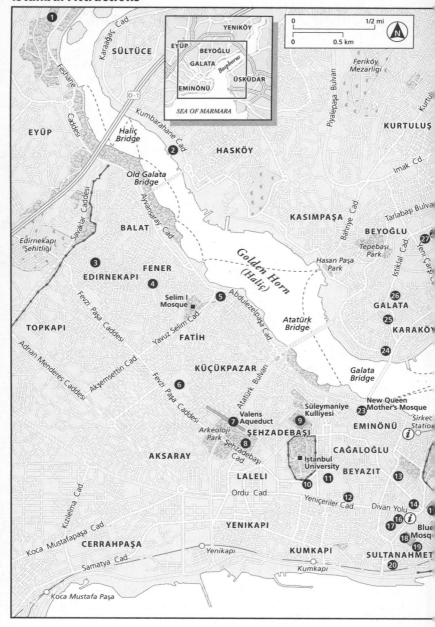

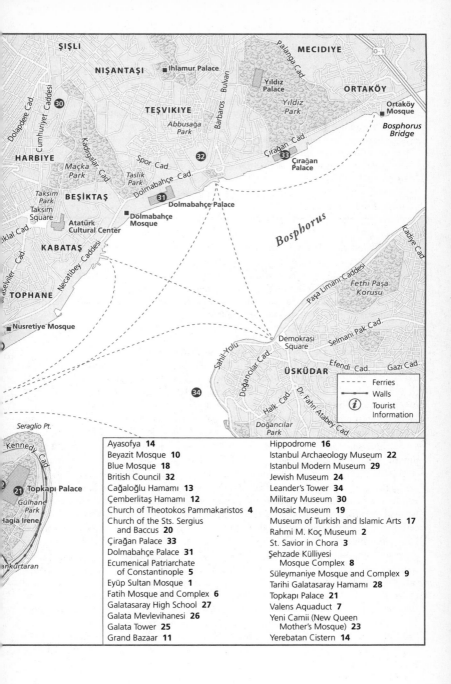

Ayasofya **14**
Beyazit Mosque **10**
Blue Mosque **18**
British Council **32**
Cağaloğlu Hamamı **13**
Çemberlitaş Hamamı **12**
Church of Theotokos Pammakaristos **4**
Church of the Sts. Sergius
  and Baccus **20**
Çirağan Palace **33**
Dolmabahçe Palace **31**
Ecumenical Patriarchate
  of Constantinople **5**
Eyüp Sultan Mosque **1**
Fatih Mosque and Complex **6**
Galatasaray High School **27**
Galata Mevlevihanesi **26**
Galata Tower **25**
Grand Bazaar **11**

Hippodrome **16**
Istanbul Archaeology Museum **22**
Istanbul Modern Museum **29**
Jewish Museum **24**
Leander's Tower **34**
Military Museum **30**
Mosaic Museum **19**
Museum of Turkish and Islamic Arts **17**
Rahmi M. Koç Museum **2**
St. Savior in Chora **3**
Şehzade Külliyesi
  Mosque Complex **8**
Süleymaniye Mosque and Complex **9**
Tarihi Galatasaray Hamamı **28**
Topkapı Palace **21**
Valens Aquaduct **7**
Yeni Camii (New Queen
  Mother's Mosque) **23**
Yerebatan Cistern **14**

Fun Fact   **I Wish I May, I Wish I Might**

According to legend, when construction of the Ayasofya reached the height of a man, the construction team set out to get a bite to eat, leaving their tools under the watch of a small boy. An angel appeared and urged the boy to fetch the men so that they could return to the work of building God's house. When the boy told the angel that he promised not to leave the tools unattended, the angel promised to keep an eye on everything until his return. After leaving the site and thus breaking his promise, the boy was never allowed to return, and the angel continues to wait for him. Go to the entrance of the basilica proper, to the left of the Imperial Door; legend has it that the angel grants a wish to all those who successfully complete a 360-degree circle with their thumb in the hole of this wish-worn column.

---

of the Mehter Band (trust me on this one, just GO. If you're running late, there's a Turkish-language repeat of the performance at 3:30), or grab a cab. After the show, take some time to visit the Military Museum (you'll have to backtrack, as the amphitheater for the Mehter Band showing is located toward the end of the exhibits). From the entrance/exit to the museum, it's but a short walk to the tony neighborhood of Nişantaşı, with a nice selection of excellent restaurants.

THE TOP SIGHTS

Ayasofya ✶✶✶   For almost a thousand years, the Ayasofya was a triumph of Christianity and the symbol of Byzantium, and until the 16th century, maintained its status as the largest Christian church in the world. The cathedral is so utterly awesome that the Statue of Liberty's torch would barely graze the top. Erected over the ashes of two previous churches using dismantled and toppled columns and marble from some of the greatest temples around the empire, the Ayasofya (known in Greek as the Hagia Sophia and in English as St. Sophia, or Church of the Holy Wisdom) was designed to surpass in grandeur, glory, and majesty every other edifice ever constructed as a monument to God. Justinian began construction soon after his suppression of the Nika Revolt, indicating that combating unemployment was high on the list as well. He chose the two preeminent architects of the day: Anthemius of Tralles (Aydın) and Isidorus of Miletus. After 5 years and 4 months, when the construction of the Ayasofya was completed in A.D. 537, the emperor raised his hands to heaven and proclaimed, "Glory to God who has deigned to let me finish so great a work. O Solomon, I have outdone thee!" Enthusiasm for this feat of architecture and engineering was short-lived, because 2 years later, an earthquake caused the dome to collapse. The new dome was slightly smaller in diameter but higher than the original, supported by a series of massive towers to counter the effects of future earthquakes. Glass fittings in the walls were employed to monitor the weight distribution of the dome; the sound of crunching glass was an early warning system indicating that the weight of the dome had shifted. Several more earthquakes caused additional damage to the church, requiring repairs to the dome (among other sections), which was increased in height thanks to the support provided by the addition of flying buttresses (additional buttresses were added at two later dates).

In 1204 the Ayasofya was sacked and stripped down to the bare bones by the Crusaders, a desecration that robbed the church of precious relics and definitively divided the Greek Orthodox and Roman Catholic churches.

After Mehmet II penetrated the city in 1453, his first official stop was to this overwhelming symbol of an empire that he had conquered, and with his head to the ground, he invoked the name of Allah, and declared the great house of worship a mosque.

In the years that followed, several adjustments were made to the building including the covering over of the frescoes and mosaics, due to the prohibition of Islam against the representation of figures. (The iconoclastic movement of the 8th and 9th centuries had similarly disavowed the use of figural depictions and icons, during which many of the frescoes and mosaics were defaced, destroyed, or cemented over; any figural representations seen today date to after this period.) A single wooden minaret was erected (and later replaced by Mimar Sinan during restorations in the 16th century), and three additional minarets were added at a later date. The altar was shifted slightly to the right to accommodate a *mihrab* indicating the direction of Mecca, and an ablution fountain, along with a kitchen, was erected in the courtyard. Along the perimeter of the church, excavations are continuing to reveal the foundations of the church built by Theodosius.

Ayasofya was converted from a mosque into a museum by Atatürk in 1935, after a painstaking restoration led by Thomas Whitmore of the Byzantium Institute of America. Mosaics and icons that were previously defaced or whitewashed were rediscovered and restored.

While this enduring symbol of Byzantium still has the power to instill awe after so many additions and reconstructions (including tombs, schools, and soup kitchens during its tour of duty as a mosque), the exterior's original architecture is marred by large and boxy buttresses; you'll get more of a representation of the intent of Justinian's original from the inside. On your way in, notice the stone cannonballs lining the gravel path of the outer courtyard. These are the actual cannonballs used by Mehmet the Conqueror in his victorious 1453 battle for the city. The main entrance to Ayasofya leads to the **exonarthex** *★*, a vaulted outer vestibule that was reserved for those not yet baptized. The **inner narthex** *★★*, or vestibule, glistens with Justinian's original gold mosaics embellished with floral and geometric patterns. The most central of the nine doors leading into the nave of the church, called the **Imperial Gate** *★*, is topped by a **mosaic** *★★★* of the Christ Pantocrator holding a book with the inscription "Peace be with you. I am the Light of the World." He is surrounded by roundels portraying the Virgin Mary, the angel Gabriel, and a bearded emperor, believed to represent Leo VI asking for forgiveness for his four marriages.

Through the Imperial Gate is a sight that brought both emperors and sultans to their knees: a soaring **dome** *★★★* that rises 56m (184 ft.) in height (about 15 stories) and spans a width of approximately 31m (102 ft.). Light filters through a crown

<hr>

Fun Fact

At 151 feet and 1 inch high, the Statue of Liberty (less the pedestal) could fit under the dome with 32 feet and 11 inches to spare.

Fun Fact Face-off in the Corner

Empress Zoë had a lot of clout in the early part of the second millennium. First she had a glorious golden mosaic, found at the end of the upper gallery, crafted in her honor, depicting Christ between herself and her first husband. When her husband died in 1034, she ordered the tiles of his face along with the inscription replaced to accommodate her second husband, repeating the procedure for the third.

---

formed by 40 windows and ribs, glittering with the gold mosaic tiles that cover the entire interior of the dome. At its decorative peak (including the side aisles, semi-domes, inner walls, and upper galleries), Ayasofya's interior mosaics covered more than 4 acres of space. Eight calligraphic discs, four of which are the largest examples of calligraphy in the Islamic world, ornament the interior and bear the names of Allah and Mohammed (above the apse); the four successive caliphs, Ali, Abu Bakr, Osman, and Omar (at each of the four corners of the dome); and Ali's sons Hassan and Huseyin (in the nave). The main nave, side aisles, apse, and semi-domes are covered with mosaics and frescoes, depicting religious and imperial motifs or floral and geometric designs. At the center of the space is a square of marble flooring called **Coronation Square,** believed to have been the location of the emperors' throne, the place of coronation, and therefore, in minds of the Byzantines (or at least the emperor), the center of the universe. Up in the southern gallery are some of the best mosaics in the church (restoration just recently completed; thus the additional entrance fee), including the **Deesis** 𝕲𝕲𝕲 (a composition depicting Christ, his mother, and St. John the Baptist), considered to be one of Byzantium's most striking mosaics, in spite of the missing lower two-thirds. This mosaic is one of the oldest, dating to the 14th century. Opposite the Deesis is **the tomb of Henrico Dandalo,** the blind Venetian doge whose success in diverting the Fourth Crusade to Constantinople resulted in his capture of the city in 1204. At the far end of the gallery near the apse are two additional mosaics: one depicting **Empress Zoë** 𝕲𝕲 with her third husband, Constantine IX Monomachus (see "Face-off in the Corner," below), separated by a figure of Christ, and a mosaic portrait of **Emperor John II Comnenus,** his wife, Empress Eirene, and their son, Prince Alexius (extended onto the panel on the wall to the right).

Exit the church through the small Vestibule of Warriors in the inner narthex opposite the ramp to the upper gallery. Previously used as an entrance, this is now an exit, so you're forced to turn around and view the mosaic lunette depicting an enthroned **Virgin Mother and Child** 𝕲𝕲𝕲, flanked by Constantine proffering a model of the city and Justinian offering a model (inaccurate) of the Ayasofya. (A mirror has been placed above the current exit to alert you to the mosaic behind you.)

Sultanahmet. ✆ 0212/522-1750. Admission 10YTL ($8.70/£4) each to the grounds/museum and the 2nd-floor gallery. Tues–Sun 9am–5pm.

Blue Mosque (Sultan Ahmet Camii) 𝕲𝕲𝕲   This grand bubble of masonry, one of the great and defining features of Istanbul's skyline, was constructed between 1609 and 1617 by Sultan Ahmet I, who was not only driven by a desire to leave behind an imperial namesake mosque, but was also determined to build a monument to rival the Ayasofya. So great was the Sultan's ambition that he had one unfortunate architect executed before finally choosing Mehmet Ağa, probably a student of Sinan, who came up with a plan commonly accepted as impossible to build. The design is a scheme of successively descending smaller domes that addresses the problem of creating a large covered interior space. The overall effect is one of such great harmony, grace, and power that it's impossible to walk away from this building unaffected.

> *Fun Fact* **Did You Know?**
>
> Approximately 21,000 tiles were used to decorate the Blue Mosque.

There are several legends associated with the construction of the **six minarets.** One says that the sultan's desire for gold minarets—*altın* in Turkish—was understood as *altı,* or six. Whatever the reasoning, the construction challenged the preeminence of the mosque in Mecca, which at the time also had six minarets. The ensuing scandal, both in and out of Istanbul, resulted in the sultan's ordering the construction of a seventh minaret at the Kaa'ba.

The mosque was completed after just over 6½ years of work and to this day remains one of the finest examples of classical Ottoman architecture. The original complex included a soup kitchen, a *medrese* (Muslim theological school), a primary school, a hospital, and a market. A *türbe,* or mausoleum, stands at the corner of the grounds near the Hippodrome and Sultanahmet Park, and houses the remains of the Sultan Ahmet I, his wife, Kösem, and three of his sons. It also contains some fine examples of calligraphy on cobalt-blue Iznik tile.

The main entrance (for worshippers; tourists must enter from a portal on the south side) is off the **Hippodrome,** beneath the symbolic chain that required even the sultan to bow his head when he arrived on horseback. Walk straight through the garden up to the main marbled courtyard of the mosque and you'll see an ablution fountain, no longer in use. The working ablution fountains are located at ground level of the northern facade facing the Ayasofya. Visitors should enter from the opposite side (from the Hippodrome entrance, follow the garden path diagonally to your right to the south side of the mosque).

If you plan your visit during the morning hours when the sun is still angled from the east, the first effect once inside will be one of blindness as the light penetrates the stained glass, creating an illusion of false darkness. As your eyes adjust, the swirling blues, greens, reds, and yellows from the tile and stained glass increase the impression of immensity and grandeur. The abundant use of decorative tile represents the pinnacle of **Iznik tile** craftsmanship, evident in the rich yet subtle blues and greens in traditional Ottoman patterns of lilies, tulips, and carnations. The overall dominance of blue prompted the mosque's early visitors to label it the Blue Mosque, a name that sticks to this day.

Lateral half **domes** resting on enormous elephantine **columns** (actually called elephant foot pillars) enhance the sense of open space, but critics contend that the pillars are too overbearing and cumbersome. The elegant **medallions** facing the *mihrab* bear the names of Allah and Mohammed; the ones opposite are decorated with the names of the first four caliphs who ruled the Islamic world.

Sultanahmet. Free admission. Daily dawn–dusk. Closed to visitors during prayer times.

Grand Bazaar (Kapalı Çarşısı)

The mother of all tourist traps, the Grand or Covered Bazaar is a vivid illustration of all that's gone wrong with the free market.

The Grand Bazaar is actually the center of a commercial area within and around the covered section of the market all the way down the hill to Eminönü. It is a vast collection of over 4,000 shops, 24 *hans* (privately owned inns or marketplaces), 65 streets, 22 gates, 2 *bedestens* (covered markets), restaurants, mosques, fountains, and teahouses within an area of 30.7 hectares (76 acres).

At the heart and soul of the bazaar are two *bedestens* (merchant centers), ordered built by Mehmet the Conqueror for the purpose of gaining revenue for the Ayasofya. These were the **Iç,** or **Inner Bedesten** (more commonly known as the Old Bedesten), and the **Sandal Bedesten.** These two rectangular structures are typical *bedestens,* meaning that they are solid, significant, and capped by rows of vaults and domes covering a perimeter of cells surrounding an inner courtyard. Ottoman merchants gravitated to this center of commerce; it is estimated that by the end of Mehmet II's rule, the bazaar had already grown to a third of its current size. Artisans tended to congregate in one area, a legacy handed down through names of streets such as Fez Makers Street (Fesçiler Sok.), Street of the Washcloth Makers (Aynacilar Sok.), and Street of Fur Makers (Kürkçüler Sok.).

There are also a number of characteristic *hans* that at one time (and now nominally) operated around a particular craft or trade. There's the **Safran Han** (stuffing/sewing pillows and mattresses), the 17th-century **Valide Han** (weaving on looms), the **Çuhacılar Hanı** (antique silver and jewelry), and the 15th-century **Kürkçüler Han,** the oldest one still in use (yarns and knitting supplies; the furs are upstairs).

Over the centuries, the shops around the bazaar fell victim to a total of 10 fires and two earthquakes; the current configuration dates to 1894, when the Minister of Public Works under Abdülhamid II reorganized the bazaar following that year's earthquake.

Today, the main drag running from the Nuruosmaniye Gate to the Beyazit Gate is **Kalpakçilar Caddesi** 𝒦, the glittering main thoroughfare lined on either side with shops of silver and gold, with anything and everything your heart's desire elsewhere in the market.

Free admission. Best entrances through the Beyazit Gate (across from the Beyazit stop on the tramway along Divanyolu) and the Nuruosmaniye Gate (from the Çemberlitaş tramway stop on Divanyolu, follow Vezirhanı Cad. to the arched entrance to the mosque grounds, which lead to the bazaar). Mon–Sat 8:30am–7pm. Closed Oct 29. Shops close early nightly during the month of Ramadan.

Hippodrome 𝒦   Watching the modestly clothed couples with their children strolling through the park on a Sunday afternoon, it's hard to imagine the centuries of rowdy chariot races, ostentatious royal celebrations, and bloody massacres that took place on these lawns. During the month of Ramadan, the trees above the park are strung with white lights, and temporary tents and imitation Ottoman houses full of

---

(*Tips* **Two Cafes in the Grand Bazaar**

Need a shot of caffeine? **Café Ist** (𝒞 **0212/527-9353;** Tarakçılar Cad.) and **Fes Café** (𝒞 **0212/528-1613;** Halıcılar Cad. 62), both located in the Grand Bazaar, are open Monday through Saturday 8:30am to 7pm, and offer sanctuary from endless cups of Nescafé with a wide selection of coffees, flavored teas, and fresh-squeezed juices. Fes also has a location just outside the Nuruosmaniye Mosque at Ali Baba Türbe Sok. 25/27 (𝒞 **0212/526-3070).**

⟨Tips⟩ Fishing for Customers: Local Shop "Commissioners"

The dregs of Turkish society mill around the entrances to the major sites in Sultanahmet (Blue Mosque, Ayasofya, Topkapı, and the Hippodrome), lying in wait to pounce on you (and a percentage of anything you buy) with apparently harmless—even helpful—offers of assistance. It's called "fishing" in local jargon, and you're the fish. The point is to gain your confidence so that you trust this person and the people/places/shops he recommends. If you don't mind the company, that's your choice. But in the event you buy, rest assured that after the transaction is completed, your new friend will find his way back to the shop (or hotel) for his cut. (Also, see "Important Tips for Single Women Travelers," in chapter 2.)

---

fast food are set up along the perimeter, while a pink-and-blue fiberglass elephant ride for toddlers wipes away any remaining stains of the Hippodrome's complex past.

Polo games and horse races were popular sports in the day. The first track was built in A.D. 203 by Septimus Severus out of the ruins of the city he sacked. Modeled on the Circus Maximus in Rome, the Hippodrome was enlarged by Constantine in 324 through the help of supporting vaults and hefty stone walls on the southern portion of the tract. The lower areas (the **Sphendome** ⭐, or retaining wall down the hill at the obelisk end of the park) were used as stables and quarters for the gladiators.

Forty rows of seats accommodated up to 100,000 people, agitated supporters divided into merchant guilds, that over time degenerated into political rivalries. These factions were known as the Blues, Greens, Reds, and Whites. The Blues and Greens put aside their disagreements to demonstrate against the emperor in 532, which resulted in a riot with protesters screaming "Nika!" (Greek for victory). In what would become known as the Nika Revolt, much of the imperial palace and the original church of Ayasofya were destroyed. Justinian eventually regained control of his throne and ordered the massacre of some 30,000 to 40,000 people as punishment. With the arrival of the Fourth Crusade, the Hippodrome fell into disuse, eventually serving as a marble quarry for the Ottomans after their conquest of the city.

At the height of its splendor, the Hippodrome was crowned with a vast collection of trophies, statues, and monuments, either crafted by local artisans or lifted from the far corners of the empire.

At the southern end of the park is the **Magnetic Column** ⭐⭐, also known as the Walled Obelisk, the Plaited Column, the Colossus, and the Column of Constantine. This column was erected in the 10th century under Constantine VII Porphyrogenitus and was faced with plaques of gilded bronze and brass plates. At one time this obelisk was used to support a pulley system for raising and lowering awnings to protect the spectators from the sun. In 1204 the bronze and brass plates were removed and smelted by the Crusaders to mint coins.

Farther along is the **Serpentine Column** ⭐⭐, a squat spiral standing 25% lower than its original 8m (26 ft.). The column was originally erected outside the Temple of Apollo at Delphi by the 31 Greek city-states to commemorate their victory over the Persians, and later brought to the city by Constantine. Made of melded bronze, the column represents three intertwining serpents and was crowned by three gold serpents' heads supporting a gold bowl, said to have been cast from the shields of the fallen Persian soldiers. The heads were lost until one resurfaced during the restoration of the Ayasofya, now in the Archaeological Museum. A second head was discovered and, like many ancient Turkish monuments, slithered its way to the British Museum in London.

The **Obelisk of Tutmosis III** ✶✶✶ is easily one of the most astounding feats of engineering in the city. This 13th-century-B.C. solid block of granite weighing over 60 tons was brought to Istanbul by Emperor Theodosius I from its place in front of the Temple of Luxor at Karnak, in Egypt. The four sides of granite are covered from top to bottom with hieroglyphics celebrating the glory of the pharaoh and the god Horus. The monument was placed in the square in A.D. 390, but *two-thirds* of the original was lost during transport. This portion, standing over 20m (66 ft.) high, was erected in under 30 days, on a Roman base depicting bas-reliefs of Theodosius's family, friends, and triumphs at the races.

At the northern end of the Hippodrome is the **Fountain of Wilhelm II (Alman Çeşmesi)** ✶✶, crafted in Germany and assembled in Istanbul to commemorate the emperor's visit to the city in 1895. Notice the initials of both the German monarch and Sultan Abdülhamid on the interior of the dome, inlaid with glittering golden mosaics.

The Hippodrome's crowning monument, long a distant memory of its original grandeur atop a disappeared imperial loggia, was a monumental **statue of four bronze horses.** In the Fourth Crusade's looting of the city in 1204, the monument was carried away to grace the facade of the Basilica of St. Marco in Venice. (Today, the ones on the facade are fake; the real ones are being protected from the elements in the Basilica of St. Marco's museum.)

Just to the north of the Hippodrome (on the corner where Divanyolu and Yere-batan Caddesi converge) is the **Million (or Milion) Stone,** the point of departure for all roads leading out of the city and essentially ground zero for all measurements. The Milion Stone was modeled after the Milliarium Aureum, erected by Julius Caesar in the Roman Forum in Rome. According to one tradition, the **True Cross** is said to have been brought from Jerusalem to Constantinople and placed by the Milion Stone during the reign of Constantine.

At Meydanı (Horse Plaza), Sultanahmet. Always open.

Istanbul Archaeology Museum (Arkeoloji Müzesi) ✶✶

The Istanbul Archaeology Museum is housed in three buildings just inside the first court of Topkapı Palace and includes the Museum of the Ancient Orient (first building on your left) and the Çinili Köşk (opposite the entrance to the main building). These museums, opened officially in 1891, owe their very existence to Osman Hamdi Bey, a 19th-century Turkish painter, archaeologist, curator, and diplomat, who fought for the Antiquities Conservation Act to combat the rampant smuggling of antiquities out of Turkey.

The Istanbul Archaeological Museum houses over one million objects, the most extraordinary of which are the sarcophagi that date back as far as the 4th century B.C. The museum excels, however, in its rich chronological collection of locally found artifacts that shed light on the origins and history of the city.

Near the entrance is a **statue of a lion** representing the only piece saved from the clutches of British archaeologists from the Mausoleum of Halicarnassus. In the halls to the left is a collection of sarcophagi found at Sidon (ancient Syria) representing various architectural styles influenced by outside cultures including Egypt, Phoenicia, and

Lycia. The most famous is the **Alexander Sarcophagus** ✿✿✿, covered with astonishingly advanced carvings of battles and the life of Alexander the Great, discovered in 1887 and once believed to have been that of the emperor himself. The discovery that the occupant was in fact Sidonian King Abdalonymos may have initially been disappointing, but it hasn't diminished the impact of this great ancient work of art. Found in the same necropolis at Sidon is the stunningly preserved **Sarcophagus of the Crying Women** ✿✿✿, with 18 intricately carved panels showing figures of women in extreme states of mourning. Don't miss the monumental **Lycian tomb** ✿✿✿, carved in a style befitting a great king and just as impressive in this exhibit as on the hills of Lycia. Farther on is the recently inaugurated Northern Wing, which rescues from storage a stunning collection of **monumental sarcophagi** ✿✿✿ and partially reconstructed **temple friezes** ✿✿✿.

On the mezzanine level is the exhibit *Istanbul Through the Ages* ✿✿✿, a rich and well-presented exhibit that won the museum the Council of Europe Museum Award in 1993. To put the exhibit into perspective, the curators have provided maps, plans, and drawings to illustrate the archaeological findings, displayed thematically, which range from prehistoric artifacts found west of Istanbul to 15th-century Byzantine works of art. The recovered **snake's head** ✿ from the Serpentine Column in the Hippodrome is on display, as is the 14th-century bell from the Galata Tower. The upper two levels, closed as of this writing, house the Troy exhibit and displays on the evolution of Anatolia over the centuries, as well as sculptures from Cyprus, Syria, and Palestine.

The newly renovated and reopened **Museum of the Ancient Orient** ✿✿ is an exceptionally rich collection of artifacts from the earliest civilizations of Anatolia, Mesopotamia, Egypt, and the Arab continent. The tour begins with pre-Islamic divinities and idols taken from the courtyard of the Al-Ula temple, along with artifacts showing ancient Aramaic inscriptions and a small collection of Egyptian antiquities. Although the individual exhibits are modest in size, the recent upgrade rivals Ankara's archaeological museum for organization and presentation.

Uncovered in the region of Mesopotamia and on display is an **obelisk of Adad-Nirari III** inscribed with cuneiform characters. Of particular significance is a series of colored **mosaic panels** ✿✿ showing animal reliefs of bulls and dragons with serpents' heads from the monumental Gate of Ishtar, built by Nebuchadnezzar, King of Babylonia. A pictorial representation on a **Sumerian devotional basin** of girls carrying pitchers of water whose contents are filling an underground source relates to the ancient Mesopotamian belief that the world was surrounded by water, a belief that has provoked questions over the origins of the biblical Great Flood.

With nothing dating more recent than the 1st century A.D., it's a real challenge to find something in this museum that is not of enormous significance. But two of the highlights are easily the fragments of the 13th-century-B.C. **sphinx** ✿ from the Yarkapı Gate at Hattuşaş (sadly underappreciated in its positioning against a passage wall) and one of the three known tablets of the **Treaty of Kadesh** ✿✿, the oldest recorded peace treaty signed between Ramses II and the Hittites in the 13th century B.C., inscribed in Akkadian, the international language of the era. (The Istanbul Archaeological Museum houses two; the third is in the Staatliche Museum in Berlin.)

Across from the Archaeology Museum is the **Çinili Köşk,** a wonderful pavilion of turquoise ceramic tiles whose facade displays eye-catching blue and white calligraphy. The mansion was originally built by Mehmet the Conqueror as a hunting pavilion, and now more appropriately houses the Museum of Turkish Ceramics. The museum, which is closed more often than not, contains a modest collection of Anatolian and Selçukian tiles, not the least of which is the 14th-century *mihrab* from the Ibrahim Bey mosque in Karaman in central Anatolia. Other highlights include some fine samples from Iznik and Kütahya, the two most important production centers for pottery, porcelain, and ceramics during the Ottoman period.

Entrance in the 1st court of Topkapı Palace (2nd portal on the left after St. Irene) and uphill at the back of Gülhane Park. ℂ 0212/520-7740. Admission 5YTL ($4.35/£2); includes the Museum of the Ancient Orient and the Çinili Köşk. Archaeology Museum and Çinili Köşk Tues–Sun 9am–5pm; Museum of the Ancient Orient Tues–Sun 9am–1pm.

Museum of Turkish and Islamic Arts ✿

Ibrahim Paşa, swept into slavery by Turkish raids in Greece, became the beloved and trusted boyhood friend of Süleyman the Magnificent. Educated and converted to Islam and eventually appointed grand vizier, Ibrahim Paşa was the sultan's only companion at mealtime, earning him the favored title *serasker sultan* (commander in chief). He also earned the sultan's sister's hand in marriage.

The palace was a gift from the sultan and was built by Sinan. From this very special palace on the Hippodrome, the sultan's family and friends had front-row seats for festivities in the square. Roxelana, the sultan's wife, managed to dispose of her rival in one of her infamous intrigues, by convincing the sultan that his grand vizier had become too big for his britches.

The palace now houses the changing exhibitions of the Museum of Turkish and Islamic Arts, a fine collection of calligraphy, peace treaties, several examples of the sultan's official seal or *tuğra,* and an insightful ethnographic section depicting the lifestyles of nomads and city-dwelling Ottomans.

Ibrahim Paşa Sarayı, on the Hippodrome, Sultanahmet. ℂ 0212/518-1805. Admission 5YTL ($4.35/£2). Tues–Sun 9am–5pm.

Topkapı Palace (Topkapı Sarayı) ✿✿✿

Residence of the sultans, administrative seat of the Ottoman Empire for almost 400 years, and the source of legend on life in the harem, Topkapı Palace should be up at the top of the list for anyone interested in the vast and exotic world behind the seraglio walls. It's impossible to rush through the palace, so you should allot at least a half-day and be prepared to encounter a few bottlenecks throughout the enclosed exhibition halls, especially in the Holy Relics Room where the ardent faithful, in their religious fervor, tend to obstruct the display cases. Built by Mehmet the Conqueror over the ruins of Constantine's Imperial Palace, Topkapı Palace occupies one of the seven hills of the city at the tip of the historic peninsula overlooking the sea. Since it is easily the most valuable real estate in the city, it doesn't take a brain surgeon to see why this spot was preferable to the original palace situated on an inland tract where the university stands today. Mehmet II began construction of the palace 9 years after his conquest of the city, where the sultans reigned continually until 1855, when Abdülmecid moved the imperial residence up the Bosphorus to Dolmabahçe Palace.

Entrance to the grounds is through the Bab-ı Hümayün Gate at the end of the Babuhümayun Caddesi (also called the Gate of Augustus, for the square outside the gate that in Byzantine times was a busy crossroads called the Forum of Augustus). Serving as the entrance through which the public would access the grounds, the gate would often display the decapitated heads of uncooperative administrators or rebels as a warning to all who entered. Just outside the gate is the **Ahmet III Fountain** ✿✿, built by Mehmet Ağa in 1729 atop an ancient source of water as a gift to Sultan

---

(Fun Fact Did You Know?

Whenever a sultan ordered the execution of someone abroad, he would require that the head be brought back to him as proof. Tradition has it that one such victim was none other than Vlad Tepes, a Wallachian nobleman and tyrant better known as Vlad the Impaler (and later, as Dracula).

Ahmet. A poem by the sultan is inscribed in the stone, inviting passersby to "drink the water and pray from the House of Ahmet."

The first courtyard, known as the **Court of the Janissaries,** is a public park of gardens and trees, just as it was in earlier days. Along the center path are the remains of a 5th-century Roman cistern. (You can save this for the way out.)

The diagonal path to the left leads to the stunning **Hagia Eirene (St. Irene)** ✿✿✿, the second-largest Byzantine church after Ayasofya, and a church that predates the arrival of Constantine's conquest of the city. The first temple on the site was dedicated to the goddess Aphrodite until it became the center of Christian activities between 272 and 398. During Constantine's pro-Christian reign, the emperor had the church enlarged; then, following its near destruction in the Nika Revolt (along with that of the Ayasofya), Justinian had it reconstructed. Excavation between 1946 and 1950 indicates that a series of buildings existed connecting the church with the Ayasofya, and the fact that both churches were completed and rededicated at about the same time indicates that these houses of worship were in some way part of a complex. The buildings were later demolished to make room for construction of the palace walls. Rumor has it that Mehmet the Conqueror's Italian consort convinced him to store the house porcelain there, where she could then secretly go and pray, but for the record, the Ottomans used the church as an arsenal. Hagia Eirene is closed to the public but is used as a venue for concerts and recitals during the International Istanbul Music Festival in the summertime. The church may be opened on special request (✆ **0212/ 520-6952**).

The ticket booths to the palace are located on the right side of the courtyard. Proceed to the Ortakapı (middle gate), known as the **"Gate of Salutation"** ✿, roughly translated from the Arabic (Turkish version) *Babüsselâm.*

Added by Süleyman the Magnificent in 1524, this gate signaled to all but the sultan to dismount before proceeding into the palace. On either side of the gate are two octagonal towers that essentially served as death row for those who fell out of favor; after a prisoner's execution, the body would be left outside the gate. To the right of the gate (facing) is a marble fountain where the executioner would wash the blood off his hands before reentering the palace.

Begin your visit with the **Palace Kitchens** ✿✿, a complex comprised of a string of lofty chambers topped by a series of chimney-domes, a narrow inner courtyard, and a smaller string of rooms. The largest in the world, the kitchens at one time employed over 1,000 servants working day and night to serve the 5,000 residents of the palace, a number that swelled to 15,000 during Ramadan. At the far end is the original wooden kitchen that survived a 16th-century fire; Sinan, who reconstructed the kitchens, added the massive conical chimneys and enlarged the original space. Suspended from the iron bars in the ceiling were the cauldrons, raised or lowered over the fire pits below according to the desired intensity of the flame. The kitchens are now

---

Fun Fact Better Safe Than Sorry

Sultans preferred to eat off celadon china, because the pigments changed color when put in contact with poisons.

---

used to exhibit the palace's rich collection of **porcelain** ✿ numbering close to 12,000 pieces, not all of which are displayed. Topkapı houses the third-most-important collection of porcelain in the world, after Beijing and Dresden, while the palace's collection of celadons surpasses that of Beijing because the Chinese destroyed all of theirs during the Cultural Revolution. Besides these 4th- and 5th-century celadons are pieces from the Sung and Yuan dynasties (9th–13th c.), pieces from the Ming Dynasty (14th and 17th c.), and porcelain from the Ching Dynasty (16th–20th c.). Many of these treasures found their way to Istanbul as gifts exchanged between the Ottomans, Chinese, and Persians as symbols of solidarity toward the maintenance and protection of the roads. There's also a rich collection of silver, particularly coffee services, candelabras, and mirrors (ornamented on the backside because of the proscription requiring the reflective side to be lain face down), and a display of Venetian glass and Bohemian crystal. The Ahmet III Fountain outside the main entrance is reproduced here in a stunning mass of silver, but there are examples of collectibles on a less grandiose scale as well.

Following a direct path along the length of the palace grounds, proceed to the **Gate of Felicity (Babüssaade)** ✿, also known as the Gate of the White Eunuchs. For 400 years, enthronement ceremonies were held at the entrance to this gate, today used as a backdrop for the annual presentation of Mozart's *Abduction from the Seraglio* during the International Istanbul Music Festival. Decapitated heads found their way above this gate as well. Only the sultan and the grand vizier were allowed past this gate into the third courtyard (while the Valide Sultan used a back gate for entrances and exits), the private quarters of the palace. Immediately inside the Gate of Felicity and acting as a visual barrier to the private quarters beyond is the **Throne Room** ✿, a pavilion used by the sultan as an audience chamber to receive (or affront) visiting ambassadors. Notice the interlocking marble used in the construction of the arched doorway; this design technique reinforced the archway and protected it against earthquakes.

Directly to the right is the Seferliler Quarters, now housing the **Palace Clothing Exhibition** or Imperial Wardrobe. Because the sultan's clothing was considered to be holy, a sultan's wardrobe would be wrapped up and preserved in the palace. This opulent display of silk, brocade, and gold-threaded clothing is only a small portion of the whole collection and includes enormously baggy costumes (to give the sultan the visual advantage of size), along with caftans and other garments showing influences from around the empire.

Past the Palace Clothing Exhibition is the Fatih Pavilion, containing a recently restored exhibition of the **Treasury** ✿✿✿, one of the greatest collections of treasures in the world. In 400 years a dynasty can amass a great quantity of wealth, supplied through spoils of war, gifts from neighboring kings and queens, and the odd impulse buy. The rooms were off-limits to everyone but the sultan, and in his absence, any visitor was required to be accompanied by at least 40 other men.

Room no. 1 of the Treasury is a collection of Ottoman objects and **ceremonial thrones** ✿✿✿, including one in pure gold, weighing in at 550 pounds, presented to

Murat III in 1585 by the Egyptian governor; an ebony throne crafted for Süleyman the Magnificent; and a jewel-encrusted throne, presented to Mahmut I by Nadir Shah of India.

The eye is immediately drawn to the jewel-studded mother-of-pearl and tortoise-shell throne of Sultan Ahmet I, crafted by the master of inlay, Mehmet Ağa, the same man commissioned by the sultan to build the Blue Mosque. (Rumor has it that during his 1995 visit, Michael Jackson requested permission to sit in one of the thrones; however, his request was denied.) Also of note in room no. 1 is the **sword** belonging to Süleyman the Magnificent, with his name and title inscribed on the blade.

Room no. 2 of the Treasury displays a collection of medals, and non-Ottoman objects and gifts (or plunder) received through the spoils of war. Immediately to the left of the exterior door is a **holy relic** 🏆—a piece of St. John the Baptist's skull and a section of his forearm, enclosed within a solid gold model. Other highlights include figurines crafted in India from seed pearls, and in the same case, a miniature tree of life and a vessel presented as gifts to the tomb of Mohammed.

The focus of room no. 3 is a pair of shoulder-high **candlesticks** 🏆 crafted of solid gold and caked with several thousand brilliants/diamonds and weighing over 105 pounds each. In a world absent of electricity, candlesticks like these would be placed on either side of the *mihrab* to provide light for the reading of the holy book. This pair was presented to the tomb of Mohammed in Medina and brought back to Istanbul after World War I. The rest of the exhibit in room no. 3, an overwhelming collection of jade, rock crystal, zinc, emeralds, and other precious gems, displays Ottoman objects made by artists and craftsmen for the sultans throughout the centuries.

Room no. 4 is the Treasury's *pièce de résistance,* a breathtaking view into the wealth of the Ottoman Empire. The famous **Topkapı Dagger** 🏆 is here, weighted down by a row of emeralds and diamonds in the hilt and on the cover. This dagger was the protagonist in the 1964 film *Topkapı* (with Peter Ustinov), an amusing film about a plot to rob the Palace Museum. The actual dagger was intended as a gift from Sultan Mahmut I to Nadir Shah to warn him of an impending conspiracy on his life, but was returned by the couriers following a bloody revolution in which the shah was killed.

You'll notice a group of people hovering around a case at the far end of room no. 4, displaying the 86-caret **Spoon Maker's Diamond** 🏆🏆, or Kaşıkdı Diamond, the fifth-largest diamond in the world glittering in a setting of 49 smaller diamonds. The diamond was actually discovered in the 17th century in a city dump by a local peddler who sold it to a jeweler for pennies.

The exhibit finishes with a stunning collection of "lesser" diamonds and gems, plus the **gold and jewel-encrusted chain mail** 🏆🏆 of Sultan Mustafa III. Also of note is the **ceremonial sword** 🏆, attributed to either Caliph Osman (7th c.) or Osman Gazi (13th c.), and used in any sultan's inauguration, usually in front of Eyüp Sultan Mosque.

Another piece of note is the **golden cradle** 🏆🏆 in which newborn sons were presented to the sultans, as well as an **emerald pendant** 🏆 with 48 strings of pearls originally sent by Sultan Abdülhamid I as a gift to the tomb of the Prophet Mohammed in Mecca. The pendant was returned to Istanbul after Mecca was no longer within the borders of the empire.

Exit the courtyard down the stairs to the right through a long passage. To the right and parallel to the sea is the second terrace, affording one of the best views in the city. Imagine the days of seaside attacks on the palace walls as you watch the maritime traffic go by. During Byzantine times, a chain, composed of links .8m (2⅔ ft.) long, was forged to span the Golden Horn and prevent enemy ships from accessing the waterway.

> **Tips   Topkapı Palace Lunch Break**
>
> After touring the Treasury, you've reached the halfway point and a good place
> to stop for lunch or drinks. The expansive **Konyalı restaurant** (✆ **0212/513-
> 9696**) includes indoor and outdoor dining rooms, as well as an outdoor cafete-
> ria-style snack bar (see "Where to Dine," earlier in this chapter).

This fourth courtyard was the realm of the sultan, and a stroll around the gardens
will reveal some lovely examples of Ottoman kiosk architecture. Near the center of the
upper level of the courtyard is the **Mustafa Paşa Kiosk,** the oldest building in the
complex, which served as the physician's quarters and as a wardrobe for the sultan
needing to effect swift changes during state functions. From the picture window overlooking the gardens, the sultan was known to observe wrestling matches, and even join
in every now and again.

Perched on the upper terrace at the northernmost corner of the palace complex is
the **Baghdad Kiosk** *✛*, magnificently sited to take best advantage of the views of the
Golden Horn. The kiosk is decorated with priceless Iznik tiles, both inside and out.
In addition to the tiles, the interior space is embellished with stained glass and
crowned by a dome decorated with a traditional Ottoman motif in gold leaf. The
kiosk served the sultan in colder weather; occupants of the kiosk were warmed by the
central brazier. The **Sofa Köşkü** is the only surviving wooden pavilion in the palace.
The golden-roofed **Iftariye Pavilion,** or "pavilion for breaking the fast," is the covered
balcony on the northern edge of the courtyard, also called the *Mehtaplık,* or "Moon
Place." This, by the way, is a fantastic spot for a photo op.

The **circumcision rooms,** rarely opened to the public, are also located in the fourth
courtyard.

Backtrack through the passage and up the steps into the third courtyard. To the
right past the Museum Directorate is the **Dormitory of the Pages of the Imperial
Treasury,** formerly used to display decorative calligraphy from the Koran as well as
jeweled Koran sets. At press time the dormitory was closed. At the far corner of the
third courtyard is the **Holy Relic Section** *✛✛✛*, the largest collection in the world of
this type, containing the personal belongings of the Prophet Mohammed, the caliphs,
and even the unexpected **staff of Moses** *✛*. The items on display were brought back
to Istanbul by Selim the Grim in 1517, following his conquest of the holy cities of
Mecca and Medina, and after declaring himself caliph. Since the Kaa'ba was restored
annually, pieces of the mosque were regularly kept as ornamentation for mosques.
This collection was off-limits to anyone but the most favored members of the sultan's
family and was only open to public viewing in 1962. The domed space is ornamented
with Iznik tiles and quotations from the Koran along with a priceless set of rain gut-
ters, an intricately carved door, and an old set of keys taken from the Kaa'ba. Directly
opposite the entrance are the **four sabers** belonging to the first four caliphs, and the
first-ever copy of the **Koran** *✛*, documented on deerskin.

To the right is the **Mohammed Chamber** *✛✛✛*, fronted by a booth in which an
imam (religious guide) has been reciting passages from the Koran continually for the
past 500 years. This tradition was started by Mehmet II and sets the stage for the collection of holy relics within. The **golden cloth** *✛* that once covered the black stone in
the central courtyard of the Kaa'ba in Mecca now hangs in this exhibit, as a new one

is richly prepared each year. Considered a gift falling from the heavens, the stone prompted Abraham to build a temple on the spot, attracting worshippers from all faiths for several hundred years. The display cases are hidden behind religious fervent communing with the spirit of the prophet through **relics** *R̂R̂* of his hair, a tooth, his footprints, and even soil from his grave. The **Holy Mantle,** the most sacred item in the collection, is contained in a **gold coffer** *R̂R̂* and sequestered in an inaccessible area of this room behind a grilled door.

Turkish and Iranian miniatures as well as portraits of Ottoman sultans are exhibited in the rooms next to the one containing the Holy Relics. While the original collection amounts to a total of 13,000 specimens, this exhibit comes nowhere near this number. The main draw is the collection of portraits (both copies and originals) modeled after those painted by some of the Renaissance's most celebrated artists (Veronese, Bellini). Lacking any record of the physical characteristics of the first 12 sultans, the Ottomans had the ones painted by the Venetians brought back to Istanbul in 1579.

In the center of the courtyard is the **Ahmet III Library,** constructed in the 16th century of white marble and recently restored and opened to the public. The bookcases are inlaid with ivory and contain about 6,000 volumes of Arab and Greek manuscripts. The stained glass is from the early 17th century; the platform divan seating is typically Ottoman, and the carpets are over 500 years old.

Return to the second courtyard, where along the right side you will come upon the **Imperial Armory,** a collection of arms and objects acquired during the various military campaigns. Mehmet the Conqueror's sword is here, as is Süleyman the Magnificent's, but it's the unattributed 2.5m (81/4-ft.) one that really impresses.

Before entering the Harem, take a peek into the **Imperial Council Hall,** or **Divan** *R̂*, constructed during the reign of Süleyman the Magnificent. State affairs were conducted here while the sultan eavesdropped from the grate above, which leads directly to the Harem. From this concealed position, the sultan could interrupt proceedings with a motion to his grand vizier and call for a private conference whenever the need arose. His wife, Roxelana, would often secretly attend these sessions, a privilege that ended in several unfortunate fatalities.

To visit the **Harem** *R̂R̂* you must purchase a ticket for one of the tours near the Carriage Gate entrance next to the Divan; your tour time will be indicated on your ticket. Tours depart on the half-hour and last about 30 minutes. Buy your ticket to the Harem at the beginning of your visit to the palace because when the tour buses arrive, the wait in both the ticket and entry lines can be very long. Of the 400 rooms, only around 20 are on the tour, with explanations that are not always audible or, for that matter, intelligible. Nonetheless, the tour is worth taking.

The Harem has three main sections: the outer quarters of the Black Eunuchs charged with guarding the Harem; the inner stone courtyard for the concubines; and the apartments facing the sea reserved for the sultan, his mother, favorite concubines, and future heirs to the throne. The tour begins at the Carriage Gate, where the sultan's mother and wives would be whisked away unseen by outsiders during exits and entrances. Past the first Guard Room is a long courtyard lined with cells that served as the Barracks of the Black Eunuchs. The upper levels were reserved for the younger eunuchs, with the lower cells housing the older ones. Winding through the maze of additions, the tour comes to the quarters of the concubines, unheated and often unsanitary rooms around a claustrophobic stone courtyard. The only way out was to be one of the very lucky few chosen by the mother for the sultan; the others were servants to the sultan, or to the girls

⟨Fun Fact⟩ **The Forbidden City**

The word *harem,* Arabic for "forbidden," conjures up images of bellybuttons, grapes, palm trees, and limitless pleasure, unless you're the one fanning the sultan. The reality was closer to a deluxe prison, a stifling hierarchy of slaves, concubines, and wives from which only a few ever emerged. It was even common practice for a new sultan to drown the concubines of his predecessor, to eliminate the possibility that one might be carrying a child with designs on the throne. The mystery enshrouding these enclosed walls was never truly lifted, and even concubines who survived kept silent.

The institution of the harem was established by Süleyman the Magnificent in 1587 following a fire in the palace in Beyazit, when the cunning Roxelana convinced him to transfer his residence over to Topkapı. Muslims are exceedingly private people, and these enclosed and restricted quarters served to maintain the "curtain" over the feminine members of his extended family.

higher up on the hierarchy. At its most crowded, the Harem housed over 800 concubines. Even if the sultan rotated every night, the numbers were against those girls, and although some were given to the harems of state officials or grand viziers, many died virgins (but who knows what really went on in there . . .).

In contrast, the **Apartment of the Valide Sultan** ⟨★★⟩, sandwiched between the girls' quarters and her son's, is a domed wonder of mother-of-pearl, ivory, tortoise shell, gold leaf, porcelain tiles, and frosted glass. The apartment consisted of a bedroom, a dining room, a chamber for prayer, and an office around a courtyard.

The **sultan's private bath** ⟨★⟩, furnished with the usual *hamam* gear but infinitely more lush, has a guarded mesh gate so that the sultan could relax without the fear of being disturbed or assassinated. The sultan's apartments are close by, and the visit continues with the **Imperial Reception Hall** ⟨★★⟩, where celebrations or evenings of entertainment took place while musicians played discreetly from the mezzanine. While the sultan presided from his throne, the women adhered to a strict hierarchy, with the most important women seated at the center of the platform.

One of the few rooms preserving the luster of its creator is the grand domed **Private Chambers of Murat III** ⟨★★⟩, built by Sinan in 1578. The walls are covered with a classic blue Iznik tile with red highlights, a prototype that was never duplicated. A frieze of calligraphy runs the perimeter of the room, and elegant panels of flowers and plums surround a bronze fireplace. The room is also called the Fountain Room because of the marble fountain that was kept running to mask conversations not intended for prying ears.

The **Reading Room** used by Ahmet I is a small but well-positioned library that affords distracting views of the convergence of the three waterways: the Golden Horn, the Marmara Sea, and the Bosphorus.

The **Fruit Room** is more of a breakfast nook added by Sultan Ahmet III to his private chambers. One look and it's not hard to figure out how this room got its name. The room is enveloped in fruit and floral overkill, but evidently the sultan's attentions were focused on the Harem pool out the window.

The next stop on the Harem tour is at the twin apartments of the crown prince, better known as **The Cage** ⟨★⟩. In the early years of the empire, a crowned prince was well prepared to fulfill his destiny as a leader, beginning his studies in these rooms and later moving on to actual field experience in one of the provinces. When the practice of fratricide was abandoned, brothers of the sultan were sequestered in these rooms, where they either went crazy or languished in the lap of luxury—or both. The opulence of the stained glass and the tile work and the mother-of-pearl inlaid cabinets belies the chambers' primary function as a jail cell, which supports a recent discovery that the actual cage was located in another part of the Harem. The tour guides continue to perpetuate the myth by billing these two rooms as the bona fide cage.

The Harem tour comes to an end at the **Courtyard of the Favorites** ✸✸, surrounded by a charming building recalling the medieval residences of Florence. The apartments on the upper floors were reserved for the members of the Harem the sultan liked best, enjoying open space and sea views as far as the Princes' Islands. The circular spot in the center of the courtyard was covered with a tent for shaded outings, and the grooves served as water channels for cooling.

The exit to the second courtyard is through the **Golden Road,** a narrow stone corridor that was the crown prince's first taste of the world beyond the stifling confines of the Harem.

Sultanahmet, entrance at the end of Babuhümayun Cad., behind the Ayasofya. © 0212/512-0480. Admission to the palace 10YTL ($8.70/£4); separate admission for both the Treasury and the Harem 10YTL ($8.70/£4) each. Wed–Mon 9am–5pm (Harem closes at 4pm).

BYZANTINE SIGHTS (OR BYZANTIUM WASN'T BUILT IN A DAY)

Church of Theotokos Pammakaristos (Joyous Mother of God Church, now the Fethiye Camii)

This church was built in 1292 by John Comnenus, probably related to the royal family, and his wife, Anna Doukaina. Later additions and renovations were made, including the construction of a side chapel in 1315 to house the remains of Michael Glabas, a former general, and his family. In 1456 the Orthodox Patriarchate moved here from the Havariyun (see Fatih Mosque and Complex, p. 131) and remained here until 1586. Five years later Murat III converted the church into a mosque and renamed it in honor of his conquest over Georgia and Azerbaijan. To accommodate a larger inner space for prayer, most of the interior walls were removed.

The interior of the church/mosque contains the restored remains of a number of mosaic panels, which, while not as varied as those at the Kariye Camii, serve as another resource for understanding 14th-century Byzantine art. In the dome is a representation of the Pantocrator surrounded by prophets (Moses, Jeremiah, Zephaniah, Micah, Joel, Zechariah, Obadiah, Habakkuk, Jonah, Malachi, Ezekiel, and Isaiah). In the apse Christ Hyperagathos is shown with the Virgin and St. John the Baptist. The Baptism of Christ survives intact to the right of the dome.

From the Kariye Camii, follow Draman Cad. (which becomes Fethiye Cad.); turn left onto Fethiyekapısı Sok. (just before the road bends sharply to the right), Fener. Ayasofya Museum Directorate at © 0212/635-1273. Admission 2YTL ($1.75/80p). Thurs–Tues 9am–5pm.

Ecumenical Patriarchate of Constantinople ✸

The Ecumenical Patriarchate of Constantinople is the surviving legacy of a religious empire that dominated the affairs of Christians worldwide for more than 1,100 years. After the fall of Rome in 476, Constantinople inherited unrivaled leadership of the Christian world under the name "Rome of the East" and "New Rome." The Greeks, Bulgarians, Serbians, Romanians, Albanians, and Georgians that adhered to the Eastern Orthodox creed were referred to as "Romans" (thus the reason why many an Istanbul church include the word

"Rum" in their title). While the Pope continued to reject the primacy of the Bishop of Constantinople (soon after given the title of Archbishop), the influence of the Patriarch of Constantinople nevertheless grew under the patronage of the Emperor. The initial seat of the Patriarchate was pre-Constantine Hagia Irene, now in the first court of Topkapı Palace. Upon Justinian's completion of the Hagia Sophia, the Church was rooted here for the next 916 years (with a brief respite when the Byzantine Court was forced to flee to Nicaea after the Fourth Crusade in 1204). The Ottoman conquest displaced the Patriarchate to the Havariyun (or Church of the 12 Apostles, now lost under Fatih Camii), before it moved to the Church of the Pammakaristos (Fethiye Camii) in 1456. In 1587, the Eastern Orthodox Church moved to the Church of the Virgin Mary in Vlah Palace, and then to St. Demetrios in Balat. The Patriarchate settled into its current spot in The Church of St. George (Ayios Yeoryios) in 1601. In the 19th century, assertions of national independence and religious autonomy whittled the influence of the Patriarchate, until its reach was constricted to the borders of the Turkish Republic and a mere handful of semi-autonomous communities abroad. Still, the Orthodox community considers the Ecumenical Patriarchate one of the two most prominent Christian institutions in the world, the other being the Holy See in Rome. Today, the Patriarch and Archbishop of Constantinople is—*primus inter pares,* or "first among equals," among the 14 autonomous and semi-autonomous Patriarchates-in-communion that make up the Eastern Orthodox Church.

The present church was built in 1720 on a traditional basilica plan. It seems to lack the grandeur one would expect of its station, but the building was constructed under the Ottoman prohibition against non-Muslim use of domes or masonry roofs on their places of worship. Instead, it is topped by a timber roof. The gilded iconostasis provides some insight into the opulence one imagines of Byzantium. The Patriarchal Throne is believed to date to St. John Chrysostom Patriarchate in the 5th century. His relics and those of St. Gregory the Theologian, which were hijacked after the 1204 Crusader sacking of the city, were brought back from Rome by Patriarch Bartholomew in 2004. In the aisle opposite these relics are the remains of the female saints, St. Euphemia, St. Theophano, and St. Solomone. There are also three invaluable gold mosaic icons, including one of the Virgin, as well as the Column of Flagellation. The small complex is comprised of the modest Cathedral, the Patriarchate Library, administrative offices, and the Ayios Harambalos spring.

Sadrazam Ali Paşa Cad. 35/3, Fener. © 0212/531-9670. Free admission. Daily 8:30am–6pm.

Galata Tower and the Galata Neighborhood ☙

The neighborhood of Galata, located on a steep hump of land north of the Golden Horn and historic peninsula, actually sits on the earliest foundations of the city, dating, as far as present-day archaeologists can tell, to Greek and Roman times. The district developed into its present form in the 13th century, when Eastern Roman Emperor Michael VIII Palaeologus granted the Genoese permission to settle here. The district became a magnet for merchants from all over Europe: Italians, Germans, Armenians, Jews, and Austrians. A stroll up and down the steep cobbled streets will reveal schools, private residences, churches, synagogues, and Ottoman-era warehouses. (There are also the ruins of a *mikva,* or Jewish bathhouse, in dire need of restoration opposite the former private mansion of the Camondo banking family, now the Galata Residence.)

The decline of Galata and its subsequent revitalization are both relatively recent phenomena. With the turn-of-the-20th-century flight of the wealthy merchant class

700 Years of Turkish Jews

Jews visiting Turkey inevitably ask for a tour of a local synagogue, and as the default working temple in the heart of Galata, Neve Shalom is usually the first and only stop. While interesting to see (particularly after sustaining recurring terrorist attacks), a visit to Neve Shalom is far from the Holy Grail of Jewish sites in Istanbul. It's also not necessarily guaranteed, since a pre-visit request accompanied by a faxed copy of your passport is the *minimum* requirement for entry. I'd recommend instead the **Jewish Museum of Turkey,** located in the restored 19th-century Zulfaris Synagogue. The museum represents the vision of the Quincentennial Foundation (named for the 500-yr. anniversary of the Jewish expulsion from Spain) and show-cases the peaceful existence of Jews in Turkey. The foundation's vision came to fruition in 2001 with this anthology of Jewish presence in Turkey begin-ning with the Ottoman conquest of Bursa, through Sultan Beyazit's invita-tion to those expelled from Spain, to the present day. The museum/synagogue is located at Karaköy Meydanı, Perçemli Sokak (© **0212/292-6333;** facing the lower entrance to the Tünel funicular, Perçemli Sok. is the first alley to your right; the museum is at the end of the street on your right). The museum is open Monday through Thursday 10am to 4pm, and Friday and Sunday from 10am to 2pm. No admission charge, but donations are encouraged.

to Istanbul's tonier neighborhoods, Galata deteriorated into a magnet for poor rural migrant families and a location of no fewer than three thriving brothels. In the 1990s, the nation's trend for historic preservation arrived in Galata with an ambitious archi-tectural revitalization project that created an inviting public square and a couple of charming and characteristic outdoor tea gardens at the base of the tower. In the past 4 or 5 years, the trend has caught fire, as local real estate gets snapped up by artists, expat journalists, and private developers and turned into galleries, cafes, hotels, and private homes. For a do-it-yourself walking tour, pick up a copy of John Freely's *Galata,* available at the Galata House (restaurant) and the bookstores listed under "Shopping," later in this chapter.

The origins of Galata Tower date back to the 5th or 6th century, but the tower that stands today is a 14th-century reconstruction by the Genoese, built in appreciation of Michael VIII Palaeologus, who granted special permission to allow them to settle the area of Galata. One condition of the agreement was that the Genoese were prohibited from putting up any defensive walls, a ban that they unceremoniously ignored.

The Galata Tower has been used as a jail, a dormitory, a site for rappelling compe-titions, and a launching pad in the 17th century when Hezarfen Ahmet Çelebi attached wings to his arms and glided all the way to Üsküdar. The tower rises 135m (443 ft.) above sea level and stands 60m (197 ft.) high, with walls that are more than 3.5m (11 ft.) thick. From the summit of the tower, you can see the Golden Horn, the Bosphorus, and the Marmara Sea, a view infinitely more splendid in the evenings when the city takes on a spectacularly romantic glow. But frankly, you can get equally spectacular views from restaurant terraces all over the city, so although the tower is used as a restaurant and nightclub for a traditional **Turkish folkloric** show (© 0212/ 293-8180), at 100YTL ($87/£40) a pop, I'd pass (and indeed I have).

Şişane. © 0212/245-1160. Historic gate daily 9am–1am (no access during the folklore show). Elevator to the top 8YTL ($6.95/£3.20).

Küçük Ayasofya Camii (Church of the Saints Sergius and Bacchus) ⋆ (Finds)

Started in A.D. 527 by Justinian in the first year of his reign, this former church represents an important stage in the process of Byzantine architecture, particularly in the support of the dome atop an octagonal base. The church took its name from two martyred Roman soldiers later elevated to the status of patron saints; the edifice later assumed the name of "Little Ayasofya" due to its resemblance to the Ayasofya in Sultanahmet Park, which was started in 532. The church was converted into a mosque in the 16th century by the chief eunuch under Beyazit II, who is buried in the garden. We know from the ancient historian Procopius that the interior of the church was covered in marble and mosaics; however, none of this remains. Opposite the entrance to the mosque is a *medrese* that encloses an uncharacteristically serene and leafy garden. An on-site eatery as well as teahouses share the arcade with a number of bookshops and **calligraphy boutiques,** and you'll find some of the most competitive prices in the city.

Lower end of Küçük Ayasofya Cad. Open at prayer times only.

Mosaic Museum ⋆   In 1933 excavators discovered a mosaic pavement below what is now the Arasta Bazaar, identified as a section of **Peristyle Courtyard** (open court with porticos) of Constantine's Great Palace. As a decorative work of the palace, it is safe to assume (as scholars have) that the creation of the mosaic flooring employed the most gifted craftsmen of the era, collected from around the empire. Because of the exceptional nature of the mosaics, there are no comparable existing Byzantine-era mosaics from which to date these. The current assumption is that they were crafted during either the reign of Constantine or of Justinian.

Archaeologists estimate that the size of the courtyard was 1,872 sq. m (20,150 sq. ft.), requiring a total of 80,000,000 *tesserae* of lime, glass, and terra cotta. Typical of Roman mosaics, the subjects depicted on the panels are representative of an earlier, pre-Christian artistic era absent of religious motifs, showing instead hunting scenes and scenes from mythology.

Entrance at Torun Sok. Across from the entrance to the Sultanahmet Palace Hotel; accessible through Arasta Bazaar to the southeast of Blue Mosque. © 0212/518-1205. Admission 4YTL ($3.50/£1.60). Tues–Sun 9am–6:30pm (to 4:30 in winter).

Take a Break in the Retaining Wall of the Hippodrome

Arranged around a mushrooming fountain with choice seating tucked into the arches of the Sphendome, the Havusbaşı Çay Bahçesi, or Pond Head Tea Garden (© 0212/638-8819), couldn't get more atmospheric. Nestle in for fresh-squeezed fruit juice, tea, or light fare well into the evening hours. In the summer, the management mounts a tiny derviş show nightly.

St. Savior in Chora (Kariye Müzesi; formerly the Kariye Camii) ⓇⓇⓇ   Much of what remained in the coffers of the Byzantine Empire was invested in the embellishment of this church, one of the finest preserved galleries of **Byzantine mosaics** as well as a detailed account of early Christian history. The original church was built in the 4th century as part of a monastery complex outside the city walls (*chora zonton* means "in the country" in Greek), but the present structure dates to the 11th century. The interior restoration and decoration were the result of the patronage of Theodore Metochites, Grand Logothete of the Treasury during the reign of Andronicus II Paleologos, and date to the first quarter of the 14th century. His benevolence is depicted in a dedicatory panel in the inner narthex over the door to the nave, which shows Metokhites presenting the Chora to Jesus.

When the church was converted into a mosque in the 16th century, the mosaics were plastered over. A 19th-century architect uncovered the mosaics but was ordered by the government to re-cover those in the section of the prayer hall. American archaeologists Whittemore and Underwood finally uncovered these masterpieces during World War II, and although the Chora became a museum in 1947, it is still often referred to as the Kariye Camii.

In total there are about 50 mosaic panels, but because some of them are only partially discernible, there seems to be disagreement on the exact count. Beginning in the exonarthex, the subjects of the mosaic panels fall into one of four themes, presented more or less in chronological order after the New Testament. Broadly, the themes relate to the cycle of the life of Christ and his miracles, stories of the life of Mary, scenes from the infancy of Christ, and stories of Christ's ministry. The panels not included in these themes are the devotional panels in the exonarthex and the narthex, and the three panels in the nave: *The Dormition of the Virgin, Christ,* and the *Virgin Hodegetria.*

The **Paracclesion** (burial section) is decorated with a series of masterful frescos completed sometime after the completion of the mosaics and were presumably executed by the same artist. The frescoes reflect the purpose of the burial chamber with scenes of Heaven and Hell, the Resurrection and the Life, and a stirring **Last Judgment** with a scroll representing infinity above a River of Fire, and a detail of Jesus saving Adam and Eve's souls from the devil.

Camii Sok., Kariye Meydanı, Edirnekapı. ⒸⒸ **0212/631-9241.** Admission 10YTL ($8.70/£4). Thurs–Tues 9:30am–6:30pm. Bus no. 90B from Beyazit or bus no. 90 from Eminönü direct to the museum; bus no. 91 from Eminönü to Edirnekapı.

Sphendome Ⓡ   The ancient retaining wall of the closed end of the Hippodrome joins the Obelisks and Spina as the only remaining relics of the early Byzantine period. Today, this enduring infrastructure supports the buildings of Marmara Technical University. The structure is best viewed from below (access down the hill along Şifa Hamamı Sok. to Nakilbent Sok.); notice the 2m-high (6½-ft.) niches that used to contain statues (now evocative of seating for an outdoor tea garden and restaurant). The high arched section served as the stables.

Southeastern end of the Hippodrome. Always open.

Valens Aqueduct (Bozdoğan Kemeri)   Now nothing more than a scenic overpass for cars traveling down Atatürk Bulvarı, the Valens Aqueduct, or "Arcade of the Gray Falcon," was started by Constantine and completed in the 4th century by Valens. Justinian II had the second tier added; even Mehmet the Conqueror and Sinan had a hand in its restoration and enlargement. The aqueduct connects the third and fourth hills of Istanbul and had an original length of about .8km (⅔ mile). Water was transported under various rulers to the Byzantine palaces, city cisterns, and then to Topkapı Palace, and the aqueduct served in supplying water to the city for a total of 1,500 years.

Bridging Atatürk Bulv. between Aksaray and the Golden Horn.

Yerebatan Cistern (Yerebatan Sarnıcı) ⭐⭐   Classical music echoing off the still water and the seductive lighting make your descent into the "Sunken Palace" seem like a scene out of *Phantom of the Opera.* The only thing missing is a rowboat, which was an actual means of transportation before the boardwalk was installed in what is now essentially a great underground fishpond and stunning historical artifact. The cistern was first constructed by Constantine and enlarged to its present form by Justinian after the Nika Revolt using 336 marble columns recycled from the Hellenistic ruins in and around the Bosphorus. The water supply, routed from reservoirs around the Black Sea and transported via the Aqueduct of Valens, served as a backup for periods of drought or siege. It was left largely untouched by the Ottomans, who preferred running, not stagnant, water, and eventually used the source to water the Topkapı Gardens. The cistern was later left to collect silt and mud until it was cleaned by the municipality and opened to the public in 1987. The water is kept clean and aerated thanks to a supply of overgrown goldfish that are replaced every 4 years or so.

Follow the wooden catwalk and notice the "column of tears," a pillar etched with symbols resembling teardrops. (An identical pattern is visible on the columns scattered along the tramway near the Universite stop, where the old Byzantine palace was once located.) At the far end of the walkway are two **Medusa heads,** one inverted and the other on its side; according to mythology, placing her this way caused her to turn herself into stone. Another superstition is that turning her upside down neutralizes her powers. Possibly, the stones were just the right size as pedestals.

Yerebatan Cad. diagonal from St. Sophia, Sultanahmet. ⓒ **0212/522-1259.** Admission 10YTL ($8.70/£4). Wed–Mon 9am–5:30pm.

HISTORIC HAMAMS (TURKISH BATHS)

The number of *hamams* in Istanbul mushroomed in the 18th century when the realization hit that they were big business. Mahmut I had the Cağaloğlu Hamamı built to finance the construction of his library near the Ayasofya, but later that century new constructions were limited because the *hamams* were using up the city's resources of water and wood. Only about 20 *hamams* have survived. One of the most visited is the palatial **Çemberlitaş Hamamı,** Vezirhan Cad. 8 (off Divanyolu at the Column of Constantine; ⓒ **0212/522-7974;** 40YTL/$35/£16 for the traditional bath, massage, and *kese* [a scrubbing using an abrasive mitt]; 28YTL/$24/£11 bath only; daily 6am–midnight with separate sections; MasterCard and Visa accepted), which was based on a design by Sinan. Also popular is the 18th-century **Cağaloğlu Hamamı,** Yerebatan Caddesi at Ankara Caddesi (ⓒ **0212/522-2424;** 36YTL/$31/£14 bath and *kese;* 68YTL/$59/£27 if you opt for the "Oriental luxury" treatment; daily 7am–10pm for men, 8am–8pm for women), which allegedly saw the bare bottoms of Franz Liszt, Edward VIII, Kaiser Wilhelm, and Florence Nightingale, and even had a part as an extra in *Indiana Jones and the Temple of Doom.*

The recently restored **Süleymaniye Hamamı** ⭐ (Mimar Sinan Cad. 20; ⓒ **0212/519-5569;** daily 7am–midnight), part of the Süleymaniye mosque complex, is another architectural and social welfare wonder of Sinan and Süleyman the Magnificent. Pickup and drop-off from your hotel is included in the price of admission, which includes the massage and kese (30€/$44/£21 or 35€/$51/£25, depending on the pickup location). One caveat: This *hamam* is coed.

The **Tarihi Galatasaray Hamamı,** Sütterazi Sok. 24, Beyoğlu (from Istiklal Cad. in front of the Galatasaray High School, it's the second street to the left of the gate; © 0212/249-4342; 40YTL/$35/£16) admission plus 5YTL/$4.35/£2) if you want the massage and *kese;* daily 7am–10pm for men, 8am–8pm for women), was built by Beyazit II as part of the Galata Sarayı school complex. The men's section is generally accepted as gay.

Probably the most spectacular *hamam* in Istanbul is the decommissioned **Haseki Sultan Hamamı,** in Sultanahmet Parkı. Built by Sinan in 1557 on a symmetrical plan that provided two separate sections of identical domed halls, the *hamam* was decommissioned in later years when it was found that the elongated layout resulted in too much heat loss. The Haseki Sultan Hamamı is now a beautifully restored exhibition center for Dösim (see "Shopping," later in this chapter) and is used for textile and carpet displays.

MONUMENTAL MOSQUES & TOMBS

Beyazit Mosque (Beyazit Camii)   Beyazit II, son of the Conqueror, is remembered kindly by history as one of the more benevolent of sovereigns, and indeed, in Turkey, he has been elevated to a saint. The mosque and complex bearing his name is the oldest surviving imperial mosque in the city (its predecessor, the Fatih Camii, succumbed to an earthquake and was reconstructed in 1766). The complex was built between 1501 and 1506 using materials taken from Theodosius's Forum of Tauri, on which it is built.

Again, the architect of Beyazit Camii looked to the Ayasofya, employing a central dome buttressed by semi-domes and a long nave with double arcades, although the mosque is half the size of the church. The Beyazit Mosque also borrows elements from the Fatih Mosque, imitating the system of buttressing and the use of great columns alongside the dome. Thanks to Sultan Beyazit II's patronage, the Ottomans found a style of their own, which served as a bridge to later classical Ottoman architecture. The sultan, who died in 1512, is buried in a simple tomb, decorated in mother-of-pearl and stained glass, at the back of the gardens.

Yeniçeriler Cad., across from the Beyazit tramway stop. No phone. Free admission. Dawn–dusk.

Eyüp Sultan Mosque (Eyüp Sultan Camii)   The holiest site in Istanbul as well as one of the most sacred places in the Islamic world, the Eyüp Sultan Mosque was erected by Mehmet the Conqueror over the tomb of Halid bin Zeyd Ebu Eyyûb (known as Eyüp Sultan), the standard-bearer for the Prophet Mohammed as well as the last survivor of his inner circle of trusted companions. It is popularly accepted that while serving as commander of the Arab forces during the siege of 668 to 669, Eyüp was killed and buried on the outskirts of the city. One of the conditions of peace after the Arab siege was that the tomb of Eyüp be preserved.

The burial site was "discovered" during Mehmet the Conqueror's siege on the city, although the tomb is mentioned in written accounts as early as the 12th century.

A little village of tombs mushroomed on the spot by those seeking Eyüp Sultan's intervention in the hereafter, and it's still considered a privilege to be buried in the

Steam Heat: Taking the *Hamam*

In characteristic socially conscious fashion, the Selçuks were the ones to adopt the Roman and Byzantine tradition of public bathing and treat it like a public work. Lacking baths or running water at home, society embraced the *hamam,* which evolved into not only a place to cleanse body and soul, but a social destination as well. Even the accouterments of the *hamam* took on symbols of status: wooden clogs inlaid with mother-of-pearl, towels embroidered with gold thread, and so on. Men gathered to talk about politics, sports, and women, while the ladies kept an eagle eye out for suitable wives for their sons.

The utility of the *hamam* evolved and fell out of daily use, probably because the neighborhood ones have a reputation for being dirty, and the historic ones come with a hefty admission charge. But when experienced properly, a visit to a *hamam* can be a cleansing one—for both mind and body. And as the spa trend takes hold in Istanbul and as new, private (hotel or club) *hamams* materialize, Turks are once again embracing the pampered pleasure of this tradition.

What to expect? The main entrance of a Turkish bath opens up to a *camekan,* a central courtyard lined with changing cubicles surrounding an ornamental marble fountain. Visitors are presented with the traditional *pestamal,* a checkered cloth worn like a sarong (up higher for women). Valuables are secured in a private locker, provided for each customer, although it's a good idea to leave the best of it at home.

The experience begins past the cooling section (and often the toilets), into the steam room, or **hararet.** For centuries architects worked to perfect the design of the *hararet:* a domed, octagonal (or square) room, often with marvelous oculi to provide entry for sunlight, and with intricate basins at various intervals and a heated marble platform, known as the **naval stone,** in the center. Often the *hamam* is covered with elaborately crafted and ornately designed tiles.

nearby cemeteries. The Girding of the Sword ceremony was traditionally held here. In this Ottoman enthronement rite, Osman Gazi's sword was passed on, maintaining continuity within the dynasty as well as creating a connection with the Turks' early ideal of Holy War.

Eyüp is a popular spot animated by the small bazaar nearby, crowds relaxing by the spray of the fountains, and little boys in blue-and-white satin celebrating their impending circumcisions. Unfortunately, it's a natural magnet for beggars as well. The baroque mosque replaces the original that was destroyed in the earthquake of 1766, but the real attraction here is the *türbe,* a sacred burial site that draws masses of pilgrims waiting in line to stand in the presence of the contents of the solid silver sarcophagus or meditate in prayer. Dress appropriately if you're planning to go in: no shorts, and heads covered for women. The line moves quickly in spite of the bottleneck inside the tomb; take a few moments to sense the power of the site. On Fridays at noon, there's an outdoor performance of the Mehter Band in the large square

Hamam protocol goes like this: You will be asked to lie on the naval stone by an attendant (who may be male or female). Many first-time visitors have questions about how much clothing to take off; in segregated *hamams* it's customary and acceptable to strip (this is a bath, after all), although I personally would reschedule if confronted with a male attendant. Step one is the scrubbing using an abrasive mitt *(kese)* aimed at removing the outer layer of dead skin and other organic detritus. The actual bath is next; the substantial and slippery soap bubbles create the perfect canvas for the accompanying massage. This is primarily where you will notice the difference between a private *hamam* (where you are the only "client") and one of the more commercial ones. In the commercial ones (listed above, all of which I have nevertheless frequented repeatedly), don't be surprised if your massage feels more like a cursory pummeling. The private *hamams* have more of a long-term stake and therefore provide high-quality service. The difference is like night and day.

The final act of the ritual is the rinsing (you may even get a relaxing facial massage), followed by a definitive tap on the shoulder followed by "You like?"—an indication that your session is over. At this point you are most likely dehydrated and sleepy, which is when the purpose of that **cold room** with the lounge chairs becomes evident. Refreshments are available and the price list is usually displayed nearby. (Refreshments are usually included in the price of a private hotel *hamam*.) In the commercial *hamams* you can go back into the *hararet* as often as you like, whereas in a hotel *hamam* a session lasts 45 minutes to an hour.

Whether you opt for the $30 version or the $75 hotel service, definitely sign up for "the works" at least once in your life and you'll forever comprehend why it was indeed good to be the sultan.

outside the mosque, and on Sundays, the plaza is filled with families parading around their little boys dressed like sultans (a pre-circumcision tradition).

Meydanı, off of Camii Kebir Cad. and north of the Golden Horn Bridge, Eyüp. No phone. Free admission. Daily dawn–dusk.

Fatih Mosque and Complex (Fatih Camii ve Külliyesi)   Faith Sultan Mehmet II had his namesake built on the ruins of the Havariyun, or the Church of Holy Apostles, which served as the seat of Christianity after the conquest, from 1453 to 1456. At that time, the church was second only to the Ayasofya in importance and therefore served as the burial place of every emperor from Constantine I to Constantius VIII (337–1028!). Alexius III Angelius looted the graves to fill his imperial coffers; the graves were again looted during the Fourth Crusade. In addition to the commanding mosque, the eight *medreses* (schools) founded by the sultan are the only surviving sections of a complex that included a caravansary, a hospital, several *hamams,* the kitchens, and a market, which combined to form a university that instructed up to

Moments A Cafe near the Eyüp Sultan Mosque

If you've made it all the way to Eyüp to visit the mosque, take a short detour to **Pierre Loti,** Gümüşsuyu Balmumcu Sok. 1 (© **0212/581-2696**), the cafe of legend and a spectacular spot for serene views of the Golden Horn. The legend goes that French naval officer Julien Viaud fell in love with Aziyade, a married Turkish woman, during his first visit to Istanbul around 1876. The young woman would sneak out of her husband's harem when he was away for the chance to spend a few fleeting moments in the arms of her lover at his house in the hills of Eyüp. After an absence from Turkey of 10 years, Viaud returned to find Aziyade had died soon after his departure. Viaud gained fame during his lifetime, and his stories are romantic accounts much like the one of legend. This cafe, on the hill of Eyüp, was a favorite of his, and for reasons unknown, became known as Pierre Loti Kahvesi. Eyüp's historic cemetery is on the hill next to the cafe. The cafe is open daily 8am to midnight; no food or alcohol is served here. Avoid weekends, when nary an empty table will be your reward for the ride up. A cable car from near the Eyüp Mosque makes the trip up to the top of the hill a little bit easier than walking up, although you may want to walk down through the old Ottoman cemetery.

1,000 students at any given time. Wanting a monument more spectacular than that of Ayasofya, the sultan cut off the hands of the architect, Atık Sinan (not Süleyman's Sinan), when the Fatih Mosque failed to surpass the height of the church, despite its position atop the fourth of the seven hills of Istanbul. The tombs of Fatih Mehmet II and his wife (mother of Beyazit II) are located outside of the *mihrab* wall.

Enter on Fevzipaşa Cad., Fatih. No phone. Free admission. Dawn–dusk.

The New Queen Mother's Mosque (Yeni Valide Camii, or just plain Yeni Camii)

Begun by Valide Safiye, mother of Mehmet III, in 1597, the foundations of this mosque were laid at the water's edge in a neighborhood slum whose inhabitants had to be paid to move out. Designed by the architect Da'ud Ağa, a pupil of Sinan, the Yeni Camii has become a defining feature of Istanbul's skyline.

The building of the mosque dragged on for over 40 years due to water seepage, funding problems, embezzlement, and the death of the sultan, which temporarily shut down operations completely. The mosque was completed by another queen mother, Valide Sultan Turhan Hattice, mother of Mehmet IV, who is buried in the valide sultan's tomb, or *türbe,* in the courtyard.

The mosque is part of a complex that included at one time a hospital, primary school, and public bath. The Mısır Çarşısı, or Egyptian Spice Market, was actually constructed as part of the complex. In the open space formed by the inner "L" of the Spice Market and the northeastern-facing side of the mosque are stalls selling garden and pet supplies, a busy and shaded tea garden, and some street vendors. At the far (northwestern) end of the mosque on the opposite corner is the *türbe,* housing, in addition to the Valide Sultan, the remains of sultans Mehmet IV, Mustafa II, Ahmet III, and Mahmut I.

Opposite the *türbe* is the house of the mosque's astronomer, or *muvakkithane,* from where the position of the sun would be monitored to establish the times of the five daily prayers. Just behind the *muvakkithane* is a ramp leading up to the entrance of the royal loge, or private prayer room. The loge is best viewed from inside the mosque; enjoying a view of the sea, it was richly decorated by tiles, a dome, a vaulted antechamber, and a private toilet.

Eminönü. No phone. Free admission. Dawn–dusk.

Şehzade Külliyesi (Crowned Prince Mosque Complex)

Sinan's first sultanic mosque and one of his early masterpieces, the Şehzade was the project that earned him the title of master builder, or *mimar.* Commissioned by Süleyman in 1543, the mosque and complex was dedicated to his favorite son, Prince Mehmet, who died of smallpox at the premature age of 21. The plan of the mosque is an important milestone in the evolution of his works, as it is a simple system of four semi-domes supported by four pillars that has been both criticized for being harsh and praised as harmonic. The use of four elephantine pillars is repeated in the Sultanahmet, or Blue Mosque.

The layout of the complex—consisting of the mosque, a *medrese,* a refectory, a double guesthouse, a caravansaray, and some tombs—follows no special plan, and indeed the primary school and public kitchens have been cut off from the rest of the complex by the main avenue. The prince's tomb is an octagonal masterpiece of arabesques, rare tiles, and stained glass housing a unique sarcophagus specially crafted out of wood lattice with ivory inlay—there is no other example like it in the empire. The smaller octagonal tomb adjacent to that of the prince is that of Rüstem Paşa.

For many years the Şehzade remained the largest building in Istanbul, but even before the mosque was completed, Süleyman ordered the construction of another, grander mosque as a monument to his reign.

Şehzadebası Cad., Vefa. No phone. Free admission. Dawn–dusk.

Süleymaniye Mosque and Complex (Süleymaniye Camii ve Külliyesi) 👁️👁️

Perched on one of the seven hills of Istanbul and dominating the skyline, this complex is considered to be Sinan's masterpiece as much as the grand monument to Süleyman's reign.

The complex covers an area of nearly 63,000 sq. m (678,126 sq. ft.), and it is here where Sinan achieves his goal of outdoing the dome of the Ayasofya. Here, the dome reaches a height of 49m (161 ft.) spanning a diameter of 27m (89 ft.) (compared to the Ayasofya's 56m-high/184-ft. dome and 34m/112-ft. diameter). The mosque was completed in 7 years (1550–1557); it is said that after the foundation was laid, Sinan stopped work completely for 3 years to ensure that the foundation had settled to his satisfaction.

Tips Catch the Ottoman Mehter Band Outdoors

That must-see **Ottoman Mehter Band** that I tout so much (p. 138) no longer requires that you head over to the Military Museum in the middle of your day. There's now a performance every Friday, an hour and a half prior to noon prayers, right in front of the Eyüp Sultan Mosque. After the music and a visit to the mosque complex, hop onto the brand-new **cable car** for the 2-minute ride up to the top of Pierre Loti Hill.

Tips　**A Sweet Shop near Galata**

Wandering around the spice bazaar, you can really work up an appetite. Across the Galata Bridge at the Karaköy seaport is the humble (but famous) **Güllüoğlu** (℃ **0212/244-4567**) sweet shop, where you'll find the best *börek*—a cheese- or meat-filled pastry that's feathery and delicious. They also keep their glass cases full of baklava.

Sinan returned to the Byzantine basilica model for the construction of the mosque with an eye to the Ayasofya. Critics have contended that this was an unsuccessful attempt to surpass the engineering feats of the church, but more than likely this was a conscious move on the part of the sultan to create a continuity and a symbolic connection with the city's past. As the Ayasofya was analogous to the Temple of Solomon in Jerusalem, so was the Süleymaniye, as the name Süleyman is the Islamic version of Solomon. After the project was completed, Sinan recounts in his "biography of the Construction" how the sultan humbly handed the keys over to him and asked him to be the one to unlock the doors, acknowledging that the masterpiece was as much the architect's as his own.

The complex includes five schools, one *imaret* (kitchens and mess hall, now a restaurant for groups), a caravansary with stables, a hospital, *hamams,* and a cemetery. The construction of the mosque and complex mobilized the entire city, employing as many as 3,000 workers at any given time, and the 165 ledgers recording the expenses incurred in the building of the mosque are still around to prove it. The great sultan is buried in an elaborate tomb on the grounds, as is his wife Hürrem Sultan (Roxelana). In the courtyard outside the entry to the cemetery and tombs are a pair of slanted marble benches used as a stand for the sarcophagi before burial.

Süleyman carried the tradition of symbolism to his grave with a system of layered domes copied from the Dome of the Rock in Jerusalem. In the garden house next to the complex is the **tomb of Sinan;** the garden house is where he spent the last years of his life. The tomb was designed by the master architect himself and is inspiring in its modesty and simplicity.

From the Grand Bazaar, cross the park of the university and follow the domes. Free admission. Daily 9:30am–4:30pm.

PALACES OF THE SULTANS

While the power and prestige of a new and modern Europe were increasing, the Ottoman Empire was on its last leg. To create an image of prosperity and modernization, Sultan Abdülmecid had the Dolmabahçe Palace constructed and abandoned Topkapı Palace along with what he considered to be the symbol of an old order. With the official and Europeanized residence of the Ottoman Empire now on the northern shores of the Bosphorus, it wasn't long before members of the court and government officials began to build mansions in the area. More palaces sprang up, and the official shifting of power from south of the Golden Horn to the waterfront of Beşiktaş was complete. If the royal palaces fail to convince you of the Ottoman Empire's extravagance during its final economic decline, they will surely convince you of its opulence.

Beylerbeyi Palace (Beylerbeyi Sarayı)　Beylerbeyi, built under Sultan Abdülaziz by another member of the talented Balyan family of architects in the European style of Dolmabahçe, was the second palace to be built on the Bosphorus and served as a summer residence and guest quarters for visiting dignitaries during their visits to the city. The shah of Iran and the king of Montenegro were guests here as well as the French Empress Eugénie, who admired the palace so much that she had the design of the windows copied on the Tuilleries Palace in Paris. It's a bit dusty, and not as grand as Dolmabahçe, but worth a visit if you're on the Asian side and looking for a diversion.

Beylerbeyi, which replaced Abdülmecid's previous palace, was completed in 1865 on a less extravagant scale than the one on the European shores, employing only 5,000 men to build it. Although less grand and weathered by time, Beylerbeyi has some features worthy of a visit, not least of all the terraced garden of magnolias at the base of the Bosphorus Bridge. The monumental staircase to this marble palace is fronted by a pool and fountain which served as much to cool the air as to look pretty, and the floors are covered with reed mats from Egypt that act as insulation against dampness. The grounds contain sumptuous pavilions and kiosks, including the Stable Pavilion, where the imperial stud was kept.

Ironically, Abdülhamid II spent the last 6 years of his life admiring Dolmabahçe from the other side of the Bosphorus, having been deposed and kept under house arrest here until his death in 1918.

Take a ferry to Üsküdar and then a bus to Çayırbaşı. ⓒ 0216/321-9320. Entrance/tour 5YTL ($4.35/£2), camera fee 10YTL ($8.70/£4). Tues–Wed and Fri–Sun 9:30am–5pm.

Çırağan Palace   From the first wooden summer mansion built on the spot in the 16th century to the grand waterfront palace that stands today, the Çırağan Palace was torn down and rebuilt no less than five times. Now a palace of deluxe suites for the adjacent Hotel Kempinski Istanbul, the palace takes its name from the hundreds of torches that lined these former royal gardens during the festivals of the Tulip Age in the latter part of the 18th century.

The foundations were laid in 1855 when Sultan Abdülaziz ordered the construction of a grand palace to be built as a monument to his reign. The architect, Nigogos Balyan, ventured as far as Spain and North Africa to find models in the Arab style called for by the sultan. The fickle Abdülaziz moved out after only a few months, condemning the palace as too damp to live in.

Murad V (who in 1876 deposed his uncle Abdülaziz), Abdulhamid II, and Mehmed V were all born in the palace, while Murad V spent the final 27 years of his life imprisoned in the palace while his brother (who deposed him shortly after Murad V bumped his uncle) kept a watchful eye on him from the Yıldız Palace next door.

Fun Fact **Bridge over Troubled Water**

In 1501, Sultan Beyazit II invited Leonardo da Vinci to construct a bridge across the Golden Horn at the mouth of the Bosphorus—a technical feat deemed impossible until then. The master submitted a plan so revolutionary that it was deemed unbuildable. (Three years later, the sultan made the same proposal to Michelangelo, but Pope Julius II refused to let him go, and he politely declined.)

After Murad V's death, the Parliament took over the building but convened here for only 2 months because of a fire in the central heating vents that spread and reduced the palace to a stone shell in under 5 hours. (Some of the original doors were given as gifts by Abdülaziz to Kaiser Wilhelm and can now be seen in the Berlin Museum.) In 1946 the Parliament handed the property over to the municipality, which for the next 40 years used it as a town dump as well as a soccer field. In 1986, the Kempinski Hotel Group saved the shell from yet another demise, using the palace as a showcase of suites for its luxury hotel next door. Since its opening, the Çırağan has laundered the pillowcases of princes, kings, presidents, and rock stars, carrying on at least a modern version of a royal legacy of the original.

The palace grounds spread along 390m (1,280 ft.) of coastline and can only be visited as part of a stop-off at the main hotel, preferably from the seaside garden terrace, which provides ample views of the Palace Sea Gate, the Palace Garden Gate, and the main building itself. A cluster of secondary palaces that now serve mainly as schools are located outside the hotel's perimeter, while the one called "Feriye" has been restored as an elegant restaurant and cinema complex (see "Where to Dine," earlier in this chapter).

Çırağan Cad. ⓒ 0212/258-3377. Free admission.

Dolmabahçe Palace (Dolmabahçe Sarayı) ⍟

Extending for almost .8km (½ mile) on a tract of landfill on the shores of the Bosphorus is Dolmabahçe Palace (appropriately translated as "filled garden"), an imperial structure that for the first time looked to Western models rather than to the more traditional Ottoman style of building. The architect of Dolmabahçe was Garabet Balyan, master of European forms and styles amid a long line of Balyan architects.

At a time of economic reform when the empire was still known as "The Sick Man of Europe," Sultan Abdülmecid II sank millions into a palace that would give the illusion of prosperity and progressiveness. The old wooden Beşiktaş Palace was torn down to make room for a more permanent structure, and the sultan spared no expense in creating a house to rival the most opulent palaces of France. While many of his subjects were living without the basics, the sultan was financing the most cutting-edge techniques, tastefully waiting until the end of the Crimean War to move in, even though the palace was completed much earlier than that.

The result is a sumptuous creation consisting of 285 rooms, four grand salons, six galleries, five main staircases, six *hamams* (of which the main one is pure alabaster), and 43 toilets. Fourteen tons of gold and 6 tons of silver were used to build the palace. The extensive use of glass, especially in the Camlı Köşk conservatory, provides a gallery of virtually every known application of glass technology of the day. The palace is a glittering collection of Baccarat, Bohemian, and English crystal as well as Venetian glass, which were used in the construction of walls, roofs, banisters, and even a crystal piano. The chandelier in the Throne Room is the largest one in Europe at 4.5 tons, a bulk that created an engineering challenge during installation but that has withstood repeated earthquake tests. The extravagant collection of objets d'art represents just a small percentage of items presented to the occupants of the palace over the years, and much of the collection is stored in the basement awaiting restoration.

Tours to the palace and harem accommodate 1,500 visitors per day per section, a stream of gaping onlookers shod in blue plastic hospital booties distributed at the entry to the palace to ensure that the carpets stay clean. Tours leave every 20 minutes and last 1 hour for the Selamlik and around 45 minutes for the Harem. If you're short on time, choose the Selamlik.

Dolmabahçe Cad. (© **0212/236-9000**. Admission and guided tour to the Selamlik (Sultan's Quarters) 10YTL ($8.70/£4); admission and guided tour to the Harem 8YTL ($6.95/£3.20). Tues–Wed and Fri–Sun 9am–5pm (last tour leaves at 4pm).

EXPLORING MODERN-DAY ISTANBUL

Istanbul pulsates with the energy of opportunity, prosperity, and optimism. Tourism is at an all-time high, foreign direct investment keeps rolling in, and the rich are getting richer. This is readily seen in Taksim, Beyoğlu, Cukurcuma, Galata, and Tünel, where you can stroll past freshly restored turn-of-the-19th-century ambassadorial palaces and barracks, converted 16th-century waterhouses, and crisp, minimalist museums, all while shopping for an expensive pair of Levi's. Below is a short list of what to look out for.

Galatasaray High School (Galatasaray Lisesi)   This school's origins date back to the 15th century, when on a hunting expedition in the area, then a thickly wooded forest, Sultan Beyazit II came upon an old man who had fought in the siege of Istanbul in 1453. At the end of this encounter, the man presented the sultan with one red and one yellow rose from his garden (the colors of the soccer team of the same name) and requested that a house of learning be built on the spot. The school was founded in 1481 as Galata Sarayı, the fourth of a network of existing palace schools. During the era of the Tanzimat, the school became a window onto the West, and much of Turkish-French relations have their origins here.

For the past 500 years, Galatasaray High School has graduated grand viziers and palace administrators, and later, prime ministers, poets, artists, and journalists. Even today, the high school continues to set the standards of learning for all of Turkey.

Istiklal Cad., across from the Galatasaray Fish Market (Balıkpazarı). (© **0212/244-3666** or 0212/249-6698. Open with prior permission from the management.

Istanbul Museum of Modern Art In a city of ancient empires, in a country whose political and economic supremacy is but a distant memory, Turkey, and in particular Istanbul, is carving itself a new niche. Only this time, it's looking forward, not back. The Istanbul Modern, opened in December 2004, occupies a crisp, utilitarian, and highly functional 86,000 square feet in a former customs warehouse just outside the cruise-ship docks. The collection of paintings, portraits, sculptures, and photographs serve to tell us, in some sense, what was going on in the minds of the Turks in the 20th century. Some pieces simply make you tilt your head in wonder. That alone makes this museum worth a look.

Meclis-I Mebusan Cad., Liman İşletmeleri Sahası, Antrepo No. 4, Karaköy. (© **0212/334-7300**. Admission 7YTL ($6.10/£2.80), free for children 11 and under. Free admission on Thurs. Tues–Sun 10am–6pm (Thurs until 8pm). Tramway to Tophane.

Military Museum Value Feared, respected, and loathed for 500 years, the Ottoman warrior was the brick on which the Ottoman dynasty was built. Indeed, it was the rising influence of industry and economics over combat and conquest that contributed to the ultimate downfall of the empire. Since war plays a pivotal role in the history and culture of Turkey, no visit to Turkey would be complete without a stopover at the Military Museum. Most people breeze through without a sideways glance, hurriedly following the arrows that direct visitors to the **Mehter Concert** . This startlingly powerful musical performance re-creates the traditional military band of the Janissaries, the elite Ottoman corps abolished when their power became too great. The musical arrangement is an unexpectedly organized cacophony of sounds that, preceding the approaching army, also served to instill terror in the opposing army.

The exhibit, housed in the former military academy where Atatürk received his education (the building was converted into a museum in 1993), contains a chronological and functional assemblage of artifacts of warfare from the Ottoman era through World War II. The exhibit is anything but dull, showcasing chain mail and bronze armor for both cavalry and horses, leather and metalwork costumes, hand-sewn leather and arrow bags, swords engraved with fruit and flower motifs or Islamic inscriptions, and even a petroleum-driven rifle. Not to be missed is the hall of tents, an unanticipated display of *in situ* elaborately embroidered and silk encampment tents used on war expeditions.

Askeri Müse ve Kültür Sitesi Komutanlığı, Harbiye/Istanbul (about .8km/½ mile north of Taksim along Cumhuriyet Cad.). ⓒ 0212/233-2720. Admission 1.50YTL ($1.30/60p). Wed–Sun 9am–5pm. Mehter Concert 3pm (English) and 3:30pm (Turkish).

SIGHTS ALONG THE BOSPHORUS

For over 2,500 years, kings and commanders have confronted the challenge of the Bosphorus, building rudimentary bridges out of boats and floating jetties to increase the size of their empires. Mandrokles of Samos crossed on huge connecting floats in 512 B.C. Persian Emperor Xerxes built a temporary bridge, as did Heraclius I of Byzantium, who crossed a chain of pontoons on horseback. Now that several bridges connect the shores of Europe and Asia, staying on the water has become more fashionable than actually crossing it. The shores are dotted with *yalıs*, or classic waterfront mansions, built as early as the 18th century: yellow, pink, and blue wooden palaces perched along the waterfront. The surrounding neighborhoods (best visited by land) retain much of their characteristic villagey feel, in stark contrast to the restored homes inhabited by the likes of ex–Prime Minister Tansu Çillar.

Cruising up the straits is a bit easier these days than when Jason and the Argonauts sailed through in search of the Golden Fleece. A number of local tour companies organize daylong or half-day boat cruises up the Bosphorus on private boats, often with a stop at the Rumeli Fortress and visits to Beylerbeyi Sarayı. Unless you've gotten a guarantee that the tour will *not* wind up on one of the public ferries, skip the tour and hop on one of the less pristine (but serviceable) city ferries and go the route yourself.

A one-way ticket on the ferry (**Istanbul Deniz Otobüsleri** website in Turkish and English **www.ido.com.tr**, or in Istanbul call their national toll-free line at ⓒ **0212/444-4436**) costs 7YTL ($6.10/£2.80). The last stop at Sarıyer is the most visited—and therefore the most touristy—but the potential for a side trip to the **Sadberk Hanım Museum** (Büyükdere Cad. 27–29, Sarıyer; ⓒ **0212/242-3813;** Thurs–Tues 10am–5pm; admission 6YTL/$5.20/£2.40) continues to make this disembarkation point one of the most popular. The museum, located in an old Ottoman house overlooking a section of the Bosphorus that was an old dockyard, houses a limited but excellent collection of artifacts representative of the progression of civilizations in Anatolia. If you're already up here, then it's worth a look; otherwise, you'll get a more comprehensive presentation of the same themes at the Museum of Anatolian Civilizations in Ankara.

A lesser appreciated alternative is to get off at Anadolu Kavağı instead, hike up the hill to the "Crusader's Castle"—named for a carved cross decoration dating to the crusader invasion but actually a Byzantine structure used as a Genoese Palace in the 14th century—and enjoy outstanding views of the European side.

The trip by sea from Eminönü (departures at 10:35am, winter only, and 1:35pm; the ferry makes a stop in Beşiktaş approximately 15 min. later) to the last stop at Anadolu Kavağı takes 2 hours (allow 6 hr. for the full round-trip excursion), with only two return departures leaving at 3 and 5pm. This schedule pretty much restricts the amount of jumping on and off you can realistically do in 1 day. Alternatively, you can take a commuter ferry from any of a number of the wharfs to the destination on the Bosphorus of your choice for 1.30YTL ($1.15/50p).

Leander's Tower (or the Maiden's Tower, or Kız Kulesi)　Rising from a rock at the mouth of the Bosphorus is the Kız Kulesi, built by Ibrahim Paşa in 1719 over the remains of a fortress built by Mehmet the Conqueror and the earliest original building constructed on the rock by Byzantine Emperor Manuel Comnenus I. The romance of the tower finds its root in an ancient myth along the lines of Romeo and Juliet: Boy (Leander) falls in love with girl (the Aphrodite Priestess Hero); boy drowns swimming to meet girl; girl finds lover's corpse; girl commits suicide. The story originated around the Dardanelles, but was too juicy not to attach to this solitary tower. Legend also has it that the tower was connected to the mainland by way of an underwater tunnel, and that there used to be a wall between the tower and the shore—a rumor not altogether implausible considering that according to a 19th-century historian, the remains of a wall could be seen in calm water.

Since as early as the 1600s, the tower has been used as a prison and a quarantine hospital. The tower is currently in service as a panoramic restaurant and tea lounge. Take advantage of the free shuttle over and get the chance both to visit the tower and enjoy a (pricey!) romantic meal, but be sure to book well ahead (© **0212/727-4095;** info@kizkulesi.com.tr).

Slightly offshore south of Üsküdar, on the Asian side of the Bosphorus.

Rumeli Fortress (Rumeli Hisarı)　This citadel was built by Mehmet the Conqueror across from the Anatolia Fortress (Anadolu Hisarı) in preparation for what was to be the seventh and final Ottoman siege of the fortified Byzantine city. Constructed

---

⟨Value⟩ See the Whirling Dervishes

The **Sufi Music Concert & Sema Ceremony** (ceremony of the Whirling Dervishes) ✪✪✪ is held on the second and last Sunday of the month at the historic Galata Mevlevihanesi, Divan Edebiyatı Müzesi, Galip Dede Caddesi, at the end of Istiklal Caddesi in Tünel (ticket office © **0535/210-4565;** foundation office © 0542/422-1544; www.emav.org). From October to April the ceremony is at 3pm; from May to September it's at 5pm. Go early for a front-row seat in this finely decorated octagonal hall. If you miss this one, there's an alternative concert of Sufi Music and a Sema Ceremony every Monday and Thursday at 7:30pm in the open hall off platform no. 1 in the train station at Sirkeci (© **0212/458-8834**). Tickets are 30YTL ($26/£12); both ceremonies last about an hour. (**Note:** Please call ahead to confirm showings, as schedules do change.)

in only 4 months, the fortress served to cut off Black Sea traffic in and out of the city, together with the Anadolu Hisarı built by his great-grandfather across the Bosphorus on the Asian shores. The Ottoman army eventually penetrated the city by carrying the Turkish galleons over land by way of a sled and pulley system, and dropping them into the Golden Horn and behind the city's defenses.

Tarabya Yeniköy Cad. north of Sariyer (some ferries make the stop at Rumeli Kavağı; otherwise, get off at Sariyer and take a *dolmuş* the rest of the way). ℂ 0212/263-5305. 2YTL ($1.75/80p). Tues–Sun 9am–5pm. Bus: 25E or 40.

LIBRARIES & CULTURAL CENTERS

The British Council, Posta Kutusu, Beşiktaş (ℂ **0212/355-5657;** www.british council.org.tr; Tues–Fri 10am–5pm, Sat 9:30am–2:30pm), is a nonprofit cultural outreach center working for educational and cultural relations. The library is one of the best resources for multilingual information on antiquities in Turkey, as well as a great reference center for translations of Turkish literary works. There's a huge collection of English-language books on all subjects, in addition to CDs, music, and videos. The center is popular with students of the English language. Its American counterpart is the American Research Institute in Turkey (Üvez Sok. 5, Arnavutköy; ℂ **0232/257-8111**).

For books and historical documents on Istanbul, the Turkish Touring and Automobile Club runs the **Istanbul Library,** located in one of the old Ottoman houses it restored on Sogukçeşme Sokagı in Sultanahmet (ℂ **0212/512-5730;** Mon–Fri 9am–noon and 1:30–5pm).

In a forgotten ancient building across from the Fener jetty on the Golden Horn is the **Women's Library** (Kadın Eserleri Kütüphanesi; ℂ **0212/534-9550;** Mon–Fri 10:30am–6:30pm; closed for religious holidays). Founded by Füsun Akatlı, a renowned Turkish writer, the library has grown into a collection of materials—mostly in Turkish—featuring female artists, photographers, directors, and artisans. There's also a section on women in Istanbul and on women in Ottoman dress. (Entrance will require you to show your passport.)

The **Istanbul Archaeology Museum,** Osman Hamdi Bey Yokuşu, Sultanahmet (ℂ **0212/520-7740**), has a library of over 60,000 volumes on the subject of archaeology and will be opened upon request. Two other archaeology-centric research centers are at the **Dutch History and Archaeology Institute Library** (Istiklal Cad. 393; ℂ **0212/293-9283**) and the **German Archaeology Institute Library** (Ayazpaşa Cami Sok. 48, Gümüşsuyu; ℂ **0212/244-0714**).

ESPECIALLY FOR KIDS

Even though Turks are notorious pushovers for their children, Istanbul isn't really a kid-friendly destination; even the most privileged and well-educated children will get bored trudging around the recesses of ancient Byzantium. Istanbul does have a series of kid-related cultural events, though, including the **Rahmi M. Koç Museum** (Hasköy Cad. 27; ℂ **0212/297-6639;** www.rmk-museum.org.tr/english), a hands-on series of exhibitions à la Smithsonian showcasing the history of human ingenuity in the areas of transportation, industry, and communications. The transparent washing machines, carburetors, decommissioned submarine bridge, trains, and aircraft will definitely push the buttons of any preteen boy (and then some) and are definitely worth a visit. Admission is 8YTL ($6.95/£3.20) for adults (4YTL/$3.50/£1.60) for students) plus an additional $4.50YTL ($3.90/£1.80; 3YTL/$2.60/£1.20 students) for entry to the (formerly free and currently overpriced) submarine exhibit. The museum is open Tuesday through Friday 10am to 5pm and Saturday and Sunday 10am to 7pm.

Miniaturk (Imrahor Cad. Sütlüce, Istanbul, on the eastern banks of the Golden Horn opposite Eyüp; ℰ **0212/222-2882;** www.miniaturk.com.tr), which opened in 2003, is an open-air minimuseum sprouting models of Turkey's most-loved monuments reconstructed here at ½₅th of their actual size. The park is open from 9am to 5pm in winter, later in summer. Admission is 10YTL ($8.70/£4).

SPECTATOR SPORTS

To say that **soccer** is a popular national sport in Turkey is to miss the point entirely. Soccer is closer to a religious experience; club rivalries are waged with an intensity comparable to the holy wars.

The three main soccer clubs in Istanbul are **Fenerbahçe, Beşiktaş,** and **Galatasaray.** Main matches are played nights at 7pm from late August to May (a few late summer matches are played at 8pm). Home matches are played every other week at **Inönü Stadium,** above Dolmabahçe Palace, for Beşiktaş; at **Alisami Yen,** in Mecidiyeköy, for Galatasaray; and at **Fenerbahçe Stadium,** near Kadıköy on the Asian side, for Fenerbahçe. Tickets run from 50YTL to 350YTL ($44–$305/£20–£140) and are available at the stadium the day of a match, or through Biletix (www.biletix.com; in English and Turkish).

6 Shopping

WHERE SHOULD I GO?
COVERED BAZAARS AND STREET MARKETS

The Grand Bazaar (Kapalıçarşı)   Perhaps it was the renown of the **Grand Bazaar** (aka the Kapalı Çarşısı, or Covered Market) that put Istanbul on the map of the world's great shopping destinations. It's certainly one of the world's major tourist traps. It's also a feast of color and texture, of glitter and glitz. It's also not to be missed. So just take a deep breath, leave your valuables (and any cash you'd rather not spend) back in the hotel safe, and dive in. Open Mon–Sat 8:30am–7pm (closes earlier during the month of Ramadan). Beyazit, Eminönü. No phone. Best entrances through the Beyazit Gate (across from the Beyazit stop on the tramway along Divanyolu) and the Nuruosmaniye Gate (from the Çemberlitaş tramway stop on Divanyolu, follow Vezirhanı Cad. to the arched entrance to the mosque grounds, which lead to the bazaar).

Arasta Bazaar   Less overwhelming in scope than the Grand Bazaar is the picturesque shopping arcade attached to the southern edge of the Blue Mosque. It's a total tourist trap, but there are a few high-quality gems mixed in with the stacks of cheap ceramics and evil eyes made in China. Open daily 9am–7pm (closes earlier in winter and during Ramadan). Sultanahmet. Entrance on Topçu Cad. (across from the Blue House hotel) and on Küçük Ayasofya Cad.

Egyptian Spice Bazaar (Mısır Carsışı) ⭑⭑⭑   A feast of the senses, the Egyptian Spice Bazaar was established in Eminönü after the Ottoman conquest of Egypt in the 16th century as a marketplace for exotic spices arriving via sea lanes by way of Egypt. Today you can find Turkish fine linens and embroidered elf slippers in addition to the barrels of herbs and spices, pistachios soaked in honey (yet another traditional Turkish aphrodisiac and "guaranteed for five times a night"), Turkish delight, and as many varieties of saffron as your heart desires. Open Mon–Sat 8:30am–6:30pm. Eminönü, opposite Galata Bridge. No phone.

Istiklal Caddesi A bustling promenade of cafes, clothing stores, blaring record shops, and bookstores, Istiklal Street from Tünel to Taksim Square may be starting to resemble an open-air mall, but it's still an essential spot for all who visit Istanbul. Be sure to pop in to the **Avrupa Pasajı** in the Balıkpazarı (near Meşrutiyet Cad. in Beyoğlu), a narrow gallery of artsy shops selling souvenirs from antique samovars to tiny harem outfits for 2-year-olds (plus merchandise like brass pepper mills at prices lower than in the Egyptian Spice Market). Istiklal Cad., Beyoğlu.

Ortaköy The **arts-and-crafts fair** on Sundays in Ortaköy is Istanbul's equivalent of "downtown." Here you'll find a mixture of street-smart jewelry, tie-dyed textiles, and revolutionary Turkish ideas. The street food here is lots of fun. Open Sun year-round. Around the Ortaköy boat landing, along the Bosporus.

MARKETS

Local markets offer a window into the vibrancy and color of the neighborhood, and provide a priceless experience in interaction with the locals. Istanbul has more than its fair share of outdoor markets, selling the usual assortment of fresh produce, household staples, sweatshirts, and maybe the odd antique. A walk through one of these provides yet another opportunity to witness another facet of this complex culture. The major markets are the Çarşamba Pazarı ("Wednesday" market), held next to the Fatih Mosque; and the Salı Pazarı ("Tuesday" market), Mahmut Baba Sokağı, Kadıköy, on the Asian side. There is also a **flea market** between Sahaflar and the Grand Bazaar, and down at Eminönü every Sunday, and an antiques market in **Horhor** (Horhor Cad. Kırk Tulumba, Aksaray; daily).

WHAT SHOULD I BUY?

The first thing that comes to mind when plotting out a plan of attack for acquisitions in Turkey is a rug, be it a *kilim,* or **tribal carpet.** Carpets, kilims, and a whole slew of related items that have lost their nomadic utility now comprise a complex industry. It is unlikely that you will get very far before being seduced by an irresistible excess of enticing keepsakes. Because the big bad city of Istanbul attracts the worst of the country's merchant opportunists, I'd recommend holding off on this purchase until you get to the heartland.

Most people are unaware that Turkey manufactures some of the best **leather items** in Europe, comparable in quality to those sold in Florence, Italy (and in some stores in Florence, the merchandise *is* Turkish). Because leather items are individually produced in-house, quality and fit may vary, but the advantage of this is that you can have a jacket, skirt, or trousers made to order, change the design of a collar, or exchange an unsightly zipper for buttons at prices far less than what you'd pay back home.

Fun Fact **Did You Know?**

The blue-and-white evil eye *(nazar boncuğu)* has its roots in Anatolian culture, although the symbol has its variants throughout the Middle East. Turks believe strongly in the power of the evil eye (if you could only see the tattoos beneath the *hijab* . . .) to ward off negative energy, especially against young children. But the evil eye transcends this culture—just check the pyramid on the backside of your U.S. dollar bill. Oh, and by the way, all of the blue evil eyes are now made in China.

(Tips **A Note About Bargaining**

That old measure by which you should offer the seller half of his initial price is old hat. They've caught on to our shopping savvy, and in fact they don't care. There are plenty of stupendously wealthy Russians and groups of cruise-ship passengers to target. I've heard that a good rule of thumb is to offer about 25% less than you're willing to pay, but in my experience, you must hold off your counteroffer for as long as you can get away with it. This method will meet with varying responses, but after a few times, you'll get the hang of it.

Also, after you've narrowed down your choice to two pieces, snub your first choice and put it down (with plans to come back to it later). Negotiate on your second choice—undoubtedly one of the finer samples in the shop and there-fore one of the pricier items on sale. Once you've established that it's out of your price range, turn to your first choice with a disappointed "and what about that one."

The entire length of Kalpakçılar Caddesi in the Grand Bazaar glitters with precious metals from the Nuruosmaniye Gate to the Beyazit Gate. But Turkish-bought **gold and silver** no longer offers the bargains it did previously, as the cost of precious metals has risen more that $300 per ounce since 2005. Still, cheap labor in China and India might keep Turkish jewelers from pricing themselves out of the market, so all hope is not lost.

Some of the world's best **meerschaum** comes from Turkey. This heat-resistant sea foam becomes soft when wet, allowing it to be carved into playful pipes that would make a collector out of the most die-hard nonsmoker. An afternoon in a historic *hamam* will expose you to some of the most beautiful traditional **white copper** objects, available as kitchen utensils as well as bathing ones, although keep in mind that you can't cook with this toxic stuff unless the inside has been coated with tin.

As far as **antiques** go, shopkeepers seem to be practiced in manufacturing bogus certificates of origin that will facilitate your trip through Customs, but beware: The certificate may not be the only counterfeit item in the shop. Collectors should keep in mind that it is prohibited by Turkish law to export anything dated prior to and through the 19th century.

Less traditional items can easily fill a suitcase, and with clever Turkish entrepreneurs coming up with new merchandise on a regular basis, you won't get bored on your second or third visit. **Pillowcases, embroidered tablecloths, ornamental tea services,** and **brass coffee grinders** are just some of the goodies that never seem to get old.

SHOPPING A TO Z
ANTIQUES & COLLECTIBLES

Objects dating to the Ottoman period make up a popular category for roving anti-quers. As a rule, all items displayed can be legally purchased and exported to your home country (unless the piece is unique, in which case you need documentation from a museum director to buy it). Objects dated prior to the Ottoman period are considered fruit from the poisonous tree. Where carpets are concerned, the cutoff is 100 years—you'll need a certificate from the shopkeeper stating the age, origin, and authenticity of the carpet. (This is standard practice anyway.) So if you're serious, your first stop should be the neighborhood along Cukurcuma in the extremely hilly neighborhood below Beyoğlu and Taksim.

Artrium This shop is one of the last holdouts in the *pasaji*, or atrium just outside the entrance to the Upper Tünel. The store stocks oldish ceramics, textiles, costume jewelry, and printed matter. Tünel Geçidi 7. ✆ 0212/251-4362.

Galeri Alfa This shop has limited-edition tin toy soldiers, inspired by several hundred years of the Ottoman Empire as well as by models from abroad. Galeri Alfa also deals in rare books and prints. Faikpaşa Yokuşu 47/2, Cukurcuma. ✆ 0212/251-1672.

Horhor Bit Pazarı One of the lesser-known and blissfully lesser-traveled markets is where you'll find dusty Turkish memorabilia from the 20th century. Merchandise includes tableware, lamps, and furniture, spread out among the more than 200 shops on six floors. Horhor Cad. Kırk Tulumba, Aksaray.

Ottomania Located in Beyoğlu just outside the Tünel atrium, Ottomania specializes in high-quality old maps and engravings. Sofyalı Sok. 30–32 (exit Tünel and walk straight through atrium). ✆ 0212/243-2157.

Ottoman Miniatures & Calligraphy Pointing is going to be your best means of communication if you're in the market for rare Ottoman and Islamic prints, or a superb original framed *tuğra*. Istiklal Cad. 6. ✆ 0212/251-1966.

BOOKS

Galeri Kayseri Anything you ever wanted to know about Istanbul or Turkey is somewhere inside this shop, or their branch across the street at no. 11. Divanyolu 58 and across the st. at no. 11, Sultanahmet. ✆ 0212/512-0456.

Homer Kitabevi Down the street from the Galatasaray High School is this absolute superlative of a bookstore, stocking a rich selection of books on Turkish issues, including politics, history, architecture, photography, travel, and religion. If you can't find it here, it's either sold out or it doesn't exist. Yeni Çarşı Cad. 28/A. ✆ 0212/ 249-5902.

Istanbul Kitapçısı Owned and operated by the Istanbul municipality, this bookstore stocks cassettes, videos, travel books, maps, and coffee table books in a variety of languages. There is also a selection of prints and posters. Istiklal Cad. 191, Beyoğlu. ✆ 0212/292-7692.

Librairie de Pera The last bookstore left on a street that was famed for its booksellers, Librairie de Pera is the little engine that could. The current owner, Ugur Güraca, presides over a multilingual collection of more than 40,000 rare books, some bound with goat skin, as well as prints, photographs, and etchings. Galip Dede Cad. 22 (opposite the Galatasaray Mevlevihanesi), Tünel. ✆ 0212/243-3991.

Nakkaş Books Aykut, the laid-back owner of the now-closed Aypa, at Mimar Mehmet Ağa Caddesi, opened a shop down the street in conjunction with some partners and owners of Nakkaş. He still carries a great selection of books on Turkish art, ceramics, history, religion, and the Ottoman Empire, some of which are rare or limited editions. The shop also carries a dizzying array of souvenirs like magnets, artistic cards, jewelry, copper, and textiles. Nakilbent Sok. 33. ✆ 0212/516-0100.

Robinson Crusoe Just before you head down to the coast for that weeklong Mediterranean vacation, stop off here to find something to read. Robinson Crusoe

Caveat Emptor! **Carpet-Buying Tips**

"Where are you from?" seems an innocuous enough question from a carpet dealer, but answer it and you're on your way to being scalped. Questions like "Where are you staying?" actually tell the salesperson about your economic status, as do "What do you do?" *(How much money do you earn?)*, "Where do you live?" *(Hey, what a coincidence! My cousin lives near you!)*, "How much time will you be staying here?" *(How much time do you have before you have to make your final decision?)*, "What are you looking for?" *(Do you even have any idea about carpets?)*, and "How long have you been here?" *(How much have you already learned about our sleazy ways?)*.

First rule of thumb: Lie about where you're staying. Take note of the name of the humblest pension near your actual hotel and file it away for future use. Also, they know that Americans are the biggest spenders of any other nationality visiting Turkey, so this is where fluency in a foreign language may come in handy. Above all, do your homework and know what you like before you arrive so you don't waste precious bargaining time overpaying for the "best sample in the shop."

Visitors traveling in groups inevitably wind up at a large roadside production center. Although these are interesting from an educational and cultural point of view, don't be had: Your tour guide, your tour company, and even the bus driver are going to each earn a hefty commission off of your sale. (Actually, the same commission system applies to almost everything you buy.)

Yes, buying a carpet in Turkey can be a very daunting task. But this is not meant to diminish your admiration of the pieces, only arm you for the negotiations, which ultimately will get you an exceptional souvenir of a wonderful country and its wonderful crafts.

stocks a limited selection of English-language fiction, travel guides, and books on Istanbul and Turkey. Istiklal Cad. 389. ✆ 0212/251-1735.

Sahaflar Çarşısı The Book Bazaar is a wonder of the printed page. Vendors carry books on Turkish subjects ranging from art to architecture to music, both old and new. Also, some of the finest examples of Ottoman art and calligraphy can be found in this book lover's mecca. Sahaflar Çarşısı, Grand Bazaar (enter from Çadırcılar Cad.).

CARPETS

When in Istanbul, my days are filled with powwows with carpet dealers proud to show me the thank-you letters received from Washington, D.C., insiders, foreign dignitaries, and vacationing journalists. Finding an honorable carpet seller is even more elusive than tracking down an honest car salesman. In a country where the minimum wage produces 455YTL ($396£182) *per month,* the business of selling carpets promises the equivalent of the American Dream, attracting the ambitious and sometimes immoral on the trail of easy money. This doesn't diminish the value of the carpets, nor does it mean that all carpet sellers are dishonest. In fact, Istanbul is full of carpet salesmen

Deconstructing the Turkish Carpet

Turkish tribal rugs are divided into **kilims,** which are flat, woven rugs, and **carpets,** which are hand-knotted using a double or Gordian Knot, a technique unique to Anatolia that results in a denser, more durable product than the single-knotted carpets found abroad. Kilims are probably more recognizable, as they are inexpensive and sold abroad.

There are four types of carpets produced currently in Turkey. **Wool-on-wool** carpets represent the oldest tradition in tribal rugs and are representative of a wide range of Anatolian regions. The earliest examples display geometric designs using natural dyes that were reliant on local resources like plants, flowers, twigs, and even insects, so that the colors of the carpets reflected the color of an individual region. Blues and reds are typical of designs originating around Bergama, which derive from the indigo root and local insects. Reds seem to be dominant in carpets made in Cappadocia. The oranges and beiges of the Üşaks are also becoming more popular among consumers.

Today the business of carpet weaving has been transformed into a mass industry. Weavers have for the most part switched over to chemical-based dyes, although the trend toward organic dyes is experiencing a rebirth.

The second type of carpet is the highly prized **silk-on-silk** samples, which developed in response to the Ottoman Palace's increasing desire for quality and splendor. Silk was a precious commodity imported from China that few could afford. In the 19th century the sultan established a royal carpet-weaving center at **Hereke** that catered exclusively to the palace. Today silk-on-silk rugs continue to outclass all others, using silk from Bursa woven into reproductions of traditional designs. (*FYI:* Silk threads cannot hold natural dyes.) Silk rugs are also produced in **Kayseri,** but these have yet to attain the high standards set by the Herekes.

A more recent development in carpet production has been the **wool-on-cotton,** which, because of the lower density of the weft, accommodates a higher ratio of knots per inch, and therefore more detail in the design. Carpets of this type come from **Kayseri, Konya (Lakık),** and **Hereke. Cotton-on-cotton** is an even newer invention, duplicating the resolution and sheen of a silk rug without the expense.

Sales tactics include an emphasis on Anatolian carpet and *kilim* weaving as a high art. This certainly applies to rare and older pieces, which command hefty sums. But modern samples—albeit handmade copies of traditional designs—are created from computerized diagrams. Finally, unless you're an expert, you should avoid buying antique rugs, which cost significantly more, and will present some challenges with Customs. The bottom line is that only antiques experts are equipped for a proper appraisal.

whose singular goal is to sell the finest-quality, most beautiful specimens for the absolute highest price they can get. The challenge for the potential buyer is not so much about avoiding fakes and scams; it's about not getting scalped. This is, after all, a business. And it's *your* business to be an educated consumer. What's a shopper to do?

Recognize that buying a carpet is an extremely labor- and time-intensive activity, and rest assured that these salesmen will find you.

CERAMICS

Art House Shop owner Fereç Zan sells a spectacular variety of urns and fireplace ornaments in his tiny shop in the Cebeci Han. Completed ceramic bowls are flown in from Kutahya and the copper is hand-worked on-site in the workshop on the second level at the back of the adjacent *Iç Cebeci Han*. Modestly sized urns sell for around 75YTL ($65/£30—significantly less than the 220 *of whatever currency* they care to quote in the Arasta Bazaar). Yağlıçılar Cad. Cebeci Han 17, Grand Bazaar. ℂ 0212/526-5509.

Istanbul Handicrafts Center The streetfront shop to the workshops in this restored 17th-century Ottoman *medrese* has a choice collection of precious ceramic and porcelain reproductions from Kütahya and Iznik. Kabasakal Cad., Istanbul Sanatları Çarşısı, next to the Yeşil Ev. ℂ 0212/517-6780.

Iznik Foundation Having revived the Ottoman-era craft of Iznik tile-making, the Iznik Foundation is now selling its wares. The trick was identifying the chemical process for achieving the vibrant blue and green pigmentation of the originals. One of the criteria was that the ceramic "canvas" had to be composed of up to 80% quartz. Kuruçeşme Öksüz Çocuk Sok. 14, Kuruçeşme. ℂ 0212/287-3243.

Kevser Located on the main street that parallels the Bosphorus on its way through Ortaköy, Kevser is an eye-catching boutique carrying fine traditional and modern ceramic pieces as well as a variety of gift items. Muallim Naci Cad. 72, Ortaköy. ℂ 0212/327-0586.

COPPER

Çadırcılar Caddesi If you simply have to have a set of those white copper *hamam* bowls or a copper platter for a table *à la Turque*, root around the slightly disheveled stalls near the book bazaar. That is, if you can't wait to get to Ankara, where copper is king. Çadırcılar Cad. (past the entrance to the book bazaar near the Grand Bazaar).

May Galeri For a more artistic presentation of copper ware, head to May Galeri in the upscale neighborhood of Nişantaşı. Süleyman Nazif Sok. Valı Konağı Cad., Nişantaşı.

CRAFTS

Evihan Handmade artistic pieces made using Turkish tiles and hand-blown glass beads are the main feature at this crafty boutique located in the up-and-coming neighborhood of Cukurcuma. Altıpatlar Sok. 8. ℂ 0212/244-0034.

Istanbul Handicrafts Center (Istanbul Sanatları Çarşısı) In another one of its commendable preservationist projects, the Touring and Automobile Club of Turkey has provided an outlet for the revival of Turkish and Ottoman crafts. Each room off the central courtyard of this restored 17th-century *medrese* serves as an atelier for a different craft. Here you can watch the creation of handmade treasures, including hand-painted silks, folk-art dolls and puppets, gilded calligraphy and miniatures, fine porcelain reproductions, and modern examples of the art of *ebru*, or marbled paper. The center is open year-round, although you may have to knock on some doors to get a personal shopping tour during the off season. Better yet, their fixed pricing takes the guesswork out of buying. Kabasakal Cad. (the side street next to the Derviş Tea Garden and across from the Blue Mosque). ℂ 0212/517-6780.

Pasabahçe The nationwide chain has recently begun making a name overseas for its elegant ceramics, hand-cut glass, and typically Ottoman tableware. The more precious pieces are trimmed in silver or gold plate. The store also stocks everyday tableware, but that's not the stuff you're going to carry home. There are 15 locations in Istanbul, including in Beyoğlu, at the Kanyon shopping center, and in Teşvikiye, the one on Istiklal Caddesi being the most convenient. Istiklal Cad. 314, Beyoğlu. ℭ 0212/244-5694.

DEPARTMENT STORES & CHAINS

So you've packed for warmer weather and the winds from the Caucasus have arrived a bit early. Head for these chains, located along Istiklal Caddesi in Istanbul, though you'll find them in major shopping areas throughout the country.

Beyman Beyman is Turkey's answer to Ralph Lauren, without the horsy patch. There's absolutely nothing cheesy about this store, carrying casual chic for men and women as well as housewares worthy of a museum. The Beymen Mega Store in Akmerkez (ℭ 0212/282-0380) is more along the lines of an upscale department store, where you can find cosmetics, stationery, and even furniture. The small outlet store in Eminönü carries reduce-priced men's shirts and ties. Akmerkez. ℭ 0212/282-0380. Abdi Ipekçi Cad. 23/1, Nişantaşı. ℭ 0212/343-0404.

Mavi Jeans These jeans started to make a showing in upscale stores in the U.S. Here, in Turkey, Mavi is more like a Turkish GAP, except that fabrics are *not* prewashed, so you should *never* put items in the dryer. Istiklal Cad. 117 (ℭ 0212/249-3758), and in the Akmerkez shopping center (see "Malls & Shopping Centers," below).

Vakko For the best designer men's and women's wear by Turkish designers, check out Vakko, Turkey's answer to Barney's New York and worth a look if only for its dazzling silver-embroidered scarves. There are a number of locations, including at the airport, in Kanyon Shopping Center, in Galleria Shopping Center, and in Nişantaşı. There's even a discount shop on Sultanhamam Caddesi, behind the Egyptian Spice Bazaar. Akmerkez. Nispetiye Cad., Etiler. ℭ 0212/282-0695.

FOOD

Hacı Bekir For the most extensive variety of Turkish delight, stop in to the legendary sweet shop with locations in Beyoğlu and Eminönü. Istiklal Cad. 129, Beyoğlu (ℭ 0212/244-2804), and Hamidiye Cad. 81–83, Eminönü (ℭ 0212/522-0666).

Kurukahveci Mehmet Turkish-coffee addicts should head to this corner behind the spice bazaar. A producer of the infamous precious brew, Kurukahveci Mehmet is also the best-known retail outlet. Tahmis Cad. 66, Eminönü.

Şutte A delight for your eyes and your stomach, Şutte is a chain of charcuteries with outlets all over the city. This location is the most central. Şutte carries rare pork

(Tips) Something Smells Fishy

Beware of anything labeled caviar. Turkey is notorious for its illegal trade in smuggled caviar, as well as for representing lower-quality replacement fish roe as high-quality caviar using counterfeit labels copied from reputable brands.

Olive Oil: Anatolia's Black Gold

Turkey's **olive oil** really doesn't get the kind of respect it deserves—an absence of effective marketing has deprived the rest of the world of one of the country's most treasured resources. But that is changing, by the looks of the gourmet shop in the airport's duty-free area. If you've been bewitched by the flaxen temptress at the bottom of your meze bowl, pick up a bottle at any local convenience-type store. The grocery store chains carry some basic brands; opt for Komili.

items like prosciutto and speck as well as hard-to-come-by wedges of *parmeggiano reggiano*. You can also take out one of the many prepared sandwiches or tempting mezes and eat them at the lone table in the Balık Pazarı. Duduodalar Sok. 21, in the Balıkpazarı (Fish Bazaar, opposite Galatasaray High School). ℂ 0212/293-9292.

GIFTS & SOUVENIRS

Abdulla Natural Products   Thou shall not covet these incredibly thick and plush towels. With two locations in and around the Grand Bazaar, Abdulla stocks goods like deliciously textured bath sheets, herbal olive-oil soaps, and all of the accouterments for a home-style *hamam* (silk pestamal, hand mitt, and so on). Halıcılar Cad. 62, inside the Grand Bazaar (ℂ 0212/527-3684), and Ali Baba Türbe Sok. 25/27, Nuruosmaniye (ℂ 0212/526-3070).

Avrupa Pasajı   A couple of shops located down this passage in the Balık Pazarı reliably stock all of those little souvenirs you can't leave Turkey without: evil eyes, copper pepper mills, hookah pipes, and scarves, all at prices much, much lower than anywhere else in town. Istiklal Cad., Balıkpazarı, Avrupa Pasajı. No phone.

Fine Art   As the distributor for Vakko in Japan, Fine Art carries their silk scarves, tablecloths, and other household textiles, as well as good-quality non-Vakko ceramics and silver jewelry. Divanyolu Cad. 13, Sultanahmet (next to McDonald's). ℂ 0212/638-9827.

HOME

Beymen Home   One could easily spend thousands of New Turkish Lira in this shop. Beymen is a candy store of contemporary home items à la Ralph Lauren or Calvin Klein. Here you'll find sleekly designed tableware, Ottoman-style copper serving platters, and sumptuously simple furniture. Boston Sok. 8, Nişantaşı. ℂ 0212/343-0404.

The Home Store   A veritable emporium of Turkish-made, stylish wear for both the home and for those who live in it, Home Store deserves a reserved corner in your luggage. Come to think of it, bring a spare bag. Akmerkez Shopping Center, Etiler. ℂ 0212/291-6297.

Mudo   Mudo is the anti-department store, carrying things you never knew you needed. A sort of cross between Pottery Barn and Next, the stores carry stylish housewares and very wearable clothing for men and women. Mudo has branched out around the country (it has 32 locations in Istanbul), with some of the stores focusing on just one "department." A Mudo Outlet is now located in the Egyptian Spice Bazaar. Rumeli Cad. 58, Nişantaşı (ℂ 0212/231-3643), Istiklal Cad., and in Akmerkez.

JEWELRY

Eller Art Gallery   Providing a more down-to-earth showcase for wearable art is this workshop (at the back) and gallery on a side street of Beyoğlu. These very Turkish designs are inspired by jewelry and other artifacts normally seen under protective glass at Ankara's Museum of Anatolian Civilizations. Istiklal Cad., Postacılar Sok. 12, Beyoğlu. © 0212/249-2364.

Pegasus   For decorative (but not too much so) silver pendants, rings, and earrings, this tiny storefront in Ortaköy is one of my favorites, and it's also gentle on the wallet. Muallim Naci Cad. Yelkovan Sok. 3/B, Ortaköy. © 0212/258-7485.

Urart Ateliers   Urart is an upscale workshop complex of designers, artists, and craftsmen dedicated to re-creating the rich traditions of Anatolian civilizations in gold and silver. Urart's precious creations are available to the public in the label's exclusive boutique in Nişantaşı. Some of their pieces are also available in the small gift shop in Topkapı Palace, in the last courtyard. In the Swissôtel (© 0212/629-0478) and at Abdi Ipekçi Cad. 18/1, Nişantaşı (© 0212/246-7194).

LEATHER GOODS

Centilmen Han   If you're looking to score some top-quality leather at bargain-basement prices, those days are long gone. Nevertheless, the fakes are pretty good these days (see below). For a good variety of leather bag manufacturers, poke around this han in the Grand Bazaar. Centilmen Han, to the right of the Çarşıkapı entrance to the Grand Bazaar. No phone.

Derimod   Locally crafted leather shoes, bags, and jackets for both men and women are sold under this Turkish national brand. Merchandise is made of fine-quality hides and crafted into traditional forms. Akmerkez Shopping Center. © 0212/282-0668.

Kayıcı Genuine Fake Bags   Just because these are not the originals doesn't mean (1) they're of inferior quality or (2) you're not going to need a full wallet to walk out of here with a little morsel. GFB carries Prada (with bargaining that begins at $250), Louis Vuitton, and other big names. Grand Bazaar. From Beyazit Gate, to the right of the leather han. © 212/526-5181.

Malls & Shopping Centers

You'd really have to have a lot of time on your hands in Istanbul to wind up at one of these shopping centers, but sometimes the lure of the florescent lighting and the chill of overtaxed air-conditioning is just too tempting to resist. The **Akmerkez Mall**, in Etiler, was actually voted the best shopping mall in Europe several years back. But clearly that wasn't enough—last year saw the opening of **Istinye Park**, an urban re-creation of a village catering to those accustomed to the stratospheres of commerce. The outdoor **Kanyon** is only a couple of years old, a Guggenheim-esque swirl of tasteful Turkish franchises and one-of-a kinders in the smart neighborhood of Levent. Other shopping malls include **Capitol Shopping Mall** in Üsküdar, **Carousel Shopping Mall** in Bakırköy, and **Galleria Shopping Mall** near the airport. **Olivium** is a newish outlet mall located halfway between the airport and Sultanahmet, where you can find various middle-of-the-range name brands at discounted prices.

Tax-Free Shopping

There's an incentive for carrying that carpet home. Foreigners (and Turkish citizens with residence abroad) are entitled to a VAT (tax) refund, worth 18% of the total amount of merchandise acquired during any one purchase. One word of caution, though: There's an ongoing scam where a merchant will ask you to sign an invoice (written in Turkish) that actually states you have already received your VAT refund at the point of purchase. Imagine handing over your paperwork at the airport (including the receipt with your signature) only to learn that you have essentially waived your own right to the refund without even knowing it. Simply put: Don't sign anything you can't read.

To receive a refund, present the merchandise and receipt to the Customs inspectors on your way out of the country (but within 3 months of purchase). Refunds are issued in the form of either a Global Refund check, redeemable at the İş Bankası branch on the Arrivals level, or as a credit to a credit card account. The Customs Tax-Free office at the airport in Istanbul, located in the International Departure Terminal, is open 24 hours a day.

7 Istanbul After Dark

Don't think that because 98% of Turks are Muslim that nobody's drinking wine with dinner. On the contrary, even in notoriously conservative Konya, bars outnumber mosques, figuratively speaking.

A typical evening on the town will involve large amounts of food accompanied by even greater amounts of raki, that aniseed-flavored spirit known as "lion's milk"—traditionally consumed in a *meyhane,* a tavern or pub where patrons gather to eat and drink. Where *meyhanes* were once the realm of men only, today they are a hybrid of the lively taverna and sophisticated restaurant, the most popular ones found primarily in the back streets of Beyoğlu. On summer evenings, the main dining room moves to the rooftops (if it's not already there), where guests are treated to the twinkling lights of a city almost without time.

The *şaraphane,* or wine bar, and the counterpart to the *birhane,* or beer hall, is the newest nightlife trend in Istanbul, a relatively recent institution that's thriving thanks to the ever-improving quality of Turkey's wines.

Live music is a staple of Turkish nightlife, and Istanbul's cafes, clubs, and Turkish Houses *(Türkü Evleri)* all offer whatever you're looking for. Bars, cafes, and nightclubs in Istanbul are generally not categorized according to the type of music they play, instead booking groups with different styles from night to night. A good rule of thumb is, the earlier the hour, the softer the music. Rock and pop resounds onto Istiklal Caddesi, where nightspots, a few of them seedy, are too numerous to cover. Another good rule is to avoid spots with neon lights and security guards and anything with the word "nightclub" or "club" in the name, as these have the reputation of being the seedy places where bad things happen to good visitors.

Safety for Single Men

Scenario #1: You're wandering around Taksim and pop into a bar for a quick beer or two. Before you know it, you're surrounded by lovely women and even doted on by the owner. But 2 hours and two beers later, the check arrives: $500. I wish that were a typo. Refuse to pay, and the big boys come out of the woodwork; you may even find your life and limb threatened. It's startling how many times this scenario plays out in seemingly innocuous-looking "establishments" around Taksim. One way to fight it, I suppose, is to dispute the charge with your credit card carrier once the bill comes in. But the best way to handle the situation is to avoid it altogether. Stay away from any place with neon and the word "nightclub" or "club" in the sign. But sadly, there is no absolute guarantee. When in doubt, follow the advice of this guidebook, or stick to the hotel bars.

Scenario #2: You're taking an innocent evening stroll through the back streets of Sultanahmet. Suddenly, you are accosted by four young boys who identify themselves as police. Having done nothing wrong and always mindful that you are in a foreign country, you cooperate. They manhandle you (perhaps looking for ID, or even drugs) and then send you packing with a shove. It all happens so fast, except that now your wallet is empty. Unfortunately, with the migration of organized crime, nowhere is safe anymore. Don't walk anywhere alone and avoid badly lit streets after dark.

Türkü Evleri are cozy little cafe/restaurants that book Turkish folk musicians performing typical Anatolian ballads to the accompaniment of the *saz* and drums. Clustered around Büyükparmakkapı Sokak in Beyoğlu, the cafes also serve basic Anatolian fare.

Meanwhile, no denizen of the night will be able to look him/herself in the mirror without having stood at the velvet ropes of one of Istanbul's **megaclubs on the Bosphorus.** While different years find these multiplexes with ever-evolving names, the themes and even the locations stay the same and invariably involve multiple candlelit restaurants, numerous bars, a dance floor, strobe lights, and fresh breezes off the Bosphorus, only inches away.

Clubs that book popular musical acts may sell tickets or impose a cover charge where normally there is none, but unless the headliner is very popular, tickets to most performing-arts events and concerts can be purchased at the location the day of the performance. For tickets to the city's main events, contact Biletix (a Ticketmaster company: **www.biletix.com**; © **0216/556-9800**).

Hotel lounges or **rooftop bars** provide a relaxing alternative to wall-to-wall smoke-filled cafes. In Sultanahmet, splendidly romantic views present themselves from almost every rooftop, or you can succumb to the dubious appeal of one of the several **Turkish night shows** around town.

The neighborhood of **Ortaköy** is particularly vibrant on summer evenings, when streets lined with outdoor vendors selling crafts, jewelry, and the like create a festival-like atmosphere. Hip, waterside restaurants and coffeehouses are open till late, or you can graze through the stalls of food and gorge yourself on stuffed mussels.

GAY ISTANBUL

Although homosexuality can be traced back to Ottoman times, there's still a stigma attached to it: The worst insult used among Turks (especially at soccer games) is *ibne,* a term referring to the receiving partner in a same-sex act. Practically speaking, homosexuality in Turkey is legal between consenting partners above the age of 18. Several *hamams* are generally accepted as gay (the men's side), including the Tarihi Galatasaray Hamamı in Beyoğlu (for hours and fees, see the section "Historic *Hamams* [Turkish Baths]," earlier in this chapter); Park Hamamı, Divanyolu, Dr. Emin Paşa Sokağı, Sultanahmet (no phone); and Aquarium, Istiklal Caddesi, Sadri Alışik Sok. 29 (© 0212/251-8926). For more specific information, log on to www.istanbulgay.com.

THE PERFORMING ARTS

Built originally as an opera house, **Atatürk Cultural Center (AKM)** in Taksim Square (© 0212/251-5600) houses the State Opera and Ballet, the Symphony Orchestra, and the State Theatre Company. Tickets are absurdly low at 7YTL to 17YTL ($6.10–$15/£2.80–£6.80) and are usually available for purchase in the month of as well as the day of the performance. During the summer months, AKM hosts the Istanbul Arts Festival but because of high demand, tickets may be hard to come by. For a schedule of performances, check out the government's website at www.kultur.gov.tr or log on to www.mymerhaba.com for upcoming events.

The annual **International Istanbul Festival** (© 0212/334-0700; www.iksv.org) is organized into four separate arts festivals averaging over 50 events yearly. The festival kicks off with the Film Festival in April, including two national and international competitions. The 2003 festival screened over 175 films in a variety of venues in Beyoğlu and Kadıköy. The theater section of the festival brings companies from all over Europe and takes place in May, with one or two offerings in English. At the end of October or in early November, selected international artists come together for the Biennale, but the big to-do takes place in June/July with the International Istanbul Music Festival, representing the worlds of opera, jazz, classical music, and ballet in evocative settings like the St. Irene, and featuring world-renowned performers like Wynton Marsalis or the traditional performance of *Der Entführung aus dem Serail (Abduction from the Seraglio),* appropriately staged in Topkapı Palace. A separate Jazz Festival, sponsored by Efes Pilsen, takes place in November in various venues around town, including local jazz clubs, cultural centers, and the open-air theater above Taksim.

Istanbul Biennale 2009

Istanbul has been celebrating a **Biennale** since 1987, but it wasn't until 2005, perhaps because of the anchorage of the new Istanbul Modern Museum, that the Biennale hit a home run. Artists were clustered around the revived neighborhood of Galata in venues that included an old apartment block, a tobacco depot, a customs warehouse, and an office building. (Previous exhibitions were housed in the Imperial Mint, in the Kız Kulesi [Maiden's Tower], in Santral Istanbul [a former electric-generating plant] on the Bosphorus Bridge, and in Çemberlitaş Hamamı.)

For information on venues, tickets, and artists, contact the Istanbul Foundation for Culture and Art (© 0212/334-0700; www.iksv.org).

THE CLUB & MUSIC SCENE

TURKISH FOLKLORE

Galata Tower   In spite of mediocre food and high prices, visitors continue to insist on a "traditional" Turkish folkloric show. Inevitably there's a belly dancer and perhaps a segment resembling a Cossack dance. The one at the Galata Tower at least comes with a fabulous view. The show runs Monday through Saturday and includes dinner. Top floor of the Galata Tower. ℂ 0212/293-8180. Admission 100YTL ($87/£40).

Orient Hotel   The belly dancers are always a crowd pleaser at the Orient Hotel, a one-stop-shop nightlife venue featuring an evening of wine, average food, and Anatolian song. It's one of the more popular of the "Turkish Nights," and easily the most convenient. Dinner starts at 8pm and the show goes on until midnight. Tiyatro Cad. 27, Beyazit (near the Grand Bazaar). ℂ 0212/517-6163. Admission 30€ ($44/£21).

Sound and Light Show   The floodlit domes and minarets of the Blue Mosque are the backdrop to a nightly (in summer) sound-and-light spectacle at the entrance to the Blue Mosque in Sultanahmet Park. The show has a charming spontaneous feel and accommodates visitors from around the globe by offering a schedule of shows with rotating languages. For information, see the Tourist Information Office in Sultanahmet Park. Sultanahmet Meydanı. ℂ 0212/518-1802.

TRADITIONAL ANATOLIAN AFTER HOURS

Türku Evi (Finds)   Backgammon, hookah pipes, and popular local singers performing the traditional yearning nomadic melodies are found at these "Turkish Houses." I confess that this listing does not refer to just one spot but instead covers the numerous cozy bars populating Hasnun Galıp Street in Beyoğlu that feature live performers singing traditional Anatolian folk songs. This is really the experience you've come all this way for. Generally, basic dinner items are served. The small space fills up with locals, who, having eaten, get up and dance in the narrow aisle between the musicians and the kilim-covered tables and banquettes. Istiklal Cad., Hasnun Galıp Sok., perpendicular to Büyükparmakkapı Sok. 18A, Beyoğlu.

Yeni Marmara (Finds)   Inconspicuously located on a little-trod street of Sultanahmet, this sleepy little teahouse and narghile cafe is one of the neighborhood's best-kept secrets. Locals relax on the back terrace jutting out above the old city walls to enjoy a game of backgammon and views of the Marmara islands. Walls and floors are covered in old rugs, and the whole space has an appealing worn vibe. Open daily 9am–1am. Küçuk Ayasofya Mah. Çayıroğlu Sok. 46, Sultanahmet. ℂ 0212/516-9013.

THE LOCAL BAR & CLUB SCENE

SULTANAHMET & THE OLD CITY

Streets of Kumkapı   The narrow warren of streets in the neighborhood opposite the fishermen's wharf of Kumkapı are crowded with restaurants which have staked their claim to individual patches of cobblestone. The atmosphere combines food and fun in a lively villagelike setting, where celebration and sometimes dancing accompany all the seafood you care to eat. Pick your poison (so to speak) and dig in. Caparız Sok., Kumkapı. Numerous restaurants.

Galata Bridge   More central and ridiculously scenic is the cluster of bars, cafes, and fish restaurants newly occupying the upper and lower levels of the Galata Bridge. While there's nothing remarkable about the restaurants per se, a couple of the venues have leapfrogged over the dining experience straight to drinks and backgammon. The east-facing and always packed **Dersaadet** (© 0212/292-7002) is the hot ticket, as it faces the minarets of the Old City. Galata Bridge, between Eminönü and Karaköy.

Meşale Çay Bahçesi   Just at the entrance to the Arasta Bazaar is an outdoor collection of benches and tables perfectly placed for a balmy summer's eve or a midday tea break in the shadow of the Blue Mosque. In summer, a lone whirling derviş "performs" nightly at 8 and 10pm. Between Nakılbend and Turun soks., at the entrance to the Arasta Bazaar. © 0212/518-9562.

Çorlulu Alipaşa Medrese   Not far from the Grand Bazaar is the outdoor living-room-cum-tea-gardens hidden in the courtyard of the old Çorlulu Alipaşa Medrese. The tree-filled garden is a perfect place to unwind, with a glass of apple tea and the essence of strawberry in your water pipe while you admire the display of carpets and souvenirs decorating the gardens of the bordering shops. The entrance to the tea gardens is on Yeniceriler Caddesi near where the road changes names from Divanyolu Caddesi. Çorlulu Alipaşa Medrese, Çarşıkapı, Yeniceriler Cad. No phone.

TAKSIM, TÜNEL & BEYOĞLU

Taksim is undeniably the heart of this city's commerce, while the entire district of Beyoğlu brings to mind characteristic back-street cafes, atmospheric bars, and stylish restaurants. While the tourists are shuttling between Taksim Square and Sultanahmet, the residents of Istanbul are making reservations in Beyoğlu. Twenty years ago this was not so, when Istiklal Caddesi looked more like the pre-Disney 42nd Street than the open-air shopping mall it is today. But tucked inside this neighborhood of opulent 19th-century mansions and former consulates are some of the classiest bars in town. Beyoğlu is still a neighborhood in transition, and the closer you get to Taksim Square, the seedier it gets.

Cezayir   The most popular locale among the new restaurants and cafes around the restored buildings of Francız Sokagı occupies an early 20th-century schoolhouse. There's a large garden shaded beneath enormous plane trees with separate corners for dining or lounging, and the food is creative without veering too far off the Turkish culinary map. There's an a la carte menu (appetizers and main courses 8YTL–28YTL/$6.95–$24/£3.20–£11) and a selection of prix-fixe menus, including a "cocktail menu" for those not in the mood for a full meal. Open daily 9am–2am. Hayriye Cad. 12 (follow Yeni Çarşı Cad. from Galatasaray High School and turn left on Hayriye Cad.). © 0212/245-9980. Reservations suggested.

Lokanta at Nu Pera/Nu Teras 𝕽𝕽𝕽   Nu Pera is actually the name of a renovated building in the neighborhood of Pera, now an utterly reborn neighborhood chock-full of cafes and restaurants. In summer the rooftop Lokanta Teras Restaurant offers an elegant and upscale atmosphere and views of a twinkling city—one of my favorite dining spots, actually. The blackboard *tapas* menu at the rear bar is a favorite. In winter, the party moves to more cramped quarters on the ground-floor level. Open daily noon–3pm and 7pm–12:30am (until 4am on weekends). Meşrutiyet Cad. 149, Tepebaşı. © 0212/245-6070.

360 Istanbul 𝕽𝕽   With views as good as this, it's no wonder that Istanbul is sprouting restaurant and bar venues in what are traditionally apartment or office buildings. 360 Istanbul takes advantage of the belfry of St. Antoine and panoramic views of the Golden Horn; on a cool summer's eve, there's really no better place to be. The decor is an unexpectedly pleasing amalgam of brick, steel, glass, and velvet; tables, alfresco banquettes, and a lounge area ensure that everybody gets something he or she wants. The Thai and Turkish menu is rather beside the point, although plenty of appetizers and finger foods will hold you over for the real meal. Go early for the best outdoor seating, or arrive late and mill about the wraparound terrace. Reservations are suggested for dinner (main courses 20YTL–34YTL/$17–$30/£8–£14). Mısır Apartment Building, Istiklal Cad. 32/311, Beyoğlu. ℭ 0212/251-1042.

Şarabı   This Istiklal wine bar looks like any other storefront cafe, but just a few steps down to the cellar—where those in the know head—is a late-19th-century underground aqueduct that people say runs from the British Embassy all the way to Tophane. The wine bar stocks more than 100 labels, including some of the better Turkish vintages. Try the Sarafin Cabernet, or the Karma Cabernet/Özküküzü blend. Open daily 11am–2am. Istiklal Cad. 80b, Beyoğlu. ℭ 0212/244-4609.

Taps   When asked for insider information on where locals go, an American-style brewery would seem an odd response. But there's the paradox: This *is* where the locals are going. (They're certainly not going to the Turkish Night show in the Galata Tower.) Taps serves seven or eight home brews, along with a typical American menu (finger foods, pizza, salads, wraps, and pasta). The original outlet is in Nişantaşı (Teşvikiye Cad. Atiye Sok. 5; ℭ 0212/296-2020), but this is more central. Sofyalı Sok. 11, Asmalımescit, Upper Tünel. ℭ 0212/245-7610.

Viktor Levi Şarap Evi   A veritable institution in Beyoğlu, Viktor Levi is one of Istanbul's oldest wine houses. The wrought iron is the first indication of the 19th-century origins of the wine bar; it's a great spot to head to if you're looking to "go where the locals go" (if there is only one such place). Impress your date by ordering a bottle of the Viktor Levi special house wine. Open daily 11am–2am. Hamalbaşi Cad. 12, Beyoğlu. ℭ 0212/249-6085.

V.S.O.P. Bar   Designed to re-create a traditional English library, V.S.O.P. is an elegant and definitely mature locale on the mezzanine level of the Marmara Istanbul. While I try to avoid hotel bars, this is actually an enjoyable spot for a drink and some conversation. Open daily noon–11pm (later on weekends). Taksim Meydanı, Taksim. ℭ 0212/251-4696.

ALONG THE BOSPHORUS

Istanbul's nightlife succumbs to the lure of the Bosphorus in the summer months (generally Apr until the end of Oct), moving alfresco and up to the seafront venues of Ortaköy and Kuruçeşme. Names tend to change seasonally, but the locations and general theme stay the same. The most popularly frequented venues at the time of writing are listed here.

Anjelique   This is a sister operation by the same people who bring us the majorly successful Vogue, Anna, A'jia, and da Mario (not all listed here). The formula seems unable to fail. Angelique takes up the top three floors above da Mario (creating a dining dilemma). Jazz and soul are played during dining hours, complementing a sensual decor backlit by the nighttime glow of the sea and sky. Dinner is served on the top two floors, while the lower floor is dedicated to the dynamic lounge. May–Oct restaurant 6pm–midnight, bar 7pm–4am. Muallim Naci Cad. Salhane Sok. 10, Ortaköy. ℭ 0212/327-2844.

Q Jazz   Q Jazz Bar cut its teeth in the cellar of the Çırağan Palace hotel before coming up to the hotel's garden terrace in summers. True to its elite lineage, Q now draws the cream of Istanbul society to its new location on the waterfront of Les Ottomans, where there's never an empty seat in the house. The bar and kitchen are open 7 nights a week, offering lobster, caviar, and other delectable appetizers. Open daily 7pm–dawn. Live music begins at 11pm. Muallim Naci Cad. 68, Kuruçeşme. © **0212/359-1500.** Cover 30YTL ($26/£12) after 11pm.

Reina   As the grande dame of after-hours entertainment, **Reina** is a multiplex of popular restaurants, a handful of waterfront dance floors, and bars, including the Zagat-rated Park Şamdan (reservations required for all restaurants). The music, as is the crowd, is eclectic; pretty much anything goes. Muallim Naci Cad. 44, Ortaköy. © **0212/ 259-5919.** Fri and Sat cover 30YTL ($26/£12).

8 Side Trips from Istanbul

BURSA: GATEWAY TO AN EMPIRE

243km (151 miles) south of Istanbul; 270km (168 miles) east of Çanakkale; 380km (236 miles) west of Ankara; 322km (200 miles) northeast of Izmir

Bursa established itself as an important center as far back as pre-Roman times, attracting emperors and rulers for its rich, fertile soil and healing thermal waters. The arrival of the Ottomans in 1326 ensured the city's prosperity as a cultural and economic center that now represents one of the richest legacies of early Ottoman art and architecture. As the first capital of the Ottoman Empire, Bursa became the beneficiary of the finest mosques, theological schools *(medreses),* humanitarian centers *(imarets),* and social services *(hans, hamams,* and public fountains). The density of arched portals, undulating domes, artfully tiled minarets, and magnificently carved *minbars* (pulpits) could easily provide the coursework for extensive study of the Ottomans, and without a doubt, fill multiple daylong walking tours.

Today Bursa is a thriving industrial and agricultural center, reputed for its fine silk and cotton textiles, and the center of Turkey's automobile industry. The nearby ski resorts at Mount Uludağ provide city dwellers with an easy weekend getaway, while others just make a special trip here to stock up on cotton towels. But many just flock here for the same reasons the Romans, Byzantines, and Ottomans did: the indulgence afforded by the density of rich hot mineral springs bubbling up all over the region.

If you plan on just a quick architectural and historical pilgrimage, you could reasonably make Bursa a day trip from Istanbul. An overnight excursion is more realistic if you want to make it a short spa getaway and leave time to wander through the exquisite *hans* (privately owned inns or marketplaces) of the early Ottoman era.

A LOOK AT THE PAST

It was common practice for a conquering king to attach his name to the cities that he founded, so the consensus is that King Prusia of Bithynia established a kingdom on the remains of a preexisting civilization here. Prusia (say it 10 times fast and it starts to sound like Bursa) of Olympus, distinguishing it from King Prusia's other conquests, was later leagued with Rome, a colonization that is attributed to the time of Eumenes II, leader of Pergamum. Bursa thrived, thanks to Rome's influence and the introduction of Christianity by the apostle Andrew. In the 6th century Emperor Justinian constructed baths and a lavish palace in the area, taking full advantage of the region's economic and thermal resources. From 1080 to 1326, Bursa bore the brunt of more than its fair share of invasions, with Selçuks, Turks, raiding Arabs, Byzantines, and Crusaders all trying to get a hold on this prosperous center. One of the Turkic tribes broke the chain when the Osmanlı tribe of Turks, led by Osman and later his son Orhan, entered Bursa in 1326 after a 10-year-long siege. Orhan established Bursa as the first permanent Ottoman capital, building a mosque and *medrese* on the site of a Byzantine monastery in what is now the Hisar District. The city expanded and thrived under sultans Murat I, Yıldırım Bayezit, Mehmet I, and Murad II. Bursa's importance began to wane when the Ottoman capital was transferred to Adrionople (present-day Edirne).

ESSENTIALS

GETTING THERE   From Istanbul's Yenikapı docks there are two ferry options for excursions to Bursa. The first is IDO's new service to the Güzelyalı port at Güzelyalı (© 0212/444-4436; www.ido.com.tr). The ferry takes 75 minutes and costs 20YTL ($17/£8) per person. There are five departures daily (six on Fri and Sun). From Güzelyalı to Bursa, take the local bus to the metro, which you will take to the last stop, arriving in the city center. Total time (including ferry, bus, and metro) from Istanbul to Bursa is about 2½ hours.

The other option from the Yenikapı docks in Istanbul is the 70-minute ferry ride (12YTL/$10/£4.80) to Yalova, north of Bursa. Ferries run every 2 hours in either direction beginning at 7:30am (last ferry 9:30pm). From the ferry landing, hop on one of the many buses lined up outside the gates; the ride to Bursa's *otogar* takes about 50 minutes and costs 7YTL ($6.10/£2.80). Bursa's *otogar* is located more than 9.5km (6 miles) out of town, so it will be necessary to either get on a municipal bus (no. 38 to Heykel or no. 96 to Çekirge) or take a taxi into town. The bus takes about half an hour and costs 1.50YTL ($1.30/60p). With luggage, this is a major stretch. Instead, a taxi is direct, quick, and cheap (expect to pay around 20YTL/$17/£8 for the 20-min. ride).

Both the ferry to Yalova and to Güzelyalı accept cars, so if you're not overly excited about the hoops you have to jump through to get there, you can shuttle yourself from the ferry docks straight into Bursa. IDO charges 60YTL ($52/£24) and 75YTL ($65/£30), respectively, for cars, plus 15YTL ($13/£6) and 10YTL ($8.70/£4) for each *additional* passenger in the vehicle.

If you prefer to do the entire journey by land, **Nilüfer Turizm** (© 0224/444-0099), which is based in Bursa, provides the most comprehensive bus service into Bursa in Turkey. The 4-hour trip costs 15YTL ($13/£6). **Metro** (© 0224/444-3455) runs buses almost hourly from Istanbul for the same price, as does **Kamil Koç** (© 0224/444-0562).

VISITOR INFORMATION   The **tourist information office** (© 0224/251-1834; fax 0224/220-1848) is hidden underneath Atatürk Caddesi in the center of town. If you're standing with Orhan Camii on your right and the Belediye (municipal building) on your left, the office is straight ahead of you at 12 o'clock. The PTT (post office) is located a few blocks west (to the right) down Atatürk Caddesi on the opposite side of the street.

All of the major bus companies have ticket offices around Heykel; tickets can also be purchased through any local travel agent or at the *otogar.*

ORIENTATION   The concentration of early Selçuk-inspired architecture is clustered in the commercial center of Bursa, in the area better known to the locals as **Heykel,** after the equestrian statue of Atatürk commanding the plaza just a few blocks to the east (*heykel* means "statue" in Turkish). Again, using the Tourist Information

---

Tips Turkish Towels & Such

If you're in the market for a few fluffy towels or one of those luscious Turkish bathrobes that sell for an arm and a leg in Bloomingdale's, the price for a selection at Bursa's **Covered Bazaar** (see "What to See & Do," below) can't be beat. The subtlest prints and plushest linens and towels are found at **Özdilek,** with branches in both the bazaar (exit the underground passage opposite the PTT and walk 1 block in) and a shopping center at Yenı Yalova Yolu 4, on the highway from the *otogar* (© **0224/219-6000**). Silk fabrics, such as scarves, blouses, and tablecloths, are available in shops on the upper level of **Koza Han,** the historic *bedesten* (covered market) next to Orhan Camii. For modern merchandise in a slick mall setting, the new glass pyramid-topped **Zafer Plaza** houses franchises such as Quicksilver, Vakko, Demirel, Mavi Jeans, and Polo Garage.

---

office for orientation, to the west/right is **Tophane Park** and the **Hisar District,** where the conquering Ottoman armies set up their capital in the 15th century. The road leads into the posher **Çekirge** section, where ambassadors and statesmen flock for the hotels and thermal hot springs. The winter ski resort of Uludağ is located about 36km (22 miles) to the south of Bursa and reachable via a funicular from the center of town.

GETTING AROUND   In all likelihood, you will spend most of your time between the Heykel and Çekirge neighborhoods. While covering small distances on foot in either neighborhood is possible, the two are just too far apart to think about walking between them. Instead, hop on a *dolmuş*—in Bursa, *dolmuşes* are group taxis—running conveniently along the main arteries. (The street names change so many times that it's useless to mention them here.) *Dolmuşes* cost around 3YTL ($2.60/£1.20) and are distinguishable from the multiple destinations marked on the roof of the car. A taxi taking the same route will cost about 10YTL ($8.70/£4).

WHAT TO SEE & DO

Bursa is so jam-packed with historic structures that it would be impossible to list them all here. In addition to the major sites named below, be sure to wander through the marketplace, spread out among open-air and covered streets. *Hans* are traditionally double-storied arcaded buildings with a central courtyard, usually occupied by an ornate fountain or pool or raised *mescit* (a small mosque). The *hans* are still used for trade and make lovely shaded retreats to take a coffee outdoors and poke amid the local merchandise. The **Fidan Han** dates to the 15th century and has a central pool topped by a *mescit.* The **Pirinç Han** (closed) was constructed by Beyazit II to earn the revenue necessary to cover the expenses of his mosque and soup kitchen in Istanbul. The **Ipek Han** is the largest *han* in Bursa and contains an octagonal *mescit* in the center of the courtyard. The revenue from this *han* was used to pay for the construction of the Yeşil Mosque. The courtyard of **Emir Han** has a graceful marble pool with exterior faucets to allow for ablutions.

Archaeology Museum (Arkeoloji Müzesi)   Constructed with the charm of any 1972 institutional project, this museum is worth the 30 minutes it will take to get through, especially if you're strolling through Çekirge or into Kültür Park. The fact that the attendant trails you to turn the lights on and off is a bit unnerving (the museum doesn't see that many tourists), obliging you to react with an appropriate level of enthusiasm. The museum houses regional artifacts dating back to the 3rd century B.C., with crude pottery and tools from as far back as the Neolithic period. Particularly impressive is the collection of ceramic and glass objects from the classical era, much of which has remained surprisingly intact. The extensive collection of coins displayed on the mezzanine is significant because notable figures had a habit of emblazoning their portraits on the face of the piece, providing a rare window of tangibility into the ancients.

Kültür Park. 🕐 **0224/220-2029**. Admission 2YTL ($1.75/80p). Tues–Sun 8:30am–noon and 1–5pm.

Atatürk Museum (Atatürk Müzesi)
This is one of those traditional timber mansions where you'd love to get a closer look. The historic rooms have been left as they were when Atatürk slept here on his visits to Bursa, down to the very last particle of dust.

Çekirge Cad., next to the Çelik Palas. 🕐 **0224/236-4844**. Free admission. Tues–Sun 8:30am–noon and 1–5pm.

Bursa Museum of Turkish and Islamic Arts (Türk Islam Eser. Müzesi) 🎯
Housed in the former *medrese* of the Green Mosque, built in 1419 by Çelebi Sultan Mehmet along with the other buildings in the Yeşil complex, this museum is worth a look, particularly because they've gone to the trouble of providing English translations. The exhibits are intimately displayed in small rooms around a central courtyard. There's a space devoted to dervish cult objects, a *hamam* (Turkish bath) room displaying silver clogs and silk embroidered bath accessories, and a model of a traditional Turkish coffeehouse, complete with barber's chair. The collection also includes Selçuk ceramics, inlaid wood pieces, and objects in iron, copper, bronze, and wood. A visit takes under 30 minutes.

Yeşil Cad., on the left just before the Green Mosque. 🕐 **0224/327-7679**. Admission 2YTL ($1.75/80p). Tues–Sun 8:30am–5pm.

Covered Bazaar (Bedesten)
The covered bazaar that stands on the site is a modern version of the original that was built by Yıldırım Bayezit in the 14th century and leveled in the earthquake of 1855. There's no glitz—or tourists—here, evidenced by the distressing concentration of satin-embroidered towels and bedspreads. Keep your eyes open for good-quality baby clothes and knockoff sportswear, and if you're looking to stuff a throw pillow, this is the place to do it, as stalls displaying fluffy unspun cotton of varying composition and quality abound.

Enter through Koza Hanı, or follow Çarşı Cad. from Ulu Camii. Daily 8:30am–7pm.

The Great Mosque (Ulu Camii) 🎯🎯
When the building was erected in 1396, architects were just beginning to dabble in the problem of covering large spaces with small domes, and the result is the first example of a monumental Ottoman multidomed mosque. The 20 domes, supported on 12 stout pillars, are better admired from within, where the final result comes together in the mosque's five naves and four bays.

The date of completion (802H—H is for *hicret,* the day Mohammed left Mecca for Medina) is inscribed on the pulpit door, but several waves of renovations were necessary after the invasion of Tamerlane, with major restorations completed after the earthquake of 1855.

The wooden *minbar* (pulpit) is a masterwork of carved geometric and floral reliefs, as are the banister work and other wood details. But the main focus of the mosque is the three-tiered **ablution fountain** beneath a large light well. Although this has its practical purposes, the result is an embracing sensation of serenity, and many worshippers remain on the raised platforms surrounding the fountain for long moments of meditation.

Bursa center. Free admission. Daily dawn–dusk.

Green Mosque (Yeşil Camii) 𝒜
Commanding a hillside terrace above the city, Yeşil Camii takes its name from the color of the green and blue tiles in the interior. Intent on leaving his mark on Bursa, Mehmet I ordered the construction of this mosque, built entirely of hewn stone and marble, as a monument to the victorious ending of his 10-year struggle for the throne. Although an architect's inscription over the portal gives the completion date as 1419, the final decorations were ordered in 1424 on the orders of Murad II, and the two minarets were added in the 19th century.

One of the first mosques to employ an inverted T-floor plan, the building signals the dawn of a new Turkish architectural tradition. The "Turkish pleat," an ingenious geometric corner detail allowing for the placement of a circular dome atop a square base, is a design device original to Turkey, while the use of multicolored ceramic tile, an influence that arrived with Tamerlane, is intricate enough to make your head spin. The high porcelain *mihrab* (a niche oriented toward Mecca) is a masterpiece of Ottoman ceramic art, difficult to miss at an understated 10m (33 ft.) high. In the center of the *mihrab* in Arabic script is the word "Allah," mounted on the wall at a later date.

The sumptuous gold mosaics and tile of the imperial loge were probably an overstated attempt at one-upping the loggia that served the Byzantine emperors; it is flanked on either side by the servants' quarters and the harem, and a closer look is at the discretion of the caretaker.

East of Heykel at the end of Yeşil Cad. Free admission. Daily dawn–dusk.

Green Tomb (Yeşil Türbesi) 𝒜𝒜
This Selçuk-influenced tomb, representing one of the noblest of its era, has become the symbol of Bursa. If you're looking for a blue building, look no further, as the tiles of this hexagonal structure are actually turquoise, topped by a lead dome resting on a plaster rim. The construction of the tomb was ordered by the tenant himself, Sultan Mehmet I, and was completed around 1421. The color glazing of the interior tile work is an outstanding example of the art, from the window pediments adorned with verses of the Koran and *hadiths* (narrations of the life of Mohammad) in Arabic script, to the tile inscriptions on the sarcophagi. It's also worth noting the workmanship of the colors of the panels on the *mihrab*, which change color according to your perspective.

East of Heykel at the end of Yeşil Cad. Free admission. Daily 8am–noon and 1–5pm.

Koza Hanı 𝒜𝒜
Meaning "Cocoon Inn," this caravansary was built in 1490 by Bayezit II to raise funds for his mosque in Istanbul. Built on two levels, the inn provided a place for the merchants to trade the last of their goods, as this was the final stop on the Silk Road from China. In the middle of the courtyard is a small **şadırvan** (ablution fountain) 𝒜 for the small *mescit* (prayer room) poised above; in the summer the verdant space becomes a peaceful tea garden. The monumental portal decorated with turquoise tiles and carvings leads into the covered bazaar. Today the Koza Hanı

continues its legacy of trading in silk with shops and boutiques stocked with scarves and fabrics at exorbitant (and extremely negotiable) prices.

Bursa Center. Free admission. Daily 8:30am–sunset.

Muradiye Complex (Muradiye Külliye) ✮✮   Constructed by Murat II between 1424 and 1426, this complex includes a mosque, a *medrese,* a soup kitchen, a bath, and a royal cemetery found within an overgrown garden of roses, magnolias, and cypress trees. Although the entrance to the grounds is open, many of the tombs and even the mosque are locked up, but the idle yet earnest ticket-window attendant will catch up with you for a private tour of the grounds, proudly locking and unlocking the royal tombs.

The Murat Paşa Mosque is a typical example of early Ottoman architecture, although the *mihrab* and *minbar* are 18th-century baroque. Reverently displayed inside on the upper-left-hand wall is an original piece from the Kaa'ba in Mecca.

To the right, beginning toward the rear of the grounds, is no ordinary cemetery. The 12 stately tombs serve as the final resting places of not only some of the first sultans, but a sobering number of members of the royal family as well, including Hüma Hatun (mother of Mehmet the Conqueror), Shehzade Ahmed (son of Beyazit II and crown prince), Sultan Murat II, Mustafa (son of Süleyman the Magnificent), and Gülşah Hatun (wife of Mehmet the Conqueror). Because succession rights relied not on heredity but on survival of the fittest, it was standard, even expected, practice for the victorious leader to cover his back by strangling his brothers with a wire cord.

The most recognizable casualty of this practice was the son of Süleyman the Magnificent: Şehzade (Prince) Mustafa, who as object of a plot spun by Roxelana for the succession of her own son was unjustly murdered at the hands of his father. Ironically, the tomb was built by Selim II, Roxelana's son and successor to the throne.

The recently restored opulence of the tomb and its outstanding porcelain tiling is indicative of why the technique for reproducing the superior Iznik tiles is impossible. In contrast, the mausoleum of Murad I, son of Orhan and third Ottoman sultan, is elegant in its simplicity. The tomb has a domed central courtyard surrounded by the traditional ambulatory. Upon the request of the sultan, an oculus was designed in the dome to allow the rains to wash over the open tomb, symbolizing his sameness with the plain folk.

After reigning for just 18 days and living the rest of his life in exile, Cem Sultan, the youngest son of Mehmed II, was brought back to Bursa to receive a royal burial in the tomb that had actually been built for Şehzade Mustafa.

The 15th-century *medrese,* now operating as a clinic, was designed around a central courtyard accessible through vaulted arches at the entrance. No one will bother you if you want to take a quick peek, but the main use for this clinic is as a tuberculosis dispensary, so it might be better to do your admiring from the outside.

The Tarihi II Murat Hamamı next to the mosque is still in operation, with separate days designated for men and women.

Çekirge (from the town center, take *dolmuş* marked MURADIYE). Free admission. Tues–Sun 8:30am–noon and 1–5pm.

Orhan Gazi Mosque (Orhan Camii) ✮✮   Constructed between 1339 and 1340 by Orhan Gazi, this is one of the most important early Ottoman constructions in Bursa. Pointed arches on the veranda show the beginnings of a particularly Ottoman detail, while the exterior brickwork recalls its Selçuk origins. The mosque was damaged in

---

Fun Fact **They Died with a Smile (or, That Joke's a Killer)**

When Sultan Orhan arrived in Bursa, he immediately set out to build his mosque. He appointed a man named **Hacıvad** as supervisor, who in turn hired a local blacksmith named **Karagöz** to oversee the installation of the iron supports. Hacıvad and Karagöz used to pass the time with clever quips and witty conversation that kept the laborers in stitches. The two eventually had the workmen doubled over in hysterics, to the point that work on the mosque came to a complete halt.

When the sultan found out about the construction delays, he had Hacıvad and Karagöz hanged (or decapitated, depending on which interpretation of the oral history you hear). The decapitated version is favored, because illustrators have had a grand time depicting the two hapless jokers approaching the sultan's throne to protest with their heads under their arms. Whichever demise, the outcome is the same: Orhan finds someone to relate the dialogues, until the sultan, too, is keeling over with laughter. Realizing his error, the sultan orders a local leather worker to create lifelike figures of the two, so that they can continue their legacy of comedy. This puppetlike shadow play gained momentum and grew into a popular cultural tradition, boasting as many as 200 characters in one presentation.

As you drive from the center of town toward Çekirge, ask your driver to point out the **Karagöz Hacıvad Memorial,** a small but colorful representation of the two folk heroes.

1413 by Karamanoğlu Mehmet Bey and repaired in 1417 by Çelebi Sultan Mehmet. Note the star-shaped decorations representing the course of the sun, and the marble embellishments on the eastern and western facades.

The surrounding complex is one of the first in the Ottoman tradition, consisting of a mosque, *medrese,* soup kitchen, bath, and inn. The cats apparently stay there free of charge, and the whole courtyard and mosque interior have a homey feel.

Bursa town center, across from the municipal building. Free admission. Daily dawn–dusk.

Tombs of Osman and Orhan ✮ This lovely park attracts local tourists as much for its tea gardens and stunning views as for the **tombs** of the two founders of the Ottoman Empire. The location in the *Hisar* (fortress), the oldest section of the city, which passed from Roman to Byzantine and finally to Ottoman hands, is a fitting one for the final resting places of Osman Gazi and Orhan Gazi.

According to Osman Gazi's wish to be "laid to rest beneath the silver dome of Bursa," his tomb was constructed on the chapel of St. Elie, the Byzantine monastery formerly on the site. The sarcophagus, surrounded by an ornate brass balustrade, is decorated with mother-of-pearl inlay. At one time, the building also contained the tomb of Orhan, but after it was partially destroyed by fire and then leveled by the 1855 earthquake, Sultan Abdülaziz had Orhan's tomb rebuilt separately. The Orhan tomb, slightly less ornate than his father's tomb, was constructed on the foundation of an 11th-century Byzantine church, from which some mosaics in the floor have survived.

Hisar District (inside the entrance to Tophane Park along Arka Sokağı, just west of the post office). No phone. Free admission. Daily dawn–dusk.

Uluumay Ottoman Museum 🟇 The restored architectural gem that is the Sair Ahmet Medrese rivals the museum within. Located in the Muradiye Complex, this assemblage of folk art was collected from around the Ottoman Empire, including the Caucuses, the Balkans, and the home territory of Anatolia. There's an ample ethnographic exhibition that features over 400 pieces of Ottoman-era jewelry, plus household items, saddlebags, silk scarves, and silver watch fobs. To name a few.

Sair Ahmet Paşa Medresesi, Muradiye Camisi Karşısı, Beşikçiler Cad., Muradiye. 🕽 **0224/225-4813.** Admission 3YTL ($2.60/£1.20). Tues–Sun 9am–6:30pm (closed at 6pm Sept–Apr).

Yıldırım Bayezit Mosque (Yıldırım Bayezit Camii) The two prominent domes, set one behind the other, represent an attempt at a design feature reminiscent of the St. Irene of Constantinople and the St. John's Basilica at Ephesus. Awkwardly juxtaposed above the three remaining domes, the larger two create a prayer hall that was to become a theme in the architecture of Ottoman mosques.

The mosque forms a part of the *külliye,* or complex, comprising a *medrese,* a *hamam,* a hospital, and the tomb of the Sultan Bayezit I, built by his son Süleyman the Magnificent in 1406.

Northeast of the town center in the Yıldırım District. Free admission. Daily dawn–dusk.

WHERE TO STAY

Hotel Çelik Palas 🟇🟇 Built in the 1930s under instructions by Atatürk, the Çelik Palas holds the title as Turkey's first five-star hotel. Until recently, this acclaimed Turkish icon was showing its dubious pedigree, but thanks to a recent upgrade, the Çelik Palas is once again at the top of its game. The best rooms—those facing the mountains—each combine the space of two rooms forming comfortably plush junior suites, with such luxuries as two bathrooms (one with a massage shower, the other a Jacuzzi tub), stylish furniture, and a sofa bed that increases the room capacity to four. Rooms in the annex are rarely used, making this end of the hotel great for groups. Best of all, there's the large, domed, **marble thermal pool,** the crown jewel of a small wellness facility that's free for guests (see "Water, Water Everywhere: Turkey's Mineral Springs," below).

Çekirge Cad. 79, 16070 Çekirge, Bursa. 🕽 **0224/233-3800.** Fax 0224/236-1910. www.celikpalasotel.com. 158 units. 270YTL ($235/£108) double; 320YTL–570YTL ($278–$496/£128–£228) suite. AE, DC, MC, V. On-site parking. **Amenities:** Restaurants; bars; large thermal pool; spa (w/Turkish bath, Jacuzzi, and sauna); concierge; tour desk; car-rental desk; shopping arcade; salon; 24-hr. room service; massage; laundry service; dry cleaning; nonsmoking rooms. *In room:* A/C, wireless Internet, cable TV, minibar, hair dryer, safe.

Kervansaray Termal Hotel 🟇 This is the preferred hotel in Bursa, one that never lets you forget you're in a town of thermal springs. There's a decorative waterfall in the modern lobby, two swimming pools, and a renovated multidomed 700-year-old *hamam.* Most rooms have a balcony with a valley, mountain, or garden view, but frankly are nothing to write home about. The health club's cleverly designed swimming pool is divided by a retractable window, providing for both indoor and outdoor swimming, and the water is supplied by nearby mineral springs.

Çekirge Meydanı, 16080 Çekirge, Bursa. 🕽 **0224/233-9300.** Fax 0224/233-9324. www.kervansarayhotels.com/ bursa. 224 units. Summer 150€ ($218/£107) double; 250€ ($363/£179) and up suite; rates lower June–Dec. Rates go up for religious festivals. AE, MC, V. **Amenities:** 2 restaurants; 2 bars; outdoor swimming pool; fitness room; historic thermal bath w/separate sections for men and women; concierge; tour desk; car-rental desk; meeting and banquet facilities; shopping arcade; salon; 24-hr. room service; massage; laundry service; dry cleaning. *In room:* A/C, satellite TV, minibar, hair dryer.

Safran Hotel The first guesthouse in Bursa, this hotel occupies a beautiful saffron-colored Ottoman mansion on a historic street across from Tophane Park. Rooms are characterized by old mattresses and worn flannel or print bedspreads, making the entire experience more like spending the weekend in a friend's garret. This of course assumes a minimum level of cleanliness, and the rattiness itself can be somewhat charming.

Ortapazar Cad. Arka Sok. 4, 16040 Bursa (near the gated entrance to the Osman and Orhan tombs). ℂ **0224/224-7216.** Fax 224/224-7219. 10 units. $90 (£45) double. AE, MC, V. **Amenities:** Children's playroom; laundry; dry cleaning; parking. *In room:* A/C, cable TV, minibar, hair dryer, safe.

WHERE TO DINE

Çiçek Izgara TURKISH/KÖFTE There's nothing worse than wandering around the center of a busy town and not knowing where to eat. Çiçek Izgara comes highly recommended by the locals, combining three floors of white linen tablecloths and impeccable service with the bright casualness of a cafeteria. Menu items include *peynerli köfte* (meatballs with cheese), *kabak dolması* (stuffed zucchini), and *cacık,* a refreshing yogurt soup.

Belediye Cad. (just after Orhan Camii on the left, 2nd floor). ℂ **0224/221-6526.** Kebaps and *köfte* 7YTL–12YTL ($6.10–$10/£2.80–£4.80). MC, V. Daily 10am–midnight.

Uludağ Kebapçısı ☆☆ ISKENDER KEBAPS The best food is often found in unremarkable, even divelike places. Although Grandpa Iskender has the historical corner on the *döner kebap* recipe, this place has perfected it. Located in two narrow storefronts near the old bus terminal, the Uludağ Kebapçısı is arguably the best place in the world to eat the Iskender *döner kebap.* You can order it with decadent slices of steak *(bonfile),* surprisingly delicious kidney *(böbrek),* or what the owner called "back" *(kantıfile)*—but don't complain to me if your cholesterol levels shoot through the roof: Uludağ goes through 18kg (40 lb.) of butter per day. Throw caution to the wind and top it all off with the *sütlü helva,* a heavenly milk pudding served mainly in the cooler months.

Garaj Karşısı Şirin Sok. 12. ℂ **0224/254-7264.** Kebaps 10YTL ($8.70/£4). MC, V. Daily 11am–midnight.

IZNIK & NICAEA: A PILGRIMAGE AND SOME PLATES

To Turks, the sleepy lakeside resort of Iznik provides a respite from the sweltering summer sun; to Christendom, Iznik sits atop modern-day **Nicaea,** the former seat of the Eastern Roman Empire and the site of the first and second Ecumenical councils. It's also synonymous with Ottoman ceramic art, which reached its pinnacle in the 15th and 16th centuries during the reign of Süleyman the Magnificent. While you're here, you should take the time to have lunch at one of the lakeside restaurants.

GETTING THERE & GETTING AROUND *Dolmuşes* regularly depart from Yalova from the main road that passes in front of the ferryboat landing (cross the street and hop on one headed south) as well as from Bursa. Once in Iznik, buses deposit passengers on the main road in front of the church. Drivers should take the car ferry from Istanbul to Yalova. From Yalova, they should follow the road to Bursa taking the first turnoff at Orhangazi to Iznik and follow the road along the north side of the lake.

Iznik retains the grid plan established in its Hellenistic era. Monuments are well signposted, but without a car, you'll be pounding the pavement for the better part of a day.

Water, Water Everywhere: Turkey's Mineral Springs

A geologic oddity-cum-spa treat with which Turkey is uncommonly blessed is the mineral spring. Thermal baths flow freely throughout the country-side, and depending on the properties and temperature of the water, are reputed to address such varied ailments as obesity, digestive problems, rheumatism, and urological disorders. Soaking in the springs and covering yourself with mineral-rich mud are some of the country's lesser-known pleasures. You can experience the thermal springs enclosed in pamper-me surroundings or in humble out-of-the-way sites. (In addition to the places listed below, see "Area Thermals," in chapter 6.)

In Bursa, history and pampering go hand in hand, and no historical pil-grimage to this city would be complete without a long soak in a mineral-rich thermal pool. The **Kervansaray Hotel's 700 year-old thermal bath** ⊛⊛, Çekirge Meydanı, 16080 Çekirge (© **0224/233-9300**), takes advantage of the **Eski Kaplica** thermal spring, an ancient source used as far back as Roman times. The bath was built in grand Ottoman style by Sultan Murat I in 1389, and a soak here (7am–11pm) is made all the more satisfying with its multi-ple domes and old stone masonry.

No one knows who originally occupied the **Yeni Kaplıca** *hamam* ⊛⊛, Yeni Kaplıca Cad. 6, Çekirge (© **0224/236-6968**; 13YTL/$11/£5.20 entrance to men's side; 10YTL/$8.70/£4 women's entrance; 6YTL/$5.20/£2.40 slough-ing; 12YTL/$10/£4.80 massage), built in 1555 and reconstructed for Süley-man the Magnificent by Grand Vizier Rüstem Paşa. The *hamam* (or at least, the men's side) still displays its original opulence, allowing wide-eyed tourists to feel like Julius Caesar for a day.

Separated from the Yeni Kaplıca building by a tea garden is the less impressive **Kaynarca,** Yeni Kaplıca Cad. 8 (© **0224/236-6955**; 6YTL/$5.20/£2.40 entrance; treatments extra), essentially a mud pit catering to women only. **Kara Mustafa Paşa Thermal Bath,** Mudanya Cad. 10 (© **0224/236-6956**), was left over from the Byzantine era and was actually the first building on the site. There are two sections, including one where you can ooze yourself into a gravelike, tile ditch full of scorching-hot mud (avoid wearing a white bathing suit for this). There are also the regular bath facilities and cubicles for changing and resting. Kara Mustafa also has rudimentary hotel accommoda-tions. Granted, it's all rather gritty, but thoroughly worth the experience. The more luxurious **Hotel Çelik Palas thermal pool** ⊛⊛, Çekirge Cad. 79, 16070 Çekirge, Bursa (© **0224/233-3800**; 30YTL/$26/£12 entrance for nonguests, free for guests), rests beneath a single multiple-skylit dome; the hotel's facil-ity offers opulence while the others excel in local character.

WHAT TO SEE & DO

Ancient Nicaea   The ancient city is enclosed along the eastern edge of Lake Iznik by about 5km (3 miles) of **ancient city walls** ⊛, made accessible through several ancient gates of which the **Istanbul Kapısı** ⊛ is the best preserved. In the center of town are the well-preserved remains of the **Church of Ayasofya** ⊛⊛ (admission

2YTL/$1.75/80p), an 11th-century church that served as the Patriarchate during the period of exile following the Fourth Crusade. The church preserves parts of the mosaic flooring and a partially exposed fresco of the Pantocrator in the niche of the left aisle. Excavations conducted in 1935, however, revealed traces of an older structure dating to the 6th century and attributed to Justinian.

Near the southwest corner of the church (across the street) are partially uncovered outdoor tile-production workshops from as early as the 15th century. Many of the **brick and mud kilns** are still intact.

The **Yeşil Cami** dates to the late 14th century and displays a minaret covered with tiles in a colorful zigzag pattern. Unfortunately, these are not originals, as the actual tiles were destroyed. Across the street is the **Nilüfer Hatun Imareti,** built by Murat I and named after his mother, wife of Orhan Gazi and a Greek princess in her own right. Originally used as a charitable foundation and soup kitchen, the well-restored *imaret* (soup kitchen) now contains the **Iznik Museum** (admission 2YTL/ $1.75/80p), housing a small collection of Roman and Byzantine artifacts and remnants from nearby burial mounds. There's also a small collection of Iznik tiles, as well as several ethnological items.

Thirty years of excavations have barely made a dent in the uncovering of the **Roman Theatre,** built by Pliny the Younger between 111 and 113 during his time as governor of Bythinia. Rather than building the theater into the side of a hill, the theater was constructed using vaults.

Iznik, Bursa.

The Iznik Foundation   Tiles, richly decorated with floral designs and colors recalling precious gems, served as architectural decoration in the palace, mosques, tombs, and other buildings with a predominantly religious function. (The sultan was also the caliph, extending religious function into the palace.) For this reason, Iznik ceramics represent one of the most important examples of Islamic art. Sadly, with the decline of the economic and political power of the Ottoman Empire, artisans and ateliers became less and less in demand, and ultimately the techniques used to make the ceramics were lost.

Thanks to the Iznik Foundation, this great artistic tradition is enjoying a steady revival. The foundation, which consists of an educational facility, a research laboratory, and a commercial center, has invested an enormous amount of energy in researching the technologies necessary for achieving success in each complex step of production. One of the first challenges is the acquisition of the raw materials, as authentic Iznik pieces contain a high ratio of quartz, a semiprecious stone. The remaining obstacles are technical, involving the proper ratio of quartz, the chemical composition of each pigment, and the correct application of heat (each pigment must be fired at a different temperature). Ottoman artisans labored their entire lives to perfect just one aspect of the product, with one person expert in the creation of coral red, another in cobalt blue, and yet another in maintaining accurate and consistent heat to a wood-fired kiln made of brick. The foundation's finished products are faithful copies of the originals that sell at prices competitive with the inferior products sold in Avanos (see "A Side Trip to Avanos," in chapter 8, "Cappadocia & the Interior"). The price of a plate or tile at the foundation can reach the stratosphere, but remember, these are made of quartz, while the fakes are made of clay. The Iznik Foundation is open to visitors and is also equipped with nine guest accommodations for those wishing to stay overnight. They also have a main office in Istanbul at Kuruçeşme Öksüz Çocuk Sok. 14, Beşiktaş (© **0212/287-3243**).

Sahil Yolu Halı Saha Arkası, Iznik. © **0224/757-6025.** Fax 0224/757-5737. www.iznik.com.

THE PRINCES' ISLANDS

The Princes' Islands are just a hop, skip, and a jump from Istanbul, and a well-received respite from the chaos and scorching sun of the city. The islands were originally used as a place of exile for members of the royalty and clergy during the age of Byzantium. It was later taken over by the more clever residents of the city as summer homes. The atmosphere is one of pure repose thanks to the prohibition against vehicles; the only form of transportation here (besides your own steam) is the characteristic and charming horse-drawn phaeton.

Thanks to the introduction of seabuses that shorten the ferry trip by an hour, the islands are only a half-hour away, making them an accessible retreat from city life.

GETTING THERE Ferries to the islands depart from the Kabataş docks adjacent to Dolmabahçe Palace and make stops at Kadıköy on the Asian side, Kınalıada, Burgazada, Heybeliada, and Büyükada. The ride all the way to Büyükada takes about 2 hours and costs 2YTL ($1.75/80p) each way. The faster catamaran shortens the trip from Kabataş to Büyükada to about 45 minutes including one stop at Heybeliada (June–Sept; © **0212/444-4436;** www.ido.com.tr). The trip costs a mere 5.50YTL ($4.80/£2.20) each way, a pittance considering that seats are reserved compared to the body shuffle inevitable on the more crowded slow boat. From Bostancı on the Asian side, there's limited direct service to Büyükada (departing at 7 and 7:30am weekdays and 9:10am on Sat and Sun). Weekend service continues on from Büyükada to the other three islands before ending at Kabataş. The one-way fare is 2.50YTL ($2.20/£1). Be sure to confirm all departure times in advance, as schedules may change.

EXPLORING THE PRINCES' ISLANDS Thanks to the absence of motorized vehicles, the islands have managed to retain their old-world charm. Horse-drawn carriages serve as local taxis, and bicycles share the meandering roads with domestic donkeys. As expected, Istanbullus inundate the islands in the summer, looking to enjoy the characteristic architecture of the many Victorian-style clapboard mansions along with a relaxing day at the beach.

Big Island, or Büyükada, is the largest of the five islands and the one most inundated during high season. There are several good beaches, diving facilities, and the old hilltop monastery of Ayayorgı (St. George), from which you can almost see all the way back to Istanbul. To get to the monastery, take a carriage to Luna Park and take the 30-minute uphill path to Ayayorgi Peak, where you can sip their homemade wine while enjoying the panorama at the monastery's simple restaurant on the hill. To better appreciate what the islands have to offer, organize your excursion for a weekday, when the ferries are not packed like sardine cans and you can still get a glimpse of the sand beneath the blankets of the other sun worshippers. In the fall a stroll along the

---

Fun Fact **Trotsky at the Beach**

Leon Trotsky spent the first years of his exile from the Soviet Union on Büyükada, from 1929 to 1933.

deserted cobblestone lanes met by the occasional donkey cart or a friendly pack of hopeful stray dogs transports you countless years back in time.

Kınalıada was the site of a major human rights infraction—the Byzantines gouged out the eyes of and exiled Romanos Diogenes IV here for his defeat by the Selçuks in the Battle of Manzikert. The monastery built for the unfortunate general is still standing. The island was raided many times by pirates and later inhabited mainly by Armenians, but because of a harsh climate, it has attracted fewer people than the other islands. Electricity first came to the island in 1946, and it wasn't until the 1980s that the island received a water supply from the municipality. Kınalıada is also the only one of the Princes' Islands without the services of the 19th-century phaetons.

Burgazada is the second of the Princes' Islands, originally settled as a Greek fishing village. In the 1950s the island attracted the wealthy Jews of Istanbul, who restored existing mansions or built their own. The island is also the home of a famous Turkish writer, Sait Faik, whose home has been turned into a museum. There are two swim clubs near the ferry landing, but if it's beaches you're after, you'll be better off on one of the other islands.

Heybeliada is the island closest to Büyükada and similar in character in that the natural beauty attracts boatloads of weekenders in the summer. The waterside promenade ensures a steady stream of visitors looking to avoid the crowds over on Büyükada, but aside from a few eateries, you'll have to make this a day trip or book a room on Büyükada anyway.

WHERE TO STAY Fantasy becomes reality on Büyükada, the biggest of the islands but not so built up that you want to avoid it. That's why the listings here are all on the "Big Island." The **Splendid Palace Hotel,** 23 Nisan Cad. (turn right at the Büyükada Princess Hotel and drop your jaw at the white domed mansion on your left; © **0216/382-6950;** fax 0216/382-6775; www.splendidhotel.net; double in summer 120YTL/$104/£48), is a palatial clapboard house with views of the Marmara with peaceful gardens, a private swimming pool, two restaurants, and an on-site patisserie. It's closed November through March. The newly renovated (2007) **Büyükada Princess Hotel,** Iskele Meydanı 2 (straight up the street from the ferry landing on the right; © **0216/382-1628;** fax 0216/382-1949; www.buyukadaprincess.com; double 110YTL–160YTL/$96–$139/£44–£64), is a more modest but gracious seaside lodge and is open year-round. There's a small pool overlooking the Marmara Sea for use in the summer months.

WHERE TO DINE Restaurants specializing in fish line the wharf to the left of the ferry landing, for breezy and atmospheric waterside dining. **Kalamar Restaurant,** Gülistan Cad. 10, Büyükada (© **0216/382-1245**), is one of the first waterside restaurants that you encounter as you make your way down the wharf. **Milano Restaurant,** Gülistan Cad. 8, Büyükada (© **0216/382-6352**), just a few doors down, has been here for more than 35 years and is the most famous restaurant on the island. More reasonable meals (minus the view) can be had in the main square at **Yıldızlar Caféteria,** Iskele Cad. 2, Büyükada (© **0216/382-4360**), actually a 100-year-old cafeteria and tea garden serving *döner kebaps,* grilled cheese sandwiches, and the Turkish fast-food favorite, *lahmacun.*

5

Çanakkale, Gallipoli & the Troad

The Troad is the ancient name for the region that included **Troy** plus nearly 100 other ancient cities (most still deprived of the light of day). Among the most important of these are **Assos, Alexandria-Troas, Dardanos,** and **Chryse,** spread out amidst olive groves, fertile plains, undulating mountains, and crystal seas. The city of **Çanakkale** presides over a region that for centuries—even millennia—was forced to defend a legacy of geographical advantage. The region became victim to the ambitions of empires, as emperors and armies swept through to stake their claims.

The lands of Turkey's Northern Aegean provided the first taste of Asia to those successful in crossing the Bosphorus or breaching the Dardanelle Straits, and the last obstacle to any attempted conquest of Istanbul, as an army's advancement into the Marmara region left the great city surrounded and isolated. Throughout history, each of these civilizations left its own personal mark, from Xerxes through Alexander the Great to Gazi Mehmet the Conqueror. The layers of culture superimposed over the pastoral countryside make for an enriching visit to any of the destinations outlined in this chapter. Plus, the Hellespont boasts some of the Aegean's most scenic beaches.

This region of the country, while popular among the city slickers of Istanbul, remains blissfully ignored by the tourist hoards, leaving you and me to still (for now) experience the Turkey of yesteryear—before its era of Europeanization. If you're crunched for time, make any of the destinations an overnight or weekend trip; literally hundreds of tour companies in Istanbul advertise affordable excursions with guides.

1 Çanakkale

15km (9⅓ miles) north of Troy; 325km (202 miles) southwest of Istanbul; 331km (206 miles) north of Izmir; 303km (188 miles) west of Bursa

This charming port in the Dardanelles is also the gateway to the battlefields of Gallipoli and the ill-fated city of Troy. When not touring, there's much to enjoy in this corner of the northern Aegean, with easy access to a handful of resort islands.

A visit to the area begins in and around the small fishing port and holiday resort of Çanakkale. There are a handful of satisfactory bed-and-breakfast-style hotels in the city center, conveniently located near transport and tour companies offering guided tours to Troy and Gallipoli (p. 174).

There's not much else to do in town except visit the Naval Museum and stroll up and down the promenade. Extremely minor highlights are of the Clock Tower; a gift from the Italian Consulate as a gift to the town; the model of the Trojan Horse used in the film *Troy,* starring Brad Pitt; and the adjacent small model of the archeological site of Troy. In the summer months, visitors can take advantage of the surrounding beaches.

ESSENTIALS
GETTING THERE
By Plane Located on the Anatolian side of the Dardanelles, **Çanakkale** is the gateway to the Northern Aegean. **Atlasjet Airlines** (© **0216/444-3387;** www.atlasjet.com) recently instituted flights from Istanbul to Çanakkale in 2007. There is only one flight a day, departing Istanbul's Atatürk Airport at 9:30pm, arriving 45 minutes later at the Çanakkale airport located 3km (1¾ miles) outside of the center of town. Fares start at 49YTL ($43/£20) for a one-way ticket. There are taxis at the airport, as well as buses heading directly to the ferry docks/clock tower in the center of town. From here you can either arrange a tour or transport to the battlefields.

By Bus The major bus companies serving Çanakkale from both Istanbul and Izmir are **Çannakale Truva** (© **444-0017**), **Metro** (© **444-3455**), and **Kamil Koç** (© **444-0562**). The ride takes about 5 to 6 hours (after a short ferry ride across the Dardanelles) with drop-offs at the Çanakkale ferry dock, located in the bull's-eye of town. Buses from Izmir and elsewhere stop at the *otogar,* about a 10-minute walk to the center of town.

By Car From Istanbul, take the E6 highway (toll road) toward Edirne. Exit at Kinali, and follow the road through Tekirdağ, Malkara, and Kesan. Follow the road through Gelibolu to the turnoff at Gelibolu for the hourly and daily car ferry to Lapseki (12YTL/$10/£4.80 per car), where you will take the coastal road south 30km (19 miles) to Çanakkale. Or, instead of taking the turnoff to Gelibolu, continue through to Eceabat, with hourly car ferry service between 7am and midnight (then every other hour) direct to Çanakkale (8.50YTL/$7.40/£3.40 per car).

VISITOR INFORMATION
The **tourist information office** (© **0286/217-1187**) is on the main square across from the ferry docks. For emergency traveler's check situations, thank the PTT (post office) for providing a kiosk next to the ferry ticket office.

ORIENTATION
The city of Çanakkale is divided by the somewhat commercialized Demircioğlu Caddesi, which leads directly to Cumhuriyet Meydanı and the ferry docks. The clock tower, 1 block in and slightly to the west of this junction, is a good meeting point for groups.

GETTING AROUND
On Foot Çanakkale revolves around the port and extends, roughly, from the Naval Museum to the south and just north of the Trojan Horse—gifted to the city of Çanakkale in 2004 by the production staff of the epic movie starring Brad Pitt. Behind the wooden horse is a model of the seven layers of Troy.

By Taxi Taxis for travel within the small city limits are metered; however, taxi rates are fixed according to the destination for travel beyond Çanakkale. If the rates seem blown out of proportion to you, try to negotiate a better rate with your driver.

WHAT TO SEE & DO
Archaeological Museum (Arkeoloji Müzesi) I'm not one to admire tchotchkes (there are more than 30,000 of them), so if you're on bone-carved hairpins and carved *stele* overload, skip this museum. The collection does contain an impressive exhibit of surprisingly detailed terra-cotta statuettes and well-preserved glass perfume bottles

salvaged from the ruins of 200 area sites, as well as a trifling fraction of the artifacts Schliemann dug up at Troy, along the coast.

Located about 1.5km (a mile) out of the town center, on the road to Troy. (C) 0286/217-3252. Admission 2YTL ($1.75/80p). Tues–Sun 9am–5pm.

Naval Museum (Deniz Müzesi), Military Museum (Askeri Müzesi), and Çimenlik Castle (Çimenlik Kalesi)　The Army Museum houses various types of war paraphernalia such as uniforms, medals, and weapons, but unless you're a war geek, the most interesting part of the exhibit is just inside the main entrance. There's a model of the Gallipoli Campaign, above which are various plaques in English with attention-grabbing anecdotes and quotes of the various battleground memorials. One recounts the story of how on August 10, 1915, Atatürk received a direct hit to the heart, but a pocket watch that he was carrying shielded him from the bullet and certain death. Other sources say it was shrapnel from the doomed 57th Regiment battle, while still others say the whole story is a load of crap. According to the debatable inscription in this museum, the shattered watch is now part of Army Commander General Limon von Sander's family collection.

Next to the Naval Museum is a replica of the 365-ton *Nusrat,* the minelayer that gets the credit for saving the day against invading British warships during the sea offensive. After the war, the underappreciated *Nusrat* was used as a lowly freight carrier and finally capsized in April 1990.

Çimenlik Castle, along with the Kilitbahir Castle on the opposite banks of the straits, was constructed by Mehmet II (the Conqueror) in the 15th century as a strategic prelude to his assault on Constantinople. The castle grounds are full of old cannons from the battles, and if you venture into one of those dark passages, you can get a glimpse of the Turkish positions, as well as the sections of the roof that were destroyed by incoming artillery.

Çimenlik Park. (C) 0286/217-1707. Admission to museums 2YTL ($1.75/80p). Museums Tues–Wed and Fri–Sun 9am–noon and 1:30–5pm. Park daily 9am–10:30pm.

WHERE TO STAY
CITY CENTER
Anzac Hotel　This hotel—not to be confused with the backpacker haven Anzac House—sits literally in the shadow of the Italianate clock tower. Rooms were renovated in 2004 and offer comfortable beds, thick satin bedcovers, and tireless hospitality.

Saat Kulesi Meydanı 8, 17001 Çanakkale (across from the clock tower). (C) 0286/217-7777. Fax 0286/217-2018. www. anzachotel.com. 27 units. $41 (£21) single; $59 (£30) double. MC, V. Free parking. **Amenities:** Restaurant; roof bar; concierge; tour desk; wireless Internet throughout hotel; 24-hr. room service; laundry service. *In room:* A/C, satellite TV, minibar.

Kervansaray　It was about time for Çanakkale to get a charming hotel, and this is it. Located just steps from everything, the Kervansaray—or at least the street-side building—was originally the stately mansion of an esteemed Ottoman judge. Now restored, rooms boast high ceilings, decorative moldings, and modern character. There's a large enclosed garden separating the house from the new addition at back, and what these rooms lack in historic character they make up for in comfort and dependability. Bathrooms in these back rooms offer comfy European sit-in tub showers, while the "main house" has rooms with showers only.

Kemalpaşa Mah. Fetvane Sok. 13, 17001 Çanakkale (down the st. from the Anzac Hotel). (C) 0286/217-8192. Fax 0286/217-2018. www.otelkervansary.com. 19 units. $51 (£26) single; $73 (£37) double. MC, V. Free parking. **Amenities:** Garden cafe; wireless Internet throughout hotel; 24-hr. room service; laundry service. *In room:* A/C, satellite TV, minibar, hair dryer.

KEPEZ & GÜZELYALİ (OUTSIDE ÇANAKKALE)

Ida Kale   Located about halfway between town (15km/9⅓ miles) and Troy (20km/ 12½ miles), the Ida Kale is a good beachfront option with easy accessibility to all of the major sites. It's owned and operated by a national tile company, a fact that plays out in the decor—bathrooms are wall-to-wall tile, as are the floors. Rooms are spacious, as are the bathrooms with large tubs.

Mola Cad. Güzelyalı, Çanakkale. ℂ 0286/232-8332. Fax 0286/232-8832. www.kaleresort.com. 84 units. $100 (£50) double (includes breakfast and dinner). MC, V. **Amenities:** 2 restaurants; bar; beach; outdoor swimming pool; fitness room; meeting facilities; wireless Internet throughout hotel; 24-hr. room service; laundry service; dry cleaning. *In room:* A/C, satellite TV, minibar, hair dryer, safe.

Kolin Hotel   Located 3km (1¾ miles) outside of town in the nearby suburb of Kepez, the five-star Kolin promises its own private beach, swimming pools (both indoor and out), and all the trimmings of a hotel of this class.

Kepez, 17100 Çanakkale. ℂ **0286/218-0808.** Fax 0286/218-0800. www.kolinhotel.com. 276 units. $135 (£67) double; $260 (£130) suite (Internet rates). MC, V. **Amenities:** 4 restaurants; 1 cafe; 5 bars; beach; outdoor swimming pool; fitness room; Turkish bath; Jacuzzi; sauna; concierge; wireless Internet throughout hotel; 24-hr. room service; babysitting, laundry service; dry cleaning; nonsmoking rooms; handicapped-accessible rooms; elevator. *In room:* A/C, satellite TV, dataport, minibar, hair dryer, safe.

Tusan Hotel   The Tusan is surrounded by pine forest and perched on a cliff overlooking the Çanakkale Straits. Each of the rooms has a balcony or patio and benefits from both sea and forest views. All rooms were renovated in 2002. During your downtime, there are billiards, a fitness room, and an assortment of private beachside terraces accessible via a footpath. The hotel serves lunch and dinner, and all meals can be taken on either the indoor or outdoor terrace. For those without a car, *dolmuşes* pass by the main road approximately every 15 minutes, or you can succumb to the taxis' exorbitant rates into town. Otherwise, the only nuisance will be the nighttime chirping of the crickets.

Güzelyalı, 17001 Çanakkale (about 9.5km/6 miles out of Çanakkale on the road to Izmir). ℂ **0286/232-8746.** Fax 0286/232-8226. www.tusanhotel.com. 64 units. 75€ ($109/£54) double. Rates lower in winter. MC, V. Free on-site parking. **Amenities:** Restaurants; fitness room; watersports (kayaking, windsurfing, diving); game room; meeting facilities; 24-hr. room service; laundry service; dry cleaning. *In room:* A/C, cable TV, minibar, hair dryer.

WHERE TO DINE

Most of the hotels located outside of the city center come with half-board. At the lower end, any *lokanta* is a good bet. While you're in town, don't pass up a taste of the creamy sweet **peynerli helvasi,** a local dessert specialty of cheese and semolina.

Gülen Pide & Kebap TURKISH   This restaurant is a bit fancier than the basic *lokantas* around town, with a menu that covers a predictable but reliable variety of grilled and stewed meats. It's the only proper establishment where you can have an informal sit-down meal without breaking the bank.

Cumhuriyet Meydanı 31, 2 blocks east of the ferry docks. ℂ **0286/212-8800.** Kebaps 6.50YTL ($5.65/£2.60). MC, V. Daily noon–midnight.

Liman Yalova Restaurant TURKISH   From a seaside shack to an institution in Çanakkale, the Yalova is reputed to have the best fish in town. The mezes and nonfish selections are also top-notch. Take advantage of dining under a beautiful sunset from the rooftop terrace.

On the quay south of the main sq., entrance on Gümrük Sok. 7. ℂ **0286/217-1045.** Appetizers 5YTL–8YTL ($4.35–$6.95/£2–£3.20); fish by weight. AE, MC, V. Daily 1pm–midnight.

2 The Gallipoli Battlefields (Gelibolu) ⭐⭐⭐

15km (9½ miles) north of Çanakkale; 310km (193 miles) southwest of Istanbul

For millennia, the Dardanelles have been a strategic point of contention—from King Xerxes of Persia, who in the 5th century B.C. created a bridge of boats to transport his troops to Greece; to Alexander the Great, who swept into Asia from the West in 334 B.C. Mehmet the Conqueror knew the tactical value of the straits as well and had two fortresses built as part of his plan to subdue Constantinople.

In modern times, Çanakkale was once again forced onto the front lines with an Allied campaign to take the Dardanelles during WWI. The battlefields of the **Gallipoli Peninsula** theater became a tragic site for all involved, with almost 200,000 fallen in 8 months. Yet at 86,000 deaths, in spite of taking the heaviest losses, the Turks, led by a gutsy lieutenant colonel named Mustafa Kemal (better known as Atatürk), ferociously repelled the assault on their homeland, and a new nation was born.

The name Gallipoli means different things to different nations. For the Australian and New Zealand Army Corps (or Anzacs), who suffered the largest numbers of Allied casualties, Gallipoli is a national icon. For Turks, Gallipoli represents above all victory by Turkish forces, many of whom were simple farmers, in defending their homeland. But the battlefields of the Gallipoli Peninsula are a solemn reminder to visitors of all nationalities of the brutality of war: jagged cliffs, pockmarked hills, and sprawling valleys where a handful of the scorched earth will most certainly bring up a piece of shrapnel. It was on these fateful shores in 1915 that Australian and New Zealand landing boats went afoul of their intended landing point, unknowingly forced northward where instead of a beach, the troops encountered impossibly vertical cliffs and enemy fire. In spite of the odds, the Anzac troops managed to grab a toehold on the heights, bravely holding out for 249 days until the massacre of the last soldier. The peninsula is now a national park home to 31 war cemeteries and a number of important monuments. The peninsula is accessible by car or bus from Istanbul, and by ferry from the nearby town of Çanakkale on the Asian side of the Dardanelles.

Tips **Leave the Driving to Them: Guided Tours to Gallipoli and Troy**

A visit to Gallipoli can either be approached as an overnight excursion from Istanbul (usually centered around Çanakkale and attached to a visit to Troy) or independently. Tours depart Istanbul at 6:30am and arrive at the battlefields around lunchtime. Most people opt in for the overnight in Çanakkale for the next morning's tour of Troy, with buses arriving back in Istanbul around 6pm. The full overnight tour costs from 120€ to 150€ ($174–$218/£86–£107), depending on the class of hotel you choose. A reliable agency offering good value for this trip in Istanbul is **Indigo Tour**, Akbıyık Cad. 24, Sultanahmet; ℂ **0212/517-7266**; www.indigotour.com). If you want to make your own arrangements (bus, car, hotel, dining) and only want a tour of the sites, contact **Hassle Free Travel Agency**, located in Çanakkale at Cumhuriyet Cad. 61 (ℂ **0286/217-5482**) and on Akbıyık Cad. 10, Sultanahmet, in Istanbul (ℂ 0212/458-9500; www.anzachouse.com). Making it easy on those visitors with only 1 day to spare, **TJ's Tours** (ℂ **0286/814-3121**; www.anzacgallipolitours.com) schedules both the Gallipoli and the Troy tour in 1 day. Tours to both run daily even in winter and cost 55YTL ($48/£22) each.

The Gallipoli Peninsula

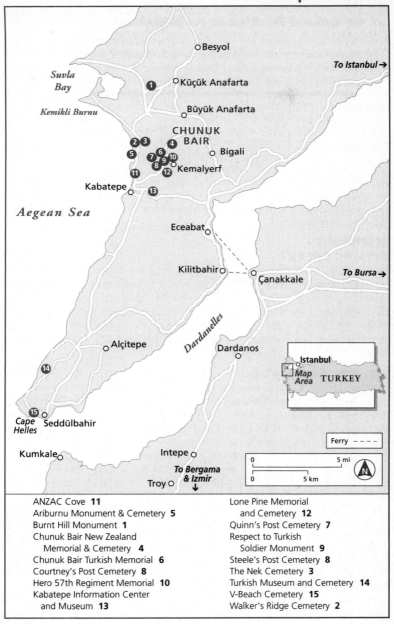

ANZAC Cove **11**
Ariburnu Monument & Cemetery **5**
Burnt Hill Monument **1**
Chunuk Bair New Zealand
   Memorial & Cemetery **4**
Chunuk Bair Turkish Memorial **6**
Courtney's Post Cemetery **8**
Hero 57th Regiment Memorial **10**
Kabatepe Information Center
   and Museum **13**

Lone Pine Memorial
   and Cemetery **12**
Quinn's Post Cemetery **7**
Respect to Turkish
   Soldier Monument **9**
Steele's Post Cemetery **8**
The Nek Cemetery **3**
Turkish Museum and Cemetery **14**
V-Beach Cemetery **15**
Walker's Ridge Cemetery **2**

Tips   Bed-and-Breakfast on the Battlefields

History buffs and pilgrims alike will jump at the chance to stay in this new guest-house overlooking the battlefields. The Gallipoli Houses (© **0286/814-2650**; www. gallipoli.com.tr) is within sight of Chunuk Bair and at most a 40-minute drive to the tip of the peninsula. The hotel was a hit as soon as it opened in May 2007.

Each year on April 25 the anniversary of the Anzacs' landing is commemorated on the battlefields. The day marks a series of memorial services at a number of the grave sites. Passenger cars are not permitted entry on this day.

For a self-guided tour of Gallipoli, you'll need a car, as the various battlefields, cemeteries, and memorials are spread out over an area of nearly 128 square miles (33,152 sq. hectares). It's also possible to sign up for guided tours (see info below) or hire a taxi (about 130YTL/$113/£52 in high season for a half-day unguided tour of the Anzac battlefields).

ESSENTIALS

GETTING THERE

By Car   It is inadvisable (and next to impossible) to rely on the ferry/*dolmuş* from Çanakkale to tour the battlefields, an expanse of approximately 28 square miles. To drive to the battlefields from Istanbul, take the E6 highway (toll road) toward Edirne. Exit Gelibolu for the hourly (daily) car ferry to Lapseki (take the coastal road south 30km/19 miles to Çanakkale) or continue through to Eceabat, with hourly car ferry service between 7am and midnight (then every other hour) direct to Çanakkale (both ferries 12YTL/$10/£4.80; 20 min).

VISITOR INFORMATION

Visitors to the park should stop at one of the two information centers at the start of their visit. The **Kabatepe Visitors Center** (© **0286/814-1297**), called Kabatepe Tan-ıtma Merkezi in Turkish, is 24km (15 miles) northwest of Eceabat, on a cliff overlooking Anzac Cove and the village of Kabatepe. This location—above Brighton Beach where the Anzac troops were supposed to land—is where you should begin your visit. The information center and memorial grounds claim the plateau that was the objective of the failed operation. The commanding hilltop was heavily fortified with Turkish artillery, but today remains eerily silent, with a few notable monuments and spectacular views of the cliffs.

There's also a visitor center at **Çamburnu** (© **0286/814-1128**), located about 1km (⅔ mile) south of Eceabat. Both have small **museums** (admission 2YTL/$1.75/80p; daily 9am–1pm and 2–6pm) housing examples of the battlefield's detritus along with uniforms and old photographs. Your time is better spent outside. Visits to the battlefields are free.

EXPLORING THE BATTLEFIELDS

In the power struggle that emerged during World War I, the Russians, who up until then were forced to sail through the icy waters of the Baltic Sea, aligned themselves with the British, hoping to gain a year-round, ice-free passage via the Dardanelles and into Europe's burgeoning commercial arena. For the Allies, control of Istanbul and the straits meant exposing the flanks of Germany and Austria-Hungary, cutting off their oil supply, and forcing Turkey out of the war (and maybe getting a little caviar from the deal as well).

The fact that Vice Admiral John de Robeck's head-on attack of the Dardanelles failed was as much due to Imperial British overconfidence as to Turkish good fortune. Assuming the enemy would crumble at the sight of the great Royal Navy, the admiral sent in a fleet of 16 ships, most of which were just shy of retirement and manned with inexperienced crews. On March 18, 1915, the battleship *Queen Elizabeth* led the fleet into battle. Four of the ships were damaged or sunk by Turkish mines. After 8 futile hours, shortly before the Turkish army would have run out of ammunition, the British Navy called it a day; however, they did not give up battle for the strait.

The resulting offensive lasted 249 days. The line of attack was simple: Secure the heights, destroy the Turkish defenses, and sail on up to Istanbul. If the current hadn't swept the Anzacs' landing boats a mile off course or if someone other than Mustafa Kemal had received the orders, then Turkey would probably be part of Greece right now and y'all would be reading another book. But tides were swift, communications were faulty, decisions were hasty, and watches were unsynchronized.

The Gallipoli campaign ended on January 9, 1916, when the Allies withdrew in the middle of the night. The Turks boast that not one life was lost in the pullout; the Anzacs, leaving on boats in the darkness, said about their fallen comrades, "I hope they don't hear us go."

The death toll was numbing: Roughly 86,000 Turkish forces and more than 160,000 Allied soldiers perished in the campaign. A staggeringly high number of Allied casualties were Anzac men—unfathomable losses for two countries with such small populations. Indeed, it's all but acknowledged that during the campaign, the Brits offered up the Anzac troops as cannon fodder; consequently, a trip to Gallipoli has become a grim pilgrimage of sorts for countless Australian and New Zealand tourists.

The entire peninsula is a national park. Turkish and Allied soldiers are buried side by side in 31 war cemeteries; several important monuments are grouped around two main areas. It's certainly possible to get to the highlights alone, but there's more to be gained by taking a tour. Tour groups are generally small and the information provided by the guides is informative and passionate; however, the real advantage of taking the tour is seeing the battlefields through the eyes of your Australian and Kiwi acquaintances.

For the locations of the monuments and cemeteries mentioned in this section, consult our map of the Gallipoli Peninsula (p. 175).

Arı Burnu Monument & Cemetery (Arı Burnu Anı ve Mezarlığı)

Shortly after 4am on the morning of April 25, 1915, after a long and cramped night in the boats, the Australian and New Zealand Army Corps landed—16,000 men in all—in the dark, expecting to set foot on level ground. The steep cliff that confronted them instead must have come as a horrific surprise; nevertheless, they hauled themselves up and grabbed at anything stable enough to hold them. Not expecting anyone stupid enough to stage a landing at such an unforgiving spot, the Turks were ill prepared to defend the cliff, allowing large numbers of confused Anzacs to gain higher ground. There was no defense at all in the hills, and by 8am, 8,000 heroic men had scrambled ashore, with three soldiers arriving halfway up the hill to strategic **Chunuk Bair,** 1.6km (a mile) away from the landing site.

The Arı Burnu cemetery is located at the northern end of Anzac Cove. On Anzac Day, a dawn memorial service is held here.

At the northern end of Anzac Cove.

Burnt Hill & Monument (Yusufçuktepe Anıtı)   Also known as Scimitar Hill, Hill 70, and Green Knoll, this ridge was one of the objectives of the Sulva Bay landings in August 1915. Skirmishes went on for 3 days, during which time control over the hill went back and forth. The final day of the attack was a fiasco for the British troops, who suffered the largest number of casualties—5,300—of the entire Gallipoli Campaign.

Cape Helles Landings & Seddülbahir   The Allied landing campaign was launched on two fronts: the beach at Kabatepe (which the Anzac boats overshot) and the village and medieval fortress of Seddülbahir at the toe of the peninsula. The Seddülbahir landings were carried out on five beaches simultaneously by British troops, but lacking the element of surprise and without even one cellphone among them, the advances were modest at best and fatal at worst.

After a violent bombardment of the village, and assuming that the beach (V Beach) was deserted, the 29th Division approached the shore. The Trojan horse–style landing was to have taken place using the cargo hold of the collier *The River Clyde,* which, once beached, would empty itself of soldiers. Like a scene out of *Saving Private Ryan,* the operation turned into a literal bloodbath, when the Turks, waiting in ambush, opened fire on the unprepared and vulnerable British army.

The landings on the other four beaches were more successful, and the troops dug in waiting for further orders. At Y Beach, a small cove with access to the cliff tops 60m (197 ft.) up, 2,000 men, a number equal to all of the Turkish forces on the tip of the peninsula that day, landed unopposed and unaware of the carnage taking place less than 6.5km (4 miles) away. The Turks finally attacked in the night, and these troops were authorized to withdraw.

Chunuk Bair Memorials (Conkbayırı)   Atatürk's arrival on the scene marks a turning point not only in the Gallipoli Campaign but also in the history of Turkey as a nascent republic. Atatürk immediately recognized the importance of the high ground of Chunuk Bair as the key to the straits.

When Atatürk and his reconnaissance team reached Chunuk Bair, Turkish soldiers were fleeing oncoming Australians, who had gained the high ground during the fateful morning of August 25. Explaining that they had run out of bullets, the soldiers were ordered by Atatürk to lie in the grass, bayonets at the ready. Fearing an ambush, the Anzac soldiers took cover, providing the Turks with the precious time needed for reinforcements to arrive. Relentless New Zealand units briefly gained the summit, but due to an unnecessarily incompetent lack of reinforcements, the troops were either slain or forced back to a lower position.

The fateful hill, visited by thousands of pensive visitors each year, is where the main New Zealand memorial shares the crest with a statue of Atatürk as a promising young officer. The Chunuk Bair cemetery is located here, and on Anzac Day, the New Zealand service is held immediately following the Dawn Service at Arı Burnu Cemetery. Nearby are the five enormous tablets of the Turkish Conkbayırı Memorial, symbolizing an outstretched hand to the heavens, and inscribed with a narration (in Turkish) of the events from the other point of view.

The Hero 57th Regiment Memorial (57 Piyade Alayı Şehitliği)   With Anzac troops attacking Chunuk Bair, and in order to gain time for reinforcements to arrive, Atatürk gave the order to his best regiment, "I'm not ordering you to attack; I'm ordering you to die. In the time which passes until we die, other troops and commanders can take our places." Stories of the 57th Regiment's courageous sacrifice, when almost 100,000 men died, are part of Turkey's proud lore, but nobody dares to touch upon the possibility that Atatürk's ambition got the better of him that day.

Oddly enough, the memorial grounds and cemetery are a fairly new addition to the national park, and it's the one place where you will run into large groups of Turks and not *one* trying to sell you any memorabilia. The lawns provide a perfect rest stop for contemplating the puzzle of war, and the ablution fountain is a welcome site for washing the grit of the trenches off of your feet.

Lone Pine (Kanlı Sırt)   The largest mass grave on the peninsula and the main memorial to the missing Australians of the campaign, Lone Pine is the final resting place of both Turks and Anzac troops, with a heavy number of gravestones reading "Believed to be buried in these trenches." About 2,200 Australians and over 4,000 Turks perished in the 3-day battle that earned Australian soldiers seven Victoria Crosses, the Australian badge of bravery and honor.

The tremendous losses at Lone Pine are even more sobering when you think that this was simply a diversionary tactic away from the main objectives of Suvla Bay and Chunuk Bair to the north. Today the hill is the site of a single pine tree rising above the scrub (the original, destroyed in a brush fire during the battle, gave seed to this one), inspiring the soldiers to name the hill after a then-current popular American hit, "On the Trail of the Lonesome Pine." Australians enter this cemetery with their heads held high, because Lone Pine embodies the spirit, character, and courage of their sons.

The Nek   Imagine the closing scene of the movie *Gallipoli,* with reinforcement after teenage reinforcement charging fearlessly into certain death. This real-life suicide mission was ordered by British commanders on August 7, 1915, to divert Turkish troops away from Sulva Bay, where a landing attempt was being made. A break in a nearby British naval bombardment had given the Turkish army the opportunity they needed to reoccupy their trenches, so when the Australian Lighthorse divisions were ordered to attack, they were summarily slaughtered.

A visit to the manicured cemetery and clean front line reveals nothing of the hardship, disease, and rotting corpses that plagued the ridge, but the wind does.

Turkish Memorial, Museum, and Cemetery (Şehitler Abidesi, Türk Şehitliği ve Müzesi)   Let's not forget that a quarter of a million Turks lost their lives defending their country from invading forces. (This is the unofficial number; the official count stands at 86,000.) This somber memorial, atop a promontory at the southern tip of the peninsula, is a fitting place to pay your final respects.

Walker's Ridge, Quinn's Post, Courtney's Post, and Steele's Post   These positions above Anzac Cove were gained in the first days of fighting. With the cliff to their backs and under constant heavy fire, the soldiers dug crude rifle pits, later deepening and connecting them into a network of trenches.

The confrontation in those first few days was ferocious, and the enemy lines were in some places only a few yards apart. The area between the enemy lines known as "no man's land" is now a modern road, and it is possible to spot overgrown trenches on your way to the cemeteries.

The Turks like to tell stories about the friendship that grew between two sides during the 8-month stalemate. If the Turks had cigarettes, the Anzacs provided the matches; when Anzac supplies failed to arrive, the Turks tossed tomatoes into the ditches. Despite the legends, the truth remains that a great respect between the Anzacs and the Turks grew out of a mutual sense of honor.

Fact or Fiction?

The **Respect to Turkish Soldier Monument (Mehmetçik Anıtı)** commemorates what some say is an apocryphal story told in the battle's aftermath. At one point during the fighting, gunfire downed an Australian soldier in the middle of an open field, and none of his compatriots had the courage to retrieve him. A Turkish soldier got up out of his trench, and both sides froze as the Turk picked up the wounded Australian and carried him over to the enemy side. He then returned to his own trench unharmed.

3 Troy ★★★

30km (19 miles) south of Çanakkale

Like the conglomerate of nearly 100 ancient cities that make up the province of Çanakkale, this is the land where the lines between history and mythology are blurred. King Priam, Helen, Agamemnon, and Odysseus were lead characters at **Troy** ★★★, made timeless by Homer in his *Illiad* and *Odyssey*. The *Iliad* and *Odyssey* have made Troy one of the most recognizable mythological events in the world, and few can resist the chance to trod among its remains.

Until 1871, when Heinrich Schliemann decided to go dig for buried treasure, finding Troy was about as likely as finding Atlantis. There was (and to a certain extent, still is) no concrete evidence that the civilization of Homer's *Iliad* existed. One of the arguments is that the poet's epic account of the Trojan War is an amalgam of battle stories based on geopolitics of the day, with a little Aaron Spelling thrown in for flavor.

Then Schliemann, a self-taught archaeologist with an ancient-Greece obsession and an even stronger lust for buried treasure, descended upon the nearby village of Hisarlık and started poking around. His shoddy excavation resulted in significant damage to the site, and when the dust settled after his looting, there was some dispute over what it was that he actually "found" there (see "Exploring the Site," below). But there's no disputing that he began the significant excavation and reconstruction process that continues to this day.

The fact that nine civilizations were built one on top of the other is no surprise, given the strategic location. Two thousand years ago, Troy was a port city at the mouth of the Dardanelles, and it would have been surprising if a war *hadn't* been fought here. While it's anyone's guess just how heroic the goings-on were on these ancient shores, the possibility of stepping into a legend is an exciting proposition—as is climbing into the belly of a wooden horse that Walt Disney would be proud of.

ESSENTIALS

GETTING THERE FROM ÇANAKKALE

By Bus   *Dolmuşes* depart from under the bridge in Çanakkale. The ride takes approximately 35 minutes and costs 2.5YTL ($2.20/£1).

By Car   From Çanakkale, follow the signs south to Troy. You can't miss it.

VISITOR INFORMATION

There is a **visitor information office** (no phone) at the entrance to the archaeological site (next to the Trojan Horse) where you can get an overview of the site as well as peruse reading materials written entirely in Turkish. At the time of this writing, the paint was drying on a world-class museum warehousing the findings from recent excavations of the site.

A TROY PRIMER

Stories about the young Schliemann paint a picture of a child prodigy on a quest from an early age. But it's entirely possible his obsession for Homer and Greek culture took root much later. It seems more likely that his main goal in life was to strike it rich; having achieved that in the California gold rush, he then set his sights on immortality.

At about 44 years old, after years of study of ancient and modern Greek and the classic epic work of Homer, Schliemann proclaimed himself an archaeologist and began digging at Pınarbaşı, which was believed at the time to be the site of Troy. Meanwhile, Frank Calvert had discovered the ruins of a palace or temple on the hill at Hisarlık, and the two agreed that this was a more likely area for the lost city.

Schliemann began bulldozing his way through the hill in 1870 and found little besides obsidian knife blades and clay tiles—which in Turkey, you can pretty much find while bending over and tying your shoe. When he finally discovered something significant—a relief of the sun god Apollo—he immediately attributed it to the ruins of Zeus's throne (and smuggled it out of the country and into his garden). It started to get interesting in August 1872 with the discovery of some gold earrings and a skeleton, and 9 months later his crew uncovered two gates guarding a stone foundation of a large building. To Schliemann, this was obviously the Scaean Gate, and the building was the palace of Priam, the last king of Troy.

Sometime later, Schliemann literally struck gold, shrewdly giving the crew the day off while he and his wife dug alone. That day's findings were monumental: a treasure of goblets; spearheads; knives; and jewelry in copper, silver, and gold, including an incredible 8,750 gold rings and buttons. Eventually Schliemann smuggled the whole lot (except for a few items now in the Archaeology Museum in Çanakkale) out of the country, initially stashing a major part of the treasure with various friends around Greece, where neither Turkish nor Greek authorities could claim ownership. He also donated a portion of the treasure to a Berlin museum, but the artifacts were stolen by the Soviets during World War II and transported to Russia. Schliemann halted and resumed excavation two more times through 1890 but never came near to the findings of that first stash, now believed to have belonged to a princess around 2000 B.C.

So the question remains: Was Schliemann a lying megalomaniac with delusions of grandeur? One biographer points to the evidence. Discrepancies between Schliemann's personal letters and diary entries show that Schliemann lied with regard to his personal life. He also reported that the site of the treasure was located in Priam's Palace, when the site of the find was actually outside the city wall. The truly incriminating evidence is in the photographs he took of Priam's treasure; several of the items "found" in 1873 appear in photos taken in 1872 of earlier finds.

⌢ Fun Fact The Looting of Troy

The bulk of Troy's valuable artifacts—more than 10,000 objects—wound up in the Berlin Museum. In the chaos at the end of World War II, the most valuable of these went to Moscow or St. Petersburg. Fifty percent, however, were damaged or went missing.

Maybe he was just nuts; there's evidence supporting that, too. Schliemann eventually retired in Athens, renamed all of his servants after characters in Greek mythology, and required them to deliver all messages to him in ancient Greek, a language he had taught himself. The inscription on the tomb he had built for himself seems to be his final word on the subject: "For the hero Schliemann."

EXPLORING THE SITE

Over a hundred years of research have revealed that the city was reconstructed at least nine times. The first settlement, referred to as Troy I, dates back to around 3000 B.C.; it lasted 5 centuries and was destroyed by fire. Schliemann's groundbreaking discovery of King Priam's treasure was found on Level II, but later research established that this civilization would have existed over 1,000 years *before* the Troy of Homer. It is unclear what caused the destruction of the successive three civilizations, but findings from the site indicate that by Troy VI, a new culture had emigrated, probably from Mycenae, expanding on the area of preceding settlements. The year 1184 B.C. is traditionally accepted as the year in which classic Troy fell, allowing archaeologists to establish that the Troy of Homer most likely took place during the existence of Troy VII-A, which was analogously destroyed by fire around 1200 B.C. Abandoned for over 400 years, the site went through repeated cycles of invasion and reconstruction until the 1st century A.D, when the city was rebuilt, apparently under the orders of Julius Caesar, and given the name Ilium Novum (hence the *Iliad* in Homer's title). The prestige of the city during the Roman period is reflected in its illustrious guests: Augustus Caesar, Hadrian, Marcus Aurelius, and Caracalla all slept here.

Archaeologists estimate that Troy is actually 10 times larger than the roughly 165-sq.-m (1,776-sq.-ft.) mound of ruins. The more significant discoveries to date are the Troy VI fortification walls, a *megaron* (aristocratic dwelling), the Temple of Athena and sacrificial altar, the Schliemann Trench (where it all started), a Roman theater, and a *bouleterion* (senate building).

Admission 10YTL ($8.70/£4). Fee for car 4YTL ($3.50/£1.60). Summer daily 8:30am–7:30pm; winter daily 8:30am–5pm.

PASSING THROUGH ALEXANDER-TROAS

Approximately 45km (28 miles) along the road southwest from Çanakkale along the coastal road toward Gülpınar, the road passes over the mountains through a handful of tiny and timeless villages (trash and all). Just past the turnoff for Dalyanköy, no sooner do you ascend the hill than the silhouettes of stones—not the ones that occur naturally—begin to emerge. The site was buried and forgotten except for its utility: **Alexander Troas** (admission, if someone appears: 4YTL/$3.50/£1.60) represents another one of those historically monumental sites looted as a building quarry. Many of the columns were removed and taken to Istanbul to use in the construction of the Yeni Valide Camii.

There seems to be conflicting information over the founding of the city (some sources say it was founded and named Antigoneia by Alexander the Great's commander, and then soon after—about a decade—renamed Alexander Troas by Alexander's other commander, Lysimachos; others lump them together and say the city was built by both commanders on the orders of Alexander the Great). In the 3rd century B.C., seven of the neighboring cities were incorporated into Alexander Troas in what became at that time one of the largest cities in Anatolia, stretching as far as Troy to the north, Gülpınar in the south, and east to Evciler. So great was Alexander Troas's position, geographically, politically, and economically, that both Julius Caesar and Constantine are said to have considered the city as the capital of their respective empires. The scattered remains of this isolated site are also frequently included on biblical tours, as there are indications that St. Paul visited three times (for more information, see Acts in the Bible).

The city walls were mapped out as part of the preliminary work to study the site in 1993, and since 1997, excavation under Elmar Schwertheim of the Westphalian Wilhelms University in Münster has been under way.

The first indication that you've arrived at the site is the sight of a neat stack of stones in the form of a tower. (There's a small spot for cars adjacent to this monument). The tower is actually part of a cornerstone section of the famously photographed intact cradle arch. The arch and "tower" are both parts of the **Herodes Atticus bath,** built in A.D. 135. With its 100m-long (328-ft.) facade, it is the largest Roman-era bath in Anatolia. Prior to the 16th century, when the site was believed to be that of Troy, the structure was called the Palace of Priam, until later, when it was thought to be a temple. Because the site is still in the very early stages of excavation, a visit will find you wading through low Mediterranean brush and past olive trees and oaks—probably accompanied only by the whispering of the wind. Some of the other structures you will stumble upon are sections of the 8km (5 miles) of city walls, interspersed by the remains of what was once a total of 44 intermittent towers. The **foundations of a temple** are visible in the clearing, where they've found a bust of Dionysius, **a theater,** and **an aqueduct** attributed to Emperor Trajan. After exploring the fields, continue down the road to the picturesque village of Dalyanköy, with its sandy beach and unpretentious waterside restaurants. This is the site of the ancient city's harbor, now a silted lagoon, artificially enclosed to protect ships from the high winds. (Fishing boats use the mooring at the adjacent Oduniskelesi.)

4 Bozcaada ⊘⋆

55km (34 miles) of the west coast of Geyikli Harbor; 50km (31 miles) southeast of Çanakkale

Off the northwestern coast of Çanakkale are two idyllic island getaways, Gökçeada and Bozcaada, second only in popularity to the Princes' Islands in the province of Istanbul.

The smaller of the two islands, **Bozcaada** ⊘⋆⋆, has the bigger role in mythology. Located opposite Troy, it was from the shelter of Bozcaada (also known as Tenedos, after Poseidon's grandson, Tenes) that Homer tells us the Greek fleet hid while staging the Trojan Horse offensive. What you'll find here today are the predictable remnants of the earlier Greeks, Venetians, and Ottomans, sparsely dotting a landscape that includes pristine stretches of beach and thermal springs. The absence of any villages, apart from the wharf, combined with the revival of a centuries-old legacy of viniculture, are what make this island so much like the original paradise. It doesn't hurt that guests get to hole up in restored Greek stone mansions set amidst the rolling landscape of vineyards (the island economy also relies, nominally, upon red poppies, used in jams and sherbet), dotted by graceful modern windmills. The island packs in visitors to the gills for the annual grape harvest festival on July 26–27 (island population swells from 2,500 to 15,000 around this time) and market day infuses the wharf with local energy every Wednesday.

Meanwhile, Gökçeada (aka Imroz), or the "Island of the God of the Seas," while also appealing in its own right, requires an additional, even heroic, effort to access (1 hr.,

45 min. by boat only 2–3 times per week). Assuming our estimable readers have limited time, such a stopover will absorb much of the time required to visit the other stellar destinations we write about in this book! We therefore regrettably don't cover Gökçeada here.

ESSENTIALS
GETTING THERE
There are currently five ferries a day departing from the Yükyeri docks west of the Geyikli town center, about 40km (25 miles) south of Çanakkale. From there, it's an easy 30 minutes to the wharf. For information, log on to www.tdi.com.tr (Turkish only) or call ℭ **0286/697-8185.** The number for the Gerikli port offices is ℭ 0286/632-0263.

WHERE TO STAY & DINE
Hotel Mauna   When traveling outside of the main touristy areas, I never underestimate the value of floor-to-ceiling bathroom tile. Or an enclosed cabin shower. This hotel has both, plus charm to boot. The Mauna is a sweet old stone house on a side street in the center of town, with a rooftop terrace bar with views to the castle and sea beyond—great for an evening aperitif.

Cumhuriyet Mah. 20 Eylül Cad., 17680 Bozcaada. ℭ **0286/697-0333.** Fax 0286/697-0273. www.otelmauna.com. 8 units. 120YTL ($104/£48) double. MC, V. Closed Nov–Mar. **Amenities:** Bar; Internet. *In room:* A/C, TV w/pay-per-view, hair dryer. No phone.

Kaikias   With a spot front and center of the water and the castle, the architect-brothers Beyildi clearly made a winning investment. They've restored this old Greek building, retaining original features like cross barrel arches, patches of decorative frieze, and some original brickwork. They've also adding breezy touches like a sailcloth ceiling to keep the relentless sun from beating down on the lobby—essentially a recently enclosed court connecting the two row houses. The dark wood of the original wide plank flooring provides a rich feel to rooms that range from simply white-washed rooms kept interesting with gilded mirrors and the odd leather armchair (standard) to regal spaces with canopied four-poster beds (suite). Bathrooms are also variable, from sleek and modern, or marble-clad with a *hamam* basin. Best to ask ahead if you have a preference.

Kale Arkası, Bozcaada. ℭ **0286/697-0250.** Fax 0286/697-8857. www.kaikias.com. 20 units. 120YTL–160YTL ($104–$139/£48–£64). MC, V. Closed Nov–Mar. In room: A/C.

WHAT TO SEE & DO
Eat, drink, and be merry. That's the point of Bozcaada. There are four main wineries on the island; you can either go directly to the factory/farms or to a little **wine-tasting tour** ⋆⋆⋆ at a number of establishments on the wharf (they make it easy here). **Talay** is a family-owned vintner established on the island in 1948 (Lale Sok. 5; ℭ **0286/697-8080**). **Ataol Farms** (also a guesthouse and restaurant) is located in Tekirbahçe (ℭ **0286/697-0384**). **Yunatcilar** (Eminiyet Sok. 24; ℭ **0286/697-8055**) has been pressing grapes since 1925. **Corvus** is a more ambitious vintner, with vineyards not only on Bozcaada, and sales points all over Turkey (ℭ **0286/697-8181**).

Admittedly, there are other reasons besides wine tasting to come to this island. Visitors flock to the most famous beach, **Ayazma Cove,** known for the cold spring that lies beneath. **Sulubahçe** and **Habbeli** are two other picture-postcard coves. Minibuses depart regularly for service to these beaches from the town center. In season (meaning

July and Aug), the lounge chairs shaded by faded straw-hat umbrellas fill up by 9am, so ideally, it's best to set aside 2 days in early summer or September/October. If you're heading here off season, keep in mind that the high winds for which Turkey's largest wind farm was erected gust over the seven rolling hills of Bozcaada.

It'll be impossible to miss the **Medieval Castle,** reconstructed by Mehmet the Conqueror in the 15th century (remember the strategic location of the island). The castle foundations were probably laid by the Phoenicians; it was later inhabited by the Venetians and Genoese. The construction of the **Church of the Virgin Mary** (Meryem Ana Kilisesi) may also date to the Venetians but the current church only dates to 1867–69.

There's also some exceptional diving around the island, including a kilometer-long reef that extends down to a depth of about 20m (66 ft.). You might even get a glimpse of the Mediterranean sea lions from **Mermer Burnu.** Special permission from the authorities is required for diving off Bozcaada; for information, contact Aganta Turizm at Belediye Dükk 7 (© **0286/697-0569;** www.aganta.net).

5 Assos ★

420km (261 miles) to Istanbul; 90km (56 miles) south of Çanakkale; 65km (40 miles) south of Troy; 160km (99 miles) north of Bergama; 250km (155 miles) north of Izmir

Several years ago, Jacque Avizou (of Les Maisons de Cappadoce, in Cappadocia) confided in me about a "little paradise" that he described as Turkey's "best-kept secret." He told me it was located far enough off the primary road system to ensure that it remained off the tourist radar, a tiny settlement of Anatolian families living atop the lofty ruins of an ancient commercial and religious center. I was intrigued and set out to plan an entire week's itinerary around the little Aegean village of Behramkale, also known by the name of the ancient city it stands on, **Assos.**

Physically, Assos/Behramkale (which I will from now on call Assos for brevity's sake) occupies the site of a conical volcanic rock on the south-facing shores of the Bay of Edremit. The Acropolis, surrounded by a 3km-long (1¾-mile) defensive wall, is crowned by the **Temple of Athena,** placed artfully, advantageously, and tactically high above the expansive Valley of the Satnioeis and the bay. The **agora, gymnasium,** and **theater,** all still in ongoing stages of excavation, are terraced down the steep slopes of the rocky landscape, making a visit to the far-flung sections of the city not just a little bit of a workout. At the base of the city (reachable via a steeply cobbled roadway) is a tiny port made up of a single breakwater and a handful of stone warehouses converted into guest accommodations. The moonlight reflecting off of the tranquil waters of the Aegean is even more romantic when you consider that this same setting served as inspiration for Aristotle during his 3-year sabbatical at Assos. Frankly, Assos has already been discovered, but is thankfully nowhere near overrun. The day that happens, though, it'll be a tight squeeze, because thanks to kryptonite-like volcanic rock upon which the village is built there's not much room—at least at the wharf—for this little village to grow.

ESSENTIALS
GETTING THERE FROM ÇANAKKALE
By Minibus   The public transport route (on one of Ayvacık Birlik *dolmuşes;* © **0286/217-2141**) from Çanakkale to Assos is a bit convoluted, but here goes: Take a *dolmuş* (minibus) from the Çanakkale *otogar* (not the *dolmuş* terminal under the

bridge) to Ayvaçık (1 hr.; 6YTL/$5.20/£2.40), and then change in Ayvaçık for another *dolmuş* to Assos (1.5 hrs.; 2.5YTL/$2.20/£1). The latter drops you off at the crossroads near the village entrance and the ancient site (but 238m/781 ft. above the wharf).

By Car From Çanakkale, follow the signs south to Ayvaçık, and then follow the (well-marked) scenic road to Assos/Behramkale.

The longer, alternative route (and the one I took) follows the road south of Çanakkale. You can make this a day of sightseeing beginning with a stop at Troy. On the road south of Troy, take the turnoff for Pınarbaşı, following the road through Mahmudiye, Ovacık, and Geyikli. After Geyikli, if you follow the road toward Dalyan you will encounter the roadside ruins of **Alexander Troas,** an enormous (and as of yet still unexcavated and/or looted) candidate for the capital city of the Roman Empire. Dalyan port is an idyllic and untouched corner of Çanakkale and a great spot to stop for a drink or a bite to eat; on your way keep your eyes open for the **Kestanbol thermal waters,** a natural and artesian hot spring bubbling up to 154°F (68°C).

South of Dalyan (from the road you turned off of) through Kösedere leads to the ancient temple of **Apollon Smyntheon at Chryse** (in the village of Gülpınar). From Gülpınar, depending on your level of stamina, you can either take the turnoff to the Ottoman castle of **Babakale** (another paradise on earth, if you ask me), constructed under Sultanahmed III to protect the villagers from frequent pirate attacks, or continue along the peninsular road to Assos/Behramkale.

The entrance to the village and the ancient Acropolis, and a number of pensions and hotels, are clustered together near the turnoff from the main road. The sea-level wharf, and additional hotels, are accessed by continuing along this same secondary cobbled road (past the entrance to the village/site) as it winds its steeply sloping way along the city's fortification walls.

VISITOR INFORMATION
You should have your information in hand before you arrive at Assos. The **Anzac Hotel** in Çanakkale (www.anzachotel.com) maintains an excellent website with information and maps to aid your way through the maze of secondary roads, olive groves, and plane trees.

WHERE TO STAY & DINE
Kervansaray The Kervansaray has been welcoming guests for nigh around 20 years now, and over the years, the management has made additional upgrades to this former customs depot, including a sauna, indoor/outdoor swimming pools, and a juice bar. The hotel is arranged around an inner atrium, following the theme of a historic caravansary. A room facing the sea will get you a tiny balcony just wide enough to seat a couple with their feet rested atop the stone balcony wall. Some of the rooms are carpeted and some have wood floors, and there's a cozy corner unit arranged around a small stone chimney. It's all very charming and comfortable, although perhaps a bit less elegant than one would expect from a hotel that bills itself as a boutique property. Still, it's the most reliable of the lot down at the wharf.

Behramkale Village Iskele (at the port), Assos/Behramkale. ℂ 0286/721-7093. Fax 0286/721-7200. www.assos kervansaray.com. 44 units. 140YTL–200YTL ($122–$174/£54–£76). Rates are for July and Aug 2007 and are for half-board. MC, V. Free parking. **Amenities:** Restaurant; bar; indoor and outdoor swimming pool; sauna; billiards; wireless Internet throughout hotel; 24-hr. room service; laundry service. *In room:* A/C, satellite TV, minibar, hair dryer.

WHAT TO SEE & DO

The city of **Assos** was established by migrants from the town of Methymna on the island of Lesbos. Over the centuries, the city was ruled as part of Lydia, by the Persians, as a member of the Athenian League in the 5th century B.C., and incorporated into the kingdom of Pergamon.

One of the rulers during the pre-Pergamon era was the freed slave and student of Plato, Hermias. From 348 to 345 B.C., Hermias's schoolmate and friend, **Aristotle,** joined him at Assos to philosophize and lecture; tradition has it that it was here that Aristotle further developed Plato's thinking on government as expounded in *The Republic.*

The ancient site comprises an **acropolis, gymnasium, theater, *bouleuterion,*** and **necropolis,** all for the most part bound by a 3.2km-long (2-mile) defensive wall, and according to leading Turkish archaeologists, the most complete fortification in the Greek world. **The Temple of Athena** was the first and only archaic temple built in Anatolia of the Doric style.

The rubble (much of the good stuff was carried off to the Boston Museum, the Louvre, and the Istanbul Archaeology Museum) is spread out over a wide and arid area littered with stones, sarcophagi, and goat droppings, so unless you're a master orienteer, your visit will be confined to the upper reaches of the acropolis. Still, the cliff-top setting of the ancient city, which produces an awe-inspiring sunset image from the temple remains over the bay, makes this pile of rocks one of the better secondary sites on the Aegean.

Behramkale. (Entrance to the site is about 150m [492 ft.] up a steep cobbled pedestrian-only road accessed from the center of the village.) No phone. Admission 4YTL ($3.50/£1.60). Daily 9am–5pm (until 4:30pm in winter).

6

The Central & Southern Aegean Coasts (Greater Izmir)

For hundreds of years, the stellar ruins at Ephesus have provided voyagers all the impetus they needed to justify a trip to this stretch of scenic coastlands. Villagers and entrepreneurs of yore were not the first to recognize the commercial value of these scenic hills and crystal waters. Historically, the central and southern Aegean coasts were crossroads for ancient trade routes. Civilization evolved out of the convergence of Eastern and Western cultures; Hellenistic settlers who fled the Dorian invasions emphasized economic expansion and forged ties with people from Egypt, Nubia, Canaan, Mesopotamia, and the Black Sea region. Welcome to the original melting pot.

At one time, the region boasted some of the most illustrious addresses in the world. The Ionian cities of Ephesus, Bergama, Miletus, and Priene served as cultural incubators in the development of Western thought, home to such philosophers and scholars as Thales Anaximenes, Anaximendros, and Heraclites. Other famous ancient Greek guests to the Anatolian coastline of the Aegean were Aristides, Strabo, Pliny, and Homer. Later (according to tradition) Mary, under the care of St. John, settled near Ephesus, permanently altering the way an entire civilization perceived Christianity while contributing to the evolution of the religion itself.

The presence of the sea becomes more insistent south of Izmir, characterized by a coastline backed by olive groves, rocky crags, and pine woods. But in recent years rampant development has been the rule and many of the region's fishing villages and farming towns have been transformed by the irresistible lure of the euro, pound sterling, and yen. The open-air museum of Ephesus, for example, is a human parking lot in August, and Bodrum in high season (mid-June through Aug) brings competition for sand, surf, and sustenance to new heights. The information in this section strives to strike a balance between lesser-traveled areas while acknowledging the fact that no one is coming to this part of Turkey to do a drive-by of Ephesus.

The destinations mentioned in this chapter are all within 3 hours of one another and buses run regularly between cities. For shorter excursions, the local *dolmuşes* (minivan-type public transportation) are reliable, though they usually call it quits in the early evening. Driving is easy and the new highways provide choice for quick excursions or the scenic route. Time can be split easily between beach activities and visiting the ancient sights. This is the place to take as much time as necessary to decompress from the worries of everyday life.

The Central & Southern Aegean Coasts

Aegean Sea

Chios
Şifne
Çeşme
Alaçatı

Bergama

Akhisar

Manisa

Izmir
Sardis

Istanbul
TURKEY
Ankara
Map Area

Samos

Kuşadası
Selçuk
Ephesus
Söke

Nazili

Hierapolis
Pamukkale

Denizli

Priene
Miletus
Didyma

GREECE

Bodrum

Karacasu

Aphrodisias
Tavas

Muğla

Halicarnassus
Kormen
Kos
Knidos

Gelibolu
Marmaris
Hisarönü
İcmeler
Datça
Turunç
Bozburun
Dalaman

Kaunos

Fethiye

Hisarönü Bay

Railway
Ruins

Rhodes (Rodos)

Mediterranean Sea

Kalkan
Kaş

1 Izmir

560km (348 miles) south of Istanbul; 70km (43 miles) north of Selçuk; 90km (56 miles) north of Kuşadası; 325km (202 miles) south of Çanakkale; 279km (173 miles) north of Marmaris

Izmir has come a long way since the late 1800s when the Ottoman elite christened the port city *Kokaryalı* (Smelly Waterfront). Today the city has earned the nobler designation of *Güzelyalı* (Beautiful Waterfront), and with the completion of a multimillion-dollar redevelopment plan that includes a green waterside park, a promenade called the **Kordon,** and the restored customs house (or **Konak Pier**) built by **Gustave Eiffel,** the name is more than appropriate.

Little was left after the fire ignited at the tail end of the War of Independence destroyed all traces of the cultural melting pot that was once Smyrna—and there's that perilous but dormant fault line to contend with. Eighty-two years after the reconstruction began, Izmir has been reinvented as a prosperous, cosmopolitan, commercial city, more livable than Istanbul, less sterile than Ankara, and filled with wide boulevards and swaying palm trees. But with the azure waters of the Aegean and the extraordinary remains of Ephesus competing for tourist attention, Izmir sadly falls short. Despite this, I actually love the place. There's plenty to do here for anyone who chooses to take an extended stay.

A LOOK AT THE PAST

The story of Izmir brings up yet another lineup of the usual suspects, beginning with the traces of an unidentified group dating from at least the 3rd millennium B.C. Excavations at the nearby site of Bayraklı in the Meles river valley have uncovered evidence of a primitive culture influenced by Hittite religious models; in fact, the Luwi word closely resembling "Smyrna" means "land of the holy mother." Somewhere along the way, the Amazon ruler Smyrna (or Myrina) added to the confusion of the origins of the city's nomenclature. Various civilizations referred to the city as Zmürni, Smyrne, Simirna, and Esmira; if you say them all 10 times *really* fast, the final outcome is the sound of the town you'll find on maps today.

Around 200 years after the disintegration of the Hittite Empire, waves of Ionian immigrants began to populate the region, creating a thriving metropolis comparable to the success and influence of its contemporary, Troy. The Lydians who moved in and trashed the place were no match for the Persian Empire, though they, too, succumbed to Alexander the Great's blaze of glory. In the 4th century B.C., Alex rebuilt an unmistakably Hellenistic city, relocating it on the hill of Pagos under the watchful protection of the Kadifekale citadel. Izmir was absorbed by General Lysimachos into his kingdom of Pergamum, but bad estate planning on the part of Attalus 200 years later resulted in the entire region becoming a Roman colony. Under the Romans and then the Byzantines, Ionia became a thriving center of trade and intellectual innovation, but the city was razed by a devastating earthquake in A.D. 178.

Control vacillated between the Byzantines and the Arabs until 1390, when the region was stabilized under Selçuk, then Ottoman, rule.

Izmir became a flourishing center of commerce in the 15th century, nurtured by the liberal policies of tolerance practiced by the Ottomans. But there was hardly a Turk in sight. The city opened its arms to waves of immigrant Jews fleeing from the Spanish Inquisition as well as Greeks and Armenians. French and other European merchants, known as the Levantines, set up customs houses here, and each enclave left its own cultural imprint on the city. After World War I, the Treaty of Sèvres assigned Greece the administration of Izmir and the surrounding region, but the Greek occupying forces got greedy and foolishly pushed eastward. The defeat of Greek forces by Atatürk's national liberation army on September 9, 1922, was the defining moment in the establishment of national sovereignty; as the Greeks were chased off the peninsula, occupying French and British forces prudently pulled out of the regions under their protection.

Depending on who tells the story, the city was destroyed by fire either by an accident of war or by angry vengeful Turks on a rampage after their victory in 1922. The city has since been rebuilt into a modern, functional, palm tree-lined, and thoroughly pleasant metropolitan city.

ESSENTIALS

GETTING THERE

BY PLANE   As the primary entry point for visits to the popular destinations of Çeşme, Ephesus, and Kuşadası, as well as a major and modern hub for international business travelers, Izmir's very modern Adnan Menderes Airport has effortlessly kept pace. In addition to **Turkish Airlines** (see below for contact information), several international and domestic airlines are now operating direct flights to Izmir. **Izmir Airlines** (© 444-4499; www.izair.rom.tr) has direct flights from Istanbul, Ankara,

Izmir

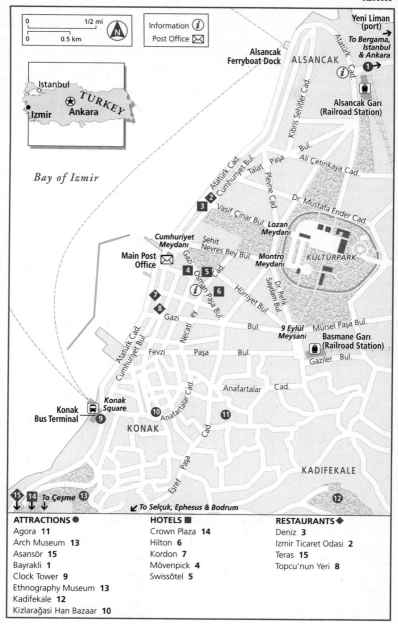

Map Labels

Yeni Liman (port)

To Bergama, Istanbul & Ankara

Alsancak Ferryboat Dock

ALSANCAK

Alsancak Garı (Railroad Station)

0   1/2 mi
0   0.5 km

N

Information ⓘ
Post Office ✉

Istanbul

TURKEY

Izmir   Ankara

Bay of Izmir

Kıbrıs Şehitler Cad.

Atatürk Cad.

Bul.

Ali Çetinkaya Cad.

Talat   Paşa

Pleyne Cad.

Atatürk Cad.
Cumhuriyet Bul.

Vasıf Çınar Bul.

Dr. Mustafa Ender Cad.

Lozan Meydanı

Şehit Nevres Bey Bul.

Cumhuriyet Meydanı

Montro Meydanı

KÜLTÜRPARK

Main Post Office ✉

Gazi Osman Paşa Cad.

Hürriyet Bul.

Dr. Refik Saydam Bul.

Gazi   ev

9 Eylül Meysanı

Mürsel Paşa Bul.

Basmane Garı (Railroad Station)

Gaziler   Bul.

Necati   ev

Fevzi   Paşa   Bul.

Atatürk Cad.
Cumhuriyet Bul.

Anafartalar   Cad.

Konak Bus Terminal

Konak Square

KONAK

Anafartalar Cad.

Anafartalar   Cad.

Eşref   Paşa   Cad.

KADİFEKALE

To Çeşme

To Selçuk, Ephesus & Bodrum

ATTRACTIONS ●

Agora **11**
Arch Museum **13**
Asansör **15**
Bayrakli **1**
Clock Tower **9**
Ethnography Museum **13**
Kadifekale **12**
Kizlarağasi Han Bazaar **10**

HOTELS ■

Crown Plaza **14**
Hilton **6**
Kordon **7**
Mövenpick **4**
Swissôtel **5**

RESTAURANTS ◆

Deniz **3**
Izmir Ticaret Odasi **2**
Teras **15**
Topcu'nun Yeri **8**

Adana, and Diyarbakır. **SunExpress** (© **0232/444-0797;** www.sunexpress.com.tr) flies twice weekly from London's Stansted Airport to Izmir in summer only. **British Airways** (© **0870/850-9850** in the U.K.; www.britishairways.com) flies direct from Gatwick 4 days a week. Other airlines offering service from Istanbul include **Atlasjet** (© **0216/444-3387;** www.atlasjet.com.tr) and **Pegasus Airlines** (© **444-0737;** www. flypgs.com). **Turkish Airlines**' Izmir office is located at Halıt Ziya Bulv. 65, Çankaya, behind the new Swissôtel Grand Efes (© **0232/484-1220;** www.thy.com). **Onur Air** (© **444-6687** or 0232/274-1939; www.onurair.com.tr) is represented locally by any number of travel agencies.

The **Havaş** shuttle (national toll-free © **0212/444-0487** or local 0232/274-2276) runs daily service from the airport into the center of Izmir with a drop-off point in front of the Grand Efes Hotel on Gaziosmanpaşa Bulvarı. Bus departure times are coordinated with domestic airlines flight arrivals; expect the ride into the city center to take about an hour. The fare is 10YTL ($8.70/£4; midnight–6am the fare increases 25%). Shuttles from the city center to the airport depart from the same spot in front of the Grand Efes daily and hourly from 3:30am to 11:30 pm.

A taxi to your hotel will cost between 35YTL and 45YTL ($30–$39/£14–£18), depending on traffic, whether or not the meter is running, or the driver's "fixed price." If you're not sure how much to spend, try out your haggling abilities on several consecutive taxis, until you figure out how much the ride should really cost. Remember that prices are more expensive between midnight and 6am.

BY BUS   Bus service is frequent and comprehensive in and out of Izmir. Service from Istanbul takes around 9½ hours; from Ankara, 9 hours; from Kuşadası, 1½ hours; from Bergama, 2½ hours; and from Bursa, about 5½ hours. As with anywhere else in Turkey, prices vary from one bus company to the next by as much as ($10/£5), so shop around before buying your ticket.

Long-distance buses arrive into Izmir's enormous and modern main *otogar* (bus station), located about 8km (5 miles) outside of town. As part of your fare, the bus companies also provide transfer minibuses into the city center. Alternatively, a taxi will cost around 10YTL ($8.70/£4).

BY TRAIN   **Turkish State Railways** (www.tcdd.gov.tr) operates three trains from Ankara: The **Karesi Ekspresi** leaves at 7:10pm for the 15-hour trip. A seat on the train costs 22YTL ($19/£8.80). You have the option of sleeping in a bed on the **Mavi Tren** departing Ankara at 6:10pm or the **9 Eylül Ekspresi** leaving at 8pm. Both trains have couchettes making that 14-hour journey a bit more pleasant. The cost is 70YTL ($61/£28) per person for single passengers, 53YTL ($46/£21) per person for two. A seat on the Mavi Tren costs 25YTL ($22/£10). From Istanbul, you'll need to get a ferry to Bandırma in order to connect to either the **6 Eylül Ekspresi** departing Bandırma at 9:45am or the **17 Eylül Ekspresi** departing at 3:45pm; the train takes about 6 hours and costs 15YTL ($13/£6). Trains arrive into Izmir's **Basmane Garı** (© **0232/484-8638** or 0232/484-5353 for reservations), about .8km (½ mile) northeast of Konak, the town center. From Basmane Garı you will need to take a bus or taxi the short ride to your hotel. *Note:* Not all trains have daily departures so confirm your itineraries well in advance.

BY FERRY   Those combining a visit to Turkey with a romp through the Greek islands may hop on a ferry in Chios for service to Çeşme, an hour-long bus ride from Izmir's *otogar*. Ferries run daily from July through September 15 with fewer runs off season. For information, contact **Ertürk** (www.erturk.com.tr), the agent located in Çeşme.

VISITOR INFORMATION

Tourist information offices are located in several high-traffic areas: Gaziosmanpaşa Bulv. 1/1 in the Swissôtel Grand Efes (*©* **0232/484-2148** or 0232/445-7390); Atatürk Cad. 418, Alsancak (*©* **0232/422-1022**); Akdeniz Mah. 1344 Sok. 2 Pasaport (*©* **0232/483-6216**); and the Adnan Menderes Airport (*©* **0232/274-2214**). There's also an ad-hoc information booth in Konak behind the Clock Tower at the entrance of Anafartalar Caddesi. Free maps are provided at the tourist information offices, at travel agents around town, and often in your hotel room.

ORIENTATION

Konak, named for the Ottoman government mansion (Hükümet Konagı) located nearby, is the area roughly containing Izmir's central district and center city, which embraces the Gulf of Izmir. A number of neighborhoods and zones are contained within Konak, including **Konak Square,** with its bustling seafront park, the little **Konak Camii,** and the **Clock Tower (Saat Kulesi),** the symbol of Izmir.

Just behind the tourist information booth at Konak Meydanı (the main square) is **Anafartalar Caddesi;** judging by the magnetic stream of people pouring in, this must be the entrance to the shopping district, also known as Kemeraltı. Winding through the oldest section of town are the narrow back streets of Izmir, where an unexpected 17th-century mosque, several synagogues, and a *bedesten* (privately owned marketplace) cohabit an area long overtaken by stores selling inexpensive gold chains.

To the north along the waterfront is **Konak Pier,** constructed as the Customs Building by Gustave Eiffel between 1875 and 1890 and reopened as a glossy shopping and dining destination. About a 15-minute walk farther up is Cumhuriyet Meydanı, punctuated by an equestrian statue of Atatürk, and the grassy waterfront park and promenade of **Kordon.** This neighborhood around Cumhuriyet Meydanı is home to a cluster of four- and five-star hotels, car-rental offices, and travel agencies. It's also part of the residential neighborhood of **Alsancak,** which boasts some restored homes, and another Atatürk Museum. **Pasaport** refers to the **historic quay** halfway between Konak Pier and Cumhuriyet Meydanı. At the northernmost tip are the harbor and ferry terminal. South of Konak Square is the neighborhood of **Karataş,** once a thriving Jewish community where you will find the Asansör and the restored houses of **Dario Moreno Sokak.**

Up on the hill is **Kadifekale,** the fortress established by Alexander the Great. The views are great, and the trip is free, but save yourself the hassle and have a drink in the Hilton Hotel's Windows on the Bay instead.

About 15km (9¾ miles) to the southwest of Konak along the coastal road is the suburban district of **Balcova,** blessed by thermal springs most recently utilized by the new and luxurious Crown Plaza.

GETTING AROUND

Much of what might hold a non-local's interest is located in convenient little clusters at various points around the city. Most of your sightseeing and shopping can be done on foot in and around Konak, which includes the museums and main-square attractions, as well as the bazaar, also known as **Kemeraltı.** From Konak, Alsancak is reachable on foot along the scenic waterfront, but for those unable or unwilling to walk,

---

Tips **Transport Made Easy with the Kentkart**

Izmir is one of an increasing number of cities to adopt an electronic payment system by way of a magnetic-stripped "city card." Like other prepay fare cards, the Kentkart offers discounts for use, so instead of paying the 1.25YTL ($1.10/50p) full fare, that ride on the bus will cost you only 95Ykr (85¢/40p). But because the Kentkart requires an initial deposit of 5YTL ($4.35/£2), buying one really only makes sense if you're planning on staying in town for the long haul. Kentkarts are available at bus ticket offices and in select shops; just look for the KENTKART logo for sales points.

---

there are municipal buses running regularly from the major bus hub at Konak (just in front of the Atatürk Cultural Center and on the street below the Archaeological Museum). If you're staying in one of the major hotels around Cumhuriyet Meydanı, you're about dead center between Konak and Alsancak. The historic Jewish quarter, today called **Asansör** for the 19th-century elevator that provides access to the cliff-top residential area, is just south of Konak and also reachable by bus. The bus fare is 1.25YTL ($1.10/50p).

At the risk of plowing through millennia of archaeological remains, Izmir has completed the first phase of construction of a brand-new one-line **metro.** The line currently runs between Bornova, a residential suburb to the northeast of town, with Üçyol just south of Konak. In-between are stops at Konak, Çankaya, Basmane, and a couple more to destinations not mentioned in this guide. The metro runs frequently between 6am and midnight Monday through Friday; service is sparser on weekends. One ride costs 1.25YTL ($1.10/50p).

A more ambitious project is in the works to connect the metro with an extension that goes all the way to Adnan Menderes Airport. Completion of the project is optimistically projected for 2008, so keep your eyes out during the 2-year shelf life of this book.

Public **ferries** crisscross Izmir's bay between Konak and the busy residential shopping area of Karşıyaka, between Pasaport (at Cumhuriyet Meydanı) and Karşıyaka, and between Pasaport and Alsancak. Fares on the ferry are about 1.25YTL ($1.10/50p) each way. Purchase your *jeton* at the ticket window prior to boarding, and double-check the destination of the boat, particularly if you're returning to Alsancak from Karşıyaka; it's a relatively long walk from Konak Square to Alsancak if you get on the wrong boat.

FAST FACTS: Izmir

Airport and Airlines Information For general airport information, call the general info line at Izmir airport at © **0232/274-2626.** For information on Turkish Airlines flights call © **0232/484-1220.** For Onur Air call © **0232/274-1939.** The number for the Havaş shuttle bus at the airport is © **0232/274-2276.**

Ambulance and Emergency Care For medical emergencies, call **Medline Ambulance** (© **0232/421-4500**) or the Greater Izmir municipality ambulance (© 0232/ 433-4949). You can also head to the Izmir Private **Karataş Hospital** (© **0232/441-4170**) at the southern end of Konak.

Car Rentals The major car-rental agencies have offices both at the airport and in downtown Izmir. **Avis** is located in the city center at Şair Eşref Bulv. 18D, Alsancak (℅ 0232/441-4417). **National Car Rental** is located both at the airport (domestic arrivals; ℅ 0232/274-3910) and in Alsancak at Şehit Nevres Bey Bulv. 11A (℅ 0232/422-7107). **Hertz** is at Kultar Mah. 1377, Sok. 8/F, Alsancak (℅ 0232/464-3440), and at the airport (℅ 0232/274-3610 for international arrivals and ℅ 0232/274-2248 for domestic arrivals).

Consulates Citizens of the **United Kingdom** have consular representation at Mustafa Bey Caddesi (℅ **0232/464-8755**). The **United States** consulate provides routine services by appointment only on Mondays and Tuesdays (for appointments call Mon and Tues 9:30–11:30am; ℅ **0232/464-8755**) and is closed Wednesday to Friday as well as Turkish and American holidays. (In an emergency, call the Ankara number: ℅ 0312/455-5555. *Note:* The State Department does not publish this address.)

Currency Exchange A *döviz,* or currency exchange office, is in the international terminal of Izmir's airport. The post office (PTT) offers extremely competitive rates of exchange, while all hotels provide exchange services. Private exchange offices typically offer better rates than banks; look for the DÖVIS sign around the Izmir Hilton Hotel and in the Konak section, around Anafartalar Caddesi. Keep in mind that hotels are notorious for offering the worst rates of exchange.

WHAT TO SEE & DO

The Agora   Constructed during the rule of Alexander the Great, the Agora is today mostly in ruins, and you'll have to walk up through a neighborhood also in ruins to get there. (Call ahead to make sure it's open, and take a taxi.) What little is left remains because of Faustina, wife of Marcus Aurelius, who had the Agora rebuilt after an earthquake devastated the original in A.D. 178. (Actually, the site is one of the best-preserved Ionian agoras because the Byzantines and Ottomans both used the space above it as a cemetery, leaving the ancient remains undisturbed.) The open-air museum—impressive at about 120m×78m (394 ft.×256 ft.)—contains the remains of three of the four main gates, some recognizable stalls, and a three-sided perimeter of porticos. Excavations of a monumental gated entrance to the Agora uncovered a treasure of statues of Greek gods and goddesses, along with more mundane figures of people and animals. More recent excavations of the Roman basilica have brought to light graffiti and drawings (in the basement), plus inscriptions of the people who provided aid after the devastating earthquake of A.D. 178.

East of Gaziosmanpaşa Bulv. (south of Anafartalar Cad.). ℅ **0232/425-5354**. Admission 2YTL ($1.75/80p). Daily 8:30am–noon and 1–5pm.

Archaeology Museum (Arkeoloji Müzesi) ⭐   This place exhibits an impressive collection of ancient and Roman artifacts recovered from area excavations, including Bergama, Iasos, Bayraklı (Izmir's original settlement), and Izmir's Agora. A service path leads you to the gate of the museum grounds, which are full of wondrously oversize amphoras dating to the Hellenistic period, and columns and capitals arranged around the gardens as impromptu seating. The lobby contains a helpful map of Turkey indicating which regions belonged to which kingdoms—a must for understanding the historical evolution of the country and for appreciating the artifacts presented in this and other exhibits. Upstairs is a chronological exhibit of pottery, ceramics, and glass, as well as funerary objects and the reconstruction of a 3rd-millennium-B.C. tomb. Larger stone and marble statues take up the lower floor, including statues of Poseidon, Demeter, and Artemis taken from the altar of Zeus in the Agora, and a river god that ornamented a fountain at Ephesus.

South of Konak Sq. in Bahri Baba Park (main entrance up the hill from Konak Sq.). © **0232/484-8324.** Admission 5YTL ($4.35/£2). Tues–Sun 9am–noon and 1–5pm.

Asansör ★★ *(Moments*   The Asansör quarter is named after the 19th-century passenger elevator installed to provide access between the upper and lower levels of this hilly neighborhood. The base of the elevator lies at the end of historic Dario Moreno Sokak, lined with old restored houses representative of the city's former Jewish neighborhood. The view from the top, 50m (164 ft.) up, is as good as anything on the Amalfi Coast, and can be made more enjoyable over a tulip-shaped glass of tea or a meal at the Teras Restaurant Café (© **0232/261-2626**).

Dario Moreno Sok., Karataş, south of Konak Sq. No phone. Elevator to the top 25Ykr (20¢/10p).

Clock Tower (Saat Kulesi)   Commanding Konak Square, this elaborately decorated clock tower has become the symbol of Izmir. Designed in a late Ottoman Moorish style, the Clock Tower was presented to the city by Sultan Abdülhamid in 1901 and stands over 24m (79 ft.) high.

Konak Sq.

Ethnography Museum (Etnoğrafya Müzesi)   This beautiful old mansion, formerly a hospital, was recovered from the Izmir Department of Public Health and put to much better use as a repository of Turkish folklore. The biggest draws are the accurate reconstruction of salons from Ottoman homes including a bridal chamber and a circumcision room. Re-created *in situ* are a number of workshops, including a pharmacy, a printing shop, a felt-making workshop, and a glassmaking atelier. Also on view is a wonderful collection of popular folkloric art, ceramics, copper utensils, and traditional costumes and decorative fabrics.

Next to the Archaeology Museum (south of Konak Sq. in Bahri Baba Park). © **0232/484-8324.** Admission 2YTL ($1.75/80p). Tues–Sun 9am–noon and 1–5pm.

Kadifekale ("Velvet Fortress")   Lysimachos, Alexander the Great's general, built this citadel at the summit of Mount Pagos—though given its strategic location, it was probably constructed on the foundations of an earlier civilization. It's now a seedy playground used by the underprivileged, making a stop up here often unpleasant; surely Alex would kick the butts of those pretzel-selling urchins were he alive today. Nevertheless, on a clear day you'll swear you can see as far as Greece from atop the remaining ramparts.

On the hilltop overlooking Izmir, just east of Konak. No phone. Sunrise–sunset. From Konak, take a city bus marked KALE; better yet, take a taxi.

Kızlarağası Han Bazaar ★   This Ottoman *bedesten* has been a successful draw since its restoration, not just because few can resist a town bazaar, but also because the prices are amazingly competitive for the stocks of sumac carpets, water pipes, camel bone, and jewelry. Better yet, some of the best coffee in Turkey is served here in the shaded center courtyard.

Kemeraltı, off Anafartalar Cad. (Start asking for directions once you get close.) Daily 9am–7pm.

Konak Pier The neighborhood of Konak was another lucky beneficiary of the redevelopment of Izmir's waterfront. Along with the neighborhood's wide-open plazas, there's this restored Customs House built by Gustave Eiffel. They've turned it into a shopping mall, but if the mall at home had views like this, I'd be a lot poorer.

Atatürk Bulv., Konak. No phone.

WHERE TO STAY

Crowne Plaza 🍴 Because this hotel is located outside of the city center (on the coastal road to Çeşme in Inciraltı), the Crown Plaza may not be the right choice for visitors with limited time and a big itinerary not centered around Izmir. Nevertheless, with a car at your disposal, it'll be easy enough to day-trip to Çeşme, Ephesus, and Sardis and be back at the hotel in time for your Exceptional Elixir Facial. The hotel, you see, is sited atop the Balcova thermal spring. The hotel is also located on the waterfront promenade of Inciraltı, and just on the doorstep of the Aegean Museum naval ship permanently docked outside the entrance. **Agamemnon Termal Spa** treatments include 14 types of massage, aroma therapies, and various skin treatments, with prices ranging from 100YTL ($87/£40) for a facial on up to 200YTL ($174/£80) for that fancy elixir one you booked before you left the hotel. Combined use of the thermal pools costs 18YTL ($16/£7.20) per day for hotel guests, 28YTL ($24/£11) for nonguests.

Inciraltı Mevkii 10, Sok. 67, Balcova, Izmir. ✆ **0232/292-1300.** Fax 0232/292-1313. www.cpizmir.com. 219 units. 242€ ($351/£173) double; 289€ ($419/£206) suite. AE, MC, V. **Amenities:** 3 restaurants; 2 bars; indoor swimming pool; health club; thermal spa; Turkish bath; sauna; concierge; tour desk; car-rental desk; business center w/secretarial services (fee-based); shopping arcade; salon; 24-hr. room service; babysitting; laundry service; dry cleaning; nonsmoking rooms; executive floors; free valet parking. In room: A/C, satellite TV w/movies, dataport, minibar, hair dryer.

Izmir Hilton 🍴 The Izmir Hilton needs no listing; they're all excellent and they're all the same. This one opened in 1992 to provide a world-class, five-star facility in a town full of wannabes. Now, however, the competition is stiff. The staff is professional and dignified; the common areas sparkle; the rooms are plush, dignified, and user-friendly; and there isn't a thing the management hasn't thought of to make your stay seamless. And in typical American-management style, there is a price tag on every extra little thing you do.

Gaziosmanpaşa Bulv. 7, 35210 Alsancak, Izmir. ✆ **800/445-8667** in the U.S., or 0232/441-6060. Fax 0232/441-2277. www.hilton.com. 381 units. From 145€ ($210/£104) double; 260€ ($377/£186) and up suite. AE, DC, MC, V. Parking garage free for guests. **Amenities:** 3 restaurants; 2 bars; indoor swimming pool; 2 tennis courts; health club; sauna; concierge; tour desk; car-rental desk; business center w/secretarial services (fee-based); shopping arcade; salon; 24-hr. room service; massage; babysitting; laundry service; dry cleaning; nonsmoking rooms; executive floors; free valet parking. In room: A/C, satellite TV w/movies, dataport, minibar, hair dryer, safe.

Kordon Hotel 🍴 It seems as if small-scale luxury hotels keep popping up all over Turkey. The Kordon, with its back to Pasaport and the Gulf of Izmir, is no exception. The hotel caters to business travelers, but you can take advantage of the textured waffle blankets, the relaxing rain showers, the designer sunken marble sinks, and views of the sea just the same. This is also the first time I've seen electronic "do not disturb" indicators.

Akdeniz Cad. 2, 35220 Pasaport, Izmir. ✆ **0232/425-0445.** Fax 0232/484-8181. www.kordonotel.com.tr. 60 units. 55€–70€ double ($77–$98/£39–£50). MC, V. **Amenities:** Panoramic rooftop restaurant; cafe; bar; banquet facilities; fitness center; concierge; business services; laundry services; dry cleaning; nonsmoking rooms. In room: A/C, satellite TV, wired and wireless Internet, minibar, coffee/tea service, hair dryer, safe.

Mövenpick   The Swiss-based Mövenpick Group, with locations all over the world, has jumped into the fray of direct competition with its compatriot, the Swissôtel Grand Efes across the street. Replacing the now-defunct Hotel Mercure, the Mövenpick is a well-respected hospitality franchise catering to business travelers on a budget, with decor and amenities pretty close to what you'll find in the Grand Efes. And with only 185 rooms (ranging from superior rooms to king suites), it's also more manageable. The facade of glass will also ensure that you get the best shot at a room with a view of the Gulf of Izmir. Because some of the rooms may still not have been completed by the opening date, keep this in mind when making your reservation.

Gaziosmanpaşa Bulv. 35210, Izmir. ⓒ 0232/484-8080. Fax 0232/484-8070. www.movenpick.com. 185 units. Check website for rates. AE, DC, MC, V. **Amenities:** Restaurant; bar; indoor swimming pool; health club; Coral Spa; Turkish Bath; wet sauna; concierge; tour desk; car-rental desk; business center w/secretarial services (fee-based); meeting and conference facilities; shopping arcade; salon; 24-hr. room service; babysitting; laundry service; dry cleaning; nonsmoking rooms; executive floors; valet parking. *In room:* A/C, satellite TV w/movies, dataport, minibar, hair dryer, safe.

Swissôtel Grand Efes 𝔸𝔸𝔸   After 4 transitional years and with the Swissôtel now at the helm, the Grand Efes can once again hold its head up as Izmir's premier five-star property. The rebuilt and refurbished hotel, convention center, and facilities are geared to a primarily business clientele. There's a state-of-the-art conference center and high-tech room amenities that feature high-speed Internet (wireless and ISDN). Suites have cordless phones, CD players, and the essential espresso machine. The modern decor is business-sleek and stylish, using tasteful woodsy tones, natural fabrics, and black accents for that designer feel. There's plenty of attention paid to relaxation, with an enormous outdoor swimming pool, a lovely palm garden, and the very soothing Amrita Spa.

Gaziosmanpaşa Bulv. 1, 35210 Izmir. ⓒ 0232/483-9761. Fax 0232/441-0494. www.izmir.swissotel.com. 402 units. Check website for rates. AE, DC, MC, V. Underground parking garage. **Amenities:** 4 restaurants; 4 bars; indoor and outdoor swimming pool; health club; Amrita Wellness Center; Turkish Bath; wet sauna; ice room; concierge; tour desk; car-rental desk; business center w/secretarial services (fee-based); shopping arcade; salon; 24-hr. room service; babysitting; laundry service; dry cleaning; nonsmoking rooms; executive floors; free valet parking. *In room:* A/C, satellite TV w/movies, dataport, minibar, hair dryer, safe.

WHERE TO DINE

Ever since the completion of the waterside promenade, the **Kordon** has become Izmir's de facto center for restaurants and breezy cafes. New ones pop up practically every day.

Deniz Restaurant 𝔸𝔸 FISH   Every city has the perfect place to celebrate special occasions or impress the boss. With a reputation that precedes it, Deniz easily earns the honors for Izmir's best restaurant. Their specialty is an adaptation of a meaty favorite: *balik kavurma,* a preparation of the flakiest Mediterranean catch in a traditional earthenware pan. There's also a fish *şiş* of the day for 35YTL ($30/£14). The fried ice cream is an unexpected delight, and the restaurant's nonsmoking room and unpretentious surroundings make the meal all the more enjoyable.

Atatürk Cad. 188/B (under Izmir Palas Oteli). ⓒ 0232/464-4499. Reservations required. Appetizers 4YTL–15YTL ($3.50–$13/£1.60–£5.20); fish by weight. DC, MC, V. Daily 11:30am–midnight.

Izmir Ticaret Odası Lokali 𝔸 KEBAPS   This unpretentious restaurant is a popular spot among local businessmen for lunch and the perfect place for dinner you've been asking around for. There are no surprises on the menu, except for the *süt kuzu* *kokoreç*—a soup of sheep's intestine (tripe, essentially), a traditional remedy for hangovers. Maybe try the grills or *pides* (flatbreads) instead.

Vasıf Çınar Bulv. 1 (on the 2nd floor opposite Deniz Restaurant). ℂ 0232/421-4249. Main courses 8YTL–16YTL ($7–$14/£3.20–£6.40). MC, V. Mon–Fri 11am–3:30pm.

Topçu'nun Yeri TURKISH   This down-to-earth eatery is a favorite among the local businessmen, and the three side-by-side restaurants and sidewalk cafes are filled to the brim with popular national actors and artists in town for the various annual fairs. On summer days when the heat becomes too much to bear, the main section has an air-conditioned dining area on the second floor, with a TV (in Turkish, of course) for a little background atmosphere. The house specialty is *çöpşiş,* cubed beef, veal, or lamb grilled on skewers; and *köfte,* the Turkish equivalent of a pressed meatball, but there is a lineup of the usual varieties of eggplant and grills on the traditional menu as well.

Kazım Dirik Cad. 3, Izmir. ℂ 0232/425-9047. Appetizers and main courses 4YTL–9YTL ($3.50–$7.85/£1.60–£3.60). MC, V. Daily noon–midnight.

IZMIR AFTER DARK

The redevelopment of Izmir's waterfront truly infuses new life into this city on the sea. The grassy **Kordon waterfront park,** which runs from Cumhuriyet Meydanı to the ferryboat docks of **Alsancak** and beyond, is rimmed by, at last count, 14 establishments, including restaurants, pubs, and Italian cafes, all with terrace seating, and facing the open park and promenade. According to the locals, they're "all good, all the same, all expensive." Check out the **Sakız Adası** (Atatürk Cad. 332/A; ℂ 0232/465-1707), a newly opened and stylish cafe celebrating the common Greek and Turkish love of mastic gum. Here you'll find drinks, liqueurs, and desserts made from the aromatic resin, infused with flavors like bergamot, quince, pistachio mandarin, and even eggplant. I hate the stuff, but you can't leave Izmir (or Çeşme) without trying it. **Sera Café** (ℂ 0232/422-1939), across from Deniz Restaurant (and below Izmir Ticaret Odası), provides live music nightly.

   The North Shield Pub (ℂ 0232/483-0720) added to its portfolio of pubs by opening up a location in Konak Pier. But tables at this location are positioned as to best enjoy the serenade of the sea and the nighttime glow of the lights bouncing off the Gulf of Izmir.

   The highly regarded **Izmir State Opera and Ballet** (ℂ 0232/484-6445) and the **Izmir State Symphony Orchestra** (ℂ 0232/425-4115; fax 0232/484-5172) perform from September to May; check with your travel agent or the official website for calendar information (www.izdob.gov.tr)—but keep your Turkish dictionary handy, as you'll need to know the names of the months. Tickets for performances cost from 7YTL to 20YTL ($6.10–$17/£2.80–£8).

2 Bergama & Pergamum (★(★

About 250km (155 miles) south of Çanakkale; 103km (64 miles) north of Izmir

The bustling city of Bergama is flanked by an industrial wasteland to the north and a forgettable series of seaside footnotes to the holiday resorts closer to Izmir. But in spite of the economic progress the city has evidently made, still no one has thought to build a decent hotel. This lack of modern accommodations has unfortunately turned Bergama into a stop, look, and leave destination—ironic given that the main attractions, the

Acropolis and Asklepion of **Pergamum** ✦✦✦, are listed among the top 100 historical sites on the Mediterranean. It's also home to one of the **seven churches of the
Apocalypse.** Still, it's a hard sell.

The ancient city of Pergamum (also written as Pergamon) dates back to the 12th
century B.C. but saw its first notable era of prosperity under Lydian King Croesus in
the 6th century B.C. Pergamum briefly fell under Persian control but was wrestled
back into Hellenistic hands in 334 B.C. by Alexander the Great. While Alexander was
out conquering other lands, Anatolia was left in the hands of his general, Lysimachus,
who had entrusted his war chest to the hands of Philataerus, commander of Pergamum. On Lysimachus's death, Philataerus founded a ruling dynasty with the late general's riches and was succeeded by his nephew, Eumenis I. Eumenis II is credited with
bringing the empire to its height, ushering in a period of economic, cultural, and artistic expansion in the 2nd century B.C. When Attalus III, the last of the ruling Attalid
dynasty, died, his ambiguous testament was interpreted by Rome as carte blanche for
the Romans to come take over. Under the Romans, Pergamum reclaimed a measure
of its former greatness, but the town was all but forgotten once the Ottomans took
control.

Most of the extraordinary buildings and monuments date to the time of Eumenes II
(197–159 B.C.), including the famed **library,** the terrace of the spectacularly sited hillside **theater,** the main **palace,** the **Altar of Zeus,** and the propylaeum of the **Temple
of Athena.** The ancient city is composed of the **Acropolis,** whose main function was
social and cultural as much as it was sacred; the **Lower City,** or realm of the lower
classes; and the **Asklepion,** one of the earliest medical and therapeutic centers on
record.

ESSENTIALS
GETTING THERE
To get to Bergama, take one of the through-buses heading from Istanbul to Izmir or
from Izmir to Çanakkale. Fares for both are around 20YTL ($17/£8). All buses go to
the new bus station located approximately 3km (1¾ miles) outside of town. From
there, either hop on a *dolmuş* (1YTL/87¢/40p) or take a taxi.

VISITOR INFORMATION
The **tourist information office** is located at Izmir Cad. 54, to the right of the government building (© **0232/633-1862**), and is open weekdays 8:30am to 12:30pm
and 2 to 5:30pm. You can pick up a map of the city, but with the city's network of
one-way streets and the narrow cobbled lanes that meander through the Old Town,
you may as well be reading Greek.

ORIENTATION
The town of Bergama has developed on and around the ancient city of Pergamum.
The heart of the modern city lies around the town's central park and municipal building while the center of Eski, or Old Bergama, with its fruit market and carpet shops,
is situated around the neighborhood of the Red Basilica. The road past the Red Basilica winds up and around for about 5km (3 miles) until it arrives at the Acropolis,
while the Asklepion is located closer to town behind the military camp. Frequently
overlooked are the original Greek houses of Eski Bergama, whose steep inclined streets
intertwine in the neighborhood above the Red Basilica.

GETTING AROUND

There is no public transportation from Bergama to either the Acropolis or Asklepion, although the latter is a reasonable walk from the town's center. A taxi to the Acropolis will cost about 15YTL to 20YTL ($13–$17/£6–£8). If you're looking for an uphill hike, there's a way to access the Acropolis on foot, saving the cost of round-trip taxi fare and the entrance fee all in one go. (Cross the Tabak Bridge and follow the path up and to the right toward the lower Agora.)

WHAT TO SEE & DO

The Acropolis 𝘨𝘨 Dominating the summit of a hill almost 300m (984 ft.) high, the Acropolis provides a humbling view of the surrounding plains, aqueducts, and reservoir below. The remains of this once-great empire are no less impressive, despite the fact that most artifacts are now on exhibit at the Pergamum Museum in Berlin. Here it's still possible to ramble around the Upper and Lower cities, amid the palaces, public and private buildings, and temples too large to cart away. Although only the foundation remains, the **Temple of Athena** was probably constructed, using the acropolis of Athens as a model, in the 3rd century B.C., in the earliest days of the Pergamene kingdom. Today you can see the architrave, along with fragments of columns, in the Berlin Museum.

Eumenis II's construction of the **great library** rivaled the one at Alexandria, provoking the Egyptians into an embargo of papyrus. Lacking such a basic essential, the people of Pergamum were forced to come up with an alternative, and parchment was invented. Ironically, when Pergamum came under Roman rule, Marc Antony gifted the entire 200,000-volume collection to Cleopatra, shipping the contents of the rival library back to Alexandria, where, tragically, the entire collection was destroyed in a fire. A 3m (9¾-ft.) statue of the goddess Athena, discovered in the area of the reading room, is now housed in the Berlin Museum.

Near the temple of Athena are the remnants of the **Palaces of the Pergamene Kings.** The smaller, northern building is believed to have been that of Attalus while the larger palace most likely belonged to Eumenes II. Mosaics discovered in the internal courtyards of the palaces are now in the Berlin Museum.

With the Romanization of Pergamum, many of the Hellenic foundations were simply adapted to suit the arriving Roman emperors and administrators. The **Temple of Trajan** 𝘨𝘨 is one example, and because of removal or looting, the temple remains dated to Hellenistic times.

The remarkable **theater** 𝘨𝘨𝘨, built into the hillside and split into three sections of tiers, was composed of 80 extraordinary levels that seated up to 10,000 people. The panorama is awe-inspiring—a fact not overlooked by Eumenes II, who had a 240m-long (787-ft.) *stoa* (covered arcade) constructed along the upper terrace of the theater. At the northern end of the terrace promenade was the **Temple of Dionysus,** which, along with the altar, is in a fairly good state of preservation. The **Temple of Dionysus** was restored by Caracalla after a fire gutted the interior.

The largest building on the Acropolis is the **Altar of Zeus,** built during the reign of Eumenes II. Fragments of the altar were recycled in the construction of the Byzantine fortification walls, but rediscovered by Carl Humann in 1871 and later reconstructed in the Berlin Museum. The reliefs (also in Berlin) depicted the mythological battle between the giants and the gods—an analogy to the Pergamene victory of the Galatians.

The **Agora** and **Agora Temple** lie to the south of the Altar of Zeus. As you head down the hill to the south, you arrive at the **Lower City,** where, up until a brush fire cleared out the overgrowth, not much more than crumbling foundations remained. Ambitious types and those heading down to town on foot should keep an eye out for what's left of the **Sanctuaries of Hera** and of **Demeter,** the **Temple of Asklepios,** several **gymnasiums,** a **House attributed to Attalos,** and a **Lower Agora.**

Hilltop; adjacent to the Garrison. ✆ 0232/631-2886. Admission 10YTL ($8.70/£4); car park 3YTL ($2.60/£1.20). Winter daily 8:30am–5:30pm; summer daily 8:30am–7:30pm.

Archaeology Museum (Arkeoloji Müzesi) ✸   The collection of statues, objects, and gravestones housed in this museum represents a fraction of the Acropolis and Asklepion ruins that the Germans didn't carry off. In spite of this, a visit here is a worthy complement to the site visits, and the curators have even been kind enough to create a faithful replica of Zeus's Altar, saving you from a trip to Berlin. Some other notable objects amid the artifacts include a statue of Hadrian taken from the Asklepion library; a 2nd-century-A.D. stone horse from the altar of Zeus; and the oldest statue in the museum, a 4th-century-B.C. *kuros,* an early example of the sculpted human form.

The ethnographic wing exhibits a collection of objects, costumes, and textiles from the surrounding region.

Zafer Mah. Cumhuriyet Cad. 10 (on left across from the BP gas station). ✆ 0232/631-2883. Admission 2YTL ($1.75/80p). Tues–Sun 8:30am–noon and 1–5pm.

The Asklepion ✸✸   This famed ancient medical center, built in honor of Asklepios, the god of healing, was also the world's first psychiatric hospital. Many of the treatments employed at Pergamum, enhanced by a sacred source of water that was later discovered as having radioactive properties, have been used for centuries, and are once again finding modern application. The treatments included psychotherapy, massage, herbal remedies, mud and bathing treatments, interpretation of dreams, and the drinking of water. The Asklepion gained in prominence under the Romans in the 2nd century A.D., but a sacred site existed prior to this as early as the 4th century B.C.

Oddly enough, everybody who was anybody was dying to get in; patients included Hadrian, Marcus Aurelius, and Caracalla. Therapy included mud baths, music concerts, and doses of water from the sacred fountain. Hours of therapy probed the meaning of the previous night's dreams, as patients believed dreams recounted a visit by the god Asklepios, who held the key to curing the illness. Galen, the influential physician and philosopher who was born in Pergamum in A.D. 129, trained and then later became an attendant to the gladiators here.

Access is via the **Sacred Way** ✸✸, which at 807m (2,648 ft.) long and colonnaded originally connected the Asklepion with the Acropolis. The Sacred Way becomes the stately Via Tecta near the entrance to the site and leads to a courtyard and fallen Propylaeum, or Monumental Gate. Don't miss the focus of the first courtyard, an **altar** inscribed with the emblem of modern medicine, the serpent. To the right of the courtyard is the Emperor's Room, which was also used as a library. The circular domed **Temple of Asklepios,** with a diameter of 23m (75 ft.), recalls the Pantheon in Rome, which was completed only 20 years earlier. Reachable through an underground tunnel is what is traditionally called the **Temple of Telesphorus** ✸, which served as both the treatment rooms and the sleeping chambers, an indication that sleep was integral in the actual healing process. At various spots in the center of the complex are a total of three pools and fountains, used for bathing, drinking, and various other forms of treatment. The semicircular **Roman Theatre** ⍟ flanks the colonnaded promenade on the northwest corner of the site.

Old Pergamum. No phone. Admission 10YTL ($8.70/£4). Winter daily 8:30am–5pm; summer daily 8:30am–7pm.

Red Basilica (Kızıl Avlu) ⍟⍟   This is one impressive pile of red brick. Built during the reign of Hadrian, this temple dedicated to the Egyptian god Serapis (the model for the Greek god Isis) was later to become one of the seven churches of the Apocalypse. The temple was destroyed in the Arab raids of A.D. 716 to 717, and then was converted by the Byzantines into a basilica. The enormous building straddles the ancient Selinus River (today the Bergama Cayı), whose two subterranean galleries provide a canal. True to the ideal that holy ground is always holy ground, a small mosque resides in one of the towers. The second tower has been recently restored and exhibits works recovered during the ongoing excavations.

Outskirts of town, at the base of the hill to the Old City and the rd. up to the Acropolis. ⓒ **0232/631-2885.** Admission 5YTL ($4.35/£2). Winter daily 8:30am–5:30pm; summer daily 8:30am–6:30pm.

WHERE TO STAY

Anıl Hotel   The Anıl Hotel is a reasonable choice for those travelers determined enough to spend the night. The lobby has some interesting Hellenistic touches, and the rooms are inoffensive. You will practically trip over the Archaeological Museum when you step out the front door, and the rooftop solarium serves up breakfast and unobstructed views of the Acropolis at no extra charge. Their second hotel, the Efsane (Atatürk Bulv. 82; ⓒ **0232/632-6350;** www.efsanehotelbergama.com), charges slightly less and comes with the added bonus of wood floors and a rooftop swimming pool.

Hafutiye Cad. 4, 35700 Bergama (Bergama center right after park behind gas station). ⓒ **0232/631-1830.** Fax 0232/632-6353. www.anilhotelbergama.com. 12 units. 50€ ($73/£36) double. 10% discount if booked via Internet site. MC, V. **Amenities:** Restaurant; bar; wireless Internet; 24-hr. room service; massage; laundry service; dry cleaning. In room: A/C, satellite TV, minibar, hair dryer.

WHERE TO DINE

Berto Sosyal Tesisleri TURKISH   Run by the Bergama Chamber of Commerce, this "social establishment" is filling the dining void with this lovely restaurant near the Ulu Mosque (sure, the town has other restaurants, but they ebb and flow with the tourist tide, as does the freshness of the dishes served). The restored building dates to 1850 and the outdoor terrace and ground-level cafe take advantage of the manicured landscaping. The menu sticks to the expected salads, meatballs, and grills.

Ulucami Mah. Büyük Alan Mevkii. ⓒ **0232/632-9641.** Appetizers and main courses 4YTL–7YTL ($3.50–$6.10/£1.60–£2.80). MC, V. Daily noon–10pm. Closed for Ramadan.

3 Highlights of the Çeşme Peninsula ⍟

81km (50 miles) west of Izmir

Given the density of cultural riches on the tried-and-true paths of the Anatolian "mainland," few foreigners venture out to Çeşme, Izmir's sun-kissed western peninsula. Perhaps now with the completion of the new superhighway, driving those scant 50 miles won't seem so insurmountable.

Çeşme, named after the many springs found in the area during the 18th and 19th centuries, is a world-class Aegean resort, blessed with picturesque beaches and thermal spas both numbering well into the double digits. When tourists discovered the haunts of the Bodrum Peninsula, the smart set migrated north to the crystalline beaches of Çeşme. Çeşme still manages to remain relatively untarnished, offering a perfect balance between sybaritic and simple pleasures, such as the appreciation of unspoiled stretches of fertile fields of aniseed, mastic trees, and olive groves.

Plan on a minimum of 2 full days to explore the beaches and baste in a thermal pool. You'll want more time if you plan on sleeping late and visiting any of the culturally rich villages.

ORIENTATION

The small resort town of Çeşme is located at the extreme western tip of the Çeşme Peninsula, located about an hour's drive out of Izmir. The highway arrives into **Çeşme Limanı (harbor),** where a left turn southward past the marina and ferry terminal heads out into the hills and arrives at some of the finest beaches in the area, namely **Pırlanta** and **Altınkum.** A right turn onto the harbor road leads into the heart of Çeşme, where a cluster of travel agents and restaurants, as well as the tourist information office, are located. Dominating the main square is the **Genovese Castle,** which together with the **Selçuk caravansary** is a striking sight from the sea. Perpendicular to the main square is the pedestrian **Inkılap Caddesi,** Çeşme's main shopping street, which heads inland from the waterfront.

From the harbor roughly to Tekke Beach at the northern end of Çeşme town, traffic moves in a one-way direction. At Tekke Beach, drivers can either circle back up and around town or follow signs for **Ayayorgı Beach** or the small port village of **Dalyan.**

About 10km (6¼ miles) before arriving in Çeşme on the highway is the turnoff for **Alaçatı the old town and bay.**

From Çeşme heading along the northeast coastal road is the beach and thermal resort of **Ilıca,** the thermals of **Şifne,** and, farther northeast along the coast, the ruins of **Erythrai** and the village of **Ildırı.** (Villages farther north such as **Karaburun**—easily 2 hours to the north—require more time than I recommend you from a short visit to Çeşme.)

ESSENTIALS
GETTING THERE
BY CAR   A toll expressway runs the length of the peninsula and connects Çeşme with Izmir and the region beyond.

BY BUS   Buses from Izmir leave from the main *otogar* outside of town, heading westward through Izmir before getting on the highway. Therefore, if you're staying around Konak, it makes more sense to get the bus near Fahrettin Altay Medyanı; ask your taxi driver to go to this secondary bus stop. Bus connections from other cities in the region must be made at the main *otogar.* The fare from Izmir's *otogar* to Çeşme is about 9.50YTL ($8.25/£3.80); from the city center it's slightly less.

Buses arriving into Çeşme arrive at the new *otogar* at the junction of the *çevreyolu* and the Izmir-Çeşme highway extension, just uphill from the main harbor. There is a taxi stand at the *otogar.*

BY FERRY   The Turkish-based **Ertürk Lines** (© **0232/712-6768;** www.erturk.com.tr; travel agency located opposite the marina) operates year-round service between Chios and Çeşme (daily service Apr–Sept departing at 6pm; contact Ertürk for off-season service). Passage costs 40€ ($58/£29) for a round-trip. There are no port taxes.

Fun Fact **Mastic: The Truth About Gum**

The resin-producing mastic tree that grows all over the Çeşme Peninsula (and the Eastern Mediterranean) has been used for centuries in many ways: to heal stomach ulcers, to clean and polish teeth, as a sunscreen and a sunburn soother, and more. In Çeşme, mastic is used in jams, to make pudding, or as a flavoring for raki (an alcoholic drink), while in the United States, the same ingredient is used chiefly as a varnish or adhesive substance. Mastic pudding, along with other cleverly bottled marmalades, is available at **Rumeli Pastanesi,** Inkılap Cad. 46, Çeşme (✆ **0232/712-6759**).

Çeşme is also one of the main ports receiving ferries from Brindisi and Ancona, Italy.

VISITOR INFORMATION

The staff at the tourist information office (✆ **0232/712-6653**), located on the waterfront across from the castle, is ready, willing, and able to provide thorough and useful information on a wide range of subjects. If I had any influence with the local municipality, I'd give these people a raise. Closed Sundays.

GETTING AROUND

With a car at your disposal, the peninsula will more readily show its special appeal, and several rental agencies can be found at the beginning and end of Inkılap Caddesi. For advance reservations (which are rarely necessary), call **Blue Rent a Car** (16 Eylül Mah. Gümrük Sok. 11; ✆ **0232/712-0939**); Ismet, the manager, speaks fantastic English and plays entirely by the book.

Sultan Rent a Car & Motorbike, Inkılap Cad. 54/C, Çeşme (✆ **0232/712-7395;** fax 0232/712-8259), rents out scooters for around 20€ to 25€ ($29–$36/£14–£18) per day—but know that technically, only drivers with an "A" class Turkish license can rent one. Still, many establishments ignore this rule at their and your peril; in the event of an accident, your home insurance may not cover losses.

Dolmuş service to points beyond operates from downtown Çeşme (in front of the municipal building at the end of Inkılap Cad., near waterfront, or from the *otogar*) to nearby beaches and sights. Fares vary only slightly and hover around 2YTL to 2.5YTL ($1.75–$2.20/80p–£1).

There's a taxi stand (✆ **0232/712-6690**) next to the castle in downtown Çeşme, but the rates are outrageous, and *dolmuşes* are fast, reliable, and cheap.

WHAT TO SEE & DO

Genovese Castle   Built in the 14th century by the Genovese to protect wine shipments, this fortress was expanded and reconstructed by the Ottoman Sultan Bayezit II in the beginning of the 16th century. It was destroyed during the wars with Venice in the 17th century, restored again in the 18th, and continued to serve as a defense system until 1833. The fortress is now the **Çeşme Archaeological Museum** housing artifacts recovered during excavations of Erythrai. The mosque that was built within the castle walls is now used as the museum's administration building.

Opposite the ferry landing. ✆ **0232/712-6609**. Admission 2YTL ($1.75/80p). Daily 8:30am–12:30pm and 1:30–5:30pm.

The Village of Ildırı and the Ancient Ruins of Erythrai   Located about a half-hour's drive (17km/11 miles) on the coastal road north from Ilıca is **Ildırı**, which enjoys the shelter of a small bay protected by a series of offshore islands. Not surprisingly, the locals, who number only about 350, make their livings on fishing boats as well as in artichoke and olive fields (and until 15 years ago, in tobacco fields, too). A number of fish restaurants line the small dock as well as the road leading to the village. On the road at the edge of town are a couple of covered shacks called restaurants—the characteristic covered, stone terraces overlook the artichoke and olive fields toward the sea. Stop here for some *gözleme* (a crepe filled with cheese, spinach, or both) and an *ayran* (a buttermilk-like salty yogurt drink), or for some fish only recently pulled out of the water.

On the edge of Ildırı is the ancient Greek city of **Erythrai** 🜨, whose remains are still mostly hidden beneath the fields of artichokes cultivated by the local villagers. Sporadic excavations conducted since 1964 have revealed a theater, dating to the 3rd century B.C. and destroyed in an earthquake in A.D. 100. There are some visible signs of a city plan, including the 6th-century-B.C. Temple of Heracles (unexcavated), a 5th-century-B.C. sacrificial altar, and 2nd-century-B.C. luxury villas and mosaic stone pavement. A climb to the top of the theater and up to the summit of the hill will reveal an old basilica-style church, as well as some of the loveliest views in the region.

About a half-hour's drive (17km/11 miles) on the coastal road north from Ilıca. No phone. Admission 2YTL ($1.75/80p). Daily 8am–5pm.

SURF, SUN & SPORTING FUN

Day boats lining Çeşme's harbor tout excursions in the Aegean for swimming, snorkeling, or simply relaxing. A day usually includes stops at **Donkey Island** (there really are donkeys there), the **Blue Lagoon,** and **Black Island.** At 30YTL ($26/£12) with lunch included, these tours are a good value. Stroll along the harbor the night before to inspect the boats.

If exploring the shipwrecks offshore is more your speed, or you just want to brush up on some rusty diving skills, contact **Dolphin Land** (✆ **0232/337-0161;** fax 0232/486-2309; www.divecesme.com) for information on their day trips around Çeşme. They also offer PADI certification with English instruction.

You'll need a car to get to **Alaçatı Bay** 🜨🜨, an expanse of water surrounded by sandy and sun-scorched hills. Thanks to year-round high winds, shallow waveless water, and wide-open space, the bay is one of the top three **windsurfing** destinations in the world and of late a popular destination for a growing number of windsurf groupies. Windsurfers from the four corners come here to participate in the Windsurf Turkey Cup, in which thrill-seekers compete in a stunt-filled challenge of wits and skill. The rest of the year, neophytes like me get out there and entertain the pros from the on-site windsurfing schools with my ineptitude. **Alaçatı Surf Paradise Club** (✆ **0232/716-6611;** www.alacati.de; closed Nov–Mar) makes it all possible by renting various models by the hour or by the day, with or without instruction. A 3-hour starter course will run you 75€ ($109/£54) including all equipment. A full-day rental without lessons costs 35€ ($51/£25 for a long board) or 60€ ($87/£43) per day for a J.P. To get there, just follow the signs; you can't miss it.

A strip of sand over 1.5km (a mile) long, **Ilıca Beach** is the longest beach on the peninsula and also the most popular. A new marina and breakwater provide direct access (no beach), and a series of semi-immersed iron ladders beckon to those wishing to dive right in. The steamy Ilıca spring bubbles up right in the middle of a rock-sheltered corner of the marina, attracting locals and visitors alike with the (free) opportunity to partake in the healing properties of the water.

Southwest of Çeşme are two of the best public beaches the peninsula has to offer. **Pırlanta Beach (Diamond Beach)** ☆☆, a pristine stretch of lily-white sand, is oriented north toward the rocky coastline. It's a bit windy here, due to the compressed winds that travel through the channel between Chios and Pirlanta Bay. The resulting foamy waves and high winds make this a perfect spot for what has become an area sports craze: **kitesurfing.** Lessons are available in English; contact www.kitesurfbeach.com.

Altınkum Beach ☆☆, named "golden" for the color of its sand, is a long stretch of beach wide open to the sea and facing south, making the waters slightly, refreshingly cooler than the other beaches on the peninsula. At these public beaches, the entrance is free and chairs and umbrellas rent for 2YTL to 3YTL ($1.75–$2.60/80p–£1.20) per person. A minibus from the yacht harbor will take you to both beaches, a distance just under 8km (5 miles). If you're driving yourself, follow the directions for the "Ionia Hotel" at the multisigned fork in the road heading toward Altınkum/Pirlanta. (**Note:** Don't confuse Altınkum with the disappointing stretch at Tursite; follow the small black sign for PLAJ.) There's also a restaurant shack on the beach at Altınkum that includes a cafeteria/bar/restaurant.

North of Çeşme, hidden amid the olive and orange groves, is **Ayayorgı Beach** ☆☆☆, an intimate and secluded bay with no actual beach—just cement piers (no sand!) and crystalline waters. Two or three beach clubs stake out their territory every year (the current ones are **Shayna Beach Club** ☎ 0232/712-1122 and **Granada** ☎ 0232/712-2253); the cover charge for a day at the beach ranges from 20YTL to 25YTL ($17–$22/£8–£10). Rent some jet skis, go wake-boarding or water-skiing, or jump on a banana ride. Hang around long enough and one or both become host to major and popular headliners or some of the area's hottest DJs. You'll need a car (or fairly expensive taxi) for the 3.5km (2¼-mile) ride from Çeşme to this beach; take the road for Dalyan and follow the signs.

A day spent roaming in and out of the leather, carpet, and silver shops of downtown Çeşme doesn't have to mean you've blown your day at the beach. **Tekke Beach,** just north of the port (and past a dizzying array of appealing waterfront fish restaurants), is the perfect escape for a quick cool-down and limited time.

AREA THERMALS

Çeşme owes its current rebirth to its thermal sources, considered sacred by the ancients. Not all the sources have been tapped, and not all of them are equal.

There may not be the luxury of the Sheraton at **Doğal Şifa Merkezi** (☎ 0232/717-2424), 3km (1¾ miles) north of Ilıca on the right in Şifne, but there's a down-to-earth sensibility in the green Astroturf runners and modest thermal pool. Doğal Şifa also has a thermal mud pit (the point is to mix it with the thermal water—though it was bone-dry during my visit) and an assortment of massage therapies conducted in spotless and stylish white rooms. Vedat Akar, the owner, pharmacist, and on-site physical therapist, can devise a plan of action for your healing needs. To get there by bus, change at Ilıca for a minibus to Şifne.

North of Ilıca on the tip of a small peninsula is a number of small coves, hidden in pine trees and rarely visited. In **Paşa Limanı** ☆☆ is **Vekamp** (☎ 0232/717-2224), which does triple duty as a beach, a thermal, and a campsite. The long rectangular thermal pool, located at the back of the property, is partially shaded in pine, and the waters averaging 104°F (40°C) cascade down a small slide onto the pebble beach just steps below.

The **Botanica Thermal Spa** ★★★ at the Sheraton in Ilıca (Şifne Cad. 35; © **0232/ 723-1240**) was devised with nothing but sheer pleasure in mind. The oriental fusion concept mixes up a luxurious stew of Buddhist, Chinese, Thai, and Balinese influences, welcoming guests to a full-service facility with four thermal pools, one saltwater and three highly sulfuric (of which one is a Jacuzzi and another is outdoor). The center also has a *hamam,* a steam room, a dry sauna, a solarium, and soothing treatment rooms surrounding the outdoor thermal pool. Spa treatments include 14 types of massage, aroma therapies, and various skin treatments, with prices ranging from 75YTL ($65/£30) for the 30-minute Botanica Ritual massage to 215YTL ($187/£86) for the Energy Lift L'Elixir facial, on up to 375YTL ($326/£150) for the Indocéane "works" (body scrub, milk bath, massage, body wrap, and relaxing tea service). Combined use of the thermal pools costs 25YTL ($22/£10) for hotel guests, 50YTL ($44/£20) for outside guests.

West of Ilıca town center is the tiny **Yıldız Peninsula;** near the point is an oddity of geology: thermal water as hot as 122° to 140°F (50°–60°C) springing forth from beneath the surface of the water. This natural phenomenon doesn't have a price tag, as there's no charge to step off the rocky point into the semi-enclosed rocky pool. (Many who have led sheltered lives come here if only to eyeball the bare flesh of women in bathing suits.) It's not uncommon, either, to see women submerged yet covered head to toe in full traditional dress.

WHERE TO STAY

The hotel listings below offer a choice of the best the Çeşme area has to offer. If you opt for one of the hotels in Çeşme town, you'll be trading beach access for convenience to the town center, which offers everything including car rentals, travel agencies, restaurants, and cafes. The buzz of visitors along the main drag out for the evening air also offers the people-watching you won't get in the other villages on the peninsula. Second to Çeşme as to level of activity is Ilıca, with one of the nicest stretches of beach around. The tiny village and cove of Dalyan has nothing more than a postcard-perfect marina lined with fish restaurants; to get around, you'll either have to rely on the services of the hotel concierge, or rustle up some authentic assistance by haggling at the marina. Alaçatı Bay is the site of development, but for now, the hotel scene (apart from the new Port Hotel at the new marina and the stodgy Süzer) is still the purview of backpacking windsurfers.

ÇEŞME TOWN
Pırıl Hotel   This hotel was a great bargain when it began as a humble three-star diamond in the rough, but the owner had a vision, and now the Pırıl is a five-star, all-inclusive hotel. The very comfortable accommodations range from standard doubles through duplex suites. The thermal center has all of the bells and whistles, but trouble is, the tile gets moldy under humid conditions—the type you find in steam rooms and *hamams.* Rates (provided in YTL to domestic clients, in U.S. dollars to Americans, and in euros to everybody else) include all meals, snacks, and drinks, and the food was actually quite good. The hotel is located .8km (½ mile) through back streets from the main drag, a distance that makes for a lovely evening walk. A private shuttle is available to and from the hotel's beach.

Çevre Yolu, 35940 Çeşme. (C) **0232/712-7574.** Fax 0232/712-7953. www.pirilhotel.com. 136 units. July–Aug 159€ ($231/£114) double; shoulder and low season 70€–119€ ($102–$173/£50–£85). Rates per person all inclusive. MC, V. Free parking. **Amenities:** Restaurant; bar; 2 outdoor swimming pools; one indoor and one outdoor thermal pool; fitness room; Turkish bath, wet sauna; Internet point; 24-hr. room service; babysitting; laundry service; dry cleaning; nonsmoking rooms; doctor on-call; free parking. *In room:* TV, minibar, hair dryer, safe.

DALYAN

Sisus Hotel ⚘⚘ Locals call this "the love hotel." This is probably because of the romantic details: white pillows wrapped up in red ribbons, tea candles in the bathroom, and colored stones accenting tabletops and consoles. Public areas are a cross between *2001: A Space Odyssey* and SoHo chic; rather than ask questions, I decided to concede that the formula works. All rooms enjoy a balcony, and design-wise, the architects thought to optimize the views by partitioning the bathrooms from the main room via glass walls. Sitting right on the charming cove that is Dalyanköy's Yat Limanı, rooms get either a sea or mountain view, while the 95-sq.-m (1,023-sq.-ft.) party "king suite" enjoys the entire rooftop deck and a downstairs foosball table. The hotel also provides a long list of amenities, not least of which is the luxurious wellness center.

Yat Limani (at the marina), Dalyanköy. International bookings in Greece: (C) **30-2810-300330.** Fax 30-2810-220785. www.lux-hotels.com/turkey/sisus. 51 units. High season 300YTL ($261/£120) double, 500YTL ($435/£200) suite ("X" Suite 1,900YTL/$1,653/£760). Rates less than half that in low season. AE, MC, V. **Amenities:** Restaurant; 5 bars; heated outdoor swimming pool; tennis court; fitness center; spa; Turkish bath; sauna; conference room; 24-hr. room service; doctor; babysitting; hairdresser. *In room:* A/C, satellite TV, CD player, Internet connection, minibar, coffee/tea service, hair dryer, safe.

ILICA

Ilıca Marina Suites Located opposite the marina and midway between the town center and natural geothermal pool, this new self-catering "apart" hotel is a reasonable option for the budget-minded. It's also practically beachfront (there's a waterfront promenade, while the actual sandy beach is a 10-min. or so walk away). Rooms look like city studios, with the bedroom at the back of the rectangular space, and a European kitchen opening to a living area. There's an indoor thermal pool on the ground floor. (They could find an alternative anti-slip solution to the AstroTurf.)

Yıldızburnu 5074 Sok. 56, 35940 Ilıca. (C) **0232/723-0200.** Fax 0232/723-3115. www.ilicamarinasuites.com. 44 units. 29YTL–39YTL ($25–$34/£12–£16) 2- to 4-person suite. Breakfast 6.60YTL ($5.75/£2.65) extra. MC, V. **Amenities:** Bar; private beach; indoor thermal pool; parking. *In room:* A/C, cable TV, kitchen (w/fridge, dishwasher, microwave), hair dryer.

Sheraton ⚘⚘ *(Kids)* Visually impressive, über-luxurious, and on the beach, this five-star facility boasts a prime spot on the peninsula's most famous beach. The new top-flight Botanica thermal spa (drawing on the sources of the local Ilıca Hot Spring) aims at nothing less than total immersion in a soothing awe. When I last visited, the hotel had added a full-service convention center.

Şifne Cad. 35, 35940 Ilıca. (C) **800/325-3535** in the U.S. and Canada, 800/325-35353 in Europe, or 0232/723-1240 in Turkey. Fax 0232/723-1856. www.sheraton.com. 373 units. From 395€ ($573/£282) double; 1,016€ ($1,473/£726) suite. Rates fluctuate according to market demand. AE, MC, V. Valet parking. **Amenities:** 3 restaurants; 3 bars; indoor and outdoor swimming pools; tennis courts; health club; thermal spa; Turkish bath; watersports; children's-center programs; game room; concierge; tour desk; car-rental desk; meeting and event facilities; shopping arcade; salon; 24-hr. room service; massage; laundry service; dry cleaning; nonsmoking rooms; executive floor. *In room:* A/C, satellite TV, dataport, minibar, hair dryer, safe.

Villa Saray   This website is too sexy for this book, but perhaps so are the villas, which ironically are a great option for families. Amenities for the villas include private swimming pools in private backyards, full American kitchens, and multiple bedrooms. Guests staying in the rooms (not reviewed here) or bungalows can retreat to the community garden or common pool area.

Izmir Cad. 5072 Sok. 2, Ilıca. ⓒ **0232/723-0266**. Fax 0232/723-3358. www.villasaray-vip.com. 36 villas. 140€ ($203/£100) bungalow; 180€–470€ ($261–$682/£129–£336) villa. MC, V. **Amenities:** Snack bar; mini market; outdoor swimming pool; kids' pool; tennis court; car park. *In room:* A/C TV, minibar.

ALAÇATI
Alaçatı Taş Hotel ⚜   This is the pioneer that has set the bar for all of the town's other guesthouses. When I say "this" I mean both the home and the homeowner, Zeynep Öziş, whose dream came true with the completion of this retreat. One feels an aura of warmth walking through this 150-year-old building, faithfully restored to accommodate the demands of today's overnight guests. Ceilings are high, the garden and salon are cozy and private, and even the smallest of the rooms are ample. Homemade pies and cakes are baked daily, furnishing goodies for the daily afternoon tea event, and even better, breakfast is served until noon.

Kemalpaşa Cad. 132; Alaçatı. ⓒ **0232/716-7722**. Fax 232/716-8517. www.tasotel.com. 8 units. Summer 130€ ($189/£93) double. Rates lower off season. MC, V. No children 11 and under. **Amenities:** Outdoor swimming pool; wireless Internet. *In room:* A/C, hair dryer, no phone.

WHERE TO DINE
ÇEŞME TOWN
Bistro Pasific Et ve Balık Restoran FISH/STEAKHOUSE   One of the newer additions to Çeşme's reclaimed waterfront is this smart bistro. It overlooks the bobbing dayboats and sun worshippers of Tekke Beach, so even if you stop in for a drink, it's well worth the atmosphere. The menu relies heavily on the local catch, which often includes *çupra,* a local sea bass special to Çeşme. For meat lovers, there's an ample selection of variously grilled steaks and kebaps.

Tekke Plajı Mevkii (on the waterfront). ⓒ **0232/712-7686**. Appetizers and main courses 5YTL–18YTL ($4.35–$16/£2–£7.20) and up for fish. MC, V. Daily noon–midnight.

Kale Lokantası HOME COOKING   This unassuming tea garden next to the castle packs up around mealtime, serving good, basic fast food at rock-bottom prices. It's much worse in the winter, when everybody has to fit into the sparsely furnished dining room. There's no menu, just steam pots full of fresh chickpea stew, vegetables with meatballs, and rice and beans. Naturally, they serve *döner kebap* (lamb roasted on a spit), but whatever you choose, a simple hearty meal couldn't be more satisfying.

Çarşı Cad. Kervansaray Yanı 11, Çeşme. ⓒ **0232/712-0519**. All items under 6YTL ($5.20/£2.40). MC, V. Daily 9am–midnight.

DALYAN
Dalyan Restaurant "Cevat'ın Yeri" ⚜⚜ FISH   This quayside restaurant was the first to open in Dalyan, when the cove was still an unmarred paradise. The three brothers, Cevat, Celal, and Mehmet, plus Arif, their brother-in-law and manager, are still at it, serving fish so fresh that its gills are still moving. It's also the only establishment on this increasingly populated waterfront that clearly identifies the price per kilo of the fish. The meze case presents a great variety, with items I've not seen at other restaurants, such as grilled cheese, stuffed calamari, and potato croquettes. The catch

of the day is fished from local waters, some of it even coming from the edge of the harbor wall where you could catch a glimpse of this evening's appetizer.

At the far end of Harbor Rd., Yacht Harbor, Dalyan, Çeşme. ⓒ 0232/724-7045. Reservations suggested. Appetizers 5YTL–15YTL ($4.35–$13/£2–£5.20); fish by weight 25YTL–100YTL ($22–$87/£10–£40). MC, V. Daily noon–1 or 2am.

ALAÇATI

Agrilia Café High ceilings, wooden tables, and city folk relaxing over the Sunday paper set the scene at this former tobacco warehouse. The cafe serves optimal Italian food without the tourist fuss as well as ample breakfasts that include local olives and an area specialty, the fresh olive bread.

Kemal Pasa Cad. 75. ⓒ 0232/716-8594. Appetizers and main courses 7YTL–23YTL ($6.10–$20/£2.80–£9.20). MC, V. Daily 9:30am–11pm (later on summer weekends).

ÇEŞME AFTER DARK

People drive from as far as Izmir and beyond for a night out at one of the beachfront restaurant/dance clubs of Çeşme. The main event usually takes place in **Ayayorgı cove.**

Istanbul's very popular Babylon venue brings the jazz to the coast in summertime. It's called **Babylon Alaçatı** (Cark Plaji at Alaçatı Bay, near the harbor; ⓒ 0232/716-6707), and it's a restaurant, cafe, bar, beach club, and concert venue all rolled into one. The box office is open Monday to Sunday 10am to 2pm.

For a more mellow evening out, perhaps dinner waterside in Dalylanköy, a drink at the stylish Sisus Hotel, or a stroll along the beach is more your speed.

A SIDE TRIP TO SARDIS

Not too many years back, a reader wrote to express his disappointment that **Sardis** 🌟🌟 was absent in the guide. So I set about to find out whether Sardis was indeed all that. Let's just start by saying that even if you have absolutely no context of the ancient city in advance of a visit, you will be wowed.

Sardis was the commercial and religious capital of the ancient kingdom of Lydia, made most famous (or infamous) for the 4th-century-B.C. ruler with the Midas touch: Croesus, who reportedly went about town with his pockets stuffed with gold pieces recovered from the nearby Pactolus River. Hmmm. Announce that there's gold in them thar hills and don't be surprised when the raiding empires arrive. Persian ruler Cyrus wrested control of Lydia from Croesus, and under Persian rule, Lydia rose to become the most powerful kingdom in all of Asia Minor. The kingdom fell to Alexander the Great in 334 B.C., and then was apportioned to the Kingdom of Pergamon after Alexander's death. The city continued to prosper through the Byzantine era (when it was a central diocese and recipient of a solid fifth of the letters to the **Seven Churches of the Revelation**), until the 14th century when it was conquered by the Ottoman Turks.

So my question is: Where are the riches? For the most part, they are all gone, stripped away by looters long ago (but short of digging a very deep hole—I looked). Actually, early in the 20th century, excavations being carried out by Princeton University uncovered a pot of gold and silver coinage, so apparently either we're late or we need bigger shovels. Excavations cosponsored by Harvard and Cornell universities have been ongoing since 1959 and have focused on unearthing the Lydian period, a tall order given that ancient Lydia sits 2m (6½ ft.) below the Roman roadways, which themselves are buried beneath meters of earth sequestered under village residences, chicken coops, and fields of wheat, barley, cotton, and corn. In the past 100 or so years of excavations, more than 11,000 artifacts have been uncovered, the more recent and notable of which (found in the Temple of Artemis) was a *4-foot-tall* marble head of what is presumed to represent either Marcus Aurelius or his son, Commodus.

The ancient city lies within an area, according to archaeologists, of "at least 3 miles of complex terrain, including the Acropolis which sits about 1,000 feet up from the plain." The monumental marble Roman avenue, partially (miniscarely, as most of it is buried beneath the asphalt road) excavated on the south side of the site, spanned a width of 19m (62 ft.), more than double the width of the current highway.

The open-air museum comprises the section of the city that served as the **Gymnasium and Bathhouse** 𝕲𝕲, a 5-acre complex that includes the **Palestra, Caldarium,** and **Frigidarium,** as well as the largest **synagogue** of the ancient world, a classically appointed space of geometrical tile mosaics occupying the southeastern corner of the palestra (gifted to the Jewish community in recognition of its value; synagogues were normally sited on the periphery of the cities). The east-facing **monumental facade** 𝕲𝕲𝕲 of the Palestra is believed to be a 3rd-century-A.D. construction of Roman emperors and brothers, Geta and Caracalla.

The **colonnaded arcade** 𝕲𝕲 that flanks the exterior of the Palestra is lined by a extended string of Byzantine-era shops, whose second stories have long disappeared, leaving stone staircases to nowhere. Several of the shops are identifiable by inscriptions on the doorway or on the odd marble basin.

Exiting from the museum and heading to the right across the main village road to the next perpendicular on the left is a road leading to the **Temple of Artemis** 𝕲𝕲. On your way to the temple the road passes an enclosed excavation that revealed (thanks to the gold dust found in the cracks of pottery found here) the Lydian mint, or the **gold refinery** where Lydia's renowned coinage was created. A bit farther along the Roman road are the ruins of a 13th-century basilica. The basilica is the only known example in Anatolia with five cupolas.

The temple of Artemis is the fourth-largest Ionic temple of the ancient world, dug out of millennia of landslides and earthquakes. The temple dates to the Hellenistic era inaugurated with Alexander's conquest. The oldest portion of the temple was constructed during this period around a **preexisting altar** of red sandstone also dedicated to Artemis, and perhaps additionally, to Cybele. In 175 to150 B.C., Zeus was added to the pantheon of the temple, along with plans to create a *dipteros,* or a double row of colonnades, surrounding the four sides of the temple. The foundations for 13 of the columns were laid along the east front, but work was discontinued; instead, two columns were brought forward and four were placed on the sides, creating an east-facing portico. Under Emperor Antonius Pius (2nd c.), the temple was divided in half providing for two separate places of worship: an east-facing sanctuary dedicated to Faustina I, wife of the emperor, and the space consecrated to Artemis. During this third period, the perimeter of columns was completed. In the 8th century, the portion of the temple dedicated to Faustina was converted into a cistern.

72km (45 miles) east of Izmir (follow the road through Türgütlü and then Ahmetli; the ancient site of Sardes is located in the village of Sart). Admission 2YTL ($1.75/80p).

4 Selçuk & Ephesus 𝕲𝕲

81km (50 miles) south of Izmir; 20km (12 miles) northeast of Kuşadası

Nobody comes to Turkey to visit poor overlooked Selçuk, relegated since ancient times to a secondary position in the shadow of Ephesus, its more illustrious neighbor.

Ephesus

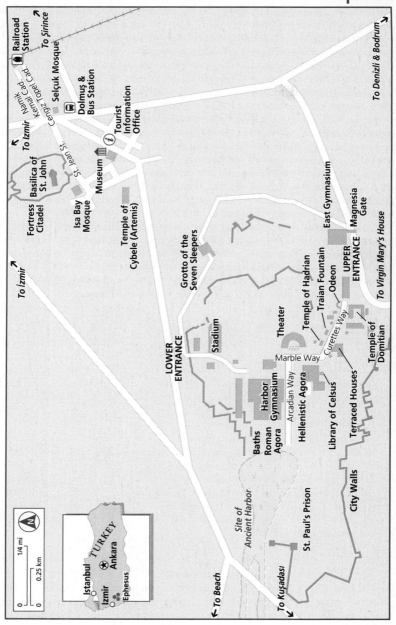

To Şirince
Railroad Station
To İzmir
Selçuk Mosque
Namık Kemal Cad.
Cengiz Topel Cad.
Dolmuş & Bus Station
Tourist Information Office
To İzmir
St. Jean St.
Basilica of St. John
Fortress Citadel
İsa Bay Mosque
Museum
Temple of Cybele (Artemis)
To İzmir
To Denizli & Bodrum
Grotto of the Seven Sleepers
East Gymnasium
Magnesia Gate
UPPER ENTRANCE
To Virgin Mary's House
Temple of Hadrian
Trajan Fountain
Odeon
Curettes Way
Temple of Domitian
LOWER ENTRANCE
Stadium
Theater
Marble Way
Arcadian Way
Harbor Gymnasium
Hellenistic Agora
Library of Celsus
Terraced Houses
City Walls
Baths
Roman Agora
Site of Ancient Harbor
St. Paul's Prison
To Beach
To Kuşadası

N

0   1/4 mi
0   0.25 km

TURKEY
Istanbul
İzmir
Ankara
Ephesus

213

But the histories of the two cities are forever intertwined; Selçuk predates Ephesus, and indeed, Selçuk *was* Ephesus.

The rise and fall of Selçuk/Ephesus, which for the purposes of this chapter refers to the combined area between and including present-day Selçuk and Mount Koressos (Bülbül Dağı, where the remains of the original city wall still stand), was directly related to the ebbs and flows of the sea. In the 7th century B.C., Cimmerian invasions relegated the Ephesians to the area around the Artemesian, at the base of Ayasoluk Hill. (Selçuk's castle occupies this hill.) Because the neighborhood of the Artemesian lies below sea level, archaeologists have been unable as of yet to excavate beyond the temple's remains. When, with the death of Alexander the Great, General Lysimachos took control of the whole of Ionia, the city of Ephesus was reestablished adjacent to the harbor. The expansion of Christianity in the 4th century A.D. saw the construction of many important religious and state buildings in Ephesus, including the castle on Ayasoluk Hill and St. John's Basilica. The silting up of the harbor resulted in the gradual decline of Ephesus as a major commercial port, leaving it vulnerable to subsequent invasions, namely the arrival of the Selçuks in the 10th century.

Today a visit to Selçuk seems only to be a necessary sidebar to the main attraction at Ephesus, just 3km (1¾ miles) away. Nevertheless, the presence of a number of noteworthy ruins—including the representative remains of one of the Seven Wonders of the World; the nearby winemaking village of Şirince, the whole of which has been declared a historic preservation site; and the beaches around Kuşadası (only 18 km/11 miles away)—make Selçuk a perfect base for a well-rounded holiday.

A LOOK AT THE PAST

Numerous legends have been attached to the founding of Ephesus, some saying the Amazons, the Lelegians, or the Carians got here first. A favorite myth attributed to the Ionians—who had arrived here by the 10th century B.C.—says that Androclus, guided by the prophesies of an oracle regarding some fish and a wild boar, founded the city.

There must be some truth behind the legend of Croesus, king of Lydia, who upon hearing of the prosperity of the trading capital decided it had to be his. The city fell under the sovereignty of Lydia in the 6th century B.C. and the Ephesians were displaced to the area around the Artemesian.

A century later, the city was once again the target of an empire, with the invasion of the Persians. For the most part absentee administrators, the Persians were subsequently thrown out by an Ionian uprising in the 5th century B.C., remaining in power until Alexander the Great's arrival. After his death, one of his generals, Lysimachos, reestablished the city between the slopes of Mount Koressos (Bülbüldağ) and Mount Pion (Panayır Dağı), and constructed the city's first fortifications, a defensive wall with a perimeter of 9km (5½ miles). The ruins of the archaeological site of Ephesus date to the city established at this time.

In the 2nd century B.C., the city reached its height as the most important port in Anatolia, and subsequent kings of Pergamum ruled here until the city was absorbed by Rome. The city opened up lucrative commercial opportunities with the exotic Middle East and it wasn't long before Ephesus was designated the capital of the Asian Provinces, attracting the likes of Brutus, Cassius, Antony, and Cicero. Under Julius Caesar, Ephesus was forced to submit to heavy taxation, but under Augustus's reign, the city of Ephesus once again became the most important commercial center on the Mediterranean. The final episode in the ebb and flow of Ephesus's prosperity came during the remarkable proliferation of Christianity, continuing through the rule of Justinian (6th c. A.D.). Many buildings of importance, including the castle on Ayasoluk Hill, date to this period.

Nevertheless, during as far back as Roman times, the port had begun to show signs of silting up, and any attempts at halting the process had proved unsuccessful. After centuries of sand and dirt depositing in the harbor, the port was little more than a marsh, and the citizens of Ephesus, by now an insignificant village under Selçuk control, moved farther inland. The swamp at the end of the Arcadian Way (Harbour Rd.) was once at the water's edge; it's now 5km (3 miles) inland.

ESSENTIALS
GETTING THERE
BY PLANE   For flight information, see "Getting There" under the Izmir heading, earlier in this chapter. From the airport, you'll need to take a minibus to the main bus station (*otogar*), and then from there, change to one of the minibuses departing about every 15 minutes for Selçuk. The ride takes about an hour and costs 6YTL ($5.20/£2.40). Visitors bound for the Kalehan have the option of taking advantage of the $70 (£35) airport transfer.

BY BUS   Long-distance buses from points within Turkey arrive at Selçuk's *otogar* opposite the park to the east side of Atatürk Caddesi. A simple inquisitive *"Selçuk otogar?"* directed at your bus *muavin* (driver's assistant) when you board will help you to know when you've arrived. (*Note:* If you're staying at the Kalehan, ask the driver to let you off at the entrance to the hotel, which is also on the main road.) Sample times and fares are: from Istanbul 35YTL ($30/£14), 10 hours; from Çanakkale 30YTL ($26/£12), 7 hours; from Antalya 30YTL ($26/£12), 7 hours.

BY CAR   From Izmir center or airport, follow the green signs for Aydın/Çevreyolu, which will take you onto the toll road. Exit at Selçuk, and then follow the local road for around 12km (7½ miles). A taxi from the airport will run you about 80YTL ($70/£32) for the half-hour journey from Izmir's airport.

VISITOR INFORMATION
The tourist information office (© **0232/892-6328**), located on the park across from the Ephesus Museum, provides free maps (and a better one for sale), as well as books on topics of local interest. They have a helpful website at www.selcuk.gov.tr.

(*Tips*   **Remember the Annual Festivals of Selçuk!**

Selçuk is the location of the infamous Camel Wrestling Festival, held during the third Sunday of January. The festival is inaugurated the day before with a parade that permits a close-up, pre-match view of the camels.

Every year on August 15, a public Mass is held at the House of the Virgin Mary. And on the second Sunday of each October, Mass is again held in celebration of the Second Ecumenical Council held at Ephesus in the year 431. Both masses commence at 10am.

ORIENTATION

Bisecting the city of Selçuk is **Atatürk Caddesi,** which runs roughly north to south, and which doubles as the highway to Izmir once you leave the center of town. The tourist attractions are all within walking distance to the west of Atatürk Caddesi, with the castle crowning the summit of **Ayasoluk Hill.** Midway down the hill to the south are the Isabey Mosque and St. John's Basilica, both accessible via **St. Jean's Sokağı.** The train station, good for excursions to Izmir, Aphrodisias, and Denizli, near Pamukkale, is located on the eastern side of town near the end of **Cengiz Topel Caddesi** (the eastern continuation of St. Jean's Sokağı to the west). This end of town acts as the hub of Selçuk's shopping and business center, with a good concentration of banks, Internet cafes, kebap houses, and tea gardens.

A green park in the center of town on the west side of Atatürk Caddesi hosts the tourist information office; on the west side of the park is the Ephesus Museum. The road to Kuşadası heads west from the *otogar,* passing the Gendarmerie and the Artemesion on the way past the turnoff for Ephesus.

The ancient city of Ephesus extends beyond the confines of the museum gates, and heartier (and well-watered) types can be seen walking single-file along the road between the Main Gate and the Cave of the Seven Sleepers. Meryemana is about 7km (4⅓ miles) up the hill from the Upper Gate, and therefore (at least for me) too far to walk.

GETTING AROUND

By Dolmuş   *Dolmuşes* leave the *otogar* for Ephesus (signs on the minibuses read EFES) every half-hour (1.50YTL/$1.30/60p). Get off at the upper gate so that you can walk through the sight heading downhill. At the exit of the site, you can either walk back into town or grab a returning *dolmuş.* You can also catch a *dolmuş* to Kuşadası (3.50YTL/$3.05/£1.40; 30 min.) or Izmir's *otogar* (6YTL/$5.20/£2.40; 1 hr.).

By Taxi   Taxis are available for quick hops from one end of town to the other (from the *otogar* to the Kalehan with luggage, for example) and, if desired, for transportation to Ephesus (10YTL/$8.70/£4 one-way) and Mary's house (11YTL/$9.55/£4.40 round-trip).

WHAT TO SEE & DO

Ephesus Museum (Efes Müzesi) ✶✶✶   The wealth of archaeological findings from the ancient city of Ephesus makes this museum one of the most important in Turkey. As in the case of many other groundbreaking sites, the first excavations were the result of a British railway engineer moonlighting as a scientist and gold digger. The British Museum became the beneficiary of the earliest artifacts, while a later Austrian expedition provided a good amount of fodder for the Kunsthistorisches Museum of Vienna. Some of the treasures actually found their way to the archaeology museums in Istanbul and Izmir, until after World War I when Turkish sovereignty was established and the municipality retained the artifacts in a newly constructed warehouse in

---

⟮Tips⟯ Alfresco Shows

Open-air concerts are staged regularly in summer in Ephesus, both at the Great Theater and at the Library of Celsus. For information and schedules, go to www.lksev.org.

the center of Selçuk. By the 1970s the warehouse was bursting at the seams with a star-tling collection of recovered items, and an expanded and renovated warehouse mor-phed into the reputable institution that you see today. The museum rooms are stocked full of treasures excavated at Ephesus, so no visit to the ancient city would be com-plete without a walk through here. Plan on about 90 minutes for the museum, a visit that will be made that much more rewarding *after* you've gained a point of reference over at Ephesus.

The exhibit opens with the Roman Period House Finds Room, displaying items recovered during excavations of the terraced houses of Ephesus's entitled class. Here you'll find examples of household items, including the bronze statue *Eros with the Dolphin* ★★ from a 2nd-century fountain, a 3rd-century fresco of Socrates, and finally the inspiration for all of those cheesy souvenir-shop models, the original statue of *Bes* ★★ attached to his exaggerated uncircumcised erect penis. Contrary to popu-lar thought, Bes, actually of Egyptian origin, was not the god of the brothel, but the protector of everything associated with motherhood and childbearing. A faded fresco of Socrates recovered from one of the homes indicates the importance of philosophy in the daily life of the citizens.

During the Roman Empire, Ephesus housed an important school of medicine; here you'll also find a collection of medical and cosmetic tools (two inseparable sciences at the time) along with a wall of portraits of several famous Ephesian physicians.

Recovered from several monumental fountains are a beautiful representation of a headless **Aphrodite** ★ and a bodiless head of **Zeus** ★ dating to the 1st century A.D. Nearby is a narration of **Polyphemus's** ★★ mythological attempt on Odysseus's life. From the Fountain of Trajan are a statue of a youthful **Dionysus with a satyr** ★, and additional statues of **Dionysus with members of the imperial family** ★. The list goes on and on. Among the mind-boggling treasures displayed in the museum, keep an eye out for the **Ivory Frieze** ★★★, discovered in an upper story of one of the Ter-raced Houses, which depicts the emperor Trajan and his Roman soldiers in battle against "the barbarians."

Many monumental artifacts are displayed in the **courtyards** ★★, including the **pediment** ★★★ from the Temple of Augustus (Isis Temple), reassembled with statues that had been moved to the pool of the Fountain of Pollio after the destruction of the temple; the **Sarcophagus with Muses** ★, dating to the 3rd century A.D.; and the **Ephesus Monument** ★, inscribed with the Customs regulations as issued by Emperor Nero in A.D. 62 and detailing the process of tax collection, typically undertaken by a third party, rather than as a state activity.

One of the most impressive and illuminating sections in the museum is dedicated to the mother goddess and dominated by two **colossal statues of Artemis** ★★★. Both statues are represented with rows of bull testicles, previously thought to be breasts or eggs, but all symbolically related to the idea of fertility.

The final exhibit contains numerous sculptures from Roman times, mostly over-shadowed by a **frieze** ★★★ recovered from the Temple of Hadrian (sections of which are in Vienna). The frieze narrates the founding of Ephesus, the birth of the cult of Artemis, and the flight of the Amazons.

On the edge of the park near the intersection of Atatürk Cad., opposite the tourist information office. ✆ **0232/ 892-6010**. Admission 2YTL ($1.75/80p). Daily 8:30am–6pm.

Tips **Academic Excellence at Ephesus**

"We had two love affairs, one with each other and one with Turkey." These are the words of Janet Crisler, speaking about her late husband, B. Cobbey Crisler, author, academic, and lecturer on biblical archaeology. Motivated by a desire to keep Crisler's legacy of academic inquisitiveness and Turcophilia alive, Janet has established the Crisler Library at Ephesos, a foundation whose mission is to support the exchange of information and ideas related to scholarship on Ephesus, and by force of the inherent influence of religion on these ancient civilizations, on biblical studies. The foundation maintains a growing library of volumes related to both areas. The Crisler Foundation is fulfilling another one of the late Crisler's goals with a collaborative excavation project with the Austrian Institute of Archaeology to unearth the Early Roman Harbor at Ephesus. After three seasons of geophysical surveys, spades went to ground on this project in the summer of 2007. The library is able to offer group lectures on the latest findings at the site (© **0252/892-8317**; www.crislerlibraryephesos.com).

The Archaeological Site of Ephesus (Efes) 🌟🌟🌟   Second only to Pompeii, a visit to Ephesus is as good an introduction as one can get to ancient Roman civilization. Almost as astonishing as the site itself is that only 20% of the ancient city has been excavated. Allot at least a half-day for just an overview of the archaeological site and a full day for a comprehensive visit. In the heat of the summer, it's best to avoid the midday sun when the reflection off the stones becomes unbearable.

The visit begins inside the Upper Entrance and basically follows a straight trajectory through the ancient city. You can get a fairly decent overview of the site by following the main street, but with so much interest located in toppled buildings lining the route, you will definitely want to scramble around a bit to get a closer look. Plan on at least 2 hours for the basic overview, and double that if you're planning to really absorb all of the main sites. Add another 30 to 45 minutes in the Terraced Houses, and still more time if you're dedicated enough to trample through every last weed to the "secondary" sites off the main street. If you're visiting during the heat of the summer, begin as early as the ticket gates will allow, and bring bottled water and perhaps a snack. There are no public toilets inside the museum, so avail yourself before entering, preferably in one of the on-site restaurants, rather than in one of the overpriced and underserviced public restrooms outside the site.

Inside the entrance immediately off to the right is the **East Gymnasium** and what's left of the **Magnesia Gate,** built by Emperor Vespasian. Rather than tap into your reserves this early in the game, head straight to the **Upper Agora** 🌟🌟, specifically to the **Odeon.** To provide some context for your visit, the Upper Agora, also known as the State Agora, was the administrative center of the city and was constructed between the reigns of Augustus and Claudius. The foundations of an early temple dedicated to the goddess Isis indicate that the site was also used for religious ceremonies. Clustered around the State Agora were the **Various Baths,** attributed to Flavius Damianus. To the south of the Agora is a monumental **Fountain,** which was fed by the River Marnas (now, Dervent) via an aqueduct about 5km (3 miles) east of Ephesus.

The **Odeon** 🌟🌟, also known as the Small Theatre, functioned as a *bouleuterion* (place for meetings of the boule, or council), although it's reasonable to believe that it served as a venue for concerts and theatrical performances as well. The structure was built in the 2nd century A.D. by Publius Vedius Antoninus, according to an inscription, and was probably covered. To the north are the remains of a covered arcade, converted, according to an inscription found on an architrave, into a **Basilica** ✿ during the reign of Augustus. Excavations beneath the basilica have revealed a single-aisle colonnade. The juxtaposition of the Basilica next to the Prytaneum and Odeon lead historians to believe that even the Basilica, in addition to religious purposes, held some state function. Next to the Odeon are the ruins of the **Prytaneum** ✿, or Town Hall, constructed by Lysimachos along with the **Altar of Hestia Boulaia** ✿, upon which burned an eternal sacred flame. The two famous statues of Artemis now on exhibit in the Ephesus Museum (in Selçuk) were found in this building. Part of the Prytaneum was scavenged in the 3rd century A.D. by a woman named Scholastikia, for building materials for her baths (see below).

At the corner of **Domitian Square** ✿✿ is an edifice referred to by archaeologists as the **Socle Structure,** and whose function is unknown. Just to the right of this is the **Pollio Fountain** ✿. The original structure was built in honor of C. Sextilius Pollio, architect of the Marnas Aqueduct; however, the fountain was actually added to the monument at a later date. Built in 97 B.C., the monument was ornamented with statues of the head of Zeus and the torso of Aphrodite, as well as the Polyphemos group of statues, narrating the story of Odysseus, now in the Ephesus Museum. At the far end of Domitian Street (below the southwest corner of the State Agora) is another **fountain,** built in A.D. 80 by Laecanius Bassus.

The **Temple of Domitian** ✿, the first temple of Ephesus built in honor of an emperor (A.D. 81–96), is located next to the Domitian Square. Not much remains of the temple, and what little information is available comes from the ruins of the foundation. A colossal statue of Domitian, 5m (16 ft.) high in a seated position, 7m (23 ft.) if you include the base, was the altar centerpiece in a cella only 9m×21m (30 ft.×69 ft.). Remains of this statue can be seen in the Ephesus Museum, while the head is on display in the Izmir Archaeological Museum (p. 195).

The **Museum of Inscriptions** takes up the underground substructure of the temple and contains a collection of stone and marble tablets that provides a rich historical record of the official decrees, state rulings, bureaucratic matters, and civil punishments. The museum is closed more often than not, providing visitors with a good excuse to skip it altogether.

At the junction to the right stand the remains of the **Monument of Memmius** ✿, built in the 1st century B.C. in honor of the grandson of the dictator Cornelius Sulla. The figures are those of Memmius, his father, Caicus, and Sulla. Next to and opposite the Monument of Memmius are two fountains: One is semicircular with a long narrow rectangular pool; the one opposite was brought here from another part of the city in the 4th century. It is decorated with garlands and a **winged Nike** ✿.

Leading away from the Upper Agora down a gently sloping street pockmarked by thousands of pounding hoofs is the famous **Curettes Way** ✿✿✿. In mythology, Curettes were demigods, a name later used by the Ephesians to designate a class of priests at first dedicated to the cult of Artemis. In Roman times, the Curettes held a place in the Prytaneum. The main thoroughfare is paved with stone and marble remnants recycled from other parts of the city, added after a 4th-century earthquake; valuable architectural elements like Doric columns and ornamental capitals are now part of the city's foundations.

About halfway down Curettes Way and blocking access to the aristocratic reaches of the Upper Agora is the **Gate of Hercules** ★★. Two of the columns show Hercules wrapped in lion skin.

Immediately on the right is the two-story **Trajan's Fountain** ★★, the point at which the star-studded section of the tour begins. Many visitors peter out because they've already spent a good portion of their time and energy before arriving at this point, so if you're resigned to the fact that you can't see everything, this is where you should begin the serious part of your tour, after having had a peek at the Odeon. Trajan's Fountain was built in the emperor's honor at the beginning of the 2nd century. The ruins have been partially restored, although only the base and a fragment of the Trajan's foot have been recovered. The fountain was decorated with statues of Dionysus, a satyr, Aphrodite, and others, now on exhibit in the Ephesus Museum.

Located after the Trajan Fountain and running perpendicular to Curettes Way past the Baths of Scholastikia is another street, paved in some places with marble slabs. The portion leading above the theater has been excavated.

The second sacred building dedicated to a ruling emperor was the **Temple of Hadrian** ★★★, one of the main attractions at Ephesus, marketed in tourist brochures almost as much as the Celsus Library. The Corinthian temple consists of a main chamber and a monumental porch; an inscription on the architrave of the porch facade indicates that temple was dedicated to the emperor by somebody named P. Quintilius. Ornamenting the semicircular arch that rests on the two inner columns of the porch facade is a bust of the goddess **Tych,** protectress of the city. In the **entablature** ★★ over the main portal is a carving of a woman; some interpretations identify the figure as Medusa, symbolically keeping the evil spirits away. The temple was partially destroyed in A.D. 400, and it was during the course of restorations that the four **decorative reliefs** ★★ were added to the lintels of the interior of the porch. (The ones in place today are plaster casts of originals now on exhibit in the Ephesus Museum.) The first three panels from the left depict the mythological foundation of Ephesus, and show representations of Androklos chasing a boar, gods with Amazons, and Amazons in a procession. The fourth panel is unrelated and shows Athena, Apollo, Androklos, Heracles, Emperor Theodosius, Artemis Ephesia, and several other historical and mythological figures.

The bases in front of the porch facade are inscribed with the names of Galerius, Maximianus, Diocletianus, and Constantius Chlorus, indicating that at one time, the bases supported statues of these emperors.

Behind the Temple of Hadrian via a stone staircase are the remains of the **Baths of Scholastikia** ★★★, constructed at the end of the 1st century and named after a rich Ephesian woman who enlarged them in the 4th. There were two entrances to the baths leading into a large main hall with niches; in one of these niches is the restored **statue of Scholastikia** ★, in its original position. During the 4th-century renovations, the original **mosaic floor** was covered over with marble slabs; some of these can be seen beneath the level of the current floor.

The original building phase of the baths included the construction of the adjacent **brothel** and the public toilets, which allowed a bit of discreet philandering.

Bizarre in its utility, the **Public Latrine** ★ provides more of a mental image into our humbler functions than one really needs. Men would sit side by side on these narrow stone benches above open troughs hidden under their robes and discuss current events as their waste washed away beneath them. A fountain occupies the center of the atrium, where running water would drown out the, well, sounds.

On the opposite side of Curettes Way is a colonnaded street flanked by a row of 12 shops and covered in a **mosaic floor** ✦✦✦ decorated with geometric patterns. The colonnade dates to the 1st century A.D.; however, the mosaics only date to the 5th century A.D. Staircases in several of the shops indicate the existence of an upper floor, probably used as sleeping quarters for employees.

However you prioritize your time at the site, don't miss the **Terraced Houses** ✦✦✦. Set on the hillside of Bülbül Dağı above the shops are five multichambered peristyle houses that have been uncovered in ongoing excavations. Since excavations of the site are ongoing, access is not guaranteed, so try to coax the caretaker to walk you through, and remember to tip. A separate ticket for entry is required (15YTL/$13/£6). (***Note to visitors with physical limitations:*** As terraced housing, access is via large exterior or interior stairways, making a visit to this exhibit somewhat challenging.)

The houses were inhabited from the 1st to the 7th centuries by the richest members of society and frequently remodeled. All of the houses had running water, sophisticated heating systems, large colonnaded inner courtyards, and rich decor. One had a private basilica. Overwhelmingly they reveal the best craftsmanship the city had to offer, in monumental arched colonnades, well-preserved mosaics, and layer upon layer of frescoes. The course of tourist visits is sure to change in the coming months; but on your way through the marked passage, keep an eye out for the spectacular collection of *in situ* 2nd-century **frescoes and mosaics** ✦✦✦.

As the poster child for Ephesus, the **Library of Celsus** ✦✦✦, whose two-tiered facade reaches us in a remarkable state of preservation, is immediately recognizable. The library was built between A.D. 110 and 135 by the Consul Julius Aquila as a mausoleum for his father, Julius Celsus Polemaeanus, governor of the Asian Provinces, whose remains remain surprisingly intact under the apsidal wall.

Three levels of niches indicate that the building had three stories, the upper two levels accessible via a horseshoe-shaped gallery. Scrolls or books were stored in the rows of niches, and reading materials were dispensed by a librarian.

In the lower niches of the facade are copies of four statues personifying wisdom, knowledge, destiny, and intelligence, the originals having been taken to Vienna. The library was abandoned after a fire of unspecified date destroyed the reading room, and around A.D. 400 the courtyard below the exterior steps was converted into a pool. The facade collapsed in an earthquake in the 10th century, but was restored and re-erected by F. Hueber of the Austrian Archaeological Institute between 1970 and 1978.

Back at the top of the steps above the library begins the **Marble Way** ✦✦✦, a 5th-century street paved entirely with—you guessed it—marble. Chariot traffic on the road was high, calling for a raised lateral platform to be built for pedestrians. Carved into the marble at about halfway down the road is the **imprint** of a footprint, a heart, and a portrait of a woman, accepted by historians as an advertisement for the brothel next door. According to the rumor mill, a large underground sewage system running beneath the street—an example of how advanced city engineering was in those days—doubled as a secret passage between the library and the brothel.

The imperial arched **Gate of Mazaeus and Mithridates** ✦✦ to the right of the library was built in 4 or 3 B.C. by two emancipated slaves of Agrippa who, according to an inscription in both Latin and Greek, had the monument erected in honor of Emperor Augustus, his wife Livia, Agrippa, and Agrippa's daughter Julia. The gate, unsuccessfully named the Gate of Augustus, was designed to provide southeastern access to the Lower or **Commercial Agora** ✦✦, a space of almost 120 sq. m (1,292 sq. ft.) of shops and colonnaded galleries on prime waterfront real estate that is lamentably off-limits indefinitely. The Agora dates to the 3rd century B.C., was expanded and altered by Augustus and Nero, and attained its final form during the reign of Caracalla. In ongoing excavations, the original foundation of the Agora was discovered about 6m (20 ft.) below current ground level. The middle of the Agora was studded with statues of Ephesian notables, and at the center, a *horologion,* or sundial.

The **Temple of Serapis,** located at the southwestern end of the Agora, is also closed off due to ongoing excavations. The temple was probably built by Egyptian traders and used as a church during Christian times.

For thespians and laypeople alike, the **Great Theatre** ✸✸✸ is a dramatic spectacle to behold. Built into the slopes of Panayır Dagı (Mt. Pion), the 30m-high (98-ft.) theater (actually, 30m/98 ft. above the level of the orchestra) required 60 years of digging to clear out a space large enough to accommodate 25,000 people, estimated at only one-tenth of the city's population. The theater was begun during the Hellenistic times (some say during the reign of Lysimachos) and was later altered and enlarged by emperors Claudius, Nero, and Trajan. Even more monumentally, St. Paul delivered his sermon condemning pagan worship from the proscenium. Even if you think it'll take an additional 60 years to hoist yourself up the steps to the upper cavea, do so, or you will be missing one of the most stunning views around.

The **Arcadian Way** ✸✸ (or Harbor Rd., also closed for excavation) is the name for the triumphal marble road leading from the harbor to the base of the Great Theatre. At 600m (1,969 ft.), the promenade was flanked by two colonnaded streets paved with mosaics and lined with elegant shops that reflected the prestige of a city of the stature of Ephesus. In fact, in the ancient world, only the wealthiest cities were lit at night, a privilege enjoyed by Ephesus, as well as Rome and Antioch. The **Theatre Gymnasium** is opposite the Great Theatre, at the junction of the Arcadian Way and the Marble Road. Complete with a bathhouse, *palestra* (gymnasium), and classrooms, the Theatre Gymnasium is the largest of its type in Ephesus. You can cut through here to rejoin the path out of the site (this leads to the Lower Entrance); just before reaching the path, turn around to face the theater, and take advantage of one of the best photo ops in the region. If you've still got any blood sugar left in you (and if this portion of the site is open to visitors, which currently it is not), you can wander around the **Verulanus Sports Arena,** the Harbor Gymnasium and Baths, and the Church of the Virgin Mary, located between the path heading out of the site and the old harbor. The arena was built during the reign of Hadrian and extends all the way to the Harbor Gymnasium, also built at this time.

The **Harbor Gymnasium and Baths** sits at the port end of the Arcadian Way and is the largest building complex in Ephesus. The building of the gymnasium is thought to have taken place during the reign of Domitian while the baths date to Constantine II. The complex has yet to be excavated.

Before exiting the Lower Entrance, follow a path and signs for the **Church of the Virgin Mary (Meryem Kilisesi)** ✸ to the left. Originally, the building was used as a Roman mercantile center, but was converted to a basilica in the 4th century. The church played an important role in the evolution of Christianity, as the first one to take Mary's name, and as the site of two important ecumenical councils in 431 and 449, in which the natures of Christ and of Mary were hotly disputed. It's a little out of the way, especially at this stage in the game, but worth the energy it'll take to trek over here (again, assuming it's not cordoned off).

A well-paved road heading east of the Vedius Gymnasium leads to **The Cave of the Seven Sleepers** ✸, about .8km (½ mile) away. According to the legend, seven young local boys (and a dog, according to one interpretation), refusing to submit to the persecutions of Emperor Decius (A.D. 249–51), fled to these caves with a group of Roman guards in hot pursuit. In characteristic Roman fashion, the guards mercilessly sealed up the cave, putting an end to yet another heretical episode. When the boys were awakened by an earthquake that also broke the cave's seals, they wandered back into town to buy some bread only to find themselves in the 5th century and 200 years older. Evidently, times had changed and Christianity was now the state religion. After their deaths, the "sleepers" were re-interred in the cave, and it wasn't long before the site became a sacred destination for pilgrimages.

This site, one of the many caves used by Seven Sleepers throughout Anatolia (there are others, located in Akhisar, Manisa, Sardes, Tarsus, and Antakya, to name a few), is actually a grouping of small churches dating to the time of the persecutions, superimposed in the rock and containing crypts carved into the walls. The actual cave site has been fenced off, but remains a draw to die-hard pilgrims. (At the time of this writing, a hole in the fence provided access.)

No phone. Admission to archaeological site 10YTL ($8.70/£4); admission to Terraced Houses 10YTL ($8.70/£4). Summer daily 8am–6:30pm; winter daily 8am–4:30pm. Follow the road from Selçuk to Kuşadası, turn left following signs for the archaeological site; the official entrance (Lower Entrance) is immediately to the right; follow signs to the Cave of the Seven Sleepers and Meryemana for the Upper Entrance.

The House of the Virgin Mary (Meryemana) ✸✸✸

According to the oral tradition of local villagers of Şirince (or Kirkince, descendants of Christians at Ephesus), Mary finished out her days in this house after migrating to Asia Minor with John. The location was "discovered" in the 19th century by Sister Anna Catherina Emmerich, a German invalid who had never left home. The discovery was in the form of a dream, from which the nun awoke with a stigmata. The site was later found as described and was visited by popes Paul VI and John Paul II, who both verified its authenticity. The validity of the site is also supported by the oral tradition of the villagers who inhabited the village in the 19th century, as they were descendants of the early Christian inhabitants.

The house is a church nowadays, with the main altar where the kitchen was situated; the right wing was the bedroom. The site, now a national park, is a requisite stop on the itineraries of Christians, Jews, and Muslims alike, and therefore always crowded. In fact, in their religious fervor, pilgrims won't think anything of elbowing you out of the way. If you get there by 7:15am you can participate in the morning Mass (10:30am on Sun); and every year on August 15 there is a Mass celebrating the Assumption. The park is also home to healing springs said to cure all sorts of ailments.

Orman Yolu. Admission to park and house 11YTL ($9.55/£4.40). Site parking 8YTL ($6.95/£3.20). Dawn–dusk. 7km (4½ miles) southwest of Selçuk; from both the Upper and Lower entrances to Ephesus, follow the signs to Meryemana, which is in a park and nature preserve.

Isabey Mosque

Built in 1375 at the direction of the Emir of Aydın and using columns and stones recycled from the ruins of Ephesus and Artemesion, the Isabey Mosque is a classic example of Selçuk architecture. It is also the oldest known example of a Turkish mosque with a courtyard. It is fitting that Isabey translates into "Jesus," as the structure owes its existence to the temples of other religions, and possibly testifies to the religious tolerance exhibited by the Selçuk Turks.

Exit the basilica entrance and turn right. Free admission. Dawn–dusk.

St. John's Basilica ★★★   After the death of Christ, St. John came with Mary to Ephesus, living most of his life in and around Ayasoluk Hill and spreading the word of Christianity as St. Paul did before him. John's grave was marked by a memorial, which was enclosed by a church of modest proportions in the 4th century. During the reign of Justinian, the emperor had a magnificent domed basilica constructed on the site. The tomb of St. John located under the main central dome elevated the site to one of the most sacred destinations in the Middle Ages. With the decline in importance of Ephesus and after repeated Arab raids, the basilica fell into ruins until the Selçuk Aydınoğlu clan converted it into a mosque in 1330. The building was completely destroyed in 1402 by Tamerlane's Mongol army.

The current entrance leads into the basilica through (or near) the southern transept. Originally, entry was through the oversize exterior courtyard atrium to the west of the nave, which led worshippers through the narthex and finally into the far end of the nave. The basilica had six domes.

The brick foundations and marble walls have been partially reconstructed; if they were fully restored, the cathedral would be the seventh largest in the world. More recent excavations east of the apse have revealed a baptistery and central pool, along with an attached chapel covered in frescoes depicting the saints.

Follow signs from Atatürk Cad.; the ruins are visible from the main road. Admission 2YTL ($1.75/80p). Daily 8:30am–4:30pm; closes later in summer.

The Temple of Artemis (Artemesion) ★   In a marshy basin just on the outskirts of town are the pitiful remains of yet another plundered Wonder of the Ancient World. Rising out of the marsh, a lone surviving column suggests the immensity of the structure, four times as large as the Parthenon and the first monumental building to be entirely constructed of marble. As an illustration of its immensity, consider that the one remaining column stands an incredible 4m (13 ft.) *below* the point of the architrave. This ancient temple, built around 650 B.C. to the cult of Artemis, was constructed on a site considered to be sacred to the Mother Goddess, Kybele.

In 356 B.C. (the year Alexander the Great was born), a psychopathic arsonist intent on immortality set fire to the temple. Twenty-two years later, during his sweep through Asia Minor, Alexander the Great offered to reconstruct the temple. In a famous refusal related by Strabo, the Ephesians thought it unfitting for one god to

---

Moments **Şirince**

Located on a hillside surrounded by apple and grape orchards is the neighboring village of Şirince. Originally settled by Greeks, the village was inhabited by the Ephesian Christians, who, displaced during the Selçuk conquests, moved up into the surrounding hills. In the Greek exchanges of 1924, Muslims from Salonica resettled here, creating a farming community highly adept at winemaking. Several years ago a couple of Turkish journalists and entrepreneurs restored several of the village's houses, which now rent out as guesthouses (see "Where to Stay," below). A few native villagers followed suit. By day, the village attracts tour buses and aggressive lace-peddling fiends. By night, however, the village settles down, the candles get lit, and several restaurants and wine houses open up. It is located 8km (5 miles) east of Selçuk in the hills (*dolmuş* service departs from the train station every 20 min. 8am–5pm).

build a temple to another god. The temple was eventually rebuilt remaining true to the original except for a raised platform, a feature of classical architecture adopted in the construction of later temples. By A.D. 263, the temple had been plundered by Nero and destroyed by the Goths. The temple was reconstructed in the 4th century, but the strengthening of Christianity condemned the structure to that of a marble quarry for St. John's Basilica and the Ayasofya in Istanbul. The site is best appreciated in the summer months, when the marshy waters are at their lowest, and the foundations of previous structures are recognizable.

Entrance off the road to Kuşadası, just past the Jandarma on the right, and a short walk out of town. No phone. Free admission. Daily 8:30am–5:30pm.

WHERE TO STAY

Given that Selçuk makes the perfect base for visits to Ephesus, and given that almost everyone who comes to Turkey passes through Ephesus, it's odd that there aren't more high-quality places to stay. One nearby alternative to Selçuk is Şirince, a pastoral village in the hills.

IN SELÇUK

Hotel Bella *Value*   Book early for a room at this friendly guesthouse, and even earlier if you want one of the street-side rooms overlooking the spotlit remains of St. John's Basilica. Bella is a recent and welcome addition to Selçuk, providing more charm on its rooftop terrace than all of the other pensions combined. Rooms are basic, simple, and comfortable, and bathrooms come equipped with showers enclosed by sliding doors. The excellent **rooftop restaurant** is open year-round; in winter, tables are sheltered from the elements by a wraparound enclosure and the heat of a briskly burning fireplace.

Atatürk Mah. St. John Sok. 7, 35920 Selçuk. ℂ 0232/892-3944. Fax 0232/892-0344. www.hotelbella.com. 12 units. 60YTL ($52/£24) double. MC, V. **Amenities:** Terrace restaurant; wireless Internet; laundry service. *In room:* A/C.

Hotel Kalehan   Located just below Selçuk's castle and St. John's Basilica, the Hotel Kalehan consists of two stately stone buildings separated by a narrow trellised lane, with the rear building standing at the back of a lush, carefully tended English-style garden. The gardens enclose a raised pool area and contain wrought-iron settees, wooden lawn chairs, and the odd cartwheel for fun. Owners Ayşe and Hakan, a brother-and-sister team, are avid collectors of antiques and have filled the inn with period furniture. Rooms are modest but lovely, in a monastic sort of way, and what they lack in luxury they certainly make up for in atmosphere. Recent upgrades include new mattresses in most of the rooms; special rooms now sport new bathrooms, mini-bars, bathrobes, and the odd extra toiletry.

Izmir Cad., 35920 Selçuk (on the main road below the castle next to the Sunoco station). ℂ 0232/892-6154. Fax 0232/892-2169. www.kalehan.com. 55 units. 70€ ($102/£50) double; 100€ ($145/£71) special room. MC, V. Free parking on-site. **Amenities:** Restaurant; bar; outdoor swimming pool; boutique; Internet point and wireless Internet. *In room:* A/C, satellite TV, fridge.

Hotel Nilya   Family-owned Hotel Nilya, located on a side street in Old Town, is easy to mistake for a private home. An imposing door with a brass plate opens onto a stone courtyard with a central fountain. Not so much as a particle of dust clutters up each room's minimalist atmosphere, where a *kilim* and striped cotton bedspread are the only embellishments. Spartan, too, are the bathrooms, with open shower stalls. The one "suite" has a little more decoration and enjoys glorious sunset views, which

---

Tips **Local hoteliers say, "We'll take you there!"**

When competition for clientele gets stiff, consumers benefit. In Selçuk, hotels and pensions are now commonly offering free rides to Ephesus as part of the price of the room.

---

can also be seen from the upper-level outdoor lounge. The American-style kitchen is wide open to the richly furnished dining room, full of period furniture and colorful geometric-patterned *kilims*. The owners don't speak much English, but lots of gesturing, a peek at the calculator, and a bit of high-school French will do you just fine.

1051 Sok. 7, 35920 Selçuk. ⓒ **0232/892-9081.** Fax 0232/892-9080. www.nilya.com. 11 units. 70YTL ($61/£28) single; 115YTL ($100/£46) double; 175YTL ($152/£70) triple. MC, V. Street parking only. Closed Nov–Mar. *In room:* A/C.

IN ŞIRINCE
Nişanyan Evleri and Kilisealtı Pansiyon ★★ *Finds*   These (illegally!) renovated houses at the top of Şirince's hillside offer total immersion into the daily rhythm of the village life. At the upper edge of the hillside is the main Köşk (pavilion), which contains the reception area and five smartly decorated rooms with nouveau Hellenistic frescoes, fresh tubs/showers, and antique furniture. Three characteristic restored houses, standing in sharp contrast to their humbler neighbors, are accessed by a stone staircase, terraced below the Köşk, with an additional five more terraced up to almost the top of the valley. Each house sleeps a minimum of two, but can comfortably accommodate four or a maximum of six people. One features a private *hamam,* another has a semi-enclosed stone veranda, and a third contains a raised-platform canopied bed—great for the kids. The spectacular success of these cottages has acted as a magnet for visitors to the village—many of whom are turned away when quoted the room rate. As a result, Nişanyan has opened the separate Kilisealtı pension, offering accommodations for much less than the price of the Evleri.

Şirince (6.5km/4 miles from Selçuk and 11km/6¾ miles from Ephesus; watch for signs on the right before entering the village, leading to a dirt road that stops at the main house). ⓒ **0232/898-3208.** Fax 0232/898-3209. www.nisanyan.com. 8 self-catering houses and 1 house with 5 rooms. 145YTL–260YTL ($126–$226/£58–£104) double in self-catering house; 120YTL–220YTL ($104–$191/£46–£84) double in hotel. MC, V. **Amenities:** Restaurant; outdoor swimming pool.

WHERE TO DINE
The hotels mentioned in this section almost all have restaurants promising superior meals to anything you might get in town (except for the Artemis Wine House in Şirince, which I highly recommend; see below). If you get sick of eating at the hotel (or any of the others; they all take "walk-ins") try one of these recommendations below.

IN SELÇUK
Okumuş Mercan Restaurant   Okumuş is the only full-menu restaurant around, with food and ambiance served under a leafy trellised canopy that shades the outdoor dining patio. Popular dishes include the *hamsi zeytinli* (anchovies in olive oil) and the *kağitta balık,* where your fish (catch of the day or fish of your choice) is cooked in paper. For a vegetarian alternative, try the *etsiz sebze yemeği* (peppers and curry).

Karşısı Hal Bina 43, opposite the PTT. ⓒ **0232/892-6196.** Appetizers and main courses 3YTL–12YTL ($2.60–$10/£1.20–£4.80). MC, V. Daily 9am–midnight.

Selçuk Köftecisi This meatball-and-kebap house succeeds in doing a brisk and humble business well away from the tourist bull's-eye of hecklers trying to fill empty tables. The menu lists a variety of meat-based kebaps and grills, plus steam pots that put out the tantalizing odor of somebody's mother's kitchen. The restaurant has an outdoor cafe in summer.

Atatürk Mah., Şehabettin Dede Cad. 10. (C) **0232/892-6696.** Appetizers and main courses 3YTL–7.50YTL ($2.60–$6.55/ £1.20–£3). MC, V. Daily noon–11pm.

IN ŞIRINCE
Artemis Wine House *Moments* Not to be confused with the Artemis winery next door (other than the fact that the wine house and restaurant make their own wine), this restaurant occupies an old schoolhouse converted into a wine house and terrace restaurant. The backdrop to your starters of creamy broccoli soup or tahini *gözleme* are the rolling hills of the valley surrounding the village. Along with the parade of usual suspects, the menu offers main courses that are equally unique. There are a variety of house wines, but apple wine is the local specialty.

On the left as you enter the village, Şirince. (C) **0232/898-3240.**

5 Kuşadası

20km (12 miles) southwest of Selçuk; 95km (59 miles) south of Izmir; 220km (137 miles) west of Pamukkale; 151km (94 miles) north of Bodrum

Only 20km (12 miles) from Selçuk, Kuşadası long ago earned the dubious honor of hosting—of all things—a steady stream of cruise ships filled with masses of tourists making the obligatory pilgrimage to Ephesus. One would never suspect that only 25 years ago, before it was discovered by the yachting set (and then exploited by mass tourism), Kuşadası was a scenic and unspoiled community of fishermen and farmers, with barely a dirt road running through it. Makes you fear for those charming villages you just came from.

In addition to patronizing the fat-cat cruisers ready to disgorge the contents of their wallets on jewelry and carpets on their way in and out of Ephesus, the town is characterized by three genres of tourism: mass tourism drawn to Ladies Beach by cheap package prices from Europe, more mass tourism clustered in cement midrise hotels in the town center, and (with a few exceptions) the more selective mass-tourism establishments north of town mushrooming up on the coastline above the yacht marina. Some of the most splendid coastline on the Aegean can still be found in the protected National Park area (see below), while the Kismet Hotel (adjacent to the yacht marina) is still a delightful oasis in a desert of commerce. If your priority is touring the area archaeological sites by day and partaking of the chaotic nightlife (with a short poolside rest in between), then Kuşadası might actually fit the bill. If rural charm is what you're after, move on.

A LOOK AT THE PAST
Nobody knows exactly when the city was founded, but at some point the Carians and Lelegians wandered westward from central Anatolia to find the advantages of the fertile soil and a gracious climate. After the usual parade of conquerors, the Ottomans laid claim to the city, and Kuşadası was given a new look by Öküz Mehmet Paşa, grand vizier under Ahmet I and Osman II. He erected several mosques and a caravansary and rebuilt the Byzantine fortress to secure the shores against attacks from the

sea. Known as "Pirate Castle," this fortress was used as a base for the exploits of the pirate Barbarossa in the 16th century. To bolster his presence in the Mediterranean, Sultan Süleyman the Magnificent put Barbarossa in command of the Ottoman fleet against Venice and Genoa, states long covetous of access to the Eastern trade routes.

The Ottomans called the city Kuşadası or "Bird Island," a name that previously referred to the offshore island, referring to its use as a stopover for pigeons during seasonal migrations. The island was renamed Güvercin Ada, or "Pigeon Island," and today is connected to the mainland by a pedestrian causeway lined with fishermen and excursion boat captains. The shady area within the castle walls provides a respite from the blazing heat of the summer sun, and it seems that tea gardens were set in and around the ramparts to take full advantage of the tremendous sunset views of the city.

ESSENTIALS
GETTING THERE
The nearest airport is Izmir's Adnan Menderes Airport, about 97km (60 miles) away. There's no convenient public transport from the airport to Kuşadası (see section 1, "Izmir," earlier in this chapter, for information on transportation out of the airport); private transfers arranged with a local company (or your hotel) in advance will run around 55€ ($80/£39, for up to three people and luggage). A taxi is about the same at 90YTL ($78/£36).

Long-distance bus service from Istanbul takes about 9 hours, 10 hours for service from Ankara. Prices vary from 45YTL to 63YTL ($39–$55/£18–£25).

Kuşadası's main *otogar* is located about .8km (½ mile) out of the town center on the main road. From there, local *dolmuşes* run through the town center on the way up the shoreline, with the names of hotels posted on the windshield. If you don't see your hotel, ask, because not all are listed.

Ferries from the Greek island of Samos arrive once daily into the main harbor from January through October ($30/£15 one-way, $35/£18 same-day return, $55/£28 round-trip with open-return ticket).

VISITOR INFORMATION
The tourist information office (© 0256/614-1103) is located across from the main harbor at Iskele Meydanı, within handy reach of disembarking cruise-ship passengers. Free maps are available, but I suggest you splurge for the better private map.

ORIENTATION
The heart of Kuşadası is found in the streets around the caravansary, across from the harbor where the shore roads of **Atatürk Bulvarı** to the north and **Liman Caddesi** to the south converge. The town's commercial thoroughfare, **Barbaros Hayrettin Caddesi,** is a pedestrian mall that heads east into the area of the old bazaar. Turn left at the post office to explore the narrow streets of the old city, lined with restaurants, bars, and souvenir shops.

Just south of the main harbor is **Güvercin Ada,** with its Byzantine fortress; farther south the shore road leads to nearby Ladies' Beach and the national park, about 20km (12 miles) away.

GETTING AROUND
If the thought of getting on a *dolmuş* was too intimidating in the big city, in Kuşadası it's going to be your best friend. Minibuses run regularly along the shore road into and out of town, as well as south to Ladies' Beach and northward along the coastal road

above the Kismet Hotel. Each ride costs 1.50YTL ($1.30/60p); to go from one end of town to the other, change *dolmuşes* in the center.

Countless storefronts up and down Atatürk Bulvarı publicize car rentals at very competitive prices. As a backup, you can contact Avis, Atatürk Bulv. 26/A (© **0256/ 614-4600**), or book your car through a reputable travel agent.

AREA BEACHES

Although Kuşadası built itself up around the idea of a beach resort, it wasn't until 2001 that the city took it upon itself to create an actual waterfront and beach. There's not much sand to speak of, and what little there is, is hardly worth a special trip, especially given the tourist element it attracts. Still, it's an improvement and the waterfront promenade makes for a great sunset stroll. Nevertheless, I recommend that you skip this beach and try the **Papaz Hamamı Beach Club** to the left of the causeway to Güvercin Ada.

The town's notorious beach has for years been universally known as **Ladies' Beach** for the overabundance of exposed boobs. This narrow stretch of sand is located about 3.5km (2¼ miles) south of town, easily reachable by any *dolmuş.*

Acting as a buffer between the Greek island of Samos less than a mile offshore and the Turkish mainland, **Dilek National Park (Dilek Milli Parkı; © 0256/614-1009)**, on the Dilek Peninsula, houses a military base as well as a mountainous natural preserve. A day trip to the quiet isolation of the park's beaches, where pine trees act as natural shelter for picnickers, is definitely a better alternative to the unexceptional beaches of central Kuşadası.

To do this, you'll really need a car to make it worth your while. Although minibus service leaves from the *otogar* every half-hour to take you the 20km (12 miles) to the park, you'll still have to get to your chosen beach, which will tack on up to an additional 9.5km (6 miles). Naturally, the closest beach, **İçmeler Köyü,** is the most crowded, with its sand and shady stretches located only .8km (½ mile) from the entrance. There are no public facilities at this beach. **Aydınlık Beach** and **Kavaklı Burun** are less frequented (5km/3 miles and 7km/4⅓ miles, respectively, from the entrance), with nothing but pebbles between you and the shoreline. Both of these have toilet and changing facilities, along with basic snack bars. The last beach, a pristine pebble stretch opposite the Greek island of Samos, is **Karasu Beach.** Freshwater showers are available, as well as toilets and changing rooms. There are snack bars open at each of the beaches during high season. The park opens daily at 8am and closes *promptly* at 6:30pm. Admission is 2YTL ($1.75/80p) per person or 7YTL ($6.10/ £2.80) per car including passengers. For a convenient dinner spot on your way back from the park, try **Değirmen** (see "Where to Dine," below).

WHERE TO STAY

Club Caravanserail (★ (*Value*   Of all the caravanseries converted into modern hotels, this is one of the most elegant, and a great opportunity to soak up real Turkish culture. The rooms have been lovingly restored, the floors and furnishings glisten with wood polish, and even the alcove fireplaces found in every room are original. The success of a place can also be judged by the tenure of its staff: Many of the employees have been at this inn for 20 years, creating a warm, familial atmosphere.

A traditional Turkish folklore show is performed in the main courtyard Thursday through Saturday (see "Kuşadası After Dark," below), but the show finishes promptly at midnight so as not to blow nonparticipating guests out of their rooms with high

Day-Tripping to Miletus, Priene & Didyma

The ancient sites of Miletus, Priene, and Didyma are three of the best-preserved Ionian settlements in Anatolia, and worth an entire day of scrambling down steps and over crumbled ruins. For the highest level of independence and flexibility, I recommend that you rent a car; at a cost as low as 33€ ($49/£24) per day, it's actually less than hiring a taxi to do the same circuit (and for little more than the price of the car, you can book a guided tour of the sites with one of the area travel agents). From Kuşadası, follow signs south to Söke, and then to Priene (38km/24 miles from Kuşadası). From Priene, it's 22km (14 miles) along the old road through miles of cotton fields to Miletus. It's another 22km (14 miles) from Miletus to Didyma, where you can either backtrack along the inland road to Söke, or continue down to Bodrum (from Didyma, 139km/86 miles; follow the more modern road via Muğla). Day tours to all three sites are available from most travel agents in surrounding towns for around 40€ ($58/£29) per person, depending on the tour company.

The ancient Greek city of Priene 🕸🕸, later inhabited and left relatively unchanged by the Romans, was the first city built on a grid plan. Formerly a port city and now stranded in the middle of acres and acres of cotton fields, Priene was once an important member of the Ionian League, around 300 B.C. The oldest remains here date to this time, and it's worth the short climb up if only for the Temple of Athena, which sits at the highest point of the city atop Mount Mykale, along with a small Greek theater. The temple was built by the architect Pytheos, the same man responsible for the construction of the Mausoleum at Halicarnassus. The theater was used for both performances and as a meeting place for the *ekklesia*—the people's parliament. Notice the first tier of seating, which is furnished with both bench-backed and "armchair" seating designated for spectators of particular importance. Another section of similar seating, called a *prohedria*, was added to the center of the fifth tier at a later date.

One of the best-preserved buildings in Priene is the *bouleuterion* (Senate House), located south of the Greek theater. The *bouleuterion* is roughly square in shape (21m×20m/69 ft.×66 ft.) with three sides of tiered seating capable of seating a mere 640 people. The building contained both a central altar and an eternal flame. Among the many private houses is one occupying a whole city block, and obviously inhabited by one of the city's wealthier citizens. The house referred to as the Alexander the Great house

decibel levels. For those wishing to attend, the management offers a meal plan that includes the show.

Atatürk Bulv. 2, 09400 Kuşadası. ✆ **0256/614-4115.** Fax 0256/614-2423. www.kusadasihotels.com/caravanserail. 26 units (all with shower). $100 double (£50); $150 (£75) suite. See website for discounts. AE, MC, V. Street parking only. **Amenities:** Restaurant and folklore show; sidewalk cafe; high-speed wired and wireless Internet throughout; laundry service; dry cleaning. *In room:* A/C, hair dryer.

is actually named for a small marble statue of Alexander (now in the Berlin Museum) that was found in another part of the city. Priene is open summer only daily 8:30am to 6:30pm; admission is 2YTL ($1.75/80p).

Miletus ⭑⭑, still for the most part buried under rubble, is actually larger than Ephesus. In fact, you'll be driving over half of it on the entry road to the Roman Theatre, one of the noteworthy ruins. Having surrendered to the silting up of four harbors, the city's fate was much the same as that of Ephesus. In fact, the hill 6.5km (4 miles) to the west of the theater was actually the island of Lade, destroyed by fire by the Persian fleet in 494 B.C.

Miletus gave the alphabet to the classical world and was also the breeding ground for many philosophers and scientists, including Thales, who calculated precisely the arrival of the solar eclipse. The archaeological site is notable for the great Roman Theatre and the Baths of Faustina, while a surprising quantity of remnants from the city's classical, Hellenistic, and Roman eras remains for the most part buried or overgrown with bone-dry shrubbery. Several maps and archaeological guides are available to help you walk through the ruins, including those sold at the entrance gate. (For more scholarly options, see "Recommended Books & Films," in chapter 2.) Miletus is open daily 8:30am to 6:30pm in summer, and until 5:30pm in winter; admission is 2YTL ($1.75/80p).

The Temple of Apollo is really all that's left of Didyma ⭑⭑, but the time spent getting to and from the site is well worth it. Didyma served as a sacred sanctuary under the custody of priests called Branchids and was connected to Miletus via a marble road, only partially excavated and visible on the opposite side of the modern road.

The temple, or Didymaion, with columns soaring over 20m (66 ft.) high, was the largest building of its time when it was erected in the 6th century B.C. (Reconstructed in the 3rd c. B.C., the temple was eclipsed in size only by those in Ephesus and Samos.) Though burned and plundered, the temple is still an amazing and inspiring sight, and much of it remains intact. The entrance to the temple is open, revealing the site of the much-revered oracle of Apollo. Don't overlook the colossal column behind the temple, which consists of layers and layers of massive stone discs supporting each other like so many felled dominoes. Didyma is open summer only, daily from 8am to 6:30pm; admission is 2YTL ($1.75/80p).

Kısmet Hotel ⭑ Co-owned by the granddaughter of the last sultan, Mehmet VI, the Kısmet Hotel occupies a small promontory sandwiched between the harbor and cliffs. In its heyday, the hotel exemplified elegance, simplicity, and nobility, but wear and tear took its toll, requiring a complete renovation of—to date—half the rooms. You'll want to book one of these (the reception could not specify which half was part of the updating); the dowdy wall-to-wall carpeting has been replaced with laminate flooring but the management has invested well in the modernized bathrooms. The swimming pool, sea views, and exclusive atmosphere provide the perfect Rx for an escape from the real world. Behind the hotel, several levels of waterfront lounging are accessible via stairs that work their way down to a cement pier and the rocky water's edge. And an expansive garden overlooking the marina provides a tranquil spot for a sunset cocktail.

Akyar Mevkii Türkmen Mah., 09400 Kuşadası. ⓒ 0256/618-1290. Fax 0256/618-1295. www.kismet.com.tr. 107 units (most with bathtub, some with minitub). 99€ ($144/£71) double; 179–299€ ($260–$434/£128–£214) suite. Tax not included in rates. AE, DC, DISC, MC, V. Parking lot on-site. Closed Nov 15–Mar 15. **Amenities:** 2 restaurants; 5 bars; outdoor swimming pool; tennis court; fitness room; Jacuzzi; shopping arcade; salon; 24-hr. room service; laundry service; dry cleaning. *In room:* A/C, satellite TV, minibar, hair dryer.

The Muses House   The house is full these days in Şirince, so it's no surprise to find another local village vying for the spillover. Kirazlı, just 14 km (9 miles) east of Kuşadası, is that up-and-comer. The restored and refurbished Greek villa–turned–hotel opened in 2006 and is hidden behind a tall whitewashed wall, a luxuriant oasis made more enjoyable because of the authenticity of the village that embraces it. The decor is a mix of modern art and antique pieces, with each of the five rooms named after a mythological muse. I wonder how long it will take for this secret to get out . . .

158 Kirazli Koyu, 09400 Kuşadası, Aydın. ⓒ 0256/667-1125. www.museshouse.com. 5 units. £50–£60 ($100–$120). MC, V. **Amenities:** Outdoor swimming pool. *In room:* A/C, satellite TV, CD and DVD players, minibar, coffee service.

WHERE TO DINE

Değirmen ★★ *Finds* *Kids* TURKISH   More than a restaurant, Değirmen is a veritable nature park located outside of Kuşadası, on the way to Dilek Milli Parkı. The restaurant proper sits at the top of a small hill surrounded by overfed rabbits and peacocks. All the food is organic, some of it grown on-site. Colossal peasant bread accompanies such dishes as *tandır kebap* (lamb cooked in an "in-ground" oven, Anatolian style) or the special *Değirmen kebap* (spareribs, chicken wings, quail, and lamb chops). Try the *erişte* (homemade egg noodles) or the *içli köfte* (meat-filled bulgur balls, either boiled or fried), and finish off with a slice of the house *künefe* (cheese-filled buttery string pastry covered in syrup and served hot).

Outside the restaurant, a cobbled path leads down from the restaurant to a duck-filled pond, over a hanging bridge, past the chickens and sheep, and straight to the riding stables, a marvelous combination for kids. The small "village store," located on the way down to the pond, is good for stocking up on basic ingredients, such as the reserve's own nuts, dried fruits, preserves, fresh eggs, olive oil, and wine. You can also buy fresh *gözleme* from a spot near the hanging bridge, or enjoy light snacks in the covered seating area down by the horses.

Davutlar Yolu (12km/7½ miles from Kuşadası on the way to the Dilek Milli Parkı). ⓒ 0256/681-2148. Reservations required to waive the park entrance fee (95Ykr/85¢/£34). Appetizers and main courses 5YTL–20YTL ($4.35–$17/ £2–£8). MC, V. Daily noon–midnight.

Tarıhı Çinar Balık FISH   From the seafront outdoor terrace, one would never know that the sights and sounds of a hectic city were just a stone's skip away. The Tarıhı Çinar has been in business for decades (first as a meat restaurant over near the national park before it switched to fish); it's been at the current location for only a handful of these years. Still, it's one of maybe two area restaurants that draws guests from beyond

Kuşadası's limits. Specials of the house are the *tuzda balık* (salt-baked fish) preceded by a plate of grilled king prawns.

Kismet Otel Yanı, Akyar, Kuşadası. ℭ **0256/618-1847**. Appetizers 8YTL–12YTL ($6.95–$10/£3.20–£4.80); fish by weight, from 40YTL ($17/£7.80) per kilo and up. AE, MC, V. Daily noon–midnight.

KUŞADASI AFTER DARK

From here, down the Aegean, Turquoise, and Mediterranean coasts, there's no way to get away from the forced partying, be it in one of the seemingly infinite clubs on **Barlar Sokağı ("Bar Street")** or in your hotel's very own discothèque.

Kuşadası's nightlife is concentrated in the old town center, in the narrow streets bordered by Barbaros Hayrettin Bulvarı and Sağlik Sokak. Kuşadası's Barlar Sokağı (walk up Barbaros Hayrettin Bulv., turn right onto Sağlık Sok., and then left under the arch into the confusion) boasts more Irish pubs per square inch than Dublin. The street is swarming with ruddy-faced boys and house touts who think that dancing on the street like Amsterdam hookers might lure somebody in for a drink. A walk-through is great for a hoot, however.

No trip to Turkey would be complete without a Turkish night folklore show, and the **Club Caravanserail,** Atatürk Bulv. 2 (ℭ **0256/614-4115**), is one of the best places to do it. The entire affair is set up like an oversize wedding banquet, with lengthy tables and long lines at the buffet. The show begins at about the time the main course arrives, and much like at a wedding, it's best to fill up on the appetizers. All in all, the mezes are adequate and the performance is fun—filled with folkloric dances from various regions, belly dancing, a spoon drummer, and the requisite lobster-red, tub-o-lard recruit for the audience-participation segment. Admission is 60€ ($87/£43) but less than half that for hotel guests.

---

6 Pamukkale ⋆⋆⋆ & Hierapolis ⋆⋆

75km (47 miles) northeast of Denizli airport; 25km (16 miles) northeast of Denizli; 652km (405 miles) south of Istanbul; 231km (144 miles) southeast of Izmir; 300km (186 miles) northeast of Bodrum

Until a few years ago, the cliff-side travertines that had become the poster child of **Pamukkale** were more like a slushy roadside pile of yesterday's snow. The terraces are the result of thousands of years of deposits left by calcium-rich natural springs coursing down the mountain. (In nearby Karahayıt, springs rich in iron and sulfur leave reddish metallic deposits at the point of exit.) But years of irresponsible tourism had turned this wonder of nature into a dismal theme park attraction, until the Turkish authorities finally in desperation called in UNESCO for backup. In an ever-evolving geological environment, it's normal that these natural springs would find new outlets, and part of UNESCO's efforts have been to divert the springs to different sections on a rotating basis to restore much-needed calcium to the upper layers of the travertines. In the 8 years since their efforts began, much of the site has been restored to its original and spectacular blinding whiteness. The travertine terraces, in concert with the plateau housing the ruins of the ancient city of **Hierapolis,** now make up a national park as well as a World Heritage Site, and a visit to one would not be complete without a look at the other.

Problem is, both Pamukkale and especially Karahayıt have become swarmed by package tourists in the market for a cheap stay. And they've found it. So there's the dilemma: The only way to enjoy the site is to stay overnight, and an overnight stay necessarily will require you to tolerate mediocre accommodations and an unbearable multitude of tourists.

If you must go, do so in the spring or fall and avoid the high-season crush. Once there, save your stroll up the travertines for just before sunset, as there's nothing quite like the glow of the setting sun reflected off the snowy landscape.

ESSENTIALS
GETTING THERE
All agencies offer day tours into the area from Izmir, Kuşadası, Bodrum, Marmaris, and Antalya (to name just a few). It's an exhausting day, requiring, at minimum, a 4-hour drive each way, plus a quickie visit.

BY BUS   The only direct service into Pamukkale by bus is provided by **Pamukkale,** the ubiquitous bus line that arrives from virtually everywhere in Turkey (© **444-3535**). Count on about 3½ to 4 hours from anywhere on the coast with fares under 30YTL ($26/£12). The bus stops in Denizli first (© **0258/261-1088**). Make sure when you buy your ticket that the final destination of Pamukkale is written on your ticket; otherwise, you may get stranded in Denizli. Once in Pamukkale, the bus arrives at the bottom of the travertines on the edge of the village of Pamukkale.

All other bus companies have Denizli as the area destination. To complete the journey into Pamukkale, take a *dolmuş* the additional 20km (12 miles) or so, a ride of about a half-hour.

BY TRAIN   A bed in a sleeper car with water basin is available on the 16-hour overnight Istanbul **Pamukkale Ekspresi** train for 68YTL ($59/£27); if you're traveling as a pair, it'll cost 52YTL ($46/£21) per person. The train leaves from Istanbul's Haydarpaşa Station on the Asian side (© **0216/336-0475**). The Denizli train station is at © **0258/268-2831.**

BY PLANE   **Turkish Airlines** (© **444-0849**) has daily evening flights from Istanbul in summer. In winter, there is one weekday early morning flight daily and one evening flight daily over the weekend.

Flights arrive into the isolated Çardak Airport (© **0258/851-2084**), about 90 minutes by private car over a desert expanse from Pamukkale. There is no ground transportation at Çardak other than the local taxi (about 100€/$145/£71 to Pamukkale). You may therefore want to arrange an airport transfer in advance with your hotel or a local travel agent. If you decide to rent a car, **Avis,** and others, will send the car to the airport.

VISITOR INFORMATION
The tourist information office is located at the top of the travertines (©/fax **0258/ 272-2077**).

ORIENTATION
The terraces lie along the base of the Çaldağ Mountains some 200m (656 ft.) above the Curuksu Plain. The upper plateau includes the ancient ruins of **Hierapolis,** a prosperous city in its heyday owing to the natural healing water sources and the local textile industry (cotton grows like weeds in these parts), the same industries that propel the local economy today.

There are two entrances to the historic and natural site, one leading from the village of Pamukkale to the southern entrance and the other about 2.5km (1½ miles) past the village up a windy road to the northern entrance. You can also walk up to the Southern Gate from the edge of the village of Pamukkale, straight uphill alongside the terraces of travertines.

If you plan to skip the Necropolis (you shouldn't), the Southern Gate is more convenient because the parking lot is closer to the travertines and some of the main attractions of Hierapolis. If you're walking in from Karahayıt, you'll be entering at the Northern Gate, which will add an extra 2.5km (1½ miles) past an impressionable cemetery (the Necropolis), a bath/basilica, and the Monumental Gate before you get to the center of the site. Admission to the ancient ruins of Hierapolis (top of the travertines, where you'll find the Pamukkale Thermal and a secondary museum) is 5YTL/$4.35/£2; admission to the enclosed archaeological museum located in the old Roman Baths is 2YTL ($1.75/80p).

GETTING AROUND

Dolmuşes ply the road from Denizli through Pamukkale up to Karahayıt regularly.

You can hire a scooter or negotiate a driver in either the village of Pamukkale or Karahayıt (good for looking into the roadside textile factories); buses and *dolmuşes* serve the solitary road between the two villages and to Denizli.

WHAT TO SEE & DO

The majority of excursions to Pamukkale can be characterized by 8 hours on a bus, split in half by a quick photo op of the **travertines** 𝕬𝕬, an hour of free time in the Sacred Pool, and lunch at some tourist buffet. With an itinerary like this, don't be surprised if you come away disappointed; an overnight in an inexpensive thermal hotel spa with a Jacuzzi, sauna, Turkish bath, and massage therapy seems to me the minimum requirement in a place known for millennia as a place of healing. Not only just what the doctor ordered, but it's also essential to factor in a morning stroll through the local village and a relaxed visit to the ancient ruins of **Hierapolis** 𝕬𝕬 after the sun has lost most of its bite.

A swim in the effervescent waters of the **Sacred Pool** 𝕬𝕬𝕬 should be at the top of the list on any travel itinerary. Scattered about at the bottom of the crystal-clear pool like so much detritus is an amazing collection of striated columns and capitals, a striking reminder of the pool's pedigree. The Sacred Pool is the main source for the springs feeding the travertines. It lies in the center of a lush garden that up until April of 2008 was enclosed within the last remaining commercial-cum-hospitality structure on the plateau (three hotels and 12 cafes were razed when UNESCO stepped in). Try to plan your visit during a fringe season (I showed up recently at 9am and couldn't even get near the place), or at least after the tour buses have trickled out.

The thermal water maintains a relatively constant temperature of about 95°F (35°C), so a dip in the middle of November is not out of the question. In addition to a high level of natural radioactivity, the water contains calcium bicarbonate, calcium sulfate, magnesium, and carbon dioxide, and after a swim, you should simply dry off and let the minerals do their magic.

The **Pamukkale Thermal** (✆ **0258/272-2024;** admission 18YTL/$16/£7.20 for adults and 7YTL/$6.10/£2.80 for children) is open from 8am to 8pm daily (until 5pm in the winter) and provides basic changing rooms, but don't forget to bring a towel.

So as not to forget that 2,000 years ago emperors and kings weekended here, the impressive remains of the ancient city-spa of Hierapolis (admission 5YTL/$4.35/£2) lie all around. The city of Hierapolis was founded in 190 B.C. by Eumenes II as part of the great Empire of Pergamum and was probably named after Hiera, the wife of the legendary founder of Pergamum. Considered a sacred site for the magic of its healing waters, Hierapolis reached its peak of development under the Romans at the end of the 2nd and 3rd centuries. During the Byzantine Era, a large church was erected to St. Philip, who was martyred here in A.D. 80.

Behind the Pamukkale Thermal are the stunning remains of the best-preserved **ancient theater** ✹✹✹ in Turkey, and the third-most-impressive theater after Ephesus and Aspendos. The theater was constructed in the middle of the 2nd century by Hadrian and adapted in the 3rd century by Septimius Severus, indicating the importance of the city during both Hellenistic and Roman times. The upper section of 25 rows, added during the restoration, is constructed of stones quarried from the ancient theater to the north of the city rather than of marble, suggesting that the city hit upon financial hardships during this era. Notice the skeleton of the mechanism below the well-preserved stage. The theater comes to life in the late spring for folklore performances during the Festival of Pamukkale.

Just down the hill are the scattered leftovers of the **Temple of Apollo,** patron of the city. If you descend the incline just inside the fence and circle to the other side of the temple's stairs, you can see the **Plutonium,** a niche believed to be sacred for the noxious carbon monoxide vapors that are emitted from a nearby underground stream. Accessible via a (closed) passageway through the temple, the temple priests were the only ones with the power (or lung capacity) to emerge alive, a thesis supported by the deaths of not just a few imprudent tourists.

A pretty good hike up the hill will lead you to the **Martyrium of St. Philip** ✹, the remains of an octagonal basilica believed to have been erected on the site where Philip was martyred.

From the Martyrium you can cut down the hill toward the **Byzantine Gate** and the **Colonnaded Street.** Crossing the city on a north-south axis for .8km (½ mile), in ancient times the street ran from the Southern Gate and ended at the monumental **Arch of Domitian** ✹, a triple arch flanked by two robust cylindrical towers constructed by Julius Frontinus, the proconsul of the Asian Provinces between A.D. 84 and 86. To the right of the gate are the pillars of the latrine, not as graphic as the toilets at Ephesus, but interesting from an architectural point of view nevertheless.

Beyond the Arch of Domitian is the **Necropolis** ✹✹✹, stretching for over 1.5km (1 mile) and ending at the northern entrance to the site. Although people traveled from all over the empire to heal their ills, it's painfully obvious from this extensive burial ground that some diseases just can't be treated by a warm bath. There are various types of sarcophagi, layers of mausoleums designed as houses for the dead, and remarkable examples of the stone cylindrical *drum tumuli* employed during Hellenistic times. Don't pass this up just because it's too hot.

On the paved road heading back to the southern entrance, notice the crumbling but imposing Roman bath, built around the end of the 2nd century and later converted into a **Byzantine basilica** ✹. From the looks of several of the archways, one more earthquake and this structure is road dust.

Next to the parking lot of the Pamukkale Thermal are a 6th-century **Christian basilica** and more **Roman baths** (these ones for the rich folk). Dating to the 1st century, the baths were constructed in the rebuilding of the city during the reign of Tiberius after a major earthquake severely damaged the city. Now a museum, the baths house artifacts from the area, including a fairly impressive marble sarcophagus, but for the most part, you can skip the exhibit and admire the baths from the outside.

WHERE TO STAY

All of the better-class accommodations are in Karahayıt close to the Northern Gate into Hierapolis, but age and neglect in some cases may tip the balance in favor of one of the dozens of family-owned pensions in Pamukkale.

Richmond Hotel and Richmond Spa   Of the few acceptable thermal hotels in the area, the Richmond seems to be the preferred choice. The hotel, consisting of two buildings sharing a large garden, has the best thermal pool from the sulfur-rich Karahayıt source, boasting the hottest spring water in the entire region. There's both indoor and outdoor swimming and thermal pools, with the temperature of the latter at a steamy 118°F (48°C). The health center smells pleasantly of witch hazel and comes equipped with a fitness room, Jacuzzi, and sauna. Rooms are bright but a bit on the small side with the bathtub sunken treacherously low into the bathroom floor. The Richmond has a ballroom, a greenhouse, and two conference rooms, which attract businesspeople and wedding celebrations, so ask for a room away from the festivities.

Karahayıt Köyü, 20027 Karahayıt. (€) **0258/271-4294.** Fax 0258/271-4078. www.richmondhotels.com.tr. 315 units (all with bathtub). 90€ ($131/£64) single; 120€ ($174/£86) double; 160€ ($232/£114) suite. MC, V. Parking on premises. **Amenities:** Restaurant; 5 bars; indoor and outdoor thermal pools; health club; Turkish bath; Jacuzzi; sauna; concierge; tour desk; car-rental desk; 24-hr. room service; massage; laundry service; dry cleaning. *In room:* A/C, satellite TV or TV/VCR or TV w/pay movies, minibar, hair dryer, safe.

WHERE TO DINE

A dinner buffet is included in the price of the hotel at all the thermal hotels, a necessary solution to the lack of alternatives in the vicinity. In many of the smaller family-run guesthouses, you'll probably be asked if you're staying for dinner (say yes!). In both villages of Pamukkale and Karahayıt, you can get a basic Turkish meal at one of the little home-style *lokantas.*

A SIDE TRIP TO APHRODISIAS ⊛⊛

Just when you think you've been saturated by amazing sights, you round another bend and behold the archaeological ruins of the ancient site of **Aphrodisias** ((€) **0256/ 448-8003;** admission 4YTL/$3.50/£1.60). The best-preserved example of a Hellenistic civilization in Turkey, Aphrodisias is still undergoing excavations, compliments of New York University. If you've got a car and time for a side trip, this is definitely worth your time.

There is almost no documentation on the early history of Aphrodisias, but it is commonly believed that the cult of the mother goddess was central to its origins. As early as the 1st century B.C., Aphrodisias was recognized as a sacred sanctuary and was awarded special privileges that began with Julius Caesar and lasted through the end of the Roman Empire. Popularity in the cult of Aphrodite hung on even as Christianity took hold, but eventually waned. After raids by Selçuk and Turcomen tribes in the 11th and 13th centuries, the city was ultimately abandoned.

The site covers an area of 520 hectares (1,285 acres). Some of the highlights of the site include the **Temple of Aphrodite** ⊛, built around the 1st century B.C. and converted into a basilica in the 5th century A.D. Excavations, however, have revealed earlier structures, dating to the 7th century B.C. The immense **Stadium of Aphrodisias** ⊛, an elongated oval of 262m×59m (860 ft.×194 ft.), rivals in grandeur the stadium of Pompeii. Before it was excavated, the truly **Olympic-size pool** 🏊🏊 was originally thought to be an agora, as it was surrounded by impressive Ionic porticos and covered a vast area. The porticos were simply aimed at creating a fabulous reflection in the pool, which is laid entirely of marble. The pool is best appreciated from the top tiers of the **theater.** Nearby is the **Portico of Tiberius,** and to the west, the **Baths of Hadrian,** who had them built.

GETTING THERE   You can get to Aphrodisias by car from Pamukkale, only 1½ hours away. Also, some day tours from Izmir and Kuşadası include a stopover in Aphrodisias, on the way to Pamukkale; just comparison-shop along the main drags in Izmir, Kuşadası, Bodrum, or Antalya for a tour to fit your needs. If you're driving from Pamukkale, Karahayıt, or Hierapolis, take the road for Denizli, and then follow the signs for Tavas. At Tavas, take the turnoff for Karacasu and follow signs for the site.

7 Bodrum 🌟🌟🌟

840km (522 miles) south of Istanbul; 240km (149 miles) south of Izmir; 180km (112 miles) west of Marmaris; 25km (16 miles) south of Bodrum Airport

When Turkish people wax lyrical over Bodrum, they are often describing the heavenly bays of the Bodrum Peninsula, namely Torba and Türkbükü. But even the center of Bodrum, with its Greek-style whitewashed houses dotting the hillside overlooking twin bays, is something to write home about.

Imagine that in 1925, shortly after the founding of the Republic and at a time when feelings of nationalism were high, Turkish writer (and Oxford-educated) Cevat Şakir Kabaağaçlı was sentenced to 3 years of imprisonment *in Bodrum* for penning an article for which he was accused of "alienating the public from military service." Okay, so he was sent to the dungeon of St. Peter's Castle, but having made a friend of the local governor, was released after a year and a half and found a house overlooking the sea in which to live out his period of exile. (His publisher wasn't so lucky; he was sent to Sinop, on the Black Sea.) The view from his home was so picturesque that it inspired him to pen piles of essays on the beauty and allure of life in what was then a backwater fishing village. It was these writings that attracted the intelligentsia of Turkey to Bodrum, a slow trickle that transformed this tiny fishing port of fewer than 5,000 inhabitants to Turkey's most popular seaside destination.

In spite of the hype, Bodrum strikes the perfect balance among whitewashed stucco hillside houses dripping in bougainvillea, magnificent vistas, historic imprints, and blowout nightlife. **St. Peter's Castle** dominates every corner of Bodrum from its spot at the middle of Bodrum's twin harbors. The crumbled yet enduring remains of the **Mausoleum,** one of the Seven Ancient Wonders of the World, also resides in Bodrum. And although it's Turkey's most popular "party destination," by day Bodrum is a quiet but thriving holiday beach resort. In the summertime the city's twin harbors become densely packed with hundreds of the wooden gulets offering trips to the nearby islands or for the *Mavi Yoluculu* (the "Blue Cruise"), Cevat's romanticized weeklong journey

---

Fun Fact **High-End Mud**

The gray mud of Kara Ada, or Black Island, off the coast of Bodrum, is the source for some of Elizabeth Arden's cosmetics.

Bodrum

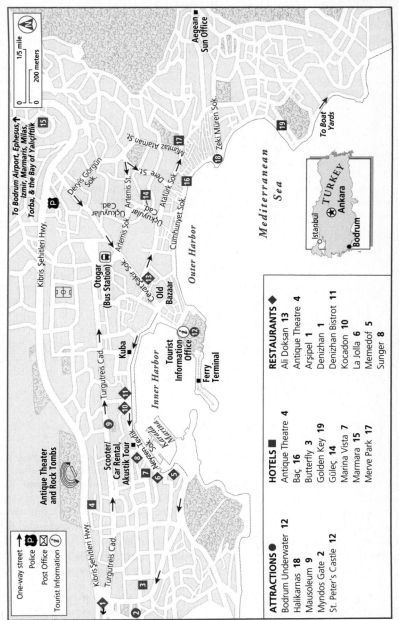

ATTRACTIONS ●
Bodrum Underwater **12**
Halikarnas **18**
Mausoleum **9**
Myndos Gate **2**
St. Peter's Castle **12**

HOTELS ■
Antique Theatre **4**
Baç **16**
Butterfly **3**
Golden Key **19**
Güleç **14**
Marina Vista **7**
Marmara **15**
Merve Park **17**

RESTAURANTS ◆
Ali Doksan **13**
Antique Theatre **4**
Arşipel **1**
Denizhan **1**
Denizhan Bistrot **11**
Kocadon **10**
La Jolla **6**
Memedof **5**
Sunger **8**

along the glorious coastlines of the Mediterranean. Meanwhile, Bodrum's nightlife—an all-night party organized by club owners each trying to outdo the excesses and spectacle of the others—is infamous throughout Turkey. By night the city becomes a maniacal stream of human flesh flowing through the narrow expanse of "Bar Street," which empties onto an open harbor of more outdoor cafes and bars, the whole sporadically illuminated by a laser show emanating from the famed Halikarnas Night Club. From every vantage point in town, there's St. Peter's Castle, illuminated by spotlights shining on the ramparts.

Bodrum's popularity seems to have no limits, and as fast as the Turkish jet set can lay its claim to a secluded cove or sandy bay, tourism follows, spurring the entitled class to seek new unspoiled hunting grounds. Examples of this can be seen all along the **Bodrum Peninsula,** in the boutique hotels and beaches of **Torba** and **Türkbükü;** in the expansive seasides at **Yalıkavak, Turgutreis, Ortakent,** and **Akyarlar;** and in the poetry of the sunken ruins and waterside fish restaurants of **Gümüşlük.** Bodrum is much more than the twin bays, and it still has quite a long way to go before becoming just another one of Turkey's overbuilt seaside resorts.

ESSENTIALS
GETTING THERE
BY PLANE   Visitors to Bodrum actually fly into Milaş, about 32km (20 miles) away and reachable in under a half-hour by way of the coastal road. **Turkish Airlines** (© 444-0849 for call center or © 0252/536-6597 at the Bodrum airport), **Onur Air** (© 444-6687 for call center or © 0252/523-0022), and **Fly Air** (© 0212/444-4359) are all competing for your business, keeping fares as low as 49YTL ($43/£20) and up to 139YTL ($121/£56) for a one-way flight. Turkish alone has five daily direct flights from Istanbul, as well as one direct flight from Ankara, and connecting flights from other major domestic cities. There are also several charter companies arriving from Germany and England; check with your local travel agent for information on when these are operating.

Havaş (© 0212/444-0487) provides transfer service by bus into Bodrum's bus station; the ride takes about 45 minutes and costs 14YTL ($12/£5.60). Havaş departures are coordinated with Turkish Airlines, Onur Air, Fly Air, and Atlasjet flight arrivals. A taxi from the airport costs about 50€ to 60€ ($73–$87/£36–£43).

BY BUS   Buses provide the cheapest and most comprehensive service into Bodrum, from pretty much everywhere in Turkey. The major bus companies serving Bodrum are **Pamukkale** (© 0252/316-6632), **Varan** (© 0252/316-7849), **Kamıl Koç** (© 0252/316-5350), and **Metro** (© 0252/313-2233), but remember that rates vary widely from company to company. **Aydın Turizm** (© 0252/316-3250) runs service along the Mediterranean coast to Ortaca, Dalyan, Dalaman, Fethiye, Ölüdeniz, and Kaş.

BY FERRY   **Bodrum Express Lines** (© 0252/316-1087; www.bodrumexpresslines. com) and the **Bodrum Ferryboat Association** (© 0252/316-0882; www.bodrum ferryboat.com) run daily hydrofoil and ferryboat service between the Greek islands of Koş and Rhodes. Bodrum Express Lines operates ferryboat service between Bodrum and Koş on Monday, Wednesday, and Friday, departing Koş at 4:30pm (Jan–May the departure is at 3:30pm) and departing Bodrum at 9:30am. The ride takes 1 hour and costs 25€ ($36/£18) one-way; passage for a small car is 100€ ($145/£71). From April through October, Bodrum Express Lines adds direct ferryboat service between Koş and Yalıkavak, Didyma, and Turgut Reis.

Bodrum Express Lines' hydrofoil service operates from April through October only. Trips between Bodrum and Koş depart daily Monday to Saturday (9:30am from Bodrum; 5pm from Koş). The ride takes 15 to 20 minutes and costs 25€ ($36/£18). The Rhodes service runs on Monday and Friday in high season, and takes 2 hours, 15 minutes. Departures from Rhodes leave at 5pm; from Bodrum, the hydrofoil leaves at 8:30am. The cost is 50€ ($73/£36) one-way. Same-day round-trips are available in summer and cost up to 10€ ($15/£7.15) above the one-way price. There is no ferry or hydrofoil service November or December.

Bodrum Express Lines also runs twice-weekly hydrofoils between Bodrum and Marmaris. Hydrofoils arrive in the charming town of Gelibolu (where BEL will complete the journey for you with a bus to Marmaris). Total travel time is 1 hour, 50 minutes (the last 20 min. are on the bus). The one-way ticket costs 25€ ($36/£18).

The **Bodrum Ferryboat Association** (© **0252/316-0882;** www.bodrumferry boat.com) also runs hydrofoil service (20 min.) to and from **Koş,** with service running once daily in July and August. Service from Koş departs at 5pm. The 9:30am departure to Koş from Bodrum allows for a short day excursion. Both the one-way and return ticket costs 25€ ($36/£18). By ferry the same journey takes 1 hour, also with a 9:30am departure (Mon–Sat); the fare is 35€ ($51/£25) one-way or round-trip. BFA also runs passenger and car-ferry service to **Datça** (2 hr.) for 20YTL ($17/£8) one-way and 30YTL ($26/£12) return with a bus transfer from Korman landing to Datça town, and 50€ ($73/£36) if you're loading a car. Children under 6 travel free; 6- to 12-year-olds pay 50%. The ferry departs in summer daily at 9am, and less frequently in winter, possibly twice a week. All tickets for ferries and hydrofoils can be purchased either at the dock, or through any travel agent in town. Allow at least 30 minutes before departure for your arrival at the docks; it can get pretty chaotic.

VISITOR INFORMATION

The tourist information office (© **0252/316-1091**) is open daily 9am to 6pm, good for little more than their collection of regional brochures and the latest copy of the *Aegean Sun*—a handy English-language publication with the only decent map available of Bodrum. Try to locate a copy of the *Bodrum Guide* as well. Stick with your hotel concierge for any significant information on Bodrum.

ORIENTATION

The white stucco town of Bodrum dots the hillside overlooking twin bays, separated by a narrow landmass from which the impressive St. Peter's Castle rises imposing above the sea. West of the castle is the **Inner Harbor,** home to the state-of-the-art Karada Marina. **Neyzen Tevfik Caddesi** runs the length of the Inner Harbor from the marina to the castle, serving as the nucleus of a neighborhood that caters mostly to the yachting crowd, and thus is quieter and more polished than the Outer Harbor. **Cevat Şakir Caddesi** bisects Bodrum, connecting downtown Bodrum with the *otogar,* the weekly market, and the highway, ending up directly at the mouth of the old bazaar.

If there are any bargains to be found in Bodrum, it's around the **Outer Harbor,** south of the castle. This is home to Bodrum's infamous nightlife and the late-night throbbings of Halikarnas Disco, so that a basic room in a pension for $13 and a sleepless night go hand in hand.

GETTING AROUND

The narrow and one-way streets of Bodrum discourage the use of a car. Although the waterfront spreads out over two harbors, downtown Bodrum is easy to cover with a pair of comfortable shoes and a bit of stamina. A scooter is a good option, because aside from solving the parking problem, you can get away with tooling around aimlessly down side streets or weaving unexpectedly through the pedestrian traffic on the waterfront promenade. For those lodging outside the city center, *dolmuşes* provide regular service along all of the major thoroughfares through the *otogar* to the city center, and from the *otogar*, you're connected to all of the bays and villages of Bodrum's scenic peninsula. A car, however, will provide the freedom to explore the spectacular nooks and crannies of the entire peninsula.

FAST FACTS: Bodrum

Airlines **Turkish Airlines** flies five times daily from Istanbul, and once daily from Ankara. The airline office in Bodrum is located in the Oasis Shopping Center northwest of town off the main road (© 0252/317-1203). THY (Turkish Airlines) also has a toll-free number: © **444-0849.**

Airport The general information line at Bodrum Airport is © **0252/536-6565.**

Car Rentals In Bodrum center the major car-rental agencies are: **Avis,** Neyzen Tevfik Cad. 92/A (© 0252/316-2333), and **National Car Rental,** Cevat Şakir Cad. 48 (© 0252/313-6110). **Budget** (© 0252/523-0271) and **Sixt** (© 0252/522-3971) have counters at Bodrum's airport and both offer pickup and delivery service. The locally based **Akustik Travel** (Neyzen Tevfik Sok. 200; © 0252/313-8964) has a small stable of cars at extremely interesting rates.

Climate Bodrum's climate is Mediterranean, with temperatures rarely falling below freezing.

Embassies & Consulates The United Kingdom has representation in Bodrum, a consular agent at Kibris Şehi tleri Caddesi (© 0252/319-0093).

Emergencies In an emergency, the **Private Hospital** (Özel Hastanesi; © 0252/313-6566; located at Mars Mabedi Caddesi, Çeşmebaşı Mevkii 22-43) and the **Medicare Private Clinic** (© 0252/316-7051; Hamam Sok. 4, Tepecik), both excellent facilities, are open for emergencies 24 hours a day, and most duty doctors speak English.

Market Day Bodrum's local market is next to the bus station and open on market days from dawn to dusk. Thursday and Friday are the days for food, Tuesday for textiles and dry goods. Wednesday is market day in Gümüşluk and Ortakent; Thursday is market day in Yalıkavak.

Newspapers & Magazines *The Bodrum Observer,* launched in January 2006, is an English-language newspaper focusing on local issues. The *Aegean Sun* is the city's free and informative publication, with articles on life in Bodrum and current tips and trends. There's also a good map inside.

Police Dial © **155** for assistance or call the station directly at © **0252/316-8080.**

Post Office The main post office is located on Cevat Şakir Caddesi and is open 24 hours a day for phone calls and other services. The change office operates on business hours, but there are several private change windows nearby.

Shopping For upscale merchandise with prices fixed to the dollar (read: expensive), the Karada Marina offers elegant shops with mainly nautical motifs. Local goods and souvenirs are hard to avoid in the maze around the castle.

Oasis, an outdoor shopping center located on the northwest side of town, comes complete with upscale shops, a cinema, and restaurants. Make a special trip here for the *lahmacun* (thin-crust dough topped with minced lamb, tomato, and onion) at **Öz Urfa** (© **0252/317-0031**), open daily 10am to 1 or 2am, or for one of their kebaps or *çiğ köfte*.

Travel Agents **Bodrum Touralpin,** Emlak Bankası Dükkanları 6, just opposite the main post office (© **0252/316-8733;** www.bodrumtouralpin.com), is the heavy hitter in town, and where most visitors go for dealings with Turkish Airlines. **Akustik Tour,** Neyzen Tevfik Sok. 200, across from the marina (© **0252/313-8964;** www.travelbodrum.com), is a professional, friendly, and English-speaking mom-and-pop outfit. Check with Tolga or Özlem at Akustik before making any hotel reservations in town; they will save you a bundle. They will also direct you to the less visited archaeological sites in the region.

WHAT TO SEE & DO

Bodrum Underwater Archaeology Museum ✶✶✶   The museum is housed in **St. Peter's Castle** ✶✶✶, the recognizable town icon. The castle juts out into the center of Bodrum's two harbors on what was once the island of Zefirya, named after Zephyros, the god of the west wind. At the time of Mausolus, there was probably a temple dedicated to Apollo on the site, as well as a palace fortress. The land structure passed to the kingdom of Pergamum and then later to Rome before winding up in the hands of the Turks. Western sources say that the Knights Hospitalers of St. John wrenched the settlement out of Selçuk Turk hands to provide a refuge to Christians and increase their influence over the west coast of Asia during the Crusades. Turkish references say that Sultan Celebi Mehmet granted permission to the Knights Hospitalers to build an outpost. The truth remains that from their base over on the island of Rhodes, the Hospitalers' mission evolved from primarily medical to mostly military. Construction on the castle began in 1402 and became a symbol of the unity of Christian Europe against the Ottoman "infidels." According to the pope, anyone contributing to the construction of the castle would go to heaven; the naming of the **castle towers** illustrates the involvement of the various European nations, as does the presence of plaques, inscriptions, armor, and other artifacts.

After the earthquake of 1522, the Hospitalers raided the Mausoleum for building stones for repairs (some of which can be seen on the outer wall of the chapel), which apparently was not as effective as the Knights had intended, as the castle was captured by Sultan Süleyman the Magnificent that same year. Under the Ottomans, the church was converted to a mosque, adding a minaret and a public bath.

Although the castle is under the auspices of the Ministry of Culture, the museum exhibitions are overseen by the Institute of Nautical Archaeology, an American non-profit organization with bases both at Texas A&M and in Bodrum. St. Peter's Castle took on double duty in 1963 as Bodrum's **Underwater Archaeology Museum** ⍟, where various shipwrecks have been reassembled for display and occupy several build-ings in the castle. In the chapel, the **East Roman Ship** ⍟ dates from the 7th century A.D.; the interesting display allows you to walk onto a full-scale reconstruction of part of the ship and the excavation site.

The **Bronze Age Shipwrecks** ⍟ exhibit displays findings recovered from sunken trading vessels discovered by local sponge divers. The artifacts, dating to the 13th and 16th centuries B.C., are indispensable for understanding the late Bronze Age. Also on display is the world's oldest known shipwreck, discovered in 1982 at **Ulu Burun,** which contained a cargo of treasures, including copper ingots, tin, exotic wooden logs, hippopotamus ivory, and precious gems. In addition to Canaanite gold jewelry, one astonishing find was a solid gold scarab attributed in hieroglyphics to one-time owner Egyptian Queen Nefertiti (scarabs, which were representations of beetles, were often carried by sailors for good luck).

Usually, archaeologists can reassemble an object from broken pieces of glass, because many of the object's pieces are often found in the same place. Not so in the Glass Wreck Hall (separate admission 4YTL/$3.50/£1.60; Tues–Fri 9am–noon and 2–4pm), which contains piles of recovered glass that defy this theory. Archaeologists deduced that the ship in question was actually transporting broken glass as cargo for recycling. This superb collection of early Islamic glass has proved important in dating similar artifacts from other medieval Islamic sites.

The **Carian Princess exhibit** (separate admission 4YTL/$3.50/£1.60; Tues–Fri 9am–noon and 2–4pm), also called the Queen Ada Hall, displays the tomb of what is commonly believed to be Queen Ada, a Hellenistic ruler of Halicarnassus, along with a gold crown and a few glass cases of other jewelry. The exhibit is hardly worth the added admission.

While ambling around the extensive castle grounds, home now to families of pea-cocks, doves, geese, and an ostrich, be sure to visit the **dungeon,** a kitschy re-creation of an amusement-park horror exhibit. The castle's two main courtyards provide respite from the relentless sun. Or you can step into medieval England and sip a glass of white wine in one of the stone alcove booths in the castle's **English Tower** ⍟.

St. Peter's Castle, Bodrum center. ⓒ 0252/316-2516. Admission 10YTL ($8.70/£4). Admission necessary for entrance to the castle. Tues–Sun 8:30am–noon and 1–7pm (last entrance at 6:30pm; closes earlier in winter).

Mausoleum of Halicarnassus   Yet another plundered Wonder of the Ancient World, the mausoleum reveals only the foundations of the original masterpiece. King Mausolus of Caria ordered the construction of the 42m (138-ft.) ornate marble mon-ument, and after his death, his wife (also his sister), Artemesia II, saw to the project's continuation. After her death the architects and artisans paid for the project out of their own pockets; it was finally completed in 350 B.C. According to historical accounts, the magnificent tomb featured pillars supporting a pyramid-shaped roof that appeared to "float" above the structure. Atop the summit was a sculpture of the king and queen riding in a chariot. In 1522, after an earthquake caused the monu-ment to collapse, the Hospitalers used the stones from the Mausoleum as building material for the reconstruction of the castle. (Look for the greenish stones on the exte-rior of the chapel just beyond the entrance to the main portion of the museum.)

> **Fun Fact** **The Maltese Falcon**
>
> After Süleyman the Magnificent's conquest of Rhodes, Charles V ended the Knights Hospitalers' 8-year exile in 1530, granting them Malta and Tripoli to block Ottoman presence in the western Mediterranean. The annual fee was one falcon, the namesake of a famous American classic, *The Maltese Falcon*.

Because of the damage caused by earthquakes, plundering, and irresponsible excavations, present-day archaeologists can only guess at the building's original appearance.

Turgut Reis Cad., up the hill off Hamam Sok. ⓒ 0252/316-1219. Admission 5YTL ($4.35/£2). Tues–Sun 8am–noon and 1–5pm.

Myndos Gate   After many years of neglect, Ericsson and Turkcell teamed up to restore the ancient walls of Hallicarnassus (7km/4⅓ miles' worth), including the remnants of the east-facing monumental Myndos Gate. In 333, the Myndos Gate succumbed to the armies of Alexander the Great, who then sacked the city leaving nothing but the Mausoleum. The gate was a three-towered Trippilion, of which the center tower is gone. According to Arrianus, the Greek historian, the tower was protected by a 15m (49-ft.) and 8m-deep (5-ft.) wide moat. The gate and its immediate surroundings have regrettably been colonized by a newish hotel; local preservationists are up in arms over the commercial sullying of a historical artifact.

Myndos Cad. (on the west side of Bodrum). No phone.

WATERSPORTS   There's nothing like a walk through the Underwater Archaeology Museum to inspire the diver in you. The waters off Bodrum are full of caverns, caves, and reefs and just recently, the Turkish Naval Forces announced plans to sink a decommissioned military boat off the coast. **Aegean Pro Dive Centre,** Kavaklısarniç Sok. Asarlık Sitesi 30, over in Bitez (ⓒ 0252/316-0737; fax 0252/313-1296; www.aegeanprodive.com; open Apr–Oct), provides a safe and easy way to get you there, running two dives a day with lunch served in between. Price for 1 day with equipment is 47€ ($68/£34). The 1-day discover scuba course is also 47€ ($68/£34). If you bring your own equipment, the price is $60 (£30). They also offer 3- and 5-day packages, group rates, snorkeling for nondiving tagalongs, and PADI certification.

It's also possible to join one of the scores of diving boats crowding the harbor just past the entrance to the castle, all of which hawk dive tours with certified divers.

If you've thrown caution to the wind ("All About the Blue Voyage," p. 42) and decided to take a last-minute Blue Cruise, contact **Aegean Yacht** (ⓒ 0252/316-1517; fax 0252/316-5749; www.aegeanyacht.com) or **Gino Group** (ⓒ 0252/316-2166; fax 0252/316-5026; www.ginogroup.com). As the main yacht agents along the Aegean and Mediterranean, both have multiple locations along the coast, hiring out their own fleet of yachts or booking gulet cabin charters. Tour boats also line the harbor for sun-and-fun day trips to nearby beaches. Day tours cost about 20€ ($29/£14), leaving around 11am, and returning by 6pm.

DAY-TRIPPING
Bodrum is perfectly situated for 1-day trips to Ephesus (usually Wed and Sat), **Pamukkale** (Mon and Fri), **Dalyan,** and **Kaunos** (Thurs and Sun). The trips are

scheduled to coincide with local market days in the respective destinations. All are easily arranged through local travel agents for around 30€ ($44/£21) per person each.

If beachgoing is the main event, a tour of the Bodrum Peninsula will offer a glimpse of fantastic bays and (as of yet) authentic seaside villages. On the northern end of the peninsula and only 8km (5 miles) from Bodrum is **Torba,** where fishermen haul in their nets and you can stroll along the beach to the remains of an old Byzantine monastery.

The simple hillside village and serene bay of **Türkbükü** ***, long a favored hideaway of Turkey's jet set, has, to date, made room for a steady stream of travelers onto this little "secret" destination. But Türkbükü may yet transform into a proletariat heaven; the local government has its sights on the exclusive, 10YTL ($8.70/£40) cup-of-coffee beach clubs that have offered luxurious cushioned wooden piers draped in sailcloth to the entitled few by threatening to dismantle the beach docks. For now, the favorite sunspots are at **Ada Beach, Maki Hotel and Beach, Maça Kızı Hotel, Bianca Beach Club,** and **Havana Beach Club** (with its open-air fitness center, all located in Türkbükü).

The wooden decks continue to jut out over Torba Bay at **Kala Beach** in Torba, Sahil Yolu, No. 191, and in Ortakent, a grassy lawn gives way to the sand and sea at **Palovera Beach.**

The new marinas at **Yalıkavak** (typical and charming) and **Turgutreis** (caters to those on the high end of the tax bracket) are meant to fill the gap for yachters traveling between Kuşadası and Bodrum, where beaches and sheltered waterfront promenades lined with restaurants and souvenir shops make for an easy and enjoyable day out.

At the westernmost tip of the Bodrum Peninsula is the enchanting fishermen's cove of **Gümüşlük** **, site of the ancient city of **Myndos,** now partially visible just under the surface of the water. The village increases in charm in the evening, when area residents choose their favorite **waterside fish restaurant** * (the best is **Gusta;** © 0252/394-4228) from the many lining the cove. Thanks to its archaeological value, Gümüşlük has rejected the onslaught of "progress," and will hopefully remain as remote, charming, and scenic in the future as it is today (no building is permitted!). The remains of ancient harbor walls are scattered at the base of the headlands just to the north and west of the village; bring a snorkel to explore the site to which Brutus and Cassius escaped in 44 B.C. after having murdered Julius Caesar. Guarding the entrance to the cove and harboring its own set of ruins is **Rabbit Island,** connected to the mainland by way of a sunken ancient city wall that allows visitors to wade over from the town center. There's also an inviting beach at the far end of the village.

As the tourist body crunch in and around Bodrum forces "regulars" to seek new and unspoiled frontiers, the little village of **Yahsı** is happy to pick up the slack. Restaurants such as **Kösem** (Yalı Mevkii 2, Ortakent; © 0252/348-3666) play host to almost exclusively Turkish clientele, and for now, prices here remain reasonable.

Other great beach destinations are **Akyarlar,** the choice of advanced windsurfers due to the strong winds; the less windy **Ortakent Beach;** and scenic **Bitez Bay,** full of windsurfing traffic and a long sandy beach.

WHERE TO STAY

The historic and cultural St. Peter's Castle draws a large share of the tourist market into the town of Bodrum, while creating a market for "cheap tourism" over at the charmless resort of Bardakçı Bay, or in a basic pension in the Outer Harbor. One such pension is **Baç Pension** (Cumhuriyet Cad. 14; © **0252/316-1602;** fax 0252/316-7917), located smack dab in the thick of the all-night body crush. But it *does* front the sea, and the windows *are* double-glazed. (*Note:* Many of the hotels listed here are only open Apr–Oct or thereabouts, as well as Christmas and New Year's.)

Choosing to lodge in one of the inspiring hideaways along the outer edges of the peninsula will certainly rejuvenate the spirit (and perhaps one or two marriages), but will also tempt you from exploring the sights and sounds of Bodrum town. One new boutique hotel not included in the listings (it was too new to make the deadline for this guide) is the **Atami Hotel** (Cennet Koyu 48, Gölköy; © **0252/357-7416;** www.atamihotel.com) in the Gölköy half of Göltürkbükü (formed by the union of two adjacent villages). The Japanese half of this joint venture has infused the hotel with delicious Far Eastern flavor and serenity.

ON (OR NEAR) THE WATERFRONT

Antique Theatre Hotel   This hotel is a sophisticated yet unpretentious hillside retreat affording truly stunning views of the castle from every room. All rooms connect to either a shared or private garden lined with trellises overgrown with bougainvillea. Bathrooms are suspiciously like the facilities you'd expect on a yacht, including the ingenious cylindrically shaped marble showers (small). Separated from the bedroom by two louvered doors, the bathroom setup is quite intimate and extremely cozy, but alas, perhaps a bit tight for those accustomed to moving around in the bathroom. The owners have taken absolute care in every detail, from the landscaping to the handmade linen bedspreads, whose creator, overwhelmed by the number ordered by the hotel, refused to sew any more when one or two regrettably wound up on a guest's plane out of Bodrum.

Kıbrıs Şehitleri Cad. 243, 48400 Bodrum (across from the ruins of the antique theater). © **0252/316-6053.** Fax 0252/316-0825. www.antiquetheatrehotel.com. 20 units (all with shower). 120€–175€ ($174–$254/£86–£125) double; 375€ ($544/£268) suite. Rates lower Nov–Apr, Christmas excluded. AE, DC, MC, V. **Amenities:** Restaurant; 3 bars; outdoor swimming pool; laundry service; dry cleaning. *In room:* A/C.

The Butterfly   This Mediterranean villa, perched atop a hill high above Bodrum, was converted from a private home to an intimate and inviting *real* boutique hotel. And it's all "green"—recycled rainwater in the pool, low-water plants, organic composting techniques, and unbleached linens. You'll be hard-pressed to choose among this boutique hotel's six uniquely styled rooms. I'm partial to the Çini Room (this is a single), with its wall of Turkish tiles, and the Bahçe Room, which benefits from its own private garden courtyard. But the jewel in the crown of what is essentially a high-end guesthouse is the sun deck, where an open cabana provides shade on one side of a smart reflecting pool, with breathtaking sunsets over Gümbet Bay.

Eskiçesme Mah., Ünlü Cad. 1512, Sok. 66, 48400 Bardakci, Bodrum. © **0252/313-8358.** Fax 0252/313-8357. www.thebutterflybodrum.com. 6 units. Apr 15–May 30 $110–$200 (£55–£100) double; June–Oct 15 $140–$250 (£70–£125) double; Oct 16–Dec 31 $90–$200 (£45–£100) double. MC, V. **Amenities:** Restaurant; bar; outdoor panoramic swimming pool; tour desk; fax service; wireless Internet; 24-hr. room service; laundry; dry cleaning. *In room:* A/C, satellite TV, minibar, hair dryer.

Hotel Güleç   Thanks to Hotel Güleç, it's still possible to get an inexpensive room in Bodrum without sacrificing a night's rest. This basic pension on a back street around the Outer Harbour has simple furniture, clean rooms, and offers a sparse breakfast. The pension hides an enormous 1,950-sq.-m (20,990-sq.-ft.) garden at the back. One of the perks is that the nearby Delphi Hotel, owned by the same family, allows guests to use its pool.

Üç Kuyular Cad. 18/A, 48400 Bodrum (from the *otogar*, turn right onto Cevat Şakir Cad., left onto Atatürk Cad., and left again onto Üç Kuyular Cad.). ℂ **0252/316-5222.** www.hotelgulec.com. 18 units (all with shower). July–Aug 52€ ($75/£37) double. Rates lower Apr–June and Sept–Nov 1. Closed Nov 2–March 30. Check with management regarding credit cards. Street parking only.

Hotel Marina Vista *Value*　Although the hotel's address on the main harbor road across from the marina may generate some suspicion as to the tranquillity of its location, the Marina Vista is nothing if not serene. The hotel is far enough from the maddening crowd but within walking distance of practically everything in Bodrum. The simple design, inspired by classic Greek pediments and details, incorporates the modern conveniences of a clean, four-star hotel, most recently renovated in 1995. Only three of the hotel's guest rooms face the marina and street, while the majority of accommodations face a quiet interior courtyard with a pool. In the summertime there's a persistent layer of flower petals dusting the poolside, but because of the management's perspective on orderliness, they regularly get swept up. For romance and breathtaking scenery, the rooftop restaurant and Havana Bar offer incredible views of the mountains, harbor, and castle.

Neyzen Tevik Cad. 226 (across from the marina), 48400 Bodrum. ℂ **0252/313-0356.** Fax 0252/316-2347. 85 units (all with tub). 85€–120€ ($123–$174/£61–£86) double. Rate range reflects seasonal fluctuations. MC, V. Street parking only. **Amenities:** 2 restaurants; 3 bars; outdoor swimming pool; fitness room; sauna; 24-hr. room service; massage; babysitting; laundry service; dry cleaning. *In room:* A/C, satellite TV, minibar, hair dryer, safe.

Merve Park Suites Hotel　Contrary to the name, this is not an all-suite hotel; in fact, there are only two. But even located this close to Halikarnas Disco, Merve Park has some appeal, namely in the museum-registered artifacts decorating the small lobby, the charming rooftop garden courtyard, and the lovely sitting areas. The antiques have also made it up to the rooms, which all have large bathrooms. The only downside to the hotel is its location in Downtown Outer Harbor, which translates into rooftop views of water towers and nighttime noise.

Atatürk Cad. 73, 48400 Bodrum. ℂ **0252/316-1546.** Fax 0252/316-1278. www.mervepark.com. 17 units. 150€ ($218/£107) double; 250€ ($363/£179) suite. Rates lower Apr–May and Oct–Nov. MC, V. Closed in winter. **Amenities:** Restaurant; bar; rooftop swimming pool; car-rental desk; 24-hr. room service; in-room massage; laundry service; dry cleaning. *In room:* A/C, satellite TV, minibar, hair dryer.

NORTH AND WEST OF TOWN

The Marmara Bodrum ✦✦✦　The Marmara Bodrum is truly a feast for the eyes. Skylit hallways, white-on-white themes (including the staff's casual "uniforms"), and an eclectic mix of really cool stuff make this place seem more like an art gallery than a hotel, with a generous dose of warmth and congeniality to remind you that you're in Turkey and not on Madison Avenue. The rooms are simultaneously deluxe and sleek, with aged bamboo closet doors, made-to-order black-on-wood consoles, wrought-iron and wicker chairs, and the finest whiter-than-white bed linens. Every room has a balcony, but the real draw is the bathroom, a glass, marble, and chrome gallery featuring a picture window between the tub and outer room.

As if a panorama of Bodrum weren't enough, the landscaping takes advantage of the rocky hilltop, incorporating the stones into the design of the outdoor space. The poolside bar tables are crafted with Iznik tiles, and the poolside lounges, chairs, and barstools are—guess what—white. Don't overlook the top-of-the-line spa facility, where a massage or an hour-long session relaxing in the flotation tank will leave you limp.

Yokuşbaşı Mevkii, PK 199, 48400 Bodrum (on the hilltop above the highway). © 0252/313-8130. Fax 0252/313-8131. www.themarmarahotels.com. 95 units (all with tub). 150€–250€ ($218–$363/£107–£179) double; 420€–650€ ($609–$943/£300–£464) suite. AE, DC, DISC, MC, V. Free parking on-site. By car from Izmir, Ephesus, Marmaris, and Bodrum airport, entering Bodrum on Kibris Sehitleri Hwy., watch for signs for the hotel entrance on the right. **Amenities:** Restaurant; bar; 2 outdoor swimming pools (1 Olympic-size); grass tennis courts; squash courts; health club; spa; Turkish bath; Jacuzzi; sauna; concierge; car-rental desk; salon; 24-hr. room service; massage; laundry service; dry cleaning; nonsmoking rooms. *In room:* A/C, satellite TV, minibar, hair dryer, safe.

IN TORBA

Queen Ada Hotel ✦✦ *(Finds*   Only 10 minutes from the castle yet worlds away in terms of tranquillity is this waterfront boutique hotel of manicured lawns and seductive hazy mountain views, backed by the ruins of an old monastery. Surrounded by land on practically all sides, the waters of Torba Bay are as serene as those in a lake. Lounges, teak settees, and a thatch-roof bar are sparse additions to the grounds, which include a waterside raised swimming pool not far from the monastery ruins. A bi-level stone building houses the guest rooms, all with access to the outdoors via a patio or balcony. The rooms are a feast of minimalist design and the contents, including multichannel CD systems, are nothing but the finest. While deciding whether to leave the property or not, you can make use of a small but effective fitness room and a selection of motorized watersports equipment (for a fee).

Kilise Mevkii 28, 48400 Torba, Bodrum. © 0252/367-1598. Fax 0252/367-1614. www.queenadahotel.com.tr. 22 units. 245€–335€ ($355–$486/£175–£239) sea-view double. Rates lower off season. Garden-view rooms approximately 25% lower. AE, MC, V. Closed Nov–Mar. **Amenities:** Restaurant; bar; heated outdoor swimming pool; fitness room; watersports; bikes; concierge; 24-hr. room service; massage; laundry service; dry cleaning. *In room:* A/C, satellite TV/VCR and CD player, minibar, coffee/tea setup, hair dryer, safe.

IN TÜRKBÜKÜ

Ada Hotel ✦✦✦ *(Finds*   Fashioned like a stately country villa, this Relais & Châteaux hotel was built from the ground up on a scrubby tract of land at the top of Türkbükü by the architect Ahmet Iğdırlıgil and designer Hakan Ezer. Using the elements of classic Ottoman design, they incorporated such features as hand-carved stonework, outdoor living spaces, and thick stone walls. The rooms are huge and luxuriously rustic, and bathrooms are embellished with plush towels (on warmers), candles, and potpourri. Although the property has no access to the bay, the luxuriant grounds—caressed by the swaying of reed plants in the breeze—along with amenities you never thought you'd need, keep your mind elsewhere. The *hamam,* reserved by the hour for private use (nonguests pay $125 for two), enjoys views of the bay via a picture window. Two of the suites share private use of an additional terrace pool. A cinema screening room provides a large selection of films and keeps young ones occupied with a huge video-game station. And the cellar restaurant, with its velours, chandeliers, stone, and ancient wood, could easily set the stage for a scene for *Camelot.* Ultimately, the Ada Hotel is in a class all itself.

Bağarası Mah. Tepecik Cad. 128, 48400 Göltürkbükü, Bodrum. © 0252/377-5915. Fax 0252/377-5379. www. adahotel.com. 14 units. Apr–June and Sept–Oct $385–$800 (£193–£400) double and suite; July–Aug $450–$900 (£225–£450) double and suite. Closed Nov–Mar. AE, DC, MC, V. **Amenities:** 2 restaurants; 2 bars; separate waterfront beach club; outdoor swimming pool; fitness room; jaw-dropping Turkish bath; Jacuzzi; sauna; bikes; movie theater and video-game station; extensive movie and music library; library lounge; concierge; tour desk; car-rental desk; Internet connection; 24-hr. room service; massage; laundry service; dry cleaning. *In room:* A/C, satellite TV/DVD player, minibar, hair dryer.

Ev ✦   The same architect who brought us the delicious Hillside Su in Antalya has created this sublime complex of 48 one- and two-bedroom apartments divided among

8 blocks (each with its own pool) terraced down the upper reaches of the hillside over-looking the bay. The waterfront is just a 3-minute drive down the hill, where the hotel operates the Ev Beach Club. Apart from the odd fuchsia accent (hangers, bath amenities), the interior design is monochromatic (blinding white, actually) and large mirrors create the feeling of even more white and more space. Oh, and there's a plasma TV in every bathroom. Meanwhile, the "whatever, whenever" concept of service emphasizes individuality, so the staff will pretty much accommodate most any (legal) need.

Türkbükü, 48400 Bodrum. (C) 0252/377-6070. Fax 0252/377-5566. www.evhotels.com.tr. 48 units. 177€ ($248/£126) double. Taxes not included. AE, MC, V. **Amenities:** Lounge; (stone) beach; 8 heated private outdoor swimming pools; fitness area; sauna; concierge; business center; meeting facilities; 24-hr. room service; massage rooms. In room:: A/C, plasma and LCD satellite TVs, CD player, fully equipped kitchen, Jacuzzi.

Maki Hotel and Maça Kızı Hotel ✦   I've combined these two unrelated properties because of their proximity and similarities. Both are stylish, relatively pricey, and waterside, although Maki Hotel does also have a bouncer to guard its front gate. Rooms in both feature smart, minimalist design. The designer consciousness spills into the bathrooms, too, which, although equipped with only a shower, sport thick muslin shower curtains and high-end toiletries. Both are recommendable for a day out on the wooden deck "beaches" of Türkbükü, and as stylish alternatives to the extraordinary (and pricier) Ada Hotel (see above). A room with a view at the Maça Kızı, which is arranged in a series of buildings standing amid terraced gardens (Maki has a garden, too), might just be more desirable, given the plush window seats in the guest rooms.

Hotel Maki. Kelesharim Mevkii, 48483 Türkbükü. (C) 0252/377-6105. Fax 0252/377-6056. www.makihotel.com.tr. 60 units. June–Sept 200€–250€ ($290–$363/£143–£179) double; 300€–650€ ($435–$943/£214–£464) suite. Rates lower off season. MC, V. **Amenities:** Restaurant; 2 bars; 2 outdoor swimming pools; fitness room; concierge; tour desk; car-rental desk; wireless Internet throughout; 24-hr. room service; massage; laundry service; dry cleaning. In room: A/C, satellite TV, minibar, hair dryer, safe.

Maça Kızı Hotel. Kesireburnu Mevkii, 48483 Türkbükü. (C) 0252/377-6272. Fax 0252/377-6287. www.macakizi.com. 46 units. 200€–250€ ($290–$363/£143–£179) double; 300€–650€ ($435–$943/£214–£464) suite. Rates reflect season. Rates lower Oct–Apr. MC, V. **Amenities:** Restaurant; bar; outdoor swimming pool; fitness room; concierge; tour desk; car-rental desk; wireless Internet throughout; 24-hr. room service; massage; laundry service; dry cleaning. In room: A/C, satellite TV, minibar, hair dryer, safe.

IN YALICIFTLIK

Kempinski Hotel Barbaros Bay ✦✦✦   This five-star property is brought to you by the same people who brought us the opulence of the Çirağan Palace in Istanbul and the new Dome in Belek, along the shoreline of Greater Antalya. Let me start by saying that almost everything about this hotel is postcard-worthy: the "fairy chimneys" emerging out of the meandering mirror pool, the placid waters of Barbaros Bay, the serene Six Senses Spa. I say "almost" because although this resort hotel is pretty close to perfect, it's a bit, well, cold. The rooms are inviting enough, what with plush beds, lazy banquettes, teak-decked terraces (or balconies), an ample dressing area, and a bathroom fit for royalty, while the common areas like the atrium lobby (which sets the tone of the hotel) remain a bit sterile. Sigh. Leave it to Frommer's to find fault in practical perfection. It's a bit of a distance from the center of Bodrum (about a 25-min. drive down a meandering Yalıciftlik road), but if it's pampering and privacy you're looking for, well, you found it.

Kizilagac Koyu, Gerenkuyu Mevkii Yaliciftlik, Bodrum. (C) 0252/311-0303. Fax 0252/311-0300. www.kempinski-bodrum.com. 173 units. 210€–383€ ($294–$536/£150–£273) double; 450€–5,250€ ($630–$7,350/£321–£3,750) suite. AE, DC, DISC, MC, V. Free parking on-site. **Amenities:** 2 restaurants; 4 bars; indoor and outdoor swimming pools; helicopter pad; marina docking; health club; spa; Turkish bath; Jacuzzi; sauna; concierge; kid's "club"; car-rental desk; free Wi-Fi; salon; 24-hr. room service; massage; laundry service; dry cleaning; nonsmoking rooms. *In room:* A/C, satellite TV, CD/DVD player, minibar, hair dryer, safe.

IN YALIKAVAK

Adahan The modern construction of this boutique bed-and-breakfast takes its form from a traditional caravansaray, placing cool stone rooms around an inner court-yard and pool. A marble torso and a smattering of antiques adorn the sitting area and outdoor cloister, creating an atmosphere of absolute serenity (ensured by their rule barring children under 12). Soothing tones of saffron and terra cotta complement the palpable warmth of the hotel, with a simplicity of decor echoed in the simple, albeit fairly large, rooms.

On the coastal road just outside the center of town. ✆ 0252/385-4759. Fax 0252/385-3575. www.adahanotel.com. 24 units. 95€–125€ ($138–$181/£68–£89) double; 150€ ($218/£107) suite. Rates lower Apr, May, Sept, and Oct. MC, V. **Amenities:** Restaurant; bar; outdoor swimming pool; 24-hr. room service; laundry service; dry cleaning. *In room:* A/C.

4Reasons 👁👁 One could easily enumerate many more than four reasons to stay at this hotel beyond the four types of oversize suite rooms dubbed "casual," "passionate," "functional," and the less inspired "junior suite." How about the breathtaking views, the fragrant breezes, the sublime swordfish carpaccio? 4Reasons is located just 2 miles out of the as-of-yet unspoiled seaside resort of Yalıkavak, which for now maintains its salt-of-the-earth roots and the possibility of a complete retreat from the world. The 4Reasons, by the way, has already been discovered by *Condé Nast Traveler.*

Bakan Cad. 2 Yalıkavak, Bodrum. ✆ 0252/385-3212. Fax 0252/385-3229. www.4reasonshotel.com. 17 units. July 1–Aug 31 160€–235€ ($232–$341/£114–£168) double. Rates lower off season. MC, V. **Amenities:** Restaurant; bar; outdoor swimming pools; concierge; car-rental desk; meeting facilities; 8am–2am room service; massage; laundry service; dry cleaning. *In room:* A/C, satellite TV, minibar, hair dryer, safe.

Lavanta Whitewashed walls, wooden shutters, and arched doors and windows characterize the look and feel of this quintessential Mediterranean bed-and-breakfast. The hotel sits on the hillside above the Aegean overlooking Yalıkavak Bay, surrounded by a fragrant and vibrant garden. The views are spectacular, while the sunsets are humbling. Rooms are decorated with elegant simplicity (not sure what to make of the different side chairs, though) and feature glazed tile, wood, and wrought iron. The hotel's restaurant is one of the more enticing ones on this end of the peninsula.

Yalıkavak, Bodrum. ✆ 0252/385-2167. Fax. 0252/385-2290. http://lavanta.com. Mid-Apr to mid-Oct. 8 units. 130€ ($189/£93) double. MC, V. **Amenities:** Outdoor swimming pool; car-rental desk; Internet; laundry service; free parking on-site. *In room:* A/C, minibar, hair dryer.

WHERE TO DINE

Ali Doksan/Sakallı Restaurant TURKISH This typical *lokanta* is a down-to-earth, trucker-type place, with the food out in large pans where you can get a look at it. Fresh bread fills the plastic canisters on the tables; it's great for wrapping around a kebap or sopping up the tasty stews, rice, and beans. Get there before the local lunch crowd packs both the indoor and outdoor tables around 1pm.

İncı (across from the post office in outdoor pedestrian mall on the left). ✆ 0232/316-6687. Vegetable or meat dishes 4YTL–9YTL ($3.50–$7.85/£1.60–£3.60). No credit cards. Daily 11am–2pm.

Antique Theatre Hotel FRENCH/MEDITERRANEAN Hosts Selmin and Zafer Başak live in Paris, where they acquired a passion for fine food and good living. But instead of withholding their know-how, they've dedicated themselves to perfecting the

---

> ### *Tips* Bodrum's Favorite Snacks
>
> Locals flock to **Tatlıcı,** hidden in the maze of streets near "Meyhane Sokak," for what they consider to be the best *börek* in town; by 10am, they're mostly all picked over. **Karadeniz Pastanesi** (Barlar Sok., near the main square) has a window full of cakes, cookies, and breads, plus sandwiches and single helpings. From the tourist information office, follow Kale Sokak, turn right onto Meyhane Sokak, and then right again into a small passageway that will put you back onto Meyhane Sokak.

---

dining experience at their Bodrum hotel and restaurant. Having already received accolades and a glowing review in the *New York Times,* the Antique Theatre's restaurant was recognized in 1999 by the Chaîne des Rotisseurs, the 58-year-old bastion of gastronomy.

Dinner is served poolside by candlelight or in the cozy dining room; poolside is best where the tables have been purposely arranged to take full advantage of the sparkling views of the city and of the castle. The aubergine (eggplant) boat filled with seafood and a Halicarnassus sauce simply whets the appetite, and just when you think you've had enough sea bass, it arrives in a sumptuous fennel-and-champagne sauce that leaves you begging for more.

Kıbrıs Şehitleri Cad. 243 (across from the ruins of the antique theater). © 0252/316-6053. Reservations required. 3-course prix-fixe menu 35€ ($51/£25). Children 6–12 eat for half-price; free for kids 5 and under. AE, DC, MC, V. Open for dinner; call to determine time.

Arşipel ☆☆ FISH   Arşipel is set in a Greek-style whitewashed building that sits in solitude on the edge of the hillside just outside of Bodrum. In summer, beachgoers use the restaurant's waterside sun deck and make use of the kitchen for lunchtime deliveries. As the sun sets, the restaurant takes on a nighttime glow that acts as a magnet for the fish below, with sea breezes adding to the romance of the spot. The restaurant specializes in the preparation of fish so fresh that several of the mezes (lagos and shrimp) are served raw in lemon, oil, and black pepper. In the cooler months, diners cozy around the fireplace in the intimate wood-beamed dining room.

Aktur Sitesi A Mah. (inside the Aktur Sitesi entrance, west of Bitez Beach). © 0252/343-1016. Appetizers 6YTL–16YTL ($5.20–$14/£2.40–£6.40); fish sold by weight. AE, MC, V. Summer daily noon–1 or 2am; winter daily 7:30pm–1am.

Denizhan ☆☆ NOUVELLE TURKISH   This rustic little spot just outside of Bodrum, opened in 1998, is where you'd take a visiting ambassador. The serving style is both elegant and flamboyant, with *şiş kebaps* (skewered lamb cubes) served at the table on skewers the length of yardsticks. The preparation goes on behind a glass-enclosed kitchen in the center of the dining room, where the only thing you won't see is the chef killing the cow. Denizhan is a carnivore's delight; sample an innovative approach to cooking meatballs (fried in a cracked-wheat crust) or try the extraordinary Denizhan special (beef baked with cheese, pistachio nuts, and garlic sprinkled with sesame seeds). Find a way to get out to this restaurant.

The management recently opened the Denizhan Bistrot in downtown Bodrum (Neyzen Tevfik Cad.), with a light menu of sandwiches, grills, pastas, and carpaccios.

Turgut Reis Yolu, about 2.5km (1½ miles) outside of town (across from the Tofaş/Fiat service station). © 0252/ 363-7674. Reservations suggested. Appetizers and main courses 7YTL–28YTL ($6.10–$24/£2.80–£11). AE, MC, V. Daily noon–midnight.

Kocadon ⭐ TURKISH/MEDITERRANEAN   A stone-cobbled courtyard, quietly nestled between two traditional stone houses, is the setting for one of Bodrum's few restaurants with longevity. The quality is consistently good; start with the buffet of cold mezes, stocked with an irresistible variety of salads and fritters—but don't go overboard yet. The kitchen puts out an ample plate of grilled calamari, and the catch of the day is prepared as you like it (try yours braised with tomatoes, peppers, and mushroom au jus). There are also some classic Ottoman dishes like the *Hünkar Beğendi* (lamb or beef stew served atop a purée of eggplant, cheese, and béchamel), which are perfectly complemented by the upper-story *cumba* and ancient candlelit olive press in the middle of the courtyard.

Set back from Neyzen Tevfik Cad. at the corner of Saray Sok. (near the mosque in the Inner Harbor). ✆ 0252/316-3705. Appetizers and main courses 9YTL–27YTL ($7.85–$23/£3.60–£11). MC, V. Daily 7pm–12:30am. Closed Nov–Apr.

La Jolla ⭐⭐ MEDITERRANEAN & SUSHI   For pasta as close to authentic Neapolitan as you can get outside of southern Italy, eat here. Owner Serdar Toprak learned the restaurant business in San Diego and then transferred himself and his magic chef's hat (he actually doesn't do the cooking) to Bodrum. The kitchen also puts out exceptional grills (filet mignon) and fish (broiled Norwegian salmon), as well as a mean paella (call ahead to order). The wine list is well thought out and the cheesecake has earned Serdar an entire peninsula's worth of friends begging for a slice.

Neyzen Tevfik Cad. 174 (across from Karada Marina). ✆ 0252/313-7660. Appetizers and main courses 4YTL–27YTL ($3.50–$23/£1.60–£11). MC, V. Daily 9am–midnight.

Memedof FISH   For fresh sea bass or sea bream right off the dock, head to the restaurant that has already firmly established itself as Bodrum's de facto fish restaurant (the traditional kind, that is). Prices are the fairest around, and Memedof has become so successful that he opened a summer-season branch in Türkbükü. One unusual thing that has everyone talking is the baked Alaska, a "gimmick" that continues to intrigue residents of the Mediterranean.

Nevzen Tevfik Cad. 234 (opposite the marina at the far end of the st.). ✆ 0252/313-4250. Appetizers and main courses 6YTL–13YTL ($5.20–$11/£2.40–£5.20); fish by weight. MC, V. Daily noon–midnight.

Sunger Pizza PIZZA/SANDWICHES   In my earlier years of visiting Bodrum, I eschewed Sunger Pizza because, from what my friends told me, it sounded so, well, un-Turkish. But after passing by the place and acknowledging that it was consistently full at all hours, I gave in. The pizza turned out to be pretty respectable. Then, on another occasion, I had to try the local favorite, *çökertme,* a sandwich of sliced sirloin on french fries with garlic yogurt (hey, you have to try these things). The rooftop terrace is extremely popular with a local clique of entrepreneurs and a favorite stop for the boating set docked across the street at the marina.

Neyzen Tevfik Cad. 218, across from Karada Marina. ✆ 0252/316-0854. Appetizers and main courses 5YTL–15YTL ($4.35–$13/£2–£6). MC, V. Daily 9am–2am. Closes earlier off season.

BODRUM AFTER DARK

Nightlife here is legendary, causing people's eyes to glaze over longingly whenever you mention Bodrum (and a different type of glazed the morning after). The games begin behind the castle along Dr. Alim Bey Caddesi, a narrow health hazard full of crowds working their way past bars, eateries, clothing shops, and booths where you can get an exaggeratedly garish temporary tattoo. This overcrowded stretch reaches full capacity

at Cumhuriyet Caddesi, the broad walkway along the Outer Harbor thick with outdoor cafes, bars, loud music, and groups of young party-seekers. But there's a sophisticated side to Bodrum, if you know where to look. With St. Peter's Castle practically
illuminating the entire bay, it's just a matter of choosing your own front seat. Several
of the hotels listed above (Antique Theatre, Marmara Bodrum, Marina Vista) take
advantage of perfectly sited terraces or rooftops. If you're feeling ambitious, drive to
the village of Gümüşlük for a romantic seafood dinner.

Café del Mare   With its back up against the waterfront and an entrance on Bar
Street, Café del Mare is a beach club, a bar, a narghile cafe, a restaurant, and a musical venue (with DJs) all rolled up into one. You can swim, eat, relax, and imbibe frozen
cocktails 24 hours a day. Cumhuriyet Cad. 164–166. ✆ 0252/316-7110.

Hadigari   Nestled at the base of Bodrum Castle, the Hadigari (Turkish for "let's go")
occupies an old powerhouse transformed into a series of inviting intimate spaces left
virtually empty on warm summer evenings, when the festivities spill out onto the
quayside terrace. An early drink at a candlelit rail-side table with classic jazz playing
in the background sets the mood for romance. Dinner is served in the restaurant
(reservations required) on the upper level from 6pm to midnight. As the night progresses the music adapts, so that by 3am the hammering of an underground beat pre-
vails. Daily 6pm to 4am. Closed Nov–May. Dr. Alim Bey Cad. ✆ 0252/313-9087 or 313-
1960. 30YTL ($26/£12) cover after midnight.

Halikarnas Night Club   Vegas on the Aegean—and yes, seeing is believing. Touted
as the biggest and best disco in the world, it's certainly the most infamous. This is
excess at its best (and worst) and a club you love to hate, but everyone is inevitably
impressed. The club's three columns tower imposingly above the harbor, a striking
backdrop to the laser show later in the evening. Old and new hits from the top of the
charts and nightly live shows are interrupted by the occasional appearances of famous
pop singers. Because the nightclub has a capacity of 5,500 people, it might be a good
idea to reserve one of the few tables the management holds for those with forethought—or work your way up to the upper level (and away from the fray), which is
lined with cushioned banquettes and fez-covered bar stools. The club opens at 10pm
but doesn't attract a soul until midnight, coaxing its clientele with theme nights like
the Foam Party (every Fri and Sat) and Turkish Pop night (Mon). Daily 10pm to 5am.
Closed Nov–Mar. Cumhuriyet Cad. 178. ✆ 0252/316-8000 or 316-1237. Cover 30YTL ($26/£12).

Küba   This open-air staple—with its hipster brand of Cuban and Latin music—
continues to draw enormous summertime crowds. The whitewashed stone courtyard
serves as the bar, enjoying moonlit (and spotlit) views of St. Peter's Castle and Karada
Marina. Nighttime revelers with an appetite can enjoy a full (and somewhat pricey)
tree-shaded alfresco meal. When the temperature dips down below what would
require a light sweater, the party heads indoors to share space with the indoor restaurant (reservations required). Daily 9pm to 4am. Closed Nov–May. Neyzen Tevfik Cad.
✆ 0252/313-4450.

Mavi   Bodrum's oldest cafe opens for breakfast, attracting intellectual types in silver-
framed eyeglasses poring over the morning papers available on the rack. By night Mavi
becomes a diminutive bar with live Turkish music and is easy to spot by the crowd
gathered around the outdoor tables. Tickets may be required for special events, but
you can usually get these at the door. Daily 7am to 2am. Closed Nov–May. Cumhuriyet
Cad. 175 (just before the incline to Halikarnas Night Club on the left). ✆ 0252/316-3932.

7

The Turquoise & Mediterranean Coasts

Brochures and photographs do scant justice to Turkey's exquisite southern coastline—a route familiar to caesars, saints, sultans, pirates, and one illustrious and infamous Egyptian queen.

The Turquoise Coast, which extends roughly from Antalya to Datça, is a slight misnomer because it ignores the emerald pools reflected at the base of thickets of pine trees and the rich sapphire of the open sea. To the west, the Toros (Taurus) Mountains tumble into the Mediterranean Sea, creating Eden-like pockets of rugged cliffs and shallow coves where land meets sea. Many of these mini-paradises are accessible only to the seafarer. Traveling east to Antalya, rocks give way to small patches of pebble beach, until they cede completely to miles and miles of sandy shoreline. And all along the length of the coastline, a short hop inland reveals long-landlocked ancient and important military and commercial port cities. The Turkish Riviera is a rich depository of layers of ancient civilizations. Mentioned in Homer's *Iliad* are the **Lycians,** a heroic people that settled the coast from the Fethiye Bay to Antalya, from **Termessos,** where both **Croesus** and **Alexander the Great** came to consult the local priests prior to waging war; **Xanthos,** the capital of Lycia for much of its heyday; the sacred cult site of **Letoon; Patara, Pinara,** and **Tlos,** three of the six principal cities of ancient Lycia; **Antiphellos,** now the modern boating and resort center of Kaş; the

mysterious **sunken city of Kekova** and the nearby ruins of **Apollonia** and **Aperla; Myra,** the birthplace of a famous bishop more commonly known as St. Nicholas, or Santa Claus; the spectacularly sited **Arycanda;** the fiery Chimeara of **Olympos;** and the scenic trifecta of harbors of **Phaselis.**

The **Carians,** whose unknown origins invoke contradictory accounts by Herodutus, Thucydides, and others, dominated the southwestern region of Anatolia from the Halicarnassus to the shores of Lake Köyçeğiz. The remains of Caria along the Mediterranean coast, some of which overlap with Lycia, bring us to the strategic harbor of ancient **Knidos** at the western extremity of the Datça Peninsula; and **Kaunos,** with its ancient theater and soaring Lycian rock tombs overlooking the scenic Dalyan River.

The legacy of these peoples can be found in the majestic tombs hewn into lofty cliffs, sarcophagi crowned with Gothic helmets, and ancient cities sunken beneath transparent waters. On a boat excursion into a secluded cove, it's practically inevitable that you will stumble upon an ancient theater, a toppled Roman bath, or the remains of a pagan temple.

Thirty years ago, the destinations in this chapter slowly began to transform from idyllic and unspoiled fishing villages into ports of call for small boats and yachts. The local population quickly caught on to the advantages of tourism,

The Lycian Way & St. Paul's Trail

The Lycian Way (Likya Yolu), a 500km (311-mile) footpath between Fethiye and Antalya, is the brainchild of Kate Clow, a British expatriate and advocate of the joys of Lycian Turkey. Over a period of time, she has researched, marked, and signposted a network of rural roads and mountain paths, which cover a variety of terrain through ancient sites and modern-day villages. Most recently, she's established a series of trails that follow (or closely parallel, where conditions require) the route taken by St. Paul on his three missionary journeys to Asia Minor. The latter three trails begin in Perge, Aspendos, and Egirdir, and take in not only Christian history, but also ancient bridges, aqueducts, canyons, lakes, and peaks. Covering the entire distance of a trail on foot could take a month, but the trails are set up for day excursions for independent outdoor enthusiasts, made more colorful with the help of her handbooks, *The Lycian Way* (Upcountry Ltd., 2000) and *St Paul Trail* (Upcountry Ltd., 2004); see "Recommended Books & Films," in chapter 2). Kate also conducts 1- or 2-week tours departing from either Fethiye or Antalya. For information on the trail, log on to www.lycianway.com.

and these days, you can usually find European amenities and boutique hotels. Unlike the polished seaside resorts of the western Mediterranean or the Greek islands, however, the Turkish Mediterranean still comes with a bit of a pleasingly rugged and untamed edge. You just may have to drive up into the mountains a bit farther to find it.

A truly satisfying visit to these parts requires a week at minimum, and that doesn't even take into account the irresistible draw of a Blue Voyage (p. 42). For the purposes of this book, I have sectioned out the primary destinations of, say, Kalkan and Kaş or Göcek and Fethiye (both only a half-hour apart by car), but it's reasonable to find a base along the coastline and do day excursions to the surrounding sites (allotted here to the section to which they are most closely located).

For those with the luxury of time, the coast should be tackled by car or *dolmuş*

(minivan-type public transportation) from end to end between Antalya and Dalaman, as both are served by airports. Ideally, you'll want to avoid the winter months, because this sunny destination is best explored at its peak (and the coastline is eerily silent in winter). For that matter, the height of summer finds this extended stretch of the Mediterranean a bit overrun, so it's best to stick to the shoulder months of April, May, early June, late September, and October. For those with limited time, I recommend the chockablock destinations of the Fethiye/Göcek or Kalkan/Kaş areas, although my heart is heavy at abandoning some of my most memorable moments in the seclusion of the Datça Peninsula, in the twilight calm at the fires of Olympos, and in the restorative settings of some of the coastline's more isolated lodgings. But then again, I'm confident that you'll come back; there's certainly enough to see.

1 Marmaris & the Datça Peninsula ⚐

590km (367 miles) west of Antalya; 165km (103 miles) southeast of Bodrum; 900km (559 miles) south of Istanbul; 185km (115 miles) southwest of Pamukkale; 120km (75 miles) northwest of Dalaman

After commissioning the construction of the castle on the hill as a preliminary to his siege on Rhodes, Süleyman the Magnificent returned from an expedition and exclaimed, *"Mimar as!"* ("Hang the architect!"). Locals use this story to explain how **Marmaris** got its name; and although this is another of those cute Turkish anecdotes, this one is particularly apt—not for the castle, but for what central Marmaris has become. Urban blight has stricken "ocean drive," characterized by seedy-looking signage and fast-food stands advertising baked potatoes to a high concentration of low-budget English tourists lazing about on the bleak public beach. It's no wonder that tour operators of Blue Cruises bypass the town altogether and provide transfers from Dalaman Airport directly to the boat. Hang the official who let this happen, I say, and all the cheap-package tourists who have made Marmaris what it is, or rather, isn't, today.

Notwithstanding central Marmaris, the majority of the Province of Marmaris offers a stunning landscape of pine-covered peaks, isolated bays and inlets, secluded beaches, and a steady expanse of Mediterranean paradise. Much of it, thankfully, is protected, including the offshore islands and sea, preserving one of Turkey's richest areas for wild flora and fauna.

The city's location midway between the heavy-hitting resorts of Bodrum and Fethiye, combined with the ease with which mass tourism from the U.K. can fly in and out for a weekend, has made Marmaris more of a necessary (and evil) way station for clients of the Blue Cruise and for the yachting set. The difficulty of land access to the hilly coastline terrain along the Datça Peninsula provides an additional deterrent for the casual visitor. The Datça Peninsula still remains somewhat underdeveloped, probably because most of its visitors sail in with their own accommodations. If it's an off-the-beaten-track excursion that you're looking for, one good option to experience what little is left of Turkey's (relatively) undiscovered western Mediterranean is to explore the sea/land route between Bodrum and Marmaris (and on to Dalyan and Fethiye, if time permits).

ESSENTIALS
GETTING THERE
BY PLANE As of this writing, a record number of airlines were offering direct domestic service: from **Istanbul** you can fly via **Turkish Airlines** (✆ 444-0849; www.thy.com), **Atlasjet** (✆ 0216/444-3387; www.atlasjet.com.tr), **Onur Air** (✆ 444-6687; www.onurair.com.tr), **Pegasus Airlines** (✆ 444-0737; www.flypgs.com), and **SunExpress** (✆ 0232/444-0797; www.sunexpress.com.tr). You can also fly from **Izmir** (Onur, Pegasus, SunExpress), from **Ankara** (Onur Air), from **Bodrum** (Martin Air, Pegasus, Onur), from **Kayseri** (Onur, Pegasus), and from **Konya** (Pegasus). Onur Air also flies direct from London and Birmingham; SunExpress also serves the London-Dalaman route. Other European-based charter airlines flying into Dalaman are **Easyjet** (www.easyjet.com), **Monarch Airlines** (www.flymonarch.com), **Thomas Cook** (www.flythomascook.com), and **British Midland** (www.flybmi.com).

Havaş (✆ 444-0487) shuttle buses will be waiting for you at the Dalaman airport to whisk you away to either Marmaris or Fethiye (separate buses for opposite directions). The bus into Marmaris (to the *otogar,* to be exact) takes 90 minutes (85km/53 miles)

The Turquoise & Mediterranean Coasts

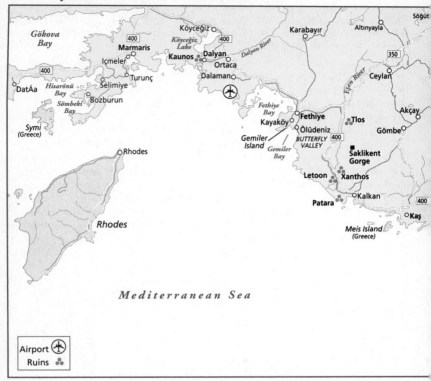

Airport ✈
Ruins ••

and costs 23YTL ($20/£9.20). There are also car-rental counters on-site, sensible if you've arrived here exclusively for a land tour. From the Marmaris *otogar*, it's a 5-minute and 1.30YTL ($1.15/50p) *dolmuş* ride to the marina; taxis will also be waiting at the *otogar*. (See "By Bus," below.) A taxi from the airport into Marmaris will cost around 110YTL ($96/£44).

BY BUS The *otogar* (station; ☎ **0252/412-3037**) is located close to the junction for the main highway, about 1.6km (1 mile) outside of the town center. If you're coming from Istanbul (14 hr.) or Ankara (10 hr.), buses depart once a day around 11pm or midnight and arrive the next day for about 65YTL ($57/£26). Service from Izmir (4¼ hr.) is more frequent, with fares as low as 25YTL ($22/£10) with Kamıl Koç. From some towns like Selçuk or Kuşadası, you may be forced to change buses in Aydın, about halfway to Marmaris. **Marmaris Koop** bus lines (☎ **0252/413-5543**) runs direct, air-conditioned minibus service to and from Bodrum (3 hr.), Ortaca/Dalyan (1½ hr.), Fethiye (3 hr.), Göcek (2½ hr.), and Antalya (7 hr.). **Pamukkale** bus company (☎ **0252/412-5586**) runs year-round direct daily service through Denizli (change to minibus for Pamukkale: 3½ hr.; 18YTL/$16/£7.20) on the way to Ankara and Bursa, in addition to Izmir, Bodrum, Fethiye, Antalya, and Kaş (summer only).

Dolmuşes (minivan-type public transportation) provide regular shuttle service from the *otogar* into town (1YTL/87¢/40p). This is a good option if the bus company you

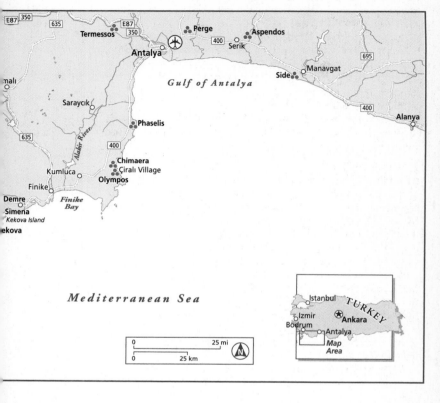

arrived on doesn't provide a free minibus transfer into town. Take a taxi (about 25YTL/$22/£10) if you're headed to the marina and instruct your driver to take you through the gates and as close as possible to your boat—otherwise, the size of the marina may force you to walk quite a distance from the gates to the mooring.

BY FERRY   A car ferry plying the route between Bodrum and Datça leaves both ports simultaneously twice daily (9am and 5pm) for the 2-hour crossing. Boats to Datça arrive at Korman, a lonesome port on the northwestern reaches of the Datça Peninsula. A one-way ticket costs 20€ ($29/£14) one-way or 30€ ($44/£21) round-trip and can be purchased at the office of **Bodrum Ferryboat Association** (© **0252/ 316-0882** in Bodrum; © **0252/712-2143** in Datça). From Korman, a shuttle bus will take you to the town of Datça, about 6.5km (4 miles) away. From Datça (assuming it's not your final destination), you can hop on a *dolmuş* for the long and varying mountain and coastal drive into Marmaris (1 hr., 15 min.).

Bodrum Express Lines (© **0252/316-1087**) also runs hydrofoils between Bodrum and Marmaris departing on Thursday and Sunday, March or April through October or November. Hydrofoils from Bodrum depart at 8am and 4pm, arriving in the charming town of Gelibolu (the transfer by bus into Marmaris is included in the price of the ticket). Total travel time is 1 hour, 50 minutes (the last 20 min. are on the bus); the trip costs 25€ ($36/£18) one-way and 30€ ($44/£21) round-trip.

Provisions Pit Stop

Not far from Iskele Meydanı on Ulusal Egemenlik Caddesi is the grocery store Targaş, indispensable for last-minute provisions like water and wine, which are generally not included in the Blue Voyage pay-one-price package.

VISITOR INFORMATION

The **tourist information office** in **Marmaris** is at Iskele Meydanı 2, across from the Atatürk statue (© **0252/412-1035;** fax 0252/412-7277). In **Datça,** it's located at the marina (©/fax 0252/712-3546).

ORIENTATION

As a chief point of departure for the Blue Voyage, the Marmaris seafront is where all of the action takes place. **Ulusal Egemenlik Caddesi** meets the Bay of Marmaris head-on at the main square proudly displaying the statue of Atatürk. The area east of **Ulusal Egemenlik Caddesi** is the older part of town, an appealing cluster of old waterfront houses crowned by the castle and well worth a look. **Kordon Caddesi** is the pedestrian continuation of Atatürk Caddesi to the east of **Iskele Meydanı,** and where the gulets (wooden boats) line the wharf each Saturday night prior to their morning departure. The wharf walk makes a semicircular loop around the base of the castle, arriving at several footbridges leading to the entrance of the marina. Within the gates of **Netsel Marina** are a few pubs and restaurants with terraces overlooking the harbor, along with an upscale outdoor shopping mall.

To the west along the shore is **Atatürk Caddesi,** which forks off and changes names several times before it exits Marmaris proper and turns into a hilly country road leading into **Içmeler,** a smaller seaside resort at the base of a beautifully crested, pine-covered mountain range. Farther west are the azure waters of the **Gulf of Hisarönü,** and the remote and magical villages of **Selimiye, Turunç,** and **Gökova,** if forced to name just a few.

About 81km (50 miles) west across a wilderness of forested mountain ranges (a little over an hour by car from Marmaris) is the oft-overlooked seaside town of **Datça** (covered in "A Side Trip to Datça," at the end of this section), the old Greek inland village of **Eski, or Old Datça,** and farther west along a slow-going road toward the tip of the peninsula, the ancient city of **Knidos.** The road west from Marmaris is in neglect, and west of Datça town it's almost nonexistent. So, if traveling by land, you may want to tackle the region of Marmaris separately from the region around Datça town—reached via ferryboat from Bodrum in under 2 hours.

GETTING AROUND

Dolmuşes ply the one main road running the length of Datça Peninsula from Marmaris to Datça town (3.75YTL/$3.25/£1.50; 90 min.) hourly in high season, reducing to five times a day off season. Within Marmaris town, *Dolmuşes* run frequently from the *otogar* along Marmaris's multinamed main road via the statue of Atatürk to points west. Transport within the city limits costs 1YTL (87¢/40p); from Marmaris to Içmeler it's 1.50YTL ($1.30/60p). Check the destination on the windshield if you're headed out of town; service runs as far as Datça.

Consider renting a car for forays into the surrounding villages and coves, or get a scooter for ease of transportation in and around the immediate reach of Marmaris town. Ask your hotel concierge if they can help you with a rental, or even ask a bellhop, who will most certainly have a friend in the vehicle-rental business. Cars rent for as little as £19 ($38), and day scooters slightly less. Agree on a model and price by phone, and a representative will deliver the vehicle to you at no extra charge.

Several taxi boats provide service between the holiday resorts of Içmeler and downtown Marmaris. Service is more frequent when demand is up, so check with your hotel to see how often they are running, if at all, and the time of day they start/finish. The ride costs 4YTL ($3.50/£1.60) each way.

A regular taxi from Içmeler to Marmaris can cost as little as 10YTL ($8.70/£4) or as much as 25YTL ($22/£10), so try to haggle a bit and agree on a price before you get in.

DAY TRIPS BY BOAT

Lining the wharves of most medium- to large-size towns are private captains touting day trips through neighboring waters. A typical excursion tools along the coastline to the south to Turunç, Umlu, Cadirgan, and Çiftlik bays, and to **Cleopatra's (Sedir) Island,** made famous for the pearly white sands the exotic queen had shipped over from Egypt. Day-boat excursions also leave from **Bozburun** and **Datça,** past scenery more beautiful than the last, where you can swim, snorkel, or just plain snooze, all for about 20YTL to 30YTL ($17–$26/£8–£12) depending on how well you bargain, lunch included. A second itinerary out of Marmaris heads a little farther out into the Mediterranean to **Dalyan** (later in this chapter), where, at **Iztuzu Beach,** you'll switch from your gulet to a motorized fishing boat for the classic tour up the Dalyan River, including a stop at Kaunos and the mud baths. Prices for this trip are a little higher, at about 30YTL ($26/£12) per person.

Certified divers with their own boats, easily spotted by the rack of wet suits and diving equipment onboard, line the wharf near Iskele Meydanı. Diving expeditions leave early in the morning; for any day-boat trip, it's important to reserve at least the evening before. Cost of a day out is about £40 ($80), including equipment, insurance, guides, and lunch. There's also the reputable **European Diving Centre** (www.europeandiving.co.uk), with outlets in both Marmaris (✆ **0252/455-4733**) and Fethiye (✆ **0252/614-9771**). EDC also offers a 1-day dive for beginners, a 3-day PADI dive course, and a 5-day PADI open-water course.

EXPLORING IN & AROUND MARMARIS

These days, Marmaris is top-heavy with cheap tourism, and it shows. But a short drive out of town reveals the original appeal that drew visitors in the first place. Leaving their mark along the peninsula is a slew of ancient civilizations, some woven into the daily fabric of humble villages, tourist marinas, and magnificent beaches. North of Marmaris on the road to Muğla is **Gökova** ★★, another stop on the yachting trail, dotted with clusters of picturesque wooden houses built in the two-story Ottoman style.

Just outside of Marmaris is the lovely resort of **Içmeler,** magnificently situated in a sheltered cove at the base of rippling pine-covered mountains. The fit and ambitious may want to sample a portion of the **scenic trail** ★★ that runs all the way from Içmeler to Değirmenyanı, about 19km (12 miles) west. The village of **Turunç** ★, farther south, sustains the charm of tradition and the comforts of modernity. A popular stop for yachts, it accommodates its visitors with handcrafted products such as honey, garden thyme, and sage tea. The long and winding road southwest to **Selimiye** ★★★ is well worth the effort. Frozen in time, this settlement is an ideal spot for enjoying local fish, village wine, and magical sunsets following a day on Sılıman Beach. Take your time traveling south from Hisarönü, though: You can walk on water at the beach of **Kızkumu** ✦ in Orhaniye, just beyond Hisarönü, where a lengthy sandbar extends 800m (2,625 ft.) into the bay. In the heat of summer, you may want to stop off at the **waterfall** ✦ near Turgut village, stroll through the Carpet Weavers Corporation, and relax over *gözleme* (a crepe filled with cheese, spinach, or both) and *ayran* (a Turkish yogurt drink).

It wouldn't be fair to finish off this section without mentioning the **Marmaris Castle Museum** (✆ 0252/412-1459), in the fortress in the old section of Marmaris. Perched above the harbor, the best access is through the bazaar behind the Atatürk statue; follow the signs through the narrow streets up the hill to the museum entrance. The exhibit isn't terribly interesting, but the views of the harbor and castle itself might be worth the 2YTL ($1.75/80p) admission fee. The museum is open daily from 8am to noon and from 1 to 5:30pm.

WHERE TO STAY
MARMARIS

Hotel Almena ✦   About 1.6km (1 mile) or so out of the center on the road to İçmeler is this boutique property of 55 smartly decorated rooms, each with a balcony. This is a good choice if you find yourself with a next-day departure. The hotel has a pool deck out back, a restaurant, and a beauty center, but alas, no beach.

Kemal Elgin Bulv. 45, 48700 Marmaris. ✆ **0252/413-8228.** Fax 0252/413-8250. www.almenahotel.com. 55 units. 85€ ($123/£61) double. MC, V. **Amenities:** Restaurant; bar; outdoor swimming pool; spa; sauna; massage. *In room:* A/C, cable and pay TV, minibar, hair dryer, safe.

Maritim Hotel Grand Azur   This property changes hands for every edition of this book. No matter. The five-star amenities remain, and it's got an expansive beachfront and manicured lawns that give it a decidedly *Great Gatsby* feel. Rooms are renovated if not a little banal, but children will love this resort for the indoor atrium kid pool, designed like a mini-jungle water park. The adult playground is even better equipped, with speedboats, jet skis, banana boats, water skis, and windsurfing equipment, not to mention the diving programs available for all levels of expertise.

Kenan Evren Bulv. 11, 48700 Marmaris. ✆ **0252/417-4050.** Fax 0252/417-4060. www.hotelgrandazur.com. 287 units. 120€ ($174/£86) double. AE, MC, V. **Amenities:** 3 restaurants; 4 bars; hotel beach; indoor and outdoor swimming pools; 3 floodlit tennis courts; fitness center; beauty center; Turkish bath; steam room; sauna; concierge; tour desk; car-rental desk; business center; Internet corner; hairdresser; shopping arcade; 24-hr. room service; babysitting; laundry service; dry cleaning; nonsmoking rooms. *In room:* A/C, satellite TV, minibar, hair dryer, safe.

Sariana Apart-Otel *Finds*   There's not much in the way of accommodations in the downtown area except for noisy backpacker-class pensions. One exception is Sariana, offering studios and one-bedroom apartments with kitchen facilities and a lovely garden, right on the marina. The floors are hydronically heated, and each unit has either a balcony or terrace.

Tepe Mah. 24, Sok. 4 (behind Netsel Marina, near the bus garage). ✆ **0252/413-6835.** Fax 0252/412-2656. www.marmarishotel.com. 50€ ($73/£36) single; 60€ ($87/£43) double; 70€ ($102/£50) triple. *In room:* A/C, satellite TV, wireless Internet, kitchenette.

İÇMELER

The hotels of İçmeler offer a lovely alternative to Marmaris. Accessible via water taxi (or if you feel like walking, there's the waterfront promenade), it's close enough to take advantage of the shopping, dining, and nightlife, yet far enough away that the coastline is once again able to enchant.

Divan Marmaris Mares   One difficulty independent travelers may encounter is that because these five-star hotels work primarily with groups, they may either be booked solid for your dates or ignore you altogether (my experience was the latter). The consolation is that the Mares is full of leisurely distractions to take your mind off of pretty much everything, and that's the point, no? Rooms are carpeted and spacious, but only a scant number of them offer sea and mountain views. There are 159 villas dotting the gardens, however, and these will provide you with optimal seclusion. The hotel organizes activities, beach parties, and live Turkish music in the evenings and there's an array of watersports activities, from diving to kayaking. Or you can just relax on the narrow sandy strip. The abundance of the breakfast buffet is without equal.

Pamucak Mevkii. ℂ **0252/455-2200.** Fax 0252/455-2201. www.mares.com.tr. 430 units. $320 (£160) double; $500 (£250) and up suite. Rates include full board and all drinks and beverages. AE, MC, V. Closed Nov–Mar. **Amenities:** 3 restaurants; 4 bars; nightclub; hotel beach; heated indoor and outdoor swimming pools; tennis, volleyball, and basketball courts; fitness center; Turkish bath; steam room; sauna; miniclub and kids' activities; concierge; tour desk; car-rental desk; heliport; business center; conference and meeting facilities; salon; shopping arcade; 24-hr. room service; babysitting; laundry service; dry cleaning; nonsmoking rooms. *In room:* A/C, satellite TV, minibar, hair dryer, safe.

Martı Resort Deluxe Hotel ⚜   Of the two hotels listed here, the Martı has the more spectacular location, nestled in the cleavage of two pine-covered mountains on a 115m-long (377-ft.) private beach. Built on the site of a 7th-century monastery (some of the ruins are visible out front), the Martı fronts an expansive playground of sand, lawns, and a duplex pool. All rooms have an outdoor entrance and a balcony. Two of the 208 standard rooms are designed for families wanting to spread out a bit into two rooms, rather than one. Villas are comprised of one or two bedrooms with mini-kitchens and a balcony or terrace, all with Jacuzzi (two are handicapped-accessible).

İçmeler Köyü. ℂ **0252/455-3440.** Fax 0252/455-3448. www.marti.com.tr. 272 units. July $105 (£53) per person half-board, add $50 (£25) per person for suite. AE, MC, V. **Amenities:** 4 restaurants; 4 bars; nightclub; hotel beach; 1 indoor and 2 outdoor swimming pools; kids' pool; tennis, volleyball, and basketball courts; fitness center; beauty center; Turkish bath; steam room; sauna; miniclub and kids' activities; movies; concierge; tour desk; car-rental desk; heliport; business center; conference and meeting facilities; hairdresser; shopping arcade; 24-hr. room service; babysitting; laundry service; dry cleaning; nonsmoking rooms. *In room:* A/C, satellite TV, minibar, hair dryer, safe.

IN BÖRDÜBET

Golden Key Bördübet ⚜ *Kids*   This place and the Golden Key Hisarönü (see below) are sister properties that sit on the edge of an undeveloped tourist frontier. What the Golden Key Bördübet lacks in waterfront, it makes up for with an unmanicured garden paradise, buried deep in the pine mountains via a bumpy 12km (7½-mile) road (6.5km/4 miles of which is a rocky dirt track). The property, shaded under a forest of lemon trees and pine, is split in half by the Bördübet Stream, which, thanks to the canoes provided by the hotel, provides direct access to the sea and to the hotel's private **"island"**—a tiny slice of heaven equipped with canoes, kayaks, wind sails, lounge chairs, and a snack bar. (This beach is also accessible by land; the hotel provides a shuttle.) In contrast to the Hisarönü property, the rooms at Bördübet are updated and stylish. The guest quarters occupy several terra-cotta-colored buildings arranged around a swimming pool. Junior suites are standard rooms with balconies, while the king suites have double the space. Duplexes are actually small albeit on two levels and enjoy small ground-floor patios. With tennis courts, bicycles at your disposal, scenic wooden bridges, a brand-new spa facility, and farm animals wandering the property, Bördübet is a great choice for parents *and* kids.

48706 Bördübet (35km/22 miles west of Marmaris). © 0252/436-9230. Fax 0252/436-9089. www.goldenkey hotels.com. 22 units. 220€–260€ ($319–$377/£157–£186) king suite. MC, V. Closed Nov–April. **Amenities:** Restaurant; 2 bars; outdoor swimming pool; watersports; bikes; concierge; car-rental desk; 24-hr. room service; dry cleaning. *In room:* A/C, satellite TV, minibar, hair dryer.

IN HISARÖNÜ

Golden Key Hisarönü ★ *Kids* A sister property of Golden Key Bördübet (see above), the hotel hugs an elevated outcropping on one of the smaller beaches of the Gulf of Hisarönü, which it shares with two teeny campsites and a family-owned restaurant. The main draw is the beachfront, backed by an expansive grassy garden strewn with lawn chairs and some kiddy paraphernalia. A swimming pool sits at the back of the property near the restaurant, along with the guest rooms, located in several buildings. At about 16 years old, the accommodations are in need of a renovation, but everything works, the beds are comfortable, the rooms are large, and the private patios are great for a late-afternoon read.

48706 Hisarönü (27km/17 miles west of Marmaris). © 0252/466-6620. Fax 0252/466-6042. www.goldenkeyhotels. com. 19 units. 160€–380€ ($232–$551/£114–£271). MC, V. Closed Nov–Mar. **Amenities:** Restaurant; 2 bars; beach; outdoor swimming pool; watersports; children's playground; car-rental desk; 24-hr. room service; dry cleaning. *In room:* A/C, satellite TV, minibar, hair dryer.

IN SELIMIYE

Palmetto Staying at the Palmetto, the most comfortable of all of the guesthouses in town, is all about appreciating the magical little fishing village of Selimiye, located 45 long and winding mountainous kilometers (28 miles) from Marmaris on the road past Hisarönü toward Bozburun. The hotel is the creation of Dr. Erol Üçer, a Turkish-born psychiatrist who has been practicing in the United States for over 30 years, and whose love for the village prompted the initiation of this little hobby. Rooms are small, spare, and simple, with neutral tones and adequate mattresses. The floors are tiled and bathrooms have showers only. Ask for one of the rooms with a balcony overlooking the pool patio to the cove to make the most of this spot, so that you can get a front-row seat to the waterfront's two harbors, the sheer rocky cliffs rising behind the minaret, and the ruins of an old church or monastery rising out of the center of the harbor.

48483 Selimiye (45km/28 miles southwest of Marmaris). © 0252/446-4299. Fax 0252/446-4301. 18 units (shower only). July–Sept 80€ ($116/£57) double. Rates drop up to 50% off season. MC, V. **Amenities:** Restaurant; bar; outdoor swimming pool; 24-hr. room service; dry cleaning. *In room:* A/C, satellite TV, minibar, hair dryer, safe.

WHERE TO DINE

Marmaris isn't hiding a grand culinary tradition, and apart from the few exceptions, the best you can hope for is a baked potato at a stand along the public beach. The several restaurants and cafes in the marina (not the ones on the wharf with menus in three languages) offer the most appealing options. For an authentic meal with views of the marina, at rock-bottom prices, head over to the diminutive two-story **Ney Restaurant** ★ in the castle (26 Sok. 24; © 0252/412-0212). If you're game and willing to head out of town, head north along the Marmaris Muğla road to the little village of Çetibeli, about 13km (8 miles) away to the little Mediterranean garden oasis of the **Çağlayan Restaurant** (Çetibeli Köyü; © 0252/426-0079). The garden has a stream running through it, with some tables accessible via a tiny footbridge. Village bread is baked daily, and available at breakfast, lunch, or dinner.

MARMARIS AFTER DARK

Nighttime activities are concentrated around the harbor, with restaurants lining the wharf from Iskele Meydanı all the way into Netsel Marina. Chaos reigns on **Hacı Mustafa Sokağı,** also known as *Barlar Sokağı,* or Bar Street, characterized by an endless lineup of bars indistinguishable from the Barlar Sokağı in countless seaside resort towns along the coast. Marmaris's version is particularly narrow, so in high season it can get claustrophobic.

More sedate and infinitely more appealing are the **art-house movies** shown in the open-air theater in Netsel Marina nightly in summer (© **0252/412-2708;** www.netsel marina.com).

SIDE TRIP TO DATÇA AND KNIDOS

Remote enough to weed out the riffraff, but easily accessible via ferryboat from Bodrum, Datça and its rugged surroundings are historic, peaceful, and most of all, unspoiled. The stunning coves of Palmut Bükü, Mesudiye, Domuzcukuru, Akvaryum, and Kargı boast some of the cleanest water in the Mediterranean, and with a 33% presence of oxygen in the air and a perfect Mediterranean climate, the elements combine to support the legendary longevity of the residents of Datça.

The proximity to the Greek islands of Rhodes and Simi can only suggest the richness of the Dorian civilization that was once here, but a look at the ancient ruins of **Knidos** ⊛⊛, whose terraced promontory rises above the site's dual harbors, certainly gives us a clue. Admission to the site is 5YTL ($4.35/£2). Excursion boats leave daily in season from Datça harbor to Knidos, making stops at a number of the more scenic coves along the way. By car, the road west of Datça is essentially a bumpy dirt path that leads to Knidos; the terrain is rugged and takes about 45 minutes.

The lovely port village of Datça is the center of activity at this end of the peninsula; in fact, Datça is the site of the original ancient city of Knidos, which moved to its current "new" position at the extreme western point of the peninsula in about 360 B.C. More recent settlements are the villages of Eski Datça and Reşadiye, located along the road between Datça and Körmen (the ferry landing about 6.5km/4 miles to the north). **Eski,** or **Old Datça** ⊛, is a landlocked village straight out of the storybooks, a minuscule cluster of old stone houses, carved doorways, and cobbled lanes dating back to when this was a Greek town. One or two coffeehouses and a pension or two hidden behind sandy stone walls add to an already thoroughly charming visit. The village of **Reşadiye** ⊛ exhibits some traditionally Turkish architecture and is worth a walk-through as well.

The road west of Datça discourages casual travel, as it is (for now) unpaved and bumpy. Not surprisingly, this end of the peninsula offers some of the most pristine bays and ancient sites, but you may want to consider arriving by boat (full-day excursions leave from Datça town daily around 9am; the cost is about 20YTL/$17/£8 per person) to make the most of the peninsula's coastal wonders.

GETTING THERE & GETTING AROUND   See "Getting There," earlier.

WHERE TO STAY & DINE   In spite of the presence of a number of holiday resorts, the pace of this end of Mediterranean Turkey promotes a more intimate, relaxed style of lodging. Charming and tranquil hardly describes the **Dede Pansiyon** (©/fax **0252/712-3951;** www.dedepansiyon.com), a quiet and flowering retreat in the heart of Eski Datça. The pension is actually a renovated Greek house, complete with a swimming pool, snack bar, and a mere six rooms. Each room is faithfully decorated according to its namesake: The Chaplin room is full of movie-related objects, the Theatre room displays masks and such, and the Chagall room contains reproductions of the famous artist's works. This is a true and unencumbered retreat. All rooms have air-conditioning and self-catering kitchens. Doubles cost 150YTL ($131/£60) in May, June, and September, and 200YTL ($174/£80) in July and August.

About .8km (½ mile) outside of Datça town is the **Marphe Hotel,** Kocatarla (© **0252/712-9030;** fax 0252/712-9172; www.hotelmarphe.com), set up like a Greek village, and constructed of whitewashed and natural stone. The Marphe consists of seven apartments (bedroom, living room, full kitchen, and balcony), seven suites, and 12 villas (two bedrooms, two bathrooms, living room, full kitchen, two balconies, and a terrace on a huge garden property in the countryside). Prices for two in a suite are 90€ ($131/£64) or 70€ ($102/£50) in low season, including breakfast. Marphe has an on-site restaurant and also offers a shuttle service into town. The **Mehmet Ali Ağa Konağı** ★★, known locally as the Koca Ev or "the big house" (Reşadiye Mah. Kavak Meydanı, Datça; © **0252/712-9257;** www.kocaev.com), can best be described as a living museum—an old Ottoman mansion owned by an aristocratic landowner prominent in Datça affairs. Ornamental archways, enamel ceilings, and antique English, French, and Viennese furniture offer a glimpse into the opulent living of the wealthy Ottoman class, and you and I now get to benefit, too. There are a scant 12 rooms, three of which are located in stone annexes. Facilities include a private beach (off-grounds), swimming pool, restaurant, and wine cave. Rates are not cheap and are listed at between 170€ and 530€ ($247–$769/£121–£379) for May through October (closed in winter).

2 Dalyan ★★ & Kaunos ★

110km (68 miles) east of Marmaris; 76km (47 miles) northwest of Fethiye

Dalyan offers the perfect refuge from the high-intensity holidays offered by back-to-back hotels and the constant whirring of jet-ski engines. What sets Dalyan apart from a coastline of Mediterranean powerhouses is its serene upriver location, its small-town character, the nearby natural treasure that is Iztuzu Beach, and a collection of some of the most stunning ancient monuments along the coast.

One of the last remaining major breeding sites on the Mediterranean for the sea turtle (loggerhead, or Caretta Caretta) and the green turtle (chelonia mydas), Dalyan rose from obscurity in 1986 when in protest against the development of a luxury hotel, environmental protectionists rallied to have the nearby beach declared a protected area. The publicity only served as a beacon for the first major wave of tourists, but even if every other street has a pension with the word "turtle" in it, Dalyan still remains, for the most part, a quiet river town. But even more monumental than the pristine pseudo-sandbar that makes up Iztuzu—better known as Turtle Beach—are the spectacular cliff-top temple-tombs soaring above the tall reeds on the opposite shores of the river. In addition to the ruins of ancient **Kaunos,** the area boasts some natural thermal sources in what has become a local ritual at the nearby mud baths. And as a delightful small village in its own right, Dalyan makes an off-the-beaten-track base for activities such as kayaking, rafting, diving, and snorkeling; exploring village life through treks, jeep tours, and bike rides; or sailing (for days) along some of Turkey's most stunning coastline. Getting around is half the fun: River *dolmuşes* shuttle people up and down the river through an incredible maze of canals enclosed within 3m (9¾-ft.) walls of reeds, past mysterious Lycian cliff tombs.

ESSENTIALS
GETTING THERE
BY PLANE   Dalaman Airport lies only 21km (13 miles) southeast of Dalyan. (Count on at least 25 min. by car; see "By Plane" under "Getting There" for Marmaris, earlier in this chapter.) It is possible to get in on your own by taking the airport coach to the crossroad in Dalaman (5km/3 miles), changing for a *dolmuş* to Ortaca (9.5km/6 miles), and then changing again for Dalyan (12km/7½ miles), an ordeal that will cost you about an hour (including waiting time) and about 5YTL ($4.35/£2). Better still is to have a trusted driver waiting for you: **Kaunos Tours** (in Dalyan center; © **0252/284-2816;** www.kaunostours.com) offers a special shuttle service for as little as £25 ($50) for a car that holds up to four people. See if you can get a local taxi to beat *that*.

BY BUS   There is no direct bus service to Dalyan. Buses will get you as far as Ortaca, located about 8km (5 miles; 15 min.; 2YTL/$1.75/80p) west on the Marmaris-to-Fethiye highway; from there you can find a taxi (25YTL–30YTL/$22–$26/£10–£12). There is also limited *dolmuş* service from Fethiye (1 hr., 10 min.) and Marmaris (1 hr., 30 min.); either trip costs around 7YTL ($6.10/£2.80).

BY BOAT   A wonderful first impression of Dalyan can be had arriving by sea. You can negotiate the cost of transportation from one of the neighboring ports—Marmaris is the closest major one—or book a cheap spot on a day excursion and take it one-way only.

VISITOR INFORMATION
The **tourist information office** (©/fax **0252/284-4235**) is located in the town center on Maraş Mahallesi.

ORIENTATION
Dalyan is situated on the **Dalyan River (Dalyan Cayı),** a river canal connecting the Köyceğiz Lake with the Mediterranean. At the mouth of the river is a natural sandbar protecting the canal from the open seas. Known as **Iztuzu Beach,** this beach peninsula divides the rough seas of the Mediterranean from the serene waters of the canal and is one of the last natural breeding grounds for the loggerhead turtle.

Majestic rock-cut temple tombs hover on the cliff face, and farther upriver on the shore opposite Dalyan are the ruins of **Kaunos,** once a thriving Lycian port town and now located slightly inland. Farther north are the open-air mud baths, and continuing upriver the thermal waters flanking the scenic **Köyceğiz Lake.** On the northern bank of the lake is the sleepy village of Köyceğiz, an alternative jumping-off point for visits to the area attractions.

The soul of Dalyan is on the river. Restaurants, waterside cafes, hotels, and pensions line the waterfront, while the business heart of the city (banks and shopping center) is located a few short steps inland. *Dolmuşes* line up near the statue of Atatürk.

GETTING AROUND
BY BOAT   Boats are the main mode of transportation in Dalyan. Dalyan's cooperative of river boatmen run river *dolmuşes* daily beginning at 9:30am to Iztuzu Beach for 5YTL ($4.35/£2) round-trip. Since the boatmen are working together, you can hop

on any one of their boats for the return trip. Upon request, they'll even pick you up at your hotel—have your hotel call ahead (© **0252/284-2094**). River *dolmuşes* run from Dalyan to Iztuzu between 9am and 1:30pm; return boats leave Iztuzu beginning at 1pm to the last run at 6pm. Don't wait until late morning to head out, though; since these are *dolmuşes,* they only leave after they've managed to pick up a reasonable number of passengers, leaving latecomers waiting indefinitely. The cooperative also runs excursion to the mud baths, the Sultaniye Thermal, and to Köyceğiz Lake daily for 15YTL ($13/£6) and transport to and from Kaunos (15YTL/$13/£6) departing at 9am and returning at 3pm daily. For all of the cooperative's trips, kids to age 6 ride free; 7 to 12 pay half-price. Meanwhile, many hotels have their own boats providing service for free or for a fee.

The more economical option for excursions is to hook up with one of the innumerable agencies around town that offer group tours of the area; this way, the cost of the private boat rental is shouldered by all participants, and the headache of filling the boat is borne by the agency. **Kaunos Tours** (© **0252/284-2816;** www.kaunostours. com), also the local representative for Europcar, runs an area day tour as well as active adventure trips (jeeps, horses, fishing, kayaking, diving, trekking), as well as a "Kids Club Day" tour.

There's an inexpensive and convenient rowboat shuttling those in the know across the river from Dalyan, at the extreme southern end of the Kordon (not far from the Dalyan Hotel) to Çandır; at only 1.50YTL ($1.30/60p), this service is extremely useful for those hearty and independent enough to brave the heat for the short walk up to the ruins of Kaunos, or the hour it will take to hike up to the mud baths.

BY DOLMUŞ   *Dolmuşes* leave regularly from the town center for Iztuzu Beach (3.50YTL/$3.05/£1.40; 20 min.), Ortaca (3.50YTL/$3.05/£1.40; 15 min.), and Köyceğiz town (3.50YTL/$3.05/£1.40; 30 min.). Fares quoted are one-way.

BY BIKE   Getting around on your own juice will give you the freedom to enjoy Iztuzu Beach, 18 hilly kilometers (11 miles) away, well after the excursion boats have cleared the docks. Scooters and bicycles are available for rental at Kaunos Moto across from the post office (© **0252/284-2816**) at reasonable daily rates.

WHAT TO SEE & DO
EXPLORING KAUNOS

The ancient site of Kaunos was a valuable port trading in salt and slaves that, much like other great cities of its time, eventually suffered the fate of rapidly receding waters. Lying on the Carian-Lycian border, Kaunos first entered the history books under Persian rule in the 6th century B.C., passing to Carian rule when the administration of the port was assigned to Carian governor Mausolus of Halicarnassus. From around 200 B.C., rule of Kaunos was passed around like a hot potato, from Ptolemy of Egypt to Rhodes, from Rhodes to Rome, from Rome back to Rhodes, and finally back to Rome in the 3rd century A.D., when Diocletian added Kaunos to the province of Lycia. The ruins of Kaunos, especially the rock tombs, reflect this cultural jumble, including Hellenistic city walls, a Roman theater, and typical Lycian tombs.

Excursion boats moor on the river's edge amid the wooden pylons of a fish farm. The mooring is about 90m (98 yd.) from the entrance to the sight, accessible by a footpath. A concession near the entrance to the ruins is your last chance to buy bottled water; be sure to avail yourself of this, because there's very little shade on the walk up.

The path that forks to the right will lead you directly up to a **Roman theater** ✯, carved into the slope of the acropolis hill. Two of the statue bases that survive are inscribed with the names of Mausolus and Hecatomnos. Farther up the hill are the fairly well-preserved remains of a **defensive sea wall** ✯, hard to imagine now that the sea is nowhere in sight. Take care hiking up to the top, as the terrain is pretty rugged, but evidently not too much of a challenge for the local mountain goats bleating in the distance. If you're not up for a treacherous climb, you can get comparable views of the marshlands (as well as what's left of the Great Harbor) from row 34 of the theater. Now a stagnant marshland, the Great Harbor was the cause of a seriously unhealthy malaria epidemic that stigmatized the locals for centuries.

Northwest of the theater are the **Roman baths** and a **Byzantine basilica** ✯; slightly above these are the remains of a **Roman temple,** recently identified as a temple to the cult of Apollo.

Two types of **rock tombs** ✯✯✯ are visible from the river as well as from the summit of the acropolis: those carved in the shapes of ornate Greek temples or simple chambers cut into the lower rock. The tombs were reused during Roman times, and all of the tombs at one time or another have fallen victim to scavengers. Admission to the site is 5YTL ($4.35/£2).

A TRIP TO IZTUZU BEACH

One of the last and most important breeding grounds for the near-extinct Caretta Caretta (loggerhead) turtle on the Mediterranean, **Iztuzu Beach** ✯✯ came to public consciousness in 1984 when conservationists mobilized against a local developer's plan for construction of a luxury hotel. Some good works backfire, and even though the developer never got around to building his hotel, the publicity only served to put the spot on the map. The Association for the Protection of Wildlife has established strict guidelines to benefit the turtles, among them: no distracting lights at night, no nighttime visitors during the summer months, and a request that sunbathers remain behind the line of wooden stakes so as not to disturb potential nests.

There are two separate beach areas: the privately run stretch receiving the tide of excursion boats, and the less crowded far end of the beach nearest the road, operated by the Dalyan municipality. With the sea at your feet, the hills over your shoulder, and the calm waters and tall reeds of the river delta at your back, pristine Iztuzu is really one of the loveliest beaches in the region.

A TRIP TO THE MUD BATHS

Most commonly reached by boat, the **Mud Baths** ✯, a rough-and-ready outdoor water pool and mud bath fed by the Sultaniye Spring, is a mandatory stop on most guided excursions. Located about 10 minutes upriver and on the bank opposite Dalyan, this idiosyncratic outdoor "spa" was last dubbed "Aqua Mia," after passing through a long line of new management. There's a sign posted with instructions on the suggested procedure, which includes slapping on fistfuls of sulfur-rich mud and embarrassed waiting periods while the mud on your skin dries. Before rinsing under one of the outdoor showers, take a look in the mirror provided, and be sure to bring a camera.

There's a lonely dockside restaurant and snack bar, and the fee for individuals (admission is included in a group price) is about 4YTL ($3.50/£1.60) *A bit of advice:* Leave that white bathing suit at home. A few minutes away by boat farther up the river toward Köyceğiz Lake is the **Sultaniye Kaplıcaları,** a thermal spring that dates to Hellenistic times with thermal water as hot as 105°F (41°C).

THE ACTIVE TRAVELER

Dalyan's accessibility makes it a good base for activity-filled day excursions. **Kaunos Tours,** across from the post office (© **0252/284-2816;** www.kaunostours.com), bills itself as "the Outdoor Specialists," offering daily adventures such as **Rafting along the Dalaman River** (Apr–Oct) through narrow gorges along rapids that can reach Grade 4 (£35/$70); a **jeep safari** (£25/$50); **sea-kayaking tours** (£25/$50); and **trekking** (£20/$40), to name the tip of their iceberg. Lunch is included on all-day tours, and children (where applicable) go along for 50% of the adult rate.

Even at the stunning natural site of Iztuzu Beach, divers and snorkelers will feel like fish out of water, because the sea floor is equally pristine below the surf—and rather boring to look at. **Diving Ekincik Bay** solves that problem, with its million-year-old caves and abundant marine life, though serious divers may want to hook up with a dive center offering day trips to the open waters around Marmaris. Kaunos Tours runs diving trips for £40 ($80) for the "discover scuba," £25 ($50) for certified divers with their own equipment for two separate dives.

Lazier days can be had with the spectacularly beautiful Göcek **12 Island Tour** 𝓚𝓚 excursion. The day trip, which is run by the Dalyan boat cooperative, departs on Wednesdays, Fridays, and Sundays at 9am, and costs 35YTL ($30/£14).

WHERE TO STAY

The village of Dalyan started out as an environmentally conscious little haven that, once discovered, spawned the conversion of many local family houses into guest pensions. It was just a matter of time before more heavy-hitting hotels changed the basic character of the village. Although construction hasn't quite gotten out of hand, Dalyan, while still somewhat isolated from the ills of mass tourism, is indeed enjoying its own bit of small-town sprawl. In a way, this is actually a good thing, because better hotels and guesthouses are sprouting up on the fringes of the town center, in contrast to the less-than-ambitious pensions that have, to date, rested on the laurels of the riverfront and rock tombs.

Club Alla Turca 𝓚𝓲𝓭𝓼   Boasting the largest pool in Dalyan (550 sq. m/5,920 sq. ft.), this 2-year-old complex consists of four new houses. The buildings were designed to replicate traditional Turkish architectural characteristics in modern materials: Wooden Ottoman *cumbas* are translated into cement, and some of the rooms are arranged in Turkish family style around an open inner courtyard. The rooms, still smelling of newness, are a delightful arrangement of greens and blues, leather accents, and inlaid marble headboards, while out-of-room amenities include an oversize TV screen and a large children's wonderland of Fisher-Price minihouses and slides. The hotel sits on a flat plain about 1km (⅔ mile) upriver from Dalyan's marina, but in exchange for the inconvenience, guests benefit from a clean, comfortable environment.

Gülpınar Mah., 48840 Dalyan. © 0252/284-4616. Fax 0252/284-4387. www.cluballaturca.com. 60 units. High season £27–£39 ($54–$78) double; low season £18–£26 ($36–$52) double. MC, V. Closed Nov 1–May 1. **Amenities:** 2 restaurants; 2 bars; outdoor swimming pool; children's pool; children's playground; game room; TV lounge; concierge; tour desk; car-rental desk; 24-hr. room service; dry cleaning. *In room:* A/C, satellite TV, minibar, hair dryer, safe.

Kano Hotel   Both modest and sublime, the Kano Hotel may lack some upgraded amenities, but it's great for its small scale and outdoor access. The hotel occupies a prime piece of riverside real estate almost directly under the watchful gaze of ancient rock-cut temples, and a small riverside "pier" makes up for the pool that the hotel doesn't have. Each room comes with one double and single bed, but only the one suite room benefits from the fantastic view.

Maraş. Mah. Sok. 142, 48840 Dalyan. ℂ 0252/284-3000. www.otelkano.com. 10 units. June–Sept 80YTL–100YTL ($70–$87/£32–£40) double. Rates lower off season. Children 12 and under stay free in parent's room. MC, V. Free parking. **Amenities:** Restaurant, bar; outdoor swimming pool w/views of the rock tombs; 24-hr. room service; dry cleaning. *In room:* A/C, plasma TV, wireless Internet, minibar, hair dryer.

Ottoman Retreat *(Kids*   The best part of this hotel is also its biggest obstacle: The scant seven one- and two-bedroom self-catering lodgings fill up well in advance of the summer season with British families down on the Turkish coast on weeklong holidays. Still, off-season availability is still a possibility, as are last-minute cancellations. The hotel is located about a 10- to 15-minute walk upriver from the center of town in the quieter, more adult (read: no frat-boy behavior) section of Dalyan. All of the units have large eat-in kitchens adequate for preparing basic meals, plus verandas with either mountain or garden views.

Gülpınar Mah. 338 Sok. 51/a. ℂ 0252/284-4498. Fax 0252/284-2239. www.ottomanretreat.com. 7 units. July–Aug £52–£89 ($104–$178) 1- and 2-bedroom apts. Rates lower off season. Open year-round. **Amenities:** Restaurant (breakfast and dinner on request); bar; outdoor and separate kids' swimming pools; Internet. *In room:* A/C, kitchen, hair dryer, safe.

Sultan Palace Hotel   When two former employees unexpectedly ran off together leaving this hotel without a chef or receptionist, the manager called her mother, Özdan, to come to the rescue in the kitchen. As fate would have it, Brit Frank Mann was staying at the hotel, having joined his family on vacation at the last minute. Three years later, Frank and Özdan were married and the proud owners of a secluded oasis of gardens and tropical plants resting at the base of a series of rocky outcroppings. The main building resembles a medieval stone tower, from which two two-story buildings radiate. The rooms are showing their age, but most of the needed improvements are cosmetic. The main detractor of the Sultan Palace is the isolated location; even though the mud baths are an easy 5-minute walk away and a hotel boat shuttles guests to Dalyan center six times a day, you may feel removed from the action. (Although Özdan's cooking is well worth the trade-off; definitely stick around for dinner.)

Horozlar Mevkii, 48840 Dalyan. ℂ 0252/284-2103. Fax 0252/284-2106. www.sultanpalasdalyan.co.uk. 26 units. £50 ($100) double B&B; £60 ($120) double half-board. MC, V. By car via the approach from Marmaris only; from Dalyan center, leave your car in the Denizatı's restaurant lot near the hotel's boat landing for transport to the opposite side of the river. **Amenities:** Restaurant; bar; outdoor swimming pool; children's pool; croquet lawn; 24-hr. room service; dry cleaning. *In room:* A/C.

WHERE TO DINE

Nothing beats a satisfying meal while seated beneath the spectacular and awe-inspiring cliff tombs across the river. There are relentless mosquitoes, however, so bring plenty of repellent when dining outdoors in Dalyan.

Ceyhan TURKISH   Ceyhan doesn't pretend to be anything other than what it is: an unpretentious assemblage of shaded tables scattered on the gravel at the water's edge. While Dalyan's other riverside restaurants are homogenous in terms of atmosphere, flavor, and price, this little gem transforms simplicity into grand appeal. The young entrepreneurs—rather, boys—who run Ceyhan have located the recipe for some of the most flavorful *yaprak dolması* (stuffed grape leaves) on the map; ditto for the decidedly unusual *fasulye* (green beans) and *patlican salatası* (eggplant salad).

Kordon Boyu (near the rowboat shuttle). ℂ 0542/895-6730. Appetizers and main courses 5.40YTL–20YTL ($4.70–$17/£2.15–£8). No credit cards. Daily 8am–2am.

Glorious Göcek

The most beautiful—and exclusive—untouched bays and coves along the Turkish Mediterranean converge in the village of **Göcek**. Göcek is recognized by the yachting community as one of the pearls of the Mediterranean, with its postcard-worthy marina, and a village with at least a few years to go before complete gentrification.

The arrival of the **Swissôtel** ⓚ at Göcek Marina made it all happen (ⓒ **800/637-9477** in the Americas or 0252/645-2760 local; fax 0252/645-2767; www.swissotel.com). Unlike the typical five-star Swissôtels, this one is a chic and luxurious mini-village, tastefully laid out on a flat plain at the foot of the mountain range. The manicured lawns give the aura of a country club—the only thing that's missing is a golf course. Doubles cost between 225€ and 320€ ($326–$464/£161–£229) in July and August. Rates are lower in shoulder season. The hotel is closed November through May. Opening in 2003 was the **Göcek Lykia Resort Hotel** (ⓒ **0252/645-2828**; fax 0252/645-2827; www.goceklykiaresort.com), with its pre-classical motifs and a "real" Lycian pool. Rates for a double from May through October are 170€ ($247/£121), 220€ ($319/£157) for a deluxe room. For a more home-style experience, consider the **Yonca Retreat** (ⓒ **0252/645-2255**; fax 0252/645-2275; www.yoncaretreat.com), a private home that's been converted into a B&B. The eight rooms have antique furnishings and cost 65€ ($94/£46) for a double. When you're not promenading down the main street, you can swim and relax in the garden pool.

Riverside Café FISH/KEBAPS   The Riverside Café, set in a private garden with tables reed-side, highlights the Turkish tradition of food preparation by grilling everything, from shrimp, calamari, and a daily selection of fresh fish, to chicken and lamb, all on an oversize outdoor charcoal barbecue. Hopefully the original Riverside will transfer some of its recipes, such as the flavorful seaweed salad, the appetizer of anchovies and sardines, and the marinated calamari, over to this location. *One caveat, however:* Bring lots of mosquito repellent.

Maraş Mah. ⓒ **0252/284-3614.** Appetizers and main courses 5.40YTL–20YTL ($4.70–$17/£2.15–£8). MC, V. Daily noon–midnight.

DALYAN AFTER DARK

Nighttime entertainment can be found all along Maraş Mahallesi, from quiet pubs to smoothie bars, headbanging beer joints, and outdoor cafes. Currently the mellower fare seems to be located farthest away from the town center.

3 Fethiye & Ölüdeniz ⓚⓚ

295km (183 miles) southwest of Antalya; 170km (106 miles) southeast of Marmaris; 290km (180 miles) southeast of Pamukkale; 15km (9⅓ miles) north of Ölüdeniz

Fethiye is much more than just the Blue Lagoon, that spectacularly turquoise poster child of Turkey's Mediterranean coast. Fethiye is rocky cliffs, pine-clad mountain

Fethiye

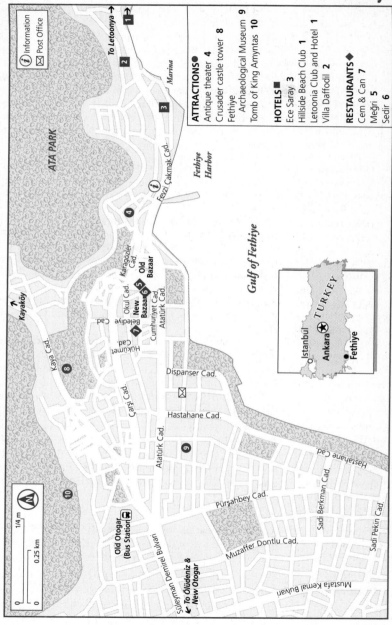

ranges, and offshore islets that speak of ancient civilizations. It's the quiet serenity of a sunset over the ghost village of Kayaköy, set in a valley amidst the piney mountains. And it's the blissful solitude of a swim in one of the innumerable unspoiled crystalline coves, many inaccessible by land. The combination is winning: The ample natural environment inspires physical activity as much as the sun-kissed coastline encourages sloth. Scuba diving, paragliding off a mountain peak, hiking ancient mountain paths, or wading slowly through an ice-cold gorge are just a few of the activities possible in and around Fethiye. As a starting point for a Blue Voyage, Fethiye is unbeatable, offering several options for day, weekend, or weeklong charters. And of course, there's the Blue Lagoon of Ölüdeniz, one of the most astonishing natural beauties in all of Turkey. If you have a week, spend it all here and more.

ESSENTIALS
GETTING THERE
BY PLANE   As a major British (and German) haven, Fethiye (via Dalaman Airport) is served by a number of regular and charter airlines from a number of cities in Europe. They are **Onur Air** (www.onurair.com.tr), **Atlasjet** (www.atlasjet.com.tr), **Easyjet** (www.easyjet.com), **Monarch Airlines** (www.flymonarch.com), **Thomas Cook** (www.flythomascook.com), and **British Midland** (www.flybmi.com). (See also "Getting There: By Plane" in the Marmaris section, earlier in this chapter, and "Getting There" in the Antalya section later in this chapter.) While there are more flights into Antalya Airport, the drive to Fethiye takes about 4 hours, so choosing Antalya will most likely be a result of fully booked flights into Dalaman, or a desire to explore the coast from east to west. Though flights are not as frequent into Dalaman Airport, it's less than 40km (25 miles) from Fethiye.

Havaş (© 444-0487) shuttle buses will be waiting for you at the Dalaman airport to whisk you away to either Marmaris or Fethiye (separate buses for opposite directions). The bus into downtown Fethiye (the marina) takes about an hour and 10 minutes and costs 17YTL ($15/£6.80).

There are also car-rental counters at both airports, sensible if you've arrived here exclusively for a land tour. A taxi from the airport will cost around 110YTL ($96/£44).

BY BUS   Ulusoy (© 444-1888) buses run once-daily service between Istanbul and Fethiye (11 hr.; 76YTL/$66/£30). **Pamukkale** (© 444-3535) connects Fethiye daily with Izmir (via Ortaca; 6 hr.; 25YTL/$22/£10) and Antalya (3½ hr.; 20YTL/$17/£8). The *otogar* is about a mile east of the town center, at the turnoff for Ölüdeniz. There is no *dolmuş* service running to the hotel listings in Fethiye town. Instead, a taxi will cost around 13YTL ($11/£5.20).

TOURIST INFORMATION
In Fethiye town, the **tourist information office** is located at Iskele Karşısı 1 (© 0252/614-1527), across from the harbor nearest the yacht marina. In Ölüdeniz, there's a "Tourism Development Cooperative" at the end of the road before the beach (© 0252/617-0438).

ORIENTATION
Downtown Fethiye, along with its busy harbor and marina, sits at the southern edge of the Gulf of Fethiye. It's hard to miss the **Antique Theatre** across from the main harbor, located on the main road that cuts through town (called **Atatürk Cad.** in the city center, Fevzi Çakmak Cad. to the west).

Çarşı Sokağı cuts through the Old Town Bazaar perpendicular to Atatürk Caddesi, forming a triangle of shopping, restaurants, and cafes known as Paspatur. The new bazaar is located on Çarşı Sokağı, which then curves around to continue east until it meets up once again with **Atatürk Caddesi** and turns into **Inönü Bulvarı. Amyntas Tomb** is southeast of the town center amid the barren brush, and farther east are the **Lycian Rock Tombs.** A few **lone sarcophagi** are scattered about town, one in the garden of the municipality building on Atatürk Caddesi, the other on Kaya Caddesi, between the old bus depot and the castle. A pedestrian promenade runs along the marina between the theater and north to Caliş Beach, and is lined with boats of all sizes touting day trips and private charters. The taxi boat to Caliş Beach is located here as well.

As you continue eastward out of Fethiye, Inönü Bulvarı intersects with the road to **Ölüdeniz,** located about 15km (9⅓ miles) up in the hills to the south. After the turnoff for Ölüdeniz, the road arrives at Hisarönü, a town that has degenerated into a stopover for mass-marketed British groups on package tours. About 4km (2½ miles) farther is the little country village of **Kayaköy,** which grew around an abandoned Greek settlement vacated in the population exchange of 1924.

Ölüdeniz, which means "Dead Sea" (but is better known as the "Blue Lagoon"), describes the beach and lagoon bearing its name and the long stretch of Belceğiz Beach. This deservedly ultra-popular seaside resort sits in a small valley at the bottom of a steep hill. Beach bums, daredevil paragliders, and at least one too many partiers base themselves in Ölüdeniz, but with a car or scooter, you can easily make this a day trip. To the left is the public beach, enclosed by the steep slopes of **Babadağ.** The beach is tastefully lined with travel agents offering adventure tours, beach restaurants, Internet cafes, and the Club Belcekız Beach Hotel at the far end. To the right is the overcrowded natural preserve with its lagoon of Mediterranean dreams, pristine and a deep shade of aqua.

GETTING AROUND

BY CAR   To really enjoy Fethiye and the surrounding areas, it's important to have your own wheels. Car-rental agencies are located near the marina, and all of the holiday resorts offer on-site car-rental services. Because the British pound sterling is the primary quoted currency of the area, the price of renting a car locally might seem a bit high. Surprisingly enough, it's better to book your vehicle from one of the major international players for the most competitive rates. The only major in town is **Avis** (Yat Limanı Körfez Apt. 9/A2; ℂ 0252/612-3719). Lesser-known firms around the yacht marina and in near the Old Town Bazaar are also a decent bet; try **Fethiye Rent-a-Car** (Atatürk Cad. 106; ℂ **0252/612-2281;** www.fethiyerentacar.com), which currently charges £27 ($54) per day for a compact.

BY SCOOTER   This is my mode of choice, but be very careful, as the roads are gravelly and the drivers are no better at the resorts than they are on the highways. Take particular care in rounding steep hilly curves, as oncoming vehicles tend to make wide turns into your lane. Otherwise, riding a scooter through the countryside is a rare joy, a good way to maintain your suntan, and the best way to solve the parking question. Most car-rental agencies have scooters available, and there are several outfitters in downtown Fethiye that will rent you a scooter for about 35YTL ($30/£14).

BY MINIBUS/DOLMUŞ   *Dolmuşes* congregate at the intersection of Atatürk Caddesi and Sedir Sokak (across from the hospital) in downtown Fethiye and provide frequent (about every 15 min.) transport to most of the sites and destinations listed in this section. The most useful routes leave for Ölüdeniz, Kayaköy, Tlos, and Sak-lıkent. A ride will cost 2YTL ($1.75/80p).

The Ölüdeniz Minibus Coop runs an hourly shuttle between Fethiye and Kayaköy (3YTL/$2.60/£1.20); less frequent are the minibuses that run about six times a day between Fethiye and Faralya/Kabak and three times daily between Fethiye and Gemiler Beach.

WHAT TO SEE & DO
ANCIENT HISTORY

Not much remains of ancient **Telmessos**, atop which modern-day Fethiye is built. In spite of centuries of destructive earthquakes, the cliff-side Lycian tombs and majestic sarcophagi never fail to draw a gasp.

The city was independent until Alexander the Great's arrival in 334 B.C. Three hundred years later the city came under Roman rule as part of the Lycian union.

The **antique theater** in the center of town dates to Roman times, although its open disposition on the hill indicates Greek influences. The amphitheater was picked apart for the reconstruction of the city after the devastating earthquake of 1957, and in 1994 restorations and further excavations to the site were begun. To the east of the municipal building is a two-story **sarcophagus** ✿ topped with a Gothic-style lid and decorated with war scenes; remains of this type of tomb are scattered about the city and hidden in private gardens.

On the hillside east of town stands the ruined **Crusader castle tower,** constructed by the Knights of St. John out of the Hellenistic and Roman stonework of an earlier acropolis.

Rock-cut tombs spot the cliff side, the most notable of which is the **Tomb of King Amyntas** ✿✿✿ in the form of a Greek temple dating to 350 B.C. The steps of the facade get a bit crowded around sunset, the favored time for a visit because of the tomb's position on the hill. Price of admission is 5YTL ($4.35/£2), or free from afar.

The nearby **Fethiye Archaeological Museum,** Fethiye Müze Müdürlüğü (✆ **0252/ 614-1150**), is small and regrettably unimportant; exhibits consist of stones and columns from the acropolis that should have been left in place. Interesting, however, is the **stele** ✿ uncovered at Letoon, with inscriptions in Lycian, Aramaic, and Greek. It proved indispensable in cracking the code of the ancient Lycian language. The museum is open Tuesday through Sunday from 8:30am to 5pm; admission is 2YTL ($1.75/80p).

Karmylassos/Kayaköy ✿✿✿   This haunting and magical place is the result of the population exchange between Turkey and Greece in 1924—in which the Turkish and Greek minorities in each country were repatriated to their "home countries," despite the incalculable suffering such a drastic uprooting caused. The Turkish village of Kayaköy sprouted up in the valley at the base of the abandoned hillside.

Originally the Lycian city of Karmylassos, the village was reestablished by Greek settlers as Levissi in either the 11th or 14th century. The houses that blanket the hills date to the 19th century. Today Karmylassos is a ghost town, and the remains of the 3,500 identical square stone houses, each positioned to afford the best views of the countryside, take on a haunting pinkish glow at sunset, the best time to visit. Although the churches and chapels have been scavenged in the search for buried sacred treasure, there's still enough of the original structures and ceramic mosaic flooring to make an impression.

Tips Drinks Are on the House

Just some years ago, Kayaköy was little more than a forgotten pile of stones. Now, along with pensions, villas, and cottages, the village once known as Levissi has not one, but two, wine houses. Mind you, these are not wine producers; however, the **Kaya Wine House** (Gökçeburun Mah. 70, Kayaköy; © 0252/618-0454) collects its fruit wines, reds, and whites from small, private vineyards, some of which are local. The **Levissi Garden** (© 0252/618-0108) keeps a wine cellar of more than 2,000 bottles from all over Turkey. Both take advantage of centuries-old stone buildings, the latter occupying a 400-year-old stone house that in 1859 housed the mayor. You can wander through the wine cellar (Levissi's is in the old stables), enjoy wine tastings, or have a multiple-course meal (with wine, of course), all for about 30YTL ($26/£12).

At the top of the ghost village, a **footpath** to Ölüdeniz continues over the hill and through some spectacular scenery. For this hike you'll need a camera, a large bottle of water, and about 2 hours; leave early in the morning to beat the heat and allow an afternoon of recovery on the pearly shores of the Blue Lagoon.

A shorter trail leads to **Cold Water Bay,** a small cove fed by icy springs, and reachable in under an hour. Be sure not to mistake one trail for the other (one unscrupulous businessman diverted hikers to his restaurant; he's since been incarcerated for tax fraud)—a mistake easily avoided by picking up a sketch map of the trails at Bülent's Place, located along the Kaya road. Eager to set people on the right path, Bülent has learned the English word for "map," and will be as helpful as he can be.

The turnoff from the Fethiye/Ölüdeniz road travels through the far-from-unspoiled enclave of **Hisarönü,** affectionately called Hiroshima by the locals who remember its age of innocence. If you follow this road for about 5 or 6.5km (3–4 miles) through the piney woods, the hollow stone houses will alert you to your arrival. A more inspiring entrance can be made by following the signs up and around Fethiye Castle for Kaya Village/Karmylassos. This winding back way leads through the upper edges of picturesque Kaya Valley, and if you're lucky, you'll get a glimpse of the nomad camp.

Dolmuşes make the 30-min. journey from Fethiye to Kayaköy daily for about 2YTL ($1.75/80p). Admission is 5YTL ($4.35/£2).

Tlos 🕭🕭 Tlos is one of the oldest and most important cites in ancient Lycia, and its position atop a rocky outpost dominates the Xanthos Valley. Hittite artifacts found here indicate the city was founded as early as 2000 B.C. After the decline of the Hittite Empire, Tlos became a Lycian city, and then was later absorbed by the Roman Empire. The city was an important bishopric during the Byzantine Era and was finally conquered by the Turks.

The most immediately impressive feature is the severe slope of the city on the rock, carved into majestic temple-like tombs, and the stone sarcophagi dotting the hillside below. A lone sarcophagus sits dramatically in the middle of a farmer's field best spotted from the stadium, located a few hundred feet up the road of the ruins near a roadside cafe graced with ice-cold springs. Take a look at the stadium first, because after the climb to the summit, it will be too much of a struggle against the heat to tack this on to the end of your tour. On the summit lie the ruins of a castle dating to the Turkish settlement, offering panoramic views of the Xanthos Valley. Excavations conducted by Antalya University have uncovered a tunnel, which seems to have provided a quick escape during times of invasion, leading to the city from the nearby village.

Follow the Fethiye/Antalya rd.; cross the bridge over the Esen Çay and look for indications to turn right onto the Saklıkent rd. The turnoff for Tlos is before Saklıkent on the left. 5YTL ($4.35/£2). Daily 8am–5pm.

Yaka Park 🌟🌟 *Kids*   This trout farm is a wonderful place to take the kids, because after ordering your food, you can try and pet one of the finger-biting swans on the upper terrace. Yaka Park takes up several outdoor terraces on a gently sloping hill, and you can choose to sit at one of the picnic tables or under a tree in an enclosed seating area on pillows and mats. There's also a bar, whose counter has been carved out and filled up with baby trout swimming along its meandering length. The trout come right out of the central pond and, once grilled, are crispy and delicious.

Yaka Köyü (about 44km/27 miles from the center of Fethiye). © 0252/634-0391. Meal of trout and all-you-can-eat appetizers around 20YTL ($17/£8). MC, V. Daily 9am–10pm. Closed Nov–Mar. Follow the Fethiye/Antalya rd. and turn right on the road to Saklıkent; turn left again toward Tlos and follow the signs for Yaka Park.

THE AREA BEACHES

The coarse sands of **Çalış Beach** lie on Fethiye Bay, 5km (3 miles) north of the downtown and stretch for about 1.6km (a mile). Çalış Beach is lined with the icons of mass tourism: side-by-side homogenous hotels set back behind the beachfront souvenir stands that keep visitors stocked in plastic flip-flops and their kids in cheap snorkels. Although I don't recommend it for the beach, the sight of some of the most magnificent sunsets behind the smaller islands to the west make Çalış Beach worth a trip at least for that event. A water taxi from Fethiye's marina crosses the bay to Çalış Beach every half-hour for 4YTL ($3.50/£1.60) each way. Or, you can take the water taxi for about the same price to the lovely beach on **Şevalye Island** (in the middle of the bay) and stumble around the Byzantine ruins.

Çalış Beach reclaims its innocence at the extreme north end known as **Koca Çalış,** where the scenery returns to its pure and natural state. Taking advantage of the high winds and shallow waters of Koca Çalış are a number of windsurfing outfitters; **Fethiye Surf Center** (P.K. 170, Fethiye; © 0252/622-0753; www.fethiyesurfcenter. com) is a family-run sports center in the rough that focuses its energies on windsurfing lessons. Şener Aykurt, founder and windsurfing instructor (when not teaching math at Anatolian High School), teaches all levels of windsurfing, beginning with 2-hour sessions for first-timers, using an on-land simulated wave apparatus. If you're not taking the lesson, you can still rent equipment. Consult their website for current rates. Şener's mom posts the menu of the day on a chalkboard on the walk of their beachfront shack; take advantage of the real home cooking or relax in the sandy tea garden.

Only 5 minutes from the center of Fethiye town is a collection of newly established public beaches practically attached to the hip of the Letoonia Club (see "Where to Stay," later). The beaches are maybe not as breathtaking as at Ölüdeniz, but they are certainly (for the moment) less crowded.

Arguably the most beautiful beach on the eastern Mediterranean, and the smallest bay in Turkey (and probably the reason you came all this way), **Ölüdeniz** 🌟🌟🌟 has become Turkey's poster child due to its extraordinary beauty. But these days, it's hard to overlook the cheap formula tourism that has overtaken this small beach resort. Still, I'd be remiss if I didn't urge you to go, if even for an off-season day on the beach. Ölüdeniz refers to both the long stretch called **Belceğiz Beach** 🌟🌟🌟 at the foot of

Babadağ, as well as the still blue waters of the **Blue Lagoon** ⟨𝕲𝕲𝕲⟩, which actually takes its name from the stagnant waters behind the natural sandbar. *Dolmuşes* leave frequently across from the hospital in Fethiye.

The exposed Belcekız Beach is ideal as a landing site for the paragliding maniacs launching themselves off the top of the mountain, although you may spot a guy flying around with a jet propulsion pack strapped to his back as well. The beach is undeveloped, the locals touting adventure trips are friendly, and the white sands and turquoise waters are hard to beat (until you walk over to the preserve).

The **Blue Lagoon** ⟨𝕲⟩ is tucked inside a natural preserve that requires an admission fee of 3.35YTL ($2.90/£1.35; though if you drive in it'll be about double with the parking fee). From the parking lot you can either follow the sandy beach around the sandbar or take the more scenic path over the pine needles and through the woods. Families who had arrived early to stake their claim are now nestled in the shade of little pine niches, and you'll pass hundreds of these picnickers as you follow the woodsy path along the shallow section of the lagoon. Keep walking, because you'll know by the color of the water when you've arrived. If you're not sure, keep going. You might want to get here early (actually, you'll want to go off season, because in summer, the crowd is crushing), because by midday the lounge chairs are all spoken for, and you may wind up piling your belongings in a heap on the pebbles and diving right in.

Make no mistake, however, the Blue Lagoon has attracted half the population of Lycia, and they've all brought their kids, so a serene afternoon of swimming and solitude is definitely out. But however overcrowded it is, this little corner of Turkey is irresistible.

With your own car, preferably a four-wheel drive, you can combine a visit to Kayaköy with a day spent tooling around **Gemiler Beach** ⟨𝕲𝕲𝕲⟩, an undeveloped cove opposite the historic ruins of Gemiler Island and some postcard views of the mountains in the distance. From the beachfront, you can swim over to the 7th-century Byzantine monastery of St. Nikola on **Gemiler Island** ⟨𝕲𝕲⟩ (site entrance 4YTL/$3.50/£1.60), hire a speedboat for a group ringo or banana boat ride, and feast on fresh fish over at the beachfront shack owned by the strange but ever harmless character, "Robinson."

Daily excursion boats offer the **"12-island tour"** ⟨𝕲𝕲⟩ (actually closer to six) around the Gulf of Fethiye, a popular diversion that can be booked directly at the dock, or through most any travel agent. In Ölüdeniz contact **Activities Unlimited** (at the Karbel Sun Hotel; ⟨ℂ⟩ **0252/617-0601**). The beauty is impossible to describe, but for about 35YTL ($30/£14), and even less off season, the trip provides an abbreviated taste of what a weeklong Blue Voyage would be like. Highlights of the cruise include stopovers at Hamam Bay, where you can swim above sunken Byzantine baths (erroneously called Cleopatra's Bath), and at Gemiler Island. There's room for a mild adrenaline rush in Turunç Bükü, where you can scale the rocks to a hanging rope and swing into the turquoise waters like Tarzan. Swimming and snorkeling around the tiny coves and bays is a high priority, and the captain is usually flexible about schedules if you decide to swim ashore to explore some medieval ruins up close.

If you haven't booked your Blue Voyage yet and would like a taste of the Lycian Coast by sea, many agencies and boat captains offer what has now become a widely marketed 4-day, 3-night **mini blue-cruise to Olympos** (if you have time, inspect the cabins of several boats before you commit), available April to mid-October. The cruise takes in some of the most stunning scenery along the coast, past Butterfly Valley, Ölüdeniz, Gemiler Island, and the beach of Patara; the final leg of the trip heads by bus overland from Demre/Myra to ancient Olympos (p. 329). Prices at the time of this writing for a cruise from July 15 to September 15 are £119 ($238) per person, including tax and three meals, but excluding drinks. Prices go down slightly off season. (There are no cruises Dec 15–Apr 1.) Most boats provide some type of snorkeling and fishing equipment. **V-GO Tourism Travel Agency,** Fevzi Çakmak Caddesi (between the marina and the Yacht Club; ℂ **0252/612-2113;** www.boatcruiseturkey.com), invented this trip, but my advice is to shop around and have a look at all of the boats available.

SPORTS & OUTDOOR ACTIVITIES
EXPLORING BUTTERFLY VALLEY　　A nature lover's paradise is located at **Butterfly Valley** 𝄐𝄐𝄐, an untouched beachfront parcel named for the rare Tiger Butterfly which breaks from its cocoon in April and May and turns the skies bright red. The colorful creatures are drawn to the smells of mint, jasmine, laurel, eucalyptus, and thyme emanating from the rich vegetation. A 45-minute hike away from the beach leads to a refreshing waterfall. Happily the valley is a First Degree Preservation Site, a designation intended to prevent the arrival of mass tourism into this isolated and pristine ecosystem.

Taxi boats leave from Ölüdeniz three times a day—at 11am, 2pm, and 6pm to the valley and at 9am, 1pm, and 5pm back to Belceğiz Beach (10YTL/$8.70/£4 roundtrip; 30 min.). An alternative for the adventurous and well-shod hiker is to follow the steep and rocky slope down from the upper rim of the valley, following the footpath from in front of "George House" pension, on the road to Faralya/Kabak (gauge about 30 min.).

For those who miss the last boat out, the spare bungalows, platform huts, and tents of the on-site Butterfly Valley "pension" (ℂ **0522/818-8570;** www.butterflyvalley. com) are your only alternatives. One night with all meals in a bungalow ranges from $19 to $27 (£9.50–£14), depending on the season (tents and platforms are $4/£2 less; closed Jan–Mar). Bathrooms and shower blocks are communal, and hot water is "available." For day-trippers, there's a basic snack bar offering the usual sparse selection of cold drinks, meatballs, and tea.

HIKING (OR WADING) SAKLİKENT GORGE　　Also known as the Canyon of the Hidden Valley, **Saklıkent Gorge** 𝄐𝄐 is a wonder of nature carved 480m (1,575 ft.) down into the canyon by the constant force of the waters flowing down from Akdağ (Ak Mt.). The water still flows, and boy, is it cold. The entrance to the gorge is down an incline off the main road, surrounded by a parking lot, ticket booth, merchant stalls, and enough tour buses to make you want to turn back.

A sturdy catwalk attached to the cliff wall leads you upstream for about 150m (492 ft.) to landfall, where the gushing waters of the **Gökçesu** and **Ulupınar** springs flow down from Babadağ into the gorge. The air is unexpectedly cold at this juncture thanks to the constant roar of the icy waters, and some clever businessman knew just how to take advantage. The **Saklıkent Gorge River Restaurant** 𝄐𝄐𝄐 (ℂ **0252/ 659-0074**) is a series of cozy wooden platforms constructed over the torrents for optimal enjoyment of a meal prepared in the stone ovens and a respite from the relentless heat. The same establishment also has a River Bar where backpacking coeds congregate for all-nighters.

A hike up the gorge through the sometimes thigh-high waters is the highlight of the trip. Enter the gorge above where the springs gush into the creek, but be prepared for the shock of water so cold you just might have gone skiing that day. Your legs will be so numb that you won't even notice that the temperature of the water stabilizes the farther away from the spring source you get. The rock face has been sanded to a silky smoothness, creating slippery slides for kids of all ages. River shoes are advisable, especially if you plan on going the full distance of 18km (11 miles).

Small group tours by minibus or jeep safari leave for Saklıkent Gorge daily in season for around £25 ($50), including a stop at the ancient city of Tlos and lunch at Yaka Park. You can also get to the gorge, located about 40km (25 miles) southeast of Fethiye (about 1 hr.), by picking up a *dolmuş* at the main terminal or flagging one down on the Fethiye/Antalya road out of town (3YTL/$2.60/£1.20). By car, follow the Fethiye/Antalya road and turn left at the road for Kemer; turn left again past Tlos and follow signs for Saklıkent. Entrance to the gorge is 5YTL ($4.35/£2); parking is free.

HORSEBACK RIDING Enjoy the scenic pine forests and mountain paths on horseback. **Activities Unlimited** (© 0252/617-0601) and **Aventura** (in the Club Belcekız Beach; © 0252/616-6427) offer daily half-day tours, with a pickup at your hotel, for around £10 ($20). You can also arrange your own outing by going directly to a stable in Kayaköy. The arrival of **Perma Ranch,** Kaya Yolu (©/fax 0252/618-0182; www.permaranch.co.uk), several years ago added two horsy Brits from Gloucestershire to the list of British expats in the area. They offer horse-riding holidays (even for travelers with limited mobility!) for £550 ($1,100) per person per week; ask to see if they are running their 3-hour excursion on horseback, which includes 2 hours of riding through the valley and mountains and a short stopover in the village neighborhood of Kınalı. The horses and tacking are in excellent shape, and use a sturdy English saddle.

PARAGLIDING Thanks to the 1,950m (6,398-ft.) drop-off of Babadağ over an open body of water, and to the gentle sea breezes and stable winds, Ölüdeniz is one of the foremost sites in the world for paragliding. Professionals come from all over to prepare for international flying competitions, an experience that is now available to the daring—and strong-stomached, as there's really nothing like puking in midair. (If you're the type to get seasick, you may want to take a pill beforehand, or carry a Ziplock bag, just in case.) Flying tandem with an experienced pilot, all of whom are certified professionals, provides a safe and easy introduction to an otherwise extreme sport.

Skysports Paragliding, located on the beach (© 0252/617-0511; fax 0252/617-0511), is the most reputable of the dozen or so outfitters touting their flights (although I'm told that pilots rotate among the companies regularly); they run five daily departures in high season, leaving by jeep at 9 and 11:30am, and 2, 4, and 6pm for the hour climb up to the summit. A 2-hour flight excursion costs $150 (£75) a head; because of limited space, book at least 1 day in advance. Check out their website at **www.skysports-turkey.com**. Other reputable organizers of paragliding jumps are Extreme Paragliding (© 0252/313-0722; www.paraglide.netfirms.com/paragliding.html), which charges $105 (£53), and **Easy Riders** (© 0252/617-0114; www.easyriderstravel.8m.com). Prices are fixed among the various companies, so don't bother trying to negotiate. Be forewarned, however, human error has been known to result in fatalities, but then again, so does driving.

SCUBA DIVING Spontaneous discovery of sunken ruins awaits you in the clear blue waters of the Gulf of Fethiye, one of the best dive sites for exploring underwater

---

Tips **Clothes Make the Woman**

Girls, listen up! Imagine a closet full of clothes designed for all occasions, all suited to you. (Clothes can be bought off the rack or made to measure.) Günsenin Günel, wife of the owner of the White Dolphin restaurant and graduate of the Chelsea School of Arts in London, is the genius behind the mannequins, which display her evening wear, trendy ensembles, and even conservative work attire tailored for real bodies. And Gün doesn't only give visiting royalty the personal-shopper experience—because when you're the only customer in the shop, it's all about you. **Günsenin Boutique** is at the entrance of the White Dolphin restaurant (and therefore usually open in the evenings, beginning at 6pm; ✆ **0252/617-0068**); another more casual shop, selling jeans, cargo pants, and beach dresses (or whatever happens to be trendy at the time), is located on the beach.

---

caves. The best outfitter in the area, with branches in Antalya, Bodrum, Kaş, Marmaris, and Dalyan, is the professionally run **European Diving Centre,** Atatürk Cad. 12/1 (opposite the main harbor; ✆ **0252/614-9771;** www.europeandiving.co.uk), offering single or multiday "dive packs" for up to £49 per day ($98; prices go down the more days you dive). Day packs include three dives, lunch, guide, tanks, weights, and weight belt. There's a £55 ($110) compulsory refresher course for divers who haven't been out in the previous 6 months. The dive center also has a 1-day "discover scuba" course, a full-day snorkel trip, and a 3-day PADI course for £145 ($290; 2–3 days). **Ocean Turizm** in the Dedeoğlu Hotel (on the Fethiye waterfront at Iskele Meydanı; ✆ **0252/612-4807**) is another local alternative, while guests of the Lykia World Hotel can dive with **Septaş Turizm** (✆ **0252/617-0200**).

WHITE-WATER RAFTING   The Dalaman River is a popular spot for rafting, kayaking, and canoeing, passing remote and breathtaking canyons through Grade 4 and 5 rapids. All of the tour companies offer the same package tour that connects with a local operator in Dalaman; a day out including all transfers and professional river guides costs 45€ ($65/£32). Tours run April through October.

WHERE TO STAY

Fethiye is the perfect base for a well-rounded holiday with plenty of forays into exploring all of the wonders the area has to offer. But with so many natural and man-made attractions, it's hard to know where to base yourself. Here are your choices: **Fethiye town** is the commercial center of the region, offering visitors travelers' convenience, shopping, nightlife, and sustenance all in a fairly tight cluster. The two properties listed here also add the option of a sea-view room, along with reasonable walkability to the town center about a kilometer down the cobbled waterfront road. **Çaliş Beach** is to the north of the center of Fethiye, a strip of beachfront pastel cement blocks standing opposite an expanse of narrow beach. Çaliş Beach could be anywhere in the world, with its cheap rates, cheap towels, and cheap blow-up rafts dangling from the rafters of ground-floor shops. The hotels of **Ölüleniz,** a resort having enough star power for the entire Turkish Mediterranean, cater to backpackers and families on a budget, and only one hotel (Club Belcekız Beach, below) actually sits on the wide shoreline. **Kayaköy** sits in a verdant valley located up in the mountains, where village life and the tourist influence have struck a tolerant balance. The choices for guest-houses and self-catering cottages have grown, and the quality of the more affordable options in lodging is gaining ground.

Hisarönü and Ovaçık are two locations on the road up from Fethiye to Kayaköy where it seems as if dozens and dozens of hotels just sprouted like mushrooms. And we all know where mushrooms like to grow. Not that the scenery is bad; although it was certainly better before the arrival of massive numbers of tourists from northern England and elsewhere on package trips. Other than the Montana Pine, I have nothing to say about either of these little hamlets, although a walk around Hisarönü can be a hoot in the evenings, as the carnival atmosphere starts cranking.

The final option for lodging around Fethiye is really a whole host of options, from an old restored farmhouse to a mountain cottage, a seafront bungalow, a beach club, or an isolated guesthouse, with one thing in common. They all enjoy a blissful level of isolation, though for some this can be maddening. With demand for this type of hotel on the rise in Fethiye, new ones are constantly forging into new uncharted landscapes. In addition to the one or two listed here, you may want to look into the Su Değirmeni (The Watermill) in Faralya (www.natur-reisen.de) and perfectly wonderful (and eco-friendly) Pastoral Vadı up in the mountains of Yaniklar (www.pastoralvadi.com).

The next challenge in identifying a hotel in and around Fethiye (and indeed, along the entire Lycian coast) is that a number of British-based holiday agents reserve all of the space in the more appealing hotels and cottages for entire seasons. One of the newer (and more sublime) exclusive properties, the Oyster Residences (www.oyster residences.com), whose reservations are appropriately managed by Exclusive Escapes (© 0208/605-3500 in the U.K.; www.exclusiveescapes.co.uk or www.hiddenturkey. com), is actually two separate properties. Both are the creations of Mehmet Bay, the owner of the illustrious Beyaz Yunuz Restaurant. The other hotel hog is Thomson Holidays (© 0870/165-0079 in the U.K.; www.thomson.co.uk), but they do sell hotels separately from their holiday packages.

FETHIYE TOWN

Ece Saray Marina & Resort *⚜⚜*   As the crown jewel of the Turquoise Coast, Fethiye has been sadly lacking in standout accommodations. Until now. The palatial Ece Saray occupies an extensive landscaped waterfront property near the western end of Fethiye's marina. Parisian-style wrought-iron balconies perch above the stunning scenery from every room. Rooms are trimmed with rosewood and embellished with the finest Vakko textiles, while bathrooms are swathed in Italian marble and come loaded with amenities such as designer soaps and plush bathrobes. The pool is surrounded by teak lounges and stunning views of the Toros Mountains. The Mrs. can while away an hour or so in the spa and wellness center (offering hydrotherapy treatments, stone therapy, and facial treatments, along with the basics), while men congregate in the terribly macho cigar room with high-backed leather chairs.

1 Karagözler Mevkii (in the Marina), 48300 Fethiye. © 0252/612-5005. Fax 0252/614-7205. www.ecesaray.net. 48 units. Sept-June 210€ ($305/£150) double; July–Aug 350€ ($508/£250) double. AE, DISC, MC, V. **Amenities:** Restaurant; waterfront cafe; 3 bars; cigar bar; full-service marina; outdoor swimming pool; fitness room; spa and wellness center; Turkish bath; Jacuzzi; sauna; small children's playground; concierge; tour desk; car-rental desk; wireless Internet; 24-hr. room service; massage; dry cleaning. *In room:* A/C, satellite TV, minibar, coffee/tea station, hair dryer, safe.

Hillside Beach Club *⚜⚜* *Kids*   Occupying one of the more sublimely isolated coves in the Fethiye area, the Hillside Beach Club promises a family-friendly structure that doesn't forget to dote on the adults. Room styles are broken up into five categories of rooms, from singles, small and regular-size doubles, and two types of triples, one of which can accommodate four. And they're not the kind that make you cringe, either: These rooms were designed as eye candy, including the sea view, which is found in all rooms. (All have balconies or terraces of varying sizes.) Rooms are also equipped with satellite TVs connected to an internal information and entertainment system, where you can while away nap time (yours or the kids') with online shopping. The hotel, which operates on an all-inclusive formula, has activities galore: aerobics, archery, windsurfing, and water polo; you can even go sailing or take out a catamaran—in fact, I can't think of anything you *can't* do here. And it's all tastefully done, and free, except for the extremely soothing spa, the ice corner (!?), the workshop, and the hairdresser. Even drinks—wine, beer, water—are gratis. The hotel has a sort of "cruise director" mentality ensuring that the resort stays at the forefront of hospitality entertainment: Expect things like symphony orchestra or opera performances, movie galas, water skiing competitions, and special activities for children such as workshops and disco parties.

Kalemya Koyu, P.O. Box 123, 48300 Fethiye (4km/2½ miles from the city center). © 0252/614-8360. Fax 0252/614-1470. www.hillsidebeachclub.com.tr. 330 units. 430€–470€ ($624–$682/£307–£336) double with up to 1 child. Check website for special offers. AE, MC, V. **Amenities:** 6 restaurants (including sushi bar); 4 bars (including fitness bar); indoor and outdoor swimming pools; 5 tennis courts (3 sand and 2 asphalt); squash; health club; Turkish bath; Balinese spa; Jacuzzi; sauna; watersports; children's playground w/separate kiddy pool; concierge; tour desk; car-rental desk; meeting and conference facilities; free Internet cafe; shopping arcade; salon; 24-hr. room service; babysitting; laundry service; dry cleaning; nonsmoking rooms. *In room:* A/C, interactive satellite TV, dataport, minibar, hair dryer, safe.

Letoonia Club and Hotel 🎣 *Kids*   Who knew Disneyland had a branch on the Mediterranean? Until I stepped foot on the grounds of Letoonia, I had no idea. This is not fundamentally a bad thing, and actually Letoonia is more like a prefabricated paradise than a cheesy venue for Mickey Mouse.

Letoonia Club is set on a cliff-side promontory on a peninsula that juts out into Fethiye Bay, enjoying splendid seclusion and three private coves. Only the orange waterslide mars the gorgeous setting of mountains and pines, but you'll be too busy taking free windsurfing lessons in one of the alternate coves to notice, although your kids definitely will. In fact, this resort caters to families not only through activities and their "miniclub," but also through the independent setup of the bungalow rooms, which are laid out with separate sleeping quarters for parents and children. To get around this massive acreage, Letoonia provides amusement-park minishuttles. Although the resort sprawls over several acres, the award-winning architect saw to it that Letoonia did nothing but complement its surroundings. If you're arriving by sea, the sight of these wooden and latticed buildings emerging from the brush will take your breath away. All rooms have a balcony, and the layout of the resort ensures that 85% of the rooms get sea views. The resort provides a free hourly shuttle to Fethiye.

P.O. Box 63, 48300 Fethiye. © 0252/614-4966. Fax 0252/614-4422. www.letoonia.com. 626 units (all bungalows w/shower). May, June, and Oct $245 (£123) double; July, Aug, and Sept $425 (£213) double. Rates all-inclusive. MC, V. **Amenities:** 5 restaurants; 10 bars; outdoor swimming pool; miniature golf; tennis courts; Turkish bath; Jacuzzi; sauna; extensive watersports; scooter rental; children's programs; game room; concierge; tour desk; car-rental desk; shopping arcade; salon; 24-hr. room service; massage; dry cleaning. *In room:* A/C, satellite TV, minibar, hair dryer, safe.

Villa Daffodil 🎣   This charming little guesthouse perched on the road across from the Gulf of Fethiye is a real attention grabber, owing to its traditional Ottoman design and wooden *cumbas* (enclosed ornamented balconies), typical of summer houses of the time. Inside, newly redecorated rooms have new mattresses, plasma TVs, and somewhat updated baths. The courtyard of the hotel doubles as an intimate breakfast and bar area, with a functioning lemon tree for a refreshing vodka tonic, and an old 19th-century horseless carriage from which you can admire the bay over the garden wall.

The owner, a retired colonel in the Turkish army, has overseen every detail of the guesthouse. The disposition of the rooms makes each type slightly different: Side rooms include a small balcony, others share a small inner courtyard, and upper-floor rooms in the back have lots of wood and attic-style ceilings. On a back garden terrace of the hotel is a small but tantalizing pool surrounded by a lush garden, perfect for a dip after a long sweaty day out and about. The owner also maintains a six-cabin gulet moored in the inlet across the street for easy guest hire.

Fevzi Çakmak Cad. 115, 48300 Fethiye. ✆ 0252/614-9595 or 0252/612-5211. Fax 0252/612-2223. www.villadaffodil.com. 27 units. $70 (£35) double; $90 (£45) with view. No credit cards. **Amenities:** Restaurant; bar; outdoor swimming pool; sauna; 6-cabin gulet for hire. *In room:* A/C, satellite TV, hair dryer.

KAYAKÖY

Kaya Cottages 🎯🎯 *Moments*   This cluster of well-appointed self-catering cottages was little more than crumbling ruins until a decade ago, when a couple of expats arrived, bought up what were essentially piles of stones for a song, and renovated them with a mind toward comfort, character, and sensitivity. The property has since been split (see "Sakli Vadi," below), leaving two cottages to another couple of British expats enchanted by the authentic rural village surroundings. The two houses are unique and reflect the property's original purpose as a farm. Up to three can stay in the "stables," a two-bedroom unit with a kitchen, fireplace, and secluded, walled-in terrace. The "smokehouse" sleeps four, an elegant sanctuary with high beams, a private patio, and a modern bathroom.

Kaya Köyü, 48304 Fethiye. ✆ 0537/579-2050. www.kaya-cottages.co.uk. 2 self-catering cottages. £350 ($700) per cottage per week plus refundable security deposit of £60 ($120). No minimum stay. May–Oct (also open during Christmas and may open during off season upon request). No credit cards. *In room:* A/C, kitchen, coffeemaker.

Misafir Evi *Value*   The former owner/manager of Kaya Cottages had her hand in getting this little inn up and running. But life changes course and now the inn is run by her good friend Filiz, who infuses the hotel with her own wonderful brand of Turkish hospitality. The rooms are simple, with twin beds under wooden roofs (on the top floor, obviously), surrounded by practical and unadorned furniture and whitewashed stone walls. The bathrooms, however, are of the type you would hope to find anywhere: floor-to-ceiling tile, a modern Roman shower separated by a glass partition, and modern fixtures. The lush garden bursts with flowers, and when not lazing drowsily in a hammock, you can be lounging poolside.

Keçiler/Kaya Köyü, 48304 Fethiye. ✆ 0252/618-0162. www.kayamisafirevi.com. 9 units. £35 ($70) double (add £5/$10 for half-board). No credit cards. **Amenities:** Restaurant; outdoor swimming pool. *In room:* A/C, no phone.

Sakli Vadi 🎯🎯 *Moments*   Jon Carter, who arrived in Kayaköy in 1993, is the helmsman behind the earliest restoration projects in the valley. With the three cottages that make up Sakli Vadi, the trend of preserving buildings' original utility continues. Here it is a "granary," comprising a rustic retreat with its own private terraced garden. The best thing about the units is that each provides an optimum level of isolation and privacy, embraced in lavender, bougainvillea, and sagebrush. A small freshwater plunge pool is shared by the three cottages, a great amenity for when the summer sun heats up the country mountain air.

Kaya Köyü, 48304 Fethiye. © **973/1779-1011** (this is a Bahrain number). www.sakli-vadi.com. 2 self-catering cottages. £350 ($700) per cottage per week. Advance payment required. See website for details. May–Oct. No credit cards. *In room:* A/C, kitchen, coffeemaker.

ÖLÜDENIZ

Club Belcekız Beach ✦   Located at the very end of Ölüdeniz Beach with Babadağ as a backdrop, Club Belcekız Beach sets the stage for a perfect seaside vacation without the fuss. Doric columns support a poolside archway, and the Cappadocian-style chimneys offer a tip of the hat to the civilizations of ancient Anatolia. Rooms are in two sections: the main garden complex and an equally nice rear garden annex. All rooms are essentially the same, with updated bathrooms and balconies or patios. The pool overlooks the beach, enjoying views of the cliffs and paragliders descending from the summit of the mountain, and the entire hotel grounds sprout with flowers and lush greenery. The property is usually booked well in advance, and usually for full-week periods, but give them a try anyway.

48300 Ölüdeniz. © **0252/617-0077.** Fax 0252/617-0372. www.belcekiz.com. 212 units (some with tub, some with shower). £60–£100 ($120–$200) double. Rates reflect seasonal differences and include breakfast and dinner. AE, MC, V. Closed mid-Nov to Mar. **Amenities:** 4 restaurants; 3 bars; outdoor swimming pool; tennis courts; fitness room; Turkish bath; sauna; children's playground; game room; concierge; tour desk; car-rental desk; meeting facilities; Internet point; salon; 24-hr. room service; massage; babysitting; laundry service; dry cleaning. *In room:* A/C, safe.

LykiaWorld ✦ *Kids*   This immense 15-hectare (37-acre) beachfront theme park supports 2,500 guests at a time. Built by the German-owned Robinsons' Club, visitors are ensured five-star amenities in a perfectly constructed artificial world of fun. It's a great family destination, and extremely gimmicky—the grounds shuttles are shaped like miniature Shining Time cruise ships and the pools and grounds feature reproductions of Lycian artifacts like sarcophagi. But this is nothing compared to the Children's Paradise, a wonderland of waterslides, mystery caves, theme playgrounds, trampolines, and supervised activities. Adults can guiltlessly get as self-absorbed as they wish; the Children's Paradise also has an area for kids under 3 years, with the option of round-the-clock babysitting (at an additional fee). Then what to do? Choose from one of the 17 pools. Relax on the resort's own private beach, arguably the nicest in Ölüdeniz. Or, go for broke in the health and beauty center by scheduling sessions for a high-pressure water massage, acupuncture, shiatsu, acupressure, or algae treatments.

Rooms in the Village are comfortable yet designed more for family function than those in the Residence, which have couples in mind. The biggest challenge? Finding your way back to the room.

P.K. 102, Ölüdeniz. © **0252/617-0400.** Fax 0252/617-0350. www.lykiaworld.com. 269 units in the Residence; 550 units in the Village. Online rates from 177€ ($257/£126) double and up depending on package and season. AE, DC, MC, V. Closed Nov–Mar. **Amenities:** 9 restaurants; 12 bars; 17 swimming pools; golf course; tennis courts; health club and spa; Turkish bath; Jacuzzi; sauna; extensive land and watersports; rentals (bike, moped, and scooter); children's center; children's programs; children's playground; cinema; game room; concierge; tour desk; car-rental desk; business center; shopping arcade; salon; 24-hr. room service; massage; babysitting; laundry service; dry cleaning; non-smoking rooms; executive floor. *In room:* A/C, satellite TV, minibar, fridge, hair dryer, safe.

Montana Pine Resort ✦   This small boutique resort was completed in 1997 and sits amid a pine forest about 1.6km (1 mile) above Ölüdeniz. The resort, a kind of complex with mini-country lodges, was built in two phases in a style that can best be described as "modern rustic." Try to stay in the newer section, placed at the back of the property far away from the poolside disco parties that blare well into the early morning hours. Every comfort has been addressed in these rooms, which sport verandas, picture windows, and spacious bathrooms. In comparison, rooms in the original section are disappointingly beige in character, and disturbingly close to the evening festivities. The two main pools are terraced and connected by a waterfall; there's also an enchanting and cozy *şark* (Oriental seating) room, with *kilims* and pillows in a private little area for pre- or post-sun relaxing. (A third pool sits behind the complex of new rooms.) The hotel provides a free shuttle service to Ölüdeniz Beach.

Ovacık Mah., 48300 Ölüdeniz, Fethiye. ℂ 0252/616-7108. Fax 0252/616-6451. www.montanapine.com. 159 units (original section with shower, newer units with tub). £110 ($220) double in mountain or valley room; £140 ($280) mountain or valley suite. Rates include breakfast and dinner but no drinks. Free airport transfer from Dalaman for stays of 7 nights or more. Rates lower for stays longer than a week. MC, V. **Amenities:** 2 restaurants; 3 bars; 3 outdoor swimming pools; miniature golf; tennis courts; fitness room; Jacuzzi; sauna; scooter rental; car-rental desk; shopping arcade; 24-hr. room service; laundry service; dry cleaning. *In room:* A/C, satellite TV, minibar, hair dryer.

Tohum   Located on 22 hectares (54 acres) of seaside cliff and brush surrounded by 140 hectares (346 acres) of forest land (the Lycian Way hiking trail passes along the road above), Tohum, which means "seed," sums up this environmentally conscious retreat. The goal, as expressed by Turkish partners Beti and Atila (based in Bernardston, Mass.), is to create a sanctuary for those wishing to reconnect with nature. A total of eight cabins dot the hillside. Half are constructed of wood beams and adobe, while the rest are made of natural wood. All are outfitted with *kilims*, mats, and crisp gingham sheets protected under a mosquito netting; all overlook the natural layer of brush out toward the sea. Meals are based on menus that recall traditional Anatolian cuisine. Offerings include a vegetarian selection using locally produced organic vegetables, grains, and beans flavored with the wild sage, basil, and oregano that perfume the air. Count on leaving your idea of a deluxe vacation behind, as this is more like an upscale camping trip; however, you're guaranteed to leave here restored and ready to take on the world.

White Cape (20 min. beyond Ölüdeniz, on the dirt road to Faralya). ℂ 413/774-4140 in the U.S. Fax 413/774-4634. www.tohum.com. $525 (£263) single sharing in a double room; $620 (£310) single in a double. $265 (£133) children 6–12. Rates are per person weekly and reflect full board; see website for updated prices, discounts, and shorter stays. No credit cards. Closed mid-Oct to Apr. Contact Tohum in advance for transfers from Fethiye.

WHERE TO DINE

Fethiye has its abundance of *pide* (flatbread) joints and kebap houses, and you certainly don't need me to point them out. Below is a small selection of the most memorable and atmospheric places in and around the three main centers.

FETHIYE

Cem & Can 👍👍 *Value* BRING-YOUR-OWN BARBECUE   Here's your chance to live abroad for an afternoon. Simply choose your fish at the fish counter (sold by weight) at the center of a bustling meat, fish, and produce market, and bring your fresh purchase over to this humble spot in the corner (nearest to Belediye Cad.). It's as no-frills as you can get, and equally authentic.

Pazaryeri/New Bazaar (between Belediye and Hükümet cads.). ℂ 0252/614-3097. Service fee w/salad and bread 5YTL ($4.35/£2). No credit cards. Daily 8am–2pm.

Meğri TURKISH   Meğri is hard to miss with its two neighboring locations in the center of Fethiye's Old Town, an unornamented *lokanta* a few steps away, and a corner cafe. The reliability of the meals makes this hands-down the most recommended restaurant in town. The main restaurant is actually two separate spaces set around the Old Town square—in summertime, tables spill out of the two stone dining rooms (one was an old converted warehouse) monopolizing the public square. Start your meal with the area's freshest, most succulent cold seafood salads with big chunks of calamari and tons of lemon, and a plateful of steamy *lavaş* on which to spread your garlic and parsley herb butter. The seafood casseroles are a local specialty, albeit a bit heavy for a sultry summer afternoon, so order your catch of the day grilled, on a *şiş,* or *kağıtta* (steamed in foil). The *lokanta,* Çarşı Cad. 26 (© **0252/614-4047**), attracts those looking for typical food without the added price, and the new location across from the old provides plenty of pleasant outdoor seating.

Paspatur Eskı Cami Gecidi Likya Sok. 8–9 (in the center of Old Town). © **0252/614-4046**. Appetizers and main courses 6.75YTL–24YTL ($5.85–$21/£2.70–£9.60). AE, DC, DISC, MC, V. Daily 9am–midnight.

Sedir *(Kids* TURKISH   This unpretentious restaurant and *lokanta* is a local favorite. Tables connect in the style of a long galley, seating you next to other hungry strangers; however, in summer most people choose to sit at one of the many outdoor tables. Hot tables provide a pleasing selection of stews served in such large portions that it's common and acceptable to order a half-portion, or you can choose from the traditional menu of meatballs, *pide,* fish, and mezes. Copycats have opened several carbon-copy restaurants adjacent to Sedir, so you can actually try a different one for each meal (**Şamdan,** Tütün Sok. 9, © **0252/614-2868; Sofra Lokantası,** Hükümet Cad. [at the corner outside the new food market], © **0252/614-3470**).

Tütün Sok. © **0252/614-1095**. Appetizers and main courses 3YTL–14YTL ($2.60–$12/£1.20–£5.60). No credit cards. Daily noon–2pm.

KAYAKÖY

Cin Bal *(Finds (Kids* MOUNTAIN GRILLS   Originally a butchery, this village garden-style eatery is a well-kept secret, serving up rustic ambience and incredible food at spectacularly low prices. You can sit at one of the few tables in the slightly overgrown valley yard or on rudimentary platforms with plump pillows while a herd of goats nibble at the nearby daffodils. After choosing from a selection of meat, fish, and wild boar, all of it fresh and succulent and in abundant portions, you grill your own food on a small, tableside barbecue. The mezes are almost unnecessary with all the food that arrives, including the essential combination of onions, tomatoes, and peppers to grill alongside the meat. The local crowd of regulars tends to make an evening of it, egged on by the roving minstrels and singing increasingly off-key as the night progresses.

Kaya Köyü. © **0252/618-0066**. Appetizers 4YTL ($3.50/£1.60); meat courses by weight, about 19YTL ($17/£7.60) per kilo. MC, V. Daily 8am–2am.

ÖLÜDENIZ

Beyaz Yunus/White Dolphin *(Moments* FISH   This is just the society destination that Ölüdeniz needed to detract from the overwhelming presence of partiers and daredevil paragliders. It commands the best spot above the far end of Belceğiz Beach, on the road that leads to Faralya and Kabak, a position on dual terraces with stunning sunset views backed by a cacophony of crashing waves. Couples may want to opt for the romantic dining terrace, a quiet and candlelit spot. Its highlight is the "G3" table, which, thanks to the best views in the house, has entertained some of the world's most privileged (having arrived by boat). Long pub tables take up the main dining terrace, with plenty of room for dishes like Mediterranean lobster and whatever the catches of the day happen to be. Mezes include the Ottoman favorite *icli köfte* (a large fried dumpling of cracked wheat surrounding a center of spiced chopped lamb) and an overwhelming variety of seafood salads. The raw whole octopus (eye included) is a house specialty prepared in the Greek style; or for the squeamish, there's stuffed grape leaves and other fresh cold starters.

Kidrak Yolu Uzeri 1 (on the cliff at the far end of Belceğiz Beach). ℂ 0252/617-0068. Appetizers 6YTL–18YTL ($5.20–$16/£2.40–£7.20); fish by weight. AE, MC, V. Daily 6pm–1am. Closed in winter.

Kumsal *Kids* TURKISH/PIDES   The nearby nighttime odor of sewage might be a major deterrent, but by day, this outdoor garden deck draped in vines and dripping bunches of grapes makes a wonderful midafternoon lunch break. It's most recognized for a variety of perfectly baked and properly doughy *pide*, with choices such as spinach and cheese, meat and cheese, or all meat or all cheese. There's also a vegetarian option topped with tomatoes, peppers, onions, and mushrooms. They've also got the usual lineup of menu items, and there's an outdoor cafe/bar, which makes this a perfect stop-off when your skin is starting to get a little too crisp.

Belceğiz Beach, near the Belcekiz Beach Hotel. ℂ 0252/617-0058. Main courses 4YTL–9.50YTL ($3.50–$8.25/ £1.60–£3.80). No credit cards. Daily 8am–1am.

Oba *Value* TURKISH/PIDES   In a sea change of restaurants that pass from owner to owner, this is the one reliable and consistent dining spot (excluding Beyaz Yunus, which is in a class all its own) in Ölüdeniz. Located 1 long block away from the beach, Oba makes for a quiet lunch or a lively dinner. The menu is traditional Turkish, but the food quality is excellent, and you get to choose between traditional Turkish platform seating or a table in the cool garden. *Pide* and pizza are only served in the evening hours.

From the Belceğiz Beach promenade, turn down the quiet side street once you see Pizza Pepino. ℂ 0252/617-0470. Appetizers and main courses 4YTL–14 ($3.50–$12/£1.60–£5.60). No credit cards. Daily 8am–1am.

FETHIYE AFTER DARK

Hotels and resorts provide the best entertainment, often drawing nonguests from the surrounding areas, with presentations of live music or some contrived line-dance activity. Look for postings around the properties for options.

The Old Town Bazaar in downtown **Fethiye** has a good number of bars, restaurants, and shops lining the ancient streets, and shops are open until as late as the money flows in.

Hisarönü, the enclave located on the road to **Kayaköy,** turns into a fun-house festival and pedestrian market on summer evenings. The streets are lined with restaurants and boisterous bars too numerous to mention (a huge draw for the local British expats), and shops selling beach souvenirs that catch your eye under fluorescent lighting.

The promenade along Belceğiz Beach down at **Ölüdeniz,** with its handful of nightspots that play music loud and louder, is absent of any real sophistication, and utterly avoidable unless you've chosen to base yourself elsewhere. There are two or three atmospheric locales where the daytime's paragliders congregate, but the best thing you can do for a quiet evening is to head up to the bar terrace of **Beyaz Yunus/White Dolphin** (p. 288). Here you can have a drink by candlelight and surf while seated in designer chairs sheltered under bougainvillea.

Buzz Beach Bar   Buzz Bar is very popular with visitors, both for the outdoor cafe along the promenade and the outdoor bar and lounge upstairs. The music is pretty good too, albeit as loud as any other bar. You can check your e-mail with a drink in hand, as they also have an Internet corner. Daily 8am to 3am. Belceğiz Beach on the promenade, Ölüdeniz. ☎ 0252/617-0045. Closed in winter.

Help Bar This ever-popular beachfront bar offers creative fun in a colorful atmosphere of odd-shaped tables (like bent dogs or bones) and hand-painted chairs named after film characters and celebrities, such as Sophia Loren and "Dirty Harry." An American-style drink and cocktail menu (read: excessively long) is complemented by light meals and starters from the restaurant's kitchen, and includes bar staples such as grilled garlic tortillas and deep-fried artichoke hearts. Daily 8 or 9am to 3am. Belceğiz Beach promenade (near the road into town), Ölüdeniz. ☎ 0252/617-0498. Closed in winter.

Ottoman Bar Türkü Evi *(Finds)* Just what the doctor ordered, Türkü Evi is that perfectly characteristic Turkish pub that's so lacking in these parts. The entrance is up the exterior stone steps to the left, which lead to a softly lit pub decorated with Anatolian carpets and serenaded by a local folk guitarist. The earlier you go, the mellower the experience; after about 11pm, locals start to pile in, light up, and dance à la turque—hands raised into the air. Daily 9pm to 3am. Barlar Sok. at Çarşı Cad., Fethiye. ☎ 0252/612-1148.

4 Kalkan ★★

81km (50 miles) southeast of Fethiye; 25km (16 miles) west of Kaş; 19km (12 miles) south of Xanthos; 18km (11 miles) east of Patara; 25km (16 miles) southeast of Letoon

When Erkut Taçkın, the famous Turkish singer from the 1960s, bought a house in Kalkan, the village's fate was sealed. For the Turkish "smart set," it had become the place to go. Ever since, Kalkan has undergone a renewal of sorts, and many of this tiny town's characteristic Ottoman and Greek structures have been brought back to life. The smart set has long moved on, replaced by British and German expats looking for inexpensive vacation and retirement homes or weeklong summertime escapes. As a result, building has sprawled almost all the way to Kalamar Bay. But while the ever-increasing influx of foreigners and visitors continues to exert pressure on this seaside village, Kalkan's terraced position below the main road prevents any palatable departure from the village's inherent small-town persona. Kalkan's center is located on a steep slope that descends into a tiny, picturesque harbor. The warren of streets leading down and around the seaside village resort are colorfully adorned with the bright colors of vacation memorabilia, handcrafted silver jewelry, locally made carpets, and terra cotta, baking under the hot sun and sharing the ambiance with the pleasant odors of grilling produce.

Contrary to its popular perception as a fishing town, Kalkan was actually settled around 150 to 200 years ago by merchants from the nearby Greek island of Meis (Castellorizo). By the turn of the last century Kalkan thrived on the production of charcoal, silk, cotton, and olive oil—it even had its own Customs house. As early as the 1950s and 1960s, the town began to attract rich English yachtspeople, leading to a trend in the 1980s of transforming dilapidated houses into characteristic whitewashed homes with shuttered windows and timber balconies.

The town's population of around 1,000 swells to 8,000 in summer, meaning that Kalkan may not be putting its best foot forward in July and August. This is when the English presence in Kalkan becomes overwhelming—even disturbing. Meanwhile, two Brit-based tour operators (Tapestry and Simply Turkey) ensure that most of the town's better hotels exclusively host their clients, thus creating a shortage of rooms for the independent traveler during the main tourist season. Nevertheless, all of this attention keeps Kalkan running at full capacity, creating demand for some of the most consistent and sophisticated menus on the Turquoise Coast.

Meanwhile, services cater to a single clientele: Chips (french fries) are the unfortunate side dish to most entrees, and mobile baked-potato kiosks are becoming a fixed part of the landscape. Price levels have been driven up to the highest level on the coast, and it shows no sign of letting up.

Kalkan's location is convenient to many historical sites—although lazy days on the beach, stunning visuals, and hours chatting with the quirky town residents are good enough reasons to base yourself here.

ESSENTIALS
GETTING THERE
Halfway between Dalaman and Antalya airports, Kalkan lies along the southwestern coast of the Mediterranean. Unless you have your own car, there's no way to avoid the long and torturous (albeit lovely) journey by land: From Antalya it's a 6-hour, rarely air-conditioned minibus ride, although the imminent completion of a new road to Kalkan should shorten this trip.

If you're arriving by long-distance bus, direct service is available year-round from Istanbul with **Pamukkale,** (© **444-3535** (12 hr.; 60YTL/$52/£24), leaving at 10pm nightly (on its way through to Kaş); and from Izmir (8 hr.; 33YTL/$29/£13), leaving at 10pm. The luxury **Kamıl Koç** (© **0800/293-1115**) also serves the long-distance routes to Istanbul, Ankara, and locally, to Ortaca and Dalaman.

Independent travelers from Dalaman Airport are up against a series of transfers, including the one from the airport to the Dalaman bus station, which must be done by taxi. From the bus station, you can either catch a through-bus headed to Izmir (double-check that it stops in Kalkan) or take a minibus. A taxi from the airport will run around 180YTL ($157/£72); from Kaş, it's about a half-hour (3YTL/$2.60/£1.20); and to/from Antalya it's about 3½ hours (15YTL/$13/£5.20).

Perhaps most convenient is to visit Kalkan as a port of call on a Blue Voyage. (If you're taking a Blue Voyage, it's worth trying to coax your captain into stopping in Kalkan for an overnight visit.)

VISITOR INFORMATION
There is no tourist information office in Kalkan. Thursday is market day.

Deniz Bank is the only bank in town, so it's a good idea to arrive in town with enough cash to get by, in case the ATM falls victim to an unexpected glitch.

At the **marina,** you can take care of the basics, such as the use of coin-operated public toilets, showers, or laundry facilities, or hire a local boat and captain for the day.

ORIENTATION
Kalkan is built on a steep hillside that descends into the bay; enclosed by rocky and rugged mountains, the village has nowhere to go but down. The main square sits at the top of the village, serving as a parking lot as well as the town's miniscule commercial center. There are two or three bus company offices, some travel agencies, a barber, a PTT, and a handful of bodegas for essential refills of water. From the tiny roundabout at the entrance to the town, a connector road leads the way out to lovely Kalamar Bay. This road is at the receiving end of most of the building boom experienced here in the past 10 or so years.

In Kalkan's compact center, the crisscross of narrow streets packed with restaurants, pensions, and shops from the main square down to the marina is known as the catchall **Yalıboyu.** This absence of definitive street addresses may at first seem odd, but even though nobody uses a street address, it's unlikely you'll get lost. All roads lead to the harbor and marina, and you will find yourself trekking up and down the steep roads countless times a day.

GETTING AROUND

Kalkan is a pedestrian village of limited size. The main square is closed to incoming traffic, requiring automobiles to circle down to the marina, turn left at the harborfront road, and left again back up the hill to the main square. Some of the hotels lining the road out of the village are still within walking distance, but anything beyond that may require wheels. If you're entering the village by car, be aware that the harbor road closes to traffic at 7pm, so you'll need to be settled in (or plan to leave your car at the top of the village) by then. If you have trouble walking up and down steep inclines, Kalkan is not for you. *Dolmuşes* depart regularly to transport you to most of the area attractions recommended here. *Note:* The Kalkan Taxi Cooperative (locally called the taxi mafia) charges the highest rates in all of Turkey: 15YTL ($13/£6) for 1.5km/ under a mile.

BY DOLMUŞ   *Dolmuşes* leave from the main square regularly (as soon as they fill up), heading east toward Kaş or west to Patara and points beyond. *Dolmuş* service back into Kalkan ends as early as 6pm, so if you pop out of town for the day, make sure you have a ride home.

BY BUS   There is a limited number of major bus companies in Kalkan, generally servicing only the longer hauls. Destinations and schedules are posted on placards outside the few minuscule ticket offices located on the main square. It's usually okay to buy your ticket at the office just prior to boarding.

If you're headed to or from any of the towns along the coast up to Antalya, catch one of **Batı Antalya Tour**'s (© **0242/844-2777**) air-conditioned buses and head out early in the morning—the lack of traffic can shorten your trip by up to an hour; from Antalya, it'll cost around 15YTL ($13/£6).

BY CAR/SCOOTER   It's almost impossible not to trip over a sign touting the rental of a scooter, car, or jeep. You'll find the scooters up in the main square across from the post office and car rentals through most travel agencies for £30 ($60) per day and up, depending on the model.

WHAT TO SEE & DO

The distinctive features of the coastline around Kalkan and the nearby Xanthos River allow for innumerable options for day trips on or near the water. Here the jagged edges of mountains meet the sea, forming a breathtaking network of islands and coves that present endless possibilities for a day of dive bombing off the roof of a boat and swimming into eerie caves. High up on your list should be a boat trip around the island of **Kekova** and the sunken city, accessible from a number of port towns along the coast (see section 5, "Kaş," later in this chapter, for further information).

AREA BEACHES

Usually, a sign reading YACHT CLUB means members only, or more accurately, not you, thank you very much. Not so here at the Kalkan Marina, where a traveler, no matter whether the arrival was by land or by sea, can venture up and over to the other side of the breakwater, to the town "beach," and rent lounges and umbrellas for about 6.75YTL ($5.85/£2.70). The Yacht Club also has an on-site watersports concession, called **Blue Marlin** (© 0242/844-2783; www.bmwatersports-kalkan.com), providing both leisurely and extreme-sports alternatives, open April through October. You'll find a snack bar with competitive prices, and can also stock up at the supermarket on the harbor.

Kalkan also boasts its very own man-made **pebble beach,** at the eastern end of town, but because it's fed by the icy spring waters channeling down from the mountain, you might want to save this for a bracing sunrise dip or a refreshing cool-off at the end of a hot and dusty day.

Kaputaş Beach ♠♠ is a tiny little sandy cove at the mouth of a colossal gorge. Only 10 minutes from Kalkan, the *dolmuş* crosses a bridge between the two sides of the formation and drops you off at the highway railing, at the top of a lofty stairway down to the beach. **Mavi Mağara (Blue Cave,** named for the hue of the boulders inside) is a short swim from Kaputaş out and to the left, but as the beach is not guarded, only strong swimmers in pairs should do this.

Over at Kalamar Bay is the **Kalamar Beach Club** ♠♠ (© 0242/844-3061), comprised of an intimate series of cement patio terraces with beach lounges, backed by a restaurant and snack bar. The guys that run the concession provide free transfers from Kalkan and make up the difference with food prices that are the highest in the area. Day rental of a lounge and umbrella is around 6.75YTL ($5.85/£2.70), and there are also showers. Boredom is kept at bay thanks to **Aquasports** (© 0242/844-2361), the on-site provider of watersports rentals. In addition to a dive concession (see the info on Kalkan Dive Centre, under "Staying Active," below), they rent jet skis and water skis (40YTL/$35/£16 per 10 min.), and also give lessons available for water-skiing. Banana boat rides are available for 20YTL ($17/£8) per person.

Area resort hotels also make their private beaches and facilities available to nonguests for a daily fee. **Club Patara** (© 0242/844-3920) is accessible via the free water taxi to the resort's platforms, where you can take advantage of the three pools and terrace lounges for around 20YTL ($17/£8). The water taxi pulls up to the pier next to the lighthouse, but keep in mind that the wait around lunchtime will be a bit longer—the captain goes AWOL for a bite to eat. Reservations are essential if you want to rent anything motorized.

Only 20 minutes away by *dolmuş* is **Patara Beach** ♠♠, the longest and certainly one of the most beautiful stretches of sand in Turkey. The beach goes on for 18km (11 miles), which makes for a pretty long surfside stroll, especially when the fierce winds are at their peak. Entrance to the beach is through the ruins of the ancient city, so if you've come by car, you'll have to pay the entrance fee of 2YTL ($1.75/80p) to the site, which includes repeat visits to the beach (keep your ticket). If you've arrived on a *dolmuş,* the beach is free, but you may want to rent an umbrella. Patara Beach is also a lesser-known nesting ground for the Caretta Caretta turtle, so it is closed after dark.

The stunning scenery and sleek minimalist pool terrace at the **Happy Hotel** at Kalamar Bay opens up its pool for a daily fee of 15YTL ($13/£6). Although there is no direct access to the sea, the views from the pool are incomparably beautiful.

EXPLORING RUINS IN THE XANTHOS VALLEY

Kalkan is a great base for day excursions to the ancient Lycian sites of the Xanthos Valley, which includes the ancient sites of Tlos (see "Fethiye & Ölüdeniz," earlier in this chapter), Xanthos, Letoon, and Patara. All of the sites are easily accessible by car with a short detour off the main road or by *dolmuşes* that run regularly from the main square. Several travel agencies in town offer excursions to one or more of the sites as part of a day tour; contact **Adda Tours,** Yalıboyu Mahallesi (© **0242/844-3610;** www.addatours.com), for the most competitive rates; **Armes Travel & Tours,** at the harbor (© **0242/844-3169**); or the Munich-based **Dardanos Travel,** Hotel Dardanos Gelemis Koyu in Patara (© **0242/843-5151** or 843-5109; www.dardanostravel.com).

The oldest and most important antique city of the region is **Xanthos** ᏝᏝ, the ancient capital of Lycia. Homer mentions this center in the *Iliad:* It was from here that Arpedonte led his troops. More tragic is the actual history of the city: On two separate and unrelated occasions, the inhabitants of Xanthos chose collective suicide rather than submission to invading armies.

The ancient city was uncovered by Sir Charles Fellows in 1838, who had much of the city dismantled and transported to the British Museum, where ruins still reside. Nevertheless, reproductions successfully evoke the originals. On your travels through Kaş/Kalkan, pick up a free map of the site; or, you can buy a book on Lycian sites at the refreshment counter. Two unforgettable monuments are on the road from the village of Kınık—the **City Gate** ᏝᏝ, dating to the Hellenistic era, and **Vespasian's Arch** ᏝᏝ, erected in honor of the Roman emperor. The **acropolis** ᏝᏝᏝ is dominated by the remains of the **Roman Theatre** ᏝᏝ, flanked by the ancient city's three most memorable sites: **Harpies' Tomb** ᏝᏝᏝ, named for the Persian General Harpagus through a controversial interpretation by Fellows of the tomb's reliefs; the **Lycian Tomb** ᏝᏝᏝ (one of several); and the **Roman Columned Tomb.** Farther back into the brush is a pillar tomb called the **Obelisk,** whose monumental contribution was lengthy inscriptions in both Lycian and Greek, which proved indispensable to deciphering and classifying the Lycian language (another inscription, found at Letoon and written in Aramaic, Greek, and Lycian, was also important).

The New Acropolis is located on the opposite side of the road and is home to the **Byzantine Church** Ꮭ, famed for the well-preserved **mosaic** Ꮭ flooring uncovered beneath layers of sand. Tour groups generally circle these major sites, overlooking entirely the overgrown path that leads along an ancient wall through to the **Necropolis** ᏝᏝ, a visit that is well worth your time. Sarcophagi are scattered or overturned; keep an eye out for the **Belly Dancer Sarcophagus** Ꮭ, named for a relief that more resembles water-bearers; the **Lion's Tomb** Ꮭ, a sarcophagus with carvings of lions and a bull in battle; and a 4th-century-B.C. **tower tomb** ᏝᏝ rising above a stone-cut Roman acropolis. Admission to the site is 2YTL ($1.75/80p).

Patara ᏝᏝ was Lycia's chief port city until the harbor silted up to form what is today an inland reed-filled marsh. If you climb to the hilltop above the **Roman Theatre** Ꮭ, the fierce winds and unrelenting lashes of sand will give you a clue why much of this ancient city still remains buried—a consequence that has kept the city in such an outstanding state of preservation. Founded according to legend by Patarus, son of Apollo and the nymph Lycia in the 5th century B.C., the site served during the winter months as one of the two most important oracles of the god, his winter months being spent at the temple at Delphi. Today the city gains its fame as the birthplace of the bishop of Myra, better known in northern and Western circles as Santa Claus (see section 6, "Demre," later in this chapter). Little by little, ongoing excavations are beginning to reveal details above and beyond the **monumental arch** ᏝᏝ that rose defiantly above the meters of earth for centuries. At the time of this writing, Patara's **main avenue** ᏝᏝ, paved with marble stone and scattered with the remains of what was probably a columned arcade, is clearly visible (albeit sometimes a bit waterlogged).

Fleeting features of the **Basilica** 🏛 poke through the ground, but perimeter excavations provide a cross section of the city's entombment.

The ruins can be easily explored in combination with a trip to Patara Beach; the road from the turnoff passes a saturated level of home-style pensions with varying degrees of charm and leads to the entrance of the archaeological site (admission 10YTL/$8.70/£4). The beach is at the end of the road.

Letoon 🏛, located less than 5km (3 miles) south of Xanthos, was the primary religious center of ancient Lycia. And while the buses are circling around Xanthos, you can escape here, smack in the middle of the Turkey you envisioned, along a pastoral village road, admiring the wind in the trees and the goats grazing in the archaeological site. Aren't you clever.

The ruins of **three temples** 🏛🏛 rise above an uneven plateau and were dedicated to the gods Apollo, Artemis, and their mother, Lato, the mythical lover of Zeus for which the sanctuary was named. The foundations of the three temples are laid out parallel to each other; the **theater** 🏛🏛 is in better shape, and it served for meetings of the Lycian Federation, religious ceremonies, and even sports events. Admission to the site is 5YTL ($4.35/£2).

STAYING ACTIVE

The waters off Kalkan provide some of the best venues for **scuba diving** along the Mediterranean. It was off nearby Uluburun that sponge divers discovered a 14th-century-B.C. shipwreck. Several outfitters organize single or multiple days of diving, as well as a "discover scuba" day for beginners. The main reliables are **Armes Travel and Tours** (Armes Travel & Tours, at the harbor; © 0242/844-3169); **Kalkan Dive Centre,** a division of Aquasports over at Kalamar Bay (© 0242/844-2456; www.kalkandiving.com), run by a couple of experienced local divers; and **Bougainville Travel** (© 0242/836-3737; www.bougainville-turkey.com), located over in nearby Kaş. A day of diving for beginners and pros starts at £25 ($50).

Canoeing along the Xanthos River is an exhilarating way to spend the day. You don't need to be a pro—the excursion organizers design tours geared toward fun rather than physical fitness. A day tour usually includes a stopover at a mud bath and a few hours of relaxation on Patara Beach. A day on the rapids runs around 55YTL ($48/£22) per person, lunch and transfers included. These and other activities are generally planned on fixed days of the week. If you don't see a tour package that suits your needs, check around the main square or down by the harbor for tours organized by other outfitters. The canoe trip with picnic lunch costs 28€ ($41/£20) per person.

A popular activity especially suited to the area is **horseback riding.** The Eşen Plain meets the sea at Patara where, riding through Roman ruins and sand dunes, you can imagine yourself in an ancient Greek countryside. Dardanos runs day and multiday trips from 38€ ($55/£27) per person.

WHERE TO STAY

One of Kalkan's more unfortunate cafes blasts its music well into the morning hours, enough to encourage one to bed down well outside of Kalkan's town center. Meanwhile, British tour companies have blocked out most of the best rooms in and around Kalkan, leaving others with sloppy seconds or the rare property unwilling to confine themselves to this type of arrangement. **Tapestry** (© 0208/995-7787; www.tapestry holidays.com) is the agent for a full stable of hotels in Kalkan, and they generally require a package deal (flight/hotel) with a full week's commitment.

Keep in mind that while a pension or special-category hotel in the center of town will at least afford some architectural integrity, don't expect a pool. But thanks to the proximity and accessibility of nearby beaches, this should by no means be a deterrent to staying in town. If your holiday style leans more toward the plush and all-inclusive, choose one of the resorts across the bay; they are connected to the village by a water shuttle.

KALKAN

Patara Prince 🏨🏨   The grounds of the Patara Prince are nothing short of a seaside paradise, set on white stone cliffs on a backdrop of verdant gardens. The complex is constructed on the steep hillside opposite Kalkan, with facilities positioned at various altitudes connected by pure-white, local stone stairways. The extremely terraced landscaping need not be a deterrent; the hotel provides a shuttle service down past the various lodging types via a service road to the waterfront.

The complex consists of traditional hotel rooms; blocks of suites of varying types, smartly decorated with features like Jacuzzis, fireplaces, and bamboo-shuttered windows separating the bathroom from the living area; and villas large enough for up to six people. The villas (some loosely associated with its timeshare operation) are charming and rustic self-catering houses complete with kitchens, living rooms, multiple bedrooms, and scenic terraces.

There are three outdoor swimming pools, one of which is a circulating seawater pool exclusively for adult use. Terraces for sunbathing step down the cliff side to waterfront platforms, where the watersports activities are organized. The hotel provides a free shuttle service to Kalkan. Note that out of high season, various hotel services go on hiatus.

P.K. 10, Kalkan. ② **0242/844-3920.** Fax 0242/844-3930. www.clubpatara.com. 60 units. 90€–220€ ($131–$319/£64–£157) double in hotel; 160€–270€ ($232–$392/£114–£193) executive and admiralty suite; 280€–1,650€ ($406–$2,393/£200–£1,179) self-catering villa. Rates reflect seasonal differences and include breakfast. AE, DC, MC, V. Parking lot on-site. **Amenities:** 4 restaurants; 4 bars; nightclub; patisserie; 4 swimming pools (3 outdoor, 1 indoor); tennis courts (2 night lit); full-service health club; extensive watersports; dive school; children's center; game room; concierge; tour desk; car-rental desk; salon, 24-hr. room service; massage; babysitting; laundry service; dry cleaning. *In room:* A/C, satellite TV, minibar, hair dryer, safe.

Rhapsody 🏨 *(Finds*   Lazing amidst cushions strewn on your own trellised sun deck is not a bad start to a Mediterranean holiday. This is your entryway into one of Kalkan's rare boutique experiences, one that replaces overused Mediterranean pastels with warm tones of lavender, sage, and powder blue, in a modern seaside interpretation of good taste. Double rooms have beech platform beds and sleek oversize headboards, but you may want to splurge for that terrace suite, which also comes with an outdoor Jacuzzi. The loft-style mezzanine suite comes in a close second, with two twin beds downstairs, separate living rooms, and Jacuzzis in the bedroom for when the kids fall asleep. The room rate includes breakfast, of course, as well as use of the Turkish bath and transfer to and from Dalaman Airport. Now that's entertainment.

Cumhuriyet Cad., Nilüfer Sok. 48, 07960 Kalkan. ② **0242/844-2575.** Fax 0242/844-2576. www.rhapsodyhotel.com. 25 units. £65 ($130) double; £85–£120 ($170–$240) suite. MC, V. **Amenities:** Restaurant; bar; outdoor swimming pool; Turkish bath; sauna; Jacuzzi.

Türk Evi 🏨 *(Value*   This guesthouse makes you feel like you've just walked into somebody's elegant country home. The Turkish and Norwegian team, along with their daughter Zirve, have created a real family atmosphere, down to the fresh farmer's butter and homemade jams. The open, farmhouselike living room, dining room, and kitchen area provide an inviting place for guests to come together, and an outdoor patio is used for family-style meals made with the freshest ingredients prepared on the outdoor barbecue (meals are for guests only). Each simple but charmingly decorated room is named after its color (the pink rooms are the ones with bathtubs), and the adjacent blue rooms provide a connecting balcony for families or friends traveling together. The owner has considerately hung mosquito netting over the beds, because in the heat of the summer, the windows must stay open. Nestled at the top of town in a woodsy setting, it's a bit of a steep climb up, so you may arrive back up from the waterfront a bit winded.

07960 Kalkan (behind the post office near the town center). © 0242/844-3129. Fax 0242/844-3492. www.kalkan turkevi.com. 9 rooms (2 with tub, 7 with shower). 30€–40€ ($44–$58/£21–£29) double. No credit cards. Parking near main road. Turn off the Kaş road into town; the entrance to the guesthouse is on the road into Kalkan immediately on the left. **Amenities:** Restaurant (for guests); laundry service; dry cleaning.

Villa Mahal 🌟🌟 *Moments*   Having already been recognized by international style magazines, the Villa Mahal could easily be called the Jewel of the Mediterranean, offering its visitors sophisticated yet unspoiled surroundings. The large property sits in the middle of an olive grove on a steep bluff overlooking Kalkan Bay and is secluded enough that nothing man-made tarnishes the view. The actual building area takes up very little of the grounds, so the brush along the cliff side provides a good level of privacy. Hotel rooms are at the top of the bluff overlooking the sea, but at 202 steps, it's a long walk down to the waterside and much longer on the way up under the fierce heat. Waterside platforms form the "beach" where there is an array of watersports and an airy and stylish seaside cafe. Villa Mahal has a very special "honeymoon suite," a chillingly romantic secluded circular building with glass walls and its very own private terrace pool overlooking the bay. A regular water shuttle runs from the platform to Kalkan's marina every 15 minutes in high season.

P.K. 4, 07960 Kalkan. © 0242/844-3268. Fax 0242/844-2122. www.villamahal.com. 14 units. 170€–310€ ($247–$450/£121–£221) double. Suites blocked by Exclusive Escapes (www.exclusiveescapes.co.uk) for 2008. Rates lower Apr–May and Oct. MC, V. Take the turn off the main road for Patara Club and follow signs for Villa Mahal. **Amenities:** Restaurant; 2 bars; 24-hr. room service; laundry service; dry cleaning. *In room:* A/C.

Zinbad Hotel   Inconspicuously located down one of Kalkan's sloped back streets, Zinbad Hotel offers spartan but clean accommodations and another one of the village's characteristic rooftop terraces. The terrace commands views of the harbor and slender minaret from the mosque, to enjoy while dining on fresh home cooking that varies daily. Half of the rooms face the harbor and are therefore preferable to the ones in the back. Rooms are spotlessly clean, with a colorful *kilim* as the only embellishment. Zinbad Hotel also has one efficiency that accommodates up to four people.

Mustafa Kocakaya Cad. 26, 07960 Kalkan. © 0242/844-3404. Fax 0242/844-3943. www.zinbadhotel.com. 30 units. June 16–Sept 15 £29 ($58) sea-view double. Rates lower out of high season and with no sea view. Closed Nov–Apr. AE, MC, V. **Amenities:** Restaurant/bar; laundry service; dry cleaning. *In room:* A/C.

KALAMAR BAY

Happy Hotel 🌟 *Value*   From the hotel's panoramic hillside terrace, enormous enough to accommodate the heated half-Olympic-size pool, the Happy (formerly the Harpy) takes full advantage of the breathtaking views of Kalamar Bay. The trade-off? The main structure is a dull glass-and-cement monster that offends its more traditional surroundings through an attempt toward innovation. The 50 rooms and suites are divided among 6 pastel-pink blocks, all with a private exterior access, and all but four rooms have a sea view, thanks to large sliding-glass doors to the terrace or balcony. Room decor is a bit 1950s, with functional taupes and hunter-green furnishings and straightforward modular furniture.

Kalamar Bay, Kalkan. ⓒ 0242/844-1133. Fax 0242/844-1132. www.happyhotel.com.tr. 50 units. July–Aug £53–£63 ($106–$126) double, £69–£79 ($138–$158) suite. Rates as low as £32 ($64) double in winter. MC, V. **Amenities:** Restaurant; 3 bars; outdoor swimming pool; children's pool; fitness center; sauna; game room; hotel cinema; business center w/secretarial services; 24-hr. room service; laundry service; dry cleaning; babysitting; mini market. *In room:* A/C, satellite TV, dataport, minibar, hair dryer, safe.

WHERE TO DINE

The problem of choice will be a tourist's major complaint when staying in Kalkan, as this village easily has the highest ratio of quality restaurants per capita on Turkey's Mediterranean coast. The trend also is that all this great "international" food comes with price tags pegged to international currencies. Unpretentious *lokanta* fare can be had at **Ali Baba** (ⓒ 0242/844-3627), up on the main square near the post office with a recently (2005) added rooftop terrace restaurant serving more substantial fare in the evenings, and at the trellis-shaded **Bezirgan's Kitchen** (ⓒ 0242/844-2106; next to the Kamıl Koç bus office).

Many of the pensions and hotels have rooftop restaurants and often serve some of the best meals using ingredients bought at market the same day. Whenever possible, I always opt for these. But as a nonguest, it's a good idea to reserve ahead (even by midmorning), to allow the cook to stock up on an adequate amount of food.

Be skeptical of restaurants advertising fresh fish; much of the fish along the Mediterranean arrives frozen—ask the waiter before you order if your selection was swimming anytime recently.

Belgin's Kitchen *(Kids)* TRADITIONAL TURKISH   Belgin's Kitchen is a longtime favorite of locals and tourists alike. Making use of a former olive factory, it's a cozy spot for a casual meal, where you can enjoy crispy fried triangular börek or painstakingly stuffed *mantı* while comfortably slouched on the mats and traditional-style floor cushions. It's not one of the town's gourmet offerings, but at least you're guaranteed a bite to eat without emptying the entire contents of your wallet. Belgin's Kitchen has local Turkish musical groups in the evening; get there early to nab the table inside the large boiled-wool traditional tent upstairs (on the roof).

Yalıboyu. ⓒ 0242/844-3614. Appetizers and main courses 4YTL–13YTL ($3.50–$11/£1.60–£5.20). MC, V. Daily 7:30am to 1 or 2am. Closed Nov–Mar.

Korsan *(Kids)* NOUVELLE TURKISH   With its white tablecloth and candlelight, the elegant Korsan, located next to the harbor, is popular among the local community of British expatriates as well as with visitors splurging on a special meal. One glance at the menu and it's obvious that this isn't going to be another banal meal of grilled lamb and green chilis. Choosing among the many mouthwatering mezes is possibly the most significant decision you will make during your vacation, with selections like chicken *şiş* with peanut sauce, fish cakes with pine nuts and berries, and humus with melted chili butter. By the time you fill up on the complimentary fresh-baked garlic bread and two or three appetizers, there is sadly no room for the Black Sea–style baked lamb in a pastry crust with mint or the barbecue fish kebap. Even the kids will be happy, with Korsan's special, less exotic children's menu. The sister restaurant, **Korsan Fish Terrace,** is on the rooftop of the owner's small hotel/pension, Patara Stone House (ⓒ 0242/844-3076), located just above the harbor.

(Finds Fishing for Condiments

About a 10-minute drive into the mountains from Kalkan is the minuscule village of Islamlar, built on the Islamlar Spring, a freshwater source that coursed down the mountain. About 10 years ago, Mahmut of Mahmut'un Yeri (the first one on the right as you enter the village of Islamar; © **0242/838-6344**) had the bright idea to harness the water in a cement pool and stock it with trout, and in no time, his neighbors were standing by in disbelief as the customers began to roll into their wild and unspoiled landscape. Today it has not only grown into a country-style restaurant with a roof terrace with views as far as the sea, but it also has spurred a parade of neighborhood imitations, all essentially identical (which means that in a small village like this one, some friends or family members are no longer on speaking terms). Little ones will love watching the trout leaping up out of the water, sometimes upstream through the mesh barrier to freedom and sometimes out of the pool to their death. For now, the price of a meal (trout, salad, and *ayran*) is about 10YTL ($8.70/£4).

At the Marina. © **0242/844-3622.** Reservations suggested. Dress smart. Appetizers and main courses 8€–18€ ($12–$26/£5.70–£13) and up for fish. MC, V. Daily noon–midnight. Closed Nov–Apr.

Patlican/Aubergine Restaurant 🕏🕏 TURKISH/OTTOMAN/INTERNA-TIONAL   *Harika* ("great" in Turkish) best describes a dining experience at this innocuous restaurant on the harborfront. Thanks to its continued success (and the fact that harborfront restaurants are no longer permitted to set up tables on the waterside promenade), Patlican recently doubled its interior space but remains cozy and delightful. First-time guests are usually drawn to the filet of wild boar, an abundant entree served with slices of eggplant, tomato, and vegetables, and slow-roasted until tender. But leave me to the grilled prawns—flavorful and slightly spicy—and a perfectly marinated swordfish *şiş* any day of the week. These are just samples of the restaurant's creativity in their special menu.

Harborside, Kalkan. © **0242/844-3332.** Reservations suggested. Appetizers and main courses 8YTL–22YTL ($11–$19/£5.70–£8.60). AE, MC, V. Daily 9am–midnight.

KALKAN AFTER DARK

Kalkan's rooftops are a special feature of its Greek houses, camouflaged behind small triangular lintels yet open to night sea breezes. They're the setting for dinner, drinks, and romance for residents and guests alike. Nightlife is also booming on the harborfront, fragrant and alive with handholding vacationers choosing from an appealing array of pubs, restaurants, and shops, while the odd narghile cafe or even sports bar will be located in the warren of streets weaving their way uphill.

Kleo Bar   Under the pagoda of a defunct Chinese restaurant is a sophisticated and utterly romantic spot for a quiet evening of music and conversation. An eclectic mix of lounge furniture is scattered outside at the far end of the harbor, with the most coveted spots—candlelit tables—closer to the water. Cocktails arrive with a fanfare of sparklers, and live music—mostly Turkish adult contemporary—is performed nightly. Daily 9pm to 3am. Next to Korsan. No phone. Closed in winter.

Yacht Club   Candlelight and music reverberate off the water in the nighttime hours at Kalkan's main "beach." There's an outdoor bar and tables, and July through September, live music acts perform until 2am. Daily 8am to 3am. In the marina. No phone. Closed in winter.

5 Kaş ★★

81km (50 miles) southeast of Fethiye; 229km (142 miles) southwest of Antalya; 25km (16 miles) east of Kalkan; 109km (68 miles) southeast of Dalaman Airport

With only 25km (16 miles) separating Kaş from Kalkan, these neighboring towns share the same stunning and broken rocky coastline, so whether you base yourself in one or the other depends on your individual character and travel style. (Keep in mind that tours run by an outfitter based in one routinely involve pickups in the other.) Kaş established itself as the more popular of the two in the 1960s and 1970s, first as a hippie hangout, and later as a stopping point for yachts and gulets on the Blue Voyage. Over the decades, the towns-proper of Kalkan and Kaş have developed their own individual character: Whereas Kalkan is contained and insular, Kaş unravels itself into the surrounding landscape. Kalkan has that provincial feel, while Kaş, in a rather carefree way, seems slightly more mature. What both share are narrow cobbled streets shadowed by the protruding balconies of the typical Ottoman houses, the DNA of antiquity, proximity to ancient and traditional places, and a front-row seat to Turkey's most breathtaking mountain and Mediterranean scenery.

In spite of its success as Turkey's second Mediterranean city, Kaş still retains a certain small-town charm. The town is built around the sparse remains of ancient **Antiphellos,** which left behind a few scattered rock tombs, a Greek theater, and an unanticipated **monumental sarcophagus** featuring four lions' heads at the upper end of one of Kaş's narrow shopping streets.

As the definition of a beach resort goes, Kaş falls somewhat short in that it lacks a proper beach. But it makes up for this with rocky terraces over crystal-clear Mediterranean waters both in town and along the peninsula. Kaş (as is Kalkan) is also an optimal jumping-off point for trips to Kekova, Myra, and some of the regions' best undiscovered mountain villages. The abundance of outdoorsy activities around Kaş has also helped to maintain its reputation as a relaxed, satisfying, and generally inexpensive holiday destination, and in the past few years, it's also developed into quite the family destination.

ESSENTIALS
GETTING THERE
Because of the proximity between Kaş and Kalkan, a selection of long-distance buses serves one, the other, or both. **Pamukkale** (© **444-3535;** 12 hr.; 60YTL/$52/£24) leaves at 10pm nightly and from Izmir (8 hr.; 33YTL/$29/£13), also leaving at 10pm. **Kamıl Koç** (© **0800/293-1115**) serves the long-distance routes from Istanbul, Ankara, and locally, from Ortaca and Dalaman.

Minibuses leave regularly from Fethiye through Kalkan and on to Kaş (1½ hr.; 12YTL/$10/£4.80). The ride by minibus from Antalya takes as little as 3½ hours (13YTL/$11/£5.20) if you leave early in the morning, longer during the day or when traffic is heavier. Kalkan is about a half-hour away (3YTL/$2.60/£1.20).

All the hotels and travel agents offer the service of airport transfers. Expect to pay 150€ ($218/£107) from Dalaman airport and slightly more for Antalya.

VISITOR INFORMATION
The **tourist information office** is located on Cumhuriyet Meydanı 5 (② **0242/836-1238**). The number for the *otogar* is ② **0242/836-1020**. There are three taxi stands in town: Liman Taksi (② **0242/836-1489**), Yat Taksi (② **0242/836-1933**), and Çakıl Taksi (② **0242/836-2448**). Friday is market day.

ORIENTATION
The *otogar* is at the north end of town. From the station, the sloping street down to the town center, the harbor, and marina is called **Atatürk Caddesi.** West of the marina (turn right before the marina at the minuscule roundabout) are the ruins of Antiphellos and the well-preserved antique theater. This road makes the circuit of the Çukurbağ Peninsula and then dumps you back onto the road into town.

In the opposite direction, up the hill past the marina to the east is **Hükümet Caddesi,** which leads to Küçükçakıl and Büyükçakı beaches.

From **Cumhuriyet Meydanı** at the harbor, the street that heads north, **Ibrahim Serin Caddesi,** is lined with shops, cafes, and bars. There are several travel agencies along this street, and the post office and banks are at the end of the commercial stretch. East of **Ibrahim Serin Caddesi** are beautiful craft and jewelry boutiques in converted traditional old wooden houses. A lone **Lycian sarcophagus** towers above the end of Uzun Çarşı Caddesi. Rock tombs are located high above town, obscured by the increased building at the top of the hill.

GETTING AROUND
Few places in Kaş are more than a 10-minute walk away, but if your accommodations are on the peninsula, you'll have to rely on a hotel transfer to get you there, because there is no minibus service, and taxi fares are uncommonly high. To get out of town to the sites mentioned in this section, you'll need to use one of the following modes of transport.

BY BUS AND DOLMUŞ Minibus service runs regularly from Kaş to Kalkan (3YTL/$2.60/£1.20 daily service 8:30am–8:30 or 9pm), which you can take for day trips to Kaputaş Beach, as well as to many of the surrounding sights.

BY TAXI In many cases, local travel agencies will provide more comfortable, air-conditioned cars or vans for lower prices than the taxi fare. Expect to pay the taxi drivers around the following fares from Kaş: Üçağız 40YTL ($35/£16), Demre 50YTL ($44/£20), Antalya Airport 175YTL–200YTL ($152–$174/£70–£80), Kaputaş Beach 50YTL ($44/£20), Kalkan 55YTL ($48/£22), and Dalaman Airport 150YTL ($131/£60).

BY BOAT Occasionally there is water-taxi service from Kaş to Üçağız (3 hr. by boat); from there you can then hire a boat to explore Kekova (10YTL/$8.70/£4 per person). Check with the tourist information office to find out if it's in operation when you get there, but most prefer to drive to Üçağız. If you prefer to get around independently and you know how to haggle effectively, head down to the harbor at any port village and see whether you can hire a boat yourself for a reasonable fee.

BY CAR With everything within walking distance, you'll need a car only to go exploring out of town. You're out of luck if you expected to earn points with Avis, Hertz, National, or Europcar; only local companies rent cars in Kaş. As a consolation for lost frequent-flier miles, the rates will be lower.

WHAT TO SEE & DO

From Kaş to Demre, archaeologists have discovered the remains of no fewer than 17 ancient Lycian sites, some of which remain interred and unidentified. These include **Teimiussa** (at the village port of Üçağız); **Simena;** and the nearby and less visited **Apollonia** and **Aperlai, Andriake,** and **Myra** (see section 6, "Demre," later). If you want to venture up where the air is a bit cooler, the site of **Arykanda,** up in the mountains, will offer you a glimpse of how the heady, pre-mortgage crisis days of antiquity may have looked to a society with very, very extravagant tastes. You could just as easily backtrack to the archaeological sites of the **Xanthos Valley** (see section 4, "Kalkan," earlier in this chapter for details), to the west of Kalkan.

The surrounding protected bays, islands, and bleached coral cliffs provide some of the best opportunities for sun-and-fun boat trips to the sunken city of **Kekova Bay,** or simple days lolling around the deck of a fishing boat or gulet. Travel agencies hopefully grabbing a piece of the tourist pie line the marina and tout day excursions to the area attractions at very competitive rates. **Bougainville Travel,** at Çukurbağlı Caddesi, the continuation of Ibrahim Serin Caddesi (© **0242/836-3142;** www.bougainville-turkey.com), a local English-speaking, British/Turkish/Dutch partnership, is a full-service travel agency and the most well-equipped outfitter for adventure travel and outdoor pursuits on the Mediterranean. Sea-kayaking trips to Kekova cost around 40€ ($58/£29) for individuals, 35€ ($51/£25) for groups. Bougainville recently added mountain-biking tours and canyoning excursions into the Salkikent or Kibris canyons to their regular offerings of sea kayaking, white-water rafting, hiking, and jeep safari trips.

BOAT TRIPS TO THE SUNKEN CITY

The region of and around **Kekova** ✫✫✫ offers a view into an unspoiled world of picturesque fishing villages and mysterious archaeological sites that long ago succumbed to burial at sea. The most visible examples of a long-gone sunken civilization lie along the northern coast of Kekova island, submerged beneath the transparent waters of **Kekova Bay.** Glass-bottom boats allow you to see fleeting details of buried amphoras or other artifacts, but the most impressive relics are the city walls and private homes visible just beneath the waterline. Swimming and snorkeling here are prohibited to preserve the location against random disappearances of archaeological findings, and it is still a mystery as to what all these walls, terraces, and pottery shards represent.

In their haste to get on a boat, many people overlook **Üçağız** ✫, a perfect example of a sleepy fishing town, with a cluster of truly remarkable **Lycian tombs** ✫✫ woven into the fabric of life at the far end of the village (some visible by sea). For now, Üçağız is only home to a couple of well-worn pensions, but if you don't mind really roughing it, you may want to consider bedding down here—truly still off the mainstream tourist radar. Visits also tend to ignore the ancient sites of **Aperlai and Apollonia,** located west of Üçağız on the mainland and accessible by boat from the sea via the Akar Pass; the effort required to get there has ensured the preservation of another "sunken city," and you can plan some time on land to explore the ruins on foot.

If you're traveling independently, you may want to arrive in Üçağız by 9 or 10am, in order to negotiate the best deals with the local fishermen for a day out on their private boat. In high season and no longer pegging their rates to a sagging dollar, boatmen are now asking for—and getting—hefty amounts of cash for a day out. Plan to arrive in Kaleköy (ancient Simena) by lunchtime for a scenic, relaxing, and simply

Finds Kaleköy (Ancient Simena)

It's almost impossible for a fishing village to retain its innocence, but the first time I visited, time seemed to have come to a complete standstill in **Simena** *ℱ*. Recently, though, and in spite of its limited access, this pastoral spot has succumbed to the onward march of commercialism. Still, there's nothing like a stroll through someone's chickens and a waterside meal of grilled fish caught hours earlier to wash away those capitalist blues.

Although it will take a little effort on your part to get to Simena, the reward will be a magical setting far removed from the modern world. There are no roads, only worn dirt paths amid the cluster of modest houses that dot the hillside. Several fish restaurants line the jetties, with comparatively excellent feasts of the freshest fish and the best location from which to stare transfixed at the one solitary stone sarcophagus poking its Gothic cap out of the bay.

Nesrin's Bademli Ev (*©* **0242/874-2170**; www.askamarine.com/bademliev. htm) is a traditional village house with three guest rooms, each with a fireplace. There's nothing but the essentials here, but all of that authenticity will run you 55€–70€ ($80–$102/£39–£50). The hotel is closed in winter.

The **Kale Pansiyon** (*©* **0242/874-2111**; fax 0242/874-2110; www.kale pansiyon.com) is a very basic family motel converted from a Greek cottage located just above the tour boat jetty. Prices are quoted at about 35€ ($51/£25) a night in July and August; otherwise, they're 30€ ($44/£21).

The **Mehtap Pansiyon** (*©* **0242/874-2146**; fax 0242/874-2261; www. mehtappansiyon.com) is more like a treehouse campsite, located on the uppermost part of the cliff with splendid views of the sea from its wooden platform on the rocky hillside. The rooms have something akin to a shower, and this is definitely a roughing-it experience, as most guests wind up sleeping on one of the beds arranged outside along the railing instead. A double is advertised as 60€ ($87/£43), but this is flexible. Mehtap also has a rustic treehouse restaurant with meals of seafood and game meats cooked by the owner himself.

marvelous meal of fresh fish. Excursions to Simena must be negotiated with the local boatmen to Kaleköy, based on a half-day rental. If you're planning on staying overnight, enlist your pension owner in getting transport over.

Check to see if the day boat out of the marina is operating (see "Getting Around," above). Otherwise, every travel agent in town offers trips to Kekova, lunch and transfers to Üçağız included. Boats depart out of Üçağız for Kekova Island in the morning, touring the bays and islands with stops for swimming and snorkeling and exploration of some area caves. Tours usually include a stopover at the untouched village of Kaleköy for a hike up the hill to the medieval Byzantine fortress of the Knights of St. John (entrance 5YTL/$4.35/£2) and a close-up of a row of sarcophagi, as well as idyllic views of the islands and bays. Sadly, these tours don't allow time for much more than that, making an all-too-hasty exit off this seaside village.

AREA BEACHES

At the end of the day in Kaş, you can collapse on a lounge at one of the cliff-side "beaches" to the southeast of town, where you're only a coral stone's throw away from a dip in some of the bluest and unspoiled waters this close to a major town. Küçükçakıl Beach ("small pebble beach") sits to the east of the marina, protected by an outcropping of rocks upon which a number of private establishments (mostly the hotels that front the coastline) provide beach lounges and umbrellas. The rocky coast forms a small inlet, into which crazy local kids dive off the low craggy rocks. Farther out about a half a mile (800m) is Büyükçakıl, or "large pebble" Beach, a small but amazing stretch of waterfront embraced and protected on three sides by low hills covered in Mediterranean brush. The beach is free and informal, but there are one or two basic facilities for showering and such, as well as lounge chairs for rent and a snack bar.

There's also the bay of **Limangazı** located on the other side of the bay and accessible only by boat. Ask a local fisherman or boat captain how much he's asking to take you there (and hopefully, back).

STAYING ACTIVE

PARAGLIDING   **Skysports,** Liman Sok. 10/A, Kaş (© **0242/836-3291;** www.skysports-turkey.com), the reputable provider of tandem flights off of Babadağ, over Ölüdeniz, runs an adjunct shop in Kaş, taking advantage of the 1,050m (3,445-ft.) summit Asaz Mountain. Pilots fly you off the ridge and over the sea, landing you safely at the marina in Kaş. A 20- to 30-minute flight (believe me, it's plenty of time) costs 100€ ($145/£71). **Bougainville Travel** (see "What to See & Do," above) recently joined the paragliding fold, with the agency's own professional tandem pilots.

SCUBA DIVING   The waters off Kaş have some of the best visibility in the Mediterranean and a wide variety of sea life. Sponge divers have been navigating these reefs for decades, and it was along the coast of Ulu Burun that a 14th-century-B.C. merchant shipwreck was discovered, now displayed in the Bodrum Underwater Archaeology Museum (p. 243). There are also several underwater caverns, of which the Mavi, near Kaputaş Beach, is most famous. Several dive outfitters with certified dive masters provide a gateway to the reefs, caves, and shipwrecks (there's even a plane wreck) for around 25€ ($36/£18), or 29€ ($42/£21) if you need to use their equipment. **Bougainville Travel** (see "What to See & Do," above) and **Barakuda Diving Center,** Hükümet Caddesi, on the hill above the harbor behind Mercan Restaurant (© **0242/836-2996;** www.barakuda-kas.de), are two of the more established agencies, while the combined team of Hakan and Rico at **Sirena Diving Center** at Doğruyol Cad. 35 (© **0242/836-3995;** www.sirenadive.com) has logged a combined 13,000 dives. All three offer much the same choices, while Barakuda also does wreck and deep-sea dives, technical dives, and nitrox dives. All can accommodate nondivers on their boats.

SEA KAYAKING   Sea kayaking offers a low-impact opportunity to experience the magical waters of the Gulf of Kekova, past partially submerged sarcophagi and over the sunken cities. The prohibition of swimming in the waters over these archaeological sites makes this sport a superb way to enjoy unhurried close-ups of the mysterious city walls, although admittedly, you'll need some imagination to visualize those vague underwater shadows. A kayak also allows you to navigate where large craft dare not go. The day trip (60YTL/$52/£24) is low-impact in either single or tandem kayaks, and sets off (after transferring from Kalkan and Kaş) from the docks at Üçağız. For information, contact **Bougainville Travel** (see "What to See & Do," above).

SHOPPING

Miles and miles of carpet shops, souvenir shops, and counterfeit sportswear have probably dulled your shopping instincts in Turkey, but Kaş restores the pleasures of dallying among unexpected treasures, long forgotten after your departure from Istanbul. The old wooden houses along the side streets house wonderful little one-of-a-kind boutiques selling new, old, and antique textiles, nautical tools and artifacts, locally designed silver and gold jewelry, copper, and of course carpets, *kilims,* and imported tribal goods. But however great the selection of inventory may be, you can be sure to expect equally monumental markups. Pity the poor arrival with a keen desire for a souvenir during a limited stopover, and no bargaining acumen. One good piece of news: It's illegal for shopkeepers to hassle you; one complaint and he/she could lose the store license.

WHERE TO STAY

True escapists of civilization have the option of lodging out on the Çukurbağ Peninsula (by car, enter Kaş's main road and turn right at the small roundabout right before the marina; all destinations on the loop road are under 5km/3 miles away), a sparsely populated collection of steep cliffs and terraced access to unspoiled waters. (Most of these hotels have been snapped up and blocked out by British-based tour operators, leaving but a handful of options for the independent traveler.) But without a car, it's undeniably more convenient to be located in the town center.

IN TOWN

Gardenia Hotel Rooms are unusually large at the Gardenia compared to other hotels in Kaş and enjoy the added benefit of stunning views of the Greek island of Meis. All have glass-front balconies so as to optimize the view. Actually, glass seems to be a running theme here; a chunky glass bathroom sink and console keep the bathroom both fresh looking and designer cool. Opt for the slight added cost of a front room with a view, or splurge for the suite, as it comes with its very own Jacuzzi. Breakfast and dinner are available to guests on the recently added dining terrace.

Hükümet Cad. 47, Küçükçakıl Mevkii, 07580 Kaş. (℃ 0242/836-2368. Fax 0242/836-1618. www.gardeniahotel-kas. com. 11 units. 130YTL–180YTL ($113–$157£52–£72) double; 255YTL ($222/£102) suite. MC, V. *In room:* A/C, satellite TV, wireless Internet, minibar, hair dryer, safe.

Hotel Club Phellos *(Kids)* Sitting on the top of the hill above the beach, Hotel Club Phellos is the best option for those looking for a full-service pseudo-resort experience. The central location makes it all the more appealing—with updated rooms that have either shower cabins or minitubs. It's all a bit formalized, but that's easy to forgive when you're perched poolside overlooking the Mediterranean or melting blissfully in the tiny yet lovely *hamam.* A bright blue waterslide spills your kids into the lower children's pool.

Doğruyol Sok. 4, Kaş. (℃ 0242/836-1953. Fax 0242/836-1890. www.hotelclubphellos.com.tr. 81 units. 80€ ($116/£57) double. MC, V. **Amenities:** Restaurant; 3 bars; outdoor swimming pool; game room; concierge; tour desk; car-rental desk; 24-hr. room service; laundry service; dry cleaning. *In room:* A/C, local TV.

Kale Otel *(Value)* This is an unexpected find: The Kale Otel offers the simple amenities of a pension in rooms that glisten. Its position on a dead-end on the hill above the ancient theater offers historical and sea views. A grassy terrace with lounges overlooking the sea makes for the perfect summertime snooze; in winter, the small sun porch offers a cozy alternative. This is also one of the recommended hotel kitchens in town, where lawn tables are set out front like a *biergarten*. Prices, however, will differ if you call speaking English as I did as opposed to Turkish for my Turkish friend.

Yenı Camii Mah., Amfitiyatro Sok. 8, Kaş. © 0242/836-4074. Fax 0242/836-2402. 26 units. May–Oct 65€–75€ ($94–$109/£46–£54) double. Rates lower in winter. No credit cards. **Amenities:** Restaurant; laundry service; dry cleaning. *In room:* A/C, no phone.

Medusa Hotel From the outside, this hotel is almost indistinguishable from the other cliff-top pensions lined up above Küçükçakıl Beach. But even though this was the first hotel to set up shop on this stretch of the beach it stays current with regular yearly renovations, in contrast to its neighbors. Like all of the hotels lining the shoreline at this end of Kaş's center, the reception is located up a long stone stairway, up past the level of the pool and restaurant. This positioning provides each of the rooms with a balcony and at least a partial sea view; reserve early and get a full view. There's an on-site restaurant, and the hotel offers the option of half-board from a buffet.

Küçükçakıl Mevkii, 07580 Kaş. © 0242/836-1440. Fax 0242/836-1441. www.medusahotels.com. 41 units. July–Sept 50€ ($73/£36) double; 85€ ($123/£61) suite. Rates lower off season. MC, V. Street parking only. **Amenities:** Restaurant; 2 bars; outdoor swimming pool; dive school; massage; laundry service; dry cleaning. *In room:* A/C, no phone.

ÇUKURBAĞ PENINSULA

Diva Residence Hotel ★★ Big stone fireplaces; unobstructed views of the Greek island of Meis; fresh, home-cooked meals. That's what you'll find at the Diva, an all-suite hotel owned and operated by a husband-and-wife team transplanted from Istanbul. Nine of the suites are spacious one-bedrooms, and the two-bedroom units can accommodate up to four. Both types have living rooms and balconies, while most (but not all) look out over an uncannily stunning view of the sea. Meals in the restaurant are served buffet style, but the kitchen will prepare special meals, including vegetarian ones, to complement the selection on the a la carte menu.

Çukurbağ Yarımadası on the Çukurbağ Peninsula, Ibrahim Cingay Sok., 07580 Kaş. © 0242/836-4255. Fax 0242/836-2509. www.divakas.com. 11 units. July–Aug 105€ ($152/£75) double, 130€ ($189/£93) family of 4. Rates lower off season. MC, V. **Amenities:** Restaurant; 3 bars; rock terrace beach; outdoor swimming pool; billiards; business center; Internet; laundry service; dry cleaning; safe; free parking. *In room:* A/C, minibar, hair dryer.

Otel Çapa ★★ *Finds* This hotel overlooks the Mediterranean from the rocky coast on the north side of the peninsula, in a serene and relaxing seafront setting enclosed in jasmine, bougainvillea, and olive and lemon trees. The grounds are terraced down toward the seafront patio, past a shaded hammock, a postcard-perfect saltwater freeform pool, a snack bar, and a fragrant thicket of low Mediterranean brush. The painted pink main building, swimming pool, rooms, and cozy open-air bar salon sit at the top.

Each room enjoys its very own balcony or terrace overlooking the pool area to the sea, keeping it breezy, light, and airy. Rooms, and bathrooms especially, are a bit on the smallish side, but the staff makes you feel like the entire property is all yours, and the result is anything but cramped. If you ever decide to leave the property, the hotel provides a shuttle to the center of Kaş (5YTL/$4.35/£2; taxis cost double) and tours to Kekova. Various motorized watersports are available for a modest fee.

Çukurbağ Yarımadası on the Çukurbağ Peninsula, 07580 Kaş. © 0242/836-3190. Fax 0242/836-3192. www.club capa.com. 22 units. $100–$120 (£50–£60) double. MC, V. Closed Nov–Mar. **Amenities:** Restaurant; 4 bars; rock terrace beach; 2 pools (1 saltwater); jet ski; boat rental; boat trips; mountain bikes; billiards; tour desk; car-rental desk; 24-hr. room service; laundry service; dry cleaning. *In room:* A/C.

WHERE TO DINE

At last count, Kaş was host to 75 restaurants, cafes, bars, and patisseries—but with the competition so steep, it's difficult to predict which ones will make it. Below is a short list. Meanwhile, some of the best meals in Kaş are prepared at your little hotel. Hotels and pensions that accept dinner reservations from nonguests are **Otel Çapa,** Çukurbağ Yarımadası (© **0242/836-3190**), offering a four- or five-course meal with table service; the **Diva Residence Hotel,** Çukurbağ Yarımadası (© **0242/836-4255**); and **Denizaltı,** also on the peninsula (© **0242/836-2741**), whose chef is formerly of Museedechanga in Istanbul. Expect to pay 25YTL to 50YTL ($22–$44/£10–£20) per person, particularly if you are ordering fish.

Bahçe and Bahçe Fish TURKISH   These two lovely gardens serve an abundant and traditional array of seafood and kebaps. The original Bahçe is famous for its mezes, while the newly opened annex across the road serves seriously good fish (and mezes, of course). Ask your waiter what's in season. The meze cases overflow with cold appetizers, such as stuffed mushrooms, vegetable pancakes, fish cakes, and *dolmalar*—flavorful stuffed grape leaves and stuffed peppers worthy of a meal in themselves, making either of these dining options a welcome alternative for vegetarians.

Anıt Mezar Karşısı 31 and Ilkokul Sok. Across from the Monumental Lycian tomb. © **0242/836-2370.** Reservations suggested. Appetizers and main courses 6YTL–14YTL ($5.20–$12/£2.40–£5.60). MC, V. Daily noon–midnight. Closed Nov–Mar.

Bi Lokma/Mama's Kitchen *Value Finds* HOMESTYLE TURKISH   The Turkish fare prepared at this little eatery is a popular draw for local diving instructors, hungry for the taste of Mom's cooking. The menu is nothing new here, but that's why everybody keeps coming back.

Hükümet Cad. 2 (on the road above the marina). © **0242/836-3942.** Appetizers and main courses 4YTL–9YTL ($3.50–$7.85/£1.60–£3.60). MC, V. Daily noon–10pm.

Chez Evi *Finds* FRENCH   This is the best meal you will have in Turkey, not only for the food, but also for the eccentricity of the chef. When Evy moved to Kaş and opened her own restaurant, it wasn't long before two ominous representatives of organized crime showed up. Evy wouldn't be intimidated and chased the two away by trashing her own bar. She's quite a rich character, and she manages to pour all of that passion into her food. Weather permitting, meals should be taken in the rear garden; if the temperature outside becomes too unbearable, opt for a table in the air-conditioned *şark* dining room surrounded by years' worth of her collectibles. The menu offers crepes and salads, and one mean chicken curry. Two of my favorite dishes are the *calmars à la Provençale* (calamari in a spicy tomato sauce) and the *filet de boeuf sauce champignons* (steak in a mushroom sauce). If you really want to ingratiate yourself, order the steak rare, because she hates to overcook a good piece of meat.

Telvı Sok. 4. © **0242/836-1253.** Reservations suggested (24-hr. advance reservation essential Nov–Mar). Main courses 25YTL–32YTL ($22–$28/£10–£13). MC, V. Daily 7pm–midnight.

Mercan TURKISH   This friendly and popular waterside restaurant also happens to be the oldest show in town; it dates back to 1956, when the owner's father did the cooking. Fish and meat dishes are staples on the traditional Turkish menu, but Mustafa (the son) has added his own special touch, creating fragrant dishes using local herbs. The Mercan Special—a split roast lamb marinated in wine and spices—is a tender and rare treat. Try the grilled swordfish kebap for a lighter, but no less filling or fulfilling, meal.

Cumhuriyet Meydanı on the marina. © 0242/836-1209. Reservations suggested. Appetizers and main courses 6YTL–16YTL ($5.20–$14/£2.40–£6.40) and up for fish. MC, V. Daily 9am–1am.

Pasha Cafe   In the center of town near the post office, tucked behind the counter of this cafe serving salads, sandwiches, and homemade sweets, is an authentic Italian espresso machine. Just visualize the swirl of milk down through the cracks between the ice cubes, and take a swig. If that's not enough to bring you by, perhaps one of their smoothies will. High tea reveals the part-British ownership of the cafe, but the relaxed atmosphere is all Mediterranean Turkish.

Öztürk Sok. © 0242/836-1389. May–Nov open daily 8am–midnight.

KAŞ AFTER DARK

Kaş takes on the glow of numerous golden lights strung throughout numerous gardens and candlelight flickering from many of the town's nooks and crannies. Keep in mind that the bars and cafes listed below are mostly closed in winter.

Café Merhaba   Catering to an international crowd, Café Merhaba is an atmospheric and cozy spot that would be inconspicuous in, say, SoHo. In Kaş, it stands out like a sore thumb, with its collection of international newspapers and magazines, in addition to the new and used paperbacks on sale. Their apple cake gets raves. Daily 8am to 1am. Closed in winter. Ibrahim Serin Cad. © 0242/836-1883.

Echo Café and Bar   Small-town partnerships often have short shelf lives, and Echo is one example. Owned by a former partner in Sun Café, Echo creates a niche by targeting the more sophisticated and groovy crowd (is that actually possible?). From one of the small balconies that look out over the harbor you can listen to a range of jazz (including some you may not like). May through October 11am to closing. Uzun Çarşı Cad., Gürsoy Sok. © 0242/836-2047.

Effendi Café and Bar   Live Turkish music emanates out of this former carpet storefront at the end of Hükümet Caddesi. The guitar and drum duet (plus vocals) is performed nightly by Özgür and Barış. There's also a terrace with views of the harbor. May through November daily 9am to closing. Cumhuriyet Meydanı 1 (at the end of Hükümet). © 0242/836-3775.

Hi Jazz Bar   It's "all jazz, all the time" at this small, bare, yet cozy bar; according to the owner, Yılmaz, the life of a New York City cab driver held no appeal, and off he went to New Orleans, where he hopped on the jazz trail. He's now here, greeting his clientele from his perch on one of the benches or small tables propped up next to the alleyway's stone wall. The music selection begins with soft jazz early in the evening and then progresses in the early hours into some hip-hop jazz. May through October 5pm to 3am. Zümrüt Sok. 3 (the st. next to Bougainville Travel). © 0242/836-1165.

Sun Café   Located across from Mercan near the marina, Sun Café is a must-do if only to toss back a drink or have a full meal next to the Lycian rock tomb at the back. The restaurant/bar is in a pavilion-type building close to the entrance, where the team of dashing, long-haired owners keep the drinks poured and the music subtle with on-and-off jazz nights. Daily 11am to 2am; closed in winter. Hükümet Cad. 3. © 0242/836-1053.

6 Demre

48km (30 miles) east of Kaş; 225km (140 miles) southwest of Antalya; 25km (16 miles) west of Finike

Taking a look around Demre—situated on a fertile coastal plain 5km (3 miles) inland from the Mediterranean Sea—it's hard to imagine a flabby, local 4th-century bishop making his rounds in 105°F (41°C) weather bundled up in a big red suit. After all, there were some lovely beaches nearby and not a mammal with antlers in sight. But somewhere during the 1,650 years that followed, several national folklores got mixed up, and legends merged that would elevate old St. Nicholas, the bishop of Myra, to the jolly international hero he is today.

The ancient city of Myra lies just on the outskirts of what is now the modern town of Demre, in a region known as Kale. (The names are sometimes used interchangeably, so this can get a bit confusing.) St. Nicholas served as bishop of Myra and earned himself a reputation of benevolence and good deeds by saving poor village girls from the fate of prostitution by dropping their dowries down the chimney. According to legend, he also rescued several village boys from the clutches of a serial killer disposed to pickling his victims in brine—but that shocking piece of history ruins the feel-good vibe altogether. The legends accumulate. Tour groups flock here for its kitsch value, while the Church of St. Nicholas continues to be a stopping-off point for religious pilgrims.

Unexpected is the **necropolis of Myra** ✹✹✹, located above the ancient site and hewn into the rock like a high-rise apartment complex for dead people. This collection of rock-cut Lycian tombs is one of the best-preserved and finest examples of its kind, as pale shades of fading pigment can still be made out against the fine details of the bas-reliefs.

Because the modern town of Demre is located inland, not many visitors stay here for longer than it takes to tour the necropolis and church. Hoping to change this trend, the local municipality has been investing in local development and preservation schemes. For now, it earns points for prettiness and charm, but still not enough to hold your interest for more than a few hours, including the area sites.

A LOOK AT THE PAST

There is not much historical evidence on Myra prior to the 1st century B.C. but rock inscriptions on the Lycian tombs date the city as far back as the 5th or 6th century B.C. We know that St. Paul visited Myra by sea on his way to Rome in A.D. 60, but Rome enters the picture officially in 42 B.C. when one of Brutus's Roman lieutenants demanded tributes for support of his civil war. The fertility of the delta and the natural protection of the river provided the city with the ingredients for thriving trade by sea, and the Romans eventually sailed past the defensive chain at the port of Andriake and, in typical style, settled into Myra permanently. The city flourished under the Pax Romana, and the fact that Emperor Germanicus and wife Agrippina paid a visit in A.D. 18 implies that this center was of major importance.

In 310, St. Nicholas was imprisoned by Diocletian for his efforts to spread Christianity but was released in 313 when Constantine ascended the throne and declared Christianity the official state religion. By the 4th century Myra had become an important Christian center for religious and administrative affairs, and with rumors spreading of the saintly Bishop Nicholas, the town gained in popularity.

They Kidnapped the Wrong Guy

In ancient times, up until the rule of Julius Caesar, pirates ran rampant in the Mediterranean and Aegean, costing empires huge sums by blocking trade routes and intercepting ships laden with riches. Even Julius Caesar had his own run-in with these sea bandits; he was captured off the coast of Miletus, on his way back from a trip to study rhetoric in Rhodes. When the pirates told Caesar that they planned on asking a ransom of 20 talents, Caesar balked and suggested 50 would be more appropriate to his stature.

In the 6 weeks that it took for the ransom to arrive from Miletus, Caesar cavorted with the pirates—joining in their games, practicing his rhetoric, and promising to have them all crucified when the time came. When the ransom arrived, the pirates kept their promise to release him. Caesar kept his as well; upon arriving in Miletus he assembled a number of galleys and surprised the pirates in their own lair. He had them all crucified, but ordered their throats cut first to spare them any unnecessary and vindictive suffering.

Subsequent years tell a story of Arab pirates, envious Italians coveting the sacred bones of the saint, and hidden treasure. In 7th-century pirate raids, a precious collection of liturgical gifts presented to the church by Justinian a century earlier was stolen, but was promptly reburied when the pirates in turn were attacked. In 1963, a local shepherd woman found the hoard while out with her goats; local smugglers got hold of a few pieces, which were eventually sold to the Dumbarton Oaks Museum at Harvard University for $1 million. Efforts to reunite the collection have been discussed between Harvard University and the Antalya Museum, but so far, the objects remain in Boston.

In 1087, hoping to redirect the flow of pilgrims back to their home, Italian merchants from Bari raided St. Nicholas's sarcophagus and transported the remains back to Italy. In their haste to get out with the goods, apparently the Barians left a few bones behind, and in 1925 the Turkish authorities were presented with a reliquary containing what was claimed to be the missing parts. Although carbon dating of the remains has proven that the bones date to the correct century, nobody knows if these are actually the bones of St. Nicholas, or where the poor guy is buried for sure. The Russians claim to have a piece of him, as does the Antalya Museum.

ESSENTIALS
GETTING THERE
BY BUS OR DOLMUŞ   Demre lies on the road that passes by the Gulf of Finike on its way around the coastline from Antalya. Minibuses and *dolmuşes* connect with Demre from Fethiye (3 hr.; 15YTL/$13/£6), Kaş (40 min.; 3YTL/$2.60/£1.20), and Finike (20–30 min.; 3YTL/$2.60£1.20) several times a day. There's also a daily connection to Üçağız, if you're headed to or from Kekova Island. Daily bus service is frequent in summer months, allowing for the spontaneity of simply showing up at the *dolmuş* stand (usually in the town center) when you're ready to go.

ORIENTATION

The Church of St. Nicholas lies smack dab in the middle of the pedestrian mall on Müze Caddesi. A turnoff onto Alakent Caddesi before the church leads to the entrance to Myra, about a mile and a half away.

Çayağzı Beach and the ancient harbor port of Andriake lie about 4km (2½ miles) to the west of the center.

GETTING AROUND

Although the necropolis of ancient Myra is only a little over a mile from the main square and easily walkable, the unrelenting heat will surely slow you down to the point where a meaningful exploration of the small site will be impossible. Do yourself a favor and take a taxi.

Dolmuşes do exist from the main square out to the beach, although you might melt while waiting for one to pass by.

WHAT TO SEE & DO
ANCIENT MYRA

Andriake & Çayağzı Beach   The port of Andriake at the mouth of Myra Creek (the Demre River) provided access to friendly merchant ships sailing up the river while the enclosed body of water protected Myra from direct attack by sea. Emperor Traian chose this harbor as a base for his expeditions to the East; it eventually fell into disuse as it silted up. The terrain can still be swampy in the spring and fall, making the area a bit challenging to explore during this time.

The ancient ruins straddle the river around what is now Çayağzı Beach, a sleepy fishing port and working boatyard. The main historical structure is Hadrian's Granary, built on the orders of the emperor as storage for grain prior to its delivery to Rome. The site includes a Roman bath supplied by a freshwater spring, and the remains of what was probably a basilica. There are a few fish stands and one restaurant from which you can enjoy wonderful sea and river views, or watch the local fishermen repair their boats.

4km (2½ miles) west of Demre center (*dolmuşes* run along Müze Cad.).

The Church of St. Nicholas (Aya Nicola Kilisesi) &   This church is an important mid–Byzantine era building, even though nothing of the original remains. The first temple on the site was built for the mother goddess Artemis, but collapsed in an earthquake in the 2nd century. A Byzantine church was built over the remains of this temple, but repeated raids and numerous earthquakes destroyed the church several times. The two domed chambers were part of a 5th- or 6th-century reconstruction and form the foundation for the domed church that was later built in the 9th century. The basilica on the site today is a 1789 reconstruction using materials that date to the 8th century, and some of the early frescoes are still visible. The honeycombed mosaic stones are originals and remain surprisingly intact, as do the domes forming the roof.

Speculation continues on which, if any, of the marble sarcophagi is the one belonging to St. Nicholas. We do know the date of his death and that his body was put in a Roman sarcophagus in the central apse on the south side of the church but was believed to have been moved after the Italian and Arab raids. The one in the west apse is believed to be that of the saint because of the reliefs of seagulls and fish scales (St. Nicholas is patron of sailors), but nobody knows anything for sure except that he's escaped to the North Pole.

Müze Cad. ℂ **0242/871-6543**. Admission 5YTL ($4.35/£2). Summer daily 8am–7pm; shorter hours in winter.

The Necropolis of Ancient Myra ★★★   Lycians believed that burying their dead high up would facilitate their rise to heaven. Until then, it seems that they expected the dead to spend some time on earth, as the tombs are carved to look like cozy old homes, complete with pediments, pillars, and support beams. Additional tombs are located to the west of the Roman theater, including the distinguishable carvings of a funerary rite decorating one tomb, known as the Painted Tomb.

The Roman theater, carved into the face of the mountain Greek-style, dates to 141 when it was rebuilt following an earthquake. The two vaults may have been added at this time for additional support against future tremors. Columns, capitals, and ill-fated theatrical heads scatter the grounds, fallen from gracing the facade of the stage.

2.4km (1½ miles) north of Müze Cad., off Alakent Cad. No phone. Admission 5YTL ($4.35/£2). Summer daily 8am–7pm; hours shorter in winter.

WHERE TO STAY

There's no reason to stay overnight in Demre, but if you get stuck, check into the **Hotel Andriake,** Finike Caddesi at the highway junction, about .8km (½ mile) south of the main square (© **0242/871-4642;** fax 0242/871-5440; www.hotelandriake.com). The hotel has the best accommodations in town at prices around 30YTL ($26/£12). You can also brave one of the pensions on the road into the marina (Andriake).

WHERE TO DINE

There are a number of restaurants on the main pedestrian street in front of the Church of St. Nick. There's really nothing special here, so if you can wait just a little longer, I'd suggest that you head down to the harbor and dine at one of the informal restaurants there, or take advantage of a roadside grill.

7 Antalya ★★

725km (450 miles) south of Istanbul; 467km (290 miles) southeast of Izmir; 298km (185 miles) northeast of Fethiye; 435km (270 miles) east of Marmaris; 634km (394 miles) southwest of Nevşehir

The city of Antalya is built on a rocky travertine plateau, formed by natural springs running down the Toros Mountains and surging off the cliffs, with the constant breathtaking silhouette of peaks and snowcaps in the distance. Meanwhile, the enormous and sun-kissed *region* of Antalya includes seaside towns well beyond the outstretched arms of the Gulf of Antalya, as far as Kaş to the west and Alanya to the east. And all along these stretches of **sandy shoreline** are more five-star, beachfront hotels than found in all of Spain.

But Antalya is much more than its beaches. Thanks to the local geological gifts that have left Antalya with rocky mountains, gushing waterfalls, soaring canyons, and lush gardens, visitors get to dive right into the **action:** Biking, hiking, cycling, canyoning, rafting, wreck diving, golfing, and even skiing are all just a stone's throw away. The city's Archaeological Museum is custodian to an incredible collection of *richesse* of antiquity collected in excavations at the nearby open-air museums of **Termessos, Aspendos,** and **Perge,** the latter two among the cities on the Anatolian Mediterranean that witnessed the arrival of St. Paul.

Only 30 years ago, Antalya was little more than a ramshackle fishing village huddled around a harbor backed by Roman and pre-Roman ruins and Byzantine ramparts. Then about 20 years ago, the trend in Turkey toward historic preservation began

Antalya

ATTRACTIONS ●
Antalya Museum **3**
Clock Tower **11**
Hadrian's Gate **13**
Hıdırlık Kulesi **18**
Iskele Mosque **7**
Mevlevihane **10**
Yivli Minare **12**

RESTAURANTS ◆
Gizli Bahçe **8**
Kral Sofrası **6**
Marina Restaurant **17**
Stella's Bistrot **20**

Beach 🏖 Information ⓘ Post Office ✉

HOTELS ■
Dedeman Antalya **5**
Atelya Pension **16**
Hillside Su **2**
Hotel Alp Paşa **15**
La Paloma Pansıon **19**
Maramara Antalya **5**
Marina Residence **17**
Ninova Pensiyon **14**
Sheraton Voyager **1**
Talya Oteli **4**
Tekeli Konakları **9**

to touch the historic quarter of **Kaleiçi,** a renaissance that has witnessed the conversion of a dusty and crumbling quarter into one of Ottoman grandeur, with timber framed manses embracing fragrant garden courtyards. But while the renewal of Kaleiçi helped to transform Antalya from the ugly duckling of the Mediterranean to its current magical Mediterranean appeal, the real show is by no means confined to the historic harbor. A renaissance has also taken root to the west of the historic city center over at **Konyaaltı,** an expansive pebbly strip of prime beachfront backed by a meandering, grassy promenade and "Beach Park," stocked full of diversions such as an aquarium, a children's playground, a paintball area, restaurants, cafes, and shops. It's this winning combination of sun, fun, cultural richness, and a conveniently located state-of-the-art international airport that has made Antalya the focal point of the Turkish Mediterranean.

ESSENTIALS
GETTING THERE
BY PLANE   As the gateway to the "Turkish Riviera," Antalya's international airport is a destination for visitors on both direct and connecting flights from dozens and dozens of cities worldwide. In 2007, the city completed a second international terminal to accommodate the continued tourist growth of the region as a whole. **Turkish Airlines** (© 444-0849; www.thy.com) and **British Airways** (© 0870/850-9850 in the U.K.; www.britishairways.com) inaugurated direct flights from London (Gatwick) to Antalya in June 2005 and April 2008, respectively. **Pegasus Airlines** (www.flypgs. com) and **SunExpress** (© 0232/444-0797 in Turkey; www.sunexpress.com.tr) soon followed suit, flying from London's Stansted Airport (summers only). The U.K.-based charter **Thomas Cook** (www.thomascookairlines.co.uk) flies year-round from London Gatwick direct to Antalya. Check with your travel agent to see about other charter flights on offer during the summer months.

Domestic service into Antalya is provided by **Turkish Airlines** (© 444-0849), **Onur Air** (© 0242/330-3432 in Antalya, or 0212/663-9176 in Istanbul), and **Atlasjet** (© 0216/444-3387; www.atlasjet.com.tr) all offering regular domestic connections between Istanbul and Antalya, and Ankara and Antalya. In summer **Fly Air** (© 444-4359; www.flyair.com.tr) resumes regular service to Antalya from Istanbul as well.

The airport is about 11km (6¾ miles) outside the city center on the road to Antalya. The **Havaş** airport shuttle (© 444-0487 or 0242/312-2956) runs round-the-clock service (approximately every 30 min.) through the city center on its way to the *otogar.* You can get off at either the Sheraton Hotel or the Turkish Airlines office on Cumhuriyet Caddesi, west of Kaleiçi. From there, you will probably need to take a taxi to your final, in-town destination. The fare is 9YTL ($7.85/£3.60).

A taxi directly from the airport to the center of town can cost anywhere from 25YTL ($22/£10) to 45YTL ($39/£18), depending on where you are staying. Nighttime rates are about 50% higher.

There are a number of car-rental windows in the domestic arrivals area, including **Europcar** (© 0242/330-3068). **Hertz** (© 0242/330-3848), **Sixt** (© 0242/330-3850), and **Budget** (© 0242/330-3326) have locations in the international terminal.

BY BUS   Antalya is a major transport hub, with 167 bus companies and 633 minibuses serving a total of 147 routes. The major bus lines serving Antalya with frequent service are Varan, Ulusöy, Kamıl Koç, Pamukkale, Uludağ, and Boss. Sample fares are: from Istanbul (12 hr.; 60YTL/$52/£24), Izmir (7–8 hr.; 35YTL/$30/£14), and Denizli (3–4½ hr.; 20YTL/$17/£8). For transport from the smaller towns along the coastline, you can hop on one of the frequent minibuses; Batı Antalya Tour is a good bet, arriving from Fethiye (21YTL/$18/£8.40), Kalkan (15YTL/$13/£6), Kaş (13YTL/$11/£5.20), and Demre (11YTL/$9.55/£4.40), to name just a few.

The dual-terminal **bus station** lies 4km (2½ miles) northwest of the town center on the highway to Burdur and is almost as user-friendly as the airport. An excruciatingly slow municipal bus is located outside the minibus/*dolmuş* terminal in front of the taxi stand, idling until its half-hourly departure. Tickets are cheap: 1YTL/87¢/40p, an amount I consider way too much for the trouble of meandering into the center of town. A taxi from the *otogar* to Kaleiçi costs around 25YTL to 35YTL ($22–$30/ £10–£14).

VISITOR INFORMATION

The **tourist information office** (© 0242/241-1747) is about a 10-minute walk west of Kaleiçi, on Cumhuriyet Caddesi, in the Özel Idare Işhanı shopping arcade right before the intersection of Anafartalar Caddesi. It's worth a visit for fliers and brochures on upcoming events. Or, save yourself a trip and pop into one of the many travel agencies lining the cobbled streets for the same information.

ORIENTATION

The city of Antalya is built upon a limestone travertine formed from the springs that run down from the mountains, so that the city meets the sea by way of breathtaking cliffs. At the center is the cliff-top fortress neighborhood of **Kaleiçi,** full of elegant garden cafes and charming ramshackle eateries, all built atop pre-Roman, Roman, and Byzantine foundations. Kaleiçi, the hassling to get you to empty your wallet notwithstanding, is a charming area of restored Greek houses, Italian villas, and Ottoman Paşa's residences, some converted into guesthouses and hotels along narrow winding streets. At the base of the cliff is the harbor and marina, built over an ancient Roman harbor and now the center of the city's resort nightlife.

About a mile and a half to the west of Kaleiçi is **Konyaaltı,** the pebbly beach beginning just west of the archaeological museum and extending (so far) for about 8km (5 miles). Development will continue up to the port, an extension that will simply put the icing on an already successful and crazily popular city/seaside resort destination. By day, beach umbrellas and lounges backed by cafes and green lawns are filled with sun-seekers; by night, the waterfront park gets strewn with oversize colored cushions and romantic lighting.

Beyond the inner city limits, Antalya spreads out to the mountainous winding roads that meander along the Lycian Coast to the west, and to the all-inclusive resort hotels along the sandy beaches sprawled out to the east, past the haphazard, poured-concrete blocks typical of Turkish towns. Clear waters and sandy coastlines also lie within walking distance of Kaleiçi, and most archaeological sites and natural phenomena are within an hour of town.

GETTING AROUND

The primarily pedestrian area around the old town and harbor is very compact, and you'll have very little need to venture far from here if this is where you're holing up for the night. The tourist information office and the archaeological museum are to the west of the city center, accessible either by tramway or about a 20-minute walk. From

Kaleiçi to Konyaaltı, it's about a 10YTL ($8.70/£4) unavoidably meandering taxi ride; it'll be cheaper on the way back because the one-way main avenue is now working in your favor.

BY TRAM   A tramway runs parallel to the coastline from the Antalya Museum to the neighborhoods east of Kaleiçi and is particularly convenient as a way to get from Kaleiçi to the museum, to Atatürk Parkı, and to Konyaaltı Beach. There's a hop-on point on Cumhuriyet Caddesi across from the clock tower, and the fare is 1YTL (87¢/40p).

BY CAR   A car in the region of Antalya is indispensable for a thorough exploration of the sights, sounds, and smells, but within the city itself, you may want to spend your energies doing something other than sitting in traffic and making sense of the one-way circuitous route through the center of town.

Although a car would be handy for a quick run to the museum, about a mile east of Kaleiçi, you'll be better off parking it and forgetting about it. The tram will take you practically door to door for 1YTL (87¢/40p) and no hassle.

All of the major companies have offices in Antalya, both at the airport (international and domestic terminals) and downtown. These include **Avis,** Fevzi Çakmak Cad. 30, in the Talya Hotel (✆ **0242/316-6148**); **Decar,** in the Dedeman Hotel (✆ **0242/ 247-0648**); and **Budget** (Gençlik Mah., Fevzi Çakmak Cad. 27/C; ✆ **0242/243-3006**).

BY TAXI   Because Kaleiçi is a walking district, a taxi is mostly useful for getting back and forth between the marina/Kaleiçi and the museum (Konyaaltı Beach, the Sheraton, and the Hillside Su are near the museum on the west side of town). Hiring a taxi is also an (albeit expensive) option for those unable or unwilling to rent wheels for day-tripping out of the city; because rates have gone through the roof and because they are quoted in a currency (the euro) that makes the dollar look like a weakling, I don't recommend this option. A tour to all of the nearby attractions will be your best bet, at this point.

FAST FACTS: Antalya

Airlines The local numbers for the main airlines are: **Turkish Airlines** (✆ **0242/ 243-4383**), **Pegasus** (✆ **0242/330-3193**), **Onur Air** (✆ **0242/330-3790**), **SunExpress** (✆ **0242/310-2727**), **Atlasjet** (✆ **0242/330-3900**), **Fly Air** (✆ **0242/248-9406**). **British Airways** does not have a local agent but can be reached in Istanbul at ✆ **0212/317-6600**.

Airport For information on departures and arrivals call your airline direct. For general airport information, the number of International Terminal 1 is ✆ **0242/ 330-3600**; International Terminal 2 is at ✆ **0242/310-5500**. The tourist information bureau at the airport may also be of some help (✆ **0242/330-3600**, ext. 1163).

Ambulance Call ✆ **112**.

Climate Antalya has four seasons: fall, winter, spring, and hell, when temperatures soar to digits even the government won't accurately report. (Everybody gets the day off when the mercury passes 104°F/40°C.) Humidity can sometimes reach into the triple digits as well.

Consulates The **U.K.** has a Vice Consulate at Fevzi Çakmak Cad. 1314, Sok. 6/8, Elif Apt. (℃ **0242/244-5313**).

Festivals Antalya hosts the **eminent Golden Orange Film Festival** in October. The Aspendos Theatre is reanimated under a moonlit sky in July, during the **International Opera and Ballet Festival.** For information on the festival schedule, tickets, or transportation, contact the **Antalya Devlet Opera ve Balesi** (℃ **0242/243-7640**; fax 0242/243-8827; www.dobgm.gov.tr) or Antalya Festivals (℃ **0242/238-2776**; www.antalyafestivals.org).

Hospitals The Antalya Private Hospital (℃ **0242/335-0000**) is at Bayindir Mahallesi 325 Sok. 8. You will also encounter English-speaking staff at the Antalya International Hospital at Kızıltoprak Mah., Meydan PTT Arkası (near the post office), ℃ **0242/311-1500** or 1501.

Post Office The PTT is open from 9am to 5pm for postal services and 24/7 for phone access. The nearest office is at the yacht harbor, on Güllük Caddesi (℃ **0242/241-5300** or 241-5381).

WHAT TO SEE & DO
A LOOK AT THE PAST
Indigenous tribes were combating the scorching heat on the rocky coastline of Antalya since prehistoric times, until eventually the Hittites migrated off the harsh Anatolian plains in search of a more gracious climate. The Hittites were succeeded by a number of independent city-states founded in the region, and today's province of Antalya covers Pamphylia and parts of Pisidya to the north, Cicilia to the east, and Lycia to the west.

Antalya officially enters the history books in the 2nd century B.C. when King Attalus II marched in to pick up the pieces of the territorial war that broke out after the death of Alexander the Great. The city was proclaimed Attaleia after the Pergamese king, later morphing into variations of Adalia, Satalia, Adalya, and Antalya by successive cultures. The city was handed over to Rome along with the rest of Pergamum, and one of the more important events in the history of the Roman city was the arrival of Emperor Hadrian, whose visit was honored with a grand monumental gate.

Sovereignty over the region passed from the Byzantines to the Selçuks and back again, and in 1103, the port became a valuable asset to the Crusaders, allowing them to avoid the treacherous overland journey from Palestine. The decline of Byzantine influence allowed the Selçuk Sultanate of Rum to annex the region around 1207 until Antalya was finally incorporated into the Ottoman Empire.

A MONUMENTAL MUSEUM
Antalya Museum (Antalya Müzesi) 𝕏𝕏𝕏   If you do only one cultural thing in Antalya, make it this. Antalya province is endowed with one of the richest cultural heritages in Turkey, and much of it can be seen at this museum. More than 5,000 archaeological works are displayed in 14 thought-provoking exhibit halls. The **Prehistory section** 𝕏𝕏𝕏 includes an amazing collection of artifacts recovered from the

Karain Cave at Burdur—the largest inhabited cave in Turkey, with findings dating back 50,000 years and representing the Paleolithic, Mesolithic, Neolithic, Chalcolithic, and Bronze ages. The **Gallery of the Gods** ✿✿✿ gives you the chance to walk among the protagonists of classic mythology, through grand statues of Zeus, Apollo, Athena, **Aphrodite** ✿, and the like, followed by statues of the emperor/gods Hadrian and Traian in the Roman Room. The **Sarcophagus Gallery** ✿✿ is a rich exhibition of intricately carved tombs, one of which was considerably returned by the J. Paul Getty Museum, after having found its way out of the country. There are also small but important exhibitions featuring the **Byzantine period,** which houses a collection of **religious icons,** and the **Selçuk and Ottoman periods,** where you'll find ceramic artifacts, calligraphy, copper, carvings, and carpets. The Antalya Museum devotes an entire room to coins; the chronological display represents 2,500 years of Anatolian history. Considering that this is such a rich collection, it's positively mind-boggling to realize that 25,000 to 30,000 artifacts are buried in storage.

About 1.6km (1 mile) to the west of town on Kenan Evren Bulv. ℂ 0242/241-4528. Admission 10YTL ($8.70/£4). Tues–Sun 9am–6pm. No large bags or backpacks allowed inside museum.

ANTALYA ATTRACTIONS

The most outstanding monument in Antalya is **Hadrian's Gate (Hadrian Kapısı)** ✿✿, halfway between Cumhuriyet Caddesi and 30 Agustos Cad., built in honor of the emperor's visit to the city in A.D. 130. A classic example of a Roman triumphal arch, Hadrian's Gate is the only remaining entrance gate into the ancient city, and a great introduction to the neighborhood of Kaleiçi.

A few steps north following Imaret Sokağı is the **Yivli Minare** ✿, built by the Selçuk Sultan Alaaeddin Keykubat in the 13th century. The fluted brick minaret stands a commanding 38m (125 ft.) high and has come to be the symbol of the city. The adjacent domed mosque (not the original) is an early example of Anatolian multidomed mosques. A small and charming cluster of souvenir stands has sprouted up in the courtyard and is at least a refreshing break from the relentless touts on the street.

The **Clock Tower (Saat Kulesi)** ✿ in nearby Kalekapısı Square rises above the outer reaches of Kaleiçi at Atatürk Caddesi and was once a part of the old city fortifications.

Past the Clock Tower, following Atatürk Caddesi, is one of the remaining outer towers of the city fortifications, standing over 15m (49 ft.) high. Just past the tower to the left is a gracefully curving building of the former **Mevlevihane,** in use today as an art gallery (Güzel Sanatlar Gelerısı; no phone; free admission) whose stark and serene interior is worth a quick detour.

At the opposite end of the quarter of Kaleiçi and dominating the edges of the cliff is the 2nd-century **Hıdırlık Kulesi** ✿. Also known as the Red Tower, the Hıdırlık Kulesi offers unobstructed panoramas of the sea, suggesting its original use as a lighthouse.

At the bottom of the stone steps leading down from Memerli Sokağı to the harbor is the **Iskele Mosque,** a simple stone structure set on four pillars over a spring. Unfortunately, the description lends more appeal to the site than the actual thing, because careless visitors have been using the small pool as a garbage dump.

The **Kaleiçi Museum,** Barbaros Mahallesi Kocatepe Sok. 25, Kaleiçi (ℂ **0242/243-4274**), takes up two buildings restored between 1993 and 1995: one a former Orthodox church, the other a traditional Turkish house. The house contains an ethnological exhibit, while the former church, built in 1863 in the name of Agios Georgios, contains different cultural and art works from the Suna-Inan Kıraç collection. The museum also sponsors a Research Institute on Mediterranean Civilizations.

CITIES OF ANTIQUITY

The Ancient City of Aspendos The city of Aspendos, commonly believed to have been settled by colonists from Argos, lies a few miles beyond Perge on the Antalya-Alanya highway. I suggest that you tackle both as a pair.

There's not much left of the ancient city, but the one remaining monument, the **Theatre of Aspendos** ⭑⭑⭑, is enough to warrant a trip. Thanks to the high-quality calcareous stone and the fact that the Selçuks reinforced the structure during its run as a caravansary, this 2,000-year-old theater is the best-preserved ancient theater in Asia Minor and the best example of a Roman theater in all of Pamphylia. The best way to visit the theater is to see it as it was meant to be, during the national opera and ballet festival in the summer (see "Fast Facts: Antalya," for info), but it's an awesome sight without the show.

Take the Antalya-Alanya hwy. east; watch for the turnoff to Aspendos on the left. ℂ 0242/735-7038. Summer daily 8am–7pm; hours shorter in winter. Admission 10YTL ($8.70/£4).

The Ancient City of Perge Three thousand years away and 11 miles east of Antalya is the ancient Pamphylian settlement of **Perge.** A clay tablet discovered in the Hittite capital of Hattuşaş shows that Perge was originally settled around 1500 B.C. under the name of "Parha." St. Paul and Barnabas came to Perge on their first missionary journey, but St. Paul preached here only upon his return from Pisidia.

The ancient city's ruins were damaged in the early 1920s when area builders treated it like the local quarry, but the city remains an impressive site. The stadium, one of the best-preserved ones of the ancient world, extends to almost 1,000 with an original capacity of around 12,000 people. It's now a modest showcase for carvings from around the city. Some finely carved marble reliefs are visible in the Greco-Roman theater, where spectacular views of the plain provide a good overview of the lower city.

Take the Antalya-Alanya hwy. east; watch for the turnoff to Perge on the left. ℂ 0242/426-2047. Summer daily 8am–7pm; hours shorter in winter. 10YTL ($8.70/£4).

AREA BEACHES

A favorite beach destination for residents of Antalya is **Konyaaltı** ⭑⭑⭑, a long stretch of pristine pebble beach backed by a meandering promenade chock-full of activities, including playgrounds and **Aqualand,** Antalya's largest water park. Kids will particularly enjoy **Dolphinland,** where for 15YTL ($13/£6) per person you can smile in wonder along with your little ones, and for an extra 75YTL ($65/£30) you can swim with the dolphins. The whole complex has been dubbed **Antalya Beach Park;** at press time, it featured 10 beach "clubs"—swaths of waterfront brightly equipped with lounges and umbrellas, and serviced by cafes, restaurants, changing cabins, and showers. Beach admission fees vary from about 4YTL to 10YTL ($3.50–$8.70/£1.60–£4) per day and include use of the facilities. Most of the beach establishments have a watersports center, with jet skis for rent by the quarter-hour, parasailing, ringo rides, water-skiing, kayaks, sea bikes, and windsurfing, to name a few. As the sun sets, beach clubs morph into stylish outdoor nightclubs, providing cushions and lounges for lots of posing and draping, and an atmosphere of high style and frivolity. Main access to the beach is down a switchback road between the archaeological museum and the park; pedestrians can enter via a series of steps and bridges behind the Sheraton Hotel or through the Hillside Su.

The sparse and sandy **Lara Beach** stretches along the coast in the opposite direction, a little over 11km (6¾ miles) east of downtown. Minibuses (nos. 18, 30, or 77) pass along the beachfront after about a half-hour or 45-minute ride. But however lovely the long stretches of sand that extend the length of Lara, it's a bit of a stretch for me to tell you to go there, given the convenience and appeal of Konyaaltı. Unless, of course, your itinerary coincides with Antalya's newly inaugurated (in 2007 it just completed its second installment) **Sand Sculpture Exhibition.** A fantasy of artistic caprice, the first exhibition took place at Lara, the second at Konyaaltı, with both lasting from late June through September. The theme in 2007 was "Arabian Nights," and it's the best thing you can lay your eyes on before the tide comes in.

Freshwater springs gushing off the mountains have found several awe-inspiring outlets in and around Antalya—a great place for a bracing, high-pressure shower. Located below Mermerli Park at the eastern end of Kaleiçi is **Memerli Plaj** ℜ (entrance through the Memerli Restaurant), a miniature beach backed by the ancient sea walls. An icy spring shoots out of the rock at the end of the beach, but the narrow sandy strip is a bit unkempt and crowded. With a little more time, you'll do better to head over to the **Lower Düden Waterfalls** ℜ, on the road to Lara Beach, where the waters plunge straight into the sea. Alternately, go an additional 13km (8 miles) to the **Upper Düden Waterfalls** ℜ, unique because you can walk behind the cascade.

Heading west by car, Antalya's sprawl dissipates and small beaches and clusters of resort hotels dot the coastal road. The planned resort village of **Kemer,** 43km (27 miles) later, takes advantage of aquamarine calm waters backed by craggy mountainous cliffs, as waves lap through the pebbles creating a relaxing munching sound. The narrow beach is equipped with lounges and umbrellas, and the overpriced shopping strip stocks enough cash registers to keep you busy after sunning.

Just 14km (8¾ miles) farther west is the ancient port city of **Phaselis** ℜℜℜ (daily summer 8am–6pm; winter 8am–4pm), nestled amid the pine trees on the edge of three pristine and scenic bays. Plan to spend the day (entrance fee 5YTL/$4.35/£2) to wade in the waters and wander through the main streets, agoras, baths, and temples of this enchanting ancient city.

The amazing caves and waterfalls around Antalya are accessible on 2-, 4-, or 6-hour **boat excursions** ℜ; crews begin hawking the next day's tours early in the evening, or you can show up at the last minute for a boat that's about to disembark. Longer tours make trips to nearby beaches and may include a guided tour of the lovely and pine-shaded ancient harbor city of Phaselis. Not all boats are created equal, though; if it's quiet you're after, ask if the crew will be blasting music all day.

STAYING ACTIVE

DIVING   In addition to a wide variety of colorful plant and sea life, the Gulf of Antalya is also a graveyard for several unlucky World War II fighter planes and at least one groundbreaking shipwreck. Maybe the *Meltem,* the winds that blow in from the Caucuses, or the rocky coastline have something to do with it, but the results are some of the most fascinating dive sites along the coast. Dive concessions are on-site at all the major hotels and resorts all up and down the region's coastline. You don't have to be a guest to sign up but a day's notice is generally necessary. **Yunus Diving,** now located within the Beach Park on Konyaaltı Beach (© **0242/238-4486** or 241-9204), offers a 2-hour discovery dive, 2-hour licensed dives, and wreck dives starting from around 40YTL ($35/£16; not including equipment rental but including the oxygen tank).

GOLF A relatively new phenomenon in Turkey, the game of golf is now catching like wildfire. Officials expect to double the number of courses by 2008 to 21, up from 11 in 2005 (three are in Istanbul and the remainder are in Antalya). Several clubs have created their very own sweet spot along the shores east of Antalya, in the secluded hills of Belek. To get to any of these, take the Antalya highway east and watch for signs for Belek on the right. All of the clubs and resorts are clearly signposted. You can book in advance by contacting the golf clubs individually, or by booking (often at a discount) through **www.bookyourgolf.net**. Book Your Golf also has a comprehensive listing, with descriptions of the courses, on its site. (*Note:* Keep your eyes peeled for the opening of **LykiaLinks,** Turkey's first seaside golf course to open in the region of Antalya, in September 2008 [www.lykiagroup.com]).

The most popular of the Antalya courses is the PGA Sultan Course at the **Antalya Golf Club,** in Belek (© **0242/725-5970;** www.antalyagolfclub.com.tr)—a par-71, 450 yd "challenge" designed by European Golf Design and David Jones. Greens fees range from 70YTL to 90YTL ($61–$78/£28–£36), depending on the season. Golfers under 16 play for 50% off.

The **Gloria Golf Club** (© **0242/715-1520**) was the first and only resort to have its very own golf course. Michel Gayon is responsible for the design of two 18-hole championship courses; there's also a 3-hole practice course for beginners. Greens fees start at £30 ($60).

The 27-hole Nick Faldo Course at **Cornelia Golf Club** (© **0242/710-1600;** www.corneliagolfresort.com) opened in 2006. It's got a dune ridge running through the course, and there are three different 18-hole combinations. Greens fees range from 59€ to 99€ ($86–$144/£42–£71), depending on the season.

The golf-obsessed may also want to check into the **Kempinski Hotel The Dome** (Uckumtepesi Mevkii, Belek; © 0242/710-1300; www.kempinski-antalya.com), sister property to the esteemed Çirağan Palace in Istanbul. It's a palatial retreat with two **PGA-endorsed courses,** and plenty of luxurious tidbits (including a ridiculously decadent spa, beach, and kids' club) for non-golfing companions.

HIKING/CAMPING Kate Clow, a British woman based in Antalya, turned a labor of love into a hiker's dream. She's mapped and marked a comprehensive network of ancient dirt roads and blissfully solitary footpaths. The first long-distance trail, called the **Lykia Yolu (Lycian Way)** 👣👣👣, connects Antalya and Fethiye; Kate has created a companion guide to go along with it (see "Recommended Books & Films," in chapter 2). The second network of trails begins along the coast around Antalya and heads over the Toros Mountains into the Lakeland around Eğirdir and on up to Antioch in Pisidia, in some cases trodding the ancient Roman roads used by St. Paul on his missionary journeys through Asia Minor. For more on the trails or for information on trekking trips, log on to **www.lycianway.com** or **www.stpaultrail.com**. If you want to rough it just a little less, Medraft Turizm, Yeşilbahçe Mahallesi Portakal Çiçeği Bulvarı, Hüseyin Kuzu Apt. 14/3, Antalya (© **0242/312-5770;** www.medraft.com), runs 3-day jeep "safaris" up into the Toros Mountains above Antalya, with overnights in their own mountain lodge. The price per person, all inclusive, is $550 (£275).

KAYAKING/RAFTING The mountainous geography and numerous rivers in the Antalya region create exhilarating white-water rafting appropriate to all levels. The Manavgat River flows through a series of lengthy gorges, but the grades 4 and 5 rapids are accessible to experienced paddlers only.

A Trip to the Mountaintop

Antalya beckons with that rare experience where it's possible to choose between a beach tan or the ski slopes. To make this even more of a reality, in 2006 Turkey inaugurated the new Tahtalı cable car, which cuts a vertical b-line from the resort of Tekirova (near Kemer) up to the summit of **Tahtalı Dağ,** 2,363m (7,753 ft.) above sea level. In 2007, the summit restaurant opened, but it'll take a bit longer before the ski slopes are complete (construction began in April 2008). So for now, the cable car's the thing, along with the breathtaking vistas that open up to passengers of the cable car during the almost 10-minute ride up the mountain—itself a protected area. The cable car runs every half-hour in both directions from April through October, hourly in winter. The cost round-trip is 40YTL ($35/£16) per person.

The Köprü River, located halfway between Antalya and Side with Grade 1 and Grade 3 rapids, is no less breathtaking but a bit more suitable to beginners. This is an ideal family day out, even if you have no experience whatsoever. **Medraft Turizm,** Yeşilbahçe Mahallesi Portakal Çiçeği Bulvarı, Hüseyin Kuzu Apt. 14/3, Antalya (© **0242/312-5770;** www.medraft.com), organizes day trips for all levels, with top professional and experienced guides, from $50 (£25) per person per day, including transfer, a full day on the water, and lunch.

WHERE TO STAY

Antalya is synonymous with sun and fun, and the holiday villages just couldn't resist the sandy beaches and plains ripe for development at the foot of the Toros Mountains. Several luxury four- and five-star playgrounds dot the coastline outward from Antalya's historic Kaleiçi area and marina, while miles and miles farther out, the several become literally *hundreds.* If what you're after is an all-inclusive resort that you never have to leave, a better option is to seek out one of the holiday villages in the newly popularized seaside stretches of Kemer and Belek, both about a half-hour to an hour's drive from Antalya. The advantages of staying farther out are mostly a matter of seclusion, as these properties tend to take up long stretches of privatized sandy beaches and hold you captive. A good compromise is in the four- and five-star hotels perched on the cliffs just outside of the city's nucleus. For those sitting on the fence, the arrival of Konyaaltı's Antalya Beach Park, backed by several full-service five-star hotels, brings new meaning to the idea of a well-rounded Mediterranean holiday.

More attuned to the desires of the independent traveler are the hotels and pensions of Antalya proper, most notably in Kaleiçi, where hotels are housed in typical restored Ottoman homes of timber or stone. The traditional Ottoman house is built around a front and rear courtyard, so that all of these hotels have at least a pool of cozy dimensions and often a serene and fragrant garden. You can also access the beach easily from Kaleiçi, or walk down the steep streets and/or steps to the harbor and hop on a day boat.

ANTALYA HOLIDAY RESORTS

Dedeman Antalya 🎿 (Kids)   The Dedeman is nothing you'd expect from a luxury hotel. It vibrates with activity and is a perfect choice for families. Rooms are decently sized but nothing special—the usual inoffensive tones, all-purpose carpeting, and wood furniture accents. One of the main attractions is the **Aquapark,** a seaside wonderland of 15 waterslides, two river rides, and a wave pool. The park is free to hotel guests and also offers restaurants, cafeterias, a swimming pool, and lounges.

On the edge of the property at the bottom of the cliff is a small natural beach area, with some of the cleanest water in the city center. If you're headed off to a day of white-water rafting or deep-sea diving, the hotel provides the services of a nursery for kids up to 6 years old (for a fee). Another big plus is that the Dedeman offers extremely competitive rates to local agents that can trickle down to you. Rooms were renovated and modernized in 2000 and remain immaculate.

Lara Yolu, 07100 Antalya. (C) 0242/321-3930. Fax 0242/321-3873. www.dedemanhotels.com. 482 units. 55€–65€ ($80–$94/£39–£46) double; 75€–115€ ($109–$167/£54–£82) suite. AE, DC, MC, V. **Amenities:** 5 restaurants; 4 bars; disco; 2 swimming pools (Olympic-size outdoor, indoor); water sports facilities; dive school; tennis courts; health club and spa; Turkish bath; Jacuzzi; sauna; extensive land and watersports; children's center; playground; water park; game room; bowling alley; concierge; tour desk; car-rental desk; meeting facilities; shopping arcade; salon; 24-hr. room service; massage; babysitting; laundry service; dry cleaning; nonsmoking rooms. *In room:* A/C, satellite TV, minibar, hair dryer, safe.

Hillside Su ★★★ (Finds)   The glorious Hillside Su manages to be both futuristic and retro at the same time. Large glass sliding doors open onto an atrium lobby and lounge where four massive disco balls dangle from the ceiling. Get the idea? The Hillside Su is the most fashion-conscious beach club on the strip, offering guests the graciousness of an array of stylish day beds and lounges, taking a page from the Delano in Miami Beach. Oh, and did I forget to mention that everything is white? Whitewashed floors, whitewashed walls, white linens and towels, white terry-cloth covers for everything. The whiteness of the hotel is offset by little accents of red: red (okay, orange) goldfish, red (or white) bedside tower lamps, and red lava lamps. Rooms are gracious in size, sporting king-size beds, a spacious sitting area with day bed, and twin ottomans. Every room has a balcony furnished with yet another bed; avoid the scorching heat of August and you just might spend the night alfresco. Bathrooms are industrial/functional, with a blocky half-exposed shower space (also constructed of cement) and bulky designer fixtures. Outside, the Hillside boasts a 53m (174-ft.) uncommonly narrow and exceptionally wonderful teak-decked swimming pool, flanked on two sides by a stylish double row of ground-level beds shaded by bamboo umbrellas. Beyond the second row of beds begin the lawns, which convert to a high-quality and reasonably priced fish restaurant by candlelight. Overall, the wonderful pretentiousness is mitigated by a disarmingly congenial and professional staff, and while the spare minimalism may be disarming to some, I found its clever and kitschy style to be simply enchanting.

Konyaaltı Cad., 07050 Antalya. (C) 0242/249-0700. Fax 0242/249-0707. www.hillside.com.tr. 294 units. 436€ ($632/£311) garden-view double; 534€ ($774/£381) sea-view double; 557€–837€ ($808–$1,214/£398–£598) suite. AE, MC, V. Free parking on-site. **Amenities:** 6 restaurants (including sushi bar); 4 bars (including fitness bar); indoor and outdoor swimming pools; 2 tennis courts; health club; squash; Turkish bath; Balinese spa; Jacuzzi; sauna; watersports; rentals (bike, moped, and scooter); excellent children's playground w/separate kiddy pool; concierge; tour desk; car-rental desk; business center w/free Internet access; shopping arcade; salon; 24-hr. room service; babysitting; laundry service; dry cleaning; nonsmoking rooms. *In room:* A/C, interactive satellite TV, dataport, minibar, hair dryer, safe, toiletries bar.

Marmara Antalya ★★★   The newest addition to the Marmara family of deluxe hotels sits atop the Falez Cliffs above the Gulf of Antalya, only 5km (3 miles) from the historic center on the Lara Beach side of the bay. The thing you want to do here is score one of the 24 rooms in the "revolving loft," an ingenious feat of engineering (the building actually floats) providing a constantly changing panorama of city, sea, and mountains. Unless you have an underwater room, that is. And thanks to the placement of furniture in the rooms, you can even enjoy the view while relaxing in the in-room bathtub. Another unique feature (gimmick?) is the "river runs through it" concept to the swimming pool and grounds, a 270m (886-ft.) canal that permits kayaking through the property. In designing the interior of the hotel, Christian Allart has created a user-friendly community space that can best be described as eclectic: a mix of beach, Bali, Provence, and ancient Egypt. There's pretty much something for everyone here.

Sirinyalı Mah. Eski Lara Cad. 136, 07160 Antalya. © **0242/249-3600.** Fax 0242/292-3318. www.themarmara hotels.com. 232 units. 179€ ($260/£128) double (add 19€/$28/£14 for sea view); 234€ ($339/£167) suite. Rates lower off season. AE, MC, V. **Amenities:** Fusion buffet-style restaurant; 4 cafe-bars; beach; indoor and outdoor swimming pools; 2 tennis courts; health club; wellness center and spa; Turkish bath; Jacuzzi; sauna; watersports; rentals (bike, moped, and scooter); concierge; tour desk; car-rental desk; business center; meeting facilities; wireless Internet; shopping arcade; salon; 24-hr. room service; babysitting; laundry service; dry cleaning; nonsmoking rooms. *In room:* A/C, cable TV, dataport, minibar, hair dryer, safe.

Sheraton Voyager 🏵🏵 *(Kids)*   The beautiful landscaped gardens and luxurious brooks that snake through the property make up for the fact that the Sheraton Voyager looks like a giant concrete seagull. But it's exactly these outstretched wings embracing the property that give 80% of the rooms panoramic sea and mountain views. And every unit has a balcony from which to enjoy them. The property is perched on the cliff top, separated from the sea by a lovely shaded public park and a pedestrian bridge that provides quick, and steep, access down to the beach. (If you don't want to walk, the hotel also provides free shuttles to the beach via the access roadway.) Room decor is homogenous, but the details—like large rooms, interactive TV and messaging system, bathrobes, slippers, and bathroom goodies—more than make up for the blandness. The outdoor swimming pool is one of the largest in the area, with two levels and a water cascade completely surrounded by palm trees. The "wellness center" offers the health- and beauty-conscious a number of sybaritic reasons to stay here.

100 Yil Bulv. © **800/325-3535** in the U.S., or 0242/238-5555. Fax 0242/243-2462. www.sheraton.com/voyager. 395 units. $175–$225 (£88–£113) double; $245 (£123) and up suite. Check website for special offers. Rates lower off season. AE, DC, MC, V. Free parking on-site. **Amenities:** 3 restaurants; 3 bars; (heated) indoor and outdoor swimming pools; adjacent golf course; lit tennis courts; health club; spa; Jacuzzi; sauna; steam room; extensive watersports; children's playground; game room; concierge; tour desk; car-rental desk; business center; meeting facilities; shopping arcade; salon; 24-hr. room service; massage; babysitting; laundry service; dry cleaning; nonsmoking rooms; executive floor. *In room:* A/C, satellite TV, dataport, minibar, hair dryer, safe.

Talya Oteli 🏵🏵   The four-star Talya Hotel, recently added to the Divan portfolio, has the comfort and character of a smaller hotel with the elegance and amenities of a five-star establishment. A six-story cement wedge, the Talya is designed in such a way that every room enjoys a balcony and direct sea views. You may never have your back to the window, but the view on the inside is of immaculate and tastefully decorated— some even sunken—rooms. An outdoor pool, splendidly heated in the mild winter months, rests atop the cliff overlooking the sea. Steps down the cliff side is the hotel's private "beach." The fitness center, accessible past a popular Internet cafe, is one of the nicest I've seen, with a Jacuzzi, tanning salon, and fabulous Turkish bath (free to guests) designed with tile and wooden benches. If you really want to pamper yourself, reserve one of the 10 bungalow-style suite rooms down on the cliff.

Fevzi Cakmak Cad. 30, 07100 Antalya. ℭ **0242/248-6800.** Fax 0242/241-5400. www.divan.com.tr. 204 units. 110€–140€ ($160–$203/£79–£100) double. AE, DC, MC, V. **Amenities:** 4 restaurants; 5 bars; outdoor swimming pool; tennis courts; health club; beautifully tiled Turkish bath; Jacuzzi; sauna; watersports; concierge; tour desk; car-rental desk; shopping arcade; salon; 24-hr. room service; massage; babysitting; laundry service; dry cleaning. *In room:* A/C, satellite TV, minibar, hair dryer, safe.

KALEIÇI

Alp Paşa   Some of the feedback I've gotten about this boutique hotel points to inhospitable management, but it's also true that complainers tend to give more feedback than happy campers. It's your call. A former merchant's inn restored from two 18th- and 19th-century *konaks,* I include this hotel as a shining example of sensitivity in historic preservation. It features wooden arches, carved ceilings, and massive fortresslike doors rescued from the original structures. Some of the more regal units have stained-glass windows and sea views, while all of the rooms, each one with its own special character, have elegant, even flamboyant, decor. Room categories are divided among standard, deluxe, and special, the last all equipped with Jacuzzis. The standards are somewhat minuscule and disappointing when held up against the higher-level units, so you may want to upgrade if your budget allows. The main drawback to staying at the Alp Paşa is the claustrophobic pool area, squashed into the entrance courtyard and surrounded by sun lounges that are just a bit too close for comfort. The entire courtyard area must be vacated to prepare for the nightly buffet dinners, so if late-afternoon poolside snoozes are an important part of your holiday, you may want to stay elsewhere.

Barbaros Mah., Hesapçı Sok. 30–32, 07100 Kaleiçi, Antalya. ℭ **0242/247-5675.** Fax 0242/248-5074. www.alppasa. com. 60 units. 100€–165€ ($145–$239/£71–£118) double; 260€ ($377/£186) suite. Rates include breakfast and buffet dinner; rates lower in spring and winter. AE, MC, V. Limited street parking. **Amenities:** Restaurant; bar; cramped outdoor swimming pool; Turkish bath; 24-hr. room service; laundry service; dry cleaning. *In room:* A/C, satellite TV, minibar, hair dryer, safe.

Atelya Pension *(Value*   This family-owned and operated collection of three Ottoman-era houses offers visitors one of the neighborhood's best values. The three buildings front a large courtyard set around a fountain and decorated in traditional Turkish style. Rooms in the older building are simple with few amenities besides the original wood plank floors and loads of character; some retain decorative niches and faded original paintings. The newer building has larger rooms, modern details, and comfortable bathrooms.

Civelek Sok. 21, 07100 Kaleiçi, Antalya. ℭ **0242/241-6416.** Fax 0242/241-2848. 21 units. 25€ ($36/£18) single; 40€ ($58/£29) double in old section; 70€ ($102/£50) double in new section. Breakfast not included. No credit cards. **Amenities:** Bar; table tennis; meals on request.

Doğan Hotel   This neighborhood long-timer is made up of three connected, elegantly restored Ottoman houses. The garden takes center stage here, surrounded by high stone walls and flanked by a soothing waterfall on one side, with a small swimming pool taking up a smaller connected courtyard. In summer, breakfast is served outside under the shade of the many orange trees. Common spaces, which include a lobby bar and "library," feature marble surfaces and touches of *kilims.* The rooms were all recently redecorated, and most have wide wooden plank floors and ceilings. If you request a *çatı odası,* you'll be happy to step foot into a room up high with a balcony and views of the harbor. Try to avoid the rooms in the rear, formerly known as the "pink building," because bathrooms are smallish.

Mermerli Banyo Sok. 5, 07100 Kaleiçi, Antalya. © **0242/241-8842**. Fax 0242/247-4006. www.doganhotel.com. 28 units. 45€–50€ ($65–$73/£32–£36) double; 75€ ($109/£54) suite. MC, V. Closed Nov–Mar. Limited street parking. **Amenities:** Lobby and garden bars; cozy outdoor swimming pool; 24-hr. room service; laundry service; dry cleaning. *In room:* A/C, satellite TV, radio, hair dryer.

La Paloma Pansion 🛱

After 15 years of flying out of Germany to spend the summer in Antalya, Hans Städter decided on a more pleasurable and cost-effective option, and invested his retirement funds into the construction of this Ottoman-style house. Completed in early 2000, La Paloma still sparkles like new—not even the bright local stone used in the construction looks weathered (no wonder, the owner is German). There are nice-size rooms with simple, tasteful decor, and ceiling fans to circulate the cooled-off air. There's the requisite swimming pool and bar, plus a children's swimming pool, in an enclosed garden courtyard. Opt for the Pavilion room and get a minibar and Jacuzzi.

Kılıçaslan Mah. Tabakhane Sok. 3, 07100 Kaleiçi, Antalya. © **0242/244-8497**. Fax 0242/247-4509. www.lapaloma pansion.com. 12 units. 50€ ($73/£36) double; 60€ ($87/£43) Pavilion room. MC, V. **Amenities:** Bar; outdoor swimming pool; 24-hr. room service; massage; laundry service; dry cleaning. *In room:* A/C.

Marina Residence 🛱

This special-category hotel is the closest you'll get to standard hotel amenities in Kaleiçi without sacrificing character. Three Ottoman Paşas' homes of differing styles were restored and redecorated, keeping embellishments like marble balustrades, wood beams, and polished trim. There's a long marble staircase to the rooms above in the main house, and all rooms are outfitted with bathtubs, comfortable duvets, and feather pillows. The terrace suite has access to its own rooftop sun terrace, offering breathtaking views of the marina (another room gets a Jacuzzi—and twin beds). Afternoons will most certainly be spent in the courtyard, an oasis of peace with a larger-than-life aquarium swimming pool, or in the new fitness room complete with a small sauna. The Marina also has one of the best restaurants in town (p. 327).

Mermerli Sok. 15, Kaleiçi, 07100 Antalya. © **0242/247-5490**. Fax 0242/241-1765. 41 units. 110€ ($160/£79) double (add 20€/$29/£14 for sea view). Rates lower Nov–Mar. AE, MC, V. **Amenities:** Restaurant; bar; courtyard swimming pool; fitness room; sauna; meeting facilities; 24-hr. room service; laundry service; dry cleaning; free valet parking. *In room:* A/C, satellite TV, minibar, hair dryer, safe.

Ninova Pension (Value

This modest but comfortable pension boasts the finest garden in Antalya, pleasantly overgrown with orange trees and an enchanting reflecting pond as a centerpiece. Rooms are basic and small; an additional four units on the upper floors are usually out of commission in the summer because of the oppressive heat. The longtime manager, a sweet woman from Istanbul, creates an atmosphere of warmth, encouraging guests to congregate in the TV room or the sitting area. Nights are blissfully silent, even though Hadrian's Gate and Atatürk Caddesi are only steps away.

Hamit Efendi Sok. 9, 07100 Kaleiçi, Antalya. © **0242/248-6114**. Fax 0242/248-9684. www.ninova-pension.com. 15 units. 40€–60€ ($58–$87/£29–£43) double. AE, MC, V. **Amenities:** Laundry service; dry cleaning. *In room:* A/C.

Tekeli Konakları 🛱

One of the more recent restorations in the walled city, Tekeli Konakları combines six traditional Turkish houses set around a common paved courtyard with several patio levels and a small pool. The rooms—each one slightly different—are elegantly yet sparsely decorated, taking advantage of architectural features such as polished wood floorboards and carved wood ceilings. Those who appreciate attention to detail will be delighted by Kutahya ceramics fashioned into door handles, the odd antique objet d'art—and in some rooms, stained-glass, Ottoman-motif artwork. The restaurant, which takes over the upper patios on summer evenings, has already earned a solid reputation, and a new indoor *pasthane* serves sweets like baklava and pudding, along with ice cream in homemade waffle cones. There's also a small boutique on the premises, stocked with high-quality textiles like embroidered table-cloths, *kilims,* and ceramics. **Early-to-bedders take note:** The neighboring disco may intrude upon your REM time.

Dizdar Hasan Sok., 07100 Kaleiçi, Antalya. © **0242/244-5465.** Fax 0242/242-6714. 8 units. Apr–Sept $112 (£56) double; Oct–Mar $75 (£38). AE, MC, V. **Amenities:** Restaurant; bar; outdoor swimming pool; 24-hr. room service; laundry service; dry cleaning. *In room:* A/C.

WHERE TO DINE

Locals flock to the eateries in the covered walkway at the intersection of Cumhuriyet Caddesi and Atatürk Caddesi, where freshly cooked *lokanta*-style cases and *döner* stands share the pavement with tiny coffee tables. It's the Turkish equivalent of the food court, and a delicious, friendly, and economical alternative to the more tourist-minded restaurants listed below.

Gizli Bahçe/Secret Garden *Moments* TURKISH/ITALIAN   This restaurant combines delicious meals with a stunning environment: Choose between a table in the romantic candlelit Italianate garden, on the cliff-top panoramic patio, or next to the ancient walls with a view that peeks through the ramparts (a few choose to sit indoors in the warmer weather). The menu is pure Turkish, with some highlights of the local kitchen, including *şakşuka,* an appetizer of eggplant, zucchini, and tomato, and special selections of the chef. Try the seafood salad served on greens with an orange sauce, or the Garden Kebap Special, a plate of sirloin strips served with tomato, yogurt, and eggplant.

Selçuk Mah., Dizdar Hasan Bey Sok. 1, Kaleiçi. © **0242/244-8010.** Dress smart. Appetizers and main courses 8YTL–28YTL ($6.95–$24/£3.20–£11). AE, MC, V. Daily 8am–midnight.

Kral Sofrası TURKISH/MEDITERRANEAN   Called the King's Table, Kral Sofrası enjoyed 20 years of success in Ankara before moving to the warmer climes of Antalya, where it was the first restaurant to open on the marina. In the summertime, meals are served on the terrace garden overlooking the rooftops and harbor, but the restaurant seems to take its name from the stately dining room inside this old Ottoman house. The Mediterranean menu offers typical Turkish harbor fare—Tygar, the owner, assures me that he rises daily at 6am to personally select the day's ingredients—with an occasional standout like the special *kiral güveç* (beef-and-vegetable casserole) or the spicy chili tahini dip. Pay your respects to the Elvis-like Atatürk shrine at the front entrance before you leave.

Yacht Harbor 35. © **0242/241-2198.** Dress smart for indoor dining. Grilled meat and fish dishes 7YTL–18YTL ($6.10–$16/£2.80–£7.20) and up for fish. MC, V. Daily 11am–1am. Closes earlier in winter.

Marina Restaurant FRENCH   The Marina Hotel has two restaurants—one in the garden and the other in the elegant main house—but the menu is so successful that it's the same one for both spots. Mouthwatering appetizers are presented as only French training will allow. To start, the chef has created a duck rillet with a walnut sauce mixed with orange and cognac and a salmon roll filled with prawns, Iranian caviar, and mustard-seed sauce. Entrees meld succulent mainstays with atypical flavors as in the T-bone steak with Madagascar chili sauce or the breast of duck with a veg-etable soufflé and cherry sauce. The Mediterranean sole stuffed with shrimp in a saf-fron sauce may not be unusual, but that doesn't make it any less yummy. The meal

---

Tips **Antalya's Festivals**

For 1 week at the beginning of September, Alexander the Great takes a back seat at the ancient theater of Phaselis to make way for Turkish jazz, folk, and classical artists. The website for the **Phaselis Festival** (© **0242/814-5911**; www. phaselisfestival.com) is currently in Turkish only, while tickets are available via Biletix (www.biletix.com), at the entrance to the ancient city of Phaselis, and some other pensions and restaurants in the immediate area surrounding the park.

---

can be completed with a selection of decadent Westernized tarts, flambés, and cakes; there's even a pear *poshet* prepared for diabetics.

Mermerli Sok. 15, Kaleiçi. © **0242/247-5490.** Reservations suggested. Dress smart. Appetizers and main courses 12YTL–34YTL ($10–$30/£4.80–£14). MC, V. Daily noon–11pm.

Stella's Bistrot ☆ *Value* MEDITERRANEAN   Far from the platforms and terraces of the tourist section, Stella's Bistrot is a welcome change from all the fish and grills. The predominantly Italian menu has been expanded to include Mediterranean dishes, but the real winner here is the authentic Italian lasagna made the way it's supposed to be, with a béchamel sauce. Salads and sandwiches are appealing alternatives for lunch, and from the sidewalk tables you can watch the tram pass by.

Fevzi Çakmak Cad. 3/C (near end of Atatürk Cad.). © **0242/243-3931.** Appetizers and main courses 6YTL–15YTL ($5.20–$13/£2.40–£6). MC, V. Daily noon–midnight.

ANTALYA AFTER DARK

Visitors to Antalya take to the streets and hidden courtyards of Kaleiçi or along the Yacht Harbor, where an ice cream and a stroll down the jetty are accompanied by sea breezes and waterside cafes. The downside is that several slow seasons have resulted in increased hassling by those idling outside their shops.

Over at Konaaltı's **Beach Park** ☆☆☆, cafes illuminated by moonlight line the seaside beach park promenade, sharing the lawns with a decadent array of cushions backed by a handful of *meyhanes.*

Meanwhile, residents looking for a quiet evening out descend on Karaalioğlu Park for a seat at one of the welcoming tea gardens dressed in bright red or for a go at a lineup of balloons with an old army rifle. When the heat and humidity become too much to bear, there's bound to be a Turkish Nights show at one of the hotels in town; standouts are listed below.

Gizli Bahçe *Finds*   The presence of two restaurants, four different dining environments, stunning views of the bay via the parapets, and a generally elegant atmosphere are just a few of the things that the Gizli Bahçe/Secret Garden has to offer. A polished and elegant bar area is a great option for a pre- or post-dinner aperitif, while live music is offered Tuesday through Sunday nights. Ask about their Turkish folk night, complete with buffet, usually scheduled for Wednesday night. Daily 8am to midnight. Closed November to mid-April. Selçuk Mah., Dizdar Hasan Bey Sok. 1, Kaleiçi. © **0242/244-8010.**

Highlander   Jolly and diminutive Fazla opened this warm-hearted pub in May 2001, which owes its name to the popular series, after Fazla spotted Christopher Lambert one day on the marina. Set slightly back from the water's edge, the outdoor cafe looks suspiciously like a Fortunoff patio display, in no small part thanks to the artificial fountain set within an outdoor round bar. Indoors, however, is pure Highlander, from the leather couches, to the dartboard, to the deep manly colors. Weekends usher in live music, but early evening hours can still be enjoyed with the house cocktail: Russian coffee with vodka and cream. Daily 8am to 3am; shorter hours in winter. Yat Limanı Iskele Cad. 2. © **0242/242-4855.**

Kale Bar   With wrought-iron patio chairs painted bubble-gum pink, the Kale Bar, located in the elegant Tütav Türk Evi, has the best views of the harbor from anywhere in town and some of the highest prices for cocktails anywhere around. Daily 11am to 2am. Closed in winter. In the Tütav Türk Evi, Memerli Sok., Kaleiçi. © **0242/248-6591.**

EXCURSIONS FROM ANTALYA
THE "MONSTER" AT OLYMPOS

One of the highlights of a visit to the Antalya coast is the **Chimaera** 🟊🟊, near the ancient city of **Olympos** 🟊 and modern-day beachfront **Çiralı** 🟊🟊. It's a good idea to combine a visit to both the natural and archaeological sites, keeping in mind that the undisturbed—even unkempt—shoreline of Çiralı is one of the best-kept natural secrets of the Mediterranean coast and a major nesting site for sea turtles.

The Chimaera, or mythical, fire-breathing monster with the head of a lion, the torso of a goat, and the rear of a snake that allegedly roams the hills is actually a series of eternal flames flickering along the rocky slopes above the ancient city of Olympos, which would account for the Lycians' worship of the fire god Hephaestos (Vulcan). But never fear: According to legend, the Chimaera was slain by Bellerophon on his winged horse, Pegasus, from his base over at Tlos. The fires are caused by the combustion of a predominantly methane gas mixture seeping out of the earth and igniting at the point of contact between serpentine and limestone rocks; though they can be extinguished briefly by covering them, they always reignite. The path up the hill to the site is at the far end of the modern village of Çiralı, about a 6- to 7km (3¾- to 4⅓-mile) hike from the beach end of the ancient city of Olympos. It's about a 20-minute hike up to the Chimaera, where a fresh pot of tea perks atop one of the flames. Although the flames are no less impressive by daylight, it's best to come at dusk, when the flames are most visible—just don't forget a flashlight.

The ancient site of Olympos hugs both sides of the Ulupınar Stream near the seashore, and dates to Hellenistic times. It's a bit overgrown and spread out on both sides of the stream, so come with a good map of the site. From 100 B.C., Olympos enjoyed the status as one of the six primary members of the Lycian League and was later absorbed as a Roman province. During this period, the area gained renown as a place of worship for the cult of Hephaestos, or Vulcan, the God of Fire.

Admission to the ancient city ruins during daylight hours (when the booth is manned) is 2YTL ($1.75/80p). There are two entrances to the site: To combine a visit to Olympos with a climb up to the Chimaera, exit the Antalya highway at the exit marked "Çiralı 7; Yanartaş 11 (Chimaera)" (Yanartaş is Turkish for "burning rock"). From here, it's a 10-minute drive along a dry stream bed bursting with oleander, wild orchids, and lavender; you can either cross the bridge and continue straight for about a mile (don't be discouraged by the poor condition of the road during the final mile or so) until you arrive at the "base camp" for the well-marked path up to the Chimaera or turn off onto the rocky road *before* the bridge into Çiralı for access to the beach. (Walk to the right to find the beach entrance to the site of Olympos.) The other main entrance to Olympos can be accessed from the turnoff from the Antalya road marked

"Olympos 11; Çavuşköy 15." *Dolmuşes* pass regularly along the Antalya highway, but transportation down to the beachfront via either turnoff is less reliable.

WHERE TO STAY & DINE   The road that loops through the village of Çiralı is lined with small, family-run pensions with varying degrees of appeal. But until that fated day when Çiralı becomes polished and unauthentic, the best place to stay is the **Olympos Lodge** ⭐⭐, Çiralı, Kemer, P.O. Box 38, Antalya (℗ **0242/825-7171;** fax 0242/825-7173; www.olymposlodge.net), just over the bridge into town (take that quick right). With only 12 rooms, this small slice of paradise is like an exclusive country club; the parking lot is consistently full of shiny Mercedes, BMWs, and collectors' Rolls-Royces. The grounds are gorgeous—a Mediterranean garden bursting with color and home to wandering chickens and peacocks abuts the beach. The rooms are rather unadorned and basic, but feature old cedar wood floorboards that reportedly repel mosquitoes. The room rate of 175€ to 200€ ($254–$290/£125–£143) for two people per night includes breakfast and dinner.

When the Olympos Lodge breaks the news that it's full, the **Arcadia** and **Arcadia 2** ⭐, Çiralı (℗ **0242/825-7340;** www.arcadiaholiday.com), located farther down the beach in a garden of flowers and lemon trees (Arcadia II is across the road in a lemon grove), offer a total of 10 spacious and extremely comfortable pine bungalows. All were built by Ahmet, the owner, assisted by Canadian-born Ann, a welcome font of local information in English. Together, they've created a cozy, romantic, and rustic environment stocked with all the creature comforts, plus coffee, a tea station, and a wine rack. Arcadia has delicious on-site dining on request; eat under the beachfront pines or relax on the shady platform *köşk*. The room rate for two people is 85€ to 110€ ($123–$160/£61–£79) and includes breakfast.

THE MOUNTAINTOP CITADEL OF TERMESSOS

Located on a natural plateau 1,050m (3,445 ft.) above sea level, the impregnable mountaintop city of **Termessos** ⭐⭐ was the only settlement not conquered by Alexander the Great. The ancient site is located about a half-hour's drive from Antalya inside the Güllük Dağ Milli Parkı (℗ **0242/423-7416**). Alex likened it to an eagle's nest; you'll think so, too, after the steep climb up. The best approach from the plateau parking area is up the main path to the city and theater for access to the lion's share of the ruins. Rather than backtracking at the end of your visit, follow the sign toward the tombs, which follows a narrow and sometimes rocky footpath past a series of rock-cut tombs and free-standing **sarcophagi,** a path that ends about 20 minutes later in the parking lot. Although the path is shady most of the way up, be sure to carry enough bottled water, as there is no concession on-site, and it can get pretty hot. The visit on foot takes as little as 2 hours (if you're well hydrated and it's early) to as much as 4 to 5 hours, if you're sluggish and really into seeing every nook and cranny.

The most impressive of the ruins is the **Greek theater,** cut into the rock with celestial views of Antalya visible through the clouds. The ability of the city's inhabitants to withstand prolonged attacks was in no small part due to the exceptional engineering of its cisterns: five tanks fed by a duct cut into the rock. Admission to the archaeological site is 5YTL ($4.35/£2) per person, plus 7YTL ($6.10/£2.80) to drive your car into the national park (don't even think about walking from the ticket gate, a hefty 9km/5½ miles downhill from the plateau parking; open daily 8am–6pm in summer and 8am–4pm in winter). If you're going by car, follow the Antalya-Burdur highway north and follow signs for the park. Tours run only about 40YTL ($35/£16) and generally include a stopover at the Duden Waterfall.

8

Cappadocia & the Interior

A stark lunar landscape. A mysterious open-air sculpture carved by Mother Nature's chisel. These common descriptions of Cappadocia really just tap-dance around the subject. So let's just get this out of the way: Those fascinating "fairy chimneys" evoke nothing so much as anatomically correct erections—and circumcised ones at that. Imagine what a field day American film censors would have had if George Lucas had succeeded in his original plan to shoot *Star Wars Episode 1: The Phantom Menace* in Cappadocia.

Nobody knows who the original inhabitants of the region were, or who first hollowed out shelters in the soft rock of these sheltered ravines and odd "chimneys." But as a largely barren area, central Cappadocia was bypassed by most armies, making it a perfect refuge for the early Christians following in the footsteps of St. Paul, who established the first Christian colonies here.

The natural land formations and huge expanses of silence are just a part of the mystery of the region. As an incubator for Christian philosophy, the monasteries, cave dwellings, and feats of underground engineering are a testament to human ingenuity. Cliff walls of the valleys are riddled with cavities that on closer inspection turn out to be centuries-old dwellings or chapels decorated with colorful frescoes and biblical images.

Cappadocian soil is extremely fertile, and a general tour of the region will reveal numerous vineyards. Famous for its local wines, Cappadocia is a major producer; you may want to veer off at a sign for ŞARAP EVI (wine house) for a leisurely tasting. The creatively named Şarap Evi, in Ürgüp, has wine tastings in the evenings, but it's just as fun to drive up to any local producer and fall into the dance of local hospitality.

1 Exploring the Region

In antiquity, Cappadocia included all of central Anatolia, stretching as far as Ankara in the north and Adana in the south (see the map of Turkey's Ancient Civilizations, on p. 385). Today the region includes the area in and around a small triangle formed by Ürgüp, Avanos, and Nevşehir, where the canyons are the deepest and the paint pigments in the rock-cut churches are the richest.

If your time is limited, it's possible to visit the major sites of the area in 2 *full* days with either your own car or the assistance of a local tour operator. Doubtless, you'll wish you had stayed longer. Tours can be either tailor-made, and therefore more pricey, or selected from a stable of standard issues. Typical day tours include (1) a visit to the open-air museums of Zelve and Göreme, overviews of the valleys from Paşabağ and Dervent, a climb up to the top of Üçhisar Fortress, and an optional pottery demonstration in Avanos; and (2) visits to the underground cities of Kaymaklı and Derinkuyu and a leisurely 4km (2½-mile) hike through the monastery-rich gorge of

Ihlara Valley. Tours may also include horseback riding; more challenging sports such as mountain biking can be easily arranged, but these are generally not advertised.

Operating with the most experience in the region is **Argeus,** Istiklal Cad. 13, Ürgüp (© **0384/341-4688;** fax 0384/341-4888; www.argeus.com.tr). Argeus is a full-service agency that, in addition to providing expert guidance on Cappadocia and Ankara, also organizes top-quality tours to destinations throughout Turkey. (For the adventurous, Argeus is also the representative for REI.) The price for a regular day tour is $110 (£55) per person for up to eight people—a bit hefty in comparison to the lower-end outfitters, but with Argeus, there are no shopping detours and all museum fees are included (private tours cost $280/£140 for one person, $240/£120 per person for two, $390/£195 for three, and so on). Argeus is also an official agent of Turkish Airlines.

Cappadocia Tours, Istiklal Cad. 19/9, Ürgüp (© **0384/341-7485;** www.cappadocia tours.com), the companion agency to Gamirasu Cave Hotel (see "Where to Stay," later), is led by Süleyman Çakır, who seeks to provide the best in "off the beaten track" tours. Think visits to local village events and historical hikes and expect to pay 160€ ($232/£114) per day for between 2 and 10 passengers including the guide and driver. For an additional 20€ ($29/£14) per person, all entrance fees will be included (these do add up), as well as vehicle expenses and an a la carte lunch, including wine.

As for more budget-minded outfitters, they come and go, and I hesitate to recommend any particular one because the last time I did, I got shocking feedback describing dubious dealings in the lean times. You'd be better off identifying a company on arrival, and be clear about what services will be included in the tour. Is lunch included? Are all of the admission fees included? Will the tour take a time-sucking detour to a carpet "production" center? (A detour to a carpet shop is not automatically a bad thing; see "*Caveat Emptor!* Carpet-Buying Tips," in chapter 4.)

THE ACTIVE EXPLORER IN CAPPADOCIA

There are few things in this world that warrant a 4:30am wake-up; usually some type of flight is involved. But chasing the sunrise above Cappadocia's spectacular landscape in a wicker basket is altogether different from boarding a 777: It's like riding on the back of a Harley with wings.

Cappadocia's climate is ideally suited to ballooning, with consistently clear summer skies and harmonious breezes. Several experienced outfitters organize hot-air balloon rides over Cappadocia. As the first in the region offering balloon rides, **Kapadokya Balloons** (© **0384/271-2442;** www.kapadokyaballoons.com) has the most flights under its belt. **Göreme Balloons** (© **0384/341-5662;** www.goremeballoons.com) showed up on the scene several years back and has an excellent track record. More recently (with the prospects of skyrocketing tourist demand and big money), there have been a number of start-ups on the Cappadocia ballooning scene. One such outfitter has the dubious achievement of having the largest hot-air balloon in the world. This pseudo air bus holds 36 passengers and goes as high as 2,000m (6,562 ft.). Too high and too cold for my taste, actually, but that's just me. But that's just one of a fleet of balloons operated by Anatolian Balloons (© **0384/271-2300;** anatolianballoons.com).

Ballooning day begins *well* before sunrise, when the flame bursts that fill the balloon provide much-needed warmth. Flights last about an hour and a half, offering otherworldly close-ups and stunning panoramas. Your heart will undoubtedly skip a beat several times throughout, including when they hand you the 230€ ($362/£184) bill. (Kapadokya Balloons calls this the regular service, Göreme has labeled this their

Cappadocia

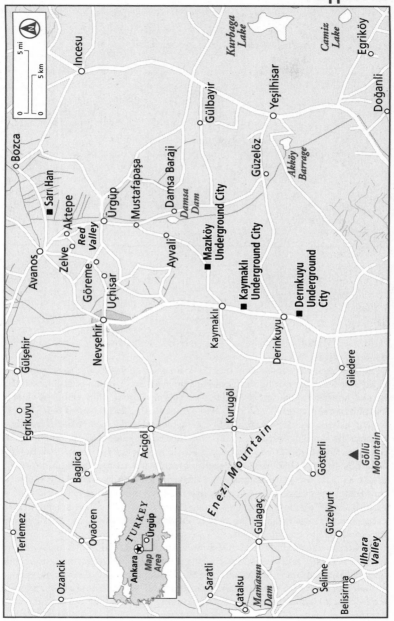

Geology 101—What's the Deal?

The erosion that carves out this fascinating topography began over 60 million years ago and can be seen in various stages even today. As the devastating 1999 earthquakes illustrated, Turkey is caught between the insistent pressure exerted from the Asian and European continental plates. The Erciyes Mountain, Melendiz Mountain, and Hasandag—all dormant or extinct volcanoes—are the result of underground forces that thrust these landmasses above water level eons ago. Recurrent volcanic eruptions blanketed the area with boulders, ash, and lava, over time creating layers of sediment, with the underneath layers more solid than the newer, softer upper levels of sediment.

The formation of the fairy chimneys is just an example of wind and water erosion in an extreme state. The early stages of erosion are visible in the graceful channels and dunes of the valleys. But as the elements carve away at the channels, the mass of tufa splits from its supports and forms pillars or pyramids. And without the protection of those teetering basalt boulders caught in the balance of gravity and time, the pillars slowly whittle down to nothing, and the crowning boulder eventually comes crashing to the ground.

"deluxe" tour, and Anatolian Balloons calls this their "long flight.") All three offer less expensive flights (160€/$252/£128), made possible by advertising fees paid by Coca-Cola, Efes Pilsen, or Mercedes-Benz in exchange for employing graphically branded balloons for flights (Anatolian Balloons is undercutting the other two companies with 225€/$354/£180 and 150€/$236/£120 flights, respectively.) Regular balloon rides run around 1½ hours; the "budget" version lasts about an hour. Reservations are essential for all flights.

Ancient Anatolian lore describes a lovelorn poet on horseback traveling through fields of irises, perpetuating the legend of Cappadocia as a "place of beautiful horses." It's still possible to replicate that equestrian journey through the region's verdant valleys and barren steppes. The **Akhal-Teke Horse Riding Center** (© **0384/511-5171**; www.akhal-tekehorsecenter.com) has clean, professionally run stables (and on-site restaurant) on the outskirts of Avanos with horses and guides for all riding levels. The charge is 35YTL ($30/£14) per hour for a ride along the Kızılirmak River; 70YTL ($61/£28) for a 2-hour ride into the mountains and natural spring; and 140YTL ($122/£56) for a 4-hour ride either up the river, through a local fishing village, and up to the Sarıhan caravansaray or through the fairy chimneys at Zelve, Paşabağ, and Çavuşin (10% discount for riders under 10 years). Daylong and several weeklong excursions are also available, and some of the overnight trips include stays in people's homes and/or overnights in tents.

Kirkit Voyage (© **0384/511-3259**; www.kirkit.com), with offices in Istanbul and Avanos, organizes activities in the area, thanks to their own horse farm in the village of Güzelyurt, near the Ihlara Valley. Horseback-riding tours for all levels of experience are available with 2- or 4-hour panoramic rides for 20€ ($29/£14) or 30€ ($44/£21), respectively. Kirkit also organizes scenic and memorable 1-, 3-, 7-, and 15-day camping treks.

As the golfing bug takes hold in Turkey, and as entrepreneurs become aware of the sums that golfing enthusiasts are willing to dump on their obsession, golf courses are mushrooming up all over, and Cappadocia is no exception, sort of. **Cross Golf**

(© **0384/271-2351;** www.crossgolfcappadocia.com), a venture of Indigo Turizm and the Museum Hotel (not listed in this book simply because each time I go, the receptionist refuses to show me any rooms), is a freestyle game of golf with no putters and with nets instead of holes. Imagine a walk through the meadows outside of Göreme through a loose course of targets.

GETTING THERE

BY PLANE   **Turkish Airlines** (© **0212/444-0849;** www.thy.com) currently has four flights daily from Istanbul to Kayseri, about 45 minutes by car from anywhere in Cappadocia. The German-based **Onur Air** (© **0212/663-9176** in Istanbul, or 444-ONUR; www.onurair.com.tr) flies to Kayseri daily from Istanbul and from Düsseldorf. **SunExpress** (© **0232/444-0797;** www.sunexpress.com.tr) flies direct four times daily from Izmir. For passengers traveling from the Asian side of Istanbul, **Pegasus** (© **444-0737;** www.flypgs.com) flies once daily from Istanbul's Sabiha Gökçen Airport. One-way fares on all of these airlines (for those who book early enough) begin at 59YTL ($51/£24).

Turkish Airlines has an office both in downtown Kayseri, at Sahabiye Mahallesi Yildirim Cad. 1 (© **0352/222-3858**), and at Kayseri's Erkilet Airport (© **0352/338-3353**). Within the Cappadocian triangle, the official representative for Turkish Airlines is **Argeus,** located at Istiklal Cad. 13, Ürgüp (© **0384/341-4688** or 341-5207). Pegasus has an office at the airport (© **0352/339-9791**).

Many local tour operators will pick you up at the airport or bus station for much less than it would cost you to take a taxi. Argeus was the first in the region to provide transfers from both airports to anywhere in the Cappadocia region in their private minivans. The fare for the 97km (60-mile) trip (1½ hr.) to/from Kayseri airport is only 9.50YTL ($8.25/£3.80). Because of the reasonable amount of competition this presents to area taxi drivers, travelers arriving and hoping to "wing it" by jumping on the Argeus bandwagon may get some resistance from the locals. To avoid misunderstandings, travelers are encouraged to *reserve space in advance* with Argeus (© **0384/341-4688;** fax 0384/341-4888; www.argeus.com.tr). Also be sure to check with your hotel first—they may pick you up for free. There are no other options for transfers in and out of Kayseri.

BY BUS   All long-distance buses into Cappadocia arrive into Nevşehir's *otogar.* If you've bought a ticket to Göreme, Ürgüp, Üçhisar, or elsewhere in the triangle, the bus company will provide a minibus transfer to that town's bus station. Some bus companies

---

⌒ Moments The Best Hikes

It's hard to find a bad hike in Cappadocia, but the journey will be all the more rewarding in this ever-changing landscape of pink, yellow, and sandy-colored "dunes," with nothing but the whisper of the wind for company. Wear good shoes and come prepared with a windbreaker or jacket, because whenever the sun plays coy behind a cloud, the temperature drops momentarily, yet precipitously. The best hikes are in the Red Valley (Kızılçukur Vadisi) from Çavuşin to the entrance of Ortahisar; in Pigeon Valley (Güvercinlik Vadisi) between Üçhisar and Göreme; and in the Uludere Valley from Uludere village to Ayvalı, where you have the option of continuing through Gomede Valley to Mustafapaşa. Also near Mustafapaşa is Kepez Valley, with its impressive cones, plus a number of churches.

simply pass through Cappadocia on the way to points east and south, in which case it is all too common that the driver will simply dump you off on the side of the highway rather than make the detour into the *otogar*. Whether your bus company is ending its journey in Cappadocia or not, if you've paid for a ticket to, say, Göreme, be sure at the time of purchasing your ticket that the terms of transport are understood. For insurance, stick to the more dependable **Nevşehir** (© **0212/444-5050**), **Metro** (© **0212/444-3455**), and **Kent** (© **0212/444-3838**) bus lines.

By bus, expect around 4 to 5 hours from Konya, 2 hours from Kayseri, 5 to 6 hours from Ankara, and 12 hours from Istanbul. If you're headed to the Aegean Coast, you'll have to change buses in either Izmir (13 hr.) or Muğla (14 hr.); for the Mediterranean coast, you'll have to take a bus to either Antalya or Muğla, and then change for minibus service to your final destination. (Certain destinations will require yet another change; for example, to Dalyan, you'll have to change in Ortaca for a *dolmuş* [minivan-type public transportation] into the center of town.)

GETTING AROUND

In most parts of Turkey, *dolmuşes* are practical. In Cappadocia, service is infrequent and at best unreliable. A local *dolmuş* follows a circuit hourly from Ürgüp bus station to Zelve, Avanos, Göreme, Üçhisar, and back; another service runs every 2 hours from Ürgüp to Avanos between 9am and 5pm.

Dolmuşes also run to the smaller villages from select main towns, so while you can get direct service from Ürgüp to, say, Mustafapaşa, you'll have to change in Nevşehir if you're headed to Derinkuyu.

A municipal bus provides service between Nevşehir and Avanos daily on the hour from 8am to 5pm.

Obviously, a day tour will solve the transportation problem (see "Exploring the Region," earlier in this chapter). For car- and scooter-rental information, see "Getting Around" in the individual sections below for details.

2 Ürgüp ★★★

23km (14 miles) east of Nevşehir; 6.5km (4 miles) east of Göreme

It's hard to believe that Ürgüp is not the capital of Cappadocia. It's certainly the region's de facto center of action. No longer a village but not quite yet a city, Ürgüp still manages to strike a balance between preserving its rural Anatolian roots and cultivating an unobtrusive yet irresistible tourist infrastructure. To meet the rising demand, hoteliers are all too eager to create perfectly charming romantic retreats for an increasingly upscale market. Crumbled hovels are becoming the exception rather than the rule, but like the transformation of Ürgüp itself, the human odors of food and sweat are being scraped away with the top layers of porous tufa. Of course, one day all of the abandoned terraced houses will have sprouted brand-new facades, a gentrification process that, while polished and attractive, will probably be devoid of the character that drew me here in the first place. But for now, Ürgüp remains a tranquil yet convenient corner of Cappadocia that makes an ideal base from which to explore the surrounding valleys.

ESSENTIALS

VISITOR INFORMATION

The **tourist information office** is in the center of town across from the police station, on Kayseri Cad. 37 (© **0384/341-4059**), and is open daily 8am to 6pm; closed

Ürgüp

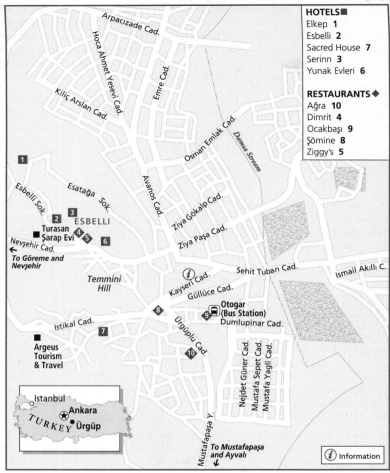

HOTELS ■
Elkep **1**
Esbelli **2**
Sacred House **7**
Serinn **3**
Yunak Evleri **6**

RESTAURANTS ◆
Ağra **10**
Dimrit **4**
Ocakbaşı **9**
Şömine **8**
Ziggy's **5**

Sunday in winter. You won't need it, though, as all of the hoteliers and agencies have good maps and even better anecdotal information.

ORIENTATION

The village fans out around the bus station and a brand-new cement-block shopping gallery, which is right in the center of town. From the main square outside the bus station running northeast is **Kayseri Caddesi,** Ürgüp's main shopping street, with a wide variety of shopping options, from overstocked antiques stores to jewelry boutiques with the finest selection of lapis lazuli, handcrafted silver, and tribal items. The information office, the police station, and the hospital can be reached down this road as well. Forking east below Kayseri Caddesi is a small street of localized travel agencies, many of which double as bike- or scooter-rental outfits. **Ahmet Refik Caddesi** heads northwest from the center, snaking around the base of the old village of partially collapsed and deserted rock homes to the left and **Temmenı Hill** to the right, on its way up the hill toward Göreme and Nevşehir. Buying a souvenir cluster of fairy chimneys is made all too easy along Ahmet Refik Caddesi, but once you've cleared the souvenir shops, rural life takes over. Near the top of the hill are the **Turasan winery** and the neighborhood of **Esbelli,** where you will find two hotels mentioned below. To re-enter town by car, turn left onto **Istiklal Caddesi,** which leads back into the town center.

GETTING AROUND

Ürgüp is easily walkable, but if you're staying in the neighborhood of Esbelli, you may want to know that the hill up from the center of town is quite steep. During the summer months when the municipality fills the streets with clouds of insect repellent to combat the irritating swarms of bees that hover over your breakfast, it's best to forgo the after-dinner stroll and take a taxi up to your hotel.

Several car-rental agencies offering low daily rates of around 61YTL ($53/£24) per day are located in the center of town, including **Avis,** Istiklal Cad. Belediye Pasaji 10 (© **0384/341-2177**); **Europcar,** Istiklal Cad. 10 (© **0384/341-8855**); and **Decar,** Istiklal Cad. 3 (© **0384/341-6760**). You may also save a few dollars by working with one of the neighboring locals. Scooters and beat-up old mountain bikes are also for rent in various shops along the market.

WHAT TO SEE & DO

With an easy blend of tradition and convenience, Ürgüp makes the perfect base for day excursions to the open-air museums of Göreme and Zelve, the nearby valleys, and neighboring villages.

The village is also a peaceful retreat for some quiet time, where you can walk around the old deserted section of town or enjoy the view from the lookout point atop windy **Temmenı Hill,** known as The Hill of Wishes, 30Ykr (25¢/10p). A mysterious tunnel (closed; don't bother with those pestering kids) almost .8km (½ mile) long leads from around the 13th-century Kebir Camii to the Selçuk tomb of Nükrettin at the top of the hill; to this day, no one knows who built it or why. The tomb was dedicated to the Selçuk leader Kılıçarslan IV, or the Sworded Lion, and a hilltop cafe allows you to relax and take it all in.

Ayvalı ✪   This is the quintessential Anatolian village, a place where life hasn't changed for centuries. A narrow ravine cuts through the bottom of the village with the trickly İçeridere River running the length of the valley all the way to Golgoli Hill, a 6.5km (4-mile) hike away. You can fill up a bottle of sparkling fresh spring water from a source on the edge of the village, while exploring eerie, untouched caves and rock-cut churches. There's a teahouse for refreshment, and if you look enough like you don't fit in, somebody in the village will feed you. But definitely try some of the fresh seasonal fruits that sell at the morning market, the only retail establishment in town (for now).

Take the road for Mustafapaşa, and then turn off on the road to Ayvalı.

Paşabağ   Wherever you see tour buses or souvenir stands, there's bound to be something interesting. Paşabağ, also known as Valley of the Monks, is a forest of cone-shaped fairy chimneys more shocking and lifelike (not life-size) than most. Not surprisingly, it's a popular stop for photo ops.

The chimneys of Paşabağ harbor a number of chapels and dwellings used by Christian hermits, the most prominent of which is a tri-level chapel with depictions of the life of St. Simeon. St. Simeon the Stylite lived a life of hardship and denial in Antioch around the 4th century, high atop a 15m (49-ft.) pillar. Later hermits were inspired to do the same, initiating a "stylite" movement of isolated living.

On the road to Zelve Valley. Free with ticket to Zelve Open Air Museum.

Sarıca Church   The Sarıca Church, located in the Kepez Valley, is the perfect example of how a monument can suffer from indifference and neglect, yet be dragged back from the brink of oblivion as a shining example of one person's dedication toward the preservation of national patrimony. Up until October 2002 when work began, this 6th- to 7th-century rock-cut basilica had been reduced to use as an organic factory warehouse for pigeon guano. Local farmers had even cut an aperture into the dome as a porthole for the pigeons. In all fairness, however, much of the deterioration in the condition of the church was due to water erosion. Today, visitors can enter through the (dry) front door—which had to be dug out—and marvel at the carved niches, arched vaults, and capitals decorated under the ochre artwork of the time.

Kepez Valley, near Mustafapaşa. No phone.

Zelve Open Air Museum ⚔   Carved into a uniquely pink tufa, Zelve was once home to one of the largest communities in the region, inhabited by a Greek population until the 1922 population exchange, when Greeks and Turks were "repatriated" to their mother countries. When Muslims took over the valley, a mosque was hewn out of the rock and stands near the entrance.

The first known inhabitants of the valley were monks, and although I can say for sure that they carved out the chapels, it's unclear who first began hollowing out the valley. The cave dwellings were used by local villagers up until 1952, when the structures were determined to be unsafe and the villagers were moved en masse over to nearby Aktepe, or New Zelve.

Now a national park, Zelve consists of three consecutive valleys whose walls are riddled with living quarters, blind tunnels, passageways, and traps for protection against attacks. Footholds chiseled into the smooth vertical tufa require an agility once aimed at keeping out unwanted visitors, but now present a fantastic challenge to modern-day rock climbers. Those interested in hiking should set aside plenty of time to explore the area, following a path over the mountain to Red Valley, about 4km (2½ miles) away. Exploring the caves can be exhilarating, challenging, and downright dangerous. Don't attempt anything fancy without a guide; Argeus (see "Exploring the Region," at the beginning of the chapter) offers excellent guided tours, but you can also arrange one through one of the many shops in town.

The road. to Zelve Valley is accessible off the Göreme-Avanos or Ürgüp-Avanos rd. ⓒ **0384/411-2525.** Admission 5YTL ($4.35/£2). Daily 8am–5:30pm.

WHERE TO STAY

There are few places on earth where you can get a good night's sleep in a cave, and Ürgüp is one of them. Besides primitive surroundings, you can expect traditionally Greek/Anatolian single-vaulted rooms with utilitarian niches cut into the rock. Because of the multilevel character of the rock, most hotels are terraced around open patios with fantastic views of the valley or of local village life.

Elkep Evi   Owned by an American couple from Miami, the Elkep Evi cave houses are built around a garden courtyard that enjoys views over Ürgüp. Its furnishings give it a warmer and cozier feel. An outdoor seating area is covered in *kilims,* while rooms are simply decorated with carpets and carved wooden headboards. They've added Jacuzzis in one of the doubles and one suite; another double and suite have Turkish baths.

Eski Turban Oteli Arkası, 50400 Ürgüp. © **0384/341-6000.** Fax 0384/341-8089. www.elkepevi.com. 14 units. $90–$150 (£45–£75) double; $140–$190 (£70–£95) suite. Free pickup from airport. MC, V. **Amenities:** Internet; laundry service; dry cleaning. *In room:* CD player, tea/coffee service, hair dryer.

Esbelli Evi *(Moments (Finds* This is the Cappadocian inn that set the standard for all others, and it's all thanks to Süha, Esbelli's gracious owner, whose genuineness and discreet hospitality are hallmarks of the hotel's warmth and exclusivity. Nine cave rooms and five multi-cave suites are chiseled in and around a cluster of contiguous cave dwellings in a breathtaking maze of stone stairways, courtyards, and outdoor terraces. The result is an irresistible collection of rooms that, thanks to polished hardwood floors, ample modern bathrooms, and thick bright white duvets, manage all at once to be prehistoric, modern, and romantic. Cave suites are meandering hideaways with strategic lighting, full kitchens, private terraces, and deliciously oversize baths, where you and that special someone can take rain showers (with two shower heads nobody gets cold) or soak in the large centerpiece bathtub. The newly installed piano "saloon" and movie theater that stocks more than 2,000 world classic and documentary films make for great distractions on those chilly winter nights.

Esbelli Sok. 8, 50400 Ürgüp. © **0384/341-3395.** Fax 0384/341-8848. www.esbelli.com.tr. 13 units. $110 (£55) single; $145 (£73) double; $320 (£160) suite. MC, V. **Amenities:** Saloon; movie theater; complimentary use of swimming pool at neighboring hotel; wireless Internet; laundry service; dry cleaning; nonsmoking rooms. *In room:* Hair dryer.

Sacred House *(* One of the newer, upscale additions to Ürgüp's already overflowing hotel landscape is this superbly decorated and ridiculously romantic hideaway on one of the more residential back streets of town. Sacred House is the dream child of the owner of Prokopi Pub, whose passion for antiques led her to create her own storage facility. Rooms reflect a sort of medieval aristocracy in the richness of the textiles draped over heavy stone walls and invaluable antiques. Rimming an open central courtyard, each room has a slightly different theme; the cleverest (and perhaps creepiest) is the altar room, reflecting the fact that the building used to be a church. The well-appointed roof terrace offers views over town; the restaurant prepares traditional Turkish cuisine with an Armenian twist.

Karahandere Mah., Barbaros Hayrettin, Sok. 25, 50400 Ürgüp. © **0384/341-7102.** www.sacred-house.com. 7 units. $130–$180 (£65–£90) double. MC, V. **Amenities:** Restaurant; rooftop bar; free airport transfer from Kayseri Airport. *In room:* Jacuzzi.

Serinn The scant five rooms that make up the Serinn superimpose a contemporary art feel on top of a prehistoric one. Seeking to carve her niche in an already flooded market, Eren Serpen, a veteran of tourism hospitality from Istanbul, engaged architect Rifat Ergör to come up with a unique and stylish blend of old and new. The result: molded plastic museum pieces and contemporary carpets on stone floors under stone barrel arches or etched cave ceilings. The newest trend in bathrooms in the area—the glass-door step-in rain shower—is featured here in all its deliciousness. And the views are as inspiring as any from the hotel's perch in Esbelli neighborhood.

Esbelli Sok. 36, Ürgüp. © **0384/341-6076.** Fax 0384/341-6096. www.serinnhouse.com. 5 units. $90–$140 (£45–£70) double. AE, MC, V. **Amenities:** Restaurant; guest laundry; parking. *In room:* Wireless Internet, hair dryer, safe.

Yunak Evleri *((Finds* The Yunak Evleri feels like an old aristocratic country guesthouse. The 27 individually sited rooms, renovated from six cave houses and one mansion, are set into the base of a dramatic and soaring outcrop, much like an amphitheater. Aiming for the high end, the owner, ex–Istanbul native Yusuf Gorurgoz, outfitted his hotel with fine accessories, such as Vakko bed runners, antique furnishings, CD sound systems (deluxe and suites only), and locally made ceramics. He personally designed the bathrooms, installing Swedish multiple-jet and steam showers to create a lavishness even the Four Seasons would be proud of. (The water pressure kicks butt as well!) All rooms enjoy either a private balcony or communal patio, and architectural niches in the main courts of the houses provide wonderful venues for barbecues or bonfires on crisp nights.

Yunak Mah., 50400 Ürgüp. © **0384/341-6920.** Fax 0384/341-6924. www.yunak.com. 17 units. $140 (£70) single; $160 (£80) double; $180 (£90) deluxe; $230 (£115) suite. Discounts for cash payment. MC, V. **Amenities:** Restaurant; laundry; dry cleaning; nonsmoking rooms. *In room:* Minibar, coffee/tea station, hair dryer, safe.

OUTSIDE OF ÜRGÜP

Gamirasu Cave Hotel 🏛🏛   Opened in 1999, Gamirasu is the project of one of the local villagers who through luck or fate obtained financial backing from some German investors. Undoubtedly this hotel will change the face of the village forever, but in the meantime, Ayvalı is still an untouched, unspoiled Cappadocian village—where women still bake bread in outdoor ovens and residents still turn a blind eye to polygamy—with not so much as a kebap house or carpet shop in sight.

The hotel is built on the edge of a wide ravine and enclosed within an unexpectedly elegant rose garden; if you walk along the creek a short way, you can bring back a pitcher of fresh bubbly mineral water. In keeping with the natural focus of the hotel, mattresses are handmade of 100% cotton and breakfast's bounty consists of locally dried apricots, pure village honey, and cream straight from the owner's cow. Guests can even participate in village activities like milking the cow or harvesting grapes with the residents. A local musician shows up regularly to serenade guests over dinner, and transportation to local sites is provided on request.

Ayvalı. © **0384/341-5825.** Fax 0384/341-7487. www.gamirasu.com. 15 units. Mar–Oct 95€ ($138/£68) double, winter 75€ ($109/£54) double; 100€–350€ ($145–$508/£71–£250) deluxe and suites. Rates include breakfast. AE, DC, MC, V. **Amenities:** Tour desk; car-rental desk; laundry service; dry cleaning. *In room:* Hair dryer.

WHERE TO DINE
IN TOWN

Ahra MANTİ/LOCAL HOME COOKING   Whenever I'm in the region, my first thought goes to *mantı*—tiny delectable dumplings topped with a buttery garlic yogurt sauce. So it was no stretch that I'd wind up at Ahra soon after they opened. I wasn't disappointed. There are a number of other notable local dishes on the menu as well; I suggest the *yağlama* (lamb "pizza" drizzled in yogurt) and perhaps a plate of the house *köfte*. The setting gets an "A" too: a homey collection of dining rooms graced with stained-glass windows, carved fireplaces, and area artifacts.

Fabrika Cad. 66 (steps from Istiklal Cad.). © **0384/341-3454.** Appetizers and main courses 3YTL–9YTL ($2.60–$7.85/£1.20–£3.60). MC, V. Summer daily 10am–11pm; winter daily 11am–9:30pm.

Oçakbaşı 🏛 *Value* BARBECUE/SOUTHERN SPECIALTIES   Most people would turn their noses up at the thought of eating a meal in the bus station, but the only upturned noses here will be the ones sniffing out the freshly grilled food on the way up the steps to the restaurant's lovely rooftop terrace. Inside and in typical style, a "barbecue bar" circles the hooded area around the charcoal grill; well-dressed tables in the dining room are also located farther away from the hot coals. Whole eggplants get roasted over the flames and then miraculously whipped up into a delectable regional specialty, the *alinazık kebap*, which is topped by chunks of flavorful grilled meat. Don't pass up the hot appetizer, *içli köfte*, mouthwatering hush puppy–like corn balls stuffed with meat and deep-fried.

In the Ürgüp *otogar*. (𝄐 **0384/341-3277**. Main courses 6YTL–13YTL ($5.20–$11/£2.40–£5.20). MC, V. Daily noon–midnight.

Şömine Café and Restaurant *(Finds* *(Value* REGIONAL TURKISH   In spite of its obvious location, this is indeed the best restaurant in Ürgüp. The marble-paved rooftop terrace overlooks Istiklal Caddesi, while on chillier evenings, you may opt for a spot inside by the cozy, fire-lit open chimney for which the restaurant is named.

The house favorite is the *testi kebap*, a lamb-and-vegetable stew cooked in a type of tandoori oven with peppers and onions. If you're leaning toward ordering this, call ahead and reserve a platter or they may be sold out by the time you get there. Another specialty is the *saç tava*, a delectable mixture of eggplant and bite-size chunks of beef prepared in an earthenware dish (ask the chef to sprinkle a layer of cheese over the top).

Ürgüp town center. (𝄐 **0384/341-8442**. Reservations suggested during high season. Appetizers and main courses 4YTL–15YTL ($3.50–$13/£1.60–£6). MC, V. Daily 9:30am–midnight.

ESBELLI

Dimrit *(Moments*   Just when you thought Cappadocia couldn't get any more romantic, something like this opens up. This is Ürgüp's newest fine-dining destination, a restaurant of regal spaces, both indoors and alfresco, all making optimal use of the region's unique cave architecture and truly breathtaking views. The menu is exactly the same as that at Şömine except that it's slightly more limited. But if it's ambiance you're after, this is the ticket.

Yunak Mah. Teyfik Fikret Cad. 40. (𝄐 **0384/341-8585**. Appetizers and main courses 4YTL–15YTL ($3.50–$13/£1.60–£6). MC, V. Daily 9:30am–midnight.

Ziggy's   If a provincial backwater could be said to have an "in" restaurant, then Ziggy's, opened in 2007, is the place of the moment. Spanning three levels on a perch atop Ürgüp's Esbelli neighborhood, the old stone building that makes up Ziggy's has an atmosphere of barrel vaults, hearths, Turkish decor, and candlelight. Turkish takes on salads and pastas include an irresistible *pastırma fettucini* and great cocktails for those late summer nights.

Yunak Mah. Tevfik Fikret Cad. 24, Ürgüp. (𝄐 **0384/341-7107**. Appetizers and main courses 6YTL–13YTL ($5.20–$11/£2.40–£5.20). MC, V. Daily 11:30am–1:30am.

IN AYVALI

Aravan *(Moments* TURKISH TANDİR   The concept of Aravan (the ancient Hittite name for the village) revolves around the *tandır*, a small cooking pit and the traditional mode of food preparation for Turks for hundreds, if not thousands, of years. The four-course meal consists of home-style recipes all prepared in the pit, from the bulgur "wedding soup," to the *kuru fasulye* (white beans in a tomato sauce), to the *güveç* (here, a succulent lamb stew). Salad and stuffed grape leaves accompany the meal, which is followed by a dessert of either fresh village apricots or local *helva*. The concept is really appealing, and the setting—the terrace of a renovated village home in summer and two cozy and carpeted Oriental-style dining rooms in crisper weather—is delightful.

Ayvalı Village. (𝄐 **0384/354-5838**. Reservations required at least 5 hr. in advance. 4-course meal 15YTL ($13/£6). MC, V. Daily noon–11pm.

A Grape for All Seasons: Cappadocia's Wines

When Kavaklıdere bought 1,600 acres for a new production center in nearby Gulşehir, it was a signal to the rest of Turkish oenophiles that Cappadocian wine had arrived. Families have been making wines in Cappadocia for centuries; a visit to one of these small producers will get you a double dose of traditional Turkish hospitality. Many of these, plus producers from around the world, convene at the International Wine Festival held annually in October. Two of the majors offer wine tastings in outposts of their vineyards; a number of wine shops in Ürgüp also arrange tasting events. Stop by **Turasan Şarap Evi** (on the Nevşehir rd. in the Esbelli section, ✆ **0384/341-4961**). May through October daily 8am to 8pm; November through April daily 8am to 6pm. **Kocabağ** (Atatürk Bulv. Göreme Yolu 69, Üçhisar; ✆ **0384/219-2979**) is a slightly smaller operation with wines that pack a nice punch.

IN MUSTAFAPAŞA

Old Greek House *(Value* REGIONAL TURKISH   This old Greek house in the ancient town of Sinassos (now Mustafapaşa), said to be the former mayor's mansion, is now a restaurant and pension. The owner's wife prepares delicious traditional dishes in the large kitchen off the side of the house; the traditional cave oven she uses for baking is visible from the inner courtyard. The five-course menu is essentially the same every day and includes stuffed eggplant with lamb, *mantı* (meat dumplings topped with sauce), white beans cooked in a tandoori oven (with or without meat), *köfte* (meatballs), and potatoes. The house retains many of its original features, and guests dine either in the main courtyard, or in one of the two upper-story rooms, where some impressive frescoes are still partially visible. Much of the wood paneling is original.

Mustafapaşa. ✆ 0384/353-5345. Reservations required for dinner. Full multicourse meal 20YTL ($17/£8). MC, V. Daily noon–midnight.

ÜRGÜP AFTER DARK

Katpatuka Café & Bistro   The name means "land of beautiful horses" in Persian; just try saying it 10 times fast after a few drinks at the bar. This open-air restaurant and cafe has good food, great ambiance, and appealing circular banquettes for those wishing to just relax and munch on pistachio nuts. There's also sporadic live music, which usually gets up and running after 10pm. Cumhuriyet Meydanı 4–5, Ürgüp. ✆ 0384/341-3002.

Prokopı Pub Bar   This bar occupies the central court of a former *han* (caravansary), in the center of town. It's unexpectedly chic, but what do you expect from an artist and a former PR executive from Istanbul? High-backed wooden stools line the island bar, but the tables for two stashed in the candlelit cave section at the back are especially romantic. There's also a breezy upper terrace, and pretty soon the cozy upstairs workshops will open as a restaurant. Summer daily 11am to 5am; winter daily 5:30pm to 3am. Cumhuriyet Meydanı 26, Ürgüp. ✆ 0384/341-4942.

3 Göreme ✶✶

15km (9⅓ miles) east of Nevşehir; 6.5km (4 miles) west of Ürgüp

With so many other charming and more characteristic villages in Cappadocia, it's a wonder that Göreme's popularity never wanes. Its name recognition has been high among backpackers, a state of affairs that led to a profusion of charmless, dormitory-style pensions and fly-by-night bars catering to a coed crowd.

As occupancy in the region in general increases, young ambitious entrepreneurs are stepping up to the plate with better-endowed pensions and outright luxury hotels. For the most part, however, the magic of the horizon is marred by the presence of modern, albeit low-rise, concrete slabs.

Ultimately, I don't usually recommend Göreme as a base, but with the prices of rooms skyrocketing in places like Ürgüp and even Üçhisar, Göreme is increasingly making sense. Staying here does have its advantages. The main appeal of Göreme, besides the Open Air Museum located on its fringes, is the village's proximity to some of the most scenic valley walks. Inconspicuous early churches dot the landscape between the town and the Open Air Museum, popping up unexpectedly at the edge of a lonely corner of a valley. In Göreme itself, one of the few villages in which the rock homes and fairy chimneys have been continually inhabited, the attractions share the spotlight with the daily lives of the locals.

Gentrification has yet to push out its natives and, with it, the authenticity of the village. In Göreme it's still common to run into a donkey delivery, or stumble upon a devout gaggle of chatty women and chickens, while staying fairly accessible to food, transportation, and Internet cafes.

ESSENTIALS

GETTING THERE

Most bus companies serving Göreme stop a few blocks from the center and provide the quick minibus transfer to the *otogar,* only 2 blocks away. If you planned on taking a taxi from the *otogar* to your hotel, you may as well grab one now. An area *dolmuş* follows a circuit hourly from Ürgüp bus station to Zelve, Avanos, Göreme, Üçhisar, and back. If you're traveling by car out of Ürgüp, you can either take the road to Avanos, turn onto the road past Zelve, and take the northern approach into Göreme; or head out of town on the Nevşehir road and take the steep cobblestone road through the Göreme Open Air Museum on your way into Göreme. The difference in mileage between the two approaches is negligible. So if your purpose is to see the town and museum, then by all means, take one road in and the other out.

VISITOR INFORMATION

The **tourist information office** is located at the *otogar* (Terminal Içi no. 1; ⓒ **0384/ 271-2124**) and mainly caters to visitors looking for accommodations. Inside is a collection of signboards of many of the pensions in town. The office is open Monday through Friday from 8:30am to 7pm, but many of the pensions have signs posted outside as well. Be on the lookout for misunderstandings relating to the cost of extras; sometimes there's a big surprise when the bill arrives. Pop into one of the several travel agencies at the *otogar* for a map of the area.

ORIENTATION

If you blink, you're bound to miss it. The road from the **Open Air Museum** leads right to the center of town over a dry creek bed; turn left onto **Uzundere Caddesi** until you get to the *otogar*. Everything you need is located here or just behind the station, including tour operators, car and scooter rentals, taxis, and the tourist information office. The **bazaar** is located behind the *otogar* around the mosque and Roman tower.

Adnan Menderes Caddesi forks off from Uzundere Caddesi closer to the turnoff from the museum; Kapadokya Balloons is on the right and the Orient Restaurant is on the left.

GETTING AROUND

Göreme is eminently walkable, especially because much of the center of town is flat. To venture a little farther out, hook up with one of the bicycle or scooter-rental shops at or around the *otogar*.

WHAT TO SEE & DO

Göreme Open Air Museum 🎔🎔🎔   Cappadocia's main attraction and the customary starting point for an overview of what the region has to offer, the Göreme Open Air Museum is a monastic complex composed of churches, rectories, and dwellings, and one of the earliest centers for religious education.

The practice of monasticism was developed by St. Basil the Great, bishop of Caesarea (Kayseri) in the 4th century, as a reaction to his increased disillusionment with the materialism of the Church. St. Basil's definition of monastic life, based on the idea that men should live in small, self-sufficient units with an emphasis on poverty, obedience, labor, and religious devotion, took root in Cappadocia, later becoming the basis for the Orthodox monastic system.

St. Basil, his brother St. Gregory of Nyssa, and St. Gregory of Nazianzoz (St. Gregorios the Theologian) greatly influenced the course of religious thought through their writings, contributing to the development of Eastern Orthodoxy. In his extensive writings St. Basil describes the nature of the Holy Spirit as a trilogy, while St. Gregory of Nyssa wrote of the dogma of the Virgin Mary, and St. Gregory of Nazianzoz developed the thesis on Jesus as a representative of the indivisible nature of the human and divine. Because of their contributions, Cappadocia became known as "the land of the three saints," but was soon divided in two in A.D. 371 when Emperor Valens rejected Basil's thesis on Jesus as the son of God.

There are at least 10 churches and chapels in the museum area dating between A.D. 900 and 1200, each one named (after a prominent attribute) by the local villagers who were exploring these caves long before there was an entrance fee. The paintings and decoration represent a flowering of a uniquely Cappadocian artistic style, while the Byzantine architectural features of the churches, like arches, columns, and capitals, are interesting in that not one of them is necessary structurally.

The best way to approach the site is to begin in a counterclockwise direction toward a clearly marked path.

During the Iconoclastic period, many of the frescoes and paintings were damaged, while the eyes of the images were scratched out by the local Turkish population superstitious of the "evil eye."

Past a small rock tower or **Monks' Convent** 🎔 is the **Church of St. Basil** 🎔, whose entrance is hollowed out with niches for small graves. This is a common feature of Cappadocian churches and it's still not uncommon to reach down and come up with a knuckle bone every now and again in the more remote valleys. Another recurring theme in Cappadocian churches is the image of St. George slaying the dragon. St.

George was considered a local hero, as local lore equated the dragon with a monster on the summit of Mount Erciyes. The church is decorated with scenes of Christ, with St. Basil and St. Theodore depicted on the north wall.

The **Church with the Apple (Elmalı Kilise)** 𝕽𝕽𝕽 is one of the smaller churches in the area, carved in the sign of a Greek cross with four irregular pillars supporting a central dome. The church was restored in 1991; however, the frescoes continue to chip off, revealing a layer of earlier paintings underneath. Paintings depict scenes of the saints, bishops, and martyrs, and to the right of the altar, a Last Supper with the symbolic fish (the letters of the word fish in Greek stand for "Jesus Christ, Son of God, the Savior"). The name of the church is believed to refer to a reddish orb in the left hand of the Archangel Michael in the dome of the main apse, although there's also speculation that there used to be an apple tree at the entrance to the church.

Santa Barbara was an Egyptian saint imprisoned by her father to protect her from the influences of Christianity. When she nevertheless found a way to practice her faith, her father tortured and killed her. The **Church of Santa Barbara** 𝕽𝕽𝕽, probably built as a tribute, is a cross-domed church with three apses, with mostly crudely painted geometrical patterns in red ochre believed to be symbolic in nature. The wall with the large locust probably represents evil, warded off by the protection of two adjacent crosses. The repetitive line of bricks above the rooster in the upper right-hand corner, symbolically warding off the evil influences of the devil, represents the Church.

The **Snake Church** 𝕽 is a simple barrel-vaulted church with a low ceiling and long nave. One fresco represents Saints Theodore and George slaying the dragon (looking suspiciously like a snake), with Emperor Constantine the Great and his mother, Helena, depicted holding the "True Cross." Legend has it that she discovered the cross upon which Jesus was crucified after seeing it in a dream, and that a piece of the cross is still buried in the foundations of the Ayasofya in Istanbul. Other sections of the cross are in the Church of the Holy Sepulchre and in St. Peter's in Rome. Another interesting portrait is the one of St. Onuphrius on the upper wall to the right of the entrance. The saint, a popular subject in medieval art, lived the life of a hermit in the Egyptian desert near Thebes and is usually depicted with a long gray beard and a fig leaf over his privates.

Until the 1950s the **Dark Church (Karanlık Kilise)** 𝕽𝕽𝕽 was used as a pigeon house. After 14 years of scraping pigeon droppings off the walls, these newly restored frescoes, depicting scenes from the New Testament, are the best preserved in all of Cappadocia and a fine example of 11th-century Byzantine art. Because light is allowed in through only one small opening, the richness of the pigments has survived the test of time. At the time of this writing, the additional 5YTL ($4.35/£2) admission fee for entry into the church had been suspended.

Cut into the same rock as the Dark Church and accessible via a metal walkway, the **Church with Sandals (Çarıklı Kilise)** 𝕽𝕽 takes its name from the two imprints on the floor inside the entrance. In the land of truth-stretching, these footprints have been given some weighty religious significance, but the fact is, they're just footprints and all of those stories are just more creative embellishment. The church is carved into a simple cross plan with intersecting barrel vaults. The frescoes, which date to the 11th century, depict the Nativity, the Baptism, the Adoration of the Magi, and other New Testament themes.

The last thing to see before exiting the museum is the **Nunnery,** or **Girls' Tower (Kızlar Kalesi)** 𝕽𝕽, a six-story convent cut into the rock with a system of tunnels, stairways, and corridors. The convent housed up to 300 nuns, whose proximity spawned rumors of a tunnel connecting the tower and the Monks' Convent to the right of the museum entrance.

About 5m (16 ft.) outside the exit to the museum site on the right is the **Buckle Church (Tokalı Kilise)** ꞌꞌꞌ, the largest rock-cut church and the one with the most sensational collection of frescoes in all of Cappadocia. Of all of the narrations of scenes from the Bible in the region, these are painted with the most detail and use the richest colors.

The Buckle Church is a complex formed of four chambers: the Old Church, the New Church, the Paracclesion, and the Lower Church. The **Old Church** dates to the 10th century, with pale hues of red and green painted in strips to represent scenes from the New Testament. Panels of rich indigo painted with pigments from the lapis stone dominate the **New Church,** carved out of the eastern wall of the Old Church and decorated with Eastern-style arches and a series of arcades. The **Paracclesion** is a chapel with a single apse, and the **Lower Church** has three aisles and a burial space, or *krypto.*

The high plateau behind **Tokalı Church** brings you to Kılıçlar Valley, named "Valley of the Swords" for the jagged formations that seem to slice into the sky. This is a favorite spot for hikers because of its high cliffs, deep ravines, and vineyards, in addition to a tunnel that forms part of an old drainage system. The cliff walls are dotted with dovecotes or pigeon houses hollowed out of the rock to harvest valuable fertilizer—pigeon droppings are rich in nitrogen—by area farmers. There are several old churches in this valley, but they are closed to the public. The best way to get to the valley is to enter along an access road from the road between the Göreme Museum and the town.

Outside of Göreme Center on the road to Üçhisar. ℂ **0384/271-2167**. Admission 10YTL ($8.70/£4). Daily 8am–5:30pm.

WHERE TO STAY

Göreme seems to have reached a saturation point of cheap accommodations, so if it's a bed in a squat chimney you're looking for, you've come to the right place. Head over from the bus station to the tourist office, where a cooperative formed by the local pension owners has organized its own little bulletin board.

Anatolian Houses ꞌꞌꞌ   Build it, and they will come. And boy, are they ever. The hotel sits inconspicuously up a narrow unassuming lane behind a high whitewashed stone wall. Jaws tend to drop upon entering, given the tiny decorative and utilitarian indoor/outdoor dipping pool. Also unexpected but stylish is the hotel's glass facade, allowing peeks into the spacious sitting room/lobby. As with almost all Cappadocian cave rooms, rooms are tucked away atop narrow and sometimes steep exterior stone stairways. If vertigo is a problem, ask for one of the rooms in the fairy chimney. Hotel decor alternates between antique collections such as terra-cotta amphorae and richly embroidered handmade bedcovers, with the odd carved nook or pair of stone columns. Fourteen rooms have Jacuzzis while four have hydromassage showers. Ask for a taste of the house wine on tap *in the wall* of the entry courtyard.

Gaferli Mah., 50180 Göreme. ℂ **0384/271-2463**. Fax 0384/271-2229. www.anatolianhouses.com. 18 units. 60€ ($87/£43) standard; 72€ ($104/£51) deluxe; 95€ ($138/£68) cave suite. Rates include breakfast. AE, DC, MC, V. **Amenities:** Restaurant; wine cellar; indoor/outdoor swimming pool; spa/wellness center; Turkish bath; sauna; business and meeting room; wireless Internet; room service (10am–midnight); laundry service; dry cleaning. *In room:* Satellite TV, minibar, kettle, hair dryer.

Göreme House ꞌ   This humble little guesthouse, converted from a century-old stately Paşa's mansion, is now in the very capable hands of new owner/managers Murat and Pınar, both veterans of Turkey's tourism industry. While before this three-story hotel was a bit sterile, now it represents small-town Turkish warmth as it should be. A few of the rooms are cut into the rock, but the majority are the typical single-vaulted rooms. Two suites are perked up with the addition of en-suite Jacuzzis. Two upper terraces, one a glass-enclosed bar and TV room and the other a spectacular open balcony, offer panoramic views of the neighboring fairy chimneys and rock-cut houses.

Eselli Mah. 47, 50180 Göreme. ⓒ 0384/271-2060. Fax 0384/271-2669. www.goremehouse.com. 13 units. 60€ ($87/£43) standard; 72€ ($104/£51) deluxe; 95€ ($138/£68) cave suite. MC, V. **Amenities:** Restaurant; bar; laundry service; dry cleaning.

Kelebek Pansiyon and Kelebek Boutique Hotel   A far cry from the scrappy backpacker's pension I first visited in 2000, Kelebek has upgraded, expanded, and grown up. The rooms in the pension rate well above pension level, with prices that give those over at the boutique hotel a run for their money. A comparative bargain—double rooms for as low as 60YTL ($52/£24)—can be had in about half of the rooms; the catch is that these units are comparatively smaller. The Kelebek's boutique hotel is an all-cave suites annex, taking up the spacious interiors of a number of fairy chimneys. Suites are decked out in Ottoman style and sport bathrooms with marble walls, Jacuzzis, and *hamam* basins.

Aydinli Mah., 50180 Göreme. ⓒ **0384/271-2531.** Fax 0384/271-2763. www.klebekhotel.com. 25 units. 60YTL– 190YTL ($52–$165/£24–£76). MC, V. **Amenities:** Restaurant; bar; laundry service; dry cleaning.

WHERE TO DINE

Alaturca   TURKISH   Newly opened in the summer of 2005, Alaturca rapidly advanced to rank among those very few Cappadocian restaurants where residents become regulars. The atmosphere is outstanding: solid wooden farmers tables under tentlike drapings of embroidered Anatolian blankets and other local handicrafts. Outside on the lawn are a smattering of beanbag chairs for partaking of tea and the wireless Internet. The restaurant, bar, and cafe serve breakfast, snacks, and meals throughout the day.

Göreme center. ⓒ **0384/271-2882.** Appetizers and main courses 6YTL–25YTL ($5.20–$22/£2.40–£10). MC, V. Daily 7am until the last person leaves.

Orient Restaurant ⭐ (Kids) TURKISH   The Orient is hands-down the most solidly consistent restaurant in Göreme. Highlights of the menu include a steak rivaling anything I've had anywhere, and an outstanding lamb rack. Orient also has an outstanding wine list that includes French imports and the best local wines (try the Öküzgözü or the Kalecik Karası). Its location at the farthest reaches of town could easily give you the impression of being in a country inn, but it's not so far as to act as a deterrent if what you're looking for is just a quick bite to eat. There are both an outdoor patio terrace and a light and airy dining room where you can grab one of the many low-to-the-ground tables with reclining-back chairs.

Göreme Center (across from Kapadokya Balloons). ⓒ **0384/271-2346.** www.orientrestaurant.net. Appetizers and main courses 5YTL–25YTL ($4.35–$22/£2–£10). MC, V. Daily 7am until the last person leaves.

4 Üçhisar ⭐⭐⭐

9km (5⅗ miles) east of Nevşehir; 6km (3¾ miles) southwest of Göreme

The sleepy troglodyte village of Üçhisar, spread out at the base of the fortress, is a place where time altogether stands still. In the valley surrounding Üçhisar, the advancement of rock formation and erosion can be seen in all of its stages. Cresting above the valley are pink-and-yellow-hued sand dunes that when under closer scrutiny reveal rocky channels. Down below, perforating the rock face of Güvercinlik Vadisi, or Pigeon Valley, are the best examples of pigeon houses, painted white to attract the birds and their valuable guano. The fortress of Üçhisar is the highest peak in the region, drawing tourists to its summit for panoramic views of this fascinating landscape with Mount Erciyes in the distance.

Not surprisingly, the quiet landscape of Üçhisar has been discovered but it's still a far cry from the polish of Ürgüp or the bustle of Göreme. Visitors can still get a taste of the elusive and authentic Cappadocian village experience before Üçhisar succeeds in renovating itself beyond recognition. Hurry.

ESSENTIALS

GETTING THERE & GETTING AROUND   Regular municipal buses run from Nevşehir to Üçhisar, but the village is close enough to Nevşehir that you could take a cab without breaking the bank. If you're coming from Göreme, you can get on one of the frequent buses running to Nevşehir. Because of its quiet, isolated nature, Üçhisar is more for the independent traveler; staying here is going to require your own wheels.

ORIENTATION   The village of Üçhisar is centered around the **fortress,** surrounded by a hillside of oddly shaped house-caves and neatly carved facades. Around Üçhisar is the spectacular scenery of Güvercinlik Valley, dotted with dovecotes and rolling rock dunes. A tea garden and outdoor restaurant occupy the center of town.

WHAT TO SEE & DO

Üçhisar has attracted its fair share of French tourists, drawn by the possibility of utter seclusion in one of the exclusive cave houses of Les Maisons de Cappadoce (p. 350). Life's frenetic pace is all but forgotten in Üçhisar, where tourists rarely venture farther than the towering rock fortress.

Üçhisar Castle   The highest peak in the region and the most prominent land formation, the Üçhisar Castle is a larger-than-life sculpture. A climb up the 120 steps to the summit of the fortress is a logical introduction to the rocky scapes of Cappadocia. In the 15th and 16th centuries, the Byzantine army took advantage of the natural elevation of three of the area's rock formations and used them as natural fortresses. Üçhisar, together with Ortahisar and a rock castle at Ürgüp (now in ruins), provided the means for an early warning system using mirrors and lights, sending messages among the fortresses and as far afield as Istanbul. Today the outer layers of Üçhisar's rock have been washed away by erosion to reveal a honeycombed structure of tunnels and cavities, rising above the man-made facades of the modern semi-troglodyte village. Recently discovered was a secret tunnel leading to the riverbed, which provided an emergency water supply in the event of an attack.

Üçhisar. ✆ **0384/219-2618.** Admission 3YTL ($2.60/£1.20). Daily 8am–sunset.

WHERE TO STAY

The latest indication of not only the general prosperity of the region as a whole, but of the advancement of this little castle village well past its status as diamond in the rough, is the arrival of the **Cappadocia Cave Resort** (Tekeli Mah. Göreme Cad. Divanli Sok. 1; ✆ **0384/219-3194**). Too new for this guide, the construction of this 85-room hotel was in progress until recently. Its three levels are built into and around four of the oldest cave houses in the village and host a swimming pool, high-end spa, sushi bar, karaoke bar, and discreet and personalized service.

Les Maisons de Cappadoce ★★ Renovated by Jacques Avizou, an expatriate French architect, these romantic cave houses look as if they stepped right out of a feature in *Maison et Jardin*. The houses are located right in the middle of a forest of fairy chimneys in the heart of the village, providing a rare opportunity for total immersion into the landscape. Closed gates and unremarkable doorways open to reveal duplex and triplex houses with breathtaking arches, stone terraces, garden courtyards, and huge fully equipped kitchens (except in the studios, which have kitchenettes). A welcome basket full of basic provisions (bread, butter, sugar, salt, eggs, and water) will be delivered on request for an additional fee. Residents are requested to provide access to the gardener or camera crews, who every now and again choose Les Maisons de Cappadoce as a location for a movie or magazine spread. The only problem with this Garden of Eden is that once you've arrived, you never want to leave. The magic of the spot is all the more evident at sunset, when the sky and chimneys turn glorious shades of red and purple.

Semiramis Aş, Belediye Meydanı 24, 50240 Üçhisar. (**C**) **0384/219-2813**. Fax 0384/219-2782. www.cappadoce.com. 5 studios, 9 houses for 4–7 people. 130€–160€ ($189–$232/£93–£114) studio; 240€–980€ ($348–$1,421/£171–£700) house. Breakfast "hamper" included in rate. Rate reduction for stays over 7 nights. MC, V. **Amenities:** Laundry service; dry cleaning. *In room:* Kitchen, fridge, coffeemaker, hair dryer.

Les Terrasses d'Üçhisar (Value (Kids For those on a budget, this is the best option in town. The hotel consists of eight cave rooms, six Anatolian-style rooms with single-barrel vaults, and one family suite in a group of adjacent stone houses. The setup is typical of the area pensions—accommodations are clean, with floors of stone and tile, and ad-hoc bathroom/shower combos that you eventually do get used to. To sweeten the deal, Les Terrasses includes breakfast and walks in the valley (and maybe a stop at their friend's place?) with the room rate. The suite can accommodate up to five people, making this a good bet for families.

Eski Göreme Yolu, 50240 Üçhisar. (**C**) **0384/219-2792**. Fax 0384/219-2762. www.terrassespension.com. 15 units. 28€ ($41/£20) single; 32€ ($46/£23) double; 72€ ($104/£51) family suite. MC, V. **Amenities:** Restaurant; bar; tour desk; laundry service; dry cleaning.

Villa Cappadocia As Göreme and Ürgüp continue to attract record numbers of visitors, new hotels are popping up in Üçhisar to accommodate the overflow. The Villa Cappadocia is one of the more recent additions—simply but artfully appointed rooms occupying a splendid site on the hillside overlooking the valley. And because it's new, the bathroom facilities—enclosed showers and plenty of modern tile—are very user-friendly. A grassy terrace shaded by some lemon trees sprawls adjacent to the hotel building, a breezy and relaxing spot for a midafternoon refreshment. The cellar restaurant (which also houses a wine cellar) is one of the more romantic spots around.

Kayabaşı Sok. 18, 50240 Üçhisar. (**C**) **0384/219-3138**. Fax 0384/219-3140. www.villacappadocia.com. 12 units. $100 (£50) double. MC, V. **Amenities:** Restaurant; bar; laundry service; dry cleaning. *In room:* Satellite TV. Closed in winter.

WHERE TO DINE

Üçhisar still has a long way to go to catch up to Ürgüp or Göreme in the dining area, but remember—that's a *good* thing. As soon as commercialism rears its ugly head in town, it'll be time to move on to another undiscovered corner of Cappadocia. Every little town has its own epicenter, and here it's the **Center Café and Restaurant,** Belediye Meydanı (© **0384/219-3117**), a leafy terrace tea garden serving standard dishes.

Elai *ℛ* EUROPEAN/REGIONAL TURKISH   Named for Kubilay, the owner, Elai is a dressy alternative to the standard eateries that litter the town centers. Housed in the former local social club (think men, tea, and *tavla,* or backgammon), the interior has been spiffed up to make the most of a soaring space of sandstone and wood beams. The kitchen prepares a combination of European and regional Turkish cuisine, offering guests a diverse menu that includes rack of lamb, duck à l'orange, and *dolmalar* (stuffed grape leaves, stuffed peppers, and so forth). Standouts during my meal were the moussaka and the *mercemek köftesi,* Mom's southeastern recipe of spicy lentil balls. Dinner or a sunset drink can also be taken on the moonlit terrace overlooking the valley and Üçhisar Castle in the distance.

Eski Göreme Cad. 61. © 0384/219-3181. Reservations suggested. Appetizers and main courses 15YTL–20YTL ($13–$17/£6–£8). MC, V. Daily 11am–11pm.

A SIDE TRIP TO AVANOS

With a tradition of pottery making that dates back to Hittite times, Avanos has made its name out of red clay. At one time, the craft so permeated the culture of the city that every household had a pottery wheel or workshop. Now the most prominent feature of the town, besides the unsightly terra-cotta sculpture in the town center, is the word "chez," as something about this particular corner of Cappadocia acts as a magnet for French nationals. As a base for explorations in Cappadocia, I couldn't recommend Avanos less. For 2 hours of poking in and out of ceramic shops, I have only slightly better things to say, if only regarding the region's distinctive terra-cotta pottery and the admittedly spectacular Ottoman ceramic reproductions.

The city, carved into the rock like so many other ancient Cappadocian towns, sits along the banks of the Kızılırmak (Red River), the longest river in Turkey. The river takes its name from the color of the water, stained by the red clay exclusive to the region, an abundant source of the raw material necessary in pottery production. Currently there are about 30 pottery shops in town, most of them boasting the same techniques used by the Hittites. But although Avanos has its own homegrown brand of terra-cotta urns, a vast majority of the classic Iznik and Kütahya designs are mass-produced using clay from Kütahya (see "Iznik & Nicaea: A Pilgrimage & Some Plates," under "Side Trips from Istanbul," in chapter 4) and marketed as valuable high-quality "Iznik reproductions." Sure, it's fascinating and fun to participate in a dirty demo on the kick-wheel, but it's all part of the sales pitch, as are the endless fabrications about quality—seems the art of Turkish salesmanship extends beyond the fringes of carpeting to the delicate surfaces of these ceramics. Worse, I have yet to successfully hand-carry a sample home, as many of the plates are much cheaper quality than the price might indicate. Charge it, have it shipped, and pay the bill only after the piece arrives safely on your doorstep.

GETTING THERE   Avanos lies at the northern tip of Cappadocia, 18km (11 miles) to Nevşehir, 9km (5⅔ miles) to Göreme, and 12km (7½ miles) to Ürgüp. Municipal buses into Avanos leave from Nevşehir hourly between 8am and 5pm. There are also *dolmuşes* leaving from Nevşehir as well as from Ürgüp to Avanos every 2 hours between 9am and 5pm.

WHERE TO DINE   Offering an unusually elegant environment for Avanos is **Bizim Ev,** Orta Mahallesi, Baklacı Sok. 1 (behind the Sarıhan; © 0384/511-5525; daily 9am–midnight), with four dining areas, including an indoor terrace, an outdoor

The Caravansaries of the Silk Road

One of the five pillars of Islam is the Koranic obligation of alms-giving, and in the fulfillment of this obligation, the Selçuks were notorious for their commitment to public works. One of the institutions created by the Selçuks in Anatolia was the *kervansaray*, or "caravan palace." Used as military bases during wartime and as inns in peacetime, these fortresses provided protection to merchants traveling along the trade routes, offering them up to 3 days of free lodging and an unprecedented system of insurance in the event of loss or injury. Caravansaries were spaced out along the trade routes at a distance of about every 49km (30 miles)—1 day's travel—and from sunset to sunrise when the main gate was closed, guests were officially under the protection of the sultan.

With control over the land trade routes and the centralization of power, Anatolia became the center of international trade under the Selçuk Empire. Thus the "Silk Road" became a great source of wealth, as taxes on overland goods continued to fill the coffers of the sultan. Spices, ivory, and fine cloth were brought from the Far East, while surprisingly, much of the trade was in slaves. The Ottoman *devşirme* system was to collect men from the Eastern lands, train them in the art of warfare, and sell them off to neighboring southern states.

Rarely did anyone travel the entire length of the route. Caravansaries also operated as marketplaces, where merchants could unload their goods, have a bath, and move on. It was unusual for anyone to stay beyond the 3-day limit, because a person's selling power was linked to the availability of new clientele, and that fizzled out after the first day. A typical journey lasted about a month before a merchant headed back home; by the time a shipment of silk brocade found its way to Istanbul, the price had been considerably marked up.

The caravansary was built according to one of three basic plans: an open courtyard, a covered building, or a combination of the two. The most opulent of the caravansaries were those reflecting the prosperity of the sultan. Called "sultanhans," these caravansaries were built on an essentially identical plan. The main portal opened onto a courtyard with a small raised mosque at the center. To the left was an arcade providing much-needed shade for protection against the scorching summer sun. On the right was a second portal leading into the apartments, which included a kitchen and *hamam*. At the back was an ornamental gate for access into the winter hall, a covered structure that shows a striking resemblance to a medieval church. The vaults in the main nave could be up to 14m (46 ft.) high, while the top of the lantern, a central domed space providing the only light in the hall, could be at a height of up to 20m (66 ft.). The walls were thick enough to provide good insulation, and tiny windows in the lantern kept out the cold. Men and camels sometimes slept in the winter section together, which, combined with the smell of spices and smoke from the oil lamps and water pipes, probably required the use of a *whole* lot of incense.

While the exterior of the fortress structure was plain, the Selçuks had a tradition of richly ornamenting the *pishtaq*, or portal. The *pishtaq*, generally limestone or marble, displayed elaborate geometrical carvings, tracery, rosettes, and inscriptions, and was hollowed out into a stalactite niche much like that of a *mihrab* (a niche that indicates the direction of Mecca).

There were also private caravansaries called *hans*, mostly located in towns that charged a fee for lodging, while the *bedesten* was typically a marketplace and workshop only. These sensational structures dot the Anatolian landscape from Istanbul to Antalya and from Erzurum to Izmir, and are used as hotels, restaurants, or the dreaded discothèque; you'll probably have the opportunity to stay in one in the course of your travels.

The best conserved of all the Selçuk *hans* is the **Sultanhanı** located about 32km (20 miles) outside of Aksaray on the road to Konya. The Sultanhanı, built by Alaeddin Keykubat I in 1229, has a highly ornamented *pishtaq* with a variety of decorative patterns applied in an unrelated, almost spontaneous manner.

Another fine example of a *sultanhan* is the **Ağzıkarahan,** located 15km (9⅓ miles) outside of Aksaray on the road to Nevşehir. The Ağzıkarahan, the third largest in the area along the Silk Road, has weathered time to remain almost intact and encloses a space of over 6,000 sq. m (64,583 sq. ft.). The open section, now used to display carpets, was built by Alaeddin Keykubat in 1231 and includes the central mosque reachable by steep and cumbersome steps. The winter section is attributed to Sultan Giyaseddin Keyhüsrev and was completed 8 years after the open section. Enormous stone vaults rise above the main aisle of the nave, flanked by raised platforms that were used for meals during the day and as sleep space at night. The camels were kept behind the raised area in the side bays. Unfortunately, the central dome has been lost.

Halfway between Aksaray and Nevşehir is the **Alay Han,** the first *sultanhan* to be built in Central Anatolia. Erected in 1192 by Sultan Kılıçarslan II, the Alay Han is threatened to become another "day facility" by the same investor who "preserved" the **Sarıhan** in Avanos. The Sarıhan, located 5km (3 miles) outside of Avanos, whose name means "yellow *han*" for the color of its stone, stands on an old trade route between Aksaray and Kayseri. Except for the mosque, which has been placed above the entrance, the caravansary follows a traditional *sultanhan* plan, with massive barrel vaults supporting the arcades and side aisles of the winter hall. It now serves as a daytime cafe and an evocative setting for a nightly staging of the *sema*, or rite of the **Whirling Dervishes,** which takes place in the winter hall or sleeping quarters. (Sarıhan is 5km/3 miles outside of Avanos center, on the road to Kaysari; ✆ **0384/511-3795;** reservations required; admission 25€/$36/£18; Apr–Oct nightly at 9:30pm, Nov–Mar at 9pm—show starts promptly, so get there early, because there's no consideration for latecomers.)

sun patio, and an upstairs "back room" mellowed by stone, arches, and *kilims*. Order the *bostan kebap,* a decadent dish of shredded beef and eggplant covered in cheese and baked in a clay pot, or the uncannily juicy *tavuk şiş* (roasted chicken), all at prices too reasonable to believe (appetizers and main courses 4YTL–12YTL/$3.50–$10/£1.60–£4.80; MasterCard and Visa accepted).

WHERE TO SHOP   Chez Galip, PTT Karşısı 24 (2 blocks east along Atatürk Cad. in a square on the left; © **0384/511-4240;** fax 0384/511-4543; www.chez-galip.com/index.htm), is probably the best-known atelier in Avanos. In the pottery business for nearly half a century, Chez Galip has gained fame (infamy?) for the creepy and diabolical hair collection in one of the back caves. My advice: Keep your hair and instead fork over a wad of New Turkish Lira for one of the fine ceramic pieces displayed throughout the seven cave rooms.

One of my personal favorites is the "special family design" creations at **Kaya Seramik House and Güray Çömlekçilik,** Eski Nevşehir Yolu 18 (from Avanos center, ceramic center is just outside of town on the old Nevşehir road on the right; © **0384/511-5091;** www.gurayseramik.com.tr). The showroom, stocked chock-full of traditional and one-of-a-kind designs, takes up 12 caves carved into the rock on the road out of town. *Note to the budget-minded:* These are far from cheap.

Sirca, Alaeddin Camii Yanı (© **0384/511-3686**), claims to have the largest collection of ceramics in Turkey, employing more than 100 people. Sirca also has an original line of Byzantine and religious decorative designs: classical repros of vases and the like decorated with symbols from Hittite mythology or in the Greek style.

5 Derinkuyu & Kaymaklı ⊛⊛⊛

Derinkuyu is 26km (16 miles) south of Nevşehir; Kaymaklı is 18km (12 miles) south of Nevşehir

While the idea of a prehistoric people seeking shelter in caves is not a foreign one, it's startling to have discovered a system of underground cities as sophisticated as those found in Cappadocia. Over 200 underground cities at least two levels deep have been discovered in the area between Kayseri and Nevşehir, with around 40 of those comprised of at least three levels or more. The troglodyte cities at Derinkuyu and Kaymaklı are two of the best examples of underground dwellings.

It remains a mystery as to who first started the digging, although Hittite artifacts found around the caves—and the fact that many of the towns' names go back to the Hittite or Sumerian language—suggest they were inhabited as far back as 3,000 to 4,000 years ago. The early Christians probably sought temporary shelter from the persecution of Roman soldiers; and after the 6th century, these dwellings provided protection from raiding Arab tribes. The crude carving of the surface levels of rock give way to a smoother, more refined face, which indicates that the levels were carved by different people at different times.

Each rock settlement had access to the safe haven of these underground dwellings by way of a secret underground passageway that would provide swift and unseen escape in times of emergency. In fact, an access tunnel can still be found on just about every villager's property. Additionally, the underground cities of Derinkuyu and Kaymaklı, about 9km (5⅔ miles) apart, are believed to be connected by an underground tunnel.

Every crucial entry point into the city was either camouflaged or blocked by a keystone, a large stone wheel that, once fixed in place, was immovable. Keystones were fixed at every level of the city as well. The labyrinth of tunnels and blind passageways

---

⸨Fun Fact **Did You Know?**

Twenty thousand people living underground produce a lot of solid waste. Lime added to cow's liver serves as a natural accelerator of the decomposition process—an important fact for those long periods underground.

---

hundreds of feet below the ground give shocking testimony to the tenaciousness of a civilization to survive and prosper by sentencing itself to months of existence deep within the earth.

GETTING THERE   Because *dolmuşes* to Kaymaklı and Derinkuyu that run out of Nevşehir require a time-consuming transfer, this is one of those times where a day tour or car rental will come in handy. The two sites are close enough to visit back-to-back, and while you're at it, you can add a side trip to the Ihlara Valley or to the evocative village of Güzelyurt.

Kaymaklı is 18km (11 miles) south of Nevşehir, with another 9km (5⅔ miles) south on the same road to get to Derinkuyu. Both cities can be reached by taking the Ürgüp Soğanlı road and taking the turnoff at Güzelöz.

VISITING THE CITIES
Going underground presents some uncomfortable conditions. Although passageways are well lit and even the lowest levels are ventilated, a few of the access ramps are long and narrow, requiring visitors to ascend or descend in single file, and in some cases, hunched over. On a busy day, problems can arise for those at the lower levels, as visitors might be stuck waiting for the last of an endless group of arrivals to clear the passageway before exiting. The visit can also be strenuous: At 204 steps, the corridor from the lowest level of Derinkuyu to the surface will cause even the most physically fit visitor to catch his or her breath and may require you to hunch over for a good part of the way.

Arrows mark the direction of the visit (red for in, blue for out). As long as you stick to the route, you should be okay, but don't wander off with a flashlight, because this labyrinth was designed to confuse intruders just like you. It's fine to veer off track in the presence of a guide—incidentally, a great and terrifying way to see how dark absolute darkness can be.

Try to avoid peak visitation hours by getting there early; tours clog the narrow one-way tunnels and cause small galleries to become loud and stuffy. Curious about the possibility of a power outage, I was told that in the event that the lights go out, a backup generator would kick in after 10 seconds.

Those with claustrophobic tendencies have mixed reactions to visiting these sites: Some find going underground to be a walk in the park, while others don't fare as well. It's really up to the individual to decide his or her own level of tolerance. For those concerned with claustrophobia or physical limitations, a good alternative to the Derinkuyu and Kaymaklı underground cities is the more modest **Mazıköy Underground City and Roman Graves** (5YTL/$4.35/£2 daily 8am–6:30pm; if the ticket window is closed during open hours, go find a local to track down the ticket taker). The underground complex is actually built *up* into the rock formation; the entrance is at ground level. More adventurous explorers should check this one out as well; access to the upper levels will require some rudimentary rock-climbing skills, a dusty experience described by friends as "epic."

Derinkuyu Underground City (Derinkuyu Yeraltı Şehri) The underground city at Derinkuyu, aptly translated as "dark well," is the largest known example of troglodyte living in Cappadocia. Eight of the levels are open to the public, with the lowest level at a depth of 54m (177 ft.). The complex is an organized and functionally advanced public space for galleries, rooms, chapels, access tunnels, water wells, and air shafts for when the communities had to dig in for the long haul. A long raised mound surrounded by trenches is thought to have been used as a school, while the stables occupied the extreme upper floors.

Only about 10% to 15% of the city's total area is available to the public, and it is thought that the city goes much farther down. Like many of the underground cities, the passageways and cavities at Derinkuyu were used as storage by local farmers until 1964, when the complex was opened to the public.

Derinkuyu. ℂ 0384/381-3194. Admission 10YTL ($8.70/£4). Daily 8am–5pm.

Kaymaklı Underground City (Kaymaklı Yeraltı Şehri) Where the sheer vastness of the underground city at Derinkuyu makes it an impressive example of a troglodyte complex, its functional nature is more easily appreciated at Kaymaklı. On the four levels that have been cleared out since 1964, kitchens, stables, and a winery have been discovered, as well as a chapel with a confessional. The complex, believed to go down 20m (66 ft.), was home to approximately 15,000 people at a time, with air shafts, water wells, and storage spaces capable of supporting the population for several months.

Practical considerations, including protection, survival, and revelry, were given to many facets of living underground. In the face of an attack, keystones were quickly moved into place; these blocked access from the outside and sealed off the various levels. Small holes were carved into the floor and used to communicate with the level above or below, so even when the keystone was pushed back, residents were saved from taking the long way around to pass on messages. The engineering of air shafts that extend beyond the lowest level and exit just below ground level provide an efficient and impressive level of air circulation that even succeeded in emptying the tunnels of the black smoke from the kitchen hearths. Because the same flues were used for communication and for water wells, the shafts did not extend all the way to the surface; this protected the water supply from contamination. Other interesting details are the grape presses that allowed for the grape juice to drain into a stone tank below. Wine was an important consideration in daily life, and probably used in religious rites as well.

Kaymaklı. ℂ 0384/218-2500. Admission 10YTL ($8.70/£4). Daily 8am–5pm.

6 The Ihlara Valley ★

97km (60 miles) southwest of Nevşehir; 49km (30 miles) southeast of Aksaray; 15km (9¹/₃ miles) southwest of Güzelyurt

A hike through the canyon is an opportunity to see the Cappadocia of more than 1,000 years ago. Only 49km (30 miles) south of Nevşehir, the barren scape of the Ihlara Valley splits open to reveal a 15km (9½-mile) fissure created by the force of the Melendez River. In contrast with the dusty expanses of the rest of Cappadocia, the bottom of the canyon, nourished by the riverbed, is verdant with vegetation supporting village life much as it did centuries ago. Local women wade along the banks of the river, their traditional baggy trousers trailing in the river's edge as they do the day's washing.

As residents are drawn to Ihlara's canyon fertility, so were the earliest Christians: The canyon is home to over 100 **churches** and an estimated 4,000 **dwellings** sculpted into the soft rock face of the valley.

The canyon descends over 90m (295 ft.) in some places, twisting and turning at the beckoning of the river along wide trails lined with poplars and pistachio trees or narrowly navigable paths. There are a number of official entry and exit points along the canyon, past modest yet viable troglodyte villages. Official entry and exit points at the villages allow for either full-day or abbreviated hikes, but you should leave time for detours to the area churches and to pet the donkeys tied to a tree along the river's edge.

ESSENTIALS

GETTING THERE & GETTING AROUND   If you come by private car, you'll probably have to leave it in the parking lot at the main entrance, which doesn't do you much good way over at the opposite end of the canyon in Belisırma or Selime. An easier way is to take a guided tour; this will make seeing the valley a whole lot richer, giving you the background information necessary to appreciate the rock churches, rather than taking just a lovely walk through the gorge. Not to be overlooked is the bonus of having someone waiting for you at the end of the canyon, thus saving you the long hike back. (You can also hike up and out to the main road and catch a rare *dolmuş* back to the main entrance.) Guides are expensive, though, so if you've got the stamina, then by all means, go it alone.

It's a 1½-hour drive from central Cappadocia to the Ihlara Valley. From central Cappadocia, follow the road through Nevşehir, to Aksaray, and then to the village of Ihlara. The traditional hike begins at the main entrance about 1.6km (1 mile) outside the village. It is not advisable to take a *dolmuş* (the only choice for public transport), because doing so will require three separate *dolmuşes* plus a taxi from the village of Ilhara to the entrance to the valley.

ORIENTATION   The main entrance to the valley is a little over 1.6km (1 mile) north of the village of Ihlara. There's a parking lot, a snack shop, and the main gate leading to the long stairway down. The cliff walls are dotted with churches and abodes on both banks of the river, with most of the sites of interest clustered around the wooden footbridge at the base of the main entrance and over near the village of Belisırma. The 3.5km (2¼-mile) hike from the main entrance to the village of Belisırma is a relatively easy one, and many people choose to have lunch at the restaurant near the riverbed and call it a day. It's also possible to begin the hike at the village of Ihlara following the left bank of the river, adding on about 3km (1¾ miles) to the total. The shorter hike takes about 1½ to 2 hours, depending on your level of fitness, while a hike up the entire canyon will take about 5 hours.

EXPLORING THE IHLARA VALLEY

Ihlara Canyon   The most common starting point to a hike into the valley is the southern entrance near the village of Ihlara, down an endless man-made serpentine stairway 400 steps to the bottom. About 3.5km (2¼ miles) away, over sometimes-rough terrain, is the village of Belisırma, an ancient center of medicine before Selçuk Sultan Kılıçarslan II transferred the school to Aksaray. The process of mummification was extensively practiced in this part of the valley; a mummy of a woman found here is on display in the Niğde Archaeological Museum.

The churches, some of which are difficult to reach, date from the 8th or 9th century while the decorative frescoes date to a later post-Iconoclastic period, somewhere between the 10th and 13th centuries. The styles of the churches are generally grouped into two categories: those with an Egyptian or Syrian influence mainly found around the main entrance, and those reflecting a typical Byzantine style bunched around Belisırma.

The first church encountered at the bottom of the steps from Ihlara is **Ağaçaltı Kilisesi** ★★★, or the Church Under the Tree, also known as the Church of Daniel or the Church of Pantassa. Designed on a Greek cross plan, the interior, which has succumbed quite a bit to the elements, may appear a bit primitive at first, but a closer inspection reveals a strong Eastern influence, visible through the use of checker patterns, medallions, and rosettes. An interesting detail is in the depiction of the Nativity; notice that the Magi are seen dressed in Phrygian-style caps. The scene of the Dormition of the Virgin recalls the mosaics of St. Savior in Chora in Istanbul, with a depiction of Jesus holding the soul of Mary in the form of an infant.

Other churches in the vicinity of the Ihlara entrance and worthy of note are the **Pürenli Seki Kilisesi (the Church with Terraces)** ★★, and the **Kokar Kilisesi (the Church That Smells!)** ★★, both to the right of the steps as you descend into the canyon.

Considered the oldest church in the valley, the **Eğritaş Kilisesi (the Church with the Crooked Stone)** ★★ was probably a funerary chapel. The vaulted chapel has a single apse and a burial chamber below, much of which has been damaged by erosion and rockslides. The badly decaying frescoes, depicting scenes from the life of Christ, are distinctive for a style that recalls Eastern pre-Iconoclastic art.

On the other side of the river over a wooden footbridge is the **Yılanlı Kilisesi (Church of the Serpents)** ★★. The church is named for the scene on the western wall, showing serpents in the act of punishing four female sinners. Women as the source of evil is a common Eastern theme taken up by later monks, and in this case, the representations probably symbolize the sin of adultery, disobedience, and slander. The most graphic of the punishments shows the fourth female sinner with two snakes biting her nipples, probably for her failure to feed her children.

Back on the left bank of the river heading in the direction of Belisırma is the **Sümbüllü Kilisesi (The Hyacinth Church)** ★★, distinctive for its ornate facade of pillars and arched niches carved directly into the rock. A set of steps leads up to the church, passing the wild growths of hyacinths that give the complex its name. The church is actually a monastery complex hollowed out of the cliff; there are spaces for both living and worship. The few surviving frescoes include a well-preserved Annunciation and a Dormition.

Kırk Damaltı Kilisesi (the Church of St. George) ★★★, one of the latest of the region, is interesting from a purely social aspect. A portrait of the donor, a female in Byzantine dress, is pictured with her husband, a man in typical Selçuk costume. The inscription reads: "This most venerable church . . . decorated through the assistance of the lady Thamar, here pictured, and of her Emir Basil Giagoupes, under his Majesty the most noble and Great Sultan Masud at the time when Sire Andronikos reigned over the Romans." It is thought to be an expression of Christian gratitude for the religious tolerance of the Selçuk Turks and dates the church to the late 13th century.

Take the Nevşehir-Aksaray rd. and turn off on the road south for Ihlara; the road leading into the canyon is signposted before the entrance to the village. (C) **0382/453-7084.** Admission 5YTL ($4.35/£2); parking extra. Daily 8am–7pm.

CAPPADOCIA TO THE COAST: A VISIT TO KONYA

Capital of the Selçuk Empire for only a scarce hundred or so years, Konya, when not described as largely resembling Detroit, exhibits one of the country's richest architectural collections of mosques, baths, caravanseries, and *medreses* (seminaries). Home of one of Islam's greatest mystical movements, the Mevlana, or Sufi sect of "Whirling Dervishes," continues to find spiritual enlightenment through the sema, or ritual whirling dance.

Konya is also Turkey's most infamously religious province, so it's a rare hotel or restaurant that serves alcohol, and the mosque entryways turn into traffic jams at prayer time. But like Turkey itself, Konya is a city of contradictions. Although the reputed spiritual center of Turkey and one of the most conservative towns in Anatolia, Konya has the highest rate of consumption of alcohol of anywhere in the country. Rebellion takes many forms, and in a city with 50,000 students, it's in the lipstick and rouge and in skirts with slits as far up as the knee—probably Konya's version of a pierced nose.

Most travelers come here to make a pilgrimage to the tomb of Mevlana, founder of the venerable Sufi sect of Islam that preaches love, charity, humility, equality, and tolerance, among other elemental principles. Members of the sect seek union with God through a meditative ceremony called the *sema*, a ritual whirling symbolizing the liberation from earthly bonds and a connection with the heavens. Ironically, all Sufi sects were banned by Atatürk in the 1920s in his far-reaching opposition to religious extremism. But Mevlana's ideals are hard to keep down, and in recent years Sufism has gained a popular following not only among Turks, but also internationally.

GETTING THERE   By Plane   Turkish Airlines (© 0212/444-0849; www.thy.com), **Pegasus** (© 444-0737; www.flypgs.com), and **Onur Air** (© 444-6687; www.onurair.com.tr) provide service from Istanbul to Konya Airport (© 0332/345-0288), located about 17km (11 miles) outside of the center of town.

By Bus   Countless bus companies run hourly service from Antalya (5 hr.). The most reliable of these are Kontur, Meram, Metro, Kontaş, and Özkaymak. These and other major bus companies offer repeated daily service from Istanbul (9 hr.; 47YTL/$41/£19), Ankara (3 hr.; 21YTL/$18/£8.40), Antalya (5 hr.; 27YTL/$23/£11), Izmir (8 hr.; 36YTL/$31/£14), and Nevşehir (4 hr.; 18YTL/$16/£7.20). Fares reflect those on Metro buses.

A taxi from the *otogar* will take about 20 minutes and cost around 10YTL ($8.70/£4), but if you don't have a lot of luggage to carry around, you may want to take the tramway (exit the main entrance, walking left along the main road toward the main intersection; the tramway is on the right corner), which takes about 45 minutes and costs 1YTL (87¢/40p). The train is marked ALAADDIN (get off at Alaaddin Hill in the center of town); from there, the Balıkçılar and Rumi are about a 10-minute walk down Alaaddin Caddesi in the direction of the Mevlana Museum, or you can hop on one of the frequent *dolmuşes* plying the length of Mevlana Caddesi. Also from the *otogar*, a *dolmuş* takes half the tramway's amount of time and costs about the same (1YTL/87¢/40p).

By Car   The Mevlana museum as well as the city's other historical sites are located at the heart of the maze of roadways leading from the periphery to the city center. Just getting in from the highway can take a half-hour, so unless you're planning an overnight, a quick stopover at the tomb of Mevlana on your way down to the coast is not going to be as easy as you might think. From Nevşehir, it's an easy 3 hours through flatlands past Aksaray. It's another easy and scenic 3 hours over the Taurus Mountains via the excellent three-lane highway from Antalya to Konya (via Seydişehir). The road via Beyşehir, passing by Lake Beyşehir, is more scenic, but takes longer.

WHERE TO STAY

Balıkçılar   It really wouldn't matter what the rooms were like at this hotel. Who cares, when they overlook the majestic and monumental Selimiye Mosque and Mevlana complex? Perhaps in preparation for the 800th birthday celebration of Rumi (in 2007), the hotel underwent a complete overhaul, upgrading what were essentially mediocre rooms to solid three-star level. But the hotel itself rates four stars, with its outstanding location, Turkish bath and sauna, and unexpected ornamental common areas. All rooms have air-conditioning, minibars, and satellite television.

Mevlana Karşısı 1, 42020 Konya. © **0332/350-9470.** Fax 0332/351-3259. www.balikcilar.com. 51 units. 120€ ($174/£86) double; 167€ ($242/£119) suite. Breakfast 12€ ($17/£8.55). MC, V. **Amenities:** Restaurant; 2 bars; Turkish bath; sauna; business center; meeting room; Internet point; 24-hr. room service; babysitter on request; laundry service; dry cleaning; free parking. *In room:* A/C, satellite TV, wireless Internet, minibar, hair dryer, safe.

Dedeman *(Kids*   For excellent, if not predictable, amenities and services, there's no place like a cookie-cutter five-star. The Dedeman is all of that. Opened in 2006, the hotel brings comforts like Jacuzzis (one in every room), a heated indoor swimming pool, spa and fitness facilities, and critical must-haves when on vacation like telephones in the bathroom and ironing boards in the room. The location isn't as convenient as the Rumi or Balıkçılar, but it's not completely off the map either.

Ozalan Mah., 42080 Selçuklu, 42020 Konya. © **0332/221-6600.** Fax 0332/221-6646. www.dedeman.com. 207 units. 130€–160€ ($189–$232/£93–£114) double. AE, MC, V. **Amenities:** 3 restaurants; 4 bars; (heated) indoor and outdoor swimming pools; tennis; health and beauty center; spa, Turkish bath; Jacuzzi; sauna; children's playground; concierge; car-rental desk; meeting facilities; free wireless Internet; shopping arcade; salon; 24-hr. room service; babysitting; laundry service; dry cleaning; nonsmoking rooms; free parking; elevator. *In room:* A/C, satellite TV, wired and wireless Internet, minibar, hair dryer, safe.

Rumi   Recently opened, the Rumi is big enough to provide the perfect combination of creature comforts, but small enough so that it doesn't have to sacrifice character. That it is located across the street from the Mevlana Museum makes choosing this hotel a no-brainer. Rooms also strike a balance between simple without going overboard to boring. Expect a bathtub or shower (except in the suites, which have Jacuzzis) and satellite TV. In between visits to the city's monuments, you can even slip in an hour in the hotel *hamam,* or sauna, at no extra charge.

Durakfakı Sok. 5, 42030 Konya (opposite the Mevlana Museum). © **0332/353-1121.** Fax 0332/353-5366. www.rumihotel.com. 33 units. $95 (£48) double; $150 (£75) suite. Tax (8%) not included. MC, V. **Amenities:** Restaurant; bar; Turkish bath; sauna; business center; meeting room; Internet point; 24-hour room service; laundry service; dry cleaning; babysitter on request; free parking. *In room:* A/C, satellite TV, minibar, hair dryer, safe.

WHERE TO DINE

Cemo *(Value (Finds*   Konya's signature dish, the *etli ekmek,* is a delectable, pseudo pizza-ish invention that tops flatbread with minced lamb. Top it with cubed spiced lamb and it becomes the Konya *boreği.* (There's a cheese version and one where you get to mix it up.) And there's no better place to try a local specialty than at the *etli ekmeçi* in town, which in this case is Cemo.

Medrese Mah. Nalçacı Cad. Karatay Sitesi Altı 2/c, Selçuklu (take Ankara Cad. north from Alaaddin Tepesi, and then take a left onto Rauf Denktaş Cad./Sille Yol. at the next major intersection). © **0332/235-4016.** Appetizers and main courses 3YTL–7YTL ($2.60–$6.10/£1.20–£2.80). MC, V. Daily 8:30am–11pm.

Mevlevi Sofrası   Adjacent to the Mevlana Museum is the Mevlevi Sofrası, which gives the tourists what they want: traditional food and ambience, several outdoor roof terraces overlooking the Mevlana Museum gardens, two indoor rooms with traditional

The "Whirling" Dervishes

Dervish sects began appearing in Islamic countries around the 9th century, with beliefs and customs as fantastic as stiletto-pierced body parts and snake eating. Some dervish sects required their followers to maintain absolute secrecy to discourage members from joining for hypocritical reasons. Others required them to wander through lands or to dress in bizarre costumes as part of their orders.

The Mevlevi order of the dervishes arose in Turkey with the spreading of Islam and is based on the philosophies of Mevlana Celaleddin-i Rumi, who was born in Balkh, the first capital of the ancient Turkish territory of Khorasan (Afghanistan) in 1207. An invitation extended by Sultan Keykübad I to his father, a man of great learning and a respected spiritual leader, brought Celaleddin to Konya at the age of 21, the -i Rumi being added upon his migration into the heart of the Selçuk Rum Empire.

The mystical order is based on the principles of universal love and the oneness of creation, which states, "to love man is to love God." While the concepts of the sect were set forth by Celaleddin-i Rumi (the *Mevlana*—Arabic for "lord"—was added to his name as a title of respect), the rites and rituals associated with the order were consolidated by his son, Sultan Veled ("sultan" here used to designate spiritual leadership). The Mevlevi philosophy eventually gained the respect of the Ottoman sultans, and Selim II, Mahmud II, and Mehmed V were among its members.

The Mevlevi ritual takes the form of the *sema*, a ritual "whirling" dance whose purpose is to create a sphere of divine reality. The Mevlevi believe that purity of heart, peace with self and the universe, and the search for perfection through ritual dance bring them closer to God. The positioning of the body during the ritual has great symbolic significance: Outstretched arms with one hand facing the heavens and the other facing the earth symbolize man as a bridge between the two spheres. The white robes worn during the *sema* are symbolic of shrouds.

Although this and other brotherhoods were officially outlawed by Atatürk's sweeping reforms, the order continues to exist. The Konya order opens the ritual *sema* to a rare public viewing every December 17 in Konya, a celebratory gathering marking the death of Mevlana Celaleddin-i Rumi.

Oriental seating, and a *sema* show nightly at 9pm. Try Konya's other specialty, *fırın kebap*—a slab of slow-cooked lamb stuffed into a roll—a messy affair in all its finger-licking, lamb fat-soaked glory. No alcohol.

Civar Mah. Şehit Nazımbey Cad. 1 (next to the Mevlana Museum). ℂ 0332/353-3341. Appetizers and main courses 4YTL–10YTL ($3.50–$8.70/£1.60–£4). MC, V. Daily 8am–11pm.

WHAT TO SEE & DO   The history of Konya dates to at least the 8th century B.C.; some of the most important archaeological findings belonging to the earliest stationary civilizations known to man were discovered at nearby **Çatalhöyük,** while Hittite artifacts have been discovered in the regions east of Konya.

Known as Iconium during the Roman and Byzantine eras, the city was the location of one of the earliest church councils. After the Selçuk victory over the Byzantine army at Malazgirt (also called Manzikert) in 1071, the Selçuks migrated west, establishing a capital on Alaeddin Hill, and setting their sights on an empire that would rival Rome—called the Sultanate of Rhum. Some of the foundations of this early Selçuk Empire are still standing on Alaeddin Hill, including the **Selçuk Palace** built for Sultan Kılıç Arslan II between 1156 and 1192, now for the most part a crumbled stone wall sheltered beneath a concrete tripod arch—the unfortunate symbol of the city. The **Alaeddin Mosque,** also built during the reign of Alaeddin Keykubat, dates to 1221; note the *minbar* (pulpit) ✿ and the *türbe,* containing the remains of eight of the ruling Selçuk sultans. The Alaeddin Hill is also an attraction in itself, home to five lovely tea gardens.

At the opposite end of Alaeddin Caddesi and about a 10-minute walk is the **Mevlana Müzesi** (Mevlana Mah.; © **0332/351-1215;** daily 9am–6pm), the original *tekke,* or lodge, of the Mevlevi Dervishes. The complex was built by Beyazit II and Selim I successively at the end of the 15th and beginning of the 16th centuries. The *tekke* includes a *semahane,* where the ritual *sema,* or whirling ceremony, takes place, a *şadırvan* for ritual ablutions, a library, living and teaching quarters, and the mausoleum housing the **tomb of Celâleddin Rumi** ✿✿, founder of the sect and later awarded the honorable title of Mevlana. The mausoleum room is highly ornamented with Islamic script and enameled bas-relief, and contains the tombs of several of the more important figures of the dervish order. The main tomb enclosed behind a silver gate crafted in 1597 is that of Mevlana. The tomb of his father, Bahaeddin Veled, is upright and adjacent to his son's, a position that signifies respect.

The adjoining room, or the *semihane,* is now a museum of Mevlana memorabilia displaying musical instruments and robes belonging to Mevlana, along with Selçuk and Ottoman objects like gold-engraved Korans from the 13th century. Among the fabulous ancient **prayer rugs** ✿✿ is the most valuable silk carpet in the world. The museum is open daily 9am to 6pm; admission is 2YTL ($1.75/80p).

As in all Muslim holy places, you must remove your shoes to visit the Mevlana Müzesi, but here the floor is bare parquet, so wear socks. Since overnight groups schedule their visits for first thing in the morning, you may want to stagger your visit to Konya by arriving here a little later. (The end of the day is a good time, as most tour buses have already left.)

On an overnight stay, there are several other sites in Konya worth a look. The **Karatay Medrese,** built during the reign of Sultan Keykavus II in 1251 by his grand Vezir, Celâleddin Karatay, houses the **Ceramic Museum (Alaattin Meydanı; © 0332/351-1914;** admission 2YTL/$1.75/80p; daily 9am–noon and 1:30–5:30pm). The museum displays a small but noteworthy collection of faience with representations from the most important centers of early ceramic arts in Anatolia. Most impressive are the 13th-century Selçuk tiles, also employed to embellish the interior space. Notice the exterior portal (street side), typical of the restrained ornamentation of Selçuk architecture. The nearby **Ince Minare** is another fine example of the ornamental use of Selçuk tiles. Admission is 2YTL ($1.75/80p); the minaret is open daily 9am to noon and 1:30 to 5:30pm.

Next to the Mevlana Museum in the park is the stately **Selimiye Mosque** ✿, a classic Ottoman building constructed between 1558 and 1587 when the future sultan Selim II was governor of Konya.

9

Ankara

Unlike Istanbul, vulnerable for centuries to neighboring countries with imperialistic motives, **Ankara** ✈ lies deep within the heartland, protected and insulated from uninvited guests. Atatürk deliberately chose Ankara for his new republic; while Istanbul was the seat of an imperial and dissolute empire, he saw Ankara as the clean-slate capital of an entirely new Turkish state. In the 80 years since Atatürk rode in on a dirt road and literally lifted Ankara out of the ashes, the city has established itself as the political and cultural center of Turkey. Ankara is almost exclusively geared toward sustaining a wide-ranging population of foreign ambassadors, visiting dignitaries, local politicians, and politically minded business enterprises. If you're looking for a good English pub, then you've come to the right place. It also boasts a number of prestigious universities and technical colleges, as well as the largest library in the country. Ankara is a center for opera, ballet, jazz, and modern dance, and is home of the Presidential Symphony Orchestra, the State Theatre, and the State Opera and Ballet.

But while Ankara buzzes with the everyday business of keeping house, you can't compare Ankara to cities like Washington, D.C., or London, even if the brilliant **Museum of Anatolian Civilizations** is worth a special detour. It's not that there's nothing to do here: The short list of worthy monuments and museums includes **Atatürk's mausoleum,** a handful of Roman-era sites, and as mentioned before, the archaeological museum. There's a predictable concentration of statues of Atatürk, and dotting the parks and avenues are monuments to inspire a strong sense of nationalism. The **Victory Monument,** in Ulus Square, honors the heroes of the War of Independence, while the **Monument to a Secure and Confident Future,** in Güvenlik Park, reminds Turks to "be proud, work hard, and have self-confidence." The **Hatti Monument** ✈, an oversize replica of a bronze solar disc, is hard to miss on Sıhhiye Square and stands as a constant reminder of the country's Anatolian roots. If none of this sounds too convincing for a stopover in the country's capital, I have to admit that the choice of whether to stop here is a dilemma borne by many. Most people choose to skip Ankara in favor of a direct transfer to Cappadocia, but with plans for a fast train from Istanbul to Ankara in the works (which will cut travel time down to just 3 hours), you should stop at least for a visit to the Museum of Anatolian Civilizations, Atatürk Mausoleum, and a stroll in and around the **ancient citadel.**

1 Orientation

454km (282 miles) southeast of Istanbul; 544km (338 miles) northeast of Antalya; 582km (362 miles) east of Izmir; 277km (172 miles) northwest of Nevşehir

GETTING THERE

BY PLANE   Ankara's new and improved **Esenboğa International Airport** is a major hub for domestic flights on Turkish Airlines (© **0312/398-0100** at the airport). Direct international flights arrive from Amsterdam, Cologne, Düseldorf, Frankfurt, Kiev, London, and Munich, as well as some other cities, with increased service in the summer.

The Esenboğa International Airport is 32km (20 miles) from the city center. **Havaş** (www.havas.com.tr) provides bus transportation from the airport daily to the Havaş City Center Office in Ulus, with departures tied to the arrival times of domestic and international flights. The ride takes about 35 minutes and costs 10YTL ($8.70/£4). Note that bus fares are 25% higher between midnight and 6am.

Half-hourly buses to the airport leave from the Havaş office (located at 19 Mayıs Stadium, Gate B, in Altındağ) daily between 3:30am and 9:30pm, and then in coordination with flight departures from 9:30pm to 3:30am. (Havaş buses also leave from the Aşti bus station, but Ulus is more convenient.) For information on Havaş buses back to the airport, call the bus station (© **0312/310-6584**). There's also a cooperative taxi arrangement at the airport that will get you and three other passengers to Ankara center for $50 (£25). Reservations must be made at least 24 hours in advance (© **0312/428-5282;** www.esenbogaairport.com/esben/index.php).

BY BUS   Virtually every city in the country, no matter how small, has at least one bus company with service to Ankara, offering almost as many fare options as buses. For example, **Varan** (© **0312/224-0043**) runs about 15 buses daily from Istanbul (travel time 5½–7 hr.; 49YTL/$43/£20), as does **Metro** (© **444-3455**), including one (5am) nonstop bus from Istanbul (5½–7 hr.; 45YTL/$39/£18). From Konya, hop on an **Özkaymak** bus (© **0312/224-0055** in Ankara, 0352/265-0160 in Konya), and from Kayseri, **Kent** (© **444-0038**) runs service daily. To get to town from Ankara's **AŞTI Otogar,** hop a cab—about 10YTL to 20YTL ($8.70–$17/£4–£8), depending on your final destination. There is a handy metro station just outside the bus entrance, but whoever designed it didn't think of travelers with luggage; you must navigate an insurmountable number of steps to get to the platform.

BY TRAIN   Of all the Turkish National Railroad trains in the country, the modern, air-conditioned, and dependable **Ankara Ekspresi** night train from Istanbul's Haydarpaşa train station to Ankara is the most reliable for service and comfort. A bunk in one of the sleeper cars costs 75YTL ($65/£30); two beds cost 50YTL ($44/£20) per person. Cabins sleep (tightly) up to three passengers, and they don't penalize you for taking up the whole cabin as a single traveler. (There's also a nominal "conductor fee" collected by the car attendant at the end of the journey; this is a legal and modest surcharge of about 2YTL/$1.75/80p.) You'll need a reservation for a spot on this train, so don't leave your ticket purchase until the last minute. The train departs nightly at 10:30pm (travel time: 9 hr., 40 min.).

There are nine additional daily departures of very slow trains heading through Ankara to points east, with fares as low as 25YTL ($22/£10), depending on which train you take. Tickets can be purchased at both Istanbul's Haydarpaşa (© **0216/336-0475**)

and Sirkeci (© **0212/527-0050**) train stations, as well as via a number of authorized ticket agents (mostly travel agencies) and post offices. The list of purchase points, as well as detailed information on routes, prices, and schedules, is now available on the TCDD's new and improved website (**www.tcdd.gov.tr**).

Remember that all trains from Istanbul to Ankara leave *from Haydarpaşa Station on the Asian side.* Ferries depart from Eminönü, Kabataş, Karaköy, and Yenikapı for the 15-minute or so trip to the train station (be sure the ferry you board is heading to the train station in Kadıköy, not to the main docks). You should book your tickets in advance from June to September either via the website (**www.ido.com.tr**) or by phone (© **0212/444-4436**). The short crossing costs 4.50YTL ($3.90/£1.80), 3.20YTL ($2.80/£1.30) with the Akbil.

VISITOR INFORMATION

There's a **tourist information office** at the airport (© **0312/398-0348**) as well as downtown at Gazi Mustafa Kemal Bulv. 121, Tandoğan (across from the Maltepe subway entrance; © **0312/231-5572**).

If you're here for an extended stay, why not think about Turkish-language classes? **Tömer** offers courses at two locations: Ziya Gökalp Cad. 18, in the neighborhood of Kızılay (© **0312/434-3090**), and Tunalı Hilmi Cad. 97, in Kavaklıdere (© **0312/426-2047**), or check out their website at www.tomer.ankara.edu.tr.

CITY LAYOUT

The city's major thoroughfare, suitably named **Atatürk Bulvarı,** runs the length of Ankara from north to south, from the Equestrian Statue of Atatürk at Ulus Meydanı all the way down to the Presidential Mansion in Çankaya, about 5km (3 miles) away.

The area around Ulus Meydanı forms the oldest section of the city. To the north of the open-statued square are remnants of ancient Rome. Immediately west of the statue runs **Cumhuriyet Bulvarı,** home to several museums and monuments to Republican Turkey. **AŞTI,** Ankara's *otogar* (bus station), is located southwest of Ulus at the end of the metro line. The **train station** is more centrally located closer to Ulus at the southwestern end of Cumhuriyet Bulvarı. Not surprisingly, the closer you get to the transport hub, the seedier it gets.

From Ulus Meydanı, located about a 5-minute walk uphill on Hisarparkı Caddesi, east of the Atatürk statue, is where you will find the **Museum of Anatolian Civilizations.** A detour from Hisarparkı Caddesi onto **Çıkrıkçılar Yokuşu** will take you through the market; eventually, all roads uphill lead to the old fortress, a living, breathing mix of modern Turkey and the Turkish heartland. The neighborhood directly opposite the main entrance to the fortress recently got a facelift thanks to the support of one of Turkey's wealthiest businessmen and a great benefactor of Turkey's patrimony; here you'll find the newly preserved **Çengelhan,** a Caravansaray dating to 1522 and housing what else but the Rahmi M. Koç Museum, along with a number of newish cafes and teahouses.

South of the starting point at the Atatürk statue along Atatürk Bulvarı is the modern section of **Kızılay,** a bustling zone of modern shopping, outdoor cafes, and bookstores. On the south side of Gazi Kemal Bulvarı is the neighborhood of **Yenişehir,** or "New City," the modern business heart of Ankara; here you'll find airline and bus-ticket offices, restaurants, and a few recommendable three- and four-star hotels.

Still farther south on Atatürk Bulvarı is **Kavaklıdere,** an old vineyard now home to the Sheraton, Hilton, residential housing, and easy living. The cluster of neighborhoods

Ankara Accommodations, Dining & Attractions

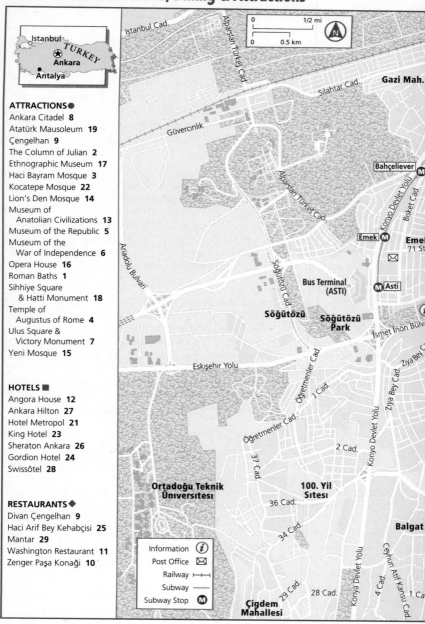

ATTRACTIONS●
Ankara Citadel **8**
Atatürk Mausoleum **19**
Çengelhan **9**
The Column of Julian **2**
Ethnographic Museum **17**
Haci Bayram Mosque **3**
Kocatepe Mosque **22**
Lion's Den Mosque **14**
Museum of
   Anatolian Civilizations **13**
Museum of the Republic **5**
Museum of the
   War of Independence **6**
Opera House **16**
Roman Baths **1**
Sihhiye Square
   & Hatti Monument **18**
Temple of
   Augustus of Rome **4**
Ulus Square &
   Victory Monument **7**
Yeni Mosque **15**

HOTELS ■
Angora House **12**
Ankara Hilton **27**
Hotel Metropol **21**
King Hotel **23**
Sheraton Ankara **26**
Gordion Hotel **24**
Swissôtel **28**

RESTAURANTS ◆
Divan Çengelhan **9**
Haci Arif Bey Kehabçisi **25**
Mantar **29**
Washington Restaurant **11**
Zenger Paşa Konaği **10**

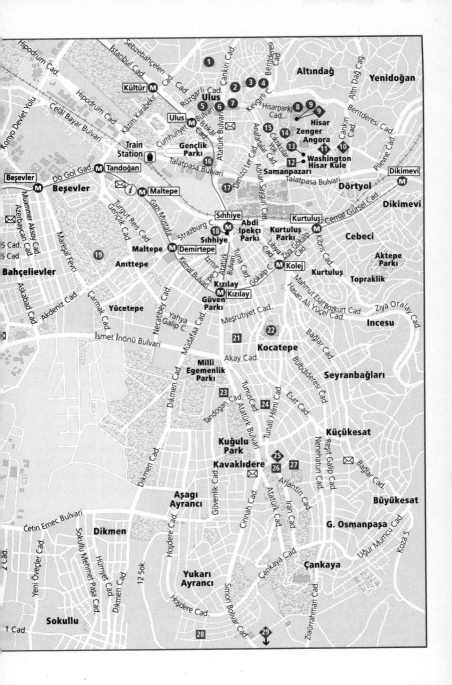

① Altındağ

Yenidoğan

Kültür Ⓜ

Ulus
⑤ ⑥ ⑦
② ③ ④

Ulus Ⓜ

Hisarparkı
Cad.
⑧ ⑨
⑨ **Hisar**

Zenger
Angora
⑮ ⑭
⑬ ⑩
Washington
⑫ **Hisar Kule**
Samanpazarı

Train
Station

Gençlik
Parkı
⑯

Talatpaşa Bulvarı

Dörtyol

Dikimevi Ⓜ

Beşevler Ⓜ

Beşevler

Ⓜ **Tandoğan**

Ⓜ **Maltepe**

⑰

Dikimevi

Sıhhiye

Abdi
İpekçi
Parkı

Kurtuluş
Parkı

Kurtuluş Ⓜ

Cebeci

Sıhhiye
⑱ Ⓜ

Maltepe **Demirtepe**

⑲

Anıttepe

Kolej

Kurtuluş

Aktepe
Parkı

Topraklık

Bahçelievler

Kızılay
Ⓜ **Kızılay**

Güven
Parkı

İncesu

Yücetepe

İsmet İnönü Bulvarı

②②

②①

Kocatepe

Seyranbağları

Milli
Egemenlik
Parkı

②③

②④

Küçükesat

Kuğulu
Park

Kavaklıdere

②⑤
②⑥ ②⑦

Aşağı
Ayrancı

Dikmen

Büyükesat

G. Osmanpaşa

Sokullu

Yukarı
Ayrancı

Çankaya

②⑧

②⑨

that includes Kavaklıdere, Çankaya, and Gaziosmanpaşa is where you'll find most of the foreign embassies, and a robust infrastructure of business-level shopping, accommodations, and dining.

GETTING AROUND

BY CAR   The Anatolian highway system is uncomplicated enough that a visitor can easily make his or her way to the greater Ankara area. Problem is, once you get there, one-way streets and avenues wind around until you unexpectedly pass your destination in a no-turn lane. And the population boom has resulted in an absence of adequate parking. If you'll be navigating by car, get your hotel to spell out the route in advance—or leave the car at the hotel in lieu of a taxi.

BY TAXI   Taking taxis makes the most sense in Ankara, especially for short stays. Gasoline costs less here and taxi fares are slightly lower than in Istanbul.

BY PUBLIC TRANSPORTATION   Ankara's rapid transit system is composed of a light metro (called the Ankaray) and the Ankara Metro. There is also a suburban rail system. Currently, construction is underway for the addition of three new metro lines (serving, roughly, areas southwest, west, and north), but the only problem is that the entire system, however efficient and clean, caters to residents of the suburbs and not tourists. So unless you need to get from Kızılay to Ulus (not a great connection, as the stop in Ulus is still a bit of a distance from the Roman ruins and the citadel) or to the AŞTİ bus station, my recommendation is don't bother. One single ride costs around 1.30YTL ($1.15/50p); a pack of 10 (10YTL/$8.70/£4) saves about 30%.

Metropolitan buses and *dolmuşes* depart from Güven Park in Kızılay and from Ulus to all points around the city, usually for under 1YTL (87¢/40p). But if you're trying to catch a bus somewhere along the middle of a route, the system can be perplexing. Unless your stay here is extended, it's not worth wasting the time to decipher the local system.

FAST FACTS: Ankara

Airline Information   Esenboğa Airport offers a new "24-hour live service" line (© 0312/428-5222). Because the information line is in Turkish, have the hotel concierge call for you. Turkish Airlines has a downtown office at Atatürk Bulv. 154, Kavaklıdere (© 0312/428-0200).

Ambulance   In a medical emergency, call **Medline** (© 0312/459-4000 in Ankara and © 444-1212 from anywhere in Turkey).

Bus Companies   Companies include **Kamıl Koç** (© 444-0562), **Kent** (© 444-0038), **Metro** (© 444-3455), **Pamukkale** (© 444-3535), **Ulusoy** (© 444-1888), and **Varan** (© 0312/426-9753 in Kavaklıdere, © 0312/224-0043 at the *otogar*).

Car Rental   **Avis** has a location in the domestic terminal (© 0312/398-0315) and at Tunus Cad. 68/2, Kavaklıdere (© 0312/467-2313); **Europcar,** also in the domestic terminal (© 0312/398-0503) and Tunus Cad. 79/2, Kavaklıdere (© 0312/426-1636); **Hertz,** Kenedi Cad. 144, Gaziosmanpaşa (© 0312/468-6290); **Budget,** Tunus Cad. 68/2 (© 0312/466-0336); and the Turkish company **Decar,** Tunus Cad. 77/1 (© 0312/426-9737, 398-2188 for the domestic terminal).

Courier Services **DHL Worldwide** (*©* 0312/444-0400), **FedEx** (*©* 444-0505), **TNT** (*©* 444-0868), and **UPS** (*©* 444-0033) all have locations in Ankara and offer convenient pickup services.

Embassies & Consulates See "Turkish Embassies & Consulates," p. 23.

Hospitals Among the private hospitals in town are **Çankaya Hospital,** Bülten Sok. 44, Kavaklıdere (*©* 0312/426-1450); **Başkent University Hospital,** Fevzi Çakmak Cad. 10, Sok. 45, Bahçelievler (*©* 0312/212-6868); and **Bayındır Hospital,** Eskişehir Yolu, Sok. 2, Söğütözü (*©* 0312/287-9000). The last also has a dental clinic on the premises.

Post Office The main post office is located in Ulus on Atatürk Bulvarı. There is another branch in Kızılay Square and countless others around town, all open from 8:30am to 5:30pm, Monday through Friday. In addition to the regular postal services, the PTT also has competitive currency exchange rates.

Telephone Dial *©* 115 for an international operator (and remember to dial 0 before a city's prefix). For calling cards and collect calls via AT&T, dial *©* 00/ 800-122-77.

Turkish Railways Ankara's Gar, or train station, is located at Talatpaşa Bulvarı at the bottom of Cumhuriyet Bulvarı. For information on schedules and trains, call *©* 0312/311-0620; for tickets and reservations, call *©* 0312/310-6515. You can also check out their website for information and schedules (now also in English) at www.tcdd.gov.tr.

2 Where to Stay

ULUS

Angora House *☆* *Finds* This restored former home of Şakir Paşa, a member of Atatürk's first parliament, provides visitors to Ankara with the only opportunity to live amid the city's early history, smack dab in the historic citadel. Virtually unscarred by tourist overdevelopment, the citadel is literally steps away from the archaeological museum. The hosts like to look after their guests (Ahmet might even play some folk music come nightfall), and each room has the character of a guest room in a private home. Of the scant six rooms, it's hard to say which is best: An antique Assyrian wardrobe stands in no. 18, no. 16 gets a latticed wooden ceiling and the only bathtub in the house, no. 22 (one of the suites) has a spacious bathroom in a hidden niche and a stunning gold-leaf ceiling, and no. 20 (the other suite) enjoys a view of Ankara from the shower. Antiques are scattered about, architectural highlights such as original prayer niches remain in place, and an inner courtyard offers the perfect opportunity for you to avail yourself of host Muammer's considerable knowledge, eke out a quick Turkish lesson, or linger over tea.

Kalekapısı Sok. 16, 06240 Ankara (in the citadel; instruct the taxi driver). *©* 0312/309-8380. Fax 0312/309-8381. 6 units. 70€ ($102/£50) double. MC, V. **Amenities:** 2 bars; laundry service; dry cleaning.

KIZILAY

Hotel Metropol Located down a quiet street near the Kocatepe Mosque, this spruced-up cement block is one of the best buys in Ankara. The interior is more inviting than the bland exterior facade would indicate, heavy on marble, wood, and leather

Father of Turkey: The Man Called Atatürk

It's impossible to overstate Atatürk's hold on this country—even 85 years after his death. His presence is unavoidable; his legacy is everywhere. Children are taught from near birth to revere the heroic, ambitious, revolutionary figure who single-handedly forged a united Turkish state from the tattered remains of the Ottoman Empire.

On May 19, 1919, Mustafa Kemal Pasha landed in the Black Sea port of Samsun, officially launching the War of Independence. Less than a year later, the Grand National Assembly convened, prompting the sultan to condemn Kemal to death. But Kemal's savvy military campaign did not falter, and 2 years later, liberation armies succeeded in clearing the mainland of all foreign presence.

Born Mustafa Kemal in Salonica in 1881, he channeled his energy into a military career at an early age. In 1905, while in the service of the sultan, he co-founded a secret organization to fight the Ottoman ruler's despotism. But unlike some power-hungry despots, Kemal's efforts resulted from a zealous love for his culture, and a refusal to see his country's sovereignty compromised. He gained widespread attention in 1915 for his pivotal role in turning back Allied forces during the long, brutal battle at Gallipoli and emerged from that campaign with the makings of a hero's reputation. At the close of World War I, Allied victors appeared ready to move in and carve up the Ottoman Empire, to the apparent indifference of the sultan. This galvanized Kemal, and he moved to harness nationalist sentiment and recruit an organized resistance.

That military victory was just the beginning, for Kemal intended no less than a societal revolution to follow. "We shall strive to win victories in such fields as culture, scholarship, science, and economics," he declared, adding that "the enduring benefits of victories depend only on the existence of an army of education." With blackboard and chalk in hand, he traveled to every corner of the country, breathing new life into this withering nation.

In his 15-year presidency, Atatürk drew his country into the 20th century through drastic and sweeping changes, not the least of which were the adoption of the Western alphabet and the insistence on a complete separation of church and state. He abolished many of the institutions that lay at the heart of Turkey, thus forcing the country to reject its Ottoman heritage. He created a new national identity, a sense of unity and pride that endures to this day. In 1934, when a law establishing surnames was instituted, the parliament gave him the name *Atatürk*—Father of the Turks. He died in 1938, 18 years after becoming president and utterly transforming his homeland.

Atatürk's influence on modern Turkey has not been without criticism, although much of this must be discreet, because *it has always been illegal to slander the Father of the Republic*. Fundamentalist critics argue that Islam as a way of life provides for all the legal needs of the country; for highly observant Muslims, the separation of mosque and state has gone too far. But Atatürk recognized that a march into the future was inevitable, and his vision lives on in a prosperous and modernizing Turkey. In his words: "Proud is he who calls himself a Turk."

details. Rooms lack air-conditioning, which might make you think twice before holing up here in the height of summer. The hotel is nestled amid restaurants and coffee shops, making this a very convenient location, but you'll have to take a taxi to visit most of the major sights.

Olgunlar Sok. 5, Bakanlıklar (just below Kızılay). ✆ 0312/417-6990. Fax 0312/417-6990. 46 units. 100€ ($145/£71) double; 123€ ($178/£88) suite. Breakfast 3.25€ ($4.70/£2.30) extra. AE, DC, MC, V. Free parking available. **Amenities:** Restaurant; bar; meeting facilities; 24-hr. room service; laundry service; dry cleaning. *In room:* Local TV.

King Hotel Güvenlik *Value* The neighborhood west of Kavaklıder is one of the more representative ones that modern, middle-class Ankara has to offer. It's located on a type of local main street and within easy walking distance to the more happening streets over on Tünalı Caddesi. The hotel boasts two on-site restaurants, a pool, a sauna, and a lovely garden. Rooms are tastefully simple without being banal, and some have en-suite kitchens. The bathrooms cover all of the comfort bases, with tub/shower combos and plenty of indigenous marble. The slightly nobler sister hotel (Piyade Sok. 17, Çankaya; ✆ **0312/440-7931**) costs only a few dollars more and is convenient to the U.N. House and to Mantar restaurant (see below).

Güvenlik Cad. 13, 06700 Aşağı Ayrancı, Ankara. ✆ 0312/418-9099. Fax 0312/417-0382. www.kinghotel.com.tr. 36 units. 50€–60€ ($73–$87/£36–£43) double. MC, V. **Amenities:** 2 restaurants; 2 bars; outdoor swimming pool; fitness center; sauna; business center; wireless Internet throughout; 24-hr. room service; laundry service; dry cleaning. *In room:* A/C, satellite TV, dataport, minibar, hair dryer, safe.

KAVAKLIDERE & ÇANKAYA

Ankara Hilton *★* The Ankara Hilton delivers the impeccable service and creature comforts that business travelers and tourists alike expect from the chain. Renovated in 2004, new multifunctional rooms sport Murphy-style beds to create a meeting environment, and an entire floor of studio suites caters to long stays. Rooms are crisp and comfortably outfitted in the inoffensive and reliable decor that Hilton is so famous for. An unfaltering American management style has provided for cable TV, laptop connections in all of the rooms, and morning delivery of the English-language *Turkish Daily News.*

Tahran Cad. 12, 06700 Kavaklıdere. ✆ 800-HILTONS (445-8667) or 0312/455-0000. Fax 0312/455-0055. www.hilton.com. 324 units. 195€–270€ ($283–$392/£139–£193) double; 360€ ($522/£257) and up suite. AE, DC, MC, V. **Amenities:** 2 restaurants; bar; indoor swimming pool; fitness center; Turkish bath; Jacuzzi; sauna; concierge; tour desk; car-rental desk; business center w/secretarial services; wired and wireless Internet; shopping arcade; salon; 24-hr. room service; laundry service; dry cleaning; executive floor. *In room:* A/C, satellite TV w/movies, fax, dataport, minibar, hair dryer, iron/ironing board, safe.

Gordion Hotel *★★* For those who prefer the intimacy of a small hotel but can't do without five-star amenities, this is the place. With its earthy tones and leather and brass detailing, the decor is a bit masculine for your typical boutique hotel. Or maybe I'm just partial to plants and silken textiles. Still, I'd stay here in a heartbeat, not least of all for the in-house beauty center and spa-like pool setting. The location is also dandy: right off the main shopping/eating district in the heart of Kavaklıdere. All rooms are wired for Internet access, and laptops, cellphones, and even PlayStations are available for rental—great for keeping kids busy during Dad's business meeting.

Büklüm Sok. 59 (just off of Tunalı Hilmi), Kavaklıdere. ✆ 0312/417-3060. Fax 0312/427-8085. www.gordion hotel.com. 44 units. 82€–148€ ($119–$215/£59–£106) double; 165€–255€ ($239–$370/£118–£182) suite. Rates include breakfast but exclude tax. MC, V. Indoor parking. **Amenities:** 2 restaurants; bar; indoor swimming pool; fitness center; steam room; sauna; meeting facilities; wireless Internet throughout hotel; salon; 24-hr. room service; massage; laundry service; dry cleaning; nonsmoking rooms. *In room:* A/C, interactive Internet TV, dataport, minibar, hair dryer, safe.

> ## *Tips* Five-Star Workouts
>
> Even if you're not staying in a five-star hotel, you can still pay to use its gym, which usually includes a swimming pool. Try the **Sheraton Ankara,** Noktalı Sokağı, Kavaklıdere (*©* **0312/468-5454**), or the **Ankara Hilton,** Tahran Cad. 12 (*©* **0312/468-2888**). Or try the more affordable private gym, **Tivolino,** on Tunali Hilmi about 4 blocks south of the Sheraton.

Sheraton Ankara ★★   I was determined not to like the Sheraton Ankara, with its tower surging arrogantly into the Ankara sky (a visual companion to the obtrusive nearby Hilton). But the bright atrium lobby, tastefully smattered with an eclectic mix of traditional and designer furniture, immediately won me over. The trendy yet inviting touches include plum-colored leather bucket chairs with stainless-steel feet and a mezzanine lounge that doubles as an art gallery.

The rooms are what you'd expect from a Sheraton, and even a little more, with spacious Turkish marble bathrooms and plush room decor. There are a few "smart" rooms for business travelers equipped with high-tech phones and faxes; modem lines have been installed in every room. The rooftop sun deck transforms itself into a movie theater on summer nights, and the hotel even serves Sunday brunch.

Noktalı Sok., Kavaklıdere. *©* 800/325-3535 or 0312/468-5454. Fax 0312/467-1136. www.sheraton.com. 307 units. $160–$400 (£80–£200) double; $595 (£298) and up suite. Breakfast and taxes may or may not be included in rate; ask for special packages. AE, DC, MC, V. Free parking in outdoor lot. **Amenities:** 3 restaurants; 3 bars (only 2 in winter); outdoor swimming pool; tennis court; squash; health club; Turkish bath; Jacuzzi; sauna; concierge; tour desk; car-rental desk; business center w/secretarial services; shopping arcade; salon; 24-hr. room service; massage; laundry service; dry cleaning; nonsmoking rooms; executive floor. *In room:* A/C, satellite TV w/pay movies, minibar, hair dryer, safe.

Swissôtel ★★★   Swissôtel thinks of things you didn't know you needed in a luxury hotel. This new property continues in the same vein. The public areas are expectedly inviting, the amenities (health club, spa features) are über-deluxe, and the rooms come equipped with LCD satellite TVs, dual electrical current (120 and 220), espresso machines, rain showers, and bathtubs. The list goes on. The hotel also features the largest Presidential Suite in Ankara.

Yıldızevler Mah. Jose Martı Cad. 2, 06550 Çankaya. *©* 0312/409-3000. Fax. 0312/409-3399. www.swissotel.com. 150 units. 175€–410€ ($254–$595/£125–£293) double. AE, DC, MC, V. **Amenities:** 3 restaurants; bar; disco; indoor and outdoor swimming pool; fitness center; wellness center; thermal spa; Turkish bath; Jacuzzi; sauna; concierge; tour desk; car-rental desk; business center w/secretarial services (fee-based); meeting facilities; wired and wireless Internet; shopping arcade; salon; 24-hr. room service; laundry service; dry cleaning; executive floor; handicapped-accessible; nonsmoking rooms. *In room:* A/C, satellite TV w/movies, fax, dataport, minibar, hair dryer, iron/ironing board, safe.

3 Where to Dine

If you're in Ankara overnight, I recommend eating dinner in one of the restaurants converted from an old Ottoman house in the citadel. Alternatively, seek out an inexpensive-to-midrange kebap joint around Kızılay or step out in style at one of the trendy restaurants along Abjantin Caddesi in Kavaklıdere or in Çankaya. Don't forget to grab a midmorning bagel-like snack of *sımıt,* a crispier version than what you'd find in Istanbul, smothered with soft cheese (found at stands everywhere in the mornings).

THE OLD FORTRESS NEIGHBORHOOD

Divan Çengelhan Brasserie 🏵🏵 TURKISH/INTERNATIONAL   The covered courtyard of this 16th-century caravansaray is an extremely atmospheric location for the Divan Brasserie. As yet another one of Koç's babies (which include the Divan group of hotels, restaurants, and patisserie), the brasserie offers best in quality and creativity with a menu that gained it membership in the prestigious culinary *Chaines des Rotisseurs*. Weekends see the restaurant hosting live music beginning at 10:30pm.

Sutepe Mah. Depo Sok. 1, Altındağ (opposite the entrance to the Citadel). 🕾 0312/309-6800. Appetizers 12YTL–28YTL ($10–$24/£4.80–£11); main courses 18YTL–36YTL ($16–$31/£7.20–£14). Tues–Sun noon–2am.

Zenger Paşa Konağı *(Kids* TRADITIONAL TURKISH   If you haven't yet tried *mantı* (Turkish ravioli), do it here. These minuscule dumplings are made on the premises right before your eyes, and served in a warm spicy garlicky yogurt sauce (sadly, it's available at lunchtime only). There's a brick oven for crunchy *pide* (flatbread) as well as the ubiquitous *gözleme*, a hearty but light crepelike treat with a selection of fillings. The kebaps arrive on a piping-hot tile. The brick-and-timber house has a back porch for a romantic twilight supper and spectacular views of the hillside below. The top-floor dining room will get you views of Ankara and the serenade of a live guitar player. Before you leave, be sure to have a look at the small collection of Turkish and Ottoman memorabilia.

Doyran Sok. 13, in the citadel. 🕾 0312/311-7070. Appetizers and main courses 6YTL–16YTL ($5.20–$14/£2.40–£6.40). MC, V. Daily 11am–midnight.

KIZILAY

Washington Restaurant 🏵 TURKISH   An institution in Ankara, the Washington Restaurant was established in 1955 with the money the owners raised while working at the Turkish Embassy in Washington, D.C. The restaurant remained in Kızılay until 1992, and then spent the next 14 years in the citadel before heading back to Kızılay. Now installed in a two-story house in Gaziosmanpaşa, Washington remains true to the menu that for years has drawn politicians, journalists, and artists for more than 50 years.

Nene Hatun Cad. 97, Gaziosmanpaşa. 🕾 0312/445-0212. Appetizers and main courses 8YTL–28YTL ($6.95–$24/£3.20–£11). AE, DC, MC, V. Daily 11:30am–midnight.

KAVAKLIDERE AND ÇANKAYA

Hacı Arif Bey Kebabçısı KEBAPS   As the Turkish Republic's flagship metropolitan city, Ankara these days is more likely to offer up modern, European translations of "World Cuisine." But if you've got a hankering for some mouthwatering *içli köfte*, eggplant salads, and tasty kebaps, then this restaurant comes highly recommended. One of the more established places on Tunalı Hilmi, Hacı Arif Bey Kebabçısı has managed to maintain a loyal clientele by consistently serving perfectly cooked grilled meats and an incredible sticky-sweet baklava every time.

Güniz Sok. 48, Kavaklıdere. 🕾 0312/467-6730. Appetizers and main courses 4YTL–13YTL ($3.50–$11/£1.60–£5.20). AE, MC, V. Daily noon–11pm.

Mantar 🏵🏵 TURKISH HOME-STYLE   A hit with the locals as well as a lunchtime favorite of U.N. employees down the road, Mantar serves grub that is good enough to bring you back again and again. Thought you'd have an outstanding *hunkar begendi* or *yaprak dolması* (stuffed grape leaves)? Try the ones here. They also serve some dishes I'd never seen elsewhere. My favorite is the *karamanmaraş köftesi* (delectable balls made of semolina); another is the *irmik* dessert (more semolina) with chocolate sauce.

4 Cad. 4/A, Yıldız. ℂ 0312/440-0978. Appetizers and main courses 5YTL–15YTL ($4.35–$13/£2–£6). MC, V. Daily 11am–midnight.

4 What to See & Do

In spite of Ankara being one of the top three cities in Turkey for work and play, my unofficial subtitle for this section is, "Give Me One Good Reason to Spend the Night in Ankara." Like any capital city, Ankara offers an endless selection of cultural institutions, activities, and events, but let's be realistic—you didn't come all this way to check out the Museum of the Centennial of History of Sports and Education now, did you? But you did come to see the Museum of Anatolian Civilizations, and you won't be disappointed. The question is, then what?

Although the Atatürk Mausoleum (Anıtkabir), set on the western side of the city, deserves a look, most of your free time should be spent in and around the citadel; it's the most picturesque and typical neighborhood of old Ankara, with some of the best views. Then head down to Tunalı Hilmi in the early evening for a walk through Ankara's version of SoHo, and grab a bite and a glass of wine.

THE TOP ATTRACTIONS

Ankara Citadel (Hisar) ℛ   The Hisar presides over an outcropping in the oldest settled part of the city. It's believed to have been built by the Galatians, but no one really knows for sure. The fortress has an inner and outer wall, the outer added during the Byzantine occupation of the city. The castle in its present state was most recently restored by the Ottomans, and dates to the Selçuk period.

Today the citadel retains much of the flavor of a small Anatolian village; from its narrow winding streets, you can catch a fleeting glimpse of the home life within. If there's any architecture worth a gander in Ankara, it's within the walls of the fortress. Many of the traditional wood-beamed houses, complete with large courtyards and gardens, have been restored and converted into marvelously atmospheric restaurants. One such establishment is the **And Café,** a welcome rest-stop just beyond the stone arched entrance to the outer citadel (with your back to the Angora House, walk right to the end; the arch is on your left; the And Café is on the second floor).

Ulus. (Follow Cumhuriyet Bulv. past the statue of Atatürk, and continue along Hisar Parkı Cad.)

Atatürk Mausoleum (Anıtkabir) ℛℛ   The Turkish psychological equivalent of the John F. Kennedy Memorial at Arlington National Cemetery in Washington, D.C., Anıtkabir draws reverent Turks from all over the country to pay their respects to the founder of the republic. Built in 1944 atop a hill overlooking the city, the memorial complex stands starkly unadorned except for the vast mosaic courtyard and the mausoleum itself, the inside of which is covered in gold leaf. Outside, soldiers are present at every corner, and if you time it right, you can witness the severe, imposing Changing of the Guard. The courtyard arcade permits entry into various rooms including the gift shop and the recently installed **Atatürk and War of Independence Museum** ℛℛ. The museum extends the entire circumference of the courtyard (lower level), and honors the founder of Turkey and the republic with sound and light dioramas of the War of Independence campaigns, portraits, and period artwork, and various exhibits highlighting the history of the republic.

Entrance on Akdeniz Cad., Anıttepe. ℂ 0312/231-7975. Free admission. Tues–Sun 9am–5pm.

Cengelhan *(Kids)* Standing at the center of what was a major commercial crossroad during the 16th and 17th centuries is this recently restored caravansaray, originally built for the daughter of Süleyman the Magnificent. The restoration, led by the ubiquitous Turkish tycoon, Rahmi Koç, was surely a labor of love. Although a major meeting place for commercial and social goings-on in its heyday, the place was in veritable ruins by the time Koç's father opened up a shop on the ground floor in 1917. The inn now houses thematic exhibits such as engineering, road transport, scientific instrumentation, medicine, and maritime pursuits. Many are interactive and should appeal particularly to fans of *The Way Things Work*.

Sutepe Mah. Depo Sok. 1, Altındağ (opposite the entrance to the Citadel). 🕾 **0312/309-6800**. Admission 4YTL ($3.50/£1.60). Tues–Sun noon–2pm.

Museum of Anatolian Civilizations (Anadolu Medeniyetleri Müzesi) *(★★★)*
This is the finest archaeological collection in all of Turkey and the primary reason Ankara is worth a stopover. Housed in a **15th-century caravansary and covered bazaar** *(★)* constructed under the reign of Mehmet the Conqueror, the museum contains a remarkable record of every civilization that passed through Anatolia as far back as the caveman.

The exhibit begins with artifacts believed to date to the Paleolithic Age and follows the progression of time throughout the museum. The most impressive Neolithic Age findings are an **8,000-year-old wall** *(★★)*, clay and ceramic representations of **bulls' heads** *(★)*, images of a fat and misshapen Mother Goddess called **Kybele** *(★★★)* (later Cybele, forerunner of Artemis and probably the Virgin Mary), and **wall paintings from Çatalhöyük** *(★)*, man's oldest known stationary civilization. The collections illustrate the first time that man tills the soil, builds homes, and takes it upon himself to decorate his surroundings. The Neolithic section gives way to artifacts recovered from Hacılar, the center of the Chalcolithic Era, and includes a large collection of stone and metal tools and decorative jewelry.

The Hatti tribes dominate the Bronze Age display with an abundance of **solar discs** *(★)*, **deer- and bull-shaped statuettes** *(★★★)*, and an evolved (and much thinner) **version of the Mother Goddess** *(★★)*. Loads of **gold jewelry** *(★)* give a rare look into the daily and religious practices of this ancient people.

Findings from the Assyrian trade colonies discovered at Kültepe, near Kayseri, are represented in the southern hall. (The Assyrians are credited with the introduction of the written word into Anatolia, much of which records transactions, receipts, and business agreements.) Over 20,000 **clay tablets** *(★★★)*, inscribed in Assyrian cuneiform, have helped reveal a priceless amount of information on this period.

The highlight of the Great Hittite Empire exhibit is the famous **relief of the God of War** *(★★★)* taken from the King's Gate at Hattuşaş, but the bronze statues of fertility gods, bulls, and deer are not to be overlooked. There are various fruit bowls and vases with animal shapes, and an infamous **vase** *(★★)* that depicts a wedding ceremony along with the popular coital position of the time. Of major significance is the Akkadian-inscribed **tablet** *(★)* (1275–1220 B.C.)—a correspondence between Egyptian Queen Nefertari (identified here as Naptera), wife of Ramses II, and Hittite Queen Puduhepa, wife of Hattuşili III, written after the treaty of Kadesh.

Around 1200 B.C. the Hittite Empire collapsed and left a vacuum in which the foundation of new city kingdoms formed. The Phrygians were one of the more important of these civilizations; most of the artifacts in this section were found in the **royal tumulus at Gordion,** the kingdom's capital. The tumulus measured 300m (984 ft.)

in diameter and 50m (164 ft.) in height. A reproduction of the **ancient tumulus** *⊛* (burial mound) in which the tomb of King Midas was believed to have been found is on display here; recent disputes have fueled speculation as to whether the tomb and tumulus are actually those of Gordius. The Phrygian section also includes carved and inlaid wooden furniture, hinged dress pins, ritual vessels in pottery and metal, and depictions of powerful animals such as lions, rams, and eagles.

Displays in the central vaulted building are rotated, but generally contain **monumental statues** *⊛* from the various collections.

On the lower lever (entrance located past the Chalcolithic display; save this for the end of your visit, circling back around to the Neolithic section and taking the stairs down) is a newer section of artifacts dating from the classical period plus a collection of objects recovered from around Ankara. The small exhibition contains some marble statues, jewelry, decorative vessels, and coins.

Near the citadel entrance, Ulus. ✆ **0312/324-3160**. Admission 10YTL ($8.70/£4). Daily 8:30am–5:30pm.

OTHER ATTRACTIONS

The Column of Julian   The column, popularly known as the Belkıs Minaresi, or Queen of Sheba monument (for reasons unknown), was erected to commemorate a visit by the Emperor Julian in A.D. 362. The Corinthian capital dates to the 6th century; the stork's nest, a permanent crowning feature, is of more recent vintage.

Near Hükümet Meydanı, Ulus. Free admission.

Hacı Bayram Mosque (Hacı Bayram Camii)   Constructed in the 15th century for the founder of the Bayrami dervish sect, a Sufi poet and composer of hymns, the Hacı Bayram Mosque is one of the most important mosques in Ankara. The mosque was built in the Selçuk style and later restored by Sinan. The ceiling is made entirely of ornamental wood, punctuated by a single hexagonal rosette, and floral and plant motifs are found throughout the mosque. The decorative Kütahya tiles were added in the 18th century.

The **Hacı Bayram Mausoleum** attracts the faithful who visit the tomb of the Sufi mystic for prayer and inspiration. The mausoleum, with its marble facade and a sturdy lead dome over an octagonal drum, was completed a year after the mosque and borders the *mihrab*'s exterior wall. The tomb's original wooden exterior and interior entrance doors are now part of the collection of the Ankara Ethnography Museum.

Ulus (from Ulus Meydanı follow Hisar Parkı Cad., turn left onto Hükümet Cad., and take the right fork). Free admission. Dawn–dusk.

Kocatepe Mosque (Kocatepe Camii)   Commanding the hill of Kocatepe, this mosque is the newest and the largest in all of Ankara, earning its place as a modern city landmark. The traditional Ottoman-style mosque was completed in 1987 and is ornamented with marble and gold leaf, stained-glass windows, decorative tile, and an enormous crystal chandelier. Enclosed in a booth in the center of the mosque is a model of the Mescid-i Nebevi mosque at Medina, presented to the Turkish President Demirel by King Fahd B. Abdulaziz of Saudi Arabia in 1993. Practicality reigns supreme in Islam, accounting for the superstore that has been opened in the cavernous basement area below.

Best access is from Olgunlar Sok., Kocatepe (southeast of Kızılay). Free admission. Dawn–dusk.

Lion's Den Mosque (Aslanhane Camii)   Named after the lion statues embedded in the wall of the tomb complex, the Aslanhane Mosque is another fine example of

Selçuk architecture, with its polychrome ceramic *mihrab*. The rows of wooden support columns are unusual, all the more because they are topped off with recycled marble Corinthian capitals.

Off Kadife Sok. (near the entrance to the citadel), Ulus. Free admission. Dawn–dusk.

Museum of the Republic   This stone building was built from 1923 to 1925 to house the Grand National Assembly, after it was transferred from its original home base just down the road. The building was abandoned from 1961 until 1982, when it was renovated to accommodate the Museum of the Republic.

The center Assembly Hall is surrounded by corridors with access to exterior rooms and constructed entirely of timber. The hall's two stories are decorated in typical Selçuk and Ottoman style, housing a minor display of documents from the early days of the republic. The exhibit is labeled exclusively in Turkish, indicating that this museum is more of a class-trip destination, but if you're in the neighborhood, it's worth a look for the Republican style of the building itself.

Atatürk Bulv., Ulus. ✆ 0312/310-7140. Admission 2YTL ($1.75/80p). Tues–Sun 8:30am–5pm.

Museum of the War of Independence (Kurtuluş Savaşı Müzesi)   This modest but dignified two-story building served as the first official seat of the Turkish Grand National Assembly. The exhibition includes documents, pictures, weapons, and objects from the War of Independence up to the founding of the republic, set in the original hall with desks straight out of a classroom scene from *Little House on the Prairie*. Lining the walls are wax figures of all of the presidents, an unusually grotesque custom of veneration repeated in the Atatürk Mausoleum.

Ulus Meydanı, Ulus. ✆ 0312/310-4960. Admission 2YTL ($1.75/80p). Tues–Sun 8:30am–5pm.

The Roman Baths   The baths were constructed during the time of Emperor Caracalla in honor of the god of medicine, Asklepios. The unusually large complex has three main divisions: a *frigidarium* (cold room), a *caldarium* (hot room), and a *tepidarium* (tepid room). The *frigidarium* had a pool and changing rooms, the *caldarium* contained a washing area and a *sudatorium* (sweating area), and the *tepidarium* was used primarily as a room for relaxing. There are also courtyards, hearths, service areas, and storage in the complex, and a renewal in funding for excavations and restoration projects will be revealing more and more.

Çankırı Cad. (just west of Cumhuriyet Bulv.), Ulus. No phone. Admission 2YTL ($1.75/80p). Daily 8:30am–noon and 1–5:30pm.

The Temple of Augustus and Rome   The temple was built by the Galatians in A.D. 10 as a tribute to Augustus during the emperor's lifetime, and later reconstructed by the Romans in the 2nd century. In anticipation of his own death, Augustus prepared a total of four documents (a list of his lifetime deeds, a financial and military accounting of the state of the empire, orders for his funeral, and his last will and testament) with instructions that the documents be dispatched and publicly displayed throughout the Roman Empire. Copies of the four documents have been found throughout ancient Rome; this temple displays the best-preserved copy of the *Res Gestae Divi Augusti,* or Deeds of Deified Augustus (written in both Greek and Latin), which represents an invaluable historical resource. Unfortunately, millennia of seismic activity and exposure to the elements have taken their toll on the temple, which is encased in decayed and rusted scaffolding and closed to the public. Inclusion in 2002 on the World Monument Fund's list of most endangered sites has afforded it renewed attention—an ambitious restoration is currently underway via a collaboration between the University of Trieste in Italy and the Middle Eastern Technical University in Ankara.

Attached to the Hacı Bayram Mosque, Ulus. No phone.

Yeni Mosque (Cenab Ahmet Paşa Camii)   This mosque was built in the 16th century by Sinan, the royal architect to Süleyman the Magnificent. It is the largest Ottoman mosque in Ankara and constructed of local red porphyry. The regal-looking *mihrab* and the *minbar* (pulpit) are of white marble.

Ulucanlar Cad. and Çankırı Sok. (just east of the citadel), Ulus. Free admission. Dawn–dusk.

ESPECIALLY FOR KIDS (OF ALL AGES)

The **Museum of Anatolian Civilizations** recently began activities that allow kids to be archaeologists for a day. Some of the activities include building models of objects on display, pressing coins as the Lydians did, and spelling their names using hieroglyphs.

The **Atatürk Farm and Zoo (Atatürk Orman Çiftliği)**, 6.5km (4 miles) south of Ankara along the road to Bursa, was originally commissioned by Atatürk to demonstrate to a skeptical populace the possibilities inherent in an apparently barren land. Thanks to his initiative, and the latest agricultural techniques (ca. 1920), the farm and zoo has become a popular afternoon-picnic destination, with its wide-open green spaces, cafes, and restaurant. The fact that the land does in fact yield fruit is proven by the excellent beer, old-fashioned ice cream, yogurt, and milk that visitors can sample. There's also an on-site replica of the house where Atatürk was born.

5 Shopping

In the bazaar area along **Çıkrıkçılar Yokuşu,** near Ulus, the strange sensation of being left alone permeates the air. In all of your travels around Turkey, you can bet that this is the *one* place you will not be accosted, hassled, harassed, or even approached. This might be due to the fact that this bazaar sees few foreign visitors. But even in the face of satin bedcovers, floor-length coats, and plastic shoes, a quiet stroll gazing at the local linens and essential items of daily life in Ankara is a lovely way to spend an afternoon.

At the end of Çıkrıkçılar Yokuşu is **Bakırcılar Çarşısı,** a street of local shops displaying a basic mix of handcrafted copper, kitchen, and hardware items. Heading left up the hill to the citadel gate is a street with a village feel and lined with spices, dried fruits, and nuts, all set out in bulk outside the shop entrances. There's also a good amount of wicker items and copper up this way, until you reach the gate of the citadel, where handicrafts give way to chintzy souvenirs.

Ankara has no shortage of modern shopping centers. Upscale shops like **Burberry's, Beymen, Calvin Klein,** and **Polo** can be found in the **Karum İş Merkezi,** the shopping mall near the Sheraton and Hilton hotels. For those looking for more ready-to-wear, step outside Karum İş Merkezi onto Tunalı Hilmi Caddesi (the street running north-south between Kocatepe and Kızılay). Don't bother with the **Atakule Tower** in Çankaya; most of the shops are of low quality or closed altogether.

In **Kızılay,** where Gazi Kemal Bulvarı and Atatürk Bulvarı meet, is a busy intersection swarming with students and office workers on their lunch breaks. The **Gima** department store offers low-priced essentials and groceries, and is a useful marker to aid you in crossing the wide boulevard over to the streets between **Tuna Caddesi** and **Gazi Mustafa Kemal Bulvarı (Ziya Gökalp Cad.,** west of Atatürk Bulv.). Opposite the Gima is the more upscale **Yeni Karamürsel,** and interspersed among the outdoor cafes and beer houses around **Sakarya Caddesi** are a number of new- and used-book stores, most with a selection of titles in English, along with a passable number of Internet cafes.

If you've got a car, head out to where most of the better shops have transferred—to the **Armada Shopping Center,** located off the eastbound side of the road to Eskisehir, or the **Mudo** megastore on the Konya road.

Even without the slightest intention of buying a sack of potatoes, it's still fun to take a walk through one of the many neighborhood *pazars* **(local markets),** where you're likely to find Polo or Banana Republic overstocks, as well as other necessary and not-so-necessary goods. The largest market is located in the center of Ankara behind the Abdi Ipekçi Park in Sıhhiye. The market operates on Wednesdays and Saturdays, and like other local markets, is open from dawn to dusk. Also on Wednesday is the covered bazaar in Aşağı Arancı, down the hill off Hoşdere Caddesi near Tomurcuk Sokak. On Mondays the **Maltepe Pazarı** spreads out behind the Maltepe Mosque, and on Fridays, the **Bahçelievler Pazarı** takes over 10 Sokak near Azerbaycan Caddesi in Bahçelievler. The **Ankara Halı** is a chaotic permanent market in Ulus, saturated with stalls of fresh fish, fruit, and vegetables. Farmers gather here in summertime to sell their own produce. The area is also full of butcher shops and charcuteries. Assembling a picnic meal of fresh cheese, meats, olives, and dried fruits is a tempting prospect; if you walk along Hisarparkı Caddesi (Fortress Park Ave.) up the hill toward the citadel, you can picnic on the grass or sit on the wall at the base of the fortress.

6 Ankara After Dark

Ankara may be a happening cultural center for the highbrow arts, but because most travelers pass through at a brisk pace, few get to actually take advantage of these events. Many do have time for a drink, though, and can select from a laundry list of pubs, wine bars, and chic cafes catering to the hefty consular population, or, at the other end of the scale, more humble diversions popular with the city's resident students. Most hotels have live music to offer as well; even Ahmet over at the Angora House will pull out his *fasıl* and perform some folk songs with little prodding.

THE PERFORMING ARTS

With Ankara's designation as capital of the new republic, the city had the responsibility of becoming a cultural capital as well. Rising out of the dust of an old village, Ankara has surpassed the other cities in Turkey to become the most active cultural center in the country.

Ankara is home to the prestigious **Presidential Symphony Orchestra,** the **State Opera and Ballet,** and a large number of theaters that feature the work of Turkish authors. The Presidential Symphony Orchestra performs twice weekly on Fridays and Saturdays during the October-to-May season, showcasing classical music by Turkish and foreign composers. Monthly programs for the State Opera and Ballet are listed in the Sunday edition of the *Turkish Daily News,* as well as on their Internet site (www.devtiyatro.gov.tr; in Turkish). Tickets can be purchased at the Opera House (© 0312/324-2210), in Opera Meydanı, Ulus, up to a month in advance of a performance.

FESTIVALS   The capital also nurtures the arts by hosting several festivals throughout the year. Ankara's **International Film Days,** in March, and the **Sevda Cenap International Arts and Music Festival,** in April and May, attract the best of Turkish and international musicians. The **Children's Festival** is held in April, with groups of children from all over the world arriving to take part in this colorful, lively event. On August 30, Ankara celebrates Victory Day with pomp and circumstance appropriate for the capital city. Ankara also organizes a series of fairs throughout the year in **Altın Park,** attracting families for an afternoon of cotton candy, piping-hot *gözleme* fresh off the cart, and the occasional kiddy ride. See "Visitor Information," earlier in this chapter, for Ankara tourist offices and information about the festivals.

THE CLUB, CAFE & BAR SCENE

Much of Ankara's nightlife is geared toward the diplomatic community, with cafes, jazz clubs, and the odd English pub clustered at the south of town. A more youthful crowd, predominantly from the nearby university, congregates in the **outdoor beer gardens** around Sakarya Caddesi in Kızılay. A few restaurants at the citadel offer nightly music, including establishments immediately to the left of the entrance that change management regularly. The **Divan Çengelhan Brasserie** (see "Where to Dine," earlier) features live music on weekends. In the neighborhood of Kavaklıdere, just off Tunalı Hilmi on **Abjantin Caddesi,** is a lineup of smart-looking, candlelit bistros; there's even a Starbucks for those of you feeling homesick. Below are a few additional and popular old reliables.

The Lord Kinross   The Lord Kinross pub is Ankara's official dart center and a popular hangout for a crowd of regular expatriates. If the clubby feel of the place doesn't intimidate you into heading out the front door, the dart league will at least provide a bit of mealtime entertainment. The menu is typical pub food, with hearty cuisine like chicken-and-mushroom pie, big steaks, and the unexpected pork sausages. Open Monday through Saturday from 6pm to midnight and Sunday from 10am to noon and 6 to 10pm. Cemâl Nadir Sok. 18, Çankaya. ℭ **0312/439-5252.**

Meyhane   Reservations are imperative at this extremely popular taverna, which serves guests a combo of Greek-influenced (or Crete-influenced) appetizers and live *fasıl* music (okay, sometimes they do Turkish pop, too) nightly. Koza Sok. 157A, Gaziosmanpaşa. ℭ **0312/446-5454.** Live music Mon–Sat 9pm–2am. Fixed menu 55YTL ($48/£22) and 60YTL ($52/£24).

The North Shield Pub   This is the Anatolian branch of a popular national chain of pubs. Patrons frequent the place as much for its imported whiskeys as for the open-air garden, open in summers. Daily noon to 1am. Güvenlik Cad. 111, Asağı Ayrancı. ℭ **0312/466-1266.**

7 A Side Trip to the Hittite Capital of Hattuşaş ⨯

Religious and political capital of the Hittite Kingdom for almost 500 years, the ancient site of **Hattuşaş** constitutes one of the most important archaeological sites in Turkey. Having imported cuneiform script from Mesopotamia and the Assyrian trade colonies, the Hittites recorded the most minute details of their civilization. Exhaustive archives of public, political, and religious life have been found in several repositories throughout Hattuşaş, and thanks to the work of a Czech linguist who succeeded in deciphering the Hittite alphabet in 1915, a wealth of information on one of the most important ancient civilizations of Anatolia is now available.

GETTING THERE   At 210km from Ankara (130 often meandering miles and easily 4½–5 hours by bus/*dolmuş*), a private car, which will cut the trip down to 2½ hours each way, is an absolute must. To get there, take highway 200-E88 out of Ankara and follow the signs for Samsun. Take the turnoff for Çorum, following past Delice and Süngürlü, and begin looking for signs for Boğazköy and the archaeological site. (The highway winds through a spectacular and desolate landscape—so be sure to fill up the tank before you go, because petrol stations in these parts pump pretty much only diesel.) The site is located at the summit of an imposing and rocky terrain high above the fertile valley of the village of **Boğazköy.**

To get there from Ankara by public transportation (if you insist), take a bus to the *center* of Süngürlü, where you'll be changing to a *dolmuş* for the remaining 14-mile ride into Boğazköy. Taxis from Süngürlü run around 25€ ($36/£18); clients of the Hattuşaş Pansiyon, Baykal Hotel, and Aşikoğlu Hotels (see "Where to Stay & Dine," below) can get a pickup for free.

VISITOR INFORMATION The only available information is a rough topographical map placed outside the ticket booth that won't do you any good once you drive away. The Hattuşaş Pansiyon has a good map of the site and the town; see **www.hattusha.com**.

There may be an "employee" at the booth offering his services or, more innocently, asking for a ride through the site, but don't be fooled—this is a local posing as a guide for tips. Although some of the locals can be knowledgeable, you'll have to weigh the fact that you'll be relinquishing your right to silence and self-discovery as you attempt to absorb the enormity of the place. All of the significant sites are signposted, so you don't have to worry about missing them.

EXPLORING THE HITTITE SITES OF HATTUŞAŞ 🏛🏛

A natural stronghold situated atop an impregnable area of steep rocky terrain, Hattuşaş had been inhabited as far back as the 3rd millennium B.C. The Hatti, an Anatolian people of unknown origin, settled here as early as 2500 B.C. Later, around 1800 B.C., King Anitta of Kushara (an ancient kingdom of similarly undetermined origins and whereabouts) invaded and set fire to the city, pronouncing it accursed, before moving on.

King Labarnas, a descendant of Anitta of Kushara, returned several generations later to reconquer and rebuild the city. Labarnas called the city Hattuşaş, or "Land of the Hatti," and changed his name to Hattusilis. Hattusilis I is accepted as the true founder of the Hittite kingdom.

From 1650 to 1200 B.C., the Hittites ruled most of Anatolia, succeeding in spreading out as far as northern Syria—much to the dissatisfaction of the Egyptian pharaohs. Tensions came to a head at the historic Battle of Kadesh, pitting the Hittite king Muwatalli II against Egypt's Ramses II. The battle essentially ended in a stalemate (with both sides claiming victory); nevertheless, for the first time in the history of mankind, a written treaty was drawn up between two warring factions. A copy of this landmark treaty was discovered in the Hattuşaş Palace Archives and is now in the Archaeology Museum in Istanbul.

The Hittites were the undisputed power in western Asia from 1400 to 1200 B.C., but a period of struggle over the ascendancy left the empire weak and vulnerable. Around 1200 B.C. the city was burned and razed by the Phrygians, who sometime between the 9th and 7th centuries B.C. established much of the fortified city that stands today. Minor settlements were later set up by the Galatians, Romans, and Byzantines.

The city was accessible through several monumental stone gates carved with reliefs of lions, sphinxes, and gods, which stand now in various states of erosion. Many of these original reliefs and statues have been moved to the Museum of Anatolian Civilizations (p. 375) in Ankara, and today there is one main entrance to the site. The first set of ruins you pass is the **Büyük Tapinak.** Located at the center of the Lower City and surrounded by a wall, this temple was the most important, consecrated to the Storm God and the Sun Goddess of Arinna, who were identified with their Hurrian equivalents, Teşup and Hepatu. The temple was constructed during the reign of the last great Hittite king, Hattusilis III (1275–1250 B.C.). The ruins of the foundations show an ample presence of storerooms, offices, and workshops; this indicates the temple was an important public building in addition to a sacred one. In some of the corners, you can still find the remains of large pottery receptacles. The actual temple is in the center, isolated from the outer sections; only the king and queen, in their roles as high priest and priestess, could enter it.

From the Büyük Tapinak, follow the road up and take the left fork where you will encounter the **Büyükkale (Great Fortress).** The royal residence occupies the highest point of a naturally rocky crest enclosed by a network of defensive walls. The palace also housed the high guard, with public rooms for the state archives, a large reception hall, and some sacred areas. Not much detail can be discerned from the remaining foundations—invisible from a lower elevation amid the grassy terraces—but a stopover at this point can provide a visual overview of the invincible position of the city.

Farther up the path on the right is **Nişantepe** ☆, an artificially smoothed rock outcropping that bears an almost 9m-long (30-ft.) inscription. Badly weathered and only partially deciphered, the inscription is most likely an accounting of the deeds of Şuppiliumus II, last of the Hattuşaş kings. Across the road to the left is a path leading to **Hieroglyphic Chamber no. 1** ☆ and the **Southern Fort,** erected several centuries after the collapse of the Hittite Empire. The Hieroglyphic Chamber dates to 1200 B.C. and is built into the side of an artificial dam. (The other end is part of the fortress.) On the back wall is the figure of a man in a long cloak. The figure, probably a god, carries a sign similar to the Egyptian *ankh* ("life") and is possibly representative of an entrance into the underworld. Few remains were found in **Hieroglyphic Chamber no. 2,** which is visible from the road but was inaccessible as this book went to press.

The best-preserved city gate at Hattuşaş is the **Kralkapı** ☆☆☆, or King's Gate, flanked by two towers with both an inner and outer portal. To the left of the inner doorway is a replica of the famous relief of the Hittite God of War. It's a stunning sight to see the relief *in situ,* even if the original is in the Museum of Anatolian Civilizations (p. 375) in Ankara.

On the road up to **Yerkapı,** over 28 temples have been uncovered. Yerkapı, which means "Earth Gate," or "Gate in the Ground," is better known as the **Sphinx Gate** ☆☆ and is the highest elevation in the area. You can either climb the stone steps to the top of the 15m-high (49-ft.) artificial bank or access the exterior of the city via the 69m (226-ft.) alternate access tunnel. The gate was named for four great sphinxes that guarded the inner gate, two of which were reconstructed from fragments and reinstalled on-site. The two remaining great sphinxes are keeping watch over the Museum of the Ancient Orient (part of Istanbul's Archaeological Museum) and a museum in Berlin. The four additional bas-relief sphinxes that were carved into the portal of the outer embankment were unfortunately not spared this end; all that remains of the originals is one badly chipped and almost indistinguishable image on the western wall.

The **Aslanlıkapı (Lion's Gate)** displays one of the best-preserved artifacts remaining on-site at Hattuşaş—symbolically warding off evil spirits. There's a hieroglyphic inscription above the head of the one on the left, but unless the sun stands at high noon, the inscription is invisible.

About 1km (⅔ mile) to the northeast (accessible by backtracking out of the entry/exit road to Hattuşaş and heading right and up the road) is the shrine of **Yazıa lıkaya** ⚡⚡, formed out of the convergence of two natural ravines and the largest known Hittite rock sanctuary. The purpose of the shrine remains a mystery, although we can speculate that it was used for annual cult celebrations or even as a royal funerary site.

In the large rock-enclosed court of **Chamber A** ⚡⚡⚡ are some of the most incredible treasures of the Hittite architectural legacy. Hewn from one end of the rock enclosure to the other is a representation of a sacred procession of deities, all of which are of Hurrian origin. Hurrian gods were given prominence by the Hittite Queen Puduhepa, wife of Hattusilis III, who was herself of noble Hurrian or Eastern origin. The cylindrical domed headdress is a symbol of divinity of Mesopotamian influence. The deities are oriented to the main scene on the back wall where the Storm God Teşup and the Sun Goddess Hepatu meet. The Storm God Teşup and Sun Goddess Hepatu, also of Hurrian origin, became the two most important deities in the Hittite pantheon, the accepted counterparts of the Hittite Storm God and the Sun Goddess of Arinna. Towering above the main scene and standing over 3.5m (11 ft.) high is a large relief of King Tudhaliya IV, son of Hattusilis III and Puduhepa.

To the right passing through a narrow rock crevice is **Chamber B** ⚡⚡, probably a memorial chapel to King Tudhaliya IV. Because the reliefs in this chamber were buried until the end of the 19th century, they are better preserved than the ones in Chamber A. The largest relief is of King Tudhaliya IV, on the main wall next to a puzzling depiction of a large sword formed by two extended lions with a divine human head for a handle. This possibly represents the God of Swords, or Nergal of the underworld. The relief on the right wall depicts a row of 12 gods bearing sickles similar to the ones in the other chamber. The number 12 as a sacred number is first seen here and repeated many times in subsequent civilizations—there were 12 gods of Olympus, 12 apostles, 12 imams of Islamic mysticism, 12 months in a year, 12 days of Christmas, and 12 to a dozen. The three niches carved into the far end of the chamber are believed to have contained the cremated remains of Hittite royalty.

No phone. Admission 2YTL ($1.75/80p). Tickets good for sites of both Hattuşaş and Yazılıkaya. Daily 8am–sunset.

WHERE TO STAY & DINE

Located 50m (164 ft.) across from the access road to the site is the motel-style **Aşikoğlu Hotel** (Çarşı Mah. 9, Boğazkale; ⓒ **0364/452-2004;** fax 0364/452-2171), with its 33 rooms all with balconies, kitchenettes, and (weak) hair dryers for 20€ ($29/£14). There's also a restaurant on-site.

The recently restored (2004) **Hattuşaş Restaurant and Pension,** on the main square (ⓒ **0364/452-2013;** fax 0364/452-2957; www.hattusha.com), offers simple rooms for 12€ ($17/£8.55) including breakfast. The family also owns the **Hotel Baykal** (same address and contact info), with double rooms for 30€ ($44/£21). For that matter, any of the campgrounds or "pansiyons" will feed you if you're hungry—and so will the locals, if you hang around long enough.

Appendix A:
Turkey in Depth

The history of Turkey reads like the history of mankind. Virtually every major Western civilization—Hittite, Greek, Roman, Byzantine, Selçuk, Ottoman—fought for control of this land and its surrounding waters. The result is a fascinating cultural and historical amalgam, and a land with countless archaeological treasures still waiting to be discovered. It's not uncommon to hike through the countryside and literally trip over a 2,000-year-old chunk of marble or the head of a statue unearthed by a farmer going about his daily business—almost too much history for one country to contain.

1 History 101

IN THE BEGINNING

In the beginning, Noah's Ark landed on Mount Ararat, or so recovered fossilized wood and boatlike support beams might indicate. Actually, the beginning in Turkey was much earlier; archaeological findings in central Anatolia indicate the presence of cave dwellers as early as 10,000 B.C. The oldest documented tribe in Anatolia was the Hatti, a nameless, faceless civilization that seems to have established small city kingdoms in central Anatolia and ruled there for about 500 years. Cuneiform tablets discovered in the regions to the east of Kayseri provide evidence of a thriving trade between these indigenous settlers and Assyrian merchants, who appear on the scene around 2000 B.C. With the arrival of the Hittites, an ancient tribe of uncertain mixed Indo-European origins, all evidence of the Hatti seems to dissolve, while commerce between the Assyrian merchants and now-ruling Hittites continues.

THE HITTITES (2000–1100 B.C.)

Who were these "Indo-European" people who subdued the indigenous Hatti kingdoms and appropriated their language, customs, and women? No one really knows (thus the hedgy term "Indo-European"). Whoever they were, the Hittites assumed Hatti names—even the term "Hittite" derives from the Hittite expression for "people in the land of the Hatti."

The Hittites built an empire of city-states in this manner, and by the mid–13th century B.C., the Hittites had taken control of a large part of Anatolia. Under Suppiluliumas I, the Hittite borders were extended to the south and east, but persistent invasions by Hittite successors created border tensions with Egypt, leading to the historic battle of Kadesh (ca. 1300 B.C.) between Hittite Emperor Muwattalis and Egyptian Pharaoh Ramses II. The Hittites are famed for their military prowess, and their revolutionary deployment of the three-wheeled chariot probably gave them a huge advantage. Although historical accounts of the battle are contradictory (both sides claimed victory), the Hittites continued their hold on Syria. Later, and for the first time in the history of mankind, a written treaty between the two countries was concluded, between Hattusil III, Muwattalis's successor, and Ramses II (ca. 1284 B.C.), who eventually married two of Hattusil's daughters to seal the pact. A copy of the treaty is in the Istanbul Archaeology Museum (p. 114). The Hittite Empire soon fell into decline and was finally destroyed by the invasion of a "Sea People."

Turkey's Ancient Civilizations

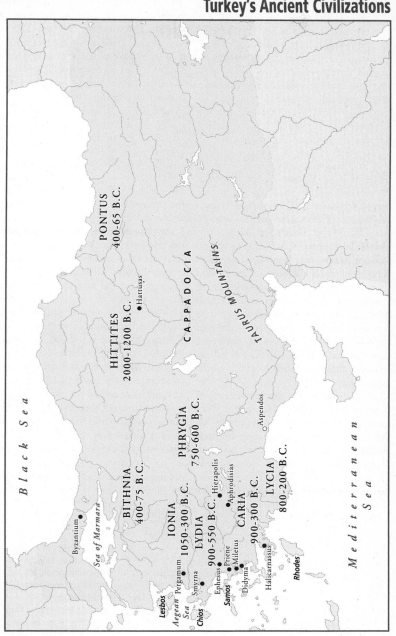

THE HELLENIC AGE

The period following the destruction of the Hittite Empire saw the immigration of and invasion by a number of civilizations. In Anatolia, what was left of the Hittite Empire fractured into independent principalities. The **Phrygians,** who were probably the "Sea People," or migrants from Thrace responsible for the destruction of the Hittite Empire, became the dominant Anatolian power in the 8th and 9th centuries B.C.

The **Phrygians** prospered up until the reign of **King Midas,** the last Phrygian king (and of the Golden Touch of mythology fame). He succumbed to invasions by the **Cimmerian** nomadic people around 725 B.C. The **Hurrians,** a native Anatolian mountain people, gave way to the **Urartians,** who, up until around 850 B.C., occupied the eastern region around Lake Van; they constructed walled citadels and an elaborate system of escape tunnels for their own defense. The **Lycians,** probably survivors of a nation of sailors or pirates—and possibly one of the Sea Peoples who caused the fall of the Hittite Empire—settled along the southwest coast.

At about the same time the Phrygians rose to power, several Hellenistic tribes were fleeing Greece to escape the invading Dorians. This group, the **Ionians,** migrated to the Aegean islands and into the central west coast of Anatolia (although the term Ionia often refers to the entire west coast). Ephesus, Miletus, and Priene are among the settlements formed during this migration; around 850 B.C., Smyrna (now Izmir) was established as their center. Originally an agricultural civilization, Ionia developed an advanced artistic and literary tradition, taking its influences from other, more advanced groups in Anatolia as well as from contact with Egyptians, Assyrians, and Phoenicians. Miletus became a vibrant center for the exchange of scientific ideas, and here you find a foundation for modern-day mathematics, geometry, astronomy, and philosophy.

Around the 7th century B.C., the **Lydians** appeared on the coast, establishing their capital at Sardis and inhabiting the inland district of western Anatolia. The Lydians were the first to coin modern money, mixing gold from the rich Pactolos Valley with silver and thus immortalizing the (apparently very rich) King Croesus. The Lydians also claim to have invented the game of dice.

Under that very rich **Croesus,** Lydia conquered and incorporated Ionia into its kingdom, but in 546 B.C., it was defeated and captured by **Cyrus the Great of Persia,** who was consolidating Persian power in Asia Minor. Cyrus the Great's successor, **Darius I,** crossed the Bosphorus and

Dateline

- ca. 10,000 B.C. Cave deposits in Antalya and surface discoveries around Ankara and Hatay regions suggest earliest cultures.
- ca. 1940–1780 B.C. Assyrian merchants from Mesopotamia establish trading colonies in central and eastern Anatolia; Indo-European people arrive, assimilating with existing Assyrian colonies.
- ca. 1750 B.C. Indo-Europeans conquer Hattuşaş, establishing the Old Hittite Kingdom.
- ca. 1300 B.C. The battle of Kadesh between Muwattalis and Ramses II; both sides claim victory.
- ca. 1284 B.C. Hattusilis III and Ramses II sign peace treaty.
- ca. 1200 B.C. Invasion by the "Sea Peoples" destroys Hittite power in Anatolia; the Trojan War.
- ca. 1200–700 B.C. Migration of Greeks to Aegean coastal regions; establishment of Phrygian, Ionian, Lycian, Lydian, Carian, and Urartu kingdoms.
- ca. 546 B.C. Persian King Cyrus the Great conquers Croesus of Lydia.

incorporated Thrace and Macedonia into the Persian Empire.

The **Carians,** mostly known as mercenaries, settled along the southwestern coast, having been chased off the Aegean islands by invading Greeks. They established, among other cities, Halicarnassus. In the 6th century B.C., Caria was incorporated into the Lydian kingdom, but later it, too, succumbed to the Persian Empire. Carian kings continued to rule as subjects of Cyrus the Great, maintaining some degree of autonomy. But 200 years of Persian domination created feelings of resentment toward Eastern ways. Many Ionians, including most of the philosophers and artists, migrated back to either Athens or Italy. The remaining Ionians regained their freedom by joining the **Delian League,** a federation of Greek city-states formed in 478 B.C. as security against the renewal of Persian aggression.

In the summer of 334 B.C., **Alexander the Great** began his war on the Persian Empire, retaking Thrace, crossing the Dardanelles, and confronting the Persian armies near Troy. He succeeded in annexing all of Anatolia under **Macedonian/Greco** rule. Alexander's untimely death in 323 B.C. was the catalyst for internal conflict among his generals, resulting in generations of clashes over the division of his territories.

During the 3rd and 2nd centuries B.C., several independent Greek states emerged in western Anatolia. The city of **Pergamum** was established and, under Eumenes II, enjoyed its greatest period of prosperity, earning itself a privileged position with Rome.

ROME & THE EASTERN PROVINCES

When Attalus III, the last of the ruling Attalid dynasty of Pergamum, died without a successor in 133 B.C., the Romans interpreted his ambiguous bequest in their favor and claimed the city, beginning the **Roman Empire**'s mass penetration into Asia Minor. The Romans claimed Pergamum and effectively absorbed the independent states of Bithynia, Cappadocia, and Pontus. Except for sporadic conflict—most notably with **Mithridates of Pontus,** who between 88 and 63 B.C. massacred over 80,000 Romans at Ephesus—the Asian Provinces enjoyed a relatively long and prosperous period of peace. It was during the 1st century A.D. that **St. Paul,** advocate of the Christian faith, began his missionary travels through Anatolia.

In A.D. 284, **Emperor Diocletian** instituted a doomed system of governmental reform, dividing the empire into two administrative units, both to be ruled by an emperor (an *Augustus*) and a designated heir (or *Caesar*). It was a system destined to collapse into civil war, but the

- **ca. 499** B.C. Persians drive out the Greeks.
- **334** B.C. Alexander the Great drives Persians out of Anatolia.
- **323** B.C. Alexander dies; Generals Lysimachos and Seleucus divide the Anatolian Empire.
- **133** B.C. Attalus III dies, leaving Pergamum to Rome; Pergamum becomes the province of Asia with its capital at Ephesus.

- **40** B.C. Mark Antony and Cleopatra marry in Antioch.
- **A.D. 47–57** St. Paul establishes first Christian community in Antioch.
- **284** Diocletian reforms Roman administrative system.
- **313** Edict of Milan establishes official tolerance of Christianity.
- **330** Constantine establishes his capital at Byzantium,

renaming it New Rome, then Constantinople.
- **476** Fall of the Roman Empire; Constantinople emerges as sole religious and cultural capital of the Eastern Roman Empire.
- **527** Justinian ascends the throne.
- **726** Leo III rejects the idea of icons.
- **1054** Catholic and Greek Orthodox churches split.

continues

Gordius, from Pauper to Prince

Legend has it that the Phrygian elders, seeking a leader to mediate quarrels and to gain status with their neighbors, consulted a local oracle for advice on how to select a king. The oracle responded that the next person to pass his shrine riding in a cart should be king, and soon enough, a farmer named Gordius rode by in his oxcart on the way to market. Gordius was proclaimed king, and the capital (near present-day Ankara) assumed his name, Gordion.

The expression "Gordion knot," which refers to a highly complex problem, takes its name from Gordius as well. Apparently, Gordius was quite proud of the fittings on his oxcart—particularly of the unusual knot he used to tie the cart's pole to the axle. He challenged all potential passersby to untie it, but the knot remained intact long after his death. When Alexander the Great arrived in Gordion more than 500 years later, he carefully studied the knot and then decisively severed it in two with his sword, before continuing on to more challenging conquests.

long-term effect was a more theological schism, as Christianity grew and took hold. In the wake of Diocletian reform, **Constantine** emerged to establish his capital at the Greek town of Byzantium, rebuilding the city to equal if not surpass the splendor of Rome. Six years later, in 330, its architectural eminence realized, the city was baptized "New Rome," then renamed Constantinopolis (or Constantinople, now Istanbul) in honor of the emperor.

By the time Constantine had established imperial Roman power in Constantinople, his acceptance of Christianity was complete, having publicly espoused the faith in the **Edict of Milan** in 313, which mandated the tolerance of Christianity within the Roman Empire. Under **Theodosius,** paganism was outlawed and Christianity, by this time already widespread, was made the official religion of the state. By Theodosius's death in 395, the eastern and western provinces had grown apart ideologically, and the Roman Empire was divided in two. When Rome fell in 476, Constantinople emerged the dominant capital of the empire.

THE AGE OF BYZANTIUM

The reign of Emperor **Justinian** and his Queen **Theodora** (527–565) inaugurated a period of great prosperity in

- **1071** Selçuks defeat Byzantine army at Malazgirt.
- **1204** Crusaders sack Constantinople.
- **1243** Mongol invasions destroy Selçuk power.
- **1261** Michael VIII Palaeologus reclaims Constantinople.
- **1326** Ottoman capital established at Bursa.
- **1453** Mehmet the Conqueror takes Constantinople.
- **1481** Reign of Bayezit II begins.

- **1492** Columbus discovers the New World.
- **1512** Reign of Selim I begins.
- **1517** Selim I captures Cairo and proclaims himself caliph.
- **1520** Reign of Süleyman begins.
- **1521** Süleyman captures Belgrade and takes Rhodes; releases surviving Knights of St. John.
- **1566** Reign of Selim II begins.

- **1570** Turks capture Cyprus.
- **1571** Turks defeated at battle of Lepanto.
- **1574** Reign of Murad III begins; Tunis is captured.
- **1622** Osman II assassinated by the Janissaries; Ahmed I restored to throne.
- **1687** Reign of Süleyman II begins.
- **1699** In the Treaty of Karlowitz, the Ottoman Empire relinquishes territory for the first time.

Anatolia. Justinian reconquered the West, and eventually regained North Africa and Italy. His construction of the incomparable Ayasofya (Church of Holy Wisdom) established Constantinople as the spiritual center of Christendom. Justinian commissioned new buildings and conducted restorations all across the empire—an undertaking so vast that it thrust the empire into economic crisis after his death. His primary legacy was the **Justinian Code**—his attempt to codify and organize the ancient system of Roman laws—that ultimately became the foundation for many modern Western legal systems.

Around the end of the 9th century, a rivalry emerged between the Orthodox Church and the Papacy over the veneration of icons. The worship of idols was first condemned by **Emperor Leo III** in 726 and then reiterated by successive emperors. In 1054, over this and other theological disagreements, the pope severed any ties that had united Byzantium with the West.

Distracted by religious and bureaucratic disputes, the Byzantines were unprepared for the arrival of nomadic Turkish warriors raiding lands to the east. The Turks (from the Chinese "Tu-Kiu") were tribes originating on the Mongolian steppes. Migrations southwestward in the 7th or 8th century put them in touch with Arab tribes centered around Baghdad, home of the caliphate, where they assimilated Islamic practices. By the 10th century, the bulk of Turks—still nomads and warriors by nature—had accepted Islam as their religion, although some Turks, such as the **Selçuks,** subscribed to the orthodox Sunni form, while others, such as the **Turkomans,** accepted the splinter Shiite sect.

These *gazi* tribes, or "warriors of the faith," marched north from Baghdad, conquering lands in the name of Islam and penetrating deep into the heart of Anatolia. The Selçuks marched northwest in a campaign to expand their territory and a desire to control the Turkoman tribes. An accidental encounter with the Byzantine army resulted in a Selçuk victory in the **Battle of Malazgirt in 1071,** opening the floodgates to a mass Turkish migration into Anatolia.

In response to the growing Turkish presence, Byzantine Emperor **Alexius Comnenus** turned to the Christians of western Europe for aid against their increasing threat. The first Crusade saw the recapturing of Jerusalem and the regaining of control of most of Anatolia.

The Selçuk Turks triumphed over the second Crusade in 1147 and eventually set up the **Sultanate of Rum,** centered around Konya, where they presided over significant cultural growth and territorial

---

- **1711** Defeat of Peter the Great at Prut River.
- **1774** Reign of Abdülhamid I begins; Treaty of Küçük Kaynarca follows defeat by Catherine the Great.
- **1789** Reign of Selim II begins; education becomes obligatory.
- **1826** Janissary massacred and corps abolished; medical and military schools opened; and Tanzimat Reforms.

- **1839** Reign of Abdülmecid begins; establishes parliamentary system and laws.
- **1854** Britain and France support Ottomans against Russia in the Crimean War.
- **1856** Treaty of Paris; Ottoman Empire accepted as a European state.
- **1861** Reign of Abdülaziz begins.
- **1875–85** Loss of most European territories, Tunisia, Egypt, and East Rumalia.

- **1876** Reign of Abdülhamid II begins, establishes first constitution; then, frustrated with parliamentary gridlock, imposes an autocracy.
- **1878** The "Sick Man of Europe" progressively deteriorates; Britain occupies Cyprus.
- **1881** Mustafa Kemal born in Salonika.
- **1908** Coup d'état led by Young Turks; Abdülhamid is deposed. *continues*

expansion. They also revived the classical Islamic system of education, attracting philosophers, poets, and craftsmen to the court. One of the most influential arrivals was the scholar **Celaleddin i-Rumi,** who founded the Order of the Mevlevi (or "Whirling") Dervishes. The Selçuks laid the foundation for modern-day Middle Eastern government with the implementation of a bureaucratic hierarchical system. They are also credited with the development of a system of way stations called *kervansarays* (caravansaries), designed to meet the needs of merchants traveling on behalf of the state, and established insurance for the loss of tradesmen.

But the Crusades were by no means a cure-all. Tensions arose because the Crusaders had no specific mandate from the pope, little sympathy toward the Greek Orthodox religion, and no agreement on the nature of their association with the Byzantine Empire. Allied with Venetian merchants who had an eye on the riches of the East, the Crusaders sacked and plundered Constantinople in 1204 in the fourth Crusade, creating the Latin Empire of Constantinople and widening the schism between the churches of the East and West. Driven from Constantinople, the Byzantines established a small empire in exile at Nicaea (now Bursa), creating a balance of power with the flourishing Selçuk Sultanate of Rum.

Michael VIII Palaeologus, ruler of the empire in exile, succeeded in reclaiming the city of Constantinople in 1261. Though their territory was drastically reduced, subsequent Byzantine emperors repeatedly tried to reunite the Orthodox and Catholic churches against the threat of invading Turks. This proved futile, and in 1453, the Ottoman Turks conquered what little remained of the Byzantine Empire and made Constantinople their capital.

OTTOMAN BEGINNINGS

Numerous independent Turkish principalities occupied the frontiers between the Selçuk Sultanate and the Byzantine Empire. These warriors traded battles and loyalties for grants of land, aiding the Selçuk rulers in their struggles against the Christians, while selling their services to hopefuls vying for the Byzantine throne. The **Osmanlıs** (or Uthmanlı, better known as the Ottomans) were particularly successful in rousing the surrounding Turkic tribes to do the same. Under the leadership of the fearless **Osman,** patriarch of the Osman (Uthman, Ottoman, whatever) clan, and his son **Orhan,** the Ottoman expansion was almost inevitable, particularly in light of the vacuum left by the Selçuk defeat at the hands of the Mongols in 1243.

The Osmanlıs (hereby referred to as the Ottomans) entered Bursa in 1326,

- ca. **1908–09** Mehmed V installed as lame duck sultan.
- **1914** Ottoman Empire enters World War I as ally of Germany.
- **1915** Under leadership of Mustafa Kemal, Turkish forces successfully repel Anzac forces at Battle of Gallipoli.
- **1918** Reign of Mehmed VI begins; Turks surrender; Allied forces enter Istanbul.

- **1919** Mustafa Kemal leads national resistance for sovereignty; occupational Greek army lands at Smyrna.
- **1920** Grand National Assembly created in Ankara with Mustafa Kemal as president.
- **1922** Greeks driven from Anatolia; sultanate abolished; Abdülmecid named as caliph only.
- **1923** Treaty of Lausanne, Mustafa Kemal establishes

the modern Republic of Turkey; Kemal is elected president; Ankara replaces Istanbul as capital.
- **1924** Caliphate abolished.
- **1924–38** Mustafa Kemal Atatürk institutes programs of modernism, secularism, and reform.
- **1934** Voting rights established for women.
- **1938** Atatürk dies in Dolmabahçe Palace; Ismet

where they set up their first permanent capital. Heading northwest, they rapidly conquered the Marmara shores, crossed the Dardanelles, and established a second fortified base at Gallipoli in 1354.

Orhan was the first Ottoman leader to assume the title of Sultan (formerly an honorary title that caliphs granted to chiefs of Islamic-influenced territories to emphasize their role as spiritual leaders). For the Ottomans, the title had military and political connotations as well. "Sultan" became the standard designation for those in power who answered to no superior other than Allah.

Orhan's son **Murat I** enjoyed one military success after another. Carving out a wide buffer circumventing Constantinople, he established a European presence at his new capital of Adrianople (now Edirne), and then directed his armies east into the Turkish emirates as well as west into the Balkans, Albania, and Bulgar territories. Finding himself surrounded, the Byzantine emperor, isolated except for sea access, became a vassal of the Sultan and was left with little recourse other than to aid the Ottomans in their conquests of the East.

Murat I defeated a Serbian coalition at the Battle of Kosovo, though he was killed in that campaign. Murat's son **Bayezit** continued his father's expansionistic tendencies, striking both west and east and earning himself the nickname of *Yıldırım,* Turkish for "lightning" or "thunderbolt." The Ottoman advance to the west began to alarm the pope, who was unable to galvanize a proper offensive, except for two dismal attempts by the French and Hungarian armies during a lull in the Hundred Years' War. The Ottomans defeated the French army at Nicopolis on the Danube in 1396, and again on the Black Sea in 1444. But their continued campaigns into the west left their eastern flanks vulnerable. The Mongols, led by **Tamerlane,** emerged as a major threat in the east, supported by Turkish emirates inflamed by Bayezit's warring on his Muslim brothers—an act expressly forbidden in the Koran. Bayezit was eventually imprisoned by Tamerlane, who restored the independent territories. Bayezit died in prison, leaving behind a 10-year power vacuum in which his sons would fight for control.

Mehmet I was the triumphant son, and he and his son **Murat II** are credited with consolidating the Ottoman territories and absorbing, either by force or by marriage, the Turkish emirates to the east. Nonetheless, they were unable to either penetrate Constantinople's defenses or cut off the city's sea routes.

Mehmet II set a nasty royal precedent by strangling his infant brother in order to solve his own problems of succession.

Inönü becomes republic's second president.
- **1945** Turkey declares war on Germany.
- **1946** Turkey becomes charter member of United Nations.
- **1950** Inönü's Republican People's Party defeated in first free election. Adnan Menderes's Democratic Party takes over.
- **1952** Turkey joins NATO.

- **1960** Military coup overthrows Menderes, who is executed the following year.
- **1961** Army restores parliamentary government.
- **1964** Turkey granted associate member status in European Union.
- **1965** Demirel's Justice Party wins elections.
- **1971** Demirel resigns after army intervention.

- **1973** Republican People's Party wins elections; Bulent Ecevit becomes prime minister.
- **1974** Turkey sends troops to northern Cyprus.
- **1980** Military coup d'état; General Kenan Evren leads government.
- **1983** Turgut Özal elected prime minister.
- **1989** Özal elected president.
- **1991** Süleyman Demirel elected prime minister.

continues

He eventually sanctioned fratricide by law: Whoever got acclaimed first was ruler and all his brothers had to die—ostensibly assuring the ascension of the most capable son.

Mehmet II set his sights immediately on Constantinople, and in 1453, in a brilliant strategy, circumvented the Byzantine defenses of the Golden Horn by carrying his fleet, ship by ship (by means of a brilliantly engineered "movable path"), over land, behind the Byzantine naval barricade. After centuries of decline and decay, the Byzantine Empire had come to an end.

THE OTTOMAN EMPIRE

With his victory over Constantinople, Mehmet II acquired the title of *fatih*, or conqueror, and established his new capital, naming the city Istanbul, probably after having heard the Greeks say *"eis ten polin"* (to the city). His troops were allowed 3 days of looting and pillaging, and then the city—by now practically unpopulated—was restored to order. He immediately began reconstruction, converting churches into mosques and repopulating the city with artisans, merchants, and farmers from all over the empire. The importance of sea power was not lost on Mehmet, who established control over the Black Sea and managed to capture some of rival

Venice's islands in the Aegean. The city's importance as a naval and trading center was confirmed. Istanbul quickly became an international city with a mixture of cultures as Christians, Greeks, Armenians, and Jews were all welcomed for the wealth of knowledge they brought with them, and of course, the tax revenues they would pay.

Having removed the final obstacle to the unity of his empire, Mehmet the Conqueror resumed his holy wars, dreaming of a world united under Islam. Soon the empire extended into Europe, with conquests of the Balkans, Greece, Albania, Serbia, and Bosnia. The Turks had suddenly become a major European presence, influencing the balance of power to the west.

Mehmet's son **Bayezit II** took up his father's sword, pursuing his empire's expansion eastward against the Safavid dynasty in Iran, a Shiite presence that would challenge the Ottomans' legitimacy for centuries. Bayezit's son **Selim the Fierce** (known as Selim the Grim in the West, for his cruelty), impatient with his father's lagging military campaigns, assassinated him and slew his brothers, along with any other possible contender for the throne. He conquered and subjugated the heretic Safavids, and then moved on to subjugate the Mamluk

---

- **1993** Özal dies; Demirel becomes president; Tansu Çiller becomes Turkey's first female prime minister.
- **1996** Çiller steps down as prime minister.
- **1999** Bulent Ecevit elected prime minister again. Kurdistan Workers Party (PKK) leader Abdullah Ocalan captured in Kenya, convicted of treason, and sentenced to

death. Two major earthquakes rock northwestern Turkey in August and November, killing an estimated 18,000 people.
- **2000** Former prime minister Necmettin Erbakan sentenced to 1 year in prison for challenging Turkey's secular rule.
- **2002** Turkey lifts bans on education and broadcasting in Kurdish.

- **2002–3 and 2005** Turkish troops join Security Assistance Force in Afghanistan.
- **2002–3** Justice and Development Party (AKP) wins landslide victory at the polls; prohibition against Recep Tayip Erdogan running for Parliament lifted; Abdullah Gül steps aside allowing Erdogan to assume post of prime minister.

sultans of Syria and Egypt. The guardian of the holy cities of Mecca and Medina wasted no time in recognizing Selim as the new spiritual leader of Islam, and he promptly proclaimed himself caliph.

The long reign of Selim's son **Süleyman** was the golden age of the Ottoman Empire, distinguished by military successes, administrative organization, economic prosperity, social order, and cultural eminence. The empire flourished under his direction; the population grew, road and caravansary networks were extended, trade prospered, and his military machine cranked out success after success. Justice was extended to the lowest members of society, protecting them from unfair governmental practices or excessive taxation; state decrees were posted publicly to discourage officials from instituting fraudulent or arbitrary laws. The people responded by hailing him as Süleyman the Lawgiver.

OTTOMAN ADMINISTRATIVE STRUCTURE

The Ottoman ruling class was organized into five imperial institutions, the most important of which was the military. Almost as important as the military were the scribes, or "men of the pen," whose primary function was the collection of revenue, in addition to their formidable duties in general record-keeping. Religion and culture were the dominion of the *ulema,* Muslim leaders educated in theology and law assigned the task of religious leadership, education, and justice. Finally, the Inner and Outer Palace Services took care of the general day-to-day administration of the palace and care of the sultan.

In theory, all lands belonged to the sultan, who by divine right could claim all titles, revenues, and property. The actual administration was bureaucratic, and the sultan's newly acquired territories were controlled through a *timer* system adapted from the Selçuks and Byzantines. A *timer* was a province assigned to a military administrator who, in exchange for the land and its revenue, provided military services and assistance in the administration of the territory. With time and expansion of the empire, the *timers* were converted into tax-paying farm units, and one-fifth of all property, goods, and captives became royal possessions.

In contrast to the Christian policy of lands passing along generational lines, *timers* were assigned according to merit. Christians and prisoners provided the sultan with a steady supply of loyal subjects under the *devşirme* (literally, collection), where teams were sent to conquered

- **2003** Terrorist bombing at Neve Shalom synagogue in Istanbul. Days later, the British Embassy and HSBC Bank are targeted. More than 250 are killed.
- **2004** Turkey abolishes death penalty.
- **2004** PKK announces end to ceasefire.

- **2005** E.U. accession talks officially launched but later put on hold because of Ankara's refusal to allow traffic from Cyprus into Turkish ports/airports.
- **2006** Ribbon cutting on new Baku Tblisi Ceyhan pipeline.
- **2007** Nomination (and subsequent election) of Abdullah

Gül for president sparks outrage between secularists and Islamists and is met with official condemnation by the military.
- **2007** Tensions heat up on the border as Turkey threatens cross-border raids into northern Iraq in response to PKK attacks on Turkish military in the south of Turkey.

Selçuk Sultans—The Rum Line

Sultan	Reign
Tugrul I Beg	1037–63
Alp Arslan	1063–73
Malik Shah I	1073–92 (battle for throne)
Süleyman I ibn Qutalmïsh	1078–86 (battle for throne)
Kılıç Arslan I	1092–1107
Malık Shah II	1107–16
Meşud I	1116–56
Kılıç Arslan II	1156–92
Giyaseddin Keyküsrev I	1192–96
Süleyman II	1196–1204
Kılıç Arslan III	1204 (child)
Giyaseddin Keyküsrev I	1204–10
Kaykavus I	1210–20
Alaaeddin Keykubat I	1220–37
Giyaseddin Keyküsrev II	1237–46

(Selçuks conquered by Mongols in 1243 and become vassals; a fight for succession of the sultanate ensued.)

Kaykavus II	1246–57
Kılıç Arslan IV	1248–65
Kaykubat II	1249–57
Kaykusrev III	1265–82

(Meşud II and Kaykubat III clash for control of throne 1282–1307 until Meşud II is deposed by Mongols in 1307.)

territories in search of the best and most promising young boys. Families often hid their children, but on the whole, the opportunity for a distinguished career of service to the sultan was appealing. Candidates between the ages of 8 and 15 were selected and sent to Istanbul, where they were converted to Islam and educated in the palace school. The finest of the *devşirme* were chosen for continued education and placement in high palace positions while the majority of the trainees entered into the elite military corps of Janissaries. By 1700 the Janissaries (*yeniçeri;* literally, "new troops") had swelled to over 100,000 from 12,000 during the reign of Mehmet the Conqueror, ultimately becoming more powerful than the government they served and inciting frequent rebellions.

The Turkish aristocracy, comprised of Muslims, Turks, Arabs, and Iranians, shared the rank of *askerî,* with the newer *devşirme* class of Christian converts making up the ruling class. During Süleyman the Magnificent's reign, this internal rivalry was expertly maneuvered to ensure honesty and obedience.

From the time of Mehmet II, sultans attended sessions of the Imperial Council, a meeting of the sultan's viziers, judges, and department heads (seated on a cushioned platform later simply known as the *divan*) in Topkapı Palace. At meetings 4 days a week, all government business

The Ottoman Sultans

Sultan	Reign
Osman I	1290–1326
Orhan	1326–59
Murat I	1359–89
Bayezit I Yıldırım (the Thunderbolt)	1389–1402
Mehmet I	1402–21
Murat II	1421–51
Mehmet II (*Fatih,* the Conqueror)	1451–81
Bayezit II	1481–1512
Selim I Yavuz (the Grim)	1512–20
Süleyman I (*Kanuni,* the Magnificent)	1520–66
Selim II	1566–74
Murat III	1574–95
Mehmet III	1595–1603
Ahmed I	1603–17
Mustafa I	1617–18
Osman II	1618–22
Ahmed I (restored)	1622–23
Murat IV	1623–40
Ibrahim	1640–48
Mehmed IV	1648–87
Süleyman II	1687–91
Ahmed II	1691–95
Mustafa II	1695–1703
Ahmed III	1703–30
Mahmud I	1730–54
Osman III	1754–57
Mustafa III	1757–74
Abdülhamid I	1774–89
Selim III	1789–1807
Mustafa IV	1807–08
Mahmud II	1808–39
Abdülmecid I	1839–61
Abdül Aziz	1861–76
Murat V	1876
Abdülhamid II (the Damned)	1876–1909
Mehmed V	1909–18
Mehmed VI	1918–22
Abdülmecid II (Caliph only)	1922–24

was conducted; public petitions and complaints were heard in the morning and executive issues were addressed in the afternoon.

Driven by the *gazi* guiding principle of *jihad* (struggle), the Ottomans had transformed themselves from plunderers into conquerors.

Süleyman the Magnificent: Pragmatic Statesman

In 1520 Süleyman ascended to the Ottoman Empire throne and immediately launched invasions into Europe. In 1521 he gained control of Belgrade and the Danube. He then turned his attention to Rhodes, the last Crusader stronghold and bastion of the Knights of St. John—the island that stood between him and his Egyptian territories, not to mention Mecca and Medina. Süleyman triumphed after a 145-day siege and mercifully released all the Knights and mercenaries, thus gaining the admiration of much of Europe (though he'd come to regret this act later in his career). Eight years later the Knights were granted Tripoli and the Island of Malta in a charter sealed by Holy Roman Emperor Charles V to thwart movement of Ottoman fleets in the Mediterranean.

Süleyman insinuated himself into the politics of Europe and attempted to destabilize both the Roman Catholic Church and the Holy Roman Empire; he believed that any power in those hands was a threat to Islam. Urged on by Francis I of France, Süleyman defeated the young Hungarian king, Louis II (nephew of Charles V), in 1526 at the battle of Mohács. In 1529, at the request of the appointed king of Hungary, he returned to confront Archduke Ferdinand of Austria. Süleyman drove Ferdinand back to Vienna but was unable to penetrate the city's defenses—a failure that would become a recurrent theme for the Ottomans.

Although Süleyman's reign was characterized by almost constant war, he brought peace to the lands that he conquered. Süleyman was said to have embodied perfectly the characteristics of *adale* (justice), much like his namesake, King Solomon. Conquered lands often fared better once he took over.

THE OTTOMAN DECLINE

Several factors, both foreign and domestic, contributed to the progressive deterioration of the Ottoman Empire over the subsequent 2½ centuries. Although Süleyman left a legacy of territories on three continents and the splendor of an empire without equal, he also left behind a scheming widow—Roxelana, the Circassian-born concubine he took as his wife and trusted advisor. Roxelana manipulated her husband, his sons, and the court with sometimes fatal results. She orchestrated events culminating in the murder of Süleyman's favorite sons, Mustafa and Bayezit, thus clearing the path of ascension for her utterly incompetent son, Selim II. Nicknamed Selim

the Sot, he preferred the pursuits of physical pleasure to governing the empire and left his grand vizier in charge of decision making. The grand vizier assumed more responsibility, but simultaneously set an unfortunate precedent of bribery, favoritism, and corruption. And taking a page from Roxelana's book, members of the harem (that is, mothers of prospective heirs) exerted more and more control over the workings of the government; this culminated in the mid–17th century with an era recognized as "The Sultanate of Women."

The abandonment of the traditional practice of fratricide contributed to the weakening of the system as well. Rather than kill off all potential heirs and risk the

Looting was forbidden, and the sultan gained respect by placing provisions along the route of a carefully planned military campaign so as not to take anything from the local peasants along the way. Kings were retained as vassals of the sultan, and as long as the tributes (taxes) were sent to Istanbul, life continued as before.

Above all, Süleyman was a pragmatic statesman. In 1536 he signed a treaty with Francis I of France, conceding commercial privileges to the French in exchange for an informal alliance against their common enemy, the Hapsburgs. With these "Capitulations," the French were exempt from Ottoman taxes and were permitted to fall under French jurisdiction. In response to this French-Turkish cooperation, the Hapsburgs urged the Persians to wage war against the sultan. Turning his attentions east, Süleyman wrestled Iraq from Persian control, arriving as far as the Persian Gulf. Here the Portuguese dominated trade with the East—a presence he was never able to repress.

The Mediterranean Sea was another source of annoyance; despite Süleyman's conquest of Tripoli in 1551, the Knights of Malta (including many of the Knights released after the sultan's victory over Rhodes) were aggressively cutting off Ottoman sea routes. Süleyman began his siege of Malta in 1565, but the Knights fought back ferociously, the battle dragged on to winter, and Süleyman was forced to stand down.

The Ottoman armor was beginning to show weakness, provoking Süleyman, at age 72, to reassert his empire's superiority by taking Vienna once and for all. But he died in his tent during the campaign on the Danube. According to tradition, his heart is buried in Szigetvár on the spot where he passed away.

endangerment of the line, sultans, beginning with Mehmet III in 1595, adopted the practice of imprisoning their sons and heirs instead of assassinating them. Isolated from daily life, inexperienced in the ways of the government or military, accustomed to excess, they either went crazy or emerged completely unprepared for the demands of leadership.

Meanwhile, in the Janissary Corps, celibacy had long been abandoned, and Selim II decreed that sons of Janissaries—who were born free Muslims—could enroll. Eventually this paved the way for other free Muslims to join, and by the mid–17th century the Janissary Corps had swelled to 200,000, squeezing the state for the payroll to support the increase in numbers. The purchasing of office undermined the merit system, and although the palace school continued to function, the *devşirme* was abandoned. During times of peace, without a paycheck, with no active duty and no prospects of conquest or booty, the Janissaries would often turn to moonlighting or to the looting of their own locally governed lands. Already feared by the state structure, they continued to exert an influence on politics to further their own financial interest. Osman II recognized this threat in 1622, but was assassinated by the Janissaries after an effort to control them. Nevertheless, the internal deterioration of the Corps was inevitable, as was the weakening of Ottoman military might.

The organization of the *timer* (feudal-like system of government) was not left unaffected by this internal degeneration. To meet the needs of an expanding empire, the *timer* system was converted to a tax-based system of farm units, requiring administrators to send a portion of their tax revenues to Istanbul. Local administrators treated the land as private property, siphoned tax monies, and removed any incentive for the peasant population to produce. The effects were not only economically disastrous, but this weakening of the centralized government also encouraged local bandit raids and peasant revolts, consequences that the government was ill-equipped to control.

With the government decentralized, corrupt, and morally hollow, the Ottomans were unable to deal effectively with outside threats or absorb the economic pressures of a Europe in Renaissance. Vasco da Gama's circumnavigation of Africa opened up new trade routes to the east; the East India Company of London could therefore sell their goods in Istanbul for less than the Ottomans would pay for direct trade with India. And with new sea trade routes, merchants no longer paid levies for passage through Ottoman territory. Meanwhile, a Western industrial revolution produced cheaper goods that flooded the Ottoman market, thanks to Süleyman's Capitulations (see "Süleyman the Magnificent: Pragmatic Statesman," above). Silver and gold mined in the Americas drove up prices, the cost of living rose, and peasants abandoned their villages, which had disastrous effects on agricultural production.

Obviously not all sultans and administrators proved to be indifferent, ineffectual, and corrupt, but those who weren't were the exceptions. Although a technically inferior Ottoman navy was defeated by a coalition of Western states at Lepanto in 1571, the Ottoman navy was able to reestablish its naval presence by taking Cyprus from Venice later the same year.

The gradual decline was arrested later that century with the reign of **Murat IV** and his grand vizier, **Köprülü**, who maintained a policy against corruption and a return to the more centralized system of government. The *gazi* spirit was reignited, inspiring decades of new campaigns toward further expansion. Köprülü was so effective that the position of grand vizier was handed down to his son and his grandson, Kara Mustafa; this was the first dynasty associated with the post.

The Ottomans were determined to capture Vienna, and in 1683 **Kara Mustafa** led the army's second doomed attempt to take the Austrian capital. The Ottomans were no match for new European artillery and were soundly defeated by an alliance of European forces—a miscalculation that Kara Mustafa paid for with his life. The army's retreat was met by ambushes and further defeats, ending in the 1699 **Treaty of Karlowitz,** which granted Austria the provinces of Hungary and Transylvania, and marked the first time in history that the Ottoman Empire actually relinquished territory.

The 18th century was, for the most part, characterized by wars with Austria and Russia. Victories against the Austrians served to stabilize borders along the Danube, but the Russians were pushing into Muslim territory in an attempt to become a Black Sea power. In the first half of the century, the Ottoman military met with many successes, not the least of which was the defeat of **Peter the Great** at the Prut River in 1711. Nonetheless, two additional clashes with Russia culminated in the **Treaty of Küçük Kaynarca,** which followed a 1774 victory by Catherine the Great. (She, as champion of the Christian Orthodox faith, actively encouraged revolt in Russian-populated Ottoman territories.) The treaty was an enormous blow to the Ottomans, demonstrating that the Ottoman Empire was no longer the great power it once was. In addition to annexing European territories, the Treaty of Küçük Kaynarca granted the Russians extensive commercial privileges in the Black Sea, a diplomatic presence in Istanbul, and the protection of the Orthodox Christian faith on Turkish soil. The desire for territorial and economic dominance, along with the trafficking of loyalties, would characterize the Russian-Turkish conflict well into the 20th century.

REFORM ATTEMPTS

It was obvious to Selim III that reform was needed. Inspired by the American and French revolutions, he created a new corps, the *nizam-i jedid* ("the new order"), on Western models, even adopting European-style uniforms. The Janissaries revolted to what they saw as a loss of power and privilege, and in a conciliatory gesture that cost him the throne, Selim dissolved the *nizam-i jedid* in 1807. In the next few years, the Janissaries executed many of the reformers as well as Selim's successor, Mustafa IV; **Mahmud II** was spared only because he was the sole surviving Ottoman prince. Proceeding with caution, Mahmud's first action was to deal with the anarchy that had taken root in the provinces, but as nationalist uprisings in Serbia, Greece, Algeria, and Romania saw the empire eroding at its borders, it was clear that the Janissaries were of little use in the defense of the empire. This allowed Mahmud to gain enough support to finally have the corps destroyed. On June 15, 1826, in a staged massacre, Mahmud II had the Janissaries surrounded and "dissolved." Taking their place was a new army trained in European techniques by German military advisors.

Finally rid of the Janissaries' influence, Mahmud II, followed by his successor, **Abdülmecid,** was able to embark on significant modernization that would last for 40 years. The period of **Tanzimat** (literally, "reordering") was ushered in, aimed at strengthening the power of the government while encouraging an economic and social structure similar to that of Europe.

Influential during this period was the arrival of telegraph lines into Istanbul in 1855, facilitating a literary renaissance that would develop into an incubator for new nationalistic ideas. Supporters of this patriotism were called "New Ottomans," whose objectives of preserving territory and limiting autocratic rule would be attainable through the adoption of a constitution. Considered dissidents, many of these supporters were forced to flee, pursuing their nationalistic aims from posts abroad.

The reforms, however, failed to alleviate a worsening financial crisis brought on by a flood of foreign products, ending in a Franco-English monopoly on tobacco, salt, alcohol, silk, and other essentials. Loans to foreign banks were bankrupting an empire that had degenerated so much as to be known as "the Sick Man of Europe." European powers used this weakness to manipulate political balances. This foreign domination was no more evident than in the Ottoman participation in the Crimean War (1854–56), when the Ottomans granted the Catholic French the right to protect Christian sites in the Ottoman-held Holy Land. The Orthodox Russians found the excuse they needed to further their territorial ambitions and declared war on the Sultanate. Britain and France entered the conflict to protect their commercial interests, and the Russians were ultimately defeated. Even though the outcome was territorially favorable to the Ottomans, the empire was demoralized, having gone from imperial power to political pawn in less than 300 years.

Abdülhamid II succeeded in temporarily reinvigorating the failing empire, but it was too little too late. In 1875 he was confronted with a rebellion by a Russian-backed pan-Slavic movement in the Balkans. Battered and driven back almost to Istanbul, the Ottomans were forced to sign the disastrous **Treaty of San Stefano** in which much of the Ottomans' European territory was lost. Anti-Russian powers swiftly united behind Britain to force a modification of the treaty in 1878 at the Conference of Berlin. Nevertheless, the damage had been done. European imperialism was costing the Ottomans more losses: Tunisia to the French in 1881, Egypt to the British in 1882, and East Rumalia to Bulgaria in 1885.

Abdülhamid II responded by reaffirming his designation as caliph and beginning a policy of reinvigorating Islamic unity. With nationalistic tendencies developing among the Arab groups and Albanians, he hoped to create a sense of solidarity geared at holding the empire together.

Succumbing to external and internal pressures, he reluctantly instituted the first written constitution establishing a parliamentary system modeled on those in the West. For the first time in the history of the empire, absolute Ottoman rule had been relinquished, but as a condition to accepting the document, Abdülhamid insisted on retaining the right as final arbiter on unresolved issues. When the opposition became too outspoken in 1877, he simply neglected to reconvene the parliament and ruled autocratically for the next 30 years. Harshly criticized for repression, censorship, and paranoia of conspiracy, he was nevertheless effective in his Westernization of the empire, concentrating on public works, economic development, education, and communications. The telegraph, which provided access to information from beyond the empire's borders, was also useful to his network of spies, providing Abdülhamid with a means for controlling potential insurgencies from within.

The strengthening of the ideal of nationalism, both within the empire and among the provinces, had important negative consequences. Armenian revolutionary groups were springing up in response to a new sense of national identity. Concerned with another separatist movement and suspicious of an Armenian allegiance with European powers, Abdülhamid suppressed these insurgencies in a series of brutal massacres in which an estimated 300,000 Armenians were killed. More separatist movements arose: Greeks in Crete demanding unification with Greece rebelled, resulting in the loss of the island, while Bulgar aggression in Macedonia was inciting unrest among the Greeks there.

European response to Abdülhamid's regime was less than positive, but the Ottomans continued to receive consistent support from the Germans, who, along with the concessionary rights to a Berlin-to-Baghdad railway, enjoyed substantial commercial privileges.

Abdülhamid's crushing policy of censorship was unable to staunch the flow of new ideas. In the late 1880s an organized movement called the Committee for Union and Progress (CUP), made up primarily of military officers and rebels in Macedonia, was organized. In the name of "Liberty, Justice, Equality, and Fraternity" these **Young Turks** orchestrated a successful nonviolent coup d'état in 1908 designed to reinstate the constitution. Abdülhamid was deposed and his brother **Mehmed V** was released from prison as token head of state.

THE YOUNG TURKS

The constitution once again in place, the Young Turks, led by a triumvirate dominated by **Enver Paşa,** had gained control but lacked a clear objective other than controlling autocratic rule and territorial integrity. Ottomanism was no longer a viable ideology given the rise of nationalistic tendencies in the troubled provinces. Solidarity based on a policy of **Pan-Islamism** was especially popular as a way to cement people across national lines, but proved to be too racially narrow. The ideal of **Pan-Turkism,** the uniting of all Turkish-speaking peoples, gained popularity but gave way to **Turkism** as the new national identity, which merged a modernized Islamic tradition with European cultural influences. In spite of these parliamentary disagreements, the effects on administration were significant: a political structure based on European models; a transformation in the role of the press; the engagement of European advisors in agricultural, law, and military matters; increased public works; and the establishment of individual and women's rights.

The social effects of these institutions were lasting, but internal conflict was seen as an opportunity by foreign powers. In 1911 Italy seized Libya and the Dodocanese Islands. Even more devastating was the loss of the remaining European territories in the first Balkan War to an alliance among Bulgaria, Serbia, Greece, and Montenegro. Some European territory was regained 2 years later in the second Balkan War, but the situation was enough for the CUP to mutate into a military dictatorship controlled by a triumvirate of Enver Pasha, Mehmet Talat, and Ahmet Cemal.

WORLD WAR I

Although the Turks favored neutrality in the conflict germinating between the Central Powers of Germany and Austria and the allied countries of England, France, and Russia, Enver Pasha, who declared himself war minister in 1914, favored cooperation with the Germans. Business is business, however, and two battleships were commissioned from the British, destined to restore pride to an outdated navy. Fearful of Turkish entente with their adversaries, the British withheld consignment of the ships, and the Germans shrewdly came to the rescue with the delivery of two battleships, the *Göben* and the *Breslau,* complete with a German crew sporting fezzes.

In the summer of 1914, Enver Pasha signed a secret peace treaty with the Germans promising naval assistance in the face of Russian aggression in the Black Sea. Two months later, flying the sultan's flag, the *Göben* and *Breslau* attacked Russian ports and the Ottoman Empire was dragged into a war. The Russians retaliated by land through the Caucuses, while the British had successfully organized Arab revolts in the eastern provinces, leaving the Turks surrounded by hostile forces. Mustafa Kemal Atatürk's legendary defense of Gallipoli in 1915 succeeded in saving the Straits, and therefore Istanbul, from invasion. Nevertheless, Turkish forces were no match for Allied tanks, automatic weapons, and airplanes and on October 30, 1918, the CUP government agreed to an armistice with England and France. Two weeks later British and French troops were occupying the sultan's palace. Enver Pasha, Mehmet Talat, and Ahmet Cemal fled the city on German warships, leaving the Allied forces to decide how to divide up the empire's few remaining territories.

Under the Treaty of Sèvres, all European territories were lost except for a small area around Istanbul. Armenia and Kurdistan gained autonomy, Greece was assigned the administration of the region around Izmir, and French and Italian troops were left to occupy portions of the rest of Anatolia. The Capitulations, suspended shortly before the war, were restored and control of Turkish finances was taken over by the Allies. The government of **Mehmet VI** signed the treaty August 20, 1920, but its destiny was to be short-lived.

THE NATIONALIST MOVEMENT

Spurred on by defeat and foreign occupation, nationalists established pockets of resistance called "Defense of Rights" groups. **Mustafa Kemal** (the name Kemal, meaning "perfection," was given to Mustafa by a school instructor for his exceptional achievement; "Atatürk" was added later) was already an active nationalist, having taken part in the CUP overthrow of 1909. He had subsequently distanced himself from the CUP, but his outspokenness had made him many enemies. Mustafa Kemal was sent to Samsun on May 19, 1919, with nebulous military orders, but instead began organizing various nationalist factions, formally resigning from military service shortly after. His goals in leading the resistance were inflexible: the recognition of a national movement and the liberation of Anatolia from foreign occupation.

That same year two important nationalist congresses were convened at Erzurum and Sivas, forming the basis for the **National Pact.** The first conference called for an independent Turkish state, while the second defined the objectives of the movement. Presiding over these meetings, Mustafa Kemal called for the rights to all remaining Ottoman territories, control of Istanbul and the Straits, the guarantee of minority rights, and rejection of foreign intervention in Turkish affairs. Unwilling to alienate the loyalists and conservatives, Mustafa Kemal reasserted the movement's allegiance to the sultan-caliphate, maintaining that until the sultan was free of foreign control, the committee would act on behalf of the people. In response, the sultan declared Mustafa Kemal a rebel, and a *fetva*—the killing of a rebel as a religious duty—was issued. Mustafa Kemal and his followers established themselves in Ankara, far from the reaches of their enemies, voting on August 23, 1920, for the creation of the **Grand National Assembly.**

In the fall of 1919, the Greeks got greedy and began moving inland, arriving as far as the Sakarya River (about 81km/50 miles west of Ankara). Troops led by **Ismet Paşa** (General) beat the Greeks back to Izmir, and in several decisive victories, Mustafa Kemal succeeded in driving the Greek troops completely off the peninsula. This last victory in the war for independence earned Kemal recognition by foreign governments as de facto leader of the Turks. The Soviet Union was the first power to sign a treaty with the nationalists in 1920, establishing set boundaries between the two countries. As nationalist troops approached Thrace, France begged off a confrontation with a complete withdrawal of French forces. Although the British remained in Thrace, they were unwilling to get caught up in a battle on behalf of the Greeks and instead arbitrated the Armistice of Mundanya, requiring the Greeks to retreat behind the Maritsa River. Kemal had succeeded in retaking possession of Istanbul, the Straits, and Thrace, essentially nullifying the Treaty of Sèvres, and it was clear that a new treaty would have to be drawn up. The Allies invited both the Ottoman government (to be represented by the sultan) and the Grand National Assembly to participate in the creation of the **Treaty of Lausanne,** but fearing that divided representation would only weaken his cause, Kemal declared the sultanate abolished and sent Ismet Paşa as sole representative of Turkey. Mehmet VI was smuggled to Malta on a British ship where he remained in exile, putting the final nail in the coffin of the Sick Man and ending 6 centuries of an empire. The role of caliph was given to his cousin Abdümecid, heir to a defunct Ottoman dynasty.

In 1923 the Treaty of Lausanne (which replaced the earlier Treaty of Sèvres and thus nullified, among other things, the formation of an independent Kurdistan) recognized Turkey as a sovereign nation. The nation's borders as proposed by the National Pact were established except for the concession of Mosul to Iraq and that of Alexandretta and Antakya (now the Hatay) to France as part of a Syrian mandate. The treaty also called for Greece and Turkey to exchange their respective minority populations, excluding those in Istanbul and western Thrace. This was meant to improve relations between the two countries in the long run, but tragically uprooted almost two million people from their adopted homelands.

Success at Lausanne was immediately followed by the Grand National Assembly's proclamation of the Republic of Turkey and the election of Mustafa Kemal as president.

MUSTAFA KEMAL ATATÜRK & THE REPUBLICAN PERIOD

At the beginning of the war for liberation, Kemal saw a country in ruins. Kemal's vision for the republic was Westernization, modernization, solidarity, secularization, and equality for all Turks. Kemal governed as an inflexible yet benevolent autocrat, asserting that a transitional period was necessary in securing effective reform. To this end he formed the Republican People's Party (RPP), which became the exclusive political vehicle for his programs. When Abdümecid indicated a desire to expand his role as caliph into the political sphere, Kemal, wary of opposition from anti-reformers and traditionalists, abolished the caliphate and banished all members of the house of Osman.

In 1924 the Grand National Assembly drew up a constitution establishing guaranteed civil rights and a legal framework for the government. Formally elected president by the assembly, Kemal selected Ismet Paşa as his prime minister, handpicked his cabinet, and set out virtually unobstructed on a path of brisk modernization.

To Kemal, secularization was essential in a modern system and vital in dealing with a European world. He closed the religious courts and ordered all religious schools secular. His rapid reforms were not without opposition—both from those who wanted a larger role for Islam in the government as well as those who

grew disillusioned with Kemal's pervasive cult of personality. The Progressive Republican Party (PRP) was formed from an opposition consisting of former supporters and associates. Kemal, in a willingness to experiment with open dialogue, admitted the party into the system, even replacing Ismet Paşa with the PRP's Fethi Bey.

An uprising in the southeast put a hasty end to this experiment. An insurgency led by Sheikh Said of the Nakshbendi Order of the Dervishes in the Kurdish southeast had broken out, intent on restoring the caliphate. Kemal responded by invoking an emergency law (the Maintenance of Order Law), reinstated Ismet Paşa as prime minister, and swiftly crushed the rebellion. The sheikh was condemned and hanged along with more than 40 other rebels; newspapers were closed down, journalists arrested, and the PRP outlawed.

Years earlier on a trip to Europe, Kemal had borne the brunt of ridicule for his tasseled red felt hat; so, in 1925 the fez, symbol of Ottoman oppression, was outlawed. Stating that "civilized men wear civilized hats," Kemal chose to wear the more modern Panama hat, much like how Mehmet the Conqueror had replaced the turban with the more "modern" fez.

Dervish orders were outlawed (but not completely suppressed). The praying at tombs was prohibited. Honorary titles were abolished. It seemed to the people that Kemal was determined to sever all ties with the past and with tradition, and the people in the outlying regions rioted. Mindful that a drastic measure such as banning the veil would enrage his critics, he opted for discouragement instead. Women in Istanbul and in the other cities began to appear in public without the veil, but the practice caught on less quickly in the rural areas.

The legal code was overhauled, taking its examples from the Swiss, Italian, and German systems. Civil law, previously the dominion of the religious leaders, was secularized, which had a particularly profound effect on women's rights. In a move toward equality, polygamy was outlawed and marriage became a civil contract, depriving husbands of the absolute right provided by Islamic law to divorce for any reason. Women were also granted equal rights in matters of custody and inheritance, while education for women on the secondary level was recognized as equal in importance to that of men. By 1934, women's rights had extended to universal suffrage, and Turkey won the distinction of being the first country in the world to have elected a woman to the Supreme Court.

Kemal's flurry of reform angered many Muslims, and in 1926 a plot to assassinate the president was uncovered. Fifteen conspirators were hanged, including members of the extinct Republican People's Party and a former deputy, while others were either tried and exiled or acquitted. In 1928 a constitutional provision declaring Islam as the state religion was deleted, completing the secularism of the Republic of Turkey.

A census, which was the first systematic accounting of the people of Turkey, brought to light gaping holes in the needs of the population. Only 10% of the people over the age of 7 were literate while even a smaller percentage of children were even in school, prompting significant reforms in education in the next few years.

Kemal's next task was aimed at both engendering Turkish pride and uniting his polyglot nation under one tongue. By the 1920s, Arabic, Persian, and French words made up 80% of language use, and Kemal ordered his scholars to the task of constructing a pure Turkish language purged of foreign influences. Arabic script was replaced with Latin characters.

To quiet the voice of his critics, Kemal personally traveled around the country teaching the new alphabet in public squares when necessary. Not even Islam was spared: In 1932 the state made it mandatory for the traditional call to prayer to be broadcast from the loudspeakers in Turkish instead of Arabic, the language of Islam.

All this modernization and bureaucratic reorganization only served to underline yet another need for change. Keeping track of all these Mohammeds, Mahmuts, and Mehmets was getting confusing, and it was obvious that a better method of identification would be necessary. Up to this point, villagers were called by their first names; now, the people were ordered to select a last name, lest they be assigned one less imaginative. Mustafa Kemal was given the name Atatürk ("father of the Turks") by the Grand National Assembly. Ismet Paşa (the Paşa meaning "general") adopted Inönü, the site of one of his victorious battles, while others selected surnames from the less original Bey ("Mr.") to something more creative along the lines of "great slayer of mountains." Old habits die hard, however, and even today it is common practice to address a person by his first name, followed by the respectful "Bey."

Atatürk's presidency was characterized by six guiding principles later to be known as the "Six Arrows." In addition to the three early principles of Republicanism, Nationalism, and Secularism, Atatürk worked toward emphasizing the ideals of Populism, Reformism, and Etatism. Populism was based on the principle that all (men) were equal, but just as important was that all men were Turks, emphasizing the sovereignty of the people over their nation. Reformism confirmed their responsibility toward rapid modernization, while Etatism embraced the government's role in economic development.

"Political and military victories cannot endure unless they are crowned by economic triumphs," said Atatürk, and in 1934 a 5-year plan for achieving economic sovereignty was inaugurated. The Ottoman economic legacy was one of agricultural stagnation and little public confidence in the quality of Ottoman products. A British saying went, "If you want to hang yourself, do it with English rope." Atatürk reversed these trends by developing agricultural and industrial production, raising Customs tariffs to protect the local industry, buying up the foreign railroad concessions, and determinedly avoiding the foreign debt trap. Nevertheless, growth was slow and the people began complaining of a low standard of living. The labor law of 1936 set up provisions for the rights of workers: Strikes were outlawed but a method of arbitration was set up. A state insurance program providing for accidents, for unexpected death, and for seniors was established, furthering the government's support of the labor force.

Atatürk fostered a policy of peaceful foreign relations, subscribing to his enduring ideal: "Peace at home, peace abroad." For the first time in Turkish history, antagonism and warfare were not central to the government's approach to its borders. He signed pacts with Greece, Romania, Yugoslavia and the Balkans, Iran, Iraq, and Afghanistan, and entered into friendly status with the Soviet Union, the United States, England, Germany, Italy, and France. In 1932 Turkey became a member of the League of Nations and in 1936, in response to Mussolini's aggression in Ethiopia, Atatürk successfully lobbied at the Montreux Convention for Turkish fortification of the Straits.

In 15 years of presidency, Atatürk transformed a feeble dictatorship into a modern, reasonably democratic, forward-thinking republic. On November 10, 1938, his efforts finally took their toll, when, after years of drinking, he died of cirrhosis of the liver, but not without naming Inönü as his successor. The League of Nations offered tribute at his death by calling him a "genius international peacemaker." Atatürk's legacy lives on and even to this day, the time of his death is always observed with a minute of silence.

FOREIGN POLICY & WORLD WAR II

Having served as prime minister from the beginning, having fought alongside Atatürk in the war of independence against the Greeks, and having represented Turkey at the Lausanne Conference, Ismet Inönü's appointment to the presidency by the Grand National Assembly the next day was a mere formality. But no sooner did Inönü take office than he was confronted with an international crisis of unprecedented proportions.

The Soviet Union's relentless lust for unfettered access to the Bosphorus Straits made it a continuous threat, while Hitler's appetite for the Balkans boded badly for Turkey. Sandwiched between two great and potentially hostile powers, Turkey entered into a "declaration of mutual guarantee" with Britain followed by a treaty of nonaggression with France. The Nazi-Soviet pact of nonaggression signed in August 1939 presented a difficult problem for Turkey, as it pitted the Soviets against Britain and France. Turkey sent an envoy to the Soviet Union in an attempt to secure a peace treaty with them, but to no avail. Betting on security in numbers, Turkey entered into a "treaty of mutual assistance" with Britain and France stipulating that no action would be required of Turkey that might lead to an eventual involvement in a war with the Soviet Union. The arrival of the Germans on Turkey's doorstep with Hitler's invasion of Greece prompted Turkey to initiate a preemptory nonaggression treaty with Germany, stipulating nonaggression with either Britain or France. Four days later Germany invaded the Soviet Union, an almost irresistible turn of events for the Turks, given their historically acrimonious relationship with the Russians. Still, Turkey managed to stay out of the fight, including denying the Germans access to the Straits or passage on or over Turkish land. After Germany's defeats in Egypt, North Africa, and Stalingrad seemed to confirm the inevitable defeat of the Germans, Turkey finally took sides when at a meeting with Roosevelt and Churchill in Cairo, Inönü relented to a request that Turkish military facilities be made available to the Allied forces.

Inönü's fence-sitting allowed Turkey to maintain its neutrality at least until February 1945, when a declaration of war on Germany became a prerequisite for admittance into the San Francisco Conference (the precursor to the United Nations, of which Turkey was one of the original 51 members).

Nevertheless, war took its toll on the Turkish economy. During the war years, inflation rose significantly, and to feed the war debt, the government imposed a capital levy on the Turkish people. Contrary to the government's posture of absolute equality, the levy was applied arbitrarily and mercilessly, and was particularly biased against rich Greek, Armenian, and Jewish merchants. Deadlines for payment were often harsh, and default was punishable by property seizures, arrest, and deportation into forced labor. To this day, Turkey acknowledges this as a shameful episode in its history, attributable to the extraordinary pressures of war.

There were postwar problems to address as well. The discovery of wartime documents revealed the Soviet Union's enduring desire for control of the Bosphorus and the Dardanelles. Historically a European issue, the United States joined with Britain to support Turkey

against Cold War pressures, expanding Turkey's scope of "Europeanization" to now include the United States. The Truman Doctrine of 1947 confirmed a United States–Turkish friendship with the United States' contribution of $400 million toward strengthening the security of Turkey and Greece against Soviet aggression. Turkey later demonstrated its support of Western policies by sending an infantry brigade to Korea to serve under United Nations command in the 1940s and 1950s.

In a postwar desire for political stability and national security against Russian aggression, Turkey pursued a policy of friendship with its neighbors, signing the Greece-Yugoslav Alliance, the Turkish-Pakistani Mutual Security Pact, and the Baghdad Pact, in addition to its membership acceptance by NATO. Turkey's recognition of Israel provoked outrage among its Arab neighbors, but because Arabs still had the stigma of being Ottoman subjects, they were simply ignored.

MUSICAL CHAIRS IN TURKEY'S POLITICS

Pressure mounted in postwar Turkey over the state's increasingly authoritarian rule. Responding to spreading dissension, Inönü yielded to his critics and authorized multiparty activity, permitting access to a democratic process. In 1946 four of the dissenters, Jelal Bayar, Adnan Menderes, Refik Koraltan, and Fuad Koprulu, founded the Democratic Party, and despite bribery, scare tactics, and even suspicious ballot handling, the Democratic Party gained unexpected popularity in the general elections and a voice in the decision-making process. By the election of May 1950, the Democratic Party had attracted enough of the displaced minorities to win a sweeping majority, appealing to private business owners, Islamic reactionaries, and the struggling rural population. In a first-time

Cyprus 101

Cyprus is another one of these divisive territorial issues not entirely dissimilar to the Northern Ireland, Palestinian, or Kashmir conflicts. Situated 65km (40 miles) off the Turkish coast, Cyprus was a part of the Ottoman Empire for centuries, with sizable migrations of Muslim Turks adding to the Orthodox Christian Greek inhabitants of the island. The island became a British colony in 1878 in exchange for support of Turkey against Russian aggression. Anti-British terrorism by Greek Cypriots in the mid-1950s incited riots in Istanbul; Turks were fearful that Greek ownership of the island would be a threat to Turkish national security. The London agreement, negotiated by Britain, Greece, and Turkey, established the independent republic of Cyprus in 1960, with a Greek president, a Turkish vice president, and a fair proportion of representatives in the government.

This bicommunal state functioned for only 3 years, as militant Greek Cypriots (backed by Greece) ousted the Turkish Cypriot members, which resulted in a series of brutal attacks on both Greek and Turkish villages. Once again, it is a case of finger-pointing about who threw the first punch. For the next 10 years, the Turkish Cypriots lived as refugees, during which time Turkey unsuccessfully sought support from a U.S. government unwilling to intervene on behalf of either the Greeks or the Turks. A Greek coup aimed at annexing the island and aided by local Greek Cypriot forces in 1974 called Turkey to action. A Turkish expeditionary force was deployed, occupying the northern third of the island, which in 1983 proclaimed itself the Turkish Republic of Northern Cyprus. Greek inhabitants of the northern territory fled south.

The United Nations has called for a unified state made up of two politically equal communities, and in 2005, Turkey voted yes for reunification. But the Greek Cypriots voted no. There have been no further attempts at negotiation as the international community pretty much waits for the dust to settle. Meanwhile, the United Nations still does not recognize the northern republic and U.N. peacekeeping forces continue to patrol the border zones between north and south. Now that the E.U. has cleared the way for accession talks with Turkey, it remains to be seen how much Cyprus will remain a thorn in the side of Turkey.

---

participating in politics until 2003. The **Justice and Development Party** (Adalet ve Kalkınma Partısı, or **AKP** in Turkish), formed in August 2001, took over where the Welfare Party left off, claiming a new, moderate stance and a willingness to work within the secular system. The AKP was propelled into power in 2002 with more than 34% of the vote, in no small part as a result of the ineptitude of the government in power to handle the 1999 earthquake, which claimed the lives of over 20,000. It is a well-publicized fact that much of the destruction caused by the earthquake could have been avoided had adequate building methods been employed, and that poorly constructed buildings were a result of corrupt business practices. The vote was also seen as a backlash against institutional corruption as well as dissatisfaction with the crumbling Turkish economy. Reccep Tayıpıp Erdoğan, the former mayor of Istanbul whose leadership of the party was delayed as a result of incendiary remarks he had made in 1997 (*"Mosques are our barracks,*

The Kurdish Question

Who are the Kurds, these people without a country? History books pinpoint their origins to western Iran, but it's more accurate to say that the Kurds have roots in many different lands. Over time, the Kurds have developed a distinctive culture, and today the Kurdish population spreads over eastern Anatolia, northeastern Iraq, Syria, and western Iran.

In the wake of World War I, Kurdish demands for an independent state were met in the Treaty of Sèvres (1920), but the treaty was nullified by Atatürk's victories over foreign occupation and replaced by the Treaty of Lausanne (1923). This new treaty made no mention of the Kurds. The Kurds have been struggling for independence ever since, suffering from repression not only in Turkey but in other countries in the region. In the 1980-to-1988 Iran-Iraq War, entire Kurdish villages were annihilated due to Iraq's use of poison gas; as a result the Turkish government allowed 100,000 refugees to flow over the border into Turkey.

In 1978 Abdullah Öcalan formed the Kurdistan Workers' Party (PKK) as an organized separatist movement, accusing the Turkish government of oppression, repression, torture, and censorship. The Turkish government labeled the PKK a terrorist organization with a limited following intent on destabilizing the Turkish nation and threatening its sovereignty. Turkey considers its Kurdish population Turkish citizens, although in practice, many of the predominantly Kurdish territories, typically in remote regions, are impoverished and lack basic public services.

The PKK took up arms in 1984, and the violence persisted until Öcalan's capture in 1999. In the 16-year armed conflict, the Turkish government estimates that over 30,000 people lost their lives, although this estimate is probably a modest one. At the end of Öcalan's trial, the PKK leader was sentenced to death; since that time, Turkey has abolished the death penalty and Öcalan can expect to live out his days in a Turkish prison.

The PKK declared an end to the cease-fire in 2003, and since then, assassinations, attacks, and counterattacks have been on the rise in the southeast. Increased tensions on the Iraqi-Turkish border don't bode well for the U.S. policy of support for Iraq's Kurdish north, as both Turkey and northern Iraq are key U.S. allies in American foreign policy in the region. For now, it's a wait-and-see situation.

---

domes our helmets, minarets our bayonets, believers our soldiers"), has been at the helm serving as prime minister since 2003, and apparently, the Turks are more than satisfied with his performance. In 2004, the AKP received an unprecedented 44% of the vote and its popularity just keeps growing. In the summer of 2007, however, the military perceived the

pendulum swinging a little too far right when Erdoğan nominated Abdullah Gül for president and released a public statement of warning. Gül's wife wears a headscarf, and this issue in itself is one of the most explosive ones in contemporary Turkish politics.

In spite of the tensions between the religious conservatives and the secular progressives, Turkey has experienced a historic level of economic stability and progress in the past few years. Erdoğan has also been at the forefront of Turkey's push for full admittance into the E.U., a process that will take at least a decade.

2 Arts, Culture & Music

First impressions of Turkey reveal a society much more European than one expects, but echoes of a strong, proud, and decidedly Oriental heritage shine through in the arts, culture, music, and folklore. Tourists flock to those "Turkish Nights" shows, expecting to cram in a few hours' worth of "authentic" folklore. But while a belly dancer in a glittery harem hat may seem the epitome of exoticism, this ritual crowd-pleasure is anything but a Turkish invention.

Turkish culture developed by absorbing the artistic traditions of conquered lands, so more than any one defining style, the Turkish arts are characterized by layers and layers of complexity. From the time the Turkish tribes spread through Anatolia in the 11th century until the end of the Ottoman Empire, the Turks had incorporated decorative and architectural styles from the Sassanids (a pre-Islamic Persian dynasty), the Romans, the early Christians, the Byzantines, and Renaissance-era Europeans.

ARCHITECTURE

The architectural and decorative arts of Turkey are closely linked to the Islamic faith, which gave major importance to mosques, *medreses* (theological schools), and mausoleums. Almost all mosques follow the plan of Mohammed's house, which was composed of an enclosed courtyard surrounded by huts, with a building at one end for prayer and an arcade to provide shade. Whereas in Mohammed's time the call to prayer was sung from the rooftops, minarets were added later for convenience and style.

The main objective reflected in Selçuk architecture was the proliferation of the purist Sunni orthodoxy, which was achieved by concentrating its efforts on the construction of *medreses* and other public works such as mosques and baths. To provide a means of safe passage for trade as well as the means for communication from one end of the empire to another, the Selçuks built a network of fortified caravansaries. Although Rum Selçuk architecture at first reflected the influences of the Iranian Selçuks, over time they developed a distinct style, incorporating features like pointed arches from the Crusaders and lofty arched spaces from Christian Armenians and Syrians employed under the sultan. They also developed the squinch, a triangular architectural device that allowed the placement of a circular dome atop a square base, laying the groundwork of what was later to become an outstanding feature of Ottoman mosque architecture. The Selçuks also combined traditional arabesque styles with indigenous Anatolian decorative motifs that literally flowered into a unique style of geometric architectural ornamentation.

A defining feature of Ottoman architecture became the dome, a form that expanded on earlier Turkish architecture but was later haunted by the feat of superior engineering accomplished in the soaring dome of the Ayasofya. As the Turks conquered Christian lands and churches were converted into mosques, traditionally Byzantine ideas were crossing cultural barriers and finding their way into the Selçuk and Ottoman vocabulary.

Ottoman architecture reached its zenith in the 16th century under Süleyman the Magnificent, in the expert hands of his master builder, Sinan. In the service of the sultan, Sinan built no fewer than 355 buildings and complexes throughout the empire, including the Süleymaniye, whose grand and cascading series of domes has become not only a defining feature of the Istanbul skyline but also a pinnacle in Ottoman architecture. (Sinan succeeded in surpassing the Ayasofya with the Selimiye in Edirne, a destination not covered in this guide.)

ART

Whereas Byzantine art featured elaborate religious interiors and the use of luxury materials like gold and silver, Islamic *hadith* frowned on the use of luxury items in its mosques, favoring instead unpretentious items like ceramics, woodcarvings, and inlay. Additionally, because of the Islamic prohibition against religious images of living creatures, Turkish decorative arts were channeled into alternative features like flowers, geometric forms, and Arabic script.

The Selçuks introduced the use of glazed bricks and tiles in the decoration of their mosques, and by the 16th century, the Ottomans had developed important centers of ceramic production at Iznik and Kütahya. Ottoman tiles incorporated a new style of foliage motif and used turquoises, blues, greens, and whites as the dominant colors. Spectacular uses of tile can be seen all over the country, in mosques, palaces, *hamams* (Turkish baths), and even private homes.

Woodworking and mother-of-pearl or ivory inlay were primarily used in the decoration of the *minbar* (pulpit), but this craft extended to the creation of Koran holders, cradles, royal thrones, and even musical instruments.

Calligraphy is intimately related to the Islamic faith and dates back to the earliest surviving Koran manuscripts. Over the centuries, different styles of calligraphy emerged, with one of the basic requirements being that the text is legible. The Selçuk period brought about a more graceful cursive script, while the earlier Arabic script was more suited to stone carving. The ornamentation of holy manuscripts became an art in itself, as seen in pages that are gilded with gold leaf or sprinkled with gold dust, and in script whose diacritical marks are accented with red ink.

Besides the use of calligraphy in religious manuscripts, under the Ottomans the application of an imperial seal, or *tuğra* (pronounced *too*-rah), on all official edicts became customary. The earliest example of a *tuğra* can be traced back to Orhan Gazi on a 1324 endowment deed, with each successive sultan creating his own distinct and personal representation. Today these seals are significant works of art, bearing price tags that stretch into the hundred- or even thousand-dollar ranges.

The art of marbled paper is another traditional Anatolian art that flourished under the Ottomans. Known as *ebru,* the art of marbling calls for natural dyes and materials, and a precise hand to create a collection of spectacular, one-of-a-kind designs.

The art of carpet weaving has a complex heritage that goes back for thousands and thousands of years. Based on the necessity of a nomadic existence, carpets had more practical functions: warmth and cleanliness. As tribes migrated and integrated, designs and symbols crossed over borders as well. Carpet designs parallel those of the other artistic media, with geometric patterns a common feature of the 13th century.

Wool carpets provided warmth for the harsh winters, while *kilims,* also placed on the ground, provided coverings for cushions in a *şark*-style (or Oriental-style) setting that could later be used to transport the contents of the tent. Prayer rugs, identifiable by a deliberate lack of symmetry (the "arrow" will always be lain in the direction of Mecca), continue to be one of the more beautiful categories of traditional Turkish rugs.

Although Turkish carpets became one of the more coveted trappings of status in Europe, appearing in the backgrounds of many a Renaissance artist such as Giovanni Bellini and Ghirlandaio, the more ornate and sophisticated designs preferred by Europeans were the creation of non-Turkic (mostly Armenian) craftsmen. Today, however, even these stunning pieces are part of the traditional Turkish carpet-weaving lexicon.

MUSIC

Much like the art, architecture, and even food of Turkey, Turkish music blends a wide range of styles and cultures, from Anatolian troubadours on horseback to the commercially successful tunes of arabesque at the top of the charts. Different combinations of styles and genres have given rise to countless new sounds that despite being modern still sound unfamiliar to a Western ear untrained in Eastern modes. An irregular meter called *akşak,* typical to Turkish folk music that originated on the Asian steppes, may sound strange to ears trained on the regular cadences of double, triple, and 4/4 time.

This style was kept alive by lovelorn troubadours singing the poetic and humanistic words of folk icons like Yunus Emre or Pir Sultan; only recently was the music written down. Folk music endures in the rural villages of Turkey and is a regular feature at wedding celebrations, circumcision ceremonies, and as part of a bar or cafe's lineup of *canlı muzik* (live music).

Classical Turkish music began as the music of the Ottoman court, and in an empire composed of a patchwork of cultures, the top composers were Greeks, Armenians, and Jews. Turkish classical music has its origins in the Persian and Arabic traditions, and eventually, the music of the Mevlevi became a major source as well.

Military music had an important role in the successes of the Ottoman Empire, with its thunderous use of percussion aimed at demoralizing an enemy before battle. The Janissary band influenced 18th- and 19th-century European music, in *alla turca* movements written by Mozart and Beethoven, and operas written by Lully and Handel.

The "Europeanization" of the Ottoman Empire in the 19th century brought many foreign musicians to the court, including Giusseppe Donizetti, brother of the more famous Gaetano Donizetti, who was given the position of head of the Imperial Band in 1831.

Pop music took hold of Turkey in the 1950s and 1960s, much as it swept the Western world. But pop in Turkey took on a different form, first with the popularity of the tango in the 1950s, and then with the re-recording of Western favorites using Turkish lyrics. It wasn't long before Turkish musicians began composing their own forms of pop. In the 1970s, as the rural population began to migrate to the cities in search of their fortunes, a widely disparaged form of music called *arabesque* swept the nation off its feet, with the sounds of unrequited love, sentimentality, and even fatalism. Arabesque was a fusion of the new pop, folk, and traditional music that developed into a new

---

Local Lingo

Walking through a bazaar or past a restaurant entrance may elicit a *"buyurun"* or *"buyurun efendem,"* both of which are expressions of courtesy. *Buyurun* has no English equivalent; it's used as an invitation to "Please feel free" (to look, to come in), or as a "You're welcome," much like the Italian *prego. Efendem* is a highly polite gender-neutral form of address that also means "Pardon?"

and highly commercial style; today, these both exotic and catchy phrases blare from every taxicab, long-distance bus, and discothèque.

LANGUAGE

Turkish is the official language of Turkey, uniting not just its citizens, but also a diaspora of Turkish-speaking peoples throughout Asia. The Turkish language originated in the highlands of the Altay Mountains of Central Asia and is heavily spoken in lands stretching from Turkey to China, including Azerbaijan, Turkmenistan, Uzbekistan, Turkistan, Kazakhstan, Kyrgyzstan, Tajikistan, and Northern Cyprus. At the height of the Ottoman Empire, the Ottoman language was a mélange of outside influences heavily infused with Arabic, the language of religion and law; Persian, the language of art and diplomacy; and French, well, just because it's French. Pure Turkish, spoken primarily in the home, was considered inappropriately informal and familiar for public use.

Atatürk was convinced that pride in one's language was critical in instilling a sense of nationalism in a people, and one of his landmark reforms was to uplift Turkish to its rightful and preeminent role as a national language. He began by purging foreign influences from the Turkish language and introducing the Latin alphabet. Words of Arabic origin still maintain a tremendous presence in daily usage, especially concerning religious matters, and knowledge of some foreign languages will nevertheless come in handy in places like the *kuaför* (coiffeur), the *asensör* (elevator, in French), or the *likör* (liquor)

store. English is slowly creeping into the language, particularly in the area of technology, with words like *telefon, Internet,* and the less high-tech *seks.*

Turkish is an agglutinative language, which means that words (and sometimes whole sentences) get formed by tacking stuff on to the root. Each suffix has some grammatical function but also provides for a discreet amount of flexibility in shades of meaning. To make matters worse, the suffix must follow rules of spelling and phonetics, so that there are eight ways of expressing the word "of."

In 1924, when Atatürk introduced the mandatory use of the Latin alphabet, Turkish became a phonetic language and is pronounced exactly as it is written, making it relatively easy to read. Is it hard to learn? Compared to what? Will a novice's pronunciation be any worse than an American's attempt at getting his lips around French? Probably not. But Turks are so uncommonly adept at languages that in all likelihood your contact with Turkish will be kept to a minimum. In most major tourist areas and many secondary ones, the local merchant population speaks English, along with French, German, Spanish, Italian, Danish, and even Russian.

Even so, it's absolutely the minimum of courtesy to put yourself out there in an attempt to communicate a few words in the native language of the country you are visiting, and knowing a few basics will help you feel less isolated and helpless. See appendix B, "A Glossary of Useful Turkish Phrases," for a glossary of common phrases and terms, with a pronunciation guide.

3 Food & Drink

As nomads, the Turks were limited by what the land offered and by what could be prepared over a crude open fire, so it's not a stretch to understand how kebaps and *köfte* became the centerpieces of Turkish cooking. Turkish food today

concentrates on simple combinations, few ingredients, and fresh produce.

With access to vast cupboards stocked with ingredients from the four corners of the empire, the palace chefs developed a more complex cuisine. The majority of these recipes, recorded in Arabic script, were regrettably lost in the language reforms. Some Ottoman favorites have made it to us nevertheless, like the *hünkar beğendi* (the sultan was pleased), *imam bayaldı* (the priest fainted; Barbara Cartland might have likened it to a woman's "flower"), and *hanım göbeği* (lady's navel), a syrupy dessert with a thumbprint in the middle. These have become staples in many run-of-the-mill restaurants, but true Ottoman cuisine is difficult to come by. Several restaurants in Istanbul have researched the palace archives to restore some of those lost delicacies to the modern table, providing a rare opportunity to sample the artistry and intricate combinations of exotic flavors in the world's first fusion food. The Turkish kitchen is always stocked with only the freshest vegetables, the most succulent fruits, the creamiest of cheeses and yogurt, and the best cuts of meat. But, unless you're a pro like the chefs to the sultans, whose lives depended on pleasing the palate of their leader, it takes a lot of creativity to turn such seemingly simple ingredients into dishes fit for a king.

A typical Turkish meal begins with a selection of cold then hot mezes, or appetizers. These often become a meal in themselves, accompanied by an ample serving of raki (see the "Drinks" section, below), that when taken together, form a recipe for friendship, laughter, and song. The menu of mezes often includes several types of eggplant, called *patlican; ezme,* a fiery hot salad of red peppers; *sigara böregi,* fried cheese "cigars"; and *dolmalar,* anything from peppers to vine leaves stuffed with rice, pine nuts, cumin, and fresh mint.

The dilemma is whether or not to fill up on these delectables or save room for the kebaps, a national dish whose stature rivals that of pasta in Italy. While *izgara* means "grilled," the catchall word *kebap,* simply put, means "roasted," and denotes an entire class of meats cooked using various methods. Typical kebaps include lamb "shish"; spicy *Adana kebap,* a spicy narrow sausage made of ground lamb; *döner kebap,* slices of lamb cooked on a vertical revolving spit; *patlican kebap,* slices of eggplant and lamb grilled on a skewer; and the artery-clogging *Iskender kebap,* layers of *pide,* tomatoes, yogurt, and thinly sliced lamb drenched in melted butter. To confuse things a bit, stews can also be called kebaps.

Turks are equally nationalistic over their *köfte,* Turkey's answer to the hamburger: flat or round little meatballs served with slices of tomato and whole green chili peppers. But even though signs for kebap houses may mar the view, Turkish citizens are anything but carnivores, preferring instead to fill up on grains and vegetables. *Saç kavurma* represents a class of casseroles sautéed or roasted in an earthenware dish that, with the help of an ample amount of velvety Turkish olive oil, brings to life the flavors of ingredients like potatoes, zucchini, tomatoes, eggplant, and beef chunks. No self-respecting gourmand should leave Turkey without having had a plate of *mantı,* a meat-filled ravioli, dumpling, or *kreplach,* adapted to the local palate by adding a garlic-and-yogurt sauce. *Pide* is yet another interpretation of pizza made up of fluffy oven-baked bread topped with a variety of ingredients and sliced in strips. *Lahmacun* is another version of the pizza, only this time the bread

You'll Never Count Sheep Again

Bus drivers in Turkey abide by an unwritten rule never to eat *cacık*—a salad of yogurt, cucumber, and garlic, often served as a soup—while on duty. The dish is believed to be a surefire, and natural, cure for insomnia.

A Restaurant Primer

The idiosyncrasies of a foreign culture can create some frustrating experiences, especially when they get in the way of eating. In Turkey, dining out in often boisterous groups has traditionally been the province of men, and a smoke-filled room that reeks of macho may not be the most relaxing prospect for a meal. A woman dining alone will often be whisked away to an upstairs "family salon," called the *aile salonu*, where—what else—families, and yes, even guys, can enjoy a night out in peace and quiet.

Restaurants are everywhere, and although the name *restoran* was a European import used for the best establishments, nowadays practically every type of place goes by that name. Cheap, simple, home-style meals can be had at a family-run place called a *lokanta*, where the food is often prepared in advance *(hazır yemek)* and presented in a steam table. The dining room is generally bare. A *meyhane* is a tavern full of those smokin' Turks I mentioned earlier, but in the major cities, these have become extremely popular places for a fun and sophisticated night out. Decor in the *meyhane* is usually as stark as in the *lokanta,* but not necessarily. A *birahane* is basically a potentially unruly beer hall.

Now that you've picked the place, it's time to sit down and read the menu, right? Wrong. Not all restaurants automatically provide menus, instead offering whatever's seasonal or the specialty of the house. If you'd feel more comfortable with a menu, don't be shy about asking, and politely say, *"Menüyü var mı?"* Mezes (appetizers) are often brought over on a platter, and the protocol is to simply point at the ones you want. Don't feel pressured into accepting every plate the waiter offers (none of it is free) or into ordering a main dish; Turks often make a meal out of an array of mezes, accompanied by raki. When ordering fish, it's perfectly acceptable (nay, advisable) to have your selection weighed for cost; if the price is higher than you planned to pay, either choose a less expensive fish or ask the waiter if it's possible to buy only half.

is as thin as a crepe and lightly covered with chopped onions, lamb, and tomatoes. Picking up some "street food" can be a great diversion, especially in the shelter of some roadside shack where the corn and *gözleme*—a freshly made cheese or potato (or whatever) crepe that is the providence of expert rolling pin-wielding village matrons—are hot off the grill.

Desserts fall into two categories: baklava and milk-based. Baklava, a type of dessert made of thin layers of pastry dough soaked in syrup, is a sugary sweet bomb best enjoyed around teatime (with ice cream,

please), although several varieties are made so light and fluffy that you'll be tempted to top off dinner with a sampling. The milk-based desserts have no eggs or butter and are a guilt-free pick-me-up in the late-afternoon hours, although there's no bad time to treat yourself to some creamy *süt-laç* (rice pudding). The sprinkling of pistachio bits is a liberal addition to these and many a Turkish dessert, while comfort food includes the *irmik helva,* a delicious yet simple family tradition of modestly sweet semolina, pine nuts, milk, and butter (okay, I lied about the guilt-free part).

> **Fun Fact Caffeined Out**
> As a result of the Ottoman's second unsuccessful siege on Vienna, many of the army supplies were left behind in the retreat, including sacks and sacks of coffee beans. Believing them to be sacks of animal waste, the Viennese began to burn the sacks, until a more worldly citizen, aware of the market value of the bean, got a whiff and promptly saved the lot. He later opened up the first coffeehouse in Vienna.

So what's the deal with Turkish delight? Otherwise known as *lokum,* this sweet candy is made of cornstarch, nuts, syrup, and an endless variety of flavorings to form a skwooshy tidbit whose appeal seems to be more in the gift-giving than on its own merit.

DRINKS

Rather than the question, "Would you like something to drink?" Turkish hospitality leaps immediately to the "What?" Tea, called *çay* (chai) in Turkish, is not so much a national drink as it is a ritual. Boil the water incorrectly and you're in for trouble. Let the tea steep without prior rinsing and you've committed an unforgivable transgression. What's amazing is that so many tea drinkers manage to maintain white teeth, and as you'll see, some don't. Tea is served extremely hot and strong in tiny tulip-shaped glasses, accompanied by exactly two sugar cubes. The size of the glass ensures that the tea gets consumed while hot, and before you slurp your final sip, a new glass will arrive. If you find the tea a bit strong, especially on an empty stomach, request that it be *"açik,"* or "opened," so that the ratio of water to steeped tea is increased.

The coffee culture is a little less prevalent (notwithstanding the current siege by Starbucks, Gloria Jean's, and Kahve Dünyası—coffee world) but no less steeped in tradition. Early clerics believed it to be an intoxicant and consequently had it banned. But the *kahvehane* (coffeehouse) refused to go away, and now the sharing of a cup of Turkish coffee is an excuse to prolong a discussion, plan, negotiate, or just plain relax. Turkish coffee is ground to a fine dust, boiled directly in the correct quantity of water, and served as is. Whether you wait for the grinds to settle or down the cup in one shot is entirely an individual choice, although if you leave the muddy residue at the bottom of the cup, you may be able to coax somebody to read your fortune.

There are two national drinks: raki and *ayran.* Raki is an alcoholic drink distilled from raisins and then redistilled with aniseed. Even when diluted with water, this "lion's milk" still packs a punch, so drink responsibly! Raki is enjoyed everywhere, but is particularly complementary to a meal of mezes.

Ayran is a refreshing beverage made by diluting yogurt with water. Westerners more accustomed to a sweet-tasting yogurt drink may at first be put off by the saltiness of *ayran,* but when mentally prepared, it's impossible to dismiss the advantages and pure enjoyment of this concoction.

A Punishment Worse Than the Crime?
In Turkey, tripe soup, called *İşkembe Çorbası,* or *Korkoreç,* is a widely accepted remedy for a hangover.

4 An Overview of Islam

The history of Islam dates to the beginning of the 7th century in the city of Mecca, in today's Saudi Arabia. At the time, Mecca contained what was believed to be the first holy shrine built by Adam and Eve. Later, after Abraham was spared the task of sacrificing his only son, he rebuilt a temple on the same spot and dedicated it to the One True God. This shrine, constructed in the shape of a simple cube (hence the word *Ka'aba*), attracted the devotion of a host of pagan cults and, by the end of the second half of the first millennium, contained over 360 types of statuettes and cult objects. Pilgrims representing a broad range of cults flocked to the city, and the wealthy and influential members of the community were delighted with the revenue that these pilgrimages brought.

Mohammed was born in Mecca around A.D. 570 (or C.E., for "Common Era") and grew up in a monotheistic family tradition. A naturally pious man, Mohammed often headed off into the hills for moments of isolated contemplation and prayer. On one of these occasions, Muslims believe that the angel Gabriel appeared with a message from God, a revelation that is accepted as the first verse of the Koran (*Koran* means "The Recitation"). The Koran forms the foundation of the Islamic faith and is believed by Muslims to be the direct word of God.

In a world of inequality, poverty, and misery, Mohammed's preachings of purity of heart, charity, humility, and justice gained a devoted following well beyond the borders of Mecca. The tribesmen of Mecca, perfectly content with the (economic benefits of the) status quo, grew alarmed and hostile at these developments, eventually forcing Mohammed and his followers to leave Mecca in fear for their lives. The town of Yathrib welcomed Mohammed and gave him an honored position as leader, changing its name to Madinat al-Nabi, or "the town of the Prophet." The town was later to become known simply as Medina.

Many of the misconceptions of Islam come from models that are related to culture and not religion. The basic principles of Islam are quite admirable, and every requirement has a practical purpose. The act of prayer sets specific time aside for the recognition of a greater power, and the act of physical prostration is a constant reminder of one's humility and man's equality. Practically speaking, regular prayer develops a sense of peace and tranquillity, of punctuality, obedience, and gratitude. Furthermore, the setting aside of 5 minutes five times a day for introspection and meditation can only have positive effects on one's overall health, especially in the face of the stresses that the modern world has to offer. The month of ritual fasting, or Ramadan (*Ramazan* in Turkish), reinforces principles of discipline and teaches people to appreciate what they have and to understand what it's like to do without. Ramadan also brings families and communities together in a feeling of brotherhood and unity.

Islam is a socially conscious religion that attends not only to inner growth but to external affairs as well. The concept of charity is implicit in Islam, which calls for a specific contribution to be made to those less fortunate (2.5%) unless doing so would cause undue hardship to the giver.

Sadly, people tend to dwell on the concepts of polygamy, unequal treatment of women, and terrorist activity associated with the Islamic idea of *jihad*. These concepts, when examined in historical context, have pure motives that have been manipulated through the ages to further the self-interest (or vision) of individuals.

(This manipulation took different forms under different authoritarian Muslim regimes.) For example, the idea of multiple wives gained ground at a time when wars were creating an abundance of widows whose only alternative for survival would have been prostitution; the humanitarian solution at the time was for a man to provide a home for as many wives as he could afford.

Islam preaches modesty, and in many societies, particularly in Saudi Arabia and Iran, this concept has been taken to extremes, requiring women to wear a black chador in public. Ironically, there is absolutely nothing in the Koran or any of the hadiths that requires a woman to wear any specific garment. In fact, the requirement of modesty applies to men as well. To force or coerce a women (or anyone) in matters of religion goes against the true spirit of Islam. (Here's a solution: Blindfold the men.)

A divisive issue in Islam dates back to the death of Mohammed and relates to the succession, an area of disagreement that spreads into ideology. **Shiite** Muslims believe that the true line of imams (or spiritual leaders) is one based on genealogy, and that the rightful representatives of Islam descend from Ali, Mohammed's cousin and son-in-law. Shiites believe that part of the imam's inheritance is divine knowledge passed between relatives. Armed with a direct line to God, Shiites often exhibit a tendency toward blind adherence.

Sunni Muslims interpret Mohammed's ideology more democratically and acknowledge the line of succession as one based on merit and "the consensus of the community."

Turkey, whose Muslims are predominantly Sunni, is the only Muslim country in the world to allow its citizens the freedom to decide their own level of observance. While the political atmosphere in Turkey represents both liberal and conservative extremes (and everything in between), Atatürk's reforms regarding secularism provided the country with the basis for personal freedoms not available to other Muslim countries where national law is based on an interpretation of *shariah* (the way of Islam).

The universal reaction of Westerners arriving in Turkey is the revelation that Islam is not synonymous with terrorism, and Muslims are just people like you and me living their lives, celebrating their families, and worrying about the bills. And they're thinking the same thing about us. While it's true that throughout the history of Islam (and Christianity, and others . . .) religion has been manipulated for political purposes, it's edifying to learn that Islam represents a generosity of spirit, a gentleness of heart, and the practice of good, clean altruistic living. The Anatolian influences in Turkish culture add some rich traditions and folklore into the mix, the result being that many Turks have found a way to adapt to the contradictions inherent in a changing world.

Appendix B:
A Glossary of Useful Turkish Phrases

1 Pronunciation Guide

VOWELS
a like the "a" in father
â like "ya" (the circumflex adds a diphthong)
e like the "e" in bed
i like the "i" in indigo
ı like the "e" in the
o like the "o" in hope
ö like the German "ö" or like the "u" in the English word further
u like the "u" in super
ü like the French "u" or like the "u" in the English word funeral

CONSONANTS
c like the "j" in Jupiter
ç like the "ch" in church
g like the "g" in gather
ğ is silent and indicates that the preceding vowel should be elongated
    (dağ becomes "daaah," meaning "mountain")
h is **always** aspirated (pronounced without the "h," the proper name
    Mahmut means "big elephant"!)
j like the "s" in pleasure
s like the "s" in simple
ş like the "sh" in share

2 Basic Vocabulary

DAYS OF THE WEEK
Sunday   **Pazar**
Monday   **Pazartesi** (literally, "the day after Sunday")
Tuesday   **Salı**
Wednesday **Çarşamba**
Thursday **Perşembe**
Friday   **Cuma**
Saturday **Cumartesi** (literally, "the day after Friday")

MONTHS OF THE YEAR

January   **Ocak**
February   **Şubat**
March   **Mart**
April   **Nisan**
May   **Mayıs**
June   **Haziran**
July   **Temmuz**
August   **Ağfustos**
September   **Eylül**
October   **Ekim**
November   **Kasım**
December   **Aralık**

EXPRESSIONS OF TIME

1 hour   **Bir saat**
Afternoon   **Öğleden sonra**
Morning   **Sabah**
Night   **Gece**
Today   **Bugün**
Tomorrow   **Yarın**
What time is it?   **Saat kaç?** (literally, "how many hours?")
Yesterday   **Dün**

NUMBERS

1	bir	30	otuz
2	iki	40	kırk
3	üç	50	elli
4	dört	60	altmış
5	beş	70	yetmiş
6	altı	80	seksen
7	yedi	90	doksan
8	sekiz	100	yüz
9	dokuz	101	yüzbir
10	on	200	ikiyüz
11	onbir	1,000	bin
12	oniki	2,000	ikibin
20	yirmi	1,000,000	birmilyon
21	yirmibir	2,000,000	ikimilyon

USEFUL SUFFIXES

ci, cı, çi, çı, cu, cü, çu, çü   indicates the seller of something
i, ı, u, ü   indicates "of something" (an "s" is added after a vowel)
ler, lar   makes a word plural
li, lı, lu, lü   indicates the presence of something; "with"
siz, sız, suz, süz   indicates the absence of something; "without"

USEFUL WORDS & PHRASES

Check, please!   **Hesap, lütfen!**

Cheers! (drinking)   **Şerefe!**

Closed   **Kapalı**

Do you have any dishes without meat?   **Etsiz yemek var mı?**

Excuse me   **Pardon** (French pronunciation) or **Afadersınız**

Gate (travel)   **Kapı**

Goodbye   **Güle güle** (said by the one staying);
   Allahai Smarladık (said by the one leaving)

Goodbye   **Hoşça kalın** (an all-purpose goodbye)

Good day   **Iyi günler**

Good evening   **Iyi akşamlar**

Good morning   **Günaydın**

Good night   **Iyi geceler**

Hello   **Merhaba**

How are you?   **Nasılsınız?**

How much?   **Kaç para?** (literally, "how much money?") or **Ne kadar?**

I'm fine, thank you.   **Iyiyim, teşekkür ederim.**

Is there . . . ?   **Var mı . . . ?** (question of availability)

Is there any meat stock in this dish?   **Içinde et suyu var mı?**

No   **Hayır** *(higher)*

One ticket, please   **Bir tane bilet, lütfen**

Open   **Açık**

Please   **Lütfen**

Pleased to meet you   **Memnun oldun**

Thank you (formal)   **Teşekkür ederim** (try to remember: "tea, sugar, a dream")

Thank you (casual)   **Sağol**

Thank you   **Mersi**

There isn't any; no; none   **Yok**

Very beautiful   **Çok güzel** (said also when the food is good)

Welcome!   **Hoş geldiniz!** (response: **Hoş bulduk**)

Well done!   **Bravo!** or **Aferin!**

Where? Where is it?   **Nerede?**

Where's the toilet?   **Tuvalet nerede?**

Yes   **Evet**

3 Glossary of Terms

~olis   Highest part of a Greek city reserved for the most important religious

~   to commanders in the Ottoman military

Bayanlar   Ladies

Baylar   Gentlemen

Bayram   Arabic term meaning "feast" denoting several of the Muslim holidays

Bedesten   Covered inn or marketplace

Bey   Turkish title of courtesy following a man's first name meaning "Mr.," as in "Mehmet bey"

Bulvarı   Boulevard

Büyük   Big

Caddesi   Avenue

Caldarium   Hottest section of a Roman bath

Caliph   Literally "successor" to the prophet Mohammad; in the past, the title was held by the religious leader of the Islamic community and was known as "commander of the faithful"

Cami/camii   Mosque; derived from the Arabic *jama* meaning "place of reunion"

Caravansary   A fortified inn; Turkish spelling is *kervansaray*

Çarşı(sı)   Market; bazaar

Celebi   Nobleman

Çeşme   Fountain

Cıkış   Exit

Cumhuriyet   Republic

Cuneiform   Linear script inscribed into tablets; used by the ancient Mesopotamians and in Asia Minor

Deniz   Sea

Dervish   A member of a mystical order of Islam

Divan   Word used to refer to the Ottoman governmental administration

Dolmuş   Minibus, minivan, or any car that operates as a group taxi

Döviz   Foreign currency

Eczane   Pharmacy

Efendi   Turkish title of courtesy following a first name meaning "sir" or "ma'am"

Emir   Arabic title for a military commander or governor of a province

Ev/evi   Home, house

Fatih   Conqueror

Frigidarium   The cold room of a Roman bath

Gar   Station

Gazi   Literally, "warrior"

Giriş   Entrance

Gişe   Ticket window

Hadith   Traditions based on the words or actions of Mohammed

Hamam(ı)   Turkish bath

Han(ı)   Inn or caravansary

Hanım   Address of respect meaning "lady"

Harem   Women's quarters of a house (literally, "forbidden")

Havaalan(ı) or **hava liman(ı)**   Airport

Hegira   Literally, "the emigration"; see *hicret*

Hicret   The date in 622 when Mohammad left Mecca for Yathrib (Medina) to escape local hostilities; this event marks the beginning of the Islamic calendar.

Hijab   From the Arabic *hajaba* meaning "to conceal"; used to mean any modest covering worn by a Muslim woman

Hisar   Fortress

Iconoclasm   8th-century Christian movement that opposed all religious icons

Imam   Literally, "leader"; an educated religious guide

Iskele(si)   Wharf, quay, or dock

Janissaries   The select corps of the Ottoman army

Jihad   Literally, "struggle" or "striving" (Arab; in Turkish: *cihad*)

Ka'aba   Muslim sacred shrine in Mecca

Kale(si)   Castle or fortress

Kat   Floor (of a building)

Kervansaray   *See* caravansary

Kilim   Flat weave rug

Kilise   Church

Konak/konağı   Mansion

Koran   The holy recitations of the Prophet Mohammed; Muslims believe that these revelations are the direct words of God

Küçük   Small

Kule   Tower

Külliye(si)   Religious and social complex consisting of mosque, school, and buildings for public use

Kümbet   Literally, "cupola" or "dome"; synonym for *türbe*

Liman(ı)   Port

Mahalle(si)   Neighborhood

Medrese   Muslim theological school

Mescit   Small prayer space; mini-mosque

Mevlana   Title of respect meaning "Lord" (Arabic)

Meydan(ı)   Public square

Meyhane   Tavern, pub, or rowdy restaurant

Mihrab   The niche in a mosque oriented toward Mecca

Minaret   The towers of a mosque from which the müezzin chants the call to prayer

Minbar   Pulpit

Müezzin   The Muslim "cantor" of the call to prayer

Necropolis   Ancient Greek or Roman cemetery

Oculus   Round "skylight" in the top of a dome

Oda(sı)   Room

Otogar   Bus station

Pansiyon   Pension, guesthouse

Paşa   Title given to commanders in the Ottoman army (close to general) and to governors of provinces

Ramadan   Islamic month of ritual fasting; Ramadan (*Ramazan* in Turkish) follows the lunar calendar so that the festival is not confined to one season

Şadirvan   Literally, "reservoir"; used for ablution fountains

Şarap   Wine

Saray(ı)   Palace

Şarcüteri   Delicatessen

Satrap   Persian governor of a province

Şehzade   Crown prince

Selamlık   In a traditional Turkish house, the part reserved for the men and the reception of guests

Sema   Mystical dance of the Mevlevi order of the dervishes

Seraglio   Sultan's palace
Sokak/sokağı   Street
Stele   Ancient tombstone
Sublime Porte   Originally the main door of the palace where meetings of the divan were held; the term was eventually used to refer to the government, and the entire Ottoman Empire in general
Tepidarium   The tepid room of a Roman bath; used for relaxation
Tuğra   Sultan's imperial seal
Türbe(si)   Turkish monumental funerary tomb
Ulu   Great
Yalı   Traditional wood Ottoman house, usually a secondary residence, built on the sea
Valide Sultan   Turkish title equivalent to Queen Mother
Yol(u)   Road (*karayolu:* highway or autobahn)
Yurt   Nomadic tent, traditionally made of felt

4 Menu Guide

WHAT IS IT?

Alabalık   Trout
Ananas   Pineapple
Ançuez   Anchovy
Balık   Fish
Barbunya   Red mullet
Beyin   Brain
Bezelye   Peas
Biber   Pepper (*kara biber:* black pepper)
Bıldırcın   Quail
Bonfile   Filet of beef
Çam fıstığı   Pine nut
Ciğer   Liver
Çilek   Strawberry
Çorba   Soup
Çupra   Sea bream
Dana   Veal
Domates   Tomato
Domuz   Pork
Dondurma   Ice cream
Ekmek   Bread
Elma   Apple
Enginar   Artichoke
Erik   Plum
Et   Meat
Fasulye   Bean
Havuç   Carrot
Hindi   Turkey
İspanak   Spinach
Istravrit   Mackerel
Jambon   Ham

Kabak   Squash (zucchini, pumpkin, and the like)
Kalkan   Turbot
Karides   Shrimp
Karnıbahar   Cauliflower
Karpuz   Watermelon
Kavun   Melon
Kayısı   Apricot
Kaz   Goose
Kefal   Gray mullet
Kılıç   Swordfish
Kiraz   Cherry
Köfte   Meatball
Kuzu   Lamb
Lağus   Grouper
Lavaş   Grilled unleavened bread
Levrek   Sea bass
Limon   Lemon
Lüfer   Bluefish
Mantar   Mushroom
Marul   Lettuce
Meyva   Fruit
Meze   Appetizer
Mezgit   Cod
Mısır   Corn
Mürekkep balığı   Squid
Muz   Banana
Ördek   Duck
Palamut   Bonito
Patates   Potato
Patlıcan   Eggplant/aubergine

Peynir   Cheese
Pide   Flat bread
Pilaf (pilâf)   Rice
Piliç   Chicken
Portakal   Orange
Salatalik   Cucumber
Sardalya   Sardine
Şeftali   Peach
Şeker   Sugar
Sığır   Beef
Soğan   Onion
Som   Salmon
Sosis   Sausage
Tarak   Scallop
Tatlılar   Sweets
Tavuk   Hen (for stewing)
Tereyağı   Butter
Ton   Tuna
Torik   Large bonito
Tuz   Salt
Un   Flour
Üzüm   Grapes
Yumurta   Eggs
Zeytin   Olive
Zeytinyağı   Olive oil

HOW IS IT PREPARED?

Buğulama   Steamed
Çevirme   Meat roasted on a spit
Çiğ   Raw
Doğranmış   Chopped
Dolma   Stuffed
Ezme   Paste
Fırın   Roasted or baked; oven
Füme   Smoked
Guveç   Earthenware dish; casseroles cooked in this pot
Haşlama   Cooked, boiled
İzgara   Grilled
Islim   Braised
Kavurma   Fried or roasted
Kebap   Roasted
Pane   Breaded and fried
Püre   Purée
Rosto   Roast meat
Saç   Iron griddle for cooking over wood fires
Sahanda   Fried
Şiş   Skewer
Sote   Sauté
Tandır   Clay lined oven
Taşım   Boiled
Tava   Fried

DRINKS

Ayran   Yogurt drink made by the addition of water and salt
Bira   Beer
Çay   Tea
Kayısı suyu   Apricot juice
Kiraz suyu   Cherry juice
Kola   Cola
Maden suyu or soda   Carbonated mineral water
Meyve suyu   Fruit juice
Portakal suyu   Orange juice

Raki   Alcoholic drink made of aniseed and diluted with water
Şarap   Wine
Şekerli   With sugar
Şekersiz   Unsweetened
Şişe suyu   Bottled water
Soğuk içecekler   Beverages
Su   Water
Süt   Milk
Suyu   Juice

APPETIZERS

Ara sıcak   Hot appetizers (translated literally, "in the middle hot")
Arnavut ciğeri   Spicy fried liver with onions
Beyin haşlaması   Boiled brain
Beyin kızartması   Fried brain
Börek   Flaky pastry, either baked or fried
Cacık   Salad of yogurt, cucumber, and garlic; often served as a soup
Çiğ köfte   Spicy raw meatballs

Çoban salatası   Salad of tomatoes, peppers, cucumbers, onions, and mint in olive oil and lemon

Ezme salatası   Spicy relish of chopped tomatoes, cucumbers, peppers, hot green chili peppers, onion, and parsley

Fesuliye piyası   White bean with onion salad

Havuç salatası   Carrot salad

Hibeş   Spread of chickpeas, red pepper, onion, and yogurt

Humus   Chickpea purée

Patlıcan salatası   Purée of roasted eggplant (also served warm; also refers to eggplant sautéed with tomatoes and peppers)

Sigara böreği   Fried filo "cigar" pastry filled with cheese

Soğuk mezeler   Cold appetizers

Su böreği   Baked filo filled with meat or cheese

Talaş böreği   Puff pastry filled with meat

Yalancı dolması   Stuffed grape leaves (no meat)

Yaprak dolması   Stuffed grape leaves (sometimes with meat)

SOUPS

Balık çorbası   Fish soup

Domatesli pirinç çorbası   Tomato and rice soup

Et suyu   Consommé

Ezo gelin çorbası   Red lentil soup with bulgur and mint

Işkembe çorbası   Tripe soup (also kokoreç)

Mantar çorbası   Mushroom soup

Mercimek çorbası   Lentil soup

Sebze çorbası   Vegetable soup

MEATS & KEBAPS

Adana kebabı   Meatballs of spicy chopped lamb flattened and grilled on a skewer

Böbrek   Kidney

Çöp kebabı   Same as *çöp şiş*

Çöp şiş   Small lamb cubes grilled on a skewer; also called *çöp kebabı*

Döner kebap   Thin slices of lamb roasted on a vertical revolving spit

İçli köfte   Corn or bulgur balls stuffed with minced lamb (boiled or fried)

Iskender kebabı   Sliced *döner kebabı* served on a layer of *pide,* tomatoes, and yogurt, and covered with melted butter

Izgara köfte   Grilled meatballs

Kadın budu köfte   "Lady's thigh," meatballs of lamb and rice, deep-fried

Karışık izgara   Mixed grill

Kuzu budu rostosu   Roasted leg of lamb

Kuzu pirzolası   Grilled lamb chops

Şiş kebabı   Marinated lamb cubes grilled on a skewer

DESSERTS

Aşure   Thick sweet pudding of whole wheat, mixed fruits, and nuts

Baklava   Flaky pastries soaked in syrup or honey

Çukulatalı pudding   Chocolate pudding

Fırın sütlaç   Baked rice pudding

Hanım göbeği   Honey-soaked flour pastry

Helva   National favorite of semolina, sesame paste or flour, sugar, and nuts

Kaymaklı kayısı tatlısı   Poached apricots stuffed with cream
Krem karamel   Crème caramel
Künefe   Butter-soaked pastry filled with melted cheese, soaked in syrup, and served hot
Muhallebi   Milk pudding
Revani   Honey-soaked semolina
Sütlaç   Rice pudding
Tatlılar   Sweets or desserts
Tavukgöğsü   Sweet chicken pudding

OTHER FAVORITE DISHES

Damat dolması   Squash stuffed with ground lamb and nuts
Domates doması   Stuffed tomatoes
Etli biber dolması   Stuffed green peppers
Gözleme   Folded savory pancake filled with potato, cheese, or meat
Hunkar beğendi   Eggplant purée topped with lamb cubes (literally, "the sultan was pleased")
Imam bayıldı   Stuffed eggplant (literally, "the imam fainted")
Lahmacun   Fast food of thin crust dough topped with minced lamb, tomato, and onion
Mantı   Meat dumplings topped with warm sauce of yogurt, garlic, and chili oil
Menemen   Wet omelet of beaten eggs, tomato, and green peppers
Musakka   Casserole of eggplant, vegetables, and ground lamb
Peynirli tost   Grilled cheese sandwich (also called *tost*)
Simit   Sesame seed-coated soft pretzel

Index

FROMMER'S® PORTABLE GUIDES

Acapulco, Ixtapa & Zihuatanejo
Amsterdam
Aruba, Bonaire & Curacao
Australia's Great Barrier Reef
Bahamas
Big Island of Hawaii
Boston
California Wine Country
Cancún
Cayman Islands
Charleston
Chicago
Dominican Republic

Florence
Las Vegas
Las Vegas for Non-Gamblers
London
Maui
Nantucket & Martha's Vineyard
New Orleans
New York City
Paris
Portland
Puerto Rico
Puerto Vallarta, Manzanillo &
    Guadalajara

Rio de Janeiro
San Diego
San Francisco
Savannah
St. Martin, Sint Maarten, Angui
    St. Bart's
Turks & Caicos
Vancouver
Venice
Virgin Islands
Washington, D.C.
Whistler

FROMMER'S® CRUISE GUIDES

Alaska Cruises & Ports of Call

Cruises & Ports of Call

European Cruises & Ports of Ca

FROMMER'S® NATIONAL PARK GUIDES

Algonquin Provincial Park
Banff & Jasper
Grand Canyon

National Parks of the American West
Rocky Mountain
Yellowstone & Grand Teton

Yosemite and Sequoia & Kings
    Canyon
Zion & Bryce Canyon

FROMMER'S® WITH KIDS GUIDES

Chicago
Hawaii
Las Vegas
London

National Parks
New York City
San Francisco

Toronto
Walt Disney World® & Orlando
Washington, D.C.

FROMMER'S® PHRASEFINDER DICTIONARY GUIDES

Chinese
French

German
Italian

Japanese
Spanish

SUZY GERSHMAN'S BORN TO SHOP GUIDES

France
Hong Kong, Shanghai & Beijing
Italy

London
New York
Paris

San Francisco
Where to Buy the Best of Everyth

FROMMER'S® BEST-LOVED DRIVING TOURS

Britain
California
France
Germany

Ireland
Italy
New England
Northern Italy

Scotland
Spain
Tuscany & Umbria

THE UNOFFICIAL GUIDES®

Adventure Travel in Alaska
Beyond Disney
California with Kids
Central Italy
Chicago
Cruises
Disneyland®
England
Hawaii

Ireland
Las Vegas
London
Maui
Mexico's Best Beach Resorts
Mini Mickey
New Orleans
New York City
Paris

San Francisco
South Florida including Miami &
    the Keys
Walt Disney World®
Walt Disney World® for
    Grown-ups
Walt Disney World® with Kids
Washington, D.C.

SPECIAL-INTEREST TITLES

Athens Past & Present
Best Places to Raise Your Family
Cities Ranked & Rated
500 Places to Take Your Kids Before They Grow Up
Frommer's Best Day Trips from London
Frommer's Best RV & Tent Campgrounds in the U.S.A.

Frommer's Exploring America by RV
Frommer's NYC Free & Dirt Cheap
Frommer's Road Atlas Europe
Frommer's Road Atlas Ireland
Retirement Places Rated